The Green Dragoon

The
Green Dragoon

The Lives of
BANASTRE TARLETON
and MARY ROBINSON

by ROBERT D. BASS

Illustrated with Photographs

Sandlapper Publishing Co., Inc.

T o

VIRGINIA WAUCHOPE BASS

CONTENTS

The Green Dragoon

1

Return of the Hero

The Black Stallion screamed and reared. The rider aimed his pistol at the charging Duke. At that moment a French uhlan drove his lance through the horse of a British dragoon. The stricken beast careened against the stallion, overthrowing both him and his rider. Stunned and broken, with his leg pinned beneath his charger, the young colonel lay helpless, while above him the Frenchmen strove again and again to drive in their lances.

As the British gave way before the uhlans, the Duke of Lauzun recognized the uniform of the Green Horse Troop, sprang from his saddle, and rushed forward to seize the prostrate Englishman. At last Washington's troops had captured Lieutenant Colonel Banastre Tarleton, hated commandant of the hated British Legion!

"Tarleton's down! Tarleton's down!" rang across the field. Without orders the reserve of the British Legion guarding the grain wagons of Lieutenant Colonel Dundas wheeled in a wild charge against the French lancers. The uhlans scattered.

"I charged without stopping," the Duke of Lauzun wrote in his Memoirs. "Tarleton picked me out, and came to me with his pistol raised. We were going to fight between our respective troops when his horse was thrown down by one of his dragoons who was being pursued by one of my lancers. I ran on him to take him prisoner. A company of English dragoons threw itself between us and protected his retreat." Boasted the Duke: "His horse was left to me."

But not the rider. "Meanwhile Tarleton escaped the enemy, and obtained another horse, when perceiving the broken state of his cavalry, occasioned by their anxiety for his safety, and which now precluded all vigorous efforts, he ordered a retreat, to afford them opportunity of recovering from their confusion," wrote Colonel Tarleton in his History *of the Campaigns of 1780 and 1781 in the Southern Provinces of North America.*

"The Duke of Lauzun's French hussars retired behind their infantry and a numerous militia who had arrived at the edge of the plain. Lieutenant Colonel Tarleton, upon receiving part of their fire from behind a rail, again ordered the retreat to be sounded."

As the bugle sounded retreat, the fighting days of Banastre Tarleton ended. The meteoric career, which rose in the North, on the battlefields from New York to Pennsylvania, and which blazed so brightly in the South, over the Carolinas and Virginia, set in the early morning of October 3, 1781, in a hot little skirmish, at the end of a lane between two rail fences, in front of the village of Gloucester, across the river from Yorktown, Virginia. But the badly mauled commandant, clinging to the saddle of a strange horse, rallied the Legion around the wagons of forage and escorted them to safety behind the British ramparts.

The French and Americans under Brigadier General de Choisy moved into the plain and tightened their lines around the dying army. At two o'clock General de Choisy dispatched a note with exciting news to Count de Rochambeau: "*Le bruit court que Tarleton a été blessé.*"

The rumor ran true—Tarleton had been wounded. As he lay among his dragoons at Gloucester, what a contrast he made with the savage rider who had conquered and tamed his black stallion, in a happier time and place, far from the battlefields around Yorktown. Said an old Tory, who as a youth had carried a message from Lord Cornwallis to Colonel Tarleton: "I have witnessed many stirring scenes, both during the Revolution and since, but I never saw one half so exciting as the one between that savage man and that savage horse!"

The young messenger from Cornwallis was excitedly looking over the camp of the Green Horse near Petersburg, Virginia.

> Just then my attention was attracted by the violent plunging of a horse which two stout grooms, one on each side, were endeavoring to lead toward the spot where we were standing. He was a large and powerful brute, beautifully formed, and black as a crow, with an eye that actually seemed to blaze with rage at the restraint put upon him. His progress was one continual bound, at times swinging the grooms clear from the earth as lightly as though they were but tassels hung on his huge Spanish bit, so that with difficulty they escaped being trampled under foot. I asked the meaning of the scene, and was informed that the horse was one that Tarleton had heard of as being a magnificent animal, but one altogether unmanageable; and so delighted was he with the description, that he sent all the way down into Moore county, where his owner resided, and purchased him at the extravagant price of one hundred guineas; and moreover, he was about to ride him that morning.

"Ride him," said I, "why one had as well try to back a streak of lightning. The mad brute will be the death of him."

"Never fear for him," said my companion, "never fear for him. His time has not come yet."

By this time the horse had been brought up to where we were; the curtain of the marquee was pushed aside, and my attention was drawn from the savage stud to rivet itself upon his dauntless rider. And a picture of a man he was! Rather below the middle height, and with a face almost femininely beautiful, Tarleton possessed a form that was a perfect model of manly strength and vigor. Without a particle of superfluous flesh, his rounded limbs and full broad chest seemed molded from iron, yet, at the same time, displaying all the elasticity which usually accompanies elegance of proportion. His dress, strange as it may appear, was a jacket and breeches of white linen, fitted to his form with the utmost exactness. Boots of russet leather were half way up the leg, the broad tops of which were turned down, the heels garnished with spurs of an immense size and length of rowel. On his head was a low crowned hat, curiously formed from the snow-white feathers of the swan, and in his hand he carried a heavy scourge with shot well twisted into its knotted lash.

After looking around for a moment or two, as though to command the attention of all, he advanced to the side of the horse, and, disdaining to use the stirrup, with one bound threw himself into the saddle, at the same time calling on the men to let him go. For an instant the animal seemed paralyzed; then, with a perfect yell of rage, bounded into the air like a stricken deer.

The struggle for mastery had commenced—bound succeeded bound with the rapidity of thought; every device which its animal instinct could teach was resorted to by the maddened brute to shake off its unwelcome burden—but in vain. Its ruthless rider proved irresistible, and clinging like fate itself, plied the scourge and rowel like a fiend. The punishment was too severe to be long withstood, and at length, after a succession of frantic efforts, the tortured animal, with a scream of agony, leaped forth upon the plain, and flew across it with the speed of an arrow.

The ground upon which Tarleton had pitched his camp was an almost level plain, something more than half a mile in circumference. Around this, after getting him under way, he continued to urge his furious steed, amid the raptures and shouts of the admiring soldiery, plying the whip and spur at every leap, until wearied and worn down with its prodigious efforts, the tired creature discontinued all exertion, save that to which it was urged by its merciless rider.

At length, exhausted from the conflict, Tarleton drew up before the tent, and threw himself from the saddle. The horse was completely subdued, and at the word of command followed him around like a dog. The victory was complete. His eye of fire was dim and lustreless, drops of agony fell from his drooping front, while from his laboring and mangled sides the mingled blood and foam poured in a thick and clotted stream. Tarleton himself was pale as death, and as soon as he was satisfied of his success, retired and threw himself on his couch. In a short time I was called into his presence, and delivered my dispatches.

As Colonel Tarleton and the cavalry of the British Legion lay hemmed-in at Gloucester, Lord Cornwallis and the infantry fared even worse at Yorktown. The troops under General Washington slowly and methodically pressed their siege. They dug trenches parallel to the breastworks. They stormed the redoubts. They poured such cannon fire directly into the British lines that on October 16 Lord Cornwallis ordered a detachment, including a grenadier company of the famed 1st Guards under Lieutenant Colonel Gerard Lake, to capture and spike the guns.

That evening Lord Cornwallis began a desperate move: to transfer his troops from Yorktown to Gloucester, to place the British Legion in front, and to fight his way to New York. Before midnight he had embarked most of the Guards in small boats and ferried them over the York River. But a violent storm arose and swept the boats from the river.

Next morning Cornwallis sent an officer under a white flag to request a parley, and on the following day commissioners drew up articles of surrender. On October 19, 1781, the remnants of the proud army that had set out from Charleston in May 1780 marched out between two lines of French and American soldiers and threw down their arms. Their flags were cased, but their band was slyly playing a popular drawing-room ballad: "The World Turn'd Upside Down." Their soldiers smiled, for they knew the tune as the old Jacobite serenade to Prince Charlie: "When the King Enjoys His Own Again"!

At the same hour at Gloucester, Lieutenant Colonel Tarleton surrendered the Guards and the British Legion to Brigadier General de Choisy. In his parley, Tarleton told De Choisy that he feared the American militiamen would kill him. Since the Waxhaws the battle cry of the militia had been "Tarleton's quarter!" Therefore De Choisy, keeping his other troops in camp, accepted the surrender with only Colonel Mercer's Virginians and the Duke of Lauzun's French Legion.

Knowing how fiercely the Americans hated him, Colonel Tarleton appealed for protection to the commander of the French forces. Count de Rochambeau gave his protection, but he sneered at the reputation of the crippled commandant of the British Legion. Said he: "Colonel Tarleton has no merit as an officer—only that bravery that every Grenadier has—but is a butcher and a barbarian."

The Colonel had been marked for death. Reported *Ruddiman's Weekly Mercury* of January 30, 1782: "Next day it was evident that Tarleton's alarm had a very justifiable foundation. The bed upon which he was to have slept had been stabbed in several places."

Lord Cornwallis and his principal officers were paroled, and then General Washington, Count de Rochambeau, and their officers offered them hospitality. Washington invited Cornwallis to his table. Others entertained British officers of their rank.

But no American invited Bloody Tarleton to dine, nor would any eat with him. Tarleton asked Marquis de Lafayette if the neglect was accidental. Lafayette referred the commandant of the hated British Legion to Lieutenant Colonel John Laurens, aide-de-camp to General Washington.

Laurens at once said, "No, Colonel Tarleton, no accident at all; intentional, I can assure you, and meant as a reproof for certain cruelties practiced by the troops under your command in the campaigns in the Carolinas."

"What, sir," scornfully rejoined Tarleton, "and is it for severities inseparable from war, which you are pleased to term cruelties, that I am to be disgraced before junior officers? Is it, sir, for a faithful discharge of my duty to my king and my country, that I am thus humiliated in the eyes of three armies?"

"Pardon me," continued Colonel Laurens. "There are modes, sir, of discharging a soldier's duty, and where mercy has a share in the mode, it renders the duty more acceptable to both friends and foes."

But the French officers, with no memories of burning homes and murdered kinsmen, were friendly. Colonel Tarleton and the Duke of Lauzun, accepting war like professional soldiers, became friends. Other Frenchmen invited him to dine.

Four days after the surrender, as Tarleton, on his way to dinner with Baron de Vioménil, rode down the main street of Yorktown, Mr. Day, steward to Sir Peyton Skipwith, recognized the horse as one taken from the stables of Sir Peyton. Contemptuous of the defeated Briton, the steward stopped him and demanded the horse. Pleading the extent of his injuries, Tarleton tried to persuade Day to allow him to continue. "I won't trust you with this horse," replied the steward and forced the Colonel to dismount. Fortunately, a French officer, seeing the humiliation and the guffawing natives, dismounted his orderly and lent the steed to Tarleton.

After the American militia had marched the British troops off to prison camps in Virginia and Maryland, Lord Cornwallis and his officers on parole sailed in the Cochran for New York. They arrived on November 19 and hastened to the headquarters of Sir Henry Clinton, commander in chief of his Majesty's forces in America. After his official report Cornwallis avoided Clinton. There was rumor that immediately after release from parole the Earl intended sending Sir Henry a challenge for not relieving Yorktown.

After the disastrous campaigns in the Southern Provinces Banastre Tarleton was glad to return to New York and the scenes of his earlier triumphs with his Green Horse. He had always found Sir Henry Clinton, a plain professional soldier, more congenial than Lord Cornwallis or Lord Rawdon. At Sir Henry's headquarters there was Major George Hanger, vice commandant of the British Legion, just returned from convalescing in Bermuda.

But there was a vacancy in Sir Henry's military family—a vacancy which called up in Tarleton's mind memories of the frolicking in the Mischianza and the stormy voyage to Tybee aboard the *Romulus*. Major John André, Tarleton's closest friend in America, had paid life's forfeit to a soldier's duty. With head erect and shoulders squared, André had marched to the gallows for his king and the honor of the British Army. Sir Henry had refused to swap Benedict Arnold for him.

While waiting for a ship bound for England, Tarleton became the friend of a prince who would one day be his king. The young Duke of Clarence, third son of King George and Queen Charlotte, had arrived in New York on August 24, 1781, aboard the man-o'-war *Prince George*. When Tarleton arrived from Yorktown the Duke went to meet him. Thereafter, dressed in his midshipman's roundabout, he walked from Rear Admiral Robert Digby's headquarters in the old Beekman house, Hanover Square, to Tarleton's quarters to dine with him.

The paroled officers did not wait long. On December 15, 1781, a convoy of 120 empty victualers, transports, and merchantmen dropped down Hudson River and headed for England. For protection against French and American privateers they were herded by the *Robust*, 74 guns, commanded by Captain Philips Cosby; and the *Janus*, 44 guns, under Captain W. H. K. O'Hara. Lord Cornwallis, with the sick and wounded officers, as well as those who were lucky when lots were drawn to determine who should remain with the troops in America, sailed aboard the *Robust*.

But men-o'-war were poor protection against the elements. On December 18 a storm of great violence overtook the convoy. Driven by the wind and waves, the ships scattered and lost their escorts. No four of them came together again. The *Janus* disappeared and weeks later limped into an English port to belie rumors that she had foundered. The *Robust* sprang a leak and by December 25 was filling at the rate of six feet an hour. With every available hand manning the pumps, Captain Cosby bore away for St. Kitts for repairs.

Before abandoning the convoy, on December 28 Captain Cosby transferred the officers from the *Robust* to humbler ships. Lord Cornwallis and General O'Hara were put aboard the lightly armed transport *Greyhound*. General Arnold and his family were sent to the *Prince Edward*. And Lieutenant Colonels Tarleton, Lake, and Dundas were transferred to an old merchantman named *London*.

News of the return from Yorktown reached England in late December when Tarleton's friend, Lieutenant Colonel John Graves Simcoe, arrived in London. On January 2, 1782, Simcoe was presented to King George at the levee at St. James's Palace.

On the same day *Ruddiman's Weekly Mercury* reported: "It must give pleasure to every lover of this country, to be assured, that by a letter from the gallant Col. Tarleton to his brother, now in Ipswich, that distinguished character was in perfect health in the middle of last month, and is daily expected in England."

Early in January ships from the scattered convoy began straggling into English ports. A dispatch from the Scilly Isles reported that on January 11 Colonel Tarleton had sailed past there aboard the *London*.

The French, too, had heard of the approach of Lord Cornwallis and his officers and had stationed about a dozen privateers off the southern coast of England. As the *London* passed Cape Lizard, the privateer *La Sensibilité* gave chase. With crowding sails lashed by a furious gale, the *London* headed for the English Channel.

La Sensibilité, lighter and more maneuverable, bore down upon the old merchantman, overhauling and capturing her without great effort. Placing a prize crew aboard the *London*, the French headed for Boulogne; but in the storm the captors and the captured were swept far up the English Channel. When they came to Dungeness, near the mouth of the Thames, Colonels Tarleton, Lake, and Dundas paid a ransom of 400 guineas and were set ashore. On January 18, 1782, they rode into the city of London.

London was gay and excited. The Queen's Birthday Ball was to be held that evening. But next morning the newspapers carried something more arresting than their usual descriptions of the costumes worn by the ladies: "Yesterday arrived from America Colonels Lake, Dundas, and Tarleton."

The *Morning Herald* carried an exclusive story. It reported that as soon as the news of the arrival of the colonels spread, his Royal Highness, the Prince of Wales, and his uncle, the Duke of Cumberland, called upon them at their hotel in King's Street. They personally conducted Colonel Lake, arm in arm, to Cumberland House where he dined with their Royal Highnesses and afterward spent the evening.

What a welcome! The Waxhaws, Guilford Courthouse, and Yorktown were only memories as Colonel Tarleton met and chatted with the heir to the throne. After the Prince and the Duke had escorted Lake off to Cumberland House, Tarleton hurried to the home of Lord George Germain, secretary of State for the Colonies, to make his report on the campaign and the capitulation at Yorktown.

As he passed along St. James's Street, he saw the beauty, the gallantry, and the wit of England converging on St. James's Palace. But the most beautiful woman in all London sat outside and watched with envy. As the *Morning Herald* remarked on January 19: "The Perdita sat in her coach for some time yesterday, in St. James Street, to see the courtly visitants pass to St. James Palace."

Perhaps, as she yearned for a glimpse of the lost Florizel, the Perdita saw instead a thin young colonel limp past in the green uniform of the British Legion.

෨

The highest social circles of London welcomed the hero of the British Legion. On January 23 Colonels Tarleton, Lake, and Dundas were escorted to St. James's Palace and presented to his Majesty. It was the first court gathering since the Queen's Birthday Ball had inaugurated the season. The assemblage was brilliant, and the Green Dragoon felt almost overwhelmed by the bishops, admirals, generals, lords, and ambassadors to whom he was introduced. Later the King granted him private audience. After noting the limp and the mangled hand, and after listening to some of Tarleton's stories, George III remarked with dull formality: "Well, Colonel Tarleton, you've been in a great many actions and had a great many escapes."

Next day the three colonels were escorted to her Majesty's drawing room in Buckingham House and presented to Queen Charlotte. There was more warmth in Tarleton's interview with his queen, for he brought a pleasing report of the Duke of Clarence, her sixteen-year-old son, romping around New York in his midshipman's suit, bluff and hearty, and enjoying himself at the headquarters of the British forces in America.

In the evening of January 24 Colonel Tarleton attended a masquerade in the Pantheon. Here he again met the Prince of Wales, slightly disguised in a black domino. "Colonel Tarleton was in a domino," said the *Morning Herald* in its gossip column on January 26, "but did not wear a vizor. On his being addressed by an unknown domino, he pleasantly replied, 'Sir, let me see your face. I fight in open day, and you attack me from a masked battery.'"

Lord George Germain assigned Tarleton work in his office, but *Ruddiman's Weekly Mercury* informed its readers: "So much does his Majesty admire the gallantry of the brave Col. Tarleton, that it is confidently reported he will soon have a very considerable promotion."

Then, to satisfy the curiosity of its readers, *Ruddiman's* added: "Col. Tarleton appears to be about five and twenty, middle sized, and has a strong resemblance to the immortal Wolfe."

Everyone inquired about the dashing dragoon. On February 2 Edward Jerningham wrote his brother: "The famous Tarleton looks as young as when you knew him at Norwich. He is much in vogue. He is invited, known or unknown, to all the assemblies; and wherever he stands a circle is formed around him."

On January 28, ten days after his arrival in London, Colonel Tarleton first sat for his portrait by Sir Joshua Reynolds. The royal artist was busy painting three other chancelings of fame, and Tarleton's sittings alternated with those of William Beckford, the wealthy eccentric remembered for his fantastic *Caliph Vathek*; George Bryan Brummell, the audacious Regency buck immortalized as Beau Brummell; and Mary Robinson, whom the scornful and the envious called "The Perdita," triumphantly returned from Paris "in perfect health and beauty."

By campfires in faraway North Carolina Banastre Tarleton had heard Mary's beauty sung by Colonel Lake. He knew that she had been trained by David Garrick, and that under the guidance of Richard Brinsley Sheridan she had become the brightest star in the firmament of Drury Lane. He knew of her portrayal of Perdita in *The Winter's Tale*, which had drawn a command performance for their Majesties. Colonel Lake had been sub-governor to the Prince of Wales and with the Prince had sat through that performance; and Lake had told him how enraptured the royal heir had been. Then came the letters which the Prince had sent to "Perdita" from "Florizel." And he knew of Mrs. Robinson's desertion of the stage and Thomas Robinson to live like a duchess with the Prince in a little house in Cork Street.

Fate led Banastre and Mary to the studio of Sir Joshua. There they met. He was dressed in a dashing new uniform of the Green Horse Troop: green coat with white piping, tan trousers, cavalryman's boots, embroidered white neckcloth, and shako of black swan's feathers. She was dressed in a bewitching fashion to look like the wife of Rubens: dark blue silk dress with low-cut neck and flouncing embroidered collar, sweeping, wide-brimmed hat, rakish with ostrich feathers, set over powdered curls, and a black ribbon around her throat, from which hung a diamond-encircled miniature of the Prince of Wales. She was even more beautiful than Lake's rapturous description.

Perhaps, as Banastre first looked into Mary's laughing blue eyes sheltered by auburn ringlets, and with a soldier's glance appraised the beautiful face, high bosom, and slender waist, he thought of the rascally lines of Peter Pindar:

> Think of the sage who wanted a fine piece:
> Who went, in vain, five hundred miles at least,
> On Laïs, a sweet *fille de joie*, to feast—
> The Mrs. Robinson of Greece.

Perhaps, as Mary gazed upon the bronzed face of the Green Dragoon, with the dark, bold eyes, hawk nose, and arrogant mouth, and appraised his handsome body, lean and hard from years of campaigning, she thought of the *bon mot* of her friend Richard Sheridan.

"Tarleton boasts of having butchered more men and lain with more women than anybody else in the army," Horace Walpole had said.

"Lain with!" cried Sheridan, remembering Tarleton from their student days at the Middle Temple. "What a weak expression! He should have said ravished. Rapes are the relaxation of murderers!"

Whatever the beautiful actress may then have thought of the handsome Colonel, years afterward she wrote of him in her novel *The False Friend*: "A being, who living only for himself, who, wrapped in flimsy garb of vanity, and considering woman as a creature formed for his amusement, marked every succeeding day with a new crime, at which, though reflection winked, humanity perpetually shuddered. To a woman of the world, a reasoning, rational, discriminating mortal, such an insect would have proved harmless; she would have admired his exterior attractions, would have contemplated his person with a mixture of admiration and pity; while her judgment would have taught her to counteract the magic, the poisonous magic, which lurked beneath the finest work of nature."

While Sir Joshua's assistants daubed in the battle flags and war horses for Tarleton's portrait, the hero set out to visit his family. Early in the evening of February 16 he stopped to exchange horses at the Red Lion Inn in Warrington. Ringing bells and general illumination announced his arrival. Soon about a thousand men, sailcloth weavers, merchants, and young gentlemen, had gathered around the Red Lion. Loosing the horses, they drew the carriage for a mile along the main street while shouting, "Long live brave Tarleton."

At the edge of town they hitched the horses again to the carriage and wished him Godspeed. Reported the *Liverpool Advertiser* on February 21, 1782: "Tarleton exclaimed, 'Don't be afraid of taking hold of my hand! Though I have lost two fingers, I can use my pen, and will draw my sword when I can be of service to my country.' "

Reaching Fairfield, the home of his sister Bridget, now Mrs. Edward Falkner, he spent the night. A messenger was dispatched to notify Liverpool of the approach of her famous son. Excitement became intense. Bonfires were lighted and shouting and singing grew boisterous. Church bells were rung all night and until church time next day. Many citizens rode out to escort him home.

At one o'clock on Sunday, Lieutenant Colonel Banastre Tarleton, commandant of the British Legion, rode triumphant into Liverpool. A great crowd, shouting acclamations and congratulations, followed him to the Exchange. The officials extended the welcome of the city. Said the *Liverpool Advertiser*: "The Colonel's politeness and affability gain him the esteem of all ranks."

From the rousing welcome at the Corn Exchange, Colonel Tarleton hurried home to a mother's kiss and a mother's tears for his mangled hand. There to welcome him were his three brothers, Thomas, John, and Clayton. Friends and relatives slipped in to gaze and chatter. Home was the hero, the soldier among his kin.

2

Banastre

$\mathcal{J}$HE TARLETON FAMILY sprang from Aigburth. This red brick manor house, on the Mersey River just below Liverpool, which in time gave its name to a flourishing suburb of that city, became the home of Edward Tarleton about the middle of the sixteenth century. Edward Tarleton had a son John, who moved from Aigburth into Liverpool. This John Tarleton had a son Edward, who remained in Liverpool and lived in the old Church Style House. Edward Tarleton was a man of considerable wealth and in the Cromwellian War fitted out and commanded the man-o'-war *Dublin*. In 1682 he was elected mayor of Liverpool.

Mayor Tarleton had a son John who became a physician. Dr. John Tarleton married Anne English, settled on Castle Street, and became a noted figure in Liverpool. His son, Thomas Tarleton (1680–1731), was a businessman of Liverpool. He married Bridget Houghton, and among their children was a son named John, who was born in 1719.

John Tarleton grew up in Liverpool, inherited his father's business, and prospered. He fell in love with Jane Parker, daughter of Banastre Parker, of Cuerdon, Lancashire. On June 25, 1751, they were married at Tarleton Chapel, Lancashire. Soon they bought and settled in the great house on the south side of Water Street, afterward famous as the King's Arms Hotel.

John and Jane Parker Tarleton had seven children. Jane, their first-born, died in infancy. Thomas was born on July 6, 1753, and then on August 21, 1754, came Banastre. Both were named after their grandfathers. John was born on October 26, 1755. William was born in 1758 and died at the age of twenty. Bridget, named for her grandmother, was born on May 26, 1760; and on September 5, 1762, Clayton was born and named for the related Clayton family.

John Tarleton, Senior, was enterprising and highly successful. He owned large shipping interests, had plantations on Jamaica, Curaçao, and several other islands of the West Indies, and with John Backhouse formed the trading firm of Tarleton and Backhouse. He considered himself a seafaring man and had his only portrait painted in the cabin of one of his ships. The foundation of his fortune was laid in the slave trade, and his West Indian property was highly profitable. Out of family pride he purchased the old seat at Aigburth, and then Bolesworth Castle, which, in the hands of his son Thomas, became the center of the Tarleton family.

As John Tarleton, Senior, prospered, he grew in popularity. Often, especially in election pasquinades, he was called "Great T." In 1764 he was elected mayor of Liverpool. There ended his popularity and his political career, for when he attempted to stand for Parliament in 1768, rioting whalemen from the Mersey used their long-handled skinning knives to prevent his appearance upon the Liverpool hustings.

The sons of Mayor Tarleton grew up and attended school in Liverpool. While the city could not boast an academy or noted public school, it supported a free school until the beginning of the nineteenth century. Undoubtedly Banastre attended that school. In presenting a petition signed by 10,000 people of Liverpool in 1795, he said before Parliament: "From the town where I was born, and by the people amongst whom I was educated, I was sent a representative to Parliament."

In school he was popular. During the campaign for Parliament in 1790, a friend, signing his letter only as "Liberty," wrote: "During the Colonel's minority, he has had frequent opportunities of gaining Friendship from his scholastic acquaintance. The author is an old school fellow of the Gallant Tarleton, and as such will do the utmost in his power to be his friend. Consider, my Brother Freemen, that as School-fellows and Citizens there is a tie that Human Nature cannot efface."

Banastre was intelligent and uncommonly strong and active. Most of his time was spent on the cricket field, where he was a noted batsman, and his playing popularized the game in Liverpool. He was not a good student, but he was well grounded in Latin. He was fond of acting and speaking, and so his father marked him for the law. When Banastre was almost sixteen his father took him to London, and there on April 10, 1770, he registered his name on the rolls of the Middle Temple.

Three sons of Mayor Tarleton were educated at Oxford. Perhaps because their father had hired a tutor to prepare them for entrance into the University, Thomas and Banastre went up to Oxford together in the fall of 1771. But they matriculated at colleges on opposite sides of High Street.

Banastre entered University College. In the *Bursar's Book*, on November 2, 1771, he wrote in a neat, firm hand:

> 1771   *Ego Banastre Tarleton filius*
> Sup.Ord: *Natu secundus Johannis de*
> Com:Nov: *Liverpool, Armigeri in Comitatu*
>   *Lancastriensis lubens subscribo*
>   *Sub tutamine Magestri Scott*
>   *Annos Natus Septen decim.*

Thomas matriculated at Brasenose College on November 4, 1771. Eight years later, on October 18, 1779, Clayton matriculated at Oriel College.

University College was in its halcyon days. The Reverend Doctor Nathan Wetherell was master and he had gathered around him a group of brilliant young dons. Outstanding were Robert Chambers, William Jones, and the brothers from Newcastle-on-Tyne, William and John Scott.

Law was the special field of the faculty of University College, and they made their college the center of law study for Oxford University. In 1762 Robert Chambers had succeeded the venerable Sir William Blackstone as the Vinerian professor of Law for the University. This professorship he held until 1773, when he was appointed judge of the Supreme Court of Bengal. William Jones, the Orientalist, had just published his *Persian Grammar*, but was now reading law, in preparation for an appointment as judge of the High Court of Calcutta. And John Scott delivered lectures as assistant to the Vinerian professor, training for the day when as the great jurist, Lord Eldon, he would become Lord High Chancellor of England.

William Scott, the most brilliant of these young professors, was appointed tutor for Banastre Tarleton. Then a teacher of Greek, Scott was soon to be elected Camden professor of History for the University. He had already received the degree of Bachelor of Laws, but was continuing his studies, to receive from the Middle Temple in 1780 the degree of Doctor of Civil Laws. Ultimately he became Lord Stowell, the international jurist and great judge of admiralty law.

In such an atmosphere law and politics became the theme of conversation and dreams, and several of Banastre's friends at University College later rose to national prominence. James Bland Burgess was elected to Parliament and supported Wilberforce against Tarleton in the great anti-slavery debates. James Plumer, after long service in Parliament, became Master of the Rolls.

The student of University College with whom Banastre remained most intimately associated throughout their lives was Francis Rawdon, oldest son of Sir John Rawdon of Moira, County Down, Ireland. The thin, gangling young Irishman had attended Harrow and on August 7, 1771, had been gazetted ensign in the 15th Regiment of Foot Soldiers. He matriculated at University College on October 23, 1771, and remained at Oxford until 1773. He then joined his regiment and sailed for

America. After his father had been created Earl of Moira in the Irish peerage, Francis became known as Lord Rawdon.

Life at University College was easy and happy. So learned and witty was the conversation in the common room that on one occasion Dr. Samuel Johnson, a warm friend of Chambers and William Scott, sat with the dons and students and drank three bottles of port "without being the worse for it."

Banastre had neither the ambition nor the temperament to strive for First Honors. Most of his time was spent on the playing fields around Oxford. He was a leading figure in riding, boxing, tennis, and cricket. Undoubtedly he swam and punted along the lazy stretches of the Cherwell. Perhaps he even pulled an oar in the University College shell on the Isis.

After two years came an abrupt end to the carefree days at Oxford. On September 6, 1773, old John Tarleton died, and in his will he left Banastre a legacy of £5000. With this small fortune Banastre, probably on the advice of tutor William Scott, posted off to London to begin the study of law in the Middle Temple. "He continued his studies for some time, but not with that assiduity which is necessary for success in such an arduous and sedentary course of life. And Congreve and Farquhar were much more his study than Coke upon Littleton, or the abridgement of the Statutes!"

This enthusiasm for Congreve and Farquhar and constant attendance upon the theater led to a hilarious impromptu. Rising from his seat in Drury Lane during an intermission, with the utter nonchalance of a seasoned prankster, Banastre leaned over the rail of his box, and, to the astonishment and delight of the audience, delivered a whimsical *eulogium* upon a near kinsman!

After two years of neglecting his studies, roistering around Drury Lane, and gambling at the Cocoa Tree, the fashionable club in St. James's Street, Tarleton abandoned law and withdrew from the Middle Temple. "Being of a lively disposition and rather involved in his circumstances, he had recourse to the Army, as a profession in which, from his natural activity and courage, he would be sure of making his fortune or dying in the pursuit of it," said the October 14, 1780, *London Chronicle*.

Maria Elizabeth Robinson was more explicit: "With a volatile disposition and a lively genius, he was soon drawn by gay companions into a vortex of fashionable amusements, and by the eager pursuit of them, exhausted his finances. In this situation he turned his thoughts to the military line, and being intimate with several gentlemen of the Army, expressed a desire to go to America."

Opportunity came quickly. In the spring of 1775 John Trotter, having purchased a commission as lieutenant, put up for sale his commission as cornet in the 1st Regiment of Dragoon Guards.

For a restless, active young man this was a rare opportunity. The 1st or King's Dragoon Guards was among the most distinguished regiments in the British Army. In the British cavalry the cornet was the commissioned officer of lowest rank, but he had the conspicuous duty of carrying the pennant, or cornet. Under the regulations established in 1765 for the sale of commissions, the price was £100 for each shilling of pay per diem. As the pay of a cornet in the Dragoon Guards was eight shillings a day, Mrs. Jane Tarleton had to offer at least £800 for the cornetcy.

Banastre Tarleton purchased his commission as cornet on April 20, 1775, and after a rousing farewell at the Cocoa Tree set out to join his regiment then quartered at Norwich. On May 2, under "Military Promotions," the London Gazette first published his name. If happy is he who finds his name correctly spelled in the dispatches, the young cornet had no cause for rejoicing: Banastre was spelled Banestier.

At Norwich, Banastre set about learning a soldier's duties. On July 24 he prepared and signed the muster roll of the 1st Company of the 1st Dragoon Guards. He passed it to Major Richard Peete, who signed it and then passed it on to their commanding officer, Lieutenant Colonel Robert Sloper. General John Mostyn was their colonel, and the King's Dragoons were locally known as Mostyn's Horse.

Cornet Tarleton's few months with Mostyn's Horse were spent in intensive and purposeful training. For on April 19, 1775, at Lexington, a village just outside Boston, Massachusetts, an aroused American militia had fired on the red-coated troops of the King. The British Army was alerted for possible duty overseas.

The Norwich Mercury kept the Dragoon Guards informed of the steps being taken to quell the unrest in the Colonies. It reported that on April 27, 1775, Major Generals William Howe, Henry Clinton, and John Burgoyne sailed for America aboard the Cerebus. General Charles Lee, who had fought in America under Braddock, resigned his commission in the English Army on June 22, renounced his half-pay, and joined the rebellion. On October 17 the Norwich Mercury reported that the 16th Regiment of Light Dragoons had been ordered to prepare for service in America. And on November 4 it reported that five regiments of infantry were to be sent out immediately under Major General Lord Cornwallis.

When Major Peete prepared the muster rolls of the First Dragoon Guards on December 24, 1775, he marked Cornet Tarleton "Absent by King's leave." The fledgling dragoon had volunteered for overseas duty under Lord Cornwallis.

On his way to embarkation at Portsmouth, the erstwhile student at the Middle Temple passed through London. Attired in the handsome uniform of the Dragoon Guards, with its scarlet coat, and wearing an enormous saber, he strutted around to the Cocoa Tree. As he and his friends discussed the prospective war in America, the conversation drifted to General Charles Lee. In a burst of excitement, Cornet Tarleton sprang to his feet, swung the great saber over his head, and, to the astonishment of the more pacific visitors to the Cocoa Tree, cried: "With this sword I'll cut off General Lee's head!"

ᴄᴛᴏ

The transports from Portsmouth and their convoying warships met in rendezvous at Cork, Ireland. Slowly the expedition assembled. Lord Cornwallis arrived and went aboard the *Bristol* with Commodore Sir Peter Parker. On February 12, 1776, the fleet hoisted sail.

After a stormy voyage it arrived at Cape Fear, North Carolina. By ten o'clock on the night of May 3 Lord Cornwallis had disembarked and was marching his troops into Fort Johnson. Cornet Tarleton, only a junior officer lost in the ruck of a great amphibious operation, left no record of his first impressions of the New World.

At Cape Fear, Sir Henry Clinton took command of the expedition and moved to subdue the Southern Colonies. On June 4, 1776, the British fleet dropped anchor off the bar of Charleston, South Carolina. The only obstruction to its immediate descent upon the city was a sorry little fort of palmetto logs and dirt near the southern end of Sullivan's Island.

In the fort lay 375 troops of the Continental line, reinforced by the South Carolina militia under Colonel William Moultrie, all under the command of General Charles Lee. On June 28 Sir Peter Parker moved his warships down the channel to reduce the fort. But the pilots grounded three ships in the van. To save her from capture the crew destroyed the *Acteon*. The terrific fire from the *Experiment* and the *Bristol* fell ineffective on the palmetto logs, but the slow, calculated fire from the fort did great damage in the ships. It killed the captain of the *Bristol*, wounded Sir Peter, and drew blood from Lord Cornwallis himself with a flying splinter. By evening there was no hope of reducing or capturing the fort, and Sir Peter drew off the fleet.

Now Cornet Tarleton had heard guns roaring and seen the dead and the dying. He had also seen delay and bungling turn victory into fiasco— an especially rewarding lesson for an ambitious young officer.

After three weeks spent in probing raids around Charleston, Sir Henry Clinton abandoned his plans; and on July 20 Sir Peter Parker headed north to join the armada gathering in New York Harbor. On August 1 he came to anchor opposite New Utrecht. Lord Cornwallis disembarked his troops on Staten Island.

In the harbor lay 400 transports and 37 warships under command of Vice Admiral Lord Richard Howe. On Staten Island 30,000 troops were concentrated under his brother, Lieutenant General William Howe. The brothers had been entrusted with negotiating a settlement with the Colonies.

But stiff-necked British pride made them address letters to "George Washington, Esquire." Washington refused to open them. He wrote to General Horatio Gates: "Lord Howe is arrived. He and the General, his brother, are appointed commissioners to dispense pardons to repenting sinners."

Washington had about 20,000 troops in the vicinity of New York. Their fortified line began at Harlem Heights, stretched across Manhattan, and ended at Brooklyn Heights, Long Island. Nearly a third of the American army lay in the fortifications around Brooklyn. After fruitless negotiations, General Howe decided to crush their left flank.

The Royal Navy ferried the Grenadier Guards over to Gravesend Bay, Long Island, on August 20, and in four days had transferred a supporting army of 20,000 soldiers. At nine o'clock on the night of August 26 General Howe began moving his army across Long Island. To the left he sent a corps under General James Grant. In the center he placed General Knyphausen and the Hessians. To the right he sent the bulk of the army under Sir Henry Clinton. And the reserve he posted in the rear under Lord Cornwallis.

With incredible luck, General Howe found Jamaica Pass unguarded and marched his army silently around the left flank and to the rear of the Americans. As soon as the battle opened and they realized that they were caught between two armies, the Americans abandoned the field and fled to their forts in Brooklyn.

Where was Cornet Tarleton? Perhaps in reserve with Lord Cornwallis. He may have seen action, for his Lordship finally rushed his troops up and joined in the pursuit. Howe contented himself with picking up Generals Sullivan, Stirling, and Woodhull. But so complete was the debacle that even the women camp followers dashed out and hauled in fleeing Americans.

General Howe delayed and attempted conciliation for more than two weeks. When this proved futile, Admiral Howe sent warships into East River to cover a landing at Kip's Bay. At daylight on September 15 assault boats began fanning out from Long Island. While the naval sharpshooters in the rigging picked off unwary Americans, the barges swept ashore and the Hessians hit the beaches.

Again panic seized the defenders. Toward Harlem Heights they fled, their speed doubled by a false cry of "Here come the dragoons!" Seeing his soldiers high-tailing across Manhattan, Washington threw his hat on the ground and cried, "Are these the men I am to defend America with?" Then spurring his horse into the fugitives, he rained blows upon men and officers. He even caned a stampeding brigadier general!

After seizing New York, the British struck at Harlem Heights, were repulsed, and then rested until October 12. Leaving Knyphausen in New York, Howe put part of his troops in boats, pushed through Hell Gate, and landed at Throgg's Neck. Having been outflanked, General Washington left 2000 men at Fort Washington in Harlem and began retreating toward White Plains.

Lieutenant Colonel William Harcourt had arrived from England with the 16th Regiment of Light Dragoons, and Tarleton immediately volunteered for duty with him. Howe used his dragoons for scouts and advance guards as he moved toward White Plains.

The flashing sabers of these horsemen spread terror among the Americans. Washington who had not yet learned their value, even though General Charles Lee wrote vehemently, "For God's sake send me some cavalry," on October 27 issued a Special Order of encouragement against the red-coated monsters. "And as an encouragement to any brave parties who will endeavor to surprise some of them, the General offers one hundred dollars for every Trooper, with his horse and accoutrements, which shall be brought in."

The reward of $100 in greenback was not worth a Continental. Next day, when they saw the light dragoons cantering in front of Howe's advancing troops, the American pickets forgot their general's Special Order and fled to the rear.

The royal gunners opened against Chatterton's Hill. The second shot tore a hole in the thigh of a Massachusetts militiaman. His screams inspired his entire regiment to join the pickets in the rear. In fifteen minutes Colonel Rall's Hessians were parading across the summit of the hill. The British had won the battle of White Plains.

Thereafter the British sat inactive while the Americans fortified and moved into North Castle. When questioned about his inactivity, General Howe pleaded political considerations. Lord Cornwallis replied: "From political motives it is impossible for either the General or myself to explain the reasons."

From White Plains General Howe turned back to reduce Fort Washington. Suspecting his purpose, Washington left General Charles Lee in command of the army. Crossing the Hudson at King's Ferry with a small contingent, he rode down to Fort Lee. From there he saw regiment after regiment of Britons and Hessians closing in on Fort Washington. On November 16 Knyphausen's Hessians carried the fortifications with the bayonet.

Washington then ordered General Nathanael Greene to abandon Fort Lee. Greene moved so reluctantly that on the night of November 19 Lord Cornwallis suddenly threw 4500 troops across the Hudson near Dobb's Ferry and marched swiftly against the fort. Greene could scarcely save his men.

Washington now began his long retreat across New Jersey with Lord Cornwallis in hot pursuit. At Brunswick the Americans paused so long that their rear guard saw the advance guard of British dragoons enter the town. Washington wrote letter after letter to General Charles Lee, urging him to bring the troops from North Castle. But Lee followed plans of his own.

After ordering Cornwallis to wait for reinforcements, Howe joined him at Brunswick. They renewed the pursuit on December 6 and on December 7 were at Trenton. But their quarry had escaped. On December 8, 1776, Washington and his troops crossed the Delaware River. Cornwallis prowled along the river for thirteen miles looking for boats. Then he sent his soldiers into winter quarters in Trenton and Princeton.

General Lee finally obeyed Washington's orders and in early December crossed the Hudson with 4000 men. By December 8 he had meandered down to Morristown, New Jersey. There he remained until December 11, meditating whether to follow Washington over the Delaware or to strike the British at Brunswick or Princeton. He moved southward. On the night of December 12 he told General John Sullivan, exchanged and again in command, to lead the army toward Philadelphia.

Lee had decided to spend that night at White's Tavern at Basking Ridge. As the tavern lay some three miles from camp, he took a guard of about a dozen Continental troops. With him were his aide, Major William Bradford, and Major James Wilkinson, a courier with dispatches from General Gates. Also with him were two French volunteers: Captain Jean Louis de Virnejoux and Lieutenant Colonel the Sieur Gaiault de Boisbertrand.

Lord Cornwallis knew of the approach of Lee's army. From Pennington, near Princeton, on December 12 he detached a scouting party and sent it northward to locate the advancing Americans. For this hazardous operation in unfamiliar country, he chose Lieutenant Colonel Harcourt, and Harcourt picked four officers and twenty-five troopers from the 16th Light Dragoons. Ensign Glyn wrote in his *Journal* on December 13: "Lt. Col. Harcourt with a party of Light Dragoons having the Cornets Geary and Tarleton with him, was detached from Trenton beyond Pennington, to gain intelligence of the Rebel General Lee's Corps, which was supposed to be about Rocky Hill."

On the morning of December 13 General Sullivan marched Lee's army off toward the juncture with the troops under Washington. Careless and unafraid, General Lee lingered at White's Tavern, catching up with correspondence. He had just written and sanded a letter to General Gates, saying of Washington: " . . . *entre nous*, a certain great man is damnably deficient—unless something which I do not expect turns up we are lost."

He was lost, even though something did turn up. Through a window Major Wilkinson saw the flash of red-coated horsemen bearing down upon the tavern in full gallop, Cornet Tarleton at their head.

There was wild shooting and loud cursing at the front door of White's Tavern. Twenty minutes later General Charles Lee was bound behind a British trooper, and with Harcourt in the van and Tarleton bringing up the rear, the 16th Light Dragoons, which Lee had once commanded so gallantly in Portugal, were riding hell-for-leather toward Princeton.

Although Banastre Tarleton had not cut off Lee's head as he had boasted he would in the Cocoa Tree, he was largely instrumental in the capture of the General known as the Palladium of America. He captured and personally escorted into camp Lieutenant Colonel Boisbertrand. The British were elated. In their celebration they even got Lee's horse drunk.

With the approach of Christmas the young Cornet had begun to feel nostalgia and on December 18 wrote a long letter to his mother. In it he gave the best account ever written of the capture of General Charles Lee.

                                                            Prince's Town Dec. 18 1776

My dear Madam

   Our Correspondence is totally stopt, so few Ships go to & come from England on Acct. of the Quantity of American Privateers that this Continent seems utterly secluded from Great Britain.

   You will with Pleasure, if you receive it, read this Letter. Lieutenant General Earl Cornwallis, under whose Command the King's Army has penetrated into the Jerseys as far as the River Delaware, being ignorant of General Lee's Motions & Situation, gave Orders on the 11th Inst. for a Party of the Queen's Light Dragoons, consisting of a Captain, 2 Subalterns & 25 Privates to be ready to march in expedition Order the next morning. Colonel Harcourt who was with the Regiment received his private Orders from Lord Cornwallis, together with Captain Eustace, his Lordship's Aid de Camp, who attended us on this Expedition. Our first Day's march was 18 miles: but barren of Incidents; we took up our Quarters at Night at Hillsborough upon the River Millstone. A Battalion of the 71st covered us at that Place—Our House caught fire at 1 o'clock in the morning & burnt to the Ground—We escaped without loss or damage—we bedded ourselves in Straw till 5 o'clock. We then received Orders to march. Col. Harcourt gave me the advanced Guard, consisting of 6 men: A Circumstance I ever shall esteem as one of the most fortunate of my Life. We marched by different & cross Roads, towards Maurice Town. We had not proceeded above 14 miles, before the advanced Guard discovered some & took one Rebel in Arms. We march'd 2 Miles forward, then Colonel Harcourt found by some People that General Lee was not above 4 or 5 Miles distant from the detachment, & at the same time heard that our Retreat was cut off by the Road we had come. He detached Captain Nash with 4 Dragoons back to prove the truth of the last information. Colonel Harcourt then order'd me to advance. We trotted on about 3 Miles when my advanced Guard seized 2 Sentrys without firing a Gun. The Dread of instant death obliged these Fellows to inform me, to the best of their Knowledge of the Situation of General Lee. They told us he was about a mile off, that his Guard was not very large & that he was about half a mile in the Rear of his Army. These men were so confused that they gave us but an imperfect idea where General Lee was. Colonel Harcourt immediately detached me with 2 men only to the top of an Eminence in the Road, to get what Intelligence I could, & if much fired upon immediately to retreat upon him. In going quick to the Ground I observ'd a Yankee Light Horseman, at whom I rush'd & made Prisoner. I brought him in to Colonel Harcourt; the Fear of the Sabre extorted great Intelligence, & he told us he had just left General Lee from whom he had an Express to carry to General Sullivan at Pukamin. He could not satisfy me exactly as to the Strength of General Lee's Guard, but confirmed the Account of the other 2 Prisoners as to his Situation.

He said he thought his guard did not consist of above 30 Men. He pointed out to us the House where he had left General Lee & mentioned that he was going to move directly.

Colonel Harcourt call'd to Eustace, to know whether he thought we were strong enough? Eustace reply'd in the Affirmative. Without further Consultation I was order'd to lead on my advanc'd Guard which consisted of only 5 Men as quick as possible. I went on at full Speed, when perceiving two Sentrys at a Door & a loaded Waggon I push'd at them, making all the Noise I cöuld. The Sentrys were struck with a Panic, dropped their Arms and fled. I order'd my Men to fire into the House thro' every Window & Door, & cut up as many of the Guard as they could. An old Woman upon her Knees begg'd for Life and told me General Lee was in the House.

This Assurance gave me Pleasure. I carry'd on my Attack with all possible Spirit & surrounded the House; tho' fired upon in front, flank & rear. Colonel Harcourt had by this time brought up the rest of the Dragoons; he pushed on to an Eminence, to observe and prevent any Surprise from General Lee's Army. He then detached Lieutenant Leigh with Dragoons to cut up all the Men in my Rear—General Lee's Aid de Camp, 2 French Colonels & some of the Guard kept up a Fire for about 8 Minutes, which we silenced. I fir'd twice through the Door of the House & then addressed myself to this effect: "I knew Genl. Lee was in the House, that if he would surrender himself, he & his Attendants should be safe, but if my Summons was not comply'd with immediately, the House should be burnt & every Person without Exception, should be put to the Sword." At this Instant I was called by one of my men to the back Door, my Attention being directly engaged by his saying that Genl. Lee was escaping that Way & I gallop'd to the Spot. The French Colonels, one of the Aid de Camp (the other being shot) & some of the Guard attempted to retreat Sword in Hand. We took one Colonel Prisoner, the rest were killed or wounded. Genl. Lee surrendered himself to the Sentry I had plac'd at the front Door, whilst we were employ'd as above. The *Prisoner* was led to Col. Harcourt, who was silencing the Fires

in my Rear & Flanks whilst I carried on the Attack upon Genl.
Lee's Quarters with the advanced Guard only. Col. Harcourt
placed his noble Prisoner upon a Horse & led him off by a different Road from that which we had come with all possible Expedition. The Bugle Horn was then sounded. I brought up the rear
of the men & the French Colonel. This Attack which continued
in the whole about 15 Minutes proved fatal to none of the Officers
or Dragoons. One Horse's Leg which was slightly graz'd & one
Saddle which was shot through the Pommel were the only Damages we sustained. We retreated afterwards 13 miles thro' an
Enemys Country without any Accident. We then forded a River,
approached Hillsborough & gave each other Congratulations with
every Symptom of Joy.

Captain Nash whom I mentioned being detached did not join
us again till Genl. Lee was our Prisoner. He was beat back from
the Place where we had passed in the morning & where they meant
to cut off our Retreat. He lost a Servant & a Horse. The Party
returned safe.

This is a most miraculous Event—it appears like a Dream. We
conducted Genl. Lee & the French Col. to Lord Cornwallis at
Penning. Our day's march only exceeded 60 Miles.

Genl. Lee is sent Prisoner to Brunswick. Colonel Harcourt's
whole Conduct was masterly—it deserves every Applause. Present
my Love, Comps. &c (I shall tire you if I write any more—).

I forgot to tell you that this Coup de Main has put an end to the
Campaign. We have not yet crossed the Delaware. The Queen's
Regt. of Lt. Dragoons are canton'd off Princes Town & Brunswick; at the former exists one who will always be proud to subscribe himself

Your affectionate Son
Banastre Tarleton

3
Mary

*W*IND WHISTLED around the dark pinnacles of the minster tower, and rain beat in torrents against the casement windows of the minster house. Inside, in her warm bedchamber, lay a woman in labor. Here, on the night of November 27, 1758, Mary Darby was born into a life of tempest and tears.

Mary was the daughter of Mr. and Mrs. John Darby, of Bristol, England. Mr. Darby was a man of wealth, a member of the mercantile firm of Miller and Elton, an adventurous American whose grandfather, in order to inherit an Irish estate, had changed the family name from Mac-Dermott. Mrs. Darby was a woman of culture, a descendant of highly respected Richard Seys, of Boverton Castle, Glamorganshire. Mary was the third of the Darby children: John, Elizabeth, Mary, William, and George.

The Darby home sat beside the crumbling old monastery of the monks of St. Augustine. The front faced a small garden opening on the minster green. The west side was bounded by the Cathedral, and the back opened on the ancient cloisters. Said Mary, "A spot more calculated to inspire the soul with mournful meditation can scarcely be found amidst the monuments of antiquity."

Mary spent her early years close to the minster. She wandered through its aisles, sat on its stairways, and dreamed childhood's dreams to the sound of its pealing organ and its chanting choir. While her brothers played on the green, she often crept into the minster and sat beneath the great eagle which held up the Bible.

At the age of five Mary entered school. She quickly learned to read and then passed delighted hours in reading and memorizing the epitaphs and inscriptions on the monuments around the minster. The melancholy and mournful fascinated her: by the time she was seven she had memorized Pope's "Lines to the Memory of an Unfortunate Lady" and Mason's "Elegy on the Death of the Countess of Coventry."

Mr. Darby gave his talented little daughter a Kirkman harpsichord, and she studied music under Edmund Broadrip. "The only melody which pleased me was that of the mournful and touching kind." Her two favorite songs were John Gay's " 'Twas When the Sea was Roaring" and Lord Lyttelton's "The Heavy Hours."

Mary next attended the famous school which Miss Hannah More and her sisters ran in Bristol. Here her playmates were the daughters of a Shakespearean actor named Powell. During the year Miss More took her pupils to see *King Lear*, in which Mr. and Mrs. Powell played Lear and Cordelia. Mary Darby saw her first Shakespearean heroine in the provincial theater in Bristol.

How happy were those days! "My clothes were sent for from London; my fancy was indulged to the extent of its caprices; I was flattered and praised into a belief that I was a being of a superior order. To sing, to play a lesson on the harpsichord, to recite an elegy, and to make doggerel verses, made the extent of my occupations, while my person improved, and my mother's indulgence was almost unexampled."

But the wheel of fortune turned. John Darby, restless, with a love for the sea in his blood, mortgaged all of his property and sailed away to start a whaling factory in Labrador. In dreams he saw it rivaling the whaling industry of Greenland. Unknown to Mrs. Darby, a "young and artful woman" named Elenor dared the voyage with him. After two years the whaling business failed, sweeping away Darby's mortgaged assets in England; and the natives destroyed his property in Labrador. By the time Mrs. Darby had heard about the scandal, John and Elenor were on their way to new adventure in America.

After an absence of several years, John Darby unexpectedly returned to England, summoned his family to London, placed John and Mary in a school in Chelsea, formally separated from Mrs. Darby, and returned to America. Said his fond daughter: "He possessed a soul brave, liberal, enlightened and ingenuous. He felt the impropriety of his conduct. Yet, though his mind was strongly organized, though his understanding was capacious, and his sense of honour delicate even to fastidiousness, he was still the dupe of his passions, the victim of an unfortunate attachment."

The school in Chelsea was run by "one of the most extraordinary women that ever graced, or disgraced society: her name was Meribah Lorrington. She was the most extensively accomplished female that I ever remember to have met," wrote Mary. She was mistress of the French and Italian languages as well as of Latin; was a mathematician and astronomer; and was a painter of skill. "All that I ever learned I acquired from this extraordinary woman."

Mary romped through the field of literature and chatted about books and authors whenever Mrs. Lorrington was sober. "I applied rigidly to study, and acquired a taste for books, which has never, from that time, deserted me. Mrs. Lorrington frequently read to me after school hours, and I to her: I sometimes indulged my fancy in writing verses, or composing rebuses; and my governess never failed to applaud the juvenile compositions I presented to her. Some of them, which I preserved and printed in a small volume shortly after my marriage, were written when I was between twelve and thirteen years of age; but as love was the theme of my poetical phantasies, I never showed them to my mother, till I was about to publish them."

After the failure of Mrs. Lorrington's school, Mrs. Darby sent Mary to a seminary run by Mrs. Leigh. But John Darby became remiss. Months passed without money from him, and, in order to support her children, Mrs. Darby set up a boarding school for girls in Little Chelsea. She rented a house and furnished it, and then she hired assistants and teachers. To Mary, now fourteen but much older in appearance, she intrusted the teaching of grammar and the selection of the readings in English prose and poetry.

Ten or twelve girls enrolled in Mrs. Darby's school. But just as it gave promise of flourishing, it was disbanded by the return of John Darby. "The pride of his soul was deeply wounded by the step which my mother had taken; he considered his name as disgraced, his conjugal reputation tarnished," wrote Mary. "At the expiration of eight months my mother, by my father's positive command, broke up her establishment, and returned to London."

John Darby and Elenor settled in Green Street, Grosvenor Square, and Mrs. Darby and her children took lodgings near Marylebone. There was scant provision, but Mrs. Darby was able to send Mary to finishing school at Oxford House.

"My early love for lyric harmony had led me to a fondness for the more sublime scenes of dramatic poetry," said Mary. She read; she memorized; she recited. "I even fancied that I could compose a tragedy, and more than once unsuccessfully attempted the arduous undertaking." Finally, Mrs. Hervey, the headmistress, mentioned Mary's flair for dramatic exhibitions to Mr. Hussey, the dancing master.

Hussey introduced his pupil to Mr. Hull, of Covent Garden Theater. Hull gave her an audition, in which Mary recited passages in the character of Jane Shore. He seemed delighted with her voice and her beauty. But Covent Garden already had a large contingent of ingenues, and nothing came of the audition. By then John Darby had returned to America, and Mrs. Darby was living in Chancery Lane, "for the advantage of the protection which a venerable and respectable friend," Mr. Samuel Cox, a solicitor, offered her. At her request, Mr. Cox, an intimate friend of the famed David Garrick, told the old actor about the ambitious girl. Garrick gave them an appointment, and Mr. Cox took Mary to the actor's home in the Adelphi.

During the evening the beautiful girl completely won Garrick's heart. Mary had just completed her fifteenth year, and he admired her tall, slender, graceful figure, and her blue eyes and her auburn hair. He liked her voice—said it reminded him of that of his favorite, Mrs. Susannah Cibber. So delighted was Garrick that he determined to introduce Mary Darby in a play at Drury Lane. For her debut he decided on the supreme test: Mary as Cordelia to Garrick's world-famed King Lear!

"My tutor was most sanguine in his expectations of my success, and every rehearsal seemed to strengthen his flattering opinion," wrote Mary. It was the year of the old veteran's retirement, but he worked eagerly with the ingenue. "He would sometimes dance a minuet with me, sometimes request me to sing the favourite ballads of the day," she recorded. "Never shall I forget the enchanting hours which I passed in Mr. Garrick's society: he appeared to me as one who possessed more power, both to awe and to attract, than any man I ever met with."

ᏣᏬ

In a house opposite that of Mrs. Darby dwelled John Vernon, a noted solicitor. With him lived several of his clerks. One of these was a well-built young man, with handsome countenance overcast by melancholy and languor. From his window he flirted sedately with the would-be actress, and Mary found him strangely attractive.

Among the Darbys' friends was a young attorney named Wayman. One evening he proposed a trip to Greenwich. For the outing Mary donned a dress of pale blue lustring and a chip hat trimmed with pale blue ribbons. When they arrived at the Star and Garter Inn at Greenwich, who should come forward to assist Mary from the carriage but the handsome young man. Said she: "I was confused: but my mother was indignant!"

Wayman introduced his friend as Thomas Robinson, Esquire. He dined with the party and remained with them until they returned to London. "During the remainder of the evening, Mr. Wayman expatiated on the many good qualities of his friend, Mr. Robinson: spoke of his future expectations from a rich old uncle; of his probable advancement in his profession; and, more than all, of his enthusiastic admiration of me."

Soon afterward Mary's brother George became dangerously ill of smallpox. Handsome young Robinson was indefatigable in his attention. "Day and night Mr. Robinson devoted himself to the task of consoling my mother, and of attending to her darling boy; hourly, and indeed momentarily, Mr. Robinson's praises were reiterated by my mother. He was the 'kindest, the best of mortals!' The least addicted to worldly follies—and the man, of all others, whom she should adore as a son-in-law."

As George recovered, Mary sickened. Instead of making her debut at Drury Lane in the character of Cordelia, she came down with small-pox. Thomas now pressed his courtship. "It was when a destructive dis-order menaced my features, and the few graces that nature had lent them, that he professed a disinterested fondness: every day he attended with the zeal of a brother; and that zeal made an impression of grati-tude upon my heart, which was the source of all my succeeding sor-rows."

The attention of Thomas Robinson and the persuasion of Mrs. Darby won Mary's consent. The marriage banns were published in St. Martin-in-the-Fields on three successive Sundays, while Mary, only fifteen years and four months old, still lay in her sickbed. The wedding day was set for April 12, 1774; but Robinson insisted that because his articles to Messrs. Vernon and Elderton still lacked three months of expiration, the wedding ceremony be kept secret. Mrs. Darby consented. She ac-companied the lovers to St. Martin's Church, and in the presence of Mrs. Darby, the clerk, and a charwoman, Thomas and Mary were mar-ried by the venerable Dr. Saunders.

"I was dressed in the habit of a Quaker, a society to which, in early youth, I was particularly partial," said Mary.

After a ten-day honeymoon at Maidenhead and Henley-upon-Thames, Thomas and Mary returned to London. Mary and Mrs. Darby took a house in Great Queen Street, Lincoln's-Inn-Fields, while Thomas con-tinued to live with Mr. Vernon. Soon the secret bride began to learn of her husband's deception. Thomas Robinson was already of age, and he still had to serve several months of his clerkship. He was not the heir to a handsome fortune, but the illegitimate son of a Mr. Harris in South Wales.

A few months after the marriage, Mrs. Darby demanded that the union be announced, for Mary had begun showing pregnancy. So Robinson set out for Wales to break the news to his father. Leaving his wife and her mother in Bristol, he went on to the home of Mr. Harris at Tregunter. Mary rejoiced to be again near the gloomy minster, with its organ, its choir, and its great brass eagle holding up the Bible. "I longed again to occupy my place beneath its expanding wings, and once I went, before the service began, to gratify my inclination."

Mr. Harris received Thomas and his bride with becoming grace, jok-ingly intimating that despite his three score and more years he should have liked Mary for his wife had she not married Tom: "I was his idol; he would dance with me; when he had taken the evening draught he would sing with me, and I was to him the most delightful of beings."

But not to his mistress and his daughter! Mrs. Molly Robinson and her daughter felt none of the enthusiasm of the old Squire of Tregunter. Miss Robinson was a sedate Methodist, and she tired of her lighthearted sister-in-law. Mrs. Molly was sullen and crabbed. "I was taunted perpetually on the folly of appearing like a woman of fortune," said Mary. According to the Robinsons: "A lawyer's wife had no right to dress like a Duchess; and that, though I might be very accomplished, a good housewife had no occasion for harpsichords and books."

Upon their return to London, Mr. and Mrs. Thomas Robinson settled at No. 13, Hatton Garden, which they furnished with elegance. They bought a handsome phaeton. Thomas bought saddle horses, and Mary purchased a wardrobe of fashionable and expensive clothes.

Then, dressing herself in a gown of light brown lustring and doing up her auburn curls without powder, the young wife put on a jaunty white chip hat and set off for Ranelagh Gardens in Chelsea.

Mary next went to the Pantheon. For the outing she wore pale pink satin trimmed with broad sable. Said she: "The splendour of the scene, the dome illuminated with variegated lamps, the music, and the beauty of the women, seemed to present a circle of enchantment."

As she sat on a sofa, she overheard a handsome young gallant ask the Marchioness Townshend, "Who is she?"

"I think I know her," replied the Earl of Northington, who had been a legal adviser of John Darby. "Miss Darby, or am I mistaken?"

Lord Northington presented Lord Lyttelton, and the nobleman, whom Mary described as "the most accomplished libertine that any age or country has produced," began pursuit of the young wife. His attentions were exciting and flattering. But Mary recorded: "His manners were overbearingly insolent, his language licentious, and his person slovenly even to a degree that was disgusting."

Mary may have found Lord Lyttelton disgusting, but she did not avoid his society. At the Pantheon, he presented Count de Belgioso, the imperial ambassador. To the Robinson home he brought many friends, among them the celebrated actor, William Brereton, and the famed duelist, Fighting Fitzgerald.

In the company of Lord Lyttelton, Thomas Robinson gambled incessantly and neglected his profession and his wife. With Lyttelton he frequented the races at Ascot and Epsom, and his style of living caused comment among Mary's friends.

But Lord Lyttelton knew what he wanted. One morning, while Robinson was away from home, he visited the young wife. "I must inform you," he confided to Mary, "that your husband is the most false and undeserving of that name! He has formed a connection with a woman of abandoned character; he lavishes on her those means of subsistence which you will shortly stand in need of."

The distraught wife drove immediately to Soho to confront her husband's mistress. The strumpet was Harriet Wilmot, and she was proudly wearing a ring which Thomas had given her.

When Mary asked her if she was acquainted with Thomas Robinson, Harriet replied, "I am. He visits me frequently."

"I have nothing more to say," Mary answered.

"You are Mr. Robinson's wife," Harriet said in a trembling voice. "I am sure you are and probably this ring was yours. Pray receive it."

Mary declined the ring and turned to go.

"I never will see him more—unworthy man—I never will again receive him," whimpered Harriet.

Mary questioned her husband about Miss Wilmot, but he "threw all the blame for his indiscretion on Lord Lyttelton."

When Lord Lyttelton called, he found Mary alone and weeping. "Now, if you are a woman of spirit you will be revenged!" tempted the libertine. "You cannot be a stranger to my motives for thus cultivating the friendship of your husband; my fortune is at your disposal. Robinson is a ruined man; his debts are considerable, and nothing but destruction can await you. Leave him! Command my powers to serve you."

But Lord Lyttelton was "the very last man in the world for whom I could have entertained the smallest partiality." And later Mary swore: "God, who judges all hearts, will know how innocent I was of the smallest conjugal infidelity."

What Lord Lyttelton failed to achieve through seduction, Fighting Fitzgerald attempted through rape. Mary found that "his manners *toward women* were beautifully interesting." During a party at Vauxhall, in Lambeth, the Robinsons sat with him until early morning. When a row started near the orchestra, both men ran to the scene. Returning in a few minutes, Fitzgerald found Mary looking for Thomas. "Let me conduct you to the door," said he; "we shall certainly find him there."

At the entrance on the Vauxhall Road, Fitzgerald stopped abruptly. "A servant opened a chaise door, there were four horses harnessed to it; and, by the light of the lamps on the side of the footpath, I plainly perceived a pistol in the pocket of the door which was open," reported Mary. At that moment "Mr. Fitzgerald placed his arm around my waist, and endeavored to lift me up the step of the chaise."

Mary resisted and demanded to know what he meant. "His hand trembled excessively, while he said in a low voice: 'Robinson can but fight me.'"

Terrified, Mary broke loose and ran. "Here he comes," exclaimed the duelist with poised nonchalance. "We have found the wrong carriage, Mr. Robinson: we have been looking for you; and Mrs. Robinson is alarmed beyond expression."

Mary was frightened beyond expression. George Robert Fitzgerald killed eighteen men before the King's officers finally hanged him. "I valued my husband's safety," Mary said. "I therefore did not mention the adventure of the evening."

Ruin came as Lord Lyttelton knew it would. Thomas Robinson ran heavily into debt, and his creditors began demanding their money. Fearing arrest and debtor's prison, he slipped out of London and, with his wife, started for the home of Mr. Harris. What a different reception awaited them at Tregunter! As Mary entered his home, Mr. Harris greeted her: "Well! So you have escaped from a prison, and now you have come here to do penance for your follies? Well! and what do you want?" The women of the family were pleased to take his greeting as their cue.

He taunted the spendthrift couple: "How long do you think I will support you? What is to become of you in a prison? What business have beggars to marry?"

The crowning humiliation he reserved until several guests, including John and Charles Morgan, members of Parliament, were at his table. Then, in reply to a pleasantry that he had just finished Tregunter House in time for a nursery, he exclaimed: "No, no. They came here because prison doors were open to receive them!"

The expectant daughter-in-law was moved to Trevecca House at the foot of Sugar Loaf Mountain. "Here I enjoyed the sweet repose of solitude: Here I wandered about woods entangled by the wild luxuriance of nature, or roved upon the mountain's side, while the blue vapours floated round its summit," wrote Mary. "O, God of Nature! Sovereign of the universe of wonders! in those interesting moments how fervently did I adore Thee!"

At Trevecca House, on November 18, 1774, Mary bore her daughter. From the memory of the two little Darby girls in the minster of Bristol, she named her Maria Elizabeth.

The common folk were eager to see "the young squire's baby, the little heiress of Tregunter." So was Mr. Harris. Two days after her birth, he called: "Well! and what do you mean to do with your child?" After a pause: "I will tell you. Tie it to your back and work for it!" And gazing at the cringing mother he continued: "Prison doors are open. Tom will die in gaol. What is to become of you?"

When Maria Elizabeth was three weeks old, letters warned Thomas Robinson that his place of concealment was known and a warrant sworn for his arrest. So the youthful parents fled to the home of Mary's grandmother in Monmouth. "We were received with genuine affection; we were caressed with unfeigned hospitality."

In Monmouth they tarried for more than a month. Mary was happy with her baby and her kindred. They entertained her pleasantly. "But the most favorite amusement I selected, was that of wandering by the river Wye, or of exploring the antique remains of Monmouth Castle, a part of which reached the garden of my grandmother's habitation."

The Robinsons spent the Christmas season of 1774 with Mary's grandmother. Friends invited them to a ball. Mary had regained her strength and spirits since the birth of her baby and she entered into the gaiety and dancing. During the evening her grandmother brought Maria Elizabeth to an anteroom, and, flushed and excited, Mary nursed her. When she returned from the ball, she found her baby in convulsions.

All night the convulsions continued, and the frantic young mother sat with her baby in her arms. The doctor despaired. But during the morning a clergyman asked permission to try a simple home remedy. After a few minutes the spasms abated, and Maria Elizabeth fell into tranquil slumber.

But not Mary. During the strain and excitement, she became seriously ill. "I was in a raging fever; the effects of not having nourished my child during twelve hours began to endanger my own existence."

After her recovery, just as they were about to flee again, an execution for a considerable sum was served on Thomas Robinson. Instead of arresting him, the friendly sheriff of Monmouth accompanied the Robinsons back to London. There Robinson compounded with his creditors, signed promissory notes, and was released from custody. He resettled his family in Hatton Garden. But having learned little restraint from their embarrassment, the young husband and wife returned to their vanities— Thomas to the gambling tables of West End, and Mary to the parades of Vauxhall and Ranelagh.

4

The Mischianza

*H*AVING DRIVEN Washington's ragamuffins south of Delaware River, General Howe ordered the British troops into cantonments in Brunswick and Princeton. Believing the rebellion largely crushed, Howe gave Lord Cornwallis leave to visit his ailing wife in England. But before his Lordship could depart, Washington crossed the Delaware in a raging blizzard on Christmas day and next morning struck a withering blow at Colonel Rall's drunken Hessians in Trenton.

Cornwallis rushed back with 8000 picked troops. But during the night of January 2, 1777, Washington outfoxed him at Assunpink Creek and marched swiftly northward. As the Americans skirted Princeton, they brushed aside a regiment of British infantry and a dismounted squadron of the 16th Light Dragoons. After Washington's brilliant maneuver to gain the highlands around Morristown, Cornwallis retreated across Jersey and concentrated his forces at Amboy and Brunswick.

Cornet Tarleton spent the winter in Brunswick. After the excitement of the fall campaign, garrison duty was boring, and he wrote telling his mother so:

Brunswick, May 25, 1777

Dear Madam,

I wrote from here in Feb'y with news of part of our winter Manoeuvres. Our leaving Princes Town & our numerous foregoing Duties were mentioned.

Winter Quarters in America are stupid & afford no Description for the Pen—

My numerous Obligations to you couched in my Brother John's Letters fill me with confusion. I am asham'd of my past Conduct & am so sensibly affect'd by your goodness that I don't know how to thank—

The accounts you send me of the whole Family's Happiness give me great Pleasure. John who is an excellent young man will pay that strict attention to you, which you so amply deserve.

We daily expect now to be set in Motion—every thing wears the Face of a lively Campaign—Genl. Washington has drawn his Army together & is encamped about nine miles from us.

Ships we hear are just arrived from England with Recruits & Supplys. Both Parties are amused with petit skirmishes but nothing material has happen'd.

I have received from England the most flattering Letters from Lord Vaughan, & the strongest Recommendations to Genl. Vaughan from whom I have pleasing Expectations. Colonel Harcourt professes Friendship & says he will move Heaven & Earth in my Favour: My attention is to a Company of Foot as the most eligible method of Rise in my Profession. I have just received a Letter from Genl. Mostyn's Regiment indulging me with 12 months more Leave, for which they apply'd to the King. The Favor was granted. They congratulate me on my good Fortune in America, & wish me success as to Promotion.

Give Mr. Thos. all Happiness in the matrimonial Line, he hesitated long before he thrust his Neck into the Marriage Yoke.

My beautiful little Sister I hope is well. She is a pleasure to her Parents I am certain. My Brother Tarleton's family Happiness encreases I hope in proportion to its Additions. To Mrs. Tarleton & him present my sincere Respects.

Your bottled Beer has arrived safe in America but I have not yet got it to Brunswick—It is a very acceptable Present.

If you could send me a few shirts & Stockings &c., at New York.

With every Duty, Love & Respect & with a Promise to write frequently I conclude myself.

Your affectionate Son & obliged humble Servant,

Banastre Tarleton

Riding patrol was no longer mere fun—the American army had ceased to be a joke. Washington no longer offered $100 Continental for captured dragoons! Lieutenant Colonel Harcourt wrote his father, Earl Harcourt: "though it was once the *ton* of this army to treat them in the most contemptible light, they are now become a formidable enemy." Against this resurgent enemy Cornet Tarleton was soon distinguished for his spirit, vigor, and capacity.

Having thrust his army within twenty miles of Philadelphia in the fall campaign, Sir William Howe, knighted and wearing the red ribbon of the Order of the Bath for capturing Long Island, now decided to take the Quaker City. Early in June, Admiral Howe began collecting warships off Amboy. General Howe began making thrusts and feints with his troops around Brunswick. Many suspected a march toward the Delaware for a decisive battle with Washington's army. But on June 30, 1777, Sir William recalled all the British troops from New Jersey.

Colonel Harcourt marched the 16th Light Dragoons to New York and on July 9 embarked them in the horse transports. Troops may be embarked for training, but horses are embarked only for action. Sir William went aboard; and on July 23 Admiral Lord Howe passed sealed orders to the captains of the 267 ships, made sail, and weighed anchor.

The voyage was hot and slow. The troops suffered, and there was great mortality among the horses. On August 10 Captain Montresor wrote in his *Journal:* "The Horse vessels in general lying too for Food from the forage vessel they being much distressed." On August 20 he continued: "Several horses thrown overboard from the different transports." Then lightning struck the transport *Henry* and crippled seven horses of the 16th Dragoons.

Few suspected its destination until the fleet dropped anchor in Delaware Bay. Scouts immediately posted off to report its presence to Washington. Finding the bay unsuitable for disembarking troops, Lord Howe swung around to Chesapeake Bay and began a slow ascent to its head. Reaching Elk River on August 25, he anchored.

Troops began moving ashore, the Hessians under Knyphausen at Cecil Courthouse and the British under Cornwallis at Elk's Ferry. As soon as the dragoons were ashore, Sir William Erskine sent patrols scouting for horses. Captain Montresor wrote that the army was in "great need of horses, owing to so long and unexpected voyage hither."

Lord Cornwallis commanded the van when the British marched from Elk River. Among his troops were the Queen's Rangers, Captain Patrick Ferguson's company of riflemen, and two troops of the 16th Light Dragoons. In second place marched Knyphausen and the Hessians, with one squadron of the 16th Light Dragoons. Among the light dragoons rode Cornet Tarleton.

The light troops began skirmishing with American patrols near Elk River. Washington, having learned of Howe's objective, had rushed southward to protect Philadelphia. The armies met at Chad's Ford on Brandywine Creek in southern Pennsylvania.

Sending Knyphausen and the Hessians to make a frontal attack at Chad's Ford, Sir William tried his favorite tactics. Under dense fog he sent Lord Cornwallis with grenadiers, infantry, and dragoons to the upper fords to turn the Americans' right flank and attack them in the rear. Having passed Jeffrey's Ford, by two o'clock Lord Cornwallis was deep in the rear of Washington's army. About four-thirty his cannon began roaring.

The Americans fought bravely, and they ran from neither Briton nor Hessian. But the result was inevitable. Outflanked, they began retreating. By twelve o'clock that night they had reached Chester.

The British camped about the Brandywine until September 16 and then headed for Philadelphia in a howling equinoctial gale. At Paoli, twelve miles from the city, they found the troops of Mad Anthony

Wayne camped in a thick wood. Howe ordered General Charles Grey to destroy the camp. Grey's adjutant, Captain John André, decided on a desperate expedient. To insure security and reliance on their bayonets he suggested that Grey order his light infantry to withdraw the powder and remove the flints from their guns.

Their attack was skillfully executed. In the darkness the British infantry bayoneted sleepy lads as they rolled from their blankets, and the dragoons sabered all who flashed their muskets. Wrote an unknown Briton of the Paoli massacre: "The Light Dragoons came on Sword in Hand. The Shrieks, Groans, Shouting, imprecations, deprecations, Clashing of Swords & Bayonets, etc., etc.!"

Next morning Harcourt's Dragoons destroyed all arms left behind at Paoli and after patrolling the Philadelphia Road brought in 150 horses. Then the army marched. On September 26, according to the *Journal* of Captain Montresor, "Lord Cornwallis, Sir William Erskine, Commissary General Weir, led by Col. Harcourt and his light dragoons with a band of music playing 'God Save the King' marched in triumph into Philadelphia."

Undoubtedly Cornet Tarleton was not the last at the barrier of the City of Brotherly Love!

The dragoons paraded to the heart of the city and went into nearby billets. The officers went to the houses assigned them. Cornwallis, with a large train of attendants, entered his quarters. The daughter of his hostess later wrote: "I well remember what we thought of the haughty looks of Lord Rawdon." Captain John André moved into the house of the absent rebel Benjamin Franklin.

Dragoons stationed near Morton's plantation broke open and ransacked the Morton house on September 28. When Mrs. Morton complained, an officer said that they would be punished. Knowing that punishment was merciless flogging, on September 30 Mrs. Morton and her son called at headquarters to beg moderation from Lieutenant Colonel Harcourt.

"The Col. upon my application, behaved unlike a gent'n by asking me 'What I wanted' in an ungenteel manner, and told me he could not attend to what I had to say, and said that the trial was coming on and I must attend to prosecute them," said young Robert Morton.

Morton told Harcourt that there was a lady who wished to speak to him. "He then came to my mother and behaved in a polite genteel manner, and assured her that he could not admit her application as the orders of the General must be obeyed, and that the soldiers were not suffered to commit such depredation on the King's subjects with impunity."

In spite of Mrs. Morton's entreaties, a court martial convicted one dragoon, and on October 1 he was severely flogged.

Before the British were firmly settled in Philadelphia, on October 4 Washington mounted a surprise attack. The Americans advanced in two columns, the column on the right under General Sullivan and that on the left under General Greene. Washington accompanied Sullivan, and their troops drove the advance guard back into the British army.

Colonel Musgrave then threw part of the 40th Regiment into the house of Chief Justice Chew, and the Americans lost momentum trying to dislodge them. Greene, too, had been checked. In its confusion a brigade on his overextended right began firing into comrades attacking the Chew House. The Americans began a general retreat, and Lord Cornwallis thrust them from Germantown with his grenadiers and dragoons. Washington retreated across Schuylkill River to the miseries of Valley Forge.

თო

Warm and snug in Philadelphia, the British kept constant watch on the ragged, shivering Americans at Valley Forge only twenty miles away. Harcourt's 16th Dragoons rode daily patrol, and Lieutenant Colonel Simcoe made frequent excursions with his Queen's Rangers. Even Lord Cornwallis occasionally moved his corps afield to collect forage and cattle from the rich farming communities in Pennsylvania and Jersey.

When not on foray or patrol, the British busied themselves only with the routine of garrison life. The younger officers lived in a round of gaiety. Such chevaliers as André, De Lancey, Musgrave, Simcoe, and Tarleton found relaxation from the saddle in readying a ballroom or hanging the silken trappings of a stage.

A revolving committee of young officers staged weekly dances at Smith's City Tavern, and to these flocked the Loyalists of Philadelphia, even the daughters of Judge Edward Shippen and Chief Justice Benjamin Chew. Bons vivants dined at the Bunch of Grapes or held supper parties at the Indian Queen.

Lord Rawdon went fowling and lost his spaniel near the Schuylkill. Hardier warriors found a cockpit in Moore's Alley, and Banastre, never reluctant to hazard a guinea on grit and steel, probably witnessed some gory mains. He lost heavily at faro and casually sent his unpaid bills to his mother.

In other matters Sir William Howe set a swift pace for his junior officers. He seized and kept for his own use Mary Pemberton's coach and horses. The older officers appeared uneasy at his conduct, and some of them freely expressed their opinions. They said that before his promotion to the chief command, he had sought the counsel and company of officers of experience and merit; but now his companions were usually a set of boys, the most dissipated fellows in the army.

From New York came Mrs. Loring, to live with Howe after he had sent her husband to a distant post. Such flagrant conduct was not overlooked by the patriots. Francis Hopkinson forever embalmed these lovers in "The Battle of the Kegs":

> Sir William, he, snug as a flea
> Lay all this time a snoring,
> Nor dreamed of harm, as he lay warm
> In bed with Mrs. Loring.

In November, Lieutenant Colonel Samuel Birch and Major Richard Crewe brought down the 17th Regiment of Light Dragoons. Sir William's example was not lost upon the newcomers. Lieutenant Colonel Birch, a man of high fashion, openly supported a mistress. Major Crewe soon found himself an elegant strumpet. There were others—all openly risking affront to the Tories.

In this fashionable circle Cornet Tarleton was one of the more riotous rakehells. Described by a contemporary Philadelphian as "below the middle size, stout, strong, heavily made," he was handsome in his red coat and form-molded breeches. He strutted about the city lively and conceited. When he was not riding exhibitions on the Common with Major Francis Gwynne, of the 16th Dragoons, he was making love to such Tory belles as Williamina Smith, Peggy Shippen, or Margaret Chew.

Out of this whirl of fun and love broke one of the worst *esclandres* of the day. It made enemies of Cornet Tarleton and Major Crewe; and some thought that, spurred by jealousy and wounded *amour-propre*, the Major would demand satisfaction from the Cornet. In plain language the London *Political Magazine* explained the affair. Cornet Tarleton "was fairly caught in bed with Major Crewe's mistress"!

◦~๑

In its profile the *Political Magazine* noted: "As General Howe seldom, or rather never, brought his cavalry to serious action, Mr. Tarleton had no decisive opportunities of displaying his character. Certain it is, however, that he was never idle." Nevertheless, Cornet Tarleton was frequently in the saddle. He was noted for his daring and admired by his seniors. Although not wealthy enough to purchase a higher commission, he won promotion by his reputation. After the surrender of General John Burgoyne at Saratoga, the War Office began raising additional regiments and recruiting Provincial troops. In this expansion Liverpool mustered a regiment, and his townsmen elected the absent Cornet one of their officers. On January 8, 1778, passing over the rank of lieutenant, Banastre Tarleton became captain of the 1st Company of the Liverpool Royal Volunteers.

Even before learning of his promotion, the intrepid young officer almost lost his life.

Washington by now had learned the value of cavalry; Moylan and Bland and Taylor had recruited regiments of light dragoons. Among the most active of these cavalrymen were Captain William Washington, cousin of the General, and Captain Henry Lee, afterward the famed "Light-Horse Harry."

Learning that Captain Harry Lee was quartered in the Spread Eagle Tavern, about six miles from Valley Forge, Sir William Erskine, commander of the British cavalry, determined to capture him. Taking 200 light dragoons on the night of January 20, 1778, a party which undoubtedly included Lieutenant Colonels Harcourt and Birch as well as Captain Tarleton, Sir William followed a circuitous route for twenty miles and swept down on the Spread Eagle at daybreak.

Captain Lee and his few men barricaded the doors of the stone house and began firing through the windows. Finding that they could not capture the tavern, the British attempted to drive off the horses of the Americans. For this dangerous mission, Sir William chose Captain Tarleton and his squadron of dragoons.

The dragoons charged. With Tarleton at their head they bore down upon the Spread Eagle as a year before they had borne down upon White's Tavern at Basking Ridge. But Harry Lee was no Charles Lee. In a loud voice he shouted: "Fire away men! Here comes our infantry. We will have them all!"

At the volley five dragoons tumbled dead from their saddles. The others wheeled and drew off. Miraculously, Banastre Tarleton escaped death. Lee's men had wounded his horse in three places. A marksman had blasted his helmet from his head. Another had put three buckshot through his light-dragoon jacket.

ↄ๛

These hard-riding, cockfighting, philandering young officers developed a passion for the theater. Congreve and Farquhar had enlivened Tarleton's days in the Middle Temple, and he became a member of the dramatic corps under John André. These amateurs established themselves in an old, deserted playhouse on South Street, and translated its Rabelaisian motto, *Totus mundus agit histrionem,* into "We act Monday, Wednesday, and Friday."

Under the direction of Captain André, assisted by Captain De Lancey, "on the 14th January, for the benefit of the widows and orphans of the army, were given the comedies of *No One's Enemy but his Own* and *The Deuce is in Him.* The characters were represented by officers of the army and navy." For the backdrop of the theater talented Captain André painted a waterfall in a forest glade. For the first performance he also composed and recited a "Prologue" replete with nostalgic echoes of the amusements of London:

Balls we have plenty, and al *Fresco* too,
Such as Soho or King-Street never knew.
Did you but see sometimes how we're arrayed,
You'd fancy we designed a masquerade.
'Twould tire your patience were I to relate here
Our rants, drums, hurricanes, and Fêtes Champêtres.
Let Ranelagh still boast her ample dome;
While heaven's own canopy, the earth's our room.
Still let Vauxhall her marshalled lamps display,
And gild her shades with artificial day;
In lofty terms old vaunting Sadler's Wells
Of her tight-rope and ladder dancing tells,
But Cunningham in both by far excells.

The success of the players was amazing. The gay life of the Quaker City responded to their productions, and play after play was performed before overflowing audiences. On February 16 they gave *The Constant Couple* and *Duke and No Duke*; on March 2, *The Inconstant* and *The Mock Doctor*; on March 25, Shakespeare's *King Henry IV, Part I*. In May they closed their theater forever with Home's *Douglas* and *The Citizen*.

In London, meanwhile, ministers had become tired of Sir William Howe's dilatory policy and had sent orders for Sir Henry Clinton to relieve him as commander in chief. Whatever faults Sir William may have had as a strategist, his younger officers adored him. To a friend in England, John André wrote: "I do not believe there is upon record an instance of a Commander-in-Chief having so universally endeared himself to those under his command or of one who received such signal and flattering proofs of their love."

Under the inspiration and direction of André, on May 19, 1778, these officers staged a farewell pageant and ball for Sir William. They called it a "Mischianza." Wrote André: "For the expenses, the whole army would have most cheerfully contributed; but it was requisite to draw the line somewhere, and twenty-two field officers joined in a subscription adequate to the plan they meant to adopt."

The Mischianza opened with a grand regatta in the Delaware River. From the river the officers and their ladies formed a procession to Wharton Villa. As they neared the villa, they passed a lawn of about twelve acres, lined with troops and prepared for tilt and tournament, according to the customs and ordinances of ancient chivalry.

The crowd was seated. With a flourish of trumpets, in rode a band of knights dressed in white and red silk, their gray chargers caparisoned in the same colors. At their head rode Lord Cathcart. Two young slaves, with sashes and drawers of blue and white silk, wearing large gold and silver clasps around their necks and arms, with breasts and shoulders bare, held his stirrups. Beside him walked his squires bearing his lance and shield: his device, Cupid riding on a lion, with a motto, "Surmounted by Love."

After him rode the six white Knights of the Blended Rose, each attended by his squire bearing his lance and shield. The third knight was Captain John André, squired by his brother Lieutenant André and come to tilt in honor of Miss Peggy Chew. His device was two game-cocks fighting, and his motto: "No Rival."

Last rode Lieutenant Sloper, in honor of Miss Peggy Shippen: his device a heart and a sword, and his motto: "Honour and the Fair."

After having made circuit of the square, these knights passed to the pavilion where sat the Ladies of the Blended Rose. Their herald advanced to the center of the square, and after a flourish of trumpets, proclaimed their challenge: "The Knights of the Blended Rose, by me their Herald, proclaim and assert that the Ladies of the Blended Rose, excel in wit, beauty, and every accomplishment, those of the *whole world*; and should any knight or knights be so hardy as to dispute or deny it, they are ready to enter the lists with them, and maintain their assertions by deeds of arms, according to the laws of ancient chivalry."

At the third challenge, the herald of the black Knights of the Burning Mountain rode forth and proclaimed his defiance: "The Knights of the Burning Mountain present themselves here, not to contest by words, but to disprove by deeds, the vain-glorious assertions of the Knights of the Blended Rose, and enter these lists to maintain, that the Ladies of the Burning Mountain are not excelled in beauty, virtue, or accomplishments, by any in the universe."

In came a band of six black knights, dressed in black and orange silk, their black chargers caparisoned in the same colors. At their head rode Captain Watson, attended by two young slaves, in black and orange livery, holding his stirrups. Beside him walked his squires, bearing his lance and shield. His device was a heart, with a wreath of flowers, and his motto: "Love and Glory."

The sixth Knight of the Burning Mountain was Captain Banastre Tarleton, on a black charger, in honor of Miss Williamina Smith, with Captain Heart his squire. His device was a light dragoon and his motto: "Swift, Vigilant, and Bold."

After the Knights of the Burning Mountain had made the circuit of the square, they drew up in front of the pavilion of the Ladies of the Burning Mountain. Then the chief of the white knights threw down his gauntlet. The chief of the black knights bade his squire pick it up.

Spurring their chargers into the center of the field, the two chiefs fought in single combat. But the Marshal of the Field, Major Gwynne, rode between them and told them that the Ladies of the Blended Rose and of the Burning Mountain were satisfied with their proofs of love. Back rode the knights to the pavilions of their ladies.

The massed bands struck up, and the company, headed by Sir William Howe, received the salute. The knights and the ladies entered the hall and opened the dancing. Then they supped, and toward the end of supper the Herald of the Blended Rose entered the room, to proclaim a health to the King, to the Queen and the Royal Family, to the Army and Navy, to the knights and their ladies, and to the ladies. Afterward they danced until dawn—even Captain Banastre Tarleton and lovely Miss Williamina Smith, daughter of the Reverend William Smith, provost of the College.

5

Susan Priscilla

$\mathcal{A}$MONG BANASTRE TARLETON's closest friends in Philadelphia was handsome Robert Bertie, the youthful Marquis of Lindsay. Two years younger than Banastre, having been born on October 19, 1756, Robert was already a seasoned veteran. He had been lieutenant in and acting colonel of the 7th Regiment, but on November 5, 1777, he purchased a commission as captain in the 15th Foot and joined that regiment.

The young marquis soon afterward requested leave to return to England, for his father, the Duke of Ancaster, was old and ill. Lord Cornwallis had again requested permission to visit his ailing wife, and as their requests were granted, on December 16, 1777, the two noblemen left Philadelphia on the *Brilliant*. On January 18, 1778, they arrived in London.

Robert's father, Peregrine Bertie, third Duke of Ancaster, was hereditary Lord Great Chamberlain of England. His mother, the Duchess of Ancaster, was Mistress of the Robes for Queen Charlotte. The Ancasters were great folk, and proudly the Duke escorted his son to the levee in St. James's Palace and presented him to his Majesty.

But Captain Bertie had little taste for court formalities. He preferred the fashionable vices he had learned while in the army in New York and Philadelphia. He fell in love with a young woman of Berkeley Square with the German name of Rebecca Krudener. Amid great drinking and frolicking, he seduced Rebecca.

Duke Peregrine Bertie died on August 12, 1778, and Robert succeeded him as fourth Duke of Ancaster. He set his house in order, bade farewell to Rebecca, and sailed for America. The *London Gazette* of October 24 reported: "The Duke of Ancaster has arrived in New York." The *London Gazette* did not report that soon thereafter Rebecca Krudener bore the Duke a daughter whom she named Susan Priscilla.

42

By this time, in the expansion of the army under Sir Henry Clinton, the Duke's old friends, Colonel Simcoe, Lord Cathcart, and Lord Rawdon each commanded his own regiment. Back to England in search of a regiment went Duke Robert. He never returned to America. On Friday, July 9, 1779, the *Morning Post* carried a brief notice: "Yesterday, at six o'clock, in the evening died Robert Bertie, Duke of Ancaster, at his house in Berkeley Square."

Next day the *Morning Post* added: "The Duke of Ancaster's death is thought to have been occasioned by so considerably overheating himself on a footrace, which he ran on Friday se'ennight past in Hyde Park. On his Grace's return home he was taken exceedingly ill. Being ill he drank five bottles of claret and champagne."

Gossipy old Horace Walpole, writing to Sir Horace Mann, impaled the young Duke forever: "The Duke of Ancaster is dead of a scarlet fever contracted by drinking and rioting at two-and twenty."

He concluded his gossip: "Though he had some excellent qualities, he was of a turbulent nature, and though of a fine figure, his manners were not noble."

The title of Duke of Ancaster and the hereditament fell to his uncle, Brownlow Bertie. But in his will Robert Bertie left his mother £800 a year from his private property and divided the rest between his sisters, Lady Priscilla Barbara Elizabeth, the wife of Sir Peter Burrell; and Lady Georgiana Charlotte, soon to be the wife of Earl Cholmondeley. To his sisters jointly fell the post of hereditary Lord Great Chamberlain of England.

The Duke's will astonished everybody. From Strawberry Hill, Horace Walpole wrote the Countess of Ossory: "Are you not sorry, Madam, for the poor Duke of Ancaster, especially since he made so noble and sensible a will? I think his attention to his mother must half kill her. I hear he has left a legacy to a very small man that was always his companion, and whom, when he was drunk, he used to fling at the heads of the company as others fling a bottle."

Robert of Ancaster cherished Rebecca Krudener. In his will he left her an annuity of £200, enough to keep her in moderate comfort until death. To their love child, little Susan Priscilla, he left the sum of £3000, with an annuity of £150 for support and education. Moreover, in his will he named his daughter Susan Priscilla Bertie, thus bequeathing her one of the proudest surnames in the English peerage.

The sudden death of her son prostrated the Duchess. She took to bed, and the doctors despaired of her life. When she recovered, she persuaded Rebecca Krudener to give her Ancaster's natural daughter. And so among her great kinfolk in Whitehall, almost in the shadow of the throne of England, little Susan Priscilla Bertie romped and slept and dreamed, innocent of the day when she would meet her father's friend, Banastre Tarleton.

6
The Green Horse

During the Mischianza the command of the British army passed from Sir William Howe to Sir Henry Clinton. Sir Henry began selecting his staff and soon announced his promotions. For aide he chose Captain William Sutherland. For adjutant general he chose Lord William Schaw Cathcart, captain in the 17th Light Dragoons.

With British and Provincial light dragoons, German chasseurs, and Simcoe's hussars under his command, Sir William Erskine needed a brigade major. Army Regulations provided that such staff officers be appointed from exemplary senior captains. Exemplary and senior captain in the Liverpool Volunteers was Banastre Tarleton. Sir William, who had seen him in action and remained one of his warmest sponsors, promoted him to brigade major. The War Office, too, on June 13, 1778, rewarded the absent major with the permanent rank of captain in his own 1st Regiment of Dragoon Guards.

This time the dispatches spelled his name Banistier.

Major Tarleton moved the 16th and 17th Light Dragoons into New Jersey on June 16. Next day Sir Henry marched the infantry to bivouacs outside Philadelphia. At three o'clock on the morning of June 18, 1778, they crossed the Delaware River at Gloucester Point and followed the dragoons on the long retreat to New York.

Parting was more than sorrow. Soldiers hid in cellars instead of leaving. About 1000 deserted before reaching New York. Several officers married and bore away their brides. Major André clipped the buttons from his coat and handed them to Miss Redman for souvenirs. Humming a little song he had composed for her—

> Return, enraptured hours,
> When Delia's heart was mine;
> When she with wreaths of flowers
> My temples would entwine—

he turned his horse's head north, waved, and rode off—toward the gallows tree.

By twelve o'clock American dragoons galloped through the streets of Philadelphia. Washington sent in General Benedict Arnold to restore order and govern the city. Arnold, still lame from wounds received at Saratoga, was dashing, handsome—and a widower. And as he joined with his fellow officers in the subdued merrymaking he· met lonely, lovely Peggy Shippen. Soon he wrote old Judge Edward Shippen: "My fortune is not large, though sufficient (not to depend upon my expectations) to make us both happy. I neither expect nor wish one with Miss Shippen." To Margaret Shippen's sorrow, her father consented to her marriage.

Slowly the British retreated toward Sandy Hook, Simcoe's Queen's Rangers and Brigade Major Tarleton's dragoons constantly patrolling and skirmishing. Washington, having rebuilt and invigorated his army during the ordeal at Valley Forge, was in close pursuit, eager for battle and harassing his enemy every mile. His line of march was parallel to but north of that of Sir Henry. Finally their routes converged in the neighborhood of Monmouth Courthouse, New Jersey.

The British rear guard camped near the courthouse on the night of June 27. There they were overtaken by the Americans. Early next morning Washington sent General Charles Lee, exchanged and restored to command, to bring on a general action.

The difficulty of the terrain, cut by deep ravines, prevented such action. But Major Tarleton, in tactical command of the dragoons, ordered the horsemen forward. With Sir Henry Clinton at their head the 16th Light Dragoons paraded across the field. Seeing the dragoons forming for battle, one of Lee's aides told him that they meant to charge. Lee ordered his troops to let them come close and then fire. The 16th Dragoons charged, received the fire, and wheeled along the American right flank.

Sensing their objective, Lee ordered the troops on his right to fall back, for "if the British cavalry had vigorously pushed on our right, they might have turned our flank, taken us in reverse, and we had been lost."

As Lee's men were retreating to positions behind a ravine, Washington rode up. Seeing the retrograde movement, he lost control of himself and began swearing with all the fire in his soldier's vocabulary.

After a severe battle, in which the infantry commanded by Lord Cornwallis stalled the American pursuit, the British continued their retreat to Sandy Hook. Here Admiral Lord Howe waited with transports to ferry them to safety in New York.

In the evening, after the battle, Lee wrote Washington and asked him about "your making use of such very singular expressions as you did."

Washington immediately replied: "What I recollect to have said, was dictated by duty, and warranted by the occasion."

The Marquis de Lafayette, with Gallic ear untrained for the nuances of Anglo-Saxon profanity, later could remember only "damned poltroon." But General Scott, who had also heard the commander in chief, testified: "Yes, sir, he swore till the leaves shook on the trees." After a moment's reflection he concluded: "He swore like an angel from heaven."

Washington ordered Lee tried by court-martial. He was convicted of disobedience to orders, misbehavior before the enemy, and disrespect to the commander in chief. He was then removed from the American service. Banastre Tarleton had not cut off Lee's head, but his dragoons had ended the career of the sometimes brilliant General.

In his report to Lord Germain, Sir Henry Clinton wrote: "I am indebted to Lord Cornwallis for his zealous services on every occasion: and I found great support from the activity of Major General Grey, Brigadier Generals Matthew, Leslie, and Sir William Erskine."

For his part Sir William Erskine had found great support in the activity of Brigade Major Tarleton.

～

Among the guides who had led the British from Elk River to Philadelphia in 1777 was Jacob James, and among their intelligence agents in Bucks County, Pennsylvania, was Richard Hovenden. Both were desperate men, well endowed to lead partisan troops in guerrilla warfare. Soon after Sir William Howe seized Philadelphia, he issued a call for volunteers for the King's Army.

Captain Richard Hovenden raised the 1st Troop of Philadelphia Light Dragoons in November and December 1777. The other officers of this troop were Lieutenants Samuel Chapman and Moore Hovenden and Cornet Thomas Miller. The company was mustered into the British service on January 8, 1778, and assigned to duty with the Queen's Rangers.

Captain Jacob James and Lieutenants Nathaniel Vernon, Jr., and Francis Gildart were commissioned in the King's Provincial troops on January 1, 1778, and sent to recruit in Chester County, Pennsylvania. On February 5, 1778, Captain James's troop of light dragoons was mustered into the British army.

Captain Thomas Sandford recruited a third company of Loyalist soldiers, and on April 24, 1778, brought to the King's Standard the Bucks County Light Dragoons. With him were Lieutenant Benjamin Hunt and Lieutenant Walter Willet.

These three troops of dragoons, sometimes called the British Legion, usually operated as guides or scouts for the Queen's Rangers or 16th and

17th Light Dragoons. By mid-February, however, the 1st was able to operate separately; and on February 17, 1778, the *Pennsylvania Evening Post* praised Hovenden's first operation: "The regular and exact performance of the orders, and the secrecy, despatch, and spirit, with which they were executed, reflect much credit on the officers and men."

In addition to these troops of dragoons the British began raising two regiments of infantry among the Pennsylvania Loyalists. Lord Rawdon issued a call to all loyal Irishmen and organized his regiment of Volunteers of Ireland. At the same time Captain William Sutherland began enlisting the Caledonian Volunteers.

After his retreat to New York, Sir Henry Clinton continued recruiting among the Loyalists. *The Royal Gazette* of New York on July 9, 1778, published an advertisement:

All Gentlemen, natives of North Britain, who are emulous of that noble spirit of loyalty and attachment, which so eminently distinguishes their countrymen at home, in the present occasion, are hereby informed, that a corps, to be titled the
Caledonian Volunteers
is now *raising*, to be commanded by their
countryman
Capt. William Sutherland
Aid de Camp to the Commander in Chief

The *London Chronicle* of September 24 reported: "The Caledonian Volunteers increase daily, owing to the activity and spirit of Capt. Sutherland."

Sir Henry Clinton had stationed Simcoe and his Queen's Rangers at Kingsbridge on the Harlem River to guard the main approach to the city of New York, and on July 15 he sent Captains Hovenden, James, and Sandford with their Provincial dragoons to join Simcoe. At the same time, he ordered the dragoons clothed in green coats to conform to those of the Queen's Rangers.

Captain Christian Huck, who had deserted his law practice in Philadelphia to follow the British to New York, became commander of Sandford's troop of dragoons. Captain David Kinlock, of the 71st Regiment, with Lieutenants Hugh Davis and John Miller, recruited a troop of horse, of which Major Tarleton was senior officer.

Captain John Mackenzie, Lieutenant Donald McBean, and Lieutenant Donald McLeod recruited a company of Scottish volunteers. Lord Cathcart was their senior member. The Caledonian Volunteers mustered only one company. Their officers were Captain Charles Stewart, 1st Lieutenant Lachland McDonald, and 2nd Lieutenant James McDonald. Major Charles Cochrane was a member of their company.

The English volunteers formed two companies. The officers of the 1st Company were Captain Kenneth McCulloch, 1st Lieutenant Donald

MacCrimmons, and 2nd Lieutenant Kenneth McLeod. The officers of the 2nd were Captain James Edwards, 1st Lieutenant John Rousselet, and 2nd Lieutenant Thomas Miller.

The American volunteers formed the 4th Company. Their officers were Captain Thomas Scott, 1st Lieutenant William Darby, and 2nd Lieutenant Donald McPherson.

From these troops of light dragoons and companies of infantry Sir Henry Clinton created a mixed regiment which he called the British Legion. On July 18, 1778, he promoted his adjutant general, Lord William Schaw Cathcart, to the colonelcy of the regiment. After looking over his junior officers for two weeks, on August 1 Sir Henry rewarded Major Banastre Tarleton for his eminent conduct of the cavalry across the Jerseys by promoting him to the rank of lieutenant colonel of the British Legion.

Colonel Tarleton still lacked three weeks of reaching his twenty-fourth birthday. Without wealth, without title, without political friends, but on valor alone, in four years he had risen from obscurity to envied rank. Both Sir William Howe and Sir Henry Clinton had been attracted by his elegant manners and his ready speech; but his undenied courage, his daring leadership, and his intuitive grasp of cavalry tactics endeared him both to Sir William Erskine and to Lord Cornwallis.

Reports of a Provincial regiment of mixed infantry and cavalry aroused curiosity in England. On January 2, 1779, the *Cambridge Chronicle and Journal* published a garbled but diverting account of the formation of the British Legion: "A noble Earl, who is now with his regiment of light dragoons in America, published in September last a kind of proclamation, inviting his countrymen to come to the royal standard, offering his Majesty's pardon, and promising to embody and head them himself against the rebels, by whom they had been deluded. In consequence thereof 400 came in from Mr. Washington's army, which his lordship immediately clothed in a new green uniform; but as there was some suspicion of them deserting back to the enemy, they were ordered to an outpost to try their fidelity, when only one attempted to desert, who was soon after taken, brought back, and tried, by his lordship's order, by a jury composed of a man out of each company, who sentenced him to die; accordingly he was executed the next morning, at the head of the regiment, which is now deemed as fine a corps as any in the Service."

∞

Lord Cathcart and Lieutenant Colonel Tarleton assembled the troops of the British Legion at Kingsbridge, where they went into bivouac with Simcoe's Queen's Rangers. But the proximity of the two regiments raised a delicate problem of military etiquette. Colonel Cathcart outranked older and senior Lieutenant Colonel Simcoe. The question of precedence came to trial when Cathcart assumed command of both the Rangers and the Legion.

Much affected, Simcoe rushed down to New York to complain directly to General Clinton. Sir Henry offered him the rank of colonel in the Provincial troops, but refused to antedate his commission so as to make him superior to Lord Cathcart. General Clinton did send Lord Cathcart and the Legion infantry to Greenwich. He also appointed him his quartermaster general, a duty his Lordship performed until he married Miss Elizabeth Eliot, daughter of the lieutenant governor of New York, and bore her in triumph to his home in Scotland.

The transfer of Cathcart left Tarleton in active command of the dragoons of the British Legion. Restless, ambitious, and not a little bored with endlessly scouring the hinterland around New York, he was almost constantly in the saddle, parading the green-clad dragoons that already were becoming famous as "Tarleton's Green Horse." Colonel Simcoe esteemed the Green Dragoon commanding the Green Horse. In his *Military Journal* Simcoe wrote that in Lieutenant Colonel Tarleton he "had a colleague, full of enterprise and spirit, and anxious of every opportunity of distinguishing himself."

These enterprising colleagues soon had a singular and narrow escape. They were scouting the front around Kingsbridge, and Simcoe was describing a private road to Tarleton. Sergeant Wright, Simcoe's orderly, alighted and took down a rail fence in Devoe's farmyard. "The Stockbridge Indians, about sixty in number, excellent marksmen, had just joined Mr. Washington's army," Simcoe wrote. "Around this farm the Indians were ambuscaded; Wright had scarce mounted his horse, when these officers, for some trivial reason, altered their intentions, and spurring their horses, soon rode out of sight and out of reach of the Indians."

Ambush is a sorry little game, but it can be played by two. Learning of cavalry stationed by day near Mamaroneck, to cover the country and protect some sick horses in the salt marshes, Simcoe determined to surprise them. The Queen's Rangers and the Legion marched during the night. Wrote Simcoe: "When they arrived at their appointed station, Lt. Col. Tarleton, with the cavalry, ambuscaded the road, on which the enemy's guard was to approach."

They waited during the early hours. "At six o'clock, as he was previously ordered, Lt. Col. Tarleton left his post, when the party of the enemy instantly appeared in his rear," said Simcoe. Every other morning the enemy had passed the point of ambush at five o'clock, but on this morning a sergeant's horse had broken loose. He had chased it an hour before his patrol could ride!

Lieutenant Colonel Andreas Emmerick's chasseurs had a brush with the Americans on August 30. They learned that among the Indian scouts was Chief Nimham. Ordering a day's provisions to be cooked,

Simcoe led the rangers, chasseurs, and dragoons out early next morning for an all-day ambuscade.

Nimham's scouts discovered Emmerick's chasseurs on the march. The Indians ambuscaded themselves behind the rail fences that lined the road. When the Chasseurs marched into range, the Indians opened fire. Hearing the firing, Simcoe rushed forward with the Queen's Rangers, and Tarleton galloped the Green Horse wide to the right and cut in behind the Indians.

Old Nimham, who had lived in England and despised Englishmen, died like a savage chief. When he saw the rangers close in upon his rear, he shouted to his braves to flee. "I am old and I will die here," he cried. Recognizing Colonel Simcoe, Nimham attacked and wounded him, but fell to the sword of Sergeant Wright.

At the command of their chief, the Indians fled. The Green Horse pursued them down Cortlandt's Ridge. Tarleton selected one of the fugitives and ran him down. Standing in his stirrups, the Green Dragoon made a powerful slash with his enormous saber. He missed. The momentum of his stroke pulled him from his horse.

With a scream the Indian sprang upon the fallen dragoon. The brave's musket had been discharged and he had no bayonet, so he reached for his knife. As he raised his arm for the death stroke, Tarleton's dragoon orderly sabered him. "That active officer had a narrow escape," Simcoe dryly wrote.

After defeating the Stockbridge Indians, Simcoe attempted to trap Colonel Gist at Babcock's House. Before daybreak on September 16 he led the Queen's Rangers, the British Legion, and the Chasseurs from Kingsbridge. "Lt. Col. Tarleton with the whole of the cavalry was to proceed to cover the right, and arrive at Valentine's hill by daylight." When the commanders sprang the trap, they were chagrined to find that Major Prueschenck had not seized Philipse Bridge, and that Gist and his troops had escaped over it. "Lt. Col. Tarleton fell in with a patrole of cavalry and dispersed it."

The *Royal Gazette*, for September 19, added details to Simcoe's narrative: "At the same time, Lt. Col. Tarleton with the dragoons, charged a body of rebels posted on Valentine's Hill; but as the enemy were near a very thick wood, they took shelter where the horse could not possibly act, which prevented their sustaining any other loss than the capture of a few of their number."

A few days later Simcoe and Tarleton patrolled as far as White Plains. Tarleton signaled that he was going to investigate an enemy picket, and Simcoe rode forward to survey and sketch the grounds Washington had occupied in the battle of White Plains. "Lt. Col. Tarleton, soon after, returned; he had put the enemy's piquet to flight, and taken some prisoners."

Thus Tarleton passed the autumn weeks in constant activity: riding, patrolling, skirmishing. It was dull and gruelling work, and without glory. His personal affairs, too, had become involved, for his family had stopped honoring his drafts upon them. He complained to his mother, then to John, and finally to Thomas:

New York Oct. 21, 1778

My dear Brother,

I wrote to you seven Days ago advising you of my Drafts I was obliged to draw in lieu of some come back—Disagreeable enough! Mr. Yates has also been my Friend.

Many many letters do I write & very few do I receive.

Nothing can equal the Compunction I feel for my Bills being dishonor'd but the shame I feel for having done a wrong thing. I have been successful as a Soldier—I have been repeatedly thank'd by the General—The Legion under my Command has taken & kill'd considerably above its numbers.

Stanley I hear is to get a Lieutenant Colonelcy in the Guards— I hope the Majority will rest with me.

Affairs would look well in this Country but great Detachments are order'd to the W. Indies from this Army. The French Connexion hurts, it does not assist the Americans. They have adopted too large a Scale & the French Policy, D'Estrange's ill fortune & overbearing manners & Demands of that Nation cause great jealousy on this Continent.

I write to my dear Mother by this Packet—I wrote to my Brother by the Duke of Ancaster. Read with them.

I am

Yours affectionately,
Ban. Tarleton

Then the Green Horse was transferred from Kingsbridge to Jericho, Long Island, and on November 1, 1778, Lieutenant Colonel Tarleton signed the first general muster roll of the British Legion. Soon Sir William Erskine ordered the Legion into winter quarters at the eastern end of the island.

During the months they lay in winter quarters, the British Legion formed part of the defensive screen on Long Island. The American army had grown so skilled and powerful that Clinton feared that Washington might attempt some kind of surprise. So the dragoons patrolled interminably through the fog and cold and snow and the infantry of the Legion maintained a vigilant lookout.

The Green Dragoon continued writing his family about his debts, and finally they wrote him again. Their letter reached him on December 24. It was a painful holiday greeting.

On Christmas afternoon Banastre replied:

Long Island New York
Province Dec. 25, 1778

My dear friends

You complain much of me, you tell me of my silence, you inform me of my folly and Dissipation—you protest my Bills—you solicit my Return to England—In answer to these various accusations & Inhibitions I confess Failings, but not so manifold as you represent—

This is a general answer—a more particular one wou'd exculpate me more—

I have wrote most frequently, wrote not short but long letters—I have addressed every Individual in the Family—I have not attempted to gloss over my Errors—I confes there are Blots in my Conduct which nothing can wipe away.

I have offer'd no Vindication but I have descended into the minutest Particulars of my Faults—vide Letter 14 Sepr.—

I have likewise offer'd Arguments why you should wrest me from Destruction & the great Probability of my restoring you the money which I have drawn for, undesir'd nay order'd to the contrary—but you have suffered Bills to return to this Country bearing with them 20 pr cent loss & bearing with them my Stigma—

I will in a few words describe to you my present Situation here. The Relation brings with it strong Reasons why I should stay in America, why you shou'd prevent my Bills returning and the probability I have of making you Restoration.

I have Lt. Col. of Dragoons Pay made up to me from Captn. of Foot. I have ten Shillings pr Day as Majr of Brigade of Cavalry; by which last Appointment I have leave to stay upon the Staff of America—put these Incomes together in England & America & Pay amounts to 34 Shillings pr Day.

These are honorable & profitable Employments—I am fortunate in my Profession—I am a *Miscreant* if ever I play again—

Sir Henry Clinton indulges me with the Command of 200 Hussars—Gl. W. Erskine to whom I act as Major of Brigade is partial to me as a Father.

If another Campaign Takes Place in America—If Gr Britain makes another Exertion which I am persuaded she will—I have advice to that Effect from England—I shall have the honorable & lucrative Employment of Lt. Col of Provincial Cavalry—The Pay & other proper Emoluments will enable me to make restitution.

Why should I return to England? My Honor as a Soldier would instantly fade & all Probability of Restitution would vanish for ever—

Besides Gl. Wm Erskine has pressed me & I have promised that if another Campaign does not ensue in this Country to wait till Spring & return with him to Europe—He extends a Hand that will be serviceable in future Life—he will introduce me to all his military Acquaintance—To be usher'd into the World by such a Man is worth Ambition & the fairest Consequences may be derived from it—

But my Infatuation yet rambles in my Heart—my cursed Itch for Play has, unless you extend your benevolent Hand totally blasted these bright Expectations.

I cannot stay if my Bills continue to come back—Ruin is Inevitable—I have already taken up 3 by the assistance of Mr. Gates to the amount of 400 £ —

I enclos'd a List in my last Letter of the 25th Octr of the Nr of Bills I have drawn—The amount is not above 2,500 £ —I would give you Triplicate but that I have not my Papers—being on Command in the Rears of the Army with the Hussars of the British legion who are on their march to the East End of Long Island—I recd your Letter of Octr by Express last night—the first Letters have rec'd for the last half Year—Its Contents are painful—When I say the Army—don't imagine I mean the whole Army. It is a Detachm't under the Command of Sr Wm Erskine who has placed me in the rear with the Command of the Hussars of the British Legion—the Intention of the move to have Forage, Flour, etc. for the whole Army quartered at New York etc. We shall remain a Month or 6 weeks on this Duty. My dear Friends I have opened myself to you as far as Time & Situation will allow—I am now to solicit you to secure me from the Storm mentioned in your Letters—make me clear & I never will gall you by a Repetition of Error or wound myself, by asking what I do not deserve—

Many Letters have miscarried not only what I have wrote to you but what I have wrote to my Acquaintance Gen. Sloper & Col. Harcourt inform'd me yesterday by letter that they never had received Letters inclosing Plans & Descriptions of the Battle of Monmouth—I *wish* this may not miscarry—

I am likewise to solicit you, my dear Friends not to suffer the Majority of the Liverpool Reg't to go over my Head during my Absence in America.

I think it more than probable, nay I have heard that Stanley is applying for a Col'y in the Guards.

With Economy & some fortunate Events I will repay you—& I will shew you all that you no longer shall reprobate my Conduct—

> I am Madame
> with the sincerest Attachment
> Your affectionate Son
> Banastre Tarleton

During the winter Banastre developed a warm friendship with his commanding officer, Brigadier General Sir William Erskine, and after the turn of the new year he found an opportunity to do him a favor. He wrote to his mother:

Sagg, Long Island
Feb. 1, 1779

My dear Madam,

I beg leave to trouble you with a few lines which contain a Request which will please you to gratify.

Sir William Erskine yesterday received a Letter from Lady Erskine informing him that she had carried Miss Erskine his Daughter to a School in Liverpool, now my Request is, that you would countenance & patronize this little woman. S. Wm. acts to me as a Father.

I wrote a very very long Letter last Packet, so long that you will scarce be able to read it before you receive this.

We live here quite retired. I keep the out Post with the Legion. A Packet has arrived. I have had no Letters.

We expect Reinforcement from England—but Affairs here are in the same Situation as when I last wrote:—How is John? I was sorry to hear of his indisposition.

With every Sentiment of Respect,
I remain Yours Most Affectionately,
Ban. Tarleton

Don't let the Majority go over my Head.

∞

In good weather Tarleton drilled his Legion. Ambitious and untiring, he had become a perfectionist, a martinet. He practiced defense against amphibious attack. He exercised and maneuvered his troops. And he developed skilful coordination between infantry and cavalry. By spring he had made the British Legion the most powerful combat team in the British army.

About the middle of May, Sir William Erskine moved the troops on Long Island back to Kingsbridge to form the advance guard for a swing through Westchester and Dutchess counties. The British Legion was at Kingsbridge on May 27, and on May 29 they moved to East Chester Heights. Sir William, with the cavalry and light troops, encamped at Dobb's Ferry on June 1. Two days later Lieutenant Colonel Tarleton crossed Croton Bridge and scattered a party of American scouts.

By June 6 Erskine had fallen back to a bivouac on Valentine's Hill. Here he remained until June 24, with his light troops scouting and patrolling. He then detached the Queen's Rangers and the British Legion for a sweep around White Plains. From White Plains, Simcoe and Tarleton marched by different routes to Croton Bridge. After routing a small patrol of Americans, they marched on and camped that night at North Castle. Next day they returned to Sir William at Valentine's Hill.

Washington's armies of veterans now had the British so tightly hemmed in around New York that they could only sweep and patrol—

or fight the deciding battle of the war. Clinton declined battle and continued his raids.

Learning that a strong party of American militiamen, Continentals,
and dragoons had encamped at Pound Bridge, near Bedford, in Westchester County, Sir Henry decided to strike them. For this hazardous
operation at a distance from his base he picked the smartest soldiers
from several regiments. Who should command them? Tarleton had
heretofore acted under Simcoe, but now Sir Henry decided that Banastre's apprentice days were over and that he could be trusted with an
independent command.

Tarleton marched his troops at eleven o'clock on the night of July 1.
He struck the Americans soon after daybreak and broke their line with
a bold charge. With his dragoons he pursued and slaughtered the fugitives. To the sword he added the torch, and burned until his foes begged
for mercy. Then, calling his troops, he retired as he had come—"Swift,
Vigilant, and Bold."

After a march of sixty-four miles in twenty-three hours, the horsemen
were back in their camp on the Bronx River. Almost exhausted, but
devoted to his duty, Banastre wrote his report to Sir Henry:

> Camp on the Brunx
> July 2, 1779, Eleven P.M.
>
> Sir,
>
> I have the honour to inform your Excellency, that I moved with
> the Detachment you were pleased to intrust me with, consisting
> of 70 of the 17th Light Dragoons, Part of the Legion Infantry and
> Cavalry, Queen's Rangers, Hussars, and some mounted yagers, in
> all about 200, at Half past Eleven o'clock last Night. The Weather
> being remarkably bad, prevented my reaching Northcastle Church
> before Four o'Clock next morning, where I received Confirmation
> of my Intelligence relative to the Numbers and situation of Shel-
> don's Regiment and 100 Continental Foot, but no tidings of
> Moiland's Regiment of Dragoons.
>
> I pursued my Route through Bedford to Pound-Bridge, without
> any material occurrence in the District of the Ridge, and within
> 300 yards of the Enemy, who were not alarmed, my Guide in
> Front mistook the Road; another Guide informed me of the Error,
> and it was rectified as soon as possible.
>
> The Enemy's Vidette had noticed to them our passing their
> Front. The whole Regiment was mounted and formed behind the
> Meeting-House. An attack was instantly made by the advanced
> Guard, consisting of the 17th Light Dragoons, the Ground not
> allowing more than Seven or Eight in Front. The Enemy did not
> stand the Charge, a general Route immediately ensued. The Diffi-
> culty of the Country, and there being no possibility of obtaining
> their Rear, enabled the Greatest Part of the Regiment to escape.

The Pursuit continued for four Miles on the Stamford and Salem Roads.

The Loss of Men in Sheldon's Dragoons, upon Inquiry and Comparison of Accounts, I estimate at 26 or 27 Killed, Wounded, and Prisoners; but their Disgrace in the Loss of the Standard of the Regiment, and of Helmets, Arms, and Accoutrements, was great. Part of the Officers' and Regimental Baggage fell into our Hands.

I have hitherto omitted mentioning the Militia, to the Amount of 120, who, together with the Continental Foot, broke and dispersed at the Approach of the King's Troops.

The Militia assembled again on Eminences and in Swamps, and before we quitted the Ground on which the first Charge was made, they fired at Great Distances. We were successful in killing, wounding, and taking 15 of them; and the rest hovered almost out of Sight.

The Inveteracy of the inhabitants of Pound-Bridge, and near Bedford, in firing from Houses and Out-houses, obliged me to burn some of their Meeting and some of their Dwelling houses with Stores. I proposed to the Militia Terms, that if they would not fire Shots from Buildings, I would not burn. They interpreted my mild Proposal wrong, imputing it to Fear. They persisted in firing until the Torch stopped their Progress; after which not a Shot was fired.

With Pleasure I relate to your Excellency, that the Loss sustained by His Majesty's Troops is trifling, 1 Hussar of the Legion killed, 1 wounded, 1 Horse of the 17th Dragoons killed; the Whole of the Detachment, except the above, being returned to Camp. The Infantry of the Legion, mounted on Horses, are extremely fatigued by a March of 64 Miles in 23 Hours.

I have the Honor to be, etc.

Banastre Tarleton

Lieutenant-Colonel, British Legion

Sensitive to criticism for his inactivity, Clinton forwarded the letter to the War Office with this covering memorandum to Lord Amherst: "I have also the honor to transmit the copy of a report made to me by Lieutenant Col. Tarleton of the Legion—whom I detached in hopes of surprising a Regt. of the Enemy's Cavalry, at Pound Bridge, to which I beg leave to refer your Lordship, for the success of this little excursion."

The War Office immediately published the report of this little success in the London Gazette. It was reprinted in many of the provincial newspapers, and it made the Green Dragoon one of the most widely known young officers in the British army.

This time the dispatches spelled his name Banastre!

Sir William Erskine, who had come to America as lieutenant colonel of the 71st or Fraser's Highlanders Regiment, obtained leave to return to Scotland. As Sir William planned to visit his daughter in Liverpool, Banastre sent a letter by him to his mother:

New York—July 4th, 1779

My dear Madam,

I wrote to you by the last Packet. I thanked you affectionately for every Good you have render'd me.

S. W. Erskine who has been my Kind Patron will deliver this to you.

You & my Brothers I am sure will thank him & treat him & the Branch of his Family with true Politeness.

I am my dear Madam exceedingly well—very happy & very fortunate in my profession.

I have nothing to amuse you with—nothing here but War—Peace I believe & hope will ensue soon.

With every affectionate Regard

I remain

Your obliged Son
Ban. Tarleton

Sir Henry Clinton spent the rest of a desultory summer marching and countermarching the British army around the ramparts of New York. They marched to Mamaroneck on July 8 and next day slogged on to Byram's Bridge. All during the rest of July they marched and camped, marched and camped. In this exercise Tarleton's British Legion always led the right van, Simcoe's Queen's Rangers the center, and Emmerick's Chasseurs the left van. By August 1, 1779, Sir Henry was satisfied, and the light troops returned to their camp at Kingsbridge.

Lieutenant Colonel Tarleton rode down to New York on August 5 for a long conference with his commander in chief and a cheerful cup with Adjutant General John André. While he was away, Simcoe led the Rangers and the Legion as far as New Rochelle, and on August 8 marched them behind the fortifications of New York. For the first time since leaving winter quarters, the dragoons were allowed to disaccouter. But the Americans were pressing so near that the infantry were not allowed to unfix their bayonets from their muskets.

Gaining intelligence that Washington was planning an attempt upon Long Island, Clinton rushed Simcoe and the Queen's Rangers to Oyster Bay. As pressure mounted, on October 19 Sir Henry transferred the British Legion from Fordham to Jericho. To forestall an American amphibious attack, Colonel Simcoe undertook to burn the boats on the Jersey shore. In a lively little skirmish at Brunswick on October 29 he had his horse shot from under him and fell prisoner to the Americans.

The loss of Simcoe left Tarleton in command of the hussars of the Queen's Rangers as well as of the dragoons of the Legion. Clinton declined to promote him, but gave him the additional title of commandant of the British Legion.

In late summer Lord Cornwallis returned from England where he had attended the last illness of Lady Cornwallis. Before departing London he had been closeted with Lord Amherst and Lord Germain and he brought back with him plans for a campaign in the Southern Provinces. Lord Cornwallis also brought with him a dormant commission to succeed Sir Henry Clinton as commander in chief of his Majesty's forces in North America.

In compliance with the directives from the War Office, Sir Henry began mustering part of his troops for embarkation. By mid-December his expeditionary force was in the transports. On December 26, 1779, a fleet of 140 ships, commanded by Vice Admiral Mariot Arbuthnot and convoyed by a flotilla of 13 battleships, broke through the thin ice in New York Harbor. They rendezvoused off Sandy Hook and turned southward.

Aboard the *Romulus*, in command of all the British cavalry and burning to distinguish himself, sailed twenty-five-year-old Banastre Tarleton, Lieutenant Colonel, commandant of the British Legion.

7

Star of Drury Lane

THOMAS AND MARY ROBINSON tripped recklessly along their way. He spent his days following the horses at Epsom or Newmarket and his nights at the faro tables of the fashionable houses around Piccadilly. Foolish, but happy, she traipsed around Vauxhall Gardens or joined the merriment under the twinkling lights of the Pantheon.

The heedless couple plunged on into debt. Soon the loan sharks began demanding their money and threatening Thomas with debtor's prison. Without funds or security of any kind, he seemed hopelessly entangled. Mary then played her ace: "My little collection of Poems, which I had arranged for publication, and which had been ready ever since my marriage, I now determined to print immediately."

Poems, by Mrs. Robinson, an octavo volume of 134 pages, was published by Parker in the spring of 1775. For it the author had selected 26 ballads, odes, and elegies, all written in the style of the poets of the late eighteenth century. *The Monthly Review* of September 1775 was kind:

Though Mrs. Robinson is by no means an Aiken or a More, she *sometimes* expresses herself decently enough on her subject:

In your own power it lies
To blend this life with joy, or care;
Ambition's idle claim despise,
Think yourself happy—and you are.

Through Mary's poems ran the theme of idyllic love, with the idealized lover as Damon, the happy shepherd:

No danger or peril I fear,
No trouble my bliss can remove,
While bless'd in the smiles of my dear,
In the smiles of the youth that I love.

59

Together we sport all the day,
  By the stream that meanders along,
Or else o'er the meadows we stray
  And Damon enchants with his song.

While Lord Lyttelton pursued Mary, teasing her as "the pretty child" and the "poetess Corry," a snide reference to her ill-starred trial as Cordelia, the young wife had bolstered her fortitude by writing an ode to virtue. It, too, appeared in *Poems.*

Ode to Virtue

I

Hail daughter of th' etherial sky,
  Hail everlasting purity,
To thee the seraphs and archangels sing,
Peace to thy altar shall her off'ring bring,
  Free from every earthly woe,
  From every ill that reigns below,
Welcome thou sweet celestial guest,
Receive me to thy gentle breast.

II

Instruct my inexperienc'd heart,
  And all thy precious gifts impart,
That my fond soul may learn of thee to prize,
Joys, which alone from thy first laws arise,
  To thee, my willing heart aspires,
  Thy name, my tender bosom fires,
Teach me, then teach me, by thy sacred rules,
To shun with scorn, the empty joys of fools.

III

Learn me to tread the paths of truth,
  And rectify my erring youth,
That under thy supreme, discerning eye,
Thy precepts my each action dignify,
  And in life's perplexing maze,
  May'st thou guide my blinded ways,
That free from art, from falsehood or disguise
Thy solid joys my soul shall learn to prize.

While Mary was busy correcting the proof sheets of her *Poems,* Thomas Robinson was arrested for debt. Detainers were lodged against him for £1200. As he had completely exhausted his resources, his creditors clapped him into the King's Bench Prison. Bravely Mary went to jail with him, carrying infant Maria Elizabeth. On the third floor they found quarters. In the cold, filth, and squalor of their rooms the young wife tried to make a home for her husband and her baby. She cooked, she washed, and she sewed. "During nine months and three weeks never once did I pass the threshold of our dreary habitation."

The English good-humoredly referred to imprisonment for debt as *captivity*. But there was nothing humorous about it to a young woman who loved gay crowds, fine clothes, and bright lights. "What I suffered during this tedious captivity! My little volume of *Poems* sold but indifferently: my health was considerably impaired; and the trifling income which Mr. Robinson received from his father was scarcely sufficient to support him."

Only Maria Elizabeth charmed the long hours. Wastrel Robinson had found other inmates more to his taste and whiled away his days with Signora Albenisi, an Italian woman of disreputable character. Nor would he work. Charitable friends sent him legal documents to copy. He scorned their aid. Eagerly Mary did the copying for the pittance she earned. As she struggled with housekeeping and fed her baby by earnings from her pen, she thought of one among the rich and powerful who might help. Neatly wrapping a copy of her *Poems*, she sent it by her brother to Georgiana, Duchess of Devonshire.

Touched with pity for the young mother sharing her husband's captivity, Georgiana, reigning queen of English society and superior to all cavil, immediately invited Mary to bring Maria Elizabeth to Devonshire House. Mary came and was overwhelmed by the beautiful Duchess whose "mildness and sensibility beamed in her eyes, and irradiated her countenance."

At their first meeting the two became friends. "She expressed her surprise at seeing so young a person, who had already experienced such vicissitude of fortune. She lamented that my destiny was so little proportioned to what she was pleased to term my desert, and with a tear of gentle sympathy requested that I would accept a proof of her good wishes."

While living on the bounty of the Duchess, Mary again turned to writing poetry. Putting into heroic couplets her experiences in and reflections on prison life, she published

Captivity
A *Poem*
and
Celadon and Lydia
A *Tale*
Dedicated, by Permission
To Her Grace, the Duchess of Devonshire
by
Mrs. Robinson

"I take the occasion of repeating my Thanks to You, for the un-merited Favors your Grace has bestowed upon me," Mary wrote in her "Dedication." Perhaps the Duchess inspired the following reflection:

> If the Benevolent, the Gen'rous few,
> Captivity, and all its horrors knew,
> Then would the Sighs of Grief ne'er heave in vain,
> Or Misery's unheeded voice complain.
> Shall the unhappy bosom, doom'd to share
> The Frowns of Fortune and the pangs of care,
> Unstained with vice, just, eloquent, and brave,
> Bow down submissive to the wealthy knave?

Mary's *Captivity* had far less merit than her earlier *Poems*. But the reviewers were again kind. The sympathetic critic for the October 1777 *Monthly Review* wrote: "Two reasons preclude criticism here. The poems are the production of a lady: and that lady is unhappy."

Ever afterward Mary Robinson loved Georgiana of Devonshire. Years later she paid her tribute to the great dame who had given bread to the ragged mother from the King's Bench Prison:

> The Nightingale with mourning lay,
>   Amid the twilight's purpling glow,
> May sweetly hymn the loss of day,
>   While echo chants her melting woe;
> But what can soothe the wounded breast,
>   And ev'ry aching sense beguile—
> Ah! what can charm the soul to rest,
>   Like Devon's voice or Devon's smile?

Thomas Robinson remained in prison for fifteen months, and the generous Duchess aided his wife in many ways. Other aid, not so generous, was offered: "Numerous messages and letters from Lords Northington and Lyttelton, from Mr. Fitzgerald, and many others were conveyed to me. But they all, except Lord Northington's, were dictated in the language of gallantry, were replete with profusions of *love*, and wishes to release me from my unpleasant and humiliating situation—and were therefore treated with contempt, scorn, and indignation."

By giving fresh securities and fresh bonds Thomas Robinson finally obtained his liberty. With his wife and daughter he left the King's Bench and, hoping to start life afresh, settled in a flat above Lyne's Confectionery Shop in Old Bond Street. Mary was radiant in her free-dom. "I felt as though I had been newly born; I longed to see all my old and intimate associates," she wrote. "The first place of public entertain-ment I went to was Vauxhall."

In the late autumn of 1776, as Thomas and Mary were walking in St. James's Park, they met William Brereton. They had not seen the actor since their captivity and they invited him to their home. After dinner their conversation turned upon a stage career for Mary. Brereton strongly recommended one, for he had seen her rehearsals with David Garrick. Shortly afterward, Brereton returned, bringing with him a friend whom he introduced to Mary as Richard Brinsley Sheridan.

Sheridan, member of a noted theatrical family from Dublin, had been a schoolfellow of Thomas Robinson at Harrow. While his family was living at Bath, the young Harrovian had a romance with Elizabeth Ann Linley, the famed concert singer, with whom he eloped to Paris and for whose honor he later fought two duels. Settling in London, he won recognition with *The Duenna*, a comic opera for which his father-in-law, Dr. Thomas Linley, wrote the music. In 1775 Sheridan rocked London with *The Rivals*.

A few months before, in company with Dr. Linley and Dr. James Ford, court physician, Sheridan had paid Garrick £ 35,000 for his half interest in the Theatre Royal in Drury Lane. As the new manager, Sheridan was scouting for talent. "At his earnest entreaty, I recited some passages from various plays," Mary wrote. "The gentleness of his manners encouraged me."

Mary found Richard Sheridan "strikingly and bewitchingly attractive." Sheridan found her an attractive and promising actress. He offered her a contract to appear in one of the popular plays of Shakespeare.

Although David Garrick had retired after selling his share in Drury Lane, he came out again to tutor Mary. He chose for her the ever popular Juliet, with Brereton playing Romeo. Garrick was "indefatigable at rehearsals; frequently going through the whole character of Romeo himself, until he was completely exhausted with the fatigue of recitation."

The Theatre Royal was crowded with the fashionables of London on the evening of December 10, 1776. Sheridan's patrons were eager to see his latest discovery. The Green Room was filled with critics and reporters. David Garrick sat quietly in the orchestra. At last the curtains parted. Mary, dressed in pale pink satin, trimmed with crepe and spangled with silver, emerged from the wings and started across the great semi-oval stage beyond the pillars of the proscenium.

"The thundering applause that greeted me, nearly over-powered all my faculties," said she. "I stood mute and bending with alarm, which did not subside till I had feebly articulated the few sentences of the first short scene, during the whole of which I never once ventured to look at the audience."

Encouraged by Sheridan from the wings and by the "penetrating eyes of Mr. Garrick, darting their lustre from the center of the Orchestra," Mary gathered strength as the play went forward. "As I acquired courage I found the applause augment; and the night was concluded with peals of clamorous approbation. I was complimented on all sides; but the praise of one object, whom I most wished to please, was flattering even to the extent of human vanity."

Mary Robinson loved old David Garrick. "I heard one of the most fascinating men and the most distinguished geniuses of the age honour me with partial approbation: a new sensation seemed to awake in my bosom."

Years later, in "Elegy to The Memory of Garrick," she wrote:

> Who can forget thy penetrating eye,
> The sweet bewitching smile, th' impassion'd look?
> The clear deep whisper, the pensive sigh,
> The feeling tear that Nature's language spoke?

The critics agreed with Garrick's approbation. Under "Drury Lane" the *Morning Post* of December 11 carried a long review:

> A Lady, whose name is Robinson, made her first appearance last night at this theatre, in the character of Juliet. Her person is genteel; her voice harmonious and admitting of various modulation; and her features, when properly animated, are striking and expressive.
> At present she discovers a theatrical genius in the rough; which, however, in elocution as well as action, seems to require a con- · siderable polishing before it can be brought to perfection. In the scene with the nurse, where she mistakes Tibalt's murder for that of her lover, Romeo, she gave an earnest of stage abilities, which if properly attended to, may prove a credit to herself and the Theatre.

Two days later the *Morning Post* confirmed its first opinion. Mrs. Robinson "has a considerable share of untutored genius, and may, under proper instruction, become an acquisition to the stage."

Next morning its rival, the *New Morning Post, or, General Advertiser*, surpassed that praise. In a sweeping generalization which included Covent Garden as well as Drury Lane, its critic said: "There has not been a lady on this, or the other stage, for some seasons, who promises to make so capital an actress." Then, sensing the qualities the public had learned to expect from Garrick, who had brought back to acting harmony and movement, gesture and grace, the critic continued: "She has eloquence and beauty: the grace of her arms is singular." He admitted that "Her walk is less pleasing," but he concluded: "We may venture to pronounce her an acquisition and an ornament."

The *Gazetteer and New Daily Advertiser* said: "The young lady who performed the part of Juliet last night was received with uncommon and universal applause."

The *Morning Chronicle and London Advertiser* noted that Mrs. Robinson had a "genteel figure, with a handsome face, and a fine masking eye. She appeared to feel the character; and although there wanted a polish in her manner of speaking and more ease in her actions and attitudes, she gave the audience a better impression of her than we can remember them to have received from any new actress for some time past."

Mary was in a dream that had blossomed into dazzling reality. No more hungry days in the King's Bench, no more disdain at Tregunter. Now London was lying at her feet! Sheridan, who kept his eyes on the box office as well as the reviews, on February 17 sent Mary back on the boards as Statira in *Alexander the Great*.

A week later, on February 24, Sheridan starred Mary as Amanda in *A Trip to Scarborough*. This he had expurgated and refurbished from Sir John Vanbrugh's *The Relapse*. As soon as the audience realized that an old play had been fobbed off on them they began to hiss.

Confusion ensued. Seasoned players began muffing their lines so badly that the *Morning Post* deferred criticism until "they are more familiar with their respective parts." Terrified, Mrs. Yates fled from the stage, leaving Mary to the fury of the audience. From the wings Sheridan implored Mary not to quit the stage. Frightened, trembling, she faced the riot and began reciting her lines. Admiring her bravery, the Duke of Cumberland, younger brother of King George, sprang up in his box and shouted to her: "It is not you, but the play they hiss."

At the Duke's shout of encouragement, Mary turned and curtsied. "That curtsy seemed to electrify the whole house, for a thundering peal of applause followed," she wrote.

Next morning, February 25, the *Gazetteer and New Daily Advertiser* exclaimed: "Mrs. Robinson's acting had certainly a just claim to the encouragement of the audience." And it concluded: "We will venture to affirm, that success cannot fail to attend her theatrical abilities."

◌◌

Enthusiasm for the plays of Shakespeare, which had been aroused by the adaptations and brilliant staging of Garrick, was now at its height. During her second season at Drury Lane, Sheridan kept Mary in Shakespearean roles. Most of the press notices about her acting continued favorable. After his production of *Hamlet*, the *Morning Chronicle* of October 1, 1777, said: "Mrs. Robinson looked Ophelia very beautifully, and for so young a theatrical adventurer, played it very pleasingly."

After her appearance in *King Richard III*, the *Morning Chronicle* of October 6 was more enthusiastic: "Mrs. Robinson's Lady Anne was a very respectable performance, and affords us strong hope that a person and face so agreeable and engaging may be well employed in the Service of the Tragic Muse."

For her Benefit, on April 30, 1778, Mary chose *Macbeth:* "To which will be added a new Farce, called *The Lucky Escape,* by Mrs. Robinson." Her Lady Macbeth was immature and left the audience displeased, but *The Lucky Escape* restored their good humor.

In reviewing Mrs. Robinson's first literary creation since her *Captivity,* the critic for the *Morning Post* of May 1 wrote of *The Lucky Escape:* "The piece was well got up, and all the players acquitted themselves with credit." And then he observed with acuteness: "There is a *prettiness* and *sentiment* in the language strongly characteristic of the author."

The reviewer for the *Morning Chronicle* was annoyed with Mrs. Robinson's operetta. "*The Lucky Escape* is evidently one of those hasty escapes from the brain, which are from time to time served up at each theatre, during the course of the benefit season, with a view to engage the attention of the publick, on the score of novelty, but which, for want of solid merit, are rarely, if ever, heard of again." Yet he confessed that "The music was chiefly compiled, and in some parts with taste. It was upon the whole rather pleasing than striking."

Said Mary: "My benefit was flatteringly attended: the boxes were filled with persons of the very highest rank and fashion; and I looked forward with delight both to celebrity and to fortune."

Having now become a star of Drury Lane, Mary received a handsome salary. But with her maids, ponies, and high living and Thomas' courtesans and race horses, the Robinsons were always in debt. All of Mary's Benefits were appropriated for Thomas' bondsmen.

In the summer of 1778, in order to patch up relations with his father, Thomas persuaded Mary to go with him again to Wales. She now found herself a heroine at Tregunter. "I was consulted as the very oracle of fashions; I was gazed at and examined with the most inquisitive curiosity," she wrote. "Mrs. Robinson, the promising young actress, was a very different personage from Mrs. Robinson who had been overwhelmed with sorrows, and came to ask asylum under the roof of vulgar ostentation."

How Mary scorned her husband's relatives for "the low taunts of uncultivated natures, the insolent vulgarity of pride, and the overbearing triumphs of a family, whose loftiest was as inferior to my stock as the small weed is beneath the tallest tree that overshades it."

Upon her return to London, Sheridan offered Mary the part of Maria in the first performance of *The School for Scandal.* "But I was now so unshaped by my increasing size that I made my excuses."

Soon afterward Mary's second daughter, Sophia, was born. Sophia lived only six weeks. During the baby's illness Sheridan offered Mary every encouragement and solicitude. "His attentions were now unremitting; he praised my talents, and he interested himself in my comforts.

When my infant died, and on the day of its dissolution, Mr. Sheridan called. I had seen many proofs of his exquisite sensibility. I had never witnessed one which so strongly impressed my mind as his countenance on entering my apartments. I had not power to speak. All he uttered was 'Beautiful little creature!' at the same time looking at my infant, and sighing with a degree of sympathetic sorrow which penetrated my soul."

Sheridan's attentions were too constant and obvious to pass unnoticed. A whispered scandal began. Yet Mary wrote: "The happiest moments I then knew, were passed in the society of this distinguished being. He saw me ill-bestowed upon a man who neither loved nor valued me; he lamented my destiny but with such delicate propriety, that it consoled while it revealed to me the unhappiness of my situation."

After her return to Drury Lane, for the season of 1778–79, Mary played only three or four roles a month. But her admirers were many. After her Palmira in Mohamet, the Morning Post of November 12, 1778, voiced its tribute: "Mrs. Robinson performed Palmira with spirit, and discovered stage powers that should be more frequently called forth by the managers."

On May 10, 1779, Sheridan presented her as Jacintha in The Suspicious Husband. Next day the Morning Post chortled: "Last night Mrs. Robinson wore the breeches for the first time (on the stage at least)." At the masquerade at Covent Garden on May 21 the beautiful actress attracted great attention by wearing Jacintha's breeches in public.

Gossips continued to revel in the stories that Sheridan was showing more than a manager's interest in the beauty. "Squib," in a letter to the Morning Post of August 25, remarked: "Mrs. Robinson is to the full, as beautiful as Mrs. Cuyler; and Mrs. Robinson has not been overlooked; the manager of Drury Lane has pushed her forward."

Finally stung by the slander, Mary replied with elaborate formality: "Mrs. Robinson presents her compliments to Squib, and desires that the next time he desires to exercise his wit, it may not be at her expense. Conscious of the rectitude of her conduct, both in public and private, Mrs. Robinson does not feel herself the least hurt, at the illnatured sarcasms of an anonymous detractor."

∞

At the age of twenty-one Mary had become the darling of the public. Every role she undertook succeeded. So Sheridan chose her to launch the 1779–80 season at Drury Lane. The production, which opened September 18, was Hamlet, and Mary played Ophelia.

"Mrs. Robinson's Ophelia was natural and affecting," said the Morning Chronicle.

The Morning Post said that "Ophelia found a more than decent representation in Mrs. Robinson, except in her singing, which was rather too discordant even for madness itself."

Next Mary appeared as Fidelia in *The Plain Dealer*, and on October 11 the *Morning Post* praised her: "Fidelia was performed with great ease and feeling by Mrs. Robinson, and is by far the best character that she has attempted."

Admirers began addressing letters to her through the daily press. After her appearance in *Twelfth Night* one of them wrote in the November 3 *Morning Post:* "I am the veriest bigot to old Shakespeare. The Genius himself could not have gazed upon you with more delight; nor have forerun your *motion, action,* and *utterance,* with more tremulous solicitude for your excellence in the character of Viola, than I did."

By now Mary was in the full sweep of the world of fashion. She bought saddle horses and kept ponies and phaeton and liveried footmen. She entertained brilliantly, and her dress became the rage of London. To the Green Room of Drury Lane came men of wealth and fame. Sheridan introduced her to the rising statesman, Charles James Fox, and orator and actress became lifelong friends.

As befitted a reigning sultana of the stage, Mary leased and moved into a spacious home in the Great Piazza situated between the Hummums and the Bedford Arms in Covent Garden. Soon Thomas moved from the Great Piazza and took up residence in Maiden Lane with a figure dancer from Drury Lane.

Among his other vices, "Mr. Robinson played more deeply than was discreet," Mary asserted. "In proportion as play obtained its influence over my husband's mind, his small portion of remaining regard for me visibly decayed." And "My salary was at times inadequate to the expenses which were incurred by an enlarged circle of new acquaintances, which Mr. Robinson had formed since my appearance in the dramatic scene."

To the young star came the distractions and temptations of popularity. "My house was thronged with visitors, and my morning levees were so crowded that I could scarcely find a quiet hour for study."

She confessed: "One of those who paid me most attention was Sir John Lade. The good natured baronet, who was then just of age, was our constant visitor."

In this first year of his manhood, Sir John, heir to a brewery fortune and former ward of Henry Thrale, Dr. Samuel Johnson's brewer friend, was brilliantly heeding the poetic admonition written by Dr. Johnson:

> Long-expected one-and-twenty,
> Ling'ring year, at length, is flown;
> Pride and pleasure, pomp and plenty,
> Great Sir John, are now your own.

•   •   •

Call the Betsies, Kates, and Jennies,
    All the names that banish care,
Lavish of your grandsire's guineas,
    Show the spirit of an heir.

      •   •   •

Wealth, my lad, was made to wander;
    Let it wander at its will;
Call the jockey, call the pander;
    Bid them come and take their fill.

      •   •   •

Should the guardian, friend or mother
    Tell the woes of wilful waste,
Scorn their counsels, scorn their pother,
    You can hang, or drown, at last.

Among the Betsies, Kates, and Jennies upon whom Sir John lavished his grandsire's guineas, none stood higher than Mary. Her home in the Great Piazza became his headquarters. Not only was he paying court to her, but he was also gambling recklessly with her husband. Of course there was gossip; news reporters noted the hardening triangle. On November 9, 1779, *The Gazetteer and New Daily Advertiser* printed:

A Theatrical Anecdote

A certain young Baronet, well known on the Turf, and famous for his high phaeton, had long laid seige to a pretty actress (a married woman) at one of our theaters; he sent her a number of letters, which after she had read (and perhaps did not like, as they might not speak to the purpose) she sent him back again; a kind of bo-peep play was kept up between them in the theatres, and from the Bedford Arms Tavern, and her window. The Baronet is shame faced, and could not address her in person, but by means of some good friend they were brought together, and on Sunday, se'ennight set out in grand cavalcade for Epsom, to celebrate the very joyful occasion of their becoming acquainted. The Baronet went first, attended by a male friend, in his phaeton, and the lady with her husband in a post coach and four, with a footman behind it; the day was spent with the greatest jollity, and the night also, if we may believe report. Since that time they are seen together in public at the theatres and elsewhere, the husband always making one of the party, between whom and the Baronet there is the greatest friendship.

As rumor spread that Lade had won the affections of the actress, whose husband showed no more jealousy than that of a street panderer, almost every rake in London began seeking the acquaintance of the beautiful Mrs. Robinson. "It was at this period that the most alluring temptations were held out to alienate me from the paths of domestic quiet," she said. "Among the list I was addressed with proposals of a libertine nature by a royal Duke, a lofty Marquis, and a City Merchant of considerable fortune, conveyed through the medium of milliners, mantua makers, etc."

The most persistent of these libertines was handsome young Charles Manners, just become Duke of Rutland. He, mistakenly thinking a bold duke could outbid a shamefaced baronet, laid his cards on the table. Said Mary: "A settlement of six hundred pounds per annum was proposed, as the means of estranging me entirely from my husband." But even if her affections could be won, they were not for sale.

തൻ

Mary was now the brightest star in the firmament of Drury Lane. To capitalize on her popularity Sheridan dusted off Garrick's altered version of Shakespeare's *The Winter's Tale*, which had been off the boards for ten years, and on November 20 presented her as Perdita. Her performance was sensational. "She was the pupil of Nature; her feelings were spontaneous, her ideas expanded, and her judgment correct," Mary wrote in her autobiographical *The Natural Daughter*. "She scorned to avail herself of the factitious mummery, that artificial, disgusting trick, which deludes the senses by exciting laughter at the expense of the understanding. She was lively and unaffected."

Recognizing incipient swagger, the *Morning Post* of November 22 growled: "Mrs. Robinson's *Perdita* would have been very decent, but for that strange kind of *niddle* and *noddle* that she now throws into every character, comic as well as tragic."

Niddle or noddle, everybody went to Drury Lane to see Perdita. The *Morning Post* noted that at the second presentation she was honored by the presence of such leaders of London society as the Duke and Duchess of Devonshire, Lord and Lady Melbourne, Lord and Lady Spencer, Lord and Lady Cranbourne, and Lord and Lady Onslow.

After this performance the *Gazetteer and New Daily Advertiser* published a long criticism:

> The piece is in general well cast and ably performed, but the dresses, on which much of the effect depends, were liable to very glaring objections. Shakespeare has been particularly attentive to the dress of Florizel and Perdita:

> > Your high self you have obscur'd
> > With a swain's wearing, and me poor lowly maid,
> > Most goddess-like, prank'd up—

> To correspond with this description Florizel and Perdita have hitherto appeared in beautiful dresses, covered with flowers of

both the same pattern, and she wore an ornamented sheep hook, instead of which Mrs. Robinson appears in a common jacket, and wears the usual red ribbons of an ordinary milk maid, and in this dress she also appears with the King to view the supposed statue of Hermione, after she is acknowledged his daughter.

While the echo from her success as Perdita was reverberating around London, Sheridan, always with his eye on the box office, sent Mary back on the boards next evening as Amanda in A Trip to Scarborough. The next night he cast her again as Perdita. This time the echo of applause swept through the halls of St. James's Palace and brought the fulfillment of all Mary's dreams: a command performance!

King George and Queen Charlotte wished to see the beautiful Mrs. Robinson as Perdita. On December 3, 1779, Richard Sheridan advertised in the London daily newspapers:

Drury Lane, by Command of their Majesties
The sixth time these ten years
At the Theatre Royal in Drury Lane
This Day will be Presented

The Winter's Tale (altered by Garrick from Shakespeare)

8
Bloody Tarleton

"*O*UR PASSAGE, with very few Exceptions," said Tarleton, "was a long Series of blustering, disagreeable Weather, from the 26 of December, when we sailed from Sandy Hook, till the first of February, when the Fleet arrived at Tybee Island." Off Cape Hatteras the fleet ran into a storm which the oldest seaman along the coast said was the worst in a generation. The ships were scattered.

When Lieutenant Colonel Tarleton arrived at Tybee aboard the *Romulus*, he was thoroughly discouraged. Admiral Arbuthnot had lost neither soldier nor sailor, but of the hundreds of trained horses so carefully embarked only 300 had survived. The others, bruised, broken, and ill, had been thrown overboard. One transport had saved only one out of thirty-one.

The commandant of the British Legion found the condition of his corps distressing. "The horses of both officers and men, which had been embarked in excellent order, were destroyed, owing to the badness of the vessels employed to transport them, or to the severity of the weather on the passage." Unfortunately there were no substitutes to be found in Georgia to remedy such a catastrophe.

To his friend John André, stationed with the troops on John's Island, near Charleston, Banastre sent a note hinting of his discouragement:

On board the Romulus off Tybee
Feb. 15, 1780

My dear André
One line & a half—The Eleanor arrived here yesterday—We are for Sava'h as soon as Weather furnishes Wind I should have said —I have trespassed but I won't relate Distresses—I hate Difficulties of any kind.

Ban. Tarleton

Then Ban set out to remedy the situation. Requisitioning the boats of the quartermaster general, he moved his men and equipment to Port Royal, South Carolina, "in order to collect at that place, from friends and enemies, by money or by force, all the horses belonging to the islands in the neighborhood."

Having thus remounted the 17th Light Dragoons and the cavalry of the Legion, Tarleton camped at Beaufort to await the arrival of General Patterson, leading an army from Savannah to Charleston. On March 18 he made a sweep around Beaufort and surprised eighty American militiamen at Salkehatchee Bridge. He killed or wounded several of them. On March 21 he joined Patterson at Horse Shoe and with him marched on to Jacksonboro. Crossing the Edisto River with his light dragoons on March 23, he moved on ahead of Patterson and struck a party of militia and dragoons at the plantation of Lieutenant Governor Thomas Bee. He killed ten and captured four of them.

During the march northward the Legion furnished scouts and vedettes for Patterson's force and on several occasions skirmished with Lieutenant Colonel William Washington's light horse or Count Pulaski's hussars. On March 25 the British Legion arrived at Stono River and was inspected by Sir Henry Clinton. Next day Tarleton advanced against Colonel Washington, who had now retreated to Governor John Rutledge's plantation, between Rantowle's Bridge and Ashley Ferry. But Washington drove back the British Legion, taking several prisoners, including Lieutenant Colonel Hamilton of the North Carolina Provincial Regiment. He almost captured Sir Henry Clinton.

On March 29, 1780, the British army, with their ferryboats protected by galleys under Captain Elphinstone of the Royal Navy, crossed the Ashley River and assembled on Charleston Neck, about twelve miles above Charleston. The following day the light infantry and yagers seized the principal road and marched down it until they were a mile and half above the city. From there they fanned out, extending their flanks to the Ashley and the Cooper rivers and thus effectually invested Charleston. On the night of April 1 they began their system of redoubts and parallels and settled down to a conventional siege.

On April 1 Major André, as deputy adjutant general, wrote a note to Tarleton relaying Sir Henry Clinton's orders for him to lead the British Legion across Ashley River: "I have, by the General's orders, just closed a letter to Brigadier-general Patterson, in consequence of which a march of cavalry, light and legion infantry will be ordered: It is to seek a passage across Ashley river, at or above Dorchester and Baycon bridge, and by this means to join the army before Charles Town. The general would not have you undertake any excursion out of your route to us, or make any other delays, after passing the river, than for the purpose of taking forage: Between your present encampment and the passage you will of course make none, as it would invite opposition."

The march and the passage across the Ashley were made without opposition, although Washington with a considerable force lay at Middleton plantation, near Goose Creek. Tarleton, with the 17th Light Dragoons and the British Legion, went into camp at the Quarter House, six miles above Charleston. On April 5 he led out 500 infantrymen and 50 horsemen in an attempt to surprise Washington, who still lay at Middleton's, but the surprise failed. Washington retreated to the 23 Mile House.

On April 12 Major Patrick Ferguson and his corps of marksmen arrived at Tarleton's camp at the Quarter House. Together they advanced ten miles up the neck to Goose Creek. Next day Lieutenant Colonel James Webster joined them with the 33rd and 64th Regiments of infantry. In the evening Tarleton and Ferguson moved on toward Moncks Corner, having intelligence that Colonel Washington had retreated from the 23 Mile House in order to join Brigadier General Isaac Huger, commanding Colonel Daniel Horry's cavalry, Count Pulaski's hussars, and other horsemen recently arrived from Virginia.

The advance guard of the Legion captured a Negro messenger bearing a letter from Huger's camp to Charleston. From the letter and the bearer Tarleton learned the disposition of the American troops at Moncks Corner. The cavalry had been posted in front of Cooper River and the militia stationed in Biggin Church, commanding Biggin Bridge. The rest of the forces had been distributed on the opposite bank of the river.

Tarleton moved his troops in silence, and at three o'clock in the morning of April 14 he struck. The Americans were completely surprised. Major Paul Vernier, commanding Pulaski's Legion, and some other officers and men who attempted to defend themselves were killed or wounded. General Huger, Colonels Washington and Jamieson, with many officers and men, fled on foot to the swamps. Major Cochrane, commanding the infantry of the British Legion, routed the Americans from Biggin Church and seized the bridge over Cooper River.

Horribly mangled by the sabers of the dragoons, Major Vernier was taken into a nearby house and thrown on a bare wooden table, where he lay bleeding and cursing. With his last breath he damned the Americans for their cowardice and God-damned the British for their barbarity in sabering him after he had surrendered and begged for quarter.

During the excitement after the battle three of Tarleton's dragoons broke into Fair Lawn, the plantation home of the distinguished Loyalist Sir John Colleton. Here women from surrounding plantations had taken refuge, and the soldiers singled out three of the fairest for rape. In the scuffle the wife of a Charleston physician received several slashes from a sword. The women finally escaped and fled to the British officers for protection.

Colonel Webster ordered the immediate arrest of their assailants. Major Ferguson, one of the most chivalrous men in the British army, demanded that they be instantly put to death. Finally the dragoons were sent to Charleston, court-martialed, and flogged without mercy.

In the affairs at Moncks Corner and Biggin Bridge, the British had an officer and 2 men wounded, but the Americans had 15 killed and 17 wounded. About 100 officers, dragoons, and hussars fell prisoner to the British Legion. More important to the British, because of the poor quality of their mounts, was the capture of 83 horses that had belonged to the American officers and their dragoons.

From Moncks Corner, Colonel Webster dispatched Tarleton and his cavalry into the country west of Cooper River to secure all the boats and to seize Bonneau's Ferry. The territory between Cooper and Ashley rivers was large. Said Tarleton: "The cavalry was kept constantly in motion, to gain intelligence of the enemy's designs, and to learn the situation of the country."

With this territory but lightly held by Tarleton's dragoons, it was still possible for the American army to evacuate Charleston, cross the Cooper, and fight its way northward. But the arrival of reinforcements from New York on April 18 enabled Clinton to send Lord Cornwallis with an army into the quarter between Cooper River and the Atlantic Ocean.

The British armies now stretched from the Edisto to the Ashley, from the Ashley to the Cooper, and from the Cooper to the Atlantic. Clinton had bottled up the American army. As he waited for General Lincoln to capitulate, he ordered Lord Cornwallis to safeguard the British rear.

Cornwallis relayed the commander's orders to Colonel Tarleton.

Camp near St. Thomas Church
April 25, 1780

Sir,

The commander in chief having directed me to use every effort to prevent supplies and reinforcements being thrown into Charles town, but particularly to guard against the garrison's escaping out of it and its dependent fortresses; I find it necessary at present to place the corps under my command on the east side of Miller's bridge, keeping a redoubt on the west side to secure a communication; I must therefore commit the care of the country between the Cooper and the Wando to your charge, with the cavalry and the infantry of the legion. The principal objects of your care will be the landing places on the west side of the Wando and in Daniel's island; and I trust in your vigilance that I shall receive the earliest information of any material movement of the enemy in that quarter; I must likewise recommend it to you to take every opportunity of procuring intelligence, either from the town, or the Santee river and back country, I leave it to your discretion to take such positions as you shall find most convenient: You will please to report to me whenever you move, that I may know where to find you. As you will be so constantly moving, you will not of course be able to embarrass yourself with the care of such stores as may fall into your hands: If you apprehend that any such may be in danger of being retaken by the enemy, and that they will be useful to them, you will please to destroy them. I must recommend it to you in the strongest manner to use your utmost endeavors to prevent the troops under your command from committing irregularities, and I am convinced that my recommendation will have weight, when I assure you that such conduct will be highly agreeable to the commander in chief.

I am, Sir,

Your most obedient, humble servant

Cornwallis

Lieut. Col. Tarleton

His Lordship's order set the pattern for most of Tarleton's future activities: keep constantly moving, secure intelligence, capture and burn all stores possible, and restrain all irregular conduct among the troops of the British Legion.

But St. Thomas offered more than campaigning. At Brabant, the plantation of Bishop Smith, many women from the surrounding parishes had taken refuge. Brabant became a constant rendezvous for the Green Dragoon. His handsome appearance, his Oxford wit, and his courtly manners endeared him to both friend and foe. In after years these ladies testified that their most courteous and gallant admirer had been Banastre Tarleton!

The American cavalry had begun to assemble north of Santee River. With fresh dragoons from the northern states, with those who had escaped capture at Moncks Corner, and with Horry's horsemen, on May 5 Colonel Anthony White crossed the Santee at Dupui's Ferry. Next morning at Wambaw, Colonel Elias Ball's plantation, near Strawberry, he found an officer and 17 men from Tarleton's command busy foraging. He captured them without resistance. Sweeping southeastward, Colonel White planned to recross the Santee at Lenud's Ferry, where Colonel Abraham Buford had been posted with 200 soldiers of the 3rd Regiment of Virginia.

Without knowledge of White's raid, Tarleton was sweeping northwestward with 150 dragoons. On the road he met a Loyalist who had witnessed the capture of the dragoons at Ball's plantation. The Tory gave the British complete information about Colonel White's forces, line of march, and apparent intention of recrossing the Santee.

Pressing rapidly forward, Tarleton overtook White at Lenud's Ferry at three o'clock in the afternoon. As soon as they spied the American vedettes, he ordered his Legion to charge them and pursue them into the main body of troops standing around the ferry.

"The corps being totally surprised, resistance and slaughter soon ceased," said Tarleton. "Five officers and thirty-six men were killed and wounded; seven officers and sixty dragoons were taken prisoners; and the whole party of light infantry were rescued, as the boat·was pushing off to convoy them to the opposite shore. All the horses, and accoutrements of the Americans were captured. Colonels White, Washington, and Jamieson, with some other officers and men, availed themselves of their swimming, to make their escape, while many who wished to follow their example perished in the river."

Sir Henry Clinton was impressed with the vigor and brilliance of the action. In his report to Lord Amherst he wrote: "The Cavalry under Lieut. Col. Tarleton had again the good fortune which Conduct and Gallantry deserve."

ᐯᑎᕮ

While Tarleton patroled the approaches and Lord Cornwallis and General Patterson protected the British flanks, Sir Henry Clinton vigorously pressed the siege. The position of the Americans had become hopeless, and on May 11, 1780, General Lincoln signed the articles of capitulation. Next day General Alexander Leslie paraded the British troops down King Street and took possession of Charleston.

Two days later Banastre rode down to see the town. While there, with friends leaving for England, he dashed off a note to his mother:

May 14 Charles Town

My dear Madam
    I have wrote often—but I write short—I am very well—very much mortified by Cr—very successful here & very much befriended by Sir Henry Clinton.
    He will by his Interest & Recommendation soon raise

Your affectionate Son
Ban. Tarleton

I shall thank you for some shirts.

In his report to Lord Amherst on the capture of Charleston, Sir Henry wrote on May 13: "And I have to give the greatest Praise to Lieut. Colonel Tarleton and the Cavalry for their Conduct, Bravery, and Eminent Services."

But Tarleton had come to headquarters to discuss a personal problem with the commander in chief. The War Office had ordered the Liverpool Volunteers to prepare for duty in Jamaica, and the commanding officer had written Tarleton to return to his regiment. When Banastre had demurred, a junior captain had been promoted over him to the rank of major.

A similar call had come to Simcoe, and so on May 15 Clinton wrote Lord Amherst, requesting that the two captains in the regular army be left as lieutenant colonels in command of their Provincial regiments. In pleading to retain them, Sir Henry wrote: "These Corps I must observe, my Lord, exist in their Chiefs; and I am persuaded that losing them, they might be reduced to the State of some other Provincial Battalions, very weak in numbers, and not trained in the same exemplary degree of Care or Discipline; tho they are now such as I can place the highest confidence in."

Sir Henry also recommended that Simcoe and Tarleton be promoted from captains to majors in the regular army: "I must add that I hope the Dates of their Promotion will leave them no Recollection of their present Suspense; and that Lieutenant Colonel Tarleton will not see the Major of the Liverpool Regiment his Senior."

Having captured the only American army in the Southern Provinces, Sir Henry Clinton began embarking many of his troops for the return to New York. Before leaving he ordered three columns to push into the back country. One was to move up the Savannah River to Augusta. The Royal Provincials under Lieutenant Colonel Nisbet Balfour were to strike boldly for the village of Ninety-Six. The most powerful force, under command of Lord Cornwallis, was ordered to cross the Santee River and march up the northeast bank in pursuit of the Americans under Colonel Buford now retreating toward North Carolina.

Earl Cornwallis, with 2500 men and five pieces of artillery, broke camp near Huger's Bridge on May 18 and marched toward Lenud's Ferry. As soon as the British Legion had crossed Santee River, Cornwallis sent Tarleton and his Green Horse to sweep the country as far as Georgetown. On May 22 the army marched from Lenud's Ferry. Although suffering from the heat, the infantry marched rapidly toward Nelson's Ferry. Since Colonel Buford and his men had passed along this road ten days earlier, Lord Cornwallis realized that it would be impossible to overtake him with the infantry. But as he had heard that Buford's regiment was escorting Governor Rutledge and a party who had escaped the encirclement of Charleston, he ordered Tarleton to select 40 men of the 17th Dragoons and 130 horsemen and 100 mounted infantry from the British Legion, to take a three-pounder, and to set out in pursuit of the Virginians.

Excited by the prospect of catching a rebel governor, on May 27 Tarleton's detachment left the army near Nelson's Ferry. Although many horses carried both a dragoon and an infantryman, Banastre began forcing his march. Across the High Hills of Santee—pausing long enough to burn a house of Colonel Thomas Sumter—and then through the swamps of the Wateree they rode. By next afternoon they had covered the sixty miles to Camden.

Here Tarleton learned that Buford and his regiment had lately encamped at Rugeley's Mill, twelve miles north of Camden. On May 26 they had broken camp and were marching with great diligence to join a corps moving from Salisbury to Charlotte. After resting his troops until two o'clock on the morning of May 29, Tarleton continued the pursuit. By daylight he had reached Rugeley's Mill. There he learned that the Americans were only twenty miles in front and retreating along the road to the settlement on the Catawba River.

What he did not learn was that Colonel Henry Rugeley, a Loyalist with a foot in each camp, had been entertaining Governor Rutledge and his party at Clermont, his home near the mill; and that upon receiving news that the British Legion had reached Camden, Rugeley had awakened his guests and sent them speeding beyond the grasp of the Green Dragoon.

At three o'clock in the sultry afternoon of May 29, 1780, near the settlement of the Waxhaws, on the line between North and South Carolina, the advance guard of the British Legion overtook Colonel Buford's regiment. Tarleton immediately wrote a summons to surrender and sent it to Colonel Buford by Captain Kinlock:

Wacsaws, May 29, 1780

Sir,

Resistance being vain, to prevent the effusion of human blood, I make offers which can never be repeated:—You are now almost encompassed by a corps of seven hundred light troops on horseback, half of that number are infantry with cannon, the rest cavalry: Earl Cornwallis is likewise within a short march with nine British battalions.

I warn you of the temerity of further inimical proceedings, and I hold out the following conditions, which are nearly the same as were accepted by Charles town: But if any persons attempt to fly after this flag is received, rest assured that their rank shall not protect them, if taken, from rigorous treatment.

1st Art. All officers to be prisoners of war, but admitted to parole, and allowed to return to their habitations until exchanged.

2nd Art. All continental soldiers to go to Lamprie's point, or any neighboring post, to remain there till exchanged, and to receive the same provisions as British soldiers.

3rd Art. All militia soldiers to be prisoners upon parole at their respective habitations.

4th Art. All arms, artillery, ammunition, stores, provisions, waggons, horses, etc., to be faithfully delivered.

5th Art. All officers to be allowed their private baggage and horses, and to have their side arms returned.

I expect an answer to these propositions as soon as possible; if they are accepted, you will order every person under your com-

mand to pile his arms in one hour after you receive the flag: If
you are rash enough to reject them, the blood be upon your head.

I have the honor to be,

Ban. Tarleton
Lieutenant Colonel, Commandant of
the British Legion

Colonel Buford, etc., etc.

Buford was in a desperate situation. His wagon train had distanced
the foot soldiers and was racing toward Salisbury. His artillery, commanded by Captain Carter, had separated from the main body and was
also racing for safety. Therefore, without halting his troops, who were
marching at double time in an effort to reach a clearing in which they
could form for battle, Buford detained Kinlock for a time and then,
with more audacity than judgment, sent him back to Tarleton with a
defiant reply:

Wacsaws, May 29, 1780
Sir, I reject your proposals, and shall defend myself to the last
extremity.

I have the honour to be, etc.

Abr. Buford, Col.

Lieut. Col. Tarleton,
Commanding British Legion

The advance guard of the Legion now charged Buford's rear guard.
A dragoon sabered Lieutenant Pearson, and as he fell, another slashed
obliquely across his face, splitting his nose, lips, tongue, and jaw. The
green horsemen wheeled back to their line, having captured a sergeant
and four American light dragoons. Both Tarleton and Buford saw the
skirmish and prepared for battle.

Colonel Buford chose to defend. He wheeled his force, consisting of
380 Continental infantry and a detachment of Colonel Washington's
cavalry, into an open wood on the right side of the road. Here he
formed his infantry in a line, with a small reserve, and placed Ensign
Cruit with his colors in the center.

Tarleton prepared to attack. He arranged his force in conventional
tactical order. To Major Cochrane he confided his right wing, consisting of 60 dragoons and about 50 infantrymen. To Captains Corbet and
Kinlock he entrusted the center, consisting of the 17th Dragoons and
part of the British Legion. He instructed them to charge the center of
the American line. To himself Tarleton assigned the left wing, consisting of 30 chosen horsemen and some infantrymen, with the plan of
assaulting the American right flank and rear.

Only three hundred yards separated the forces, and Tarleton was surprised to hear the American officers shouting to their men to hold fire

until the dragoons were within ten paces. He knew that a horseman can cover ten yards in one second. Said he: "This forbearance in not firing before the dragoons were within ten yards of the object of their attack, prevented their falling into confusion on the charge, and likewise deprived the Americans of the further use of their ammunition."

The British charged. Tarleton swung around the right flank of the Americans and raced for their standard bearer. He sabered Cruit even as the young ensign raised the white flag. A Continental fired at Tarleton and killed his horse. Before he could mount another, his dragoons were victorious and out of control.

The Americans soon sued for quarter. A few, notwithstanding, continued to fire. The British swung their sabers indiscriminately until all had grounded arms.

As Captain John Stokes used his sword to protect his head from the saber of a dragoon, another rode past and sliced off his right hand with one stroke. Stokes seized his sword in his left hand and fought until another stroke split his left arm from wrist to shoulder. Another stroke laid his head open the whole length of his crown down to his eyebrows.

"Do you ask quarter?" shouted an infantryman to the prostrate officer.

"I do not; finish me as soon as possible," replied Stokes.

Twice the soldier drove his bayonet through the helpless American. Another infantryman repeated the question and received the same answer. Twice he transfixed Stokes with his bayonet. Finally a humane British sergeant offered his protection. As he carried the officer to safety, he was obliged to lay him down and stand over him to protect him from the inflamed Legionnaires.

Dr. Stapleton, surgeon of the British Legion, refused to touch Stokes until he finished bandaging the wounded British. Finally Lieutenant Pateschall of the 17th Dragoons, himself bleeding profusely, ordered Stapleton to dress the most severely wounded Americans. The surgeon grudgingly stuffed rough tow into their wounds. Incredibly, Cruit, Stokes, and Pearson lived.

The infantrymen continued to sweep over the ground, plunging their bayonets into any living American. Where several had fallen together, they used their bayonets to untangle them, in order to finish off those on the bottom. In this massacre was born the American battle cry of "Tarleton's quarter!"

Flushed with blood and victory, Tarleton rushed a note to Lord Cornwallis:

May 29, 1780

My Lord

I am extremely fatigued with overtaking the Enemy & beating them—I summoned the Corps—they refused my terms—I have cut

170 Off'rs and Men to pieces—2 six pounders 2 pair culverin 2 Royals & all their Baggage have fallen into my Hands—

I have lost 2 Off'rs killed one wounded & between 10 & 20 men killed and wounded with a number missing.

I shall collect a regular report for your Lordship upon my arrival at C—— to which place I shall proceed in case I do not meet with satisfactory intelligence concern'g Mr. Gos'n & of another I have out—

> I have the Honor to be
> Your most devoted
> B. Tarleton

Next morning the commandant of the British Legion wrote a full battle report:

My Lord,

I have the honour to inform you, that yesterday at three o'clock, P.M. after a march of one hundred and five miles in fifty-four hours, with the corps of cavalry, the infantry of the legion, mounted, on horses, and a three pounder, at Wacsaw, near the line which divided North from South Carolina, the rebel force, commanded by Colonel Buford, consisting of the 11th Virginia and detachments of other regiments, from the same province, with artillery, and some cavalry, were brought to action.

After the summons, in which terms similar to those accepted by Charles town were offered, and positively rejected, the action commenced in a wood; the attacks were pointed at both flanks, the front, and reserve, by two hundred and seventy cavalry and infantry blended, and at the same instant all were equally victorious, few of the enemy escaping, except the commanding officer by a precipitate flight on horseback.

It is above my ability to say any thing in commendation of the bravery and exertion of officers and men. I leave their merit to your lordship's consideration.

> I have the honour to be, etc.
> Ban. Tarleton.
> Lieutenant-colonel, commandant
> of the British legion.

Lieutenant-general Earl Cornwallis, etc., etc.

Appended to this letter were detailed lists of the killed and wounded on both sides, the prisoners, and the captured equipment and supplies.

Lord Cornwallis rushed Tarleton's first letter from Waxhaws off to Sir Henry Clinton in Charleston. With Tarleton's battle report he dispatched a letter of encomium:

Camden, June 2, 1780

Sir,

In my letter of the 30th of last month, I enclosed a note from Lieutenant Colonel Tarleton, wrote in great haste from the field of action, and I explained my reasons for sending the detachment under his command in pursuit of the enemy.

I have now the honour of transmitting to you his account of the march and engagement, with the loss on both sides.

I can only add the highest encomiums on the conduct of Lieutenant-colonel Tarleton. It will give me the most sensible satisfaction to hear that your Excellency has been able to obtain for him some distinguishing mark of His Majesty's favor.

I have the honour to be, etc.

Cornwallis

His Excellency Sir Henry Clinton,
K.B., etc.

Sir Henry immediately forwarded the letters from both Tarleton and Cornwallis to Lord George Germain, with a lukewarm covering letter:

Romulus, off Charles town bar,
June 5, 1780

My Lord,

I have just received from Earl Cornwallis a letter, enclosing a more particular report than has yet been received from Lieutenant-colonel Tarleton, of the affair at Wacsaw. I have the honour to enclose both, together with a return of the killed and wounded, and of the artillery and other implements taken.

Your lordship will observe, that the enemy's killed and wounded, and taken, exceed Lieutenant-colonel Tarleton's numbers with which he attacked them.

I have the honour to be, etc.

H. Clinton

All of these letters were published in a *London Gazette Extraordinary* on July 5, 1780. English newspapers everywhere reprinted them. From an unsung lieutenant-colonel of Provincial troops, Banastre Tarleton soared into a popular hero. The *London Chronicle* of July 18 epitomized the national feeling toward the massacre of Waxhaws: "Col. Tarleton knew, that having taken a command of the King's troops, the duty he owed to his country directed him to fight and conquer."

But to Americans he became the most hated man in the British army: a savage and a butcher, cruel and merciless, forever to bear the hated name of Bloody Tarleton.

9

Along Black River

$\mathcal{A}$FTER THE MASSACRE at the Waxhaws, Lieutenant Colonel Tarleton and his troops buried their dead and rode leisurely back to Camden. In one bloody stroke they had destroyed the last organized force in South Carolina. Never was victory more complete. Never did the path of conquest seem easier than when they went into bivouac beneath the live oaks on the edge of the village.

Lord Cornwallis and the main army joined the Legion on June 1, and at Logtown, about a mile away, his Lordship established a camp and a supply depot for operations in upper South Carolina. To overawe the Whigs and protect the Loyalists, he had already posted Lieutenant Colonel Balfour and a regiment of Royal Provincials at Ninety-Six. From Camden he now sent Lord Rawdon and the Volunteers of Ireland to the Waxhaws. A few days afterward he sent Lieutenant Colonel George Turnbull with the New York Volunteers and Captain Christian Huck's troop of green dragoons to Rocky Mount. And then to complete his line of posts along the frontier he sent Major Archibald McArthur with the 71st Regiment to Cheraw.

To Tarleton and the British Legion his Lordship assigned the task of keeping open communications between these strong points. For the first weeks the rebels were quiescent, and the Green Horse tramped unmolested from Georgetown to Cheraw and on to Camden and Ninety-Six. So peaceful was the back country that the work of the couriers became routine. And so about the middle of June, at the request of Lord Cornwallis, who wished his dragoons augmented and re-equipped before the campaign into North Carolina, Banastre turned the command of the Legion over to Major Cochrane and rode down to the British headquarters in Charleston.

When the Green Dragoon reached the capital city, he was quartered in the home of a leading Whig. The husband was with the American troops, and Ban let his poor hostess keep only one room of the house for herself and her children. The others he kept for himself, his orderlies, bodyguards, and friends. When he began making merry, the lady remonstrated and asked for another room. With firm politeness he scrawled her a note saying that "reflection convinces me that enemies should not be allowed any conveniences."

Among the merriest of his friends was George Hanger. As a captain in the Hessian Yagers, Hanger had been stationed in Savannah. When General Patterson had marched from Savannah to join Sir Henry Clinton for the attack on Charleston, Hanger had commanded a battalion of Hessians. When the British Legion joined Patterson's corps at Beaufort, the commandant of the Legion renewed his friendship with the Captain.

Sir Henry had needed a German-speaking Englishman for liaison with the Hessians, and so he appointed Hanger an aide-de-camp. Noted for his recklessness, Hanger served Clinton well. He personally scouted the defenses of Charleston and advised Sir Henry where to strike.

Before his return to New York, Clinton gave the Captain an assignment of which he informed Lord Cornwallis, in a letter dated Charles Town, June 1, 1780: "Having Judged it to be for the good of his Majesty's Service that some fit and qualified persons should be appointed to superintend the Militia in the Southern Provinces, I have made choice of Major Ferguson of the 71st regiment and Captain Hanger of the Corps of Jagers, for that Service. And I have accordingly given them Commissions appointing Major Ferguson Inspector of Militia and Major Commandant of the First Battalion of Militia to be raised, and Captain Hanger Deputy Inspector with the Brevet rank of Major of Militia."

George Hanger was the third son of Gabriel, Lord Coleraine. After attending a preparatory school, George matriculated at Eton, where he became a noted hellion. "At that early period," he confessed in his memoirs, "I had a most decided preference for female society, and passed as much time in the company of women as I have ever done since. A carpenter's wife was the first object of my early affections; nor can I well express the nature of my obligations to her. Frequently have I risked breaking my neck in getting over the roof of my boarding-house at night, to pass a few hours with some favorite grisette of Windsor. During the latter part of my time at Eton, to perfect my education, I became attached to, and was very much enamoured of, the daughter of a vendor of cabbages."

After George loitered through the Sixth Form at Eton, Lord Coleraine sent him to the University of Göttingen. After learning to speak German, he deserted the University for the army of Frederick the Great. Here he learned cavalry tactics under the eye of famed General von

Luckner. Returning to England in January 1771 he purchased a commission as ensign in the 1st Regiment of Footguards.

The Guardsman was harum-scarum, extravagant, and irascible. Falling in love with one whom he called "the lovely Egyptea of Norwood," a gypsy who had a sweet voice and played charmingly on the dulcimer, he married her according to the rites of her gypsy tribe. Then Ensign and Mrs. Hanger settled in London, where he introduced her to his fellow officers, bragged of her love and fidelity, and remained enchanted until he awoke one morning to find that his lovely Egyptea had run off with a bandy-legged tinker.

Hanger consoled himself by plunging into the world of fashion. He became a macaroni. His older brother, William, Lord Coleraine, popularly known as Blue Hanger from the light blue color he affected in his clothes, was recognized in the London clubs as perhaps the best-dressed man of his age. George rivaled William in sartorial extravagance.

"For one winter's dress-clothes only it cost me £900," he admitted. Then he bragged about his wardrobe for the birthday balls of the King and Queen. "I was always handsomely dressed at every birthday; but for one in particular I put myself to a very great expense, having two suits for that day. My morning vestments cost me near £80, and those for the ball above £180. It was a satin coat *brode en plain et sur les coutures*; and the first satin coat that had ever made its appearance in this country."

Ensign Hanger was also noted for a hot temper. Before his twenty-first birthday he had fought three duels. Between his flirting and fighting, he neglected his duties, and in 1776 a junior was promoted over him. Angry and disgusted, he resigned his commission in the Footguards. Soon afterward, however, King George began hiring troops from Hesse-Cassel to fight in America, and Hanger purchased a commission as captain in the yagers and sailed for America with the Hessians under General Wilhelm von Knyphausen.

Captain Hanger loved the Hessian uniform, with its short blue coat ornamented with gold frogs and with its broad sword belt. He had swaggered around New York in it, gambled, and became a hardened roué. In Charleston he still played the dandy. With the family upon whom he had been quartered he was notorious for the train of strumpets, dogs, and monkeys he kept in his rooms.

Tarleton admired Hanger. As commandant of the British Legion, Banastre had decided that Major Cochrane should devote all of his time to its infantry. He now decided that Major Hanger would make a daring leader of its dragoons. So, even before broaching the subject to Lord Cornwallis, Ban went over his Lordship's head in a secret letter to Major John André, who had returned to New York, and suggested that André ask Sir Henry Clinton to assign Hanger to the British Legion.

Charles Town June 21, 1780

My dear André,

I beg you will make the following request immediately made known to his Excellency and I rely upon your interest & Friendship—

My Lord Cornwallis has ordered the Troops of Cavalry to be Completed & then Augmented—No service requiring more, I shall require an addition of Officers—

It will be pleasing to Major Hanger & highly pleasing to me to have him appointed Major to the Cavalry of the. Legion which Step will neither interfere with Major Cochrane or any other Person.

I once mentioned this affair to Sir Henry Clinton. He seemed to attend to it & gave assent to its Execution, since which I have not had the Honour of conversing further on the Subject with his Excellency.

I have many material things to say to you, but I devote this Letter to the Subject which most interests me. I shall send a duplicate & triplicate in case of Accident but pray send an early Answer that my Friend may join us soon if appointed.

I am yours with the greatest Esteem & Regard

Ban. Tarleton

On June 1, 1780, Sir Henry Clinton and Admiral Mariot Arbuthnot had offered the rebels in South Carolina "pardon for their past treasonable offenses, and a reinstatement in their rights and immunities heretofore enjoyed, exempt from taxation, except by their own legislature." Because of this conciliation, men began flocking into Charleston for pardon. Even such leaders as Joseph Kershaw, Isaac Hayne, and Andrew Pickens came in and signed their paroles.

With such good augury, Lord Cornwallis decided to re-establish civil government in South Carolina. Entrusting the command of the army at Camden to Lord Rawdon, early on June 21 his Lordship rode off toward Charleston. Arriving in the capital, he established headquarters at Drayton Hall, the magnificent home of William Henry Drayton, a Congressman then in Philadelphia. From there he began directing both civil and military affairs.

Among the petty military problems laid on his desk was that of changing Hanger's assignment. Although commander in chief in the Southern Provinces, Cornwallis was reluctant to countermand any order left by Clinton.

But Tarleton wheedled, and on August 6 his Lordship wrote Sir Henry: "Poor Hanger is always willing to do his best, but he did not think that he should be very useful, in collecting the lists, fixing the Officers, and establishing the militia in the different districts; and as He found that the Attempt would take him up many months & would be entirely a civil employment, He beg'd that he might act as a Volunteer Major of

Tarleton's Cavalry: as Tarleton seemed to wish it very much, I have given my consent until your pleasure shall be known."

ᴄⱷᴕ

Soon after Colonel Turnbull had encamped at Rocky Mount, an insurrection broke out among the Presbyterians along Fishing Creek west of the Catawba. Turnbull dispatched Captain Huck and his dragoons to allay the trouble. With violence and profanity, on Sunday morning, June 11, the Philadelphian set out to capture the Reverend John Simpson, Presbyterian minister of the congregations of Upper and Lower Fishing Creek. Near the church his troops shot and killed pious young William Strong as he trudged along with his Bible under his arm. Hearing the shot, Mrs. Simpson and her children ran into the orchard and hid. From there they watched Huck give a warning to other disturbers of the King's peace by burning the manse. Finding that Preacher Simpson had deserted his pulpit and joined the rebels under Captain John McClure, Captain Christian Huck exclaimed: "God Almighty has turned rebel, but if there are twenty Gods on their side, the rebels shall be conquered."

But relief from Huck's depredation was massing under General Sumter. In the early years of the Revolution, Thomas Sumter, a Virginian who had settled in South Carolina, became colonel of the 2nd Regiment of South Carolina. He had resigned his commission in 1778, but upon the fall of Charleston and Tarleton's burning his home in the High Hills of Santee, Sumter took to the field. Riding to the angry settlement in the New Acquisition, which lay west of the Catawba, he began reviving the militia. So great was the respect paid him that on June 15, 1780, the soldiers assembled at Hagler's Branch elected Sumter their *general*.

With his reputation growing, General Sumter went recruiting through the Up Country. He stopped at the settlement of the Gillespies, good Presbyterian brothers who were noted for their fighting cocks. They prided themselves upon the chicks from a blue game hen. None had ever shown a white feather, and Old Tuck had never lost a fight. Sumter found the Gillespies crouched around a bloody main, watching their feathered hero. When he approached them about enlisting, promising to show them a battle of men, the Gillespies swore that Sumter was another Old Tuck. They proclaimed him a Chick of the Blue Hen. Soon recruits were flocking to the crow of this "Gamecock"!

Sumter established a camp at Clem's Creek on the east of the Catawba and began calling the militia colonels to his standard. To him came William Bratton, William Hill, Edward Lacey, Thomas Taylor, and Richard Winn.

From Rocky Mount, Turnbull dispatched Captain Huck, with a detachment of 35 dragoons of the British Legion, 20 mounted infantry of the New York Volunteers, and 60 Loyalists, to seek out and punish these rebels. On July 11 Huck surprised the plantation of Captain McClure and caught young James McClure and his brother-in-law, Edward Martin, melting down pewter dishes and molding bullets. He ordered them hanged at sunrise. When Mrs. McClure pleaded for the boys, the captain called Christian slapped her with the flat of his sword.

But Mary McClure slipped from the house, saddled a horse, and galloped to Sumter's camp. That evening Captain McClure and Colonel Bratton mustered 150 volunteers and set out to rescue their wives and children. As they rode, Colonel Lacey joined them. Soon their ranks had swollen to 500 volunteers. But before they had ridden twenty miles half their number had drifted away.

When he reached home, Colonel Bratton learned that during the day Captain Huck had stopped at his plantation and demanded that Mrs. Bratton and her family of rebels prepare a meal for him and his troops.

"Where is your husband?" Huck asked.

"In Sumter's army," replied Mrs. Bratton. A trooper slashed at her throat with a reaping hook.

Bratton also learned from his wife that after dinner Huck had marched only a quarter of a mile away and was encamped on the plantation of James Williamson. Bratton's scouts reported that the enemy had pitched their tents between the rail fences along the lane to Williamson's house. Here they lay in great insecurity, without patrols or pickets and with only a couple of sentinels posted along the road at the end of the lane.

Colonel Bratton divided the troops with Colonel Lacey. The two parties swung around through the fields and approached on opposite sides of the lane. At daybreak they struck. The surprise was so complete that their troops opened fire at seventy-five paces. The British sprang to arms, formed, and thrice charged with their bayonets. But they were trapped between the fences. Captain Huck dashed from Williamson's house, sprang upon a horse, and tried to rally his men. A marksman named Campbell toppled him from his saddle, blood spurting from a gaping bullet hole in his neck.

Turnbull and then Rawdon sent their fleetest messengers racing to Charleston with news of Bratton's bloody slaughter of Huck and his dragoons. On July 15 Lord Cornwallis wrote Sir Henry Clinton an account of the affair. Soberly he concluded: "Captain Huck, encouraged by meeting no opposition, encamped in an unguarded manner, and was totally surprised and routed. The Captain was killed, and only twelve of the Legion, and as many of the militia, escaped."

Banastre Tarleton's reaction to the news of the slaughter of his beloved Legionnaires was violent. He went straight to General Cornwallis

and remonstrated bitterly against Colonel Rawdon's detaching small
units of the British Legion for dangerous missions. Cornwallis listened,
agreed, and ordered Tarleton to return to Camden and the command
of the British Legion. He wrote a sharp letter to Rawdon: "Cavalry acts
chiefly upon the nerves, and if used it loses its terror; it loses its greatest
force. Tarleton will join in a few days. In the meantime let me conjure
you to take care of the Cavalry and give the most positive orders against
small detachments."

Next day Banastre wrote to John André. For the first time there
crept into his correspondence a note of bitterness against both Rawdon
and Cornwallis:

> Ever since the affair at Waxhaw, the Troops of the Legion (not-
> withstanding my Remonstrances, Petition, & openly pointing out
> the dangers of Detachment into N. Carolina) have been sent out
> at great hazard—
>
> And since my Lord Cornwallis sent me here to prepare accou-
> trements etc for augmentation & the next Campaign, I have had
> the mortification to hear that 70 men of the Legion have never
> been kept together—Detachment after Detachm't either by my
> Lord Cornwallis or my Lord Rawdon to the great Detriment of
> the Corps—& a very ill requital for their service during the Cam-
> paign—In short they have meant to defend the Frontier as a man
> would do who being placed in a House and ordered to defend it
> had lopped off his arms & legs & placed them in different windows
> and Apartments—In like manner detachment is equally dishearten-
> ing & useless.
>
> Capt'n Huck, Lt. Hunt and 50 Men have been cut up—12 are
> returned—(I hope (this long expected Event by me) will stop
> Detachment)—I am going up the Country immediately.

But the Green Dragoon did not go upcountry immediately. Suddenly
he felt nausea. His teeth began to chatter and his limbs to tremble.
Across his bed he sprawled, his temples throbbing and his forehead
burning with the high fever of malaria.

As Banastre lay in bed in the almost tropical heat of August, he felt
the glory ooze out of war. Ahead of him lay only weary miles of riding
and fighting. His fevered thoughts wandered back to the cool streets of
Liverpool.

Perhaps there was a way out. Personal popularity had elected him
first captain in the Liverpool Royal Volunteers. Could a hero's popularity elect him to Parliament? Off to his family went a letter soliciting
aid in placing the name of Banastre Tarleton before the voters in the
coming election. And the son of the old Tory lord mayor of Liverpool,
even though he was becoming the scourge of the Whigs in Carolina,
offered himself as a candidate of the Whig Party.

∾

To receive submissions and dispense pardons in eastern Carolina, Admiral Arbuthnot sent John Plumer Ardesoife, his flag captain, to Georgetown aboard the 64-gun battleship *Europe*. In late June Captain Ardesoife anchored in Winyah Bay and, with the village overawed by the bristling guns of the *Europe*, went ashore and established headquarters. Soon he had the submission of the inhabitants on the plantations about Waccamaw, Winyah, and lower Santee.

But thirty miles above Georgetown lay a district known as Williamsburg. This district had been colonized by Scotch-Irish Presbyterians who cleared plantations along Black River, built schools and churches, and founded the town of Kingstree. They had prospered and expanded their settlement up Black River, along Lynches River, and through the basin of the Pedee.

These Scotch-Irish settlers loved liberty, and they hated the English Church. They also hated the kings of the German house of Hanover and continued their allegiance to the royal family of Stewart. In the early days of trouble between England and her colonies, they were among the first to join the Liberty Associations. At the outbreak of hostilities, many of them enlisted in the South Carolina regiments and served in and around Charleston.

Among the most distinguished of these soldiers was Major John James. A substantial planter, an elder in the Indiantown Presbyterian Church, and the commanding officer of the Williamsburg militia, Major James was chosen to visit Georgetown and inquire about the terms offered by Ardesoife.

Dressed in the plain garb of a planter, without any military display, the Major rode his horse "Thunder" down to Georgetown, visited headquarters, and explained his mission to Captain Ardesoife.

"The submission must be unconditional," replied the Captain.

"Must the men of Williamsburg take up arms against their countrymen?"

"Although you have rebelled against his Majesty," responded Ardesoife, "he offers you a free pardon, of which you are undeserving, for you ought all to be hanged. But as he offers you a free pardon, you must take up arms in support of his cause."

"I do not think the men I represent will accept such terms," replied the Major.

At the word *represent* Ardesoife sprang to his feet. "You damned rebel, if you speak in such language I will immediately order you to be hanged up to the yard-arm!"

Ardesoife wore a sword, so James seized a chair. He brandished it in the Captain's face and backed through the door. Minutes later he was aback Thunder and streaking toward Kingstree.

News of Ardesoife's threat and James's escape flew through Williamsburg. The stubborn Scotch-Irish decided to fight. As they assembled and argued, messengers sped among them. They brought heartening tidings that on June 20 Baron de Kalb had crossed from Virginia into North Carolina and was marching southward with an army of 2000 Continentals.

Major James called out the militia. They assembled under Captains John James (of the Lake), John McCauley, William McCottry, and Henry Mouzon. James posted the company under McCottry—the men prided themselves on the name of "McCottry's Rifles"—at Witherspoon's Ferry on Lynches River, athwart the great post road from Savannah to Philadelphia. He then sent a messenger speeding northward to implore De Kalb to send an experienced officer to serve as commander of the men of Williamsburg.

"The whole country between Pedee and Santee has ever since been in an absolute state of rebellion, every friend of Government has been carried off, and his plantation destroyed," wrote Lord Cornwallis. "This unfortunate business, if it should have no worse consequence, will shake the confidence of our friends in this province and make our situation very uneasy until we can advance."

Lord Cornwallis believed the sovereign remedy for rebellion to be Banastre Tarleton. He ordered him to collect all the convalescent dragoons in Charleston, and, against the approach of De Kalb, to join Lord Rawdon at Camden. First he should have a look at Kingstree. "With the assistance of Major Hanger, who was lately appointed to the cavalry, thirty dragoons and forty mounted militia were assembled," said Tarleton in his *Campaigns*.

With these horsemen Tarleton and Hanger left Charleston before day on August 1. But because of rains and flooded creeks, they spent five days traversing forty miles. On August 5 they reached Lenud's Ferry. That evening Tarleton wrote Cornwallis that "the incessant rains having raised the waters and dislodged the creek bridges" he had found "the journey rather tedious." He also reported that "Colonel Ball is here, his militia is not numerous—He will I believe be able to furnish me with about 25 young men to assist in allaying the commotion near Black River."

Next morning the dragoons rode on to Black River. Crossing at the Lower Bridge, they swept into Kingstree and went into bivouac on the village green, "in order to punish the inhabitants in that quarter for their late breach of paroles and perfidious revolt. A necessary service was concealed under this disagreeable exertion of authority: The vicinity of the rivers Santee and Wateree, and of all the Charles town communications with the royal army, rendered it highly proper to strike terror into the inhabitants of that district," said Tarleton.

Major James sent messengers galloping with orders for his militia to advance. But after dark Mrs. John Hamilton, wife of the most hated Tory in Kingstree, slipped into the British camp to warn Tarleton that

James was advancing with 500 men. Rousing his horsemen, the Green Dragoon crossed over the Kingstree Bridge and disappeared up the west bank of Black River. Soon McCottry's Rifles, mounted on farm horses, rode up and with much rearing and swearing set off in pursuit. Even the most sanguine of McCottry's Calvinistic friends felt that it was God's Providence that these militiamen did not overtake Tarleton's professional soldiers.

Guided by Ball's Tories, the dragoons recrossed the river near Frierson's plantation. Straight to the home of Captain Henry Mouzon on Pudding Swamp rode the British. They drove the family and slaves of the absent militiaman from their beds and burned the fourteen buildings in the messuage. Then turning northward they rode for thirty miles, pausing only after reaching the peaceful community of Salem.

From Ball's militia Tarleton had learned that the Whigs in Williamsburg were expecting De Kalb to answer their petition by sending them Lieutenant Colonel William Washington. The militia were eager to serve under the fearless young dragoon who bore the magic name of Washington. And from his guides Banastre had also learned that in Salem the leader of this movement was old James Bradley, a Whig representative in the General Assembly of South Carolina.

As befitted a friend and disciple of John André, Banastre was often a ham and on occasion a consummate actor. He knew that during the siege of Charleston André had repeatedly doffed his uniform and, dressed in the homespun of a back countryman, had passed through the American lines. In the city André had posed as a Virginian, connected in a civil capacity with the Virginia Continentals, and as such he had strolled unmolested down King Street. He had stood in the shadow of St. Michael's Church and gazed seaward from the Battery. Even his host, good Loyalist Edward Shrewsbury, never dreamed that André was a spy!

As he had neared Salem Tarleton decided to impersonate William Washington. With great glee he told Hanger and the other dragoons to assume the ranks and names of American soldiers. Under the August sun the red and green coats of the British had already been cast aside. So, dressed in a white linen shirt and cavalryman's tan trousers, the Green Dragoon walked boldly up to the Bradley house and introduced himself as Colonel William Washington.

The Bradleys were naïve country folk who had never seen William Washington. They fell for the ruse. Mrs. Bradley hustled off to prepare a plantation dinner for the hungry Colonel, while Mr. Bradley, as Tarleton reported in the *Campaigns*, "was severe in his denunciations against the British officers and soldiers, and warm in commendation of the heroic spirit of his supposed friends and guests."

After dinner the stranger with elegant manners and a Lancashire accent asked Bradley to guide his troops over two difficult fords on the

main branches of upper Black River. He planned, he hesitatingly confided to Bradley, to strike Lord Rawdon in Camden.

Bradley entered heartily into the plan. He called some neighboring
militiamen and led the British across both Bradley's and Nelson's fords.
After his dragoons had safely passed Megirt's Swamp and were approaching the familiar Santee road, Banastre suddenly clapped his pistol to the
head of the astounded old man. Throwing off their pretense the British
seized all the Americans and conducted them to Camden where they
slapped them into jail.

As Bradley lay in chains, with shackles on his wrists and gyves around
his ankles, old Mrs. Bradley, called by friends "one of the most humane,
gentle, and affectionate of her sex," unable to believe that the handsome young Colonel who had eaten her bread could be such a barbarian, packed a basket with food, saddled a horse, and rode the sixty
miles to Camden. Unfortunately, she found Banastre in a surly mood.
He refused her permission to carry her basket to her husband. For her
tears and entreaties he called her the vilest names in a dragoon's billings-
gate.

10

Camden and Fishing Creek

*U*PON THEIR ARRIVAL at Camden, Tarleton and Hanger found only convalescents at Logtown. Lord Rawdon, having moved fourteen miles to the east and deployed the army along Little Lynches Creek, was disputing the passage of the American army under General Horatio Gates. Since the two dragoons had left Charleston, General Gates, the hero of Saratoga, had overtaken the American army, superseded Baron de Kalb as commander, and begun a rapid advance toward Camden.

The commandant of the British Legion was shocked and angered at the condition of his corps. "He had evident proof that the Legion cavalry were nearly destroyed by the constant duties of detachment and patrole," he wrote in the *Campaigns*. But "he collected all the dragoons at that post and in the neighborhood, and joined Lord Rawdon at Lynches Creek on the 10th day of August."

During the American advance across South Carolina, Lord Rawdon had dispatched messenger after messenger to warn Lord Cornwallis. But General Patterson, commandant of Charleston, was desperately ill of malaria, and Cornwallis awaited the arrival of Colonel Balfour whom he had recalled from Ninety-Six. Rawdon had also begun calling in British troops from their advanced bases and concentrating them around Camden. Before leaving for Charleston, Balfour had sent four companies of light infantry which arrived at Camden on August 13.

The news of the approach of a formidable American army had also roused General Sumter. On July 17 he had written Baron de Kalb that 1500 men could take Nelson's and Murray's ferries and force the British back upon Charleston. To begin this drive, the Gamecock collected 500 men, crossed the Catawba at Blair's Ford, and on August 1 summoned Colonel Turnbull to surrender the post at Rocky Mount.

Turnbull replied that Sumter "might come and take it." The General began his attack. His men climbed the mount and infiltrated the stockade. For eight hours they battled. After great gallantry and exertion they set one of the blockhouses on fire. But just as the roof blazed, a violent thunderstorm extinguished every spark. The Americans then retreated, as Colonel Hill lamented, "under as great a mortification, as ever any number of men endured."

In the *Campaigns* Tarleton wrote of Sumter: "This active partisan was thoroughly sensible, that the minds of men are influenced by enterprise, and that to keep undisciplined people together, it is necessary to employ them. For this purpose, he again surveyed the state of the British posts upon the frontier, and on minute examination he deemed Hanging Rock the most vulnerable."

Knowing that the recall of the regular troops to Camden had left the post weak, at seven o'clock on the morning of August 6 Sumter attacked Hanging Rock. His troops routed the defending Tory militia under Colonel Samuel Bryan. Twice they were repulsed by the flashing bayonets of Captain Rousselet's company of British Legion infantry.

Sumter's men then turned upon and decimated Major Carden's Prince of Wales's American Regiment. In grim hand-to-hand fighting they killed Captain McCulloch, the gallant senior captain of the infantry of the British Legion. At that point Major Carden lost his nerve. He resigned the command of the British to Captain Rousselet.

At the height of this savage fighting came unexpected support for Rousselet. Captains Stewart and McDonald, with forty mounted infantry of the British Legion, moving from Rocky Mount toward the concentration at Camden, heard the firing. They swung around and galloped eastward on the high road toward upper Lynches Creek. Reaching the battle, they used an old stratagem of extending their horsemen in a long line and charging into the thickest of the fight. The Americans gave ground, but in turn Major William Davie charged these mounted infantrymen with his dragoons and drove them to the protection of the infantry of the Legion.

By now Sumter's men had seized and were plundering the British camp. They were hungry, and they gobbled down the enemy's field rations with gusto. They were thirsty, and they drained the enemy's enormous puncheons. Hearing many of his cockerels begin to crow from old Jamaica rum, the Gamecock wisely ordered a retreat. "Boys," he said, "it is not good to pursue a victory too far."

The British now evacuated both Hanging Rock and Rocky Mount. As they retired toward Camden, Sumter followed and seized all the passes over the Wateree from Elkin's Ford to Whitaker's Ferry five miles below Camden. Trying to coordinate his movements with those of the main army, on August 12 he wrote General Gates. He suggested that a powerful corps be thrown behind Camden. For the second time he urged that a strong detachment be sent to the High Hills of Santee or to Nelson's Ferry to cut the British supply route and to prevent their expected retreat toward Charleston.

On August 3 Gates had crossed the Pedee at Mask's Ferry and marched straight for Camden. At Little Lynches Creek he paused, for Rawdon was posted on high ground. After consulting his guides, on August 11 Gates wheeled his army to the right, forded the creek, and began a flanking movement. Rawdon ordered a retreat, his retrogression being covered by Tarleton's dragoons. As the British retired toward their fortifications at Logtown, the advance guard of the Americans came to rest at Rugeley's Mill.

Meanwhile, after having turned the command in Charleston over to Colonel Balfour, Lord Cornwallis left Drayton Hall on horseback in the evening of August 10. By riding night and day he arrived in Camden during the night of August 13. Next morning he decided to fight Gates. "I saw no difficulty in making good my retreat to Charleston, with the troops that were able to march," he wrote Lord Germain on August 21, "but in taking that resolution I must have not only left near 800 sick and a great quantity of stores at this place, but I clearly saw the loss of the whole province except Charlestown, and of all Georgia except Savannah, as immediate consequences, besides forfeiting all pretensions to future confidence from our friends in this part of America."

Lord Cornwallis began shifting and strengthening his corps in preparation for the battle. Still fuming at Rawdon for having destroyed his horses, Tarleton appealed directly to Cornwallis. "Upon application from Lieutenant-colonel Tarleton, he ordered all the horses of the army, belonging both to regiments and departments, to be assembled. The best were selected for the service of the cavalry, and, upon the proprietors receiving payment, they were delivered up to the British Legion," wrote Tarleton.

On August 15 the King's troops were ready. In the afternoon Cornwallis sent Tarleton and the Legion to reconnoiter the Americans and gain intelligence of their movements. About ten miles from Camden, on the road to Rugeley's, Banastre picked up three American soldiers. During interrogation they told him that they were convalescent and had been "directed to join the American army, on the high road, that night, as General Gates had given orders for his troops to move from Rugeley's mills to attack the British camp next morning near Camden."

Mounting his prisoners behind dragoons, Tarleton galloped back to headquarters. When examined by Lord Cornwallis, the three soldiers repeated their stories, confirming other intelligence gained during the day. Thus forewarned of Gates's move, Cornwallis circulated an order for the British to stand by their arms. "I determined to march at ten o'clock on the night of the 15th," Cornwallis wrote Lord Germain, "and to attack at daybreak, pointing my principal force against their continentals, who from good intelligence, I knew to be badly posted, close to Colonel Rugeley's house."

At ten o'clock the army set out on the main road to Rugeley's. Colonel Webster commanded the front division. As his advance guard he deployed twenty dragoons and twenty infantrymen from the British Legion under Lieutenant Donovan. Lord Rawdon commanded the center, which consisted of infantry, including the infantry of the Legion. The rear division, for use as reserves, consisted largely of the 71st Regiment. And Tarleton and his Green Horse formed the rear guard.

In the meantime, General Gates, encamped at Rugeley's, had formulated his plans for striking the British. Arrogant, without adequate knowledge of the army which he commanded, and quite heedless of General Charles Lee's admonition not to allow his Northern laurels to turn to Southern willows, Gates believed that Cornwallis was only another Burgoyne and that he was on the verge of another Saratoga.

On August 14 he ordered Colonel Thomas Woolford, with 100 Continentals and 300 North Carolina militiamen, to cross the Wateree and join in Sumter's march behind Camden. And to prevent the escape of any of the British whom he planned to defeat, he ordered Lieutenant Colonel Francis Marion, former commanding officer of the 2nd Regiment of South Carolina, to ride to Williamsburg, take command of James's militia, and burn the ferryboats on the Santee.

From Camp Clermont at Rugeley's on August 15 Gates issued an order for his Grand Army to march at ten o'clock that night. For his advance guard the General chose the dragoons of Armand's Legion. But Gates had seen the Green Horse wheeling around Rawdon's retreating column and he feared them. This fear he communicated to Colonel Armand in his order: "In case of an attack by the enemy's cavalry, in front, not only to support the shock of the enemy's horse, but to rout them; and to consider the order, to stand the attacks of the enemy's cavalry, be their numbers what they may, as positive."

About halfway between Rugeley's and Camden at two-thirty on the morning of August 16 the advance guards of the armies collided. The British charged. In spite of their positive orders to stand, Armand's dragoons broke and retreated. But Lieutenant Donovan had been wounded, and his Legionnaires also retreated. Colonel Webster quickly threw his infantry across the road. After desultory firing for a quarter of an hour, both sides became silent as General Gates and Lord Cornwallis disposed their forces for the coming battle.

From his guides Lord Cornwallis learned that his position was decidedly advantageous. His army was on a wooded sand ridge between two deep swamps. Behind him ran Saunders' Creek. So at dawn he deployed the 23rd and 33rd Regiments under Webster to the right, their line extending from the road to a swamp. To the left he sent Lord Rawdon with the Volunteers of Ireland, the Legion infantry, and Hamilton's North Carolinians. Their line extended from the road to a swamp on the left. For reserve he posted a battalion of the 71st Regiment behind each wing.

Tarleton and the cavalry of the British Legion were posted in column, "on account of the thickness of the woods, to the right of the main road, close to the first battalion of the 71st, with orders to act offensively against the enemy, or in defense of the British troops, as opportunity offered, or necessity required."

In contrast to the calmness with which Lord Cornwallis prepared for battle, General Gates showed astonishment when Colonel Armand struck the British advance guard. He immediately called his generals to a council. When Colonel Otho Williams, the adjutant general, came to summon De Kalb, the old Baron inquired: "Has the General given you orders to retreat the army?"

Gates asked his assembled generals: "Gentlemen, what is best to be done?"

After a long silence General Stevens replied: "Gentlemen, is it not too late now to do anything but fight?"

Gates began deploying the American troops. Opposite Rawdon on his right he posted the Continentals from Maryland under General Mordecai Gist and from Delaware under Baron de Kalb. In his center he stationed the North Carolina militia under General Caswell. And to his left he sent the Virginia militia under General Stevens.

Colonel Williams then suggested that Stevens should make a brisk attack upon Webster's forming line.

"That's right, sir. Let it be done," replied Gates.

As Stevens' skirmishers moved forward, Lord Cornwallis, observing their movement, sent Captain Alexander Ross, his aide, to order Rawdon to advance. Cornwallis then rode forward and in person ordered Webster to begin the attack.

With loud cheering the British advanced, their long red line steady and their bayonets gleaming in the hazy, smoky morning light. Terrified, the Virginians threw down their loaded guns and fled. The North Carolinians followed. "At least two thirds of the army fled without firing a shot," said Colonel Williams.

Instead of pursuing the militia, Colonel Webster wheeled his veterans around and began rolling up the left flank of the Continentals. The Maryland and Delaware regiments fought with utmost gallantry. Old Baron de Kalb, unhorsed and fighting on foot beside the Marylanders, received eleven wounds. As he fell, Lieutenant Colonel du Buysson, his aide, embraced the General and into his own body received the bayonets pointed at his superior. Inspired by such heroism, the reserve of the Maryland and Delaware regiments continued firing, but "a part of the British cavalry, under Major Hanger, was ordered to charge their flank, while Lieutenant Colonel Tarleton, with the remainder of his regiment, completed their confusion."

Rout and slaughter ensued. Said Tarleton: "The continentals, the state troops, and the Militia, abandoned their arms, their colors, and their cannon, to seek protection in flight, or to obtain it from the clemency of the conquerors." All through the terrible heat of a mid-August day, Tarleton and the cavalry of the British Legion pursued the fleeing Americans. Finally, sated with blood and death, horses and riders overcome by exhaustion, they halted at Hanging Rock twenty-two miles from the battlefield.

Fearful of falling into the hands of the Green Dragoon, Gates fled like a poltroon. Meeting Major Davie, he yelled for him to fall back toward Charlotte or the Green Horse would be upon him.

"My men are accustomed to Tarleton and do not fear him," answered Davie. When he met General Isaac Huger, the Major asked him how far he ought to obey General Gates.

"Just as far as you please," replied Huger, "for you will never see him again."

Davie sent a messenger after Gates, saying that if the General wished, he would go and bury the dead.

"I say retreat," yelled the General, spurring his horse toward Charlotte. "Let the dead bury their dead!"

ତ୦

As soon as Colonel Woolford joined him, Sumter began operations. On the west side of Wateree Ferry the British under Colonel Carey had erected a small redoubt. On August 15 Sumter sent Colonel Taylor and his regiment to surprise Fort Carey. Taylor captured the British Colonel, 30 troops, and 36 wagons loaded with rum, clothes, and food. Later in the day Taylor captured 50 troops bringing supplies from Ninety-Six, six wagons loaded with baggage, 300 head of cattle, and some sheep. Hearing that the British were preparing to cross over to retake their comrades and stores, Sumter began retreating up the Wateree.

At daybreak Sumter heard the guns of the battle of Camden, but he remained ignorant of the victor. After seeing Gates fleeing from the battlefield, Major Davie sent Captain Nathaniel Martin and two dragoons to Sumter to report the debacle and to appoint a rendezvous near Charlotte. The Gamecock marched all day and all night, but his progress was slow, for the weather was sultry and his troops were cumbered with prisoners and captured wagons.

In the meantime Lord Cornwallis marched part of his army on to Rugeley's where they occupied the camp forfeited by the Americans.

Late in the afternoon Tarleton and the dragoons of the Legion, trailing back from Hanging Rock, entered Camp Rugeley. Although the British were loaded with booty and glutted with prisoners—at least 1000 had fallen into their hands—there was still more marching and fighting for the light infantry and the British Legion. Cornwallis had learned the whereabouts of Sumter. He told Tarleton to be ready to move at dawn.

Early on the morning of August 17, Banastre, with 350 men and one small cannon, marched up the east side of the Wateree. By late afternoon he had information that Sumter was on a parallel course on the opposite side of the river. Reaching the ferry at Rocky Mount at dusk, he saw campfires about a mile beyond the river. Hoping that Sumter might cross the river in front of them, the British Legion went into bivouac in silence and without fires. At dawn it was evident that the Americans had decamped. British vedettes soon returned and reported that they had seen their rear guard leaving Rocky Mount.

Putting the infantry and cannon into the boats, Tarleton and his dragoons swam their horses across the Wateree. All morning the British trailed the Americans over the rough sandy roads, in the near-tropical heat of August. By twelve o'clock they had reached Fishing Creek, some forty miles above Camden. Here the exhausted infantry complained that they could march no farther. Posting them on high ground, Tarleton selected 100 dragoons and 60 foot soldiers, whom he mounted behind the dragoons, and pushed on after Sumter.

For five miles there were fresh tracks. Then two of Sumter's vedettes fired upon the advance guard of the British Legion. They killed a dragoon. His companions cut the vedettes to pieces with their sabers. A sergeant and four men rode to the crown of a nearby hill, peered over, and waved frantically for their commander. Spurring his horse, Tarleton ascended the hill and saw before him what few commanders have ever seen: the enemy bivouac in absolute disorganization, quiet, and peace. With arms stacked, Sumter's men were resting. Some were cooking, some were sleeping in the shade, and some were bathing in Fishing Creek.

"The decision, and the preparation for the attack were momentary. The cavalry and infantry were formed into one line, and giving a general shout, advanced to the charge," said Tarleton. Before the surprised Americans could move, the British dragoons had ridden between them and their arms and were swinging their great sabers in carnage. "Universal consternation immediately ensued throughout the camps; some opposition was, however, made from behind the waggons, in front of the militia."

Sumter, exhausted by the heat and marching, lay fast asleep under a wagon. Awakened by the fighting around him, he risked one peep. Then, forgetting his coat and his command, he sneaked out, leaped astride a horse without a saddle, and, as Tarleton reported, "in the general confusion, made his escape." Two days later he reached Major Davie's camp, sans officer, sans soldier, sans servant.

Captain Charles Campbell, who had burned Sumter's home in the High Hills, was slain in the rally at the wagons.

With 300 prisoners, 100 released British troops, and 44 wagons loaded with recaptured stores, Tarleton and his Legionnaires reached Camden on August 21. Cornwallis was elated. The action at Fishing Creek, which had destroyed the rebel militia, was too brilliant for commentary. His Lordship immediately completed his battle reports and hastened them to London by Captain Alexander Ross.

Weary from five days of riding and fighting, Banastre dashed off a note to his brother John and sent it to England by Captain Ross:

> Camp Camden Sth Carolina
> Augst ye 21st 1780
>
> My dear Brother
>
> I have received your long letter, I thank you sincerely for every proof of your Affection—The public prints will announce two Glorious Actions for Britain within a few days—I had the Honor of a great Command in the first Action—the last was wholly entrusted to me—I received a Slight Wound which did not require a dressing—Two days afterwards I fought with every success and Honor my best Friends would Wish—Lord Cornwallis's public Letters will name the Circumstances—the defeat of Horatio Gates —and the Laurels gathered in the Field—I enclose you a certificate of my being Alive not signed by Church Wardens or attested before Ministers but with the respectable Signature of Earl Cornwallis Lord Rawdon and Gov Martin—Ministers of Heaven or Church Wardens We have not with us—such Friends & Attestations as I have I send unto you—from the Well fought Field the Clergy and Wardens are far distant—When I shall arrive at a place inhabited by Priests or Wardens again the Lord knows, but I hope this Campaign will be a long and conclusive one to America—I empower you my good Brother to receive the Legacy left me by my Aunt Parker—Brevet Rank is all I Wish—give up the 79th Company— Major or Lieutenant Colonel I must be by this time—yours
>
> most Affectionately
> remember me in the same manner to my Mother and all other Friends—
>
> Ban. Tarleton

Captain Ross bore dispatches for both Lord Amherst and Lord Germain. In his letter to Amherst, Lord Cornwallis was flattering in his praise of the Green Dragoon. "Your Lordship will see the account of the brilliant action of Lt. Colonel Tarleton: I think it is my Duty to declare that he is one of the most promising officers I ever knew; I have no private connexion with him nor any motive for recommending him but the desire of seeing extraordinary merit rewarded and of placing him in such rank as may enable him to render the most essential services to his King and Country."

In his letter to Germain, Lord Cornwallis reported the battle of Camden, praising the officers and men, and concluding: "The capacity and vigour of Lieutenant Colonel Tarleton, at the head of the cavalry, deserve my highest commendation."

His Lordship then reported the action at Fishing Creek. "On the morning of the 17th I detached Lieutenant-colonel Tarleton with the legion cavalry and infantry, and the corps of light infantry," he wrote. "Lieutenant-colonel Tarleton executed this service with his usual activity and military address."

And after recounting the events, he concluded, indirectly calling the attention of the King to the prowess of the commandant of the British Legion: "This action was too brilliant to need any comment of mine, and will, I have no doubt, highly recommend Lieutenant-colonel Tarleton to his Majesty's favour."

Lord Germain showed the Cornwallis dispatch to King George. His Majesty was delighted with the valor of his soldiers in Carolina. To Lord Cornwallis, on November 9, 1780, Germain relayed the approval of their sovereign: "It is therefore particularly pleasing to me to obey His Majesty's commands by signifying to your Lordship His Royal Pleasure that you do acquaint the Officers and Soldiers of the brave Army under your Command that their behaviour upon that glorious day is highly approved by the Sovereign, and you will particularly express to Lord Rawdon, Lieutenant colonels Webster and Tarleton His Majesty's approbation of their judicious and spirited Conduct. The latter indeed has a double Claim of Praise for his great Alertness in overtaking General Sumter's detachment before they were apprized of Gate's defeat, and by their destruction rendering the Victory at Camden still more decisive."

The valor of Banastre Tarleton had at last been brought to the notice of his king! His brilliance had won royal approbation. And when Lord Germain published the Cornwallis report in a *London Gazette Extraordinary* of October 9, 1780, the English people made the Green Dragoon their national hero.

11

The Swamp Fox

"Our sickness is great, and truly alarming," Cornwallis wrote Clinton on August 23, 1780. "The Officers are particularly affected; Doctor Hayes, and almost all the Hospital Surgeons are laid up. Every person of my family, and every Public Officer of the Army, is now incapable of doing his duty."

Having fought Gates in order to protect the 800 British troops ill of malaria and yellow fever, Lord Cornwallis found that victory only enhanced his problem. He had hundreds of wounded and some 1000 prisoners to tax further the meager facilities at Camden. So he decided to send all able-bodied prisoners to Charleston before they came down with chills and fever. To protect their line of march the British commander sent Major James Wemyss with troops of the 63rd Regiment to the High Hills of Santee and Lieutenant Colonel Tarleton with a detachment of the British Legion and Hamilton's Loyalist militia to Ratcliffe's Bridge on Lynches River.

In the meantime, Lieutenant Colonel Francis Marion, after peeling off from the American army at Rugeley's Mill, had hastened to Williamsburg, taken command of Major James's militia, and ridden on a boat-burning foray along Santee River. Having been privately informed of the destruction of the American army, he concealed the news from his troops and continued to ride and burn. On August 23 he destroyed the flatboats at Murray's Ferry and on August 24 those at Nelson's Ferry.

Here Marion learned that the first batch of 150 prisoners bound for Charleston had encamped at the empty plantation house of General Sumter at Great Savannah, six miles above Nelson's. He decided to surprise them, and before daylight on August 25 he captured Captain Roberts and thirty-eight escorts and released the Americans. Then hearing that Tarleton's dragoons were sweeping the country between Ratcliffe's and Kingstree, Marion and his militia fled back along the Santee. They slipped through Kingstree, crossed Pedee River, and went into hiding in Britton's Neck.

To chase Marion's guerrillas from his supply line to Charleston, Cornwallis ordered Major Wemyss to march the 63rd Regiment from the High Hills of Santee to Kingstree. His Lordship's orders of August 28 read: "I should advise your sweeping the country entirely from Kingstree Bridge to Pedee, and returning by the Cheraws. I would have you disarm in the most rigid manner, all Persons who cannot be depended upon and punish the concealment of Arms and ammunition with a total demolition of the plantation."

On September 5 the 63rd, indifferently mounted on horses they had rustled in the High Hills, rode on their mission of sword and fire. They went straight to the home of Major James. Locking Mrs. James and her children in their house, for three days Wemyss tried to badger them into revealing the hiding place of the Major.

Wemyss court-martialed Captain John James, the Major's oldest son, for having broken his parole. As the loyal slaves refused to testify against him, the British were cheated of a hanging. But not of a burning. They laid the James home in ashes.

Adam Cusac was less fortunate. Convicted of having broken his parole by firing across Black River into the plantation of Loyalist John Brockington, Cusac was hauled away to Long Bluff. Mrs. Cusac and the children followed their loved one to the place. Wemyss personally supervised the hanging; and as the noose slipped over Cusac's head, in anguish and terror his family threw themselves upon the ground in front of Wemyss' horse. The enraged Major seized his rein and spurred his horse to trample them into the dust. A young officer snatched the bridle and held him back.

But Wemyss was a demon. He burned a swath fifteen miles wide along the seventy-mile road from Kingstree to Cheraw. His men broke up every loom, burned every gristmill or blacksmith shop, and bayonetted every sheep. James Wemyss became the second most hated man in the British army.

თ

"Our sickness at present is rather at a Stand, the Recovery's nearly Keeping Pace with the falling down," Lord Cornwallis wrote Clinton on August 29 in announcing the start of his invasion of North Carolina. "I dread the Convalescents not being able to march; but it is very tempting to try it, as a Move of forty or fifty miles would put us in a much better Climate."

Cornwallis wrote to Major Innes on September 6: "I shall move with part of the Troops Tomorrow to Waxhaw, & Tarleton will be stationed between the Catawba & Broad River. I shall probably remain there some days."

He broke camp on September 8, and the main army slowly marched up the east side of the Wateree toward the settlement on the Waxhaws. But Lieutenant Colonel Tarleton and the British Legion crossed the Wateree and marched up the western side. Said Tarleton: "The scarcity of forage in the district of the Wacsaws was the principal reason for this temporary separation."

The British Legion moved briskly toward Charlotte. But at Fishing Creek, Tarleton became violently ill. Carried to the home of Mrs. White, for several days he lay helpless and delirious with yellow fever. "He cannot be moved," wrote Cornwallis to Balfour on September 20, "and I am obliged to leave his Corps there for his protection."

As Tarleton lay ill, the invasion of North Carolina faltered. Cornwallis encamped his own corps at the Waxhaws. From there on September 20 he sent an appeal to Lieutenant Archibald Campbell: "I am very anxious for the next account of Colonel Tarleton. I beg you will send twice a day at least."

From the Waxhaws on September 21 his Lordship wrote Balfour: "I informed you in my last letter that Tarleton was gone towards Charlotte, but I soon after heard that instead of having marched, he was very dangerously ill. I have been very uneasy about him until this morning; his Fever has now intermitted and I hope he is safe."

Banastre was safe from yellow jack. But in the swamps along Fishing Creek lurked the men who had killed Captain Huck. They were daring and desperate. His Legion closed ranks around him and waited.

Lord Cornwallis ended his letter to Balfour: "Tarleton's Illness is of the greatest Inconvenience to me at present, as I not only lose his Services, but the whole Corps must remain quite useless in order to protect him."

On September 22 Cornwallis wrote Sir Henry Clinton: "If nothing material happens to obstruct my plan of operation, I mean, as soon as Lieutenant-colonel Tarleton can be removed to proceed . . . . to Charlotte-town."

With his entire campaign in peril, all because of the illness of one man, Lord Cornwallis decided he had to move. On September 22 he dispatched Major McArthur and the 71st Regiment to protect Tarleton and the other ill and convalescent at Blair's Mill. He then placed Major George Hanger in command of the British Legion, ordered him to cross the Catawba at Blair's Ferry, and form the advance guard for the march to Charlotte.

To Balfour next day Cornwallis wrote: "Tarleton is vastly better. I got him conveyed this morning to Blair's Mill on the East side of Catawba, and his corps will pass this evening."

But the British General was like a man defending himself with his left hand while guarding his paralyzed right arm. Marion had erupted again in Williamsburg. Sumter was rousing the Up Country. Colonel Isaac Shelby and his Back Water men were already trailing Major Patrick Ferguson. And the only British officer capable of dispersing these rebels lay on a cot at Blair's, still too weak to sit a horse. Cornwallis bitterly confided to Balfour: "His illness has been truly unfortunate; it has prevented our demolishing the Militia while it was assembling."

On September 23 his Lordship wrote a letter to Major Ferguson: "Tarleton is better, and was moved today in a litter."

On the day that Banastre Tarleton was moved out of the Valley on a litter, John André began his descent into the Shadows. He had tried an old trick once too often. Near Tarrytown, on the far-off Hudson, he was caught in civilian clothes behind the American lines and arrested as a spy.

Marching into Charlotte along the Steel Creek road on September 24, Major Hanger found the enemy. Major Davie had posted his North Carolina troops around the courthouse and behind a wall and the garden fences flanking the road. Here he was ready to dispute the advance of the British army.

Hanger formed the British Legion to dislodge them. Sending infantry skirmishers ahead to draw the American fire, he led the cavalry of the Legion in a charge toward the courthouse. The American fire was so hot that the dragoons recoiled.

Hanger formed them again on the village green. They charged. A second time they recoiled. As dissension spread among the Green Horse, Lord Cornwallis, feeling the absence of Tarleton keenly, rode up and shouted: "Legion! Remember you have everything to lose, but nothing to gain!"

Again Hanger led them in a charge. Webster's infantry had dislodged the troops of Davie, and the Legionnaires, taunted about losing their reputation, drove them from Charlotte.

Afterward Cornwallis wrote Balfour: "Indeed the whole of them are very different when Tarleton is present or absent."

Now Hanger sickened. The doctors placed him and five other officers with yellow fever in a wagon filled with straw and sent them to Camden. The others died and were buried in the woods. Hanger was so desperately ill on reaching Camden that for weeks he lived on opium and port wine.

While Hanger and Tarleton lay ill, Major Patrick Ferguson and his corps of well-drilled Loyalist militia were marching eastward from Tryon County to join Cornwallis at Charlotte. It was known that Shelby was gathering Americans to prevent this juncture, but there was no great apprehension for Ferguson, even after Lord Cornwallis received this appeal: "I am on my march towards you, by a road leading from the

Cherokee Ford, north of King's Mountain. Three or four hundred good Soldiers, part dragoons, would finish the business. Something must be done soon."

On October 6 his Lordship replied: "Tarleton shall pass at some of the upper Fords, and clear the Country; for the present both he and his Corps want a few days rest."

On the eve of the battle of King's Mountain the fate of the British cause trembled in the balance; and Banastre Tarleton, having been hauled into Charlotte on a sling strung across a wagon, was still too weak to ride.

By the evening of October 9 Lord Cornwallis had fugitive reports that on October 7 Colonel Shelby and his horsemen had overtaken and slain Ferguson and destroyed his corps at King's Mountain. That evening Major Money wrote Balfour: "If his Lordship hears nothing from him during the Night he means to detach Tarleton with the Legion tomorrow at Daybreak toward Ninety-Six."

Money also revealed the reason for the paralysis among the British. Lord Cornwallis was too ill to command. "Lord Cornwallis desired me to acquaint you that his having a feverish cold upon him prevents his writing you by this express."

At dawn of October 10 Tarleton was strong enough to ride. Cornwallis ordered him "to reinforce Ferguson wherever he could find him, and to draw his corps to the Catawba, if after the junction, advantage could not be obtained over the mountaineers," said Tarleton in the *Campaigns*. "Accordingly Tarleton marched to Smith's Ford, below the forks of the Catawba, where he received certain information of the melancholy fate of Major Ferguson. This mortifying intelligence was forwarded to Charlotte Town, and the light troops crossed the river, to give protection to the fugitives, and to attend the operation of the enemy."

After the destruction of Ferguson and his troops, Lord Cornwallis altered his plans for the winter campaign. The growing power of the Partisan corps and the exposed position of the British army, away from its base of supply, determined his Lordship to contract his lines. He decided to retreat into central South Carolina. Recalling Tarleton to the Catawba, he abandoned Charlotte on the evening of October 14 and marched the army toward the Catawba Ford.

The British army remained at the Catawba settlement for a week, for Lord Cornwallis was now too ill of fever to be moved. The command fell upon Lord Rawdon. He led the army across the Catawba, near Twelve Mile Creek, on October 21, without difficulty or opposition. Then he sent Banastre and his dragoons to scout the country between the Broad and the Catawba rivers.

After riding through the territory, Tarleton recommended Winnsboro as the site for the winter camp. Later he wrote: "Wynnesborough presented the most numerous advantages: Its spacious plantations yielded a tolerable post; its centrical situation between the Broad river and the Wateree afforded protection to Ninety Six and Camden; and its vicinity to the Dutch fork, and a rich country in the rear, promised abundant supplies of flour, forage and cattle."

ono

As soon as the army had encamped on the high, rolling grounds of the Mount Zion Academy and his officers had settled in the mansions of the Winns, Lord Cornwallis turned his attention to suppressing the Partisans of South Carolina. Among the most troublesome was Colonel Marion. "Mr. Marion, by his zeal and abilities, showed himself capable of the trust committed to his charge," wrote Tarleton. "He collected his adherents at the shortest notice, in the neighborhood of Black river, and, after making incursions to the friendly districts, or threatening the communications, to avoid pursuit, he disbanded his followers."

Marion's attacks frequently delayed supplies between Charleston and Camden. From Charleston Balfour wrote: "But the numbers, & spirits of the rebell partys so far outbalances our Militia, that a post, at the High Hills of Santee or Kingstree Bridge, is now absolutely necessary, otherwise communication is at an end betwixt the army and this town."

Galloping suddenly up from Snow's Island, on October 28 Marion struck and dispersed the Tory militia assembled under Colonel Tynes at Tearcoat Swamp. Then, emerging from the swamps of upper Black River, he passed through the High Hills of Santee and came to rest at Singleton's Mills, with his troops athwart the British supply line.

From Camden on November 1 Turnbull wrote Tarleton to bring his dragoons from Winnsboro and drive off Marion. As Banastre prepared his British Legion for a campaign, he sent Turnbull's letter to Lord Cornwallis. On November 2 his Lordship replied: "I can make nothing of Turnbull's letter to you, as he only seems to describe Parties of ten or twelve Rebels, which of course it is not intended to employ the Legion to hunt." But he gave Tarleton permission to go, saying: "You will of course not be long absent and let me hear from you constantly."

Tarleton passed the Wateree on November 3. From Camden he reported to Cornwallis: "Col. Turnbull has informed me of People assembling at Singleton's on Wateree. I can't believe it, but have sent to learn Facts which I shall receive tomorrow Morning at 6 o'clock."

By the same express Turnbull reported to Lord Cornwallis: "Two men have arrived this morning from Black Creek who assure us that Marion and Snipes have their quarters at Singleton's Mills. We have sent a spy who we expect to be back by Morning, and Tarleton will regulate his Route accordingly. We can never fix the numbers with those country fellows."

That night in his bivouac as Banastre prepared his report to Lord Cornwallis, he thought of Liverpool and his family. To his mother he scrawled a note:

Camp near Camden November 3, 80

My dear Madam—
   I am extremely obliged to you for your kind Present & Letter.
   I have been visited with the Fever of the Country but am now most perfectly recovered.
   I am Madam, with most dutiful Respect

Your affectionate Son
Ban. Tarleton

From Winnsboro on November 5 Lord Cornwallis answered his favorite dragoon: "I received yours yesterday, and most sincerely hope you will get at Mr. Marion. I am always sanguine when you are concerned."

Turnbull ordered Major Harrison and his Provincials to serve as guides, and on November 4 Tarleton rode from Camden. At Singleton's Mills he found no rebels. But from there on November 5 he reported to Cornwallis: "A Negro has just told me of a Party at Jack's Creek. I shall proceed to General Richardson's, and if I get no satisfactory intelligence before I arrive there, I shall take post and destroy the Country between there & Kingstree, down to Nelson's, &c &c."

After learning that Marion's troops lay at Jack's Creek, Tarleton divided his dragoons into several patrols and spread rumors that the main body had returned to Camden. Said he: "Not withstanding the divisions scattered throughout the country, to impose upon the enemy, Lieutenant-colonel Tarleton took care that no detachment should be out of reach of assistance; and that the whole formed, after dusk every evening, a solid and vigilant corps during the night."

This stratagem almost lured Marion to attack. During the evening of November 7 Tarleton's troops lay in full battle order at the plantation of the widow of General Richard Richardson. They had even emplaced their three-pounder. Having heard of a small party at the widow's, Marion rode forward to surprise them. But Mrs. Richardson sent her son, Colonel Richard Richardson, who had been ill and was hiding on the plantation, to warn him of the ambuscade.

Marion had advanced to within two miles of Richardson's. He immediately wheeled his troops around, crossed the Woodyard Swamp, and never halted until he had ridden Richbourg's mill dam across Jack's Creek, six miles away. After putting a miry swamp and a large millpond between his troops and the British, he exclaimed: "Now we are safe!"

Before daylight an escaped prisoner reached the British and reported Marion's flight. Tarleton immediately sent forward a patrol. It returned with the report that the trap had been discovered and that Marion's men had retreated with great confusion and rapidity.

William Dobein James, the fifteen-year-old son of Major James, was with Marion. "Next morning, Marion, knowing the vigilance of his foe, decamped betimes," wrote James, "and pursuing his route down Black river, for thirty-five miles, through woods and swamps and bogs, where there was no road, encamped the following night on advantageous ground, at Benbow's ferry, about ten miles above Kingstree, on the east side of Black river."

In his *Campaigns* Tarleton wrote that he pursued Marion "for seven hours through swamps and defiles." Under the guidance of Harrison, the British Legion rode from Jack's Creek on the Santee, around the miry Woodyard, and then eastward across twenty-six miles of fields, woods, and swamps.

Not having had so much as a glimpse of Marion's men, at Ox Swamp on Black River, twenty-three miles above Kingstree, Banastre Tarleton paused. He looked at his tired horses and at the roadless bog. Then he cried in the thick accents of Lancashire: "Come, my boys! Let us go back and we will find the gamecock. But as for this damned old fox, the devil himself could not catch him."

The Green Dragoon swung back toward Nelson's Ferry and rode another ten miles without stopping. He spent November 9 and 10 suppressing disloyalty with the torch. He burned Sumter's mills on Jack's Creek and rode on for vengeance upon Widow Richardson.

His mood was blacker than the mourning band he wore for André. In sheer ghoulishness, although many thought he was looking for the family silver, he dug up old General Richardson who had lain in the plantation graveyard for some six weeks. He ripped open the coffin in order that he might "look upon the face of such a brave man."

And his final vandalism provoked Governor Rutledge on December 8 to write the South Carolina delegates in Congress: "Tarleton, at the house of the widow of General Richardson, exceeded his usual barbarity; for having dined in her house, he not only burned it after plundering it of everything it contained, but having driven into the barns a number of cattle, hogs and poultry, he consumed them, together with the barn and the corn in it, in one general blaze."

Next morning the British Legion trotted toward the High Hills. At Singleton's the Green Dragoon issued a proclamation to the inhabitants in the district along the Santee:

Singleton's Mills, Nov. 11, 1780

Be it known to all People concerned in the late Revolt, between Nelson's Ferry, Kingstree Bridge, & Santee Hills, that a general and free Pardon, is held out to all the said Delinquents, in case they will return Home between the Date hereof & twenty-fifth of this

Month—upon their arrival at Home they must separately acquaint the Officers of the Loyal Militia of their Intention to live peaceably at their Plantations, and in Case of a future Insurrection and Invasion to give Notice thereof; which Declaration (of the assembled People) the said Officers of Loyal Militia must Transmit to the Officer commanding his Majesty's Troops at Camden—

It is not the wish of Britain to be cruel or to destroy, but it is now obvious to all Carolina that Treachery, Perfidy, and Perjury will be punished with instant Fire and Sword.

Ban. Tarleton
Lt. Col. Com. B.L.

After posting his Proclamation, the Commandant of the British Legion set about writing his official report. On November 8 Lord Cornwallis, having heard rumors that Tarleton's promotion to the permanent rank of lieutenant colonel in the British Army had come from the War Office, had written his favorite dragoon: "You say nothing to me about your Rank of Lieut.Col., which if it is true that you have it, I take very ill, as you must be convinced that it is an Event in which I feel myself much interested."

In one of the longest letters he ever wrote his commanding officer, Banastre answered:

Singleton's Mills, Nov. 11, 1780

My Lord

I have the Honor to inform you that I have so far returned from my Expedition after Col. Marion, Horry etc. The Insurrection would have been general & dangerous to Camden & the Communications of the army had it not been nipped before it arrived at maturity—The Enemy had just issued a Proclamation saying your Lordship was dead, that the whole cavalry with 600 infantry and your humble Servant were cut to pieces, and that Camden was passed by a Northern Army.

No Intelligence to be depended upon can I possibly obtain of the Enemy's Situation or Number. Every Inhabitant between Santee Hills, Nelson's Ferry, and Kingstree Bridge, besides as many from Saint Stephens Parish, had either joined thro affection, hid themselves through dislike to, or were Prisoners to Marion & his Adherents.

I was disappointed in my attack at Singleton's Mills, the Place where 4000 were said to be collected. I kept my Numbers concealed, advanced on the Roads, fell back again, showed Tokens of Fear, by leaving Camp abruptly & Provisions cooked, in order to draw the Enemy of whom I could gain no news either to attack or approach me. I so far deceived Marion that he would undoubtedly have attacked on the 7th instant in the Evening had he not been prevented by some treacherous Women (Mrs. Richardson, &), with him 400 or 500 men—A Prisoner who escaped from him in the Night came in to my Camp just before Day on Nov. 8th & informed me that he would have attacked me had he not obtained Intelligence of number at Richardson's, but on that account he had altered his Route in Confusion. The Corps under my command were ordered under Arms immediately and made a rapid march of 26 miles through Swamps, Woods, & Fastnesses toward Black River without a Halt. The Enemy by being all mounted, obtaining so much time previous to the pursuing & owing to the Difficulties of the Country could not be brought to Action. I had the Mortification not to fight them, but I had the Pleasure in a great Measure to disperse them.

A few Prisoners were taken from the Swamps by Col. Harrison's Corps. I returned on my Steps & laid the Houses & Plantations of violent Rebels Waste about Richardson's & Jack's Creek. The country seems now convinced of the error of Insurrection. People join me from the Swamps. The Torch is stopped & I have issued the enclosed Proclamation. Thus my Lord I have used my best Ability to settle the Affairs of this part of the Province, but if there had been one individual of the Country attached to our Cause & exempt from Fear the total Destruction of Mr. Marion had been accomplished. I am to acknowledge the honor of your Lordship's letters of the 4, 5, & 8 dates, in your last you chide me for not informing you of my Advancement—A letter from Liverpool by a private Ship from a near Relation dated 10th Aug't. says "that the King has honored you with the Rank of Lt.Col. in the Army & your Brevet is on board the S. Carolina Packet."

Your Praises my Lord have exalted me. I hope my future Services will merit your just Commendations. Those Actions ought to be the best which are founded on gratitude.

Ban. Tarleton

Francis Marion, trailing back along the Santee road a few days later, gazed at the ruin and desolation. The sight almost overwhelmed him. Of Banastre Tarleton he wrote: "It is distressing to see women and children sitting in the open air around a fire, without a blanket, or any clothing but what they had on, and women of family, and that had ample fortunes; *for he spares neither Whig nor Tory.*"

On November 17 Balfour wrote Lord Cornwallis about Banastre's cossacking along the Santee: "But after his dissipating and dispersing account of Marion, I am sorry to say that in a few days afterwards, he appeared with 500 men before Georgetown, where I am sorry to say he now is, within a few Miles."

Cornwallis answered good-humoredly: "As to Marion, I do not think that Tarleton flattered himself that he had done more than stopping his immediate progress and preventing the Militia from joining him, and if the accounts I hear from that Country are true his visit has not been ineffectual."

Balfour replied: "Marion's movements I by Tarleton may be remembered of—it is no joke to us."

Sensible generals do not report pique and jealousy among their subordinates: their careers are enhanced by victories alone. In his report to Sir Henry Clinton, dated at Winnsboro on December 3, 1780, Lord Cornwallis wrote: "Colonel Marion had so wrought on the minds of the people, partly by the terror of his threats and cruelty of his punishments, and partly by the promise of plunder, that there was scarcely an inhabitant between the Santee and Pedee that was not in arms against us. I therefore sent Tarleton, who pursued Marion for several days, and by convincing the inhabitants that there was a power superior to Marion, who could likewise punish and reward, so far checked the insurrection, that the greatest part of them have not dared openly to appear in arms against us since his expedition."

12

The Gamecock

*H*IS FIGHT WITH SUMTER came sooner than Tarleton had expected. In dull routine Lord Cornwallis wrote on November 8: "The enemy is, I believe, in no great force, and Marion is cautious and vigilant. If a blow could be struck at any body of the rebels it might be attended with good consequences; but I do not see any advantage we can derive from a partial destruction of the country."

Next morning his Lordship sent an express racing headlong toward the Santee. To Turnbull at Camden he wrote: "Pray forward the enclosed immediately by an Officer to Tarleton whose Presence in these Parts is absolutely necessary."

> Wynnesborough,
> November 9, 1780

Dear Tarleton,

Major Wemyss attacked Sumpter at Fish Dam at one o'clock this morning, contrary to his plan, which was to wait until day light; the consequences is that Wemyss is wounded and left, and about twenty men: Lieutenant Hovenden is wounded, but I believe the legion has not lost much—Must beg of you to return immediately leaving some horses for mounting men at Camden. I am under the greatest anxiety for Ninety Six, and trust you will lose no time in returning to me.

> I am
> Yours sincerely
> Cornwallis

Lieutenant-colonel Tarleton

In early October, Major Wemyss had ended his burning, plundering foray into the Pedee country and had returned to Camden. Later he had joined Cornwallis at Winnsboro, and when Tarleton rode off after

Marion, his Lordship began using the mounted infantry of Wemyss' 63rd as if they were dragoons. In his sweeps on November 7 Wemyss discovered that General Sumter had camped at Moore's house about thirty miles above Winnsboro.

Wemyss wished to surprise Sumter. "As the defeating so daring and troublesome a man as Sumter and dispersing such a banditti, was a great object," said Cornwallis, "I consented to his making the trial on the 9th at daybreak, and gave him forty of the dragoons which Tarleton had left with me, desiring him, however, to put them neither in the front, nor to make any use of them during the night."

With his mounted 63rd and the Legion dragoons Wemyss marched on November 8. Unknown to him Sumter had advanced five miles to Fishdam Ford and was encamped in the woods and gullies on both sides of the road, with his rear against Broad River. About one o'clock Wemyss stumbled upon Sumter's vedettes while leading his men. The vedettes fired five shots: one broke the Major's arm and another ripped into his knee.

When Wemyss fell from his saddle, Lieutenant Stark, not knowing the instructions of Cornwallis, led a cavalry charge along the road into Sumter's camp. The silhouettes of the horsemen made excellent targets, and Colonel Winn's marksmen drove them back in disorder. There followed confused fighting in the dark. Neither could tell who had the advantage, so both sides withdrew.

Five dragoons had been deputized to kill or capture Sumter. Led by a Tory guide named Sealy, they found his tent. But when two dragoons entered the marquee, Sumter ducked under the back, leaped a fence, and crawled under the riverbank. Not knowing who was in possession of the silent battlefield, the coatless Gamecock sat until daylight with his head under an overhanging tussock and shivered through the November frost.

Lieutenant Stark abandoned his dead and left Major Wemyss and other wounded with a sergeant major under a flag of truce. The sergeant said later that no rebels were seen for two hours after sunrise. About noon Sumter returned and took the paroles of the British. In Wemyss' pocket was a list of the men he had hanged and the houses he had burned along the Pedee. After glancing over it, Sumter threw the list into the fire. He tumbled the wounded Major into a wagon and for several days trundled it in the wake of his militia.

∾

From Singleton's Mills the green horsemen of the British Legion had started racing toward Winnsboro. On November 13 Lord Rawdon, who with the Volunteers of Ireland had relieved Turnbull at Camden, reported them in bivouac eight miles below the village. Here a courier delivered another letter from Lord Cornwallis to Tarleton: "You will have received my letter of yesterday, since which we have intelligence that Sumpter has passed the Broad River, and joined Clarke, Brannen, etc. They talk of expecting some of the mountaineers; as they have excellent horses, we cannot hurt them; and unless they receive some check they will be very troublesome."

Soon after breaking camp, Tarleton received a third summons. In it was the highest laudation: "I wish you would get three Legions, and divide yourself in three parts: We can do no good without you."

In his next letter Lord Cornwallis ordered his horsemen to swing north of Winnsboro:

> Winnsborough, Nov. 13, 1780
> seven o'clock P M

Dear Tarleton

Sumpter is at Hawkins Mill on Tyger River with what he calls a thousand men; bragging much of his Victory, our friends are all in the utmost Terror and running down to the Congarees as fast as possible. I shall be glad to see you but your Corps must keep at a distance as they would consume our whole substance in half an hour. I rather think the Legion had better march up the Wateree as you will then threaten Lacy, Smallwood & Sumpter & perhaps inert the two former. I believe you can subsist, I may probably see you the day your Corps passes the Ferry. Lord Rawdon & England will explain to you all my wishes, my expectations & personal difficulties; amongst which the establishing a post on Black River is not the least—I fancy that you will have found that Morgan and Washington are quite out of your reach.

> I am Dear Tarleton
> Most sincerely yo'rs
> Cornwallis

Then to Major McArthur, guarding Brierly's Ferry on Broad River with the 71st Regiment, Lord Cornwallis wrote: "Tarleton is advanced to Camden & I hope we shall soon put a stop to Mr. Sumpter's bragging."

Next day Cornwallis ordered the British Legion to march directly to Brierly's. Tarleton forced his march, and at about nine o'clock on the morning of November 18 reached McArthur's camp. His exhausted troops went down to the edge of the Broad River to refresh themselves. While they were washing up and cleaning their horses, a troop of about 150 horsemen dashed up to the opposite bank and began firing across the river. They knocked over a horse and wounded a soldier of the 63rd. Tarleton opened with his cannon and sent them scampering.

Then, concealing the green uniforms of the British Legion and displaying the red coats of McArthur's 71st infantry, so that spies and scouts could not discover his return from the lower Santee, Tarleton sent his men over the ferry. The Legion cavalry crossed at a ford three miles below the ferry, and about ten o'clock the whole corps went into camp some miles beyond Brierly's.

That evening Tarleton received intelligence that General Sumter, with about 1000 men under their militia colonels Brandon, Bratton, Clarke, Few, Hill, Lacey, Myddleton, Taylor, Twiggs, and Winn, was marching toward the house of Colonel James Williams. This was a fortified post on Little River, about fifteen miles above Ninety-Six. It was held by Loyalist militia under the renegade Colonel Moses Kirkland.

At daybreak on November 19 the Green Dragoon set out to surprise the Gamecock. All day his troops marched with diligence, directing their course along Indian Creek and encamping that night near Enoree River. During the evening a malcontent of the 63rd deserted, stole a horse, and reached Sumter's camp before midnight.

Tarleton resumed his pursuit at dawn. Before ten o'clock his scouts reported that Sumter had turned back from Williams' and was retreating in great haste up the Enoree. Doubling their tempo, the British marched until they approached a ford. Here the dragoons of the advance guard charged a detachment of Americans under Captain Patrick Carr, who were guarding some Tory prisoners. Sumter's men fled, but the green horsemen swooped down and cut the Tories to pieces before realizing their mistake.

From a survivor Banastre learned that only two hours earlier the Gamecock had crossed the Enoree and was forcing his march toward the Tyger. With his cavalry, his infantry, and his three-pounder in a compact body, he pursued the Americans until four o'clock. Realizing that he could not overtake them before dark or before they had crossed the Tyger River, Tarleton ordered the infantry to slacken and march at their own pace. He then started after Sumter with 80 mounted infantrymen of the 63rd Regiment and 190 dragoons of the British Legion.

Before five o'clock the advance guard of the Legion charged the rear guard of the Americans. But about this time a woman who had viewed the British line of march from a wood, rode into Sumter's ranks to inform him that the British cavalry was unsupported by infantry or cannon.

Sumter had reached the Tyger, but he knew that should he attempt to cross, Tarleton would cut his rear guard to pieces. At bay, but in an almost impregnable position, he turned to face his pursuer. On his left was an open field of about fifty acres, with five log houses sitting above the river on an eminence known as Blackstock's Hill. On his right was a thick wood, flanking the road and rising up the side of a long, steep hill. At his back flowed the river. And before him the terrain sloped down to a shallow spring branch.

Sumter's position was strong and his disposition of his troops was judicious. On his left he formed the Georgians, under Colonel Twiggs, posting their sharpshooters in the jams of the rail fence near Black-stock's house and extending their line across the field and into the woods. To defend Blackstock's house and barns he assigned Colonel Hampton and his riflemen. The right wing Sumter commanded in person, stationing the troops of Colonels Bratton, Hill, McCall, and Taylor from the great road to the high hill. On his extreme right he placed Colonel Lacey's mounted infantry. And the reserve and rear guard under Colonel Richard Winn he posted along the Tyger.

Tarleton did not wish to pit 270 regulars against 1000 militiamen. He wanted to lie close, pin them against the river, and harass them until the arrival of his cannon and infantry. So he ordered the 63rd to dismount and to take position at the end of the clearing on the right of the road and facing downhill to the branch. To the left of the road, with their flank against the wood and their front facing downhill, he formed the dragoons of the Legion.

Sumter opened the battle by sending 400 infantrymen downhill, across the branch, and uphill to attack the 80 men of the 63rd. His troops delivered their fire at too great a distance, and while they were reloading the 63rd counterattacked with the bayonet. In hand-to-hand fighting, with the odds five to one, they drove the Americans back uphill and into the wood beyond Blackstock's house.

As this fighting raged across the eastern end of Blackstock's field, Sumter ordered Lacey to flank Tarleton's left and strike the idle dragoons. The horsemen were so intent on watching the infantry push the foe across the valley below that Lacey rode unperceived to within seventy-five yards of them. At Lacey's fire 20 dragoons fell. "Lt. Skinner bravely repulsed the detachment which threatened the flank," said Tarleton in the *Campaigns*.

Sumter, with his aides, Colonel Henry Hampton and Captain Robert McKelvey, had ridden into the woods to encourage Lacey's attack. While returning to his command post in the center, Sumter was struck by a ball that pierced his right shoulder, ripped through the shoulder blade, and chipped a splinter from his backbone.

When they reached the command post, Captain McKelvey heard a sprinkling on the dry November leaves. Looking quickly at Sumter, the Captain saw blood trickling down his coat and spattering the ground.

"General, you are wounded!" he cried.

"I am wounded," Sumter replied. "Say nothing about it."

With his right arm hanging limp, Sumter asked Colonel Hampton to put his sword into the scabbard and to get a man to lead off his horse. "Say nothing about it," he told his aides. "Request Colonel Twiggs to take the command."

By now the British infantry was in trouble. "The ardour of the 63rd carried them too far, and exposed them to a considerable fire from the buildings and the mountain," wrote Tarleton. "Though the undertaking appeared hazardous, Lieutenant-colonel Tarleton determined to charge the enemy's center with a column of dragoons, in order to cover the 63rd, whose situation was now become dangerous."

Tarleton charged at the head of his Green Horse. They swept Sumter's cordon from the road. But the musket fire from the fence jams and the log houses toppled horses and riders so fast that they choked the way. The dragoons turned back from this barrier of screaming, dying flesh. Their flashing sabers had freed the 63rd and allowed them to rally.

Lieutenants Cope and Gibson had been killed and Major Money lay mortally wounded.

As darkness settled over the field, both horse and infantry, having driven the enemy back into their stronghold, returned to their original positions. Tarleton then led them into a bivouac on a hill two miles from Blackstock's.

The Chick of the Blue Hen had won, but he was unable to stand and scarcely able to speak. Colonel Twiggs knew that Tarleton waited only for daylight before striking again, so he abandoned the field. Leaving Colonel Winn to keep bright campfires burning through the night, the colonels forded the Tyger. Then each went his way and disbanded his troops.

About a hundred men remained under arms as a bodyguard for their helpless General. Stretching an uncured bull hide between two horses, they formed a crude litter, and into this they gently laid the Gamecock. His escort paused at Goudelock's near Grindal Shoals on Pacolet River only long enough for a doctor to dress his wound. Then an escort of five men hurried him on to his camp at Colonel Samuel Watson's on Steel Creek in the New Acquisition, twenty miles below Charlotte.

To stop Tarleton from chivvying his troops, Sumter had turned and provoked a battle. He had repulsed the British. He had seized most of their dead and wounded. But even though Tarleton had been defeated in his tactics, he had succeeded in his strategy and achieved his objective. He had deflected the blow from Williams' house and Ninety-Six. He had overtaken, battered, and dispersed the rebels. And he had sent their elected general from the field a speechless, helpless, bloody mass wrapped in a bull hide.

As propaganda to inspirit the militia, Colonel Charles S. Myddelton officially reported for Sumter that Tarleton had left 92 dead and 100 wounded British upon the field. For the Americans he reported 3 killed and 3 wounded, besides General Sumter. In his secret report to Lord Cornwallis after recovering his dead and wounded, the commandant of the British Legion made neither false claims nor admissions. The fate of every British soldier was recorded in the great quarterly muster rolls:

Camp at Blackstokes
Tyger River
Nov. 22 Tuesday 1780
7 o'clock A. M.

My Lord

I have no baggage consequently no cypher—I trust for this short letter no accident—I yesterday cut Sumpter's rear guard to pieces on Ennoree—I pursued his trail with great rapidity & had an action on this ground last night with the Cavalry & 63rd only—

Sumpter is defeated, his Corps dispersed, & himself dangerously wounded—The ground was difficult—But night came on & for want of our infantry I could not immediately pursue the Blow—Three young men who were of Ferguson's Corps have promised to fix Sumpter immediately—I have promised them for the Deed 50 gs. each in case he falls into our Hands.

But my Lord I have lost men—50 killed & wounded & Officers which are losses to the public Service—Poor Money is wounded but not dangerously—Gibson & Cope killed—Also numerous Legion wounded & every officer I have my own included killed or wounded—The Rebels were commanded by Sumpter—Clarke Lacey Brannon also were present—1000 in all & were attacked by 190 Cav'y & 90 Inf'y on most unapproachable ground—I have written to McArthur to pass & bring my Baggage—I shall take every immediate step boldly to suppress Insurrection.

I have the Honor
to be your most
Obedient Serv't.
Ban. Tarleton

N.B. The Enemy attacked the 63rd & forced me to action before the cannon, Legion and light Inf'y could be brought up.

B.T.

From Blackstock's a horseman raced the sixty miles to Winnsboro and delivered Tarleton's report to Lord Cornwallis. Immediately his Lordship answered:

Wynnesborough Nov'r 22, 1780

My Dear Tarleton,

I most heartily wish you joy of your success. But wish it had not cost you so much: I have ordered M'Arthur to proceed to Calley's ford on Ennoree, and to wait for your orders with his battalion, sending on the baggage with a captain and fifty men: If you should want him, it will make but little delay; if not, it will save him a long march. I have sent Stewart to assist your wounded; I am happy to hear that Money is in no danger; I most sincerely rejoice in your escape, as well on my account, as on that of your country: That success and every happiness may attend you, is the sincere wish

> Of your most faithful
> And affectionate friend,
> Cornwallis.

In a postscript the commanding general of his Majesty's forces in the Southern Provinces pledged his invincible dragoon: "I will not tire you with a repetition of my obligations to you: I trust you will find that I shall never forget *them*."

After sending orders for Major McArthur to advance to Blackstock's to protect his wounded and hold his prisoners, Tarleton crossed the Tyger and started pursuing the Americans. For two days he trailed Sumter. He bagged stragglers and collected members of the 63rd and Ferguson's corps who had eluded their captors. At Pacolet River he stopped, and having been convinced that the colonels had dismissed their militia and that Sumter had died, he started leisurely back.

During his countermarch, he wrote a second report on the battle of Blackstock's. In it Ban's usual laconic style was enhanced by lack of proper writing paper:

	Near the Head of
Sumpter's wound	Tiger Wednesday
is thru both shoulders—	Nov'r. 24, 1780
People this instant have	10 o'clock a.m.
reported him dead.	

My Lord

I believe my last action had very good consequences. The Rebels have disbanded. Sumpter is mortally wounded. One colonel of theirs killed & about 120 militia wounded and prisoners—of the rebel army—Night & want of Inf'y prevented a pursuit—Many prisoners came in yesterday who had escaped them during the engagement. Several of them have sent in for terms. One Adj't & 12 men submitted themselves yesterday.

There is a report of Colonel Selvey but is I am persuaded a rebel one—All the people about him say that their whole force was at Blackstoke's 10 Colonels, 1000 men, & &.

It was difficult for me to maneuvre for want of intelligence and I had to pass the Ennoree three miles before I could strike at Sumpter—You will see my Lord by my letter of yesterday that I could only bring up 80 of 63d and 190 cavalry—I did not mean to attack Sumpter, only to harass and lie close to him till I could bring up the rest of the Corps, as he could never pass the Tiger if I had attacked.

The 63d were attacked by the Enemy which brought on the affair—I will write more fully when I get more Paper—I ordered Major McArthur to Blackstokes on leaving as I did with our waggons full of wounded.

> Ban. Tarleton

Several of Fergusons have made their escape & some of 63d taken at Fish Dam—Money is as well as can be expected.

In his rampage through the heart of South Carolina the Green Dragoon had lost count of the days: he dated his letters as of November 22 and 24 instead of November 21 and 22. Nor did he stop to inquire the correct spelling of Blackstock, Brierly, Cunningham, or Shelby, but wrote these names as they sounded in his Lancashire brogue: Blackstokes, Byerly, Coningham, and Selvey.

Lieutenant General Cornwallis warmheartedly answered: "I have no doubt but your victory will be attended with as good consequences to our affairs as it is with honour and credit to yourself; I shall be very glad to hear that Sumpter is in a condition to give us no further trouble; he certainly has been our greatest plague in this country."

In his report to Sir Henry Clinton, Lord Cornwallis lauded the fearless dragoon who had fought, defeated, and chased the rebels from Goose Creek to Pacolet River. Proudly he wrote: "It is not easy for Lieutenant Colonel Tarleton to add to the reputation he has acquired in this province; but the defeating one thousand men, posted on very strong ground, and occupying log houses, with one hundred and ninety cavalry and eighty infantry, is proof of that spirit and those talents which must render the most essential services to his country."

On November 25 Tarleton reported: "I hope tomorrow to complete the destruction of our enemies in this district—Sumpter is now reported dead—Colonels Thomas, Clark & Chandler are dead." Then in supressing rebellion he hanged a feckless Whig named Johnson.

Tarleton's putting the Gamecock *hors de combat* stilled the commotion in the Up Country. But the Swamp Fox continued to raid the supply line between Charleston and Camden and to animate the correspondence of Balfour and Rawdon. On November 25 Lord Cornwallis wrote Balfour: "We have lost two great plagues in Sumpter and Clarke. I wish your friend Marion was as quiet."

Upon his return over the Tyger, Tarleton learned that Lord Cornwallis, in anxiety for his own weak garrison in Winnsboro, had recalled McArthur posthaste to Brierly's and had ordered the British Legion to march to Williams'. Tarleton visited Brigadier General Robert Cunningham, "a man of spirit and conduct," and reviewed the freshly embodied militia. In ordering this embodiment, on November 25, Cornwallis wrote Colonel Cruger: "I should wish to have as many of the Militia as possible sent to Colonel Tarleton. If anybody can put spirit into them he will."

Having obtained paper and his cipher device from his baggage brought up by McArthur, the Green Dragoon now sent a coded message to Lord Cornwallis reporting the end of the campaign against the

Gamecock (The use of cipher in military communications is hereafter indicated by italics):

28 Nov'r 6 o'clock a.m.

My Lord

All affairs in this district are settled—Macarthur is a day & a half march on his return—I march this day and leave Coningham with proper orders.

I have the Honor
to be
Your Lordship's
Most devoted Serv't
Ban Tarleton

The Green Dragoon returned to his camp at Woodward's plantation near Brierly's Ferry about December 1. Soon he rode on to Winnsboro to see Lord Cornwallis and to visit the sick and wounded from his Legion.

His dragoons spent the mild days of early December in rest and recuperation. Some rode patrols and others went foraging. The farriers shod the horses. "At present we are very busy," Tarleton wrote Cornwallis on December 5. "No Iron for shoes to be obtained here. I am obliged to send for it from Camden."

Tarleton wrote that forage for his horses had become scarce around Woodward's. Cornwallis suggested that the dragoons move into a new section: only in the Dutch Fork, lying between the Broad and the Saluda rivers and stretching away to the Congaree, was there an abundance of food and forage. The dragoon replied:

Woodward's Dec. 14, 1780

My Lord

I am still upon my old ground. Yesterday patroles were sent into the neighborhood in order to review the stock of forage.

The officer who was detached to the Country above Byerley's Ferry reports that there was not above six loads of forage for seven miles above that place. It is full as convenient to the Corps to remain here as to move except to the Congarees, that I fear is too far.

I have this morning detached Lt. Willett with 160 guineas in his Pocket to buy horses—I hope he will be successful & accomplish this business without any References or Disputes.

After having delivered all the supposed Friends of Government that the real ones could point out, I am still enlarged with prisoners that Blackstokes threw into my Hands; I have therefore sent them on to your Lordship's camp in order that they may be transmitted on, or receive such doom as your Lordship shall judge right.

I have the Honor
to be
Your Lordship's
Most devoted Serv't,
Ban. Tarleton

"I have no material intelligence," Cornwallis answered next day, "and I am sorry to say, none that I can depend on from the enemy on our front. If you can meet with any persons more enterprising than those I can find, I beg you will employ them. No news from Ninety Six or General Cunningham since you left us. I saw yesterday your convalescents; some of them I hardly thought fit to join; and there were rather more black attendants, both male and female, than I think you will like to see."

In these days of leisure, the Green Dragoon relaxed, read his letters, and dreamed of home. From Liverpool had come news good and bad. Even though he was a hero among his townsmen, he had failed to win support for his candidacy in the parliamentary election in November. His brother John had been unable to collect the legacy his Aunt Parker had left Ban to pay his debts. And John had sent him a keg of wine for Christmas. In a cheerful mood Ban wrote a note of thanks:

Winnsboro Dec. 16 1780
South Carolina

My dear Brother—

Several Letters have I received from you—accept my thanks for all the Trouble you experienced on my Account last Summer—

My Lord Amherst is averse to American Promotion but I think he cannot stop mine—

My Lord Cornwallis's Letters & Report of the Carolina Affairs, must remove every Obstruction to my Preferment—I have not yet heard, but suppose my Rank of Lt.Col. beyond Doubt.

I have had many hair breadth Escapes since my last—my good Genius still smiles—I hope will hover around me till I once more see my native Country.

About my worldly affairs I have wrote to you very frequently— My Debts may be now paid to Advantage, that is compromised or otherwise easily disposed of—Griffeth of the Cocoa Tree can best inform you.

My Aunt Parkers Legacy I have impowered you to receive— Letters of Attorney I cannot obtain—my Lord Cornwallis' Signature I have sent—I have not been within a hundred Miles of Charles Town these 6 months—no Attorney in this County except in Arms—Law always breeds Rebellion.

The Duke of Newcastle Earl Lincoln & Collyer I shall write to thank—

It is a terrible Affair my not coming in for Liverpool—Ambition could not have had a fairer Path, had I obtained that Election.

We are just going against the Enemy in N Carolina with a compleat & Gallant Army, much may be expected. Event only can determine—I have the Advanced Guard—My Lord Cornwallis confers Honors & Affectionate Obligations upon me.

I thank you for your Present of Wine & with every kind wish I remain—

Your most afft. Broth.

Ban Tarleton

13

Perdita

"Ꮟ Y JOVE, MRS. ROBINSON, you will make a conquest of the Prince; for tonight you look handsomer than ever," exclaimed Gentleman Smith as Mary stood in the wings ready to play Perdita before the royal family.

At that moment young Ford, son of one of the proprietors, presented Viscount Malden to the waiting actress. As they chatted, she observed that the Prince of Wales, attended by his sub-governor, Colonel Gerard Lake, was watching them. He was a good-looking youth of seventeen, of medium height and stocky build, with Germanic features and a florid complexion accentuated by his high white neckerchief and the quantity of powder in his hair.

"I hurried through the first scene, not without much embarrassment, owing to the fixed attention with which the Prince of Wales honoured me," said Mary. And as flattering remarks from the Prince drifted to her ear, the performers again teased the star about her conquest. On the last curtsy, the royal family returned a bow to the performers. In her *Memoirs,* Mary Darby Robinson tenderly recorded: "But just as the curtain was falling, my eyes met those of the Prince of Wales: and, with a look that I *never shall forget,* he gently inclined his head a second time; I felt the compliment, and blushed my gratitude."

As Mary left the theater, she met the royal family crossing the stage. "I was again honored with a very marked and low bow from the Prince of Wales."

At a supper party at her home in the Great Piazza, Mary's guests reminded her of the flattering attention of the Prince; and the conversation of the whole evening centered around his person, graces, and amiable manners.

Several days later Lord Malden called upon Mary. He was nervous, awkward, embarrassed. He attempted to speak, but paused, hesitated, apologized. Finally he drew a small letter from his pocket and thrust it at the actress. It was addressed only "Perdita." Inside was a brief love letter signed "Florizel."

"Well, my Lord, and what does this mean?" asked the half-angry wife of Thomas Robinson, knowing that in *The Winter's Tale* it is Florizel who wins Perdita.

"Can you not guess the writer?" countered Malden.

"Perhaps yourself, my Lord."

"Upon my honor, no," replied his Lordship. "I should not have dared so to address you on so short an acquaintance."

"Then from whom does the letter come?"

Malden hesitated. He stuttered. Finally he blurted out: "I could not refuse, for the letter is from the Prince of Wales."

With skepticism born of experience, Mary returned a formal answer. But she pressed the Prince's note to her bosom: "A thousand times did I read this short but expressive letter."

The next day Lord Malden brought a second letter, with instructions for Mrs. Robinson to attend the Oratorio at the Opera House, where by sign the Prince would "convince me that he was the writer of the letters." To the Oratorio went the giddy young actress. With craftiness she rented a box opposite and above that of the royal family. Nervously she waited.

Soon the Prince of Wales and the Duke of York entered and seated themselves in the front of their box. The Prince slowly scanned the audience. When he found Mary, he bowed and began flirting ostentatiously. He held the playbill before his face. He drew his hand across his forehead. Along the edge of the box he moved his hand as if writing a letter.

The Prince pointed out Mary to the Duke, and as the princes gazed and whispered, the audience also looked toward Mary's box and began whispering. Nor were the hungry news reporters less observant. Next day the *Morning Post* quoted a chorus from Dryden's "Alexander's Feast," which seemed appropriate for a Prince who

> Gazed on the fair
> Who caused his care
> And sigh'd, and look'd, and sigh'd again.

Sparkling with intrigue, the star of Drury Lane shone brilliantly during the Christmas season. She was now acknowledged the première Shakespearean actress of her generation, and the London audience supported her with enthusiasm. On December 21 she opened the festivities by donning the male disguise of Viola in *Twelfth Night, or What You Will*. She drew capacity audiences on December 24, 25, and 27 as Juliet in *Romeo and Juliet*. And on December 31, 1779, Mary closed the year again attired as the handsome youth who arouses the tender passion of Countess Olivia.

To Mary the new year brought increasing popularity. Five or six times a month she appeared on the stage at Drury Lane. On one evening she was the shepherdess Perdita and on the next she was Viola. Realizing her attractiveness in men's clothing, on January 28 Sheridan sent Mary upon the boards in the elegant page-boy trappings of Rosalind in *As You Like It*.

The critic for the *Morning Chronicle* of January 29, 1780, noticed that under the royal ogling the actress had begun to preen and strut: "Mrs. Robinson last night acquitted herself very respectably in the character of Rosalind in Shakespeare's beautiful comedy *As You Like It*. Her figure was perfectly proper, and her deportment sufficiently graceful. She will, however, improve her performance of the part, if she in the future uses less labour in her oratory, and does not aim at the emphatic so much."

All London soon knew that the emphatic was centered upon one person. Neither Prince nor actress concealed their infatuation until it aroused the ire of the King and Queen. On February 11 Mary went to the Oratorio to gaze upon the Prince. But, according to the *Morning Post*, she met with humiliating reproof: "A circumstance of rather embarrassing nature happened at last night's oratorio. Mrs. R——, decked out in all her finery, took care to post herself in one of the upper boxes immediately opposite the Prince's, and by those airs peculiar to herself contrived at last to *basilisk* a certain heir apparent, that his fixed attention to the beautiful object above became generally noticed, and soon after astonished their Majesties; who, not being able to discover the cause, seemed at a loss to account for the extraordinary effect. No sooner, however, were they properly informed, than a messenger was instantly sent aloft, desiring the *dart-dealing* actress to withdraw; which she complied with, though not without expressing the utmost chagrin at her mortifying removal."

"The *Maids of Honour* were thrown into the utmost consternation by the alarming occasion," scoffed the *Morning Post*. And remembering that on the previous evening Mary had played Perdita at Drury Lane, it counseled:

> Queen it not an inch further
> But milk thy ewes and weep!

Almost every day now Lord Malden delivered a letter from Florizel. Each was fraught with love and begged for an assignation, but Mary refused to meet with his Royal Highness. "I was not insensible to all his powers of attraction; I thought him one of the most amiable of men," she wrote. "There was a beautiful ingenuousness in his language, a warm and enthusiastic adoration, expressed in every letter, which interested and charmed me."

One day his Lordship brought Mary a copy of Meyer's painting of the Prince in a miniature set with diamonds. "This picture is now in my possession," she wrote in her *Memoirs*. "Within the case was a small heart cut in paper, which I also have; on one side was written, '*Je ne change qu'en mourant*.' On the other: 'Unalterable to my Perdita through life.' "

Volatile and excitable throughout her career, Mary could bear only so much. And now, as the Prince pleaded, and Malden wheedled, and gossip mounted, Mary broke under the strain. On March 9 the *Morning Post* said: "Mrs. Robinson, of Drury Lane Theatre, lies dangerously ill at her home in Covent Garden."

Florizel was even more tender than before to his Perdita. He wore Lord Malden out with carrying royal messages. His Lordship complained to Mary and regretted his task. But he confided to her that the Duke of Cumberland had come to his home to warn him that the Prince was most wretched on account of Mrs. Robinson.

∽

As spring advanced, the story of Paolo and Francesca quickened in the land of Lancelot and Guinevere. "Lord Malden again lamented that he had engaged himself in the intercourse," Mary wrote afterward, "and declared that he had himself conceived so violent a passion for me that he was the most miserable and unfortunate of mortals."

Thus importuned by a miserable prince and an unfortunate viscount, Mary was in her own inferno. But gossip assigned to Lord Malden the reward expected by the Prince. After the masquerade on April 3 the *Morning Post* saluted her as his mistress. "Mrs. R——n, with a pink jacket and coat, with loose gauze thrown over it, appeared melancholy from the prevailing inattention of the company, retired with her pliant spouse on one side, and the Malden hero on the other, who sympathetically sulked with his acknowledged half."

The *Morning Post* of April 19 again reported Lord Malden and Mrs. Robinson together at a masquerade at the Pantheon. Later Maria Elizabeth Robinson wrote: "The constant devoirs of Lord Malden, whose attentions were as little understood as maliciously interpreted, conspired to distract a young creature, whose exposed situation, whose wavering and unformed character, rendered her but too obnoxious to a thousand errors and perils."

The *Morning Post* reported that Sir John Lade, having been replaced in Mary's retinue by Lord Malden, was in such gallant pursuit of Miss Brown, an actress of Covent Garden, that the little brunette had fled to her house in the country "Yesterday was held a grand *Jubilee* at

R——n Lodge, next door to the *Bedford Arms*, Covent Garden, in consequence of the little *Brunette* having evacuated all her town *breastworks* in favor of the heroine of the said *Lodge:* Lord Mal——n, Sir J—— L——, and various other *young gentlemen*, it is said, honoured this convivial meeting with their presence."

A letter to the editor, from a "Brunette-ite to Mrs. Robinson," chided Mary for having lost Sir John to Miss Brown: "You talk much of your *education and superior understanding*; but how useless are they, when through pique, we find you abusing the pretty *Brunette of Covent Garden*, bell, book, and candle! for depriving you of the most *promising gull* that followed in your flock of admirers."

But Mary was too busy to hold promising gulls. Sheridan staged Lee's *The Rival Queens*, and she played Statira, the second wife of Alexander the Great. Again and again she was Amanda in *A Trip to Scarborough.* So thoroughly had Sheridan cleansed the bawdy and blasphemous from Vanbrugh's *The Relapse, or Virtue in Danger* that the wits now called it *A Relapse, or Drury in Danger*, but the theatergoers loved her in the play. They even forgot the expurgated lines of Berinthia's feigned anger as she was being borne away by Loveless, Amanda's husband: "Help, help! I'm ravished, ruined, undone. O Lord, I shall never be able to bear it."

The drawing power of Mary's trim breeches figure continued. Choosing Wycherley's *The Plain Dealer*, Sheridan cast her as Fidelia, a young lady who cherished such passion for Manly, the plain dealer, that she followed him to sea in man's clothing. As Jacintha in Hoadley's *The Suspicious Husband* Mary again donned breeches and again escaped with virtue.

Passion now bore Mary and the Prince to the inevitable climax. Cooped up in Buckingham House by his parents' orders, his Royal Highness could not attend the Masked Ridotto at Covent Garden on May 1. But from Grey's he sent jewels, and next day the *Morning Post* reported: "Mrs. Robinson shone with unusual lustre, exhibiting a rich suit of diamonds contrasting with a ruby head."

Having seen Mary wear the breeches of Viola and Rosalind, and of Fidelia and Jacintha, the Prince proposed that she come disguised as a boy to his apartment in Buckingham House. She refused. But as his courtship advanced she became less obstinate. Said she: "The unbounded assurances of lasting affection which I received from his Royal Highness in many scores of the most eloquent letters, the contempt which I experienced from my husband, and the perpetual labor I underwent for his support, at length began to weary my fortitude. Still I was reluctant to become the theme of public animadversion, and still I remonstrated with my husband on the unkindness of his conduct."

As Perdita's consent trembled in the balance, Florizel threw in a Royal makeweight. "Previous to my first interview with his Royal Highness, in one of his letters I was astonished to find a bond of the most solemn and binding nature, containing a promise of the sum of twenty thousand pounds, to be paid at the period of his Royal Highness's coming of age."

"This paper was signed by the Prince, and sealed with the royal arms," wrote Mary. "It was expressed in terms so liberal, so voluntary, so marked by true affection, that I had scarcely the power to read it. My tears, excited by the most agonizing conflicts, obscured the letters, and nearly blotted out those sentiments, which will be impressed upon my mind till the latest period of my existence."

Across the boards of Drury Lane she strode as Lady Anne in *King Richard III*, a queenly exemplar that love is every woman's price. Then as Imogen in *Cymbeline* she gazed over the footlights toward the royal box and rapturously declaimed:

> "He is
> A man worth any woman; overbuys me
> Almost the sum he pays."

The Prince suggested that Mary meet him at the home of Lord Malden. She thought that too dangerous. After long and agitated arranging, she agreed to meet him in the palace yard at Kew.

On a soft spring evening, at the trysting hour, Mary and Lord Malden waited on the bank across the Thames from the old palace. Just as the dusk crept into darkness, Mary saw a white handkerchief waving from the courtyard. Crossing over quickly in a boat, she and Lord Malden saw the Prince of Wales and the Duke of York.

The Prince ran to meet them. Mary laid her trembling hand in the hand of Prince George; and after Malden and the Duke wandered off among the roses, theirs became a passionate lovers' meeting. "Words of the most affectionate nature were uttered by the Prince," said Mary. "The rank of the Prince no longer chilled into awe that being, who now considered him as the lover and the friend. The graces of his person, the irresistible sweetness of his smile, the tenderness of his melodious yet manly voice, will be remembered by me till the vision of this changing scene shall be forgotten."

Many and frequent were the assignations at this romantic spot. Sometimes the lovers remained together until midnight, guarded from intrusion by Lord Malden and the Duke of York. "Often have I lamented the distance which destiny had placed between us: how would my soul have idolized such a *husband!*"

Beautiful actresses have often been the private province of kings and princes, even those of England, but scandal belongs in the public domain. Gossip about her princely conquest heightened interest in the beautiful

Mrs. Robinson. She now became the cynosure of Drury Lane, and Richard Sheridan capitalized on the scandal. In debt, the director of Drury Lane watched the sale of seats: box seats at six shillings, the pit at three, the gallery at two, and the upper gallery at a shilling. How he drove the actress who drew the shillings!

On April 1 Mary played Jacintha in *The Suspicious Husband*. During the remainder of the season she performed almost nightly. On May 4 she was Mrs. Brady in *The Irish Widow*. On May 18 she changed to Perdita, on May 19 she again turned into Mrs. Brady, and on May 20 she was Viola. On May 22 she played Rosalind, and on May 24 she played both leads in a double bill: Perdita in *The Winter's Tale* and Sir Harry Revell (or Eliza) in Lady Craven's *The Miniature Picture*. On May 26, 27, and 29 she was Sir Harry in *The Miniature Picture*.

Madly in love, or at least passionately infatuated, Mary suddenly displayed such power that even the niggling critic for the *Morning Chronicle* of May 27 became rapturous: "Mrs. Robinson's Eliza does her infinite credit: she displays a degree of acting merit in the breeches scenes of the character, infinitely superior to any sample of professional talent she has before shown, and stands eminently distinguished from the other performers."

Caustic old Horace Walpole, writing to the Reverend William Mason, reported going to see Lady Craven's play, "and Mrs. Robinson (who is supposed to be the favourite of the Prince of Wales) thought on nothing but her own charms and him."

Then came the finale. On May 31, 1780, the evening that Drury Lane closed for the summer, Mary Robinson closed her stage career forever. But not without tears. After the final curtain, she entered the Green Room with bravado, singing the epilogue from *The Irish Widow*:

> "Oh, joy to you all in full measure,
> So wishes and prays Widow Brady!"

A moment later she was sobbing hysterically.

ᲡᎳ

Next day Mary slipped away for a tryst with the Prince, she to lodgings in Old Windsor and he with the royal family to Windsor Castle. Then with all the pride of seventeen years, he escorted her everywhere, even into St. James's Palace. On June 4 he brought her to the palace for the King's Birthday Ball, and though he dared not bring another man's wife into the ballroom, he bade Mary watch from the Chamberlain's box. As the Prince opened the dancing with Lady Augusta Campbell, Mary saw her select two rosebuds and hand them to him, a love symbol before all the proud scions of Albion.

The Prince beckoned the young Earl of Cholmondeley and by him sent the rosebuds to Mary. "I placed them in my bosom, and, I confess, felt proud of the power by which I thus mortified an exalted rival."

The scandal dripped from everybody's tongue. Letters to the editor piled up. But the newspapers, even the gossip-mongering *Morning Post*, were afraid to mention the affair. The laws of libel were too harsh, as the Reverend Henry Bate, editor of the *Morning Post*, found out. For on June 27 he had published a libelous letter attacking the Duke of Richmond, and on July 10 a bailiff had waited on him with a subpoena. For his libel the reverend editor served a year in prison.

By July 18, however, the *Morning Post* was ready to publish the scandal. As an introduction, it used that British adjunct to the newspaper, a letter to the editor:

Windsor, July 14

Mr. Editor,

And so the Theatrical Perdita of Drury Lane is laboring night and day to insinuate to the world, that an amour has taken place, or is to take place, between her and a certain young illustrious character. If such a report, may, in the smallest contribute to the fair lady, in her other pursuits and designs, it would be a pity to contradict the report; but otherwise, Mr. Editor, it may be friendly in you to whisper in her ear, that if the young gentleman had really any penchant for her, which, however, is not the case, her present system of vain boasting must give his heart a very speedy quietus.

Yours, etc.

Ovid

Then the *Morning Post* forever linked the names of Mary Robinson and Prince George as Perdita and Florizel:

Anecdote

In the last solemn season of Lent, whenever *Florizel* was present at the Oratorio, *Perdita* never failed to testify her taste for sacred music, or something else, by being there also. It was her custom to seat herself as nearly opposite *Florizel* as she could contrive. They were apt to exchange looks: and they were remarked. *Florizel*, in consequence, was admonished; and measures were taken, though ineffectual, to prevent *Perdita's* future admittance. When *Perdita* next presented herself at the door, she was given to understand, that a certain *Liberty*, which, in common with some others, she had long enjoyed, was now denied her. *Perdita*, without the least discomfiture, and with that bewitching indifference for which she is admired—turned to her husband, who always accompanies her to public places, and said—*Pay your guinea*. *Perdita* ascended to her box; she did the usual execution; and when the entertainment was over, she placed herself at the back of the stage, in a situation where *Florizel* must view her as he passed to his chair. *Florizel* gazed, and he departed, in all the grandeur of regal pomp. *Perdita* calmly retired to the carriage of a late American *Plenipo*; to which she was carefully handed by the most convenient of husbands.

Two days later the *Morning Post* returned to the scandal: "A certain young actress who leads the TON appeared in the side-box at the Haymarket Theatre a few evenings since, with all the grace and splendour of a Duchess, to the no small mortification of the female world, and the astonishment of every spectator!!"

‿

"The writer has paid the highest compliments to the young lady in question, who could make a conquest in the heart of a young and illustrious personage, at the very moment when he is surrounded by all the beauties of the British Court, vying with each other to capture and ensnare him," an anonymous correspondent wrote the *Morning Post* on July 22.

"Mrs. Robinson now appeared in indecent splendour, rendered still more scandalous by the vile participation of her husband," wrote an anonymous biographer of George IV. "Her house was openly frequented by the Prince and his friends. Though refused admission to all good company in private houses, she mingled with the most distinguished on all other occasions."

The Prince gave a grand ball for Mary at Weltjie's. His guests included lords and ladies of the proudest lineage. The Prince opened the dancing with the Duchess of Devonshire. Georgiana was no philosopher, but she must have registered astonishment at the sight of Mary clinging to the arm of the Prince. Could this be the same creature she had thrown crumbs to in the King's Bench Prison just four years ago? Truly *Amor vincit omnia!*

Lady Harriet Spencer, in a letter to Mrs. Shipley, wife of the Bishop of Asaph, wrote of the gossip: "The thing which is most talked at present is the Prince of Wales, who keeps Mrs. Robinson *en maitresse declose, c'est toute a fait un etablissement*; she wears his picture about her neck, and drives about with four nag tailed horses and two servants behind her."

Whenever Mary appeared in public, she became the center of curiosity. Said she in her *Memoirs*: "I was frequently obliged to quit Ranelagh, owing to the crowd which staring curiosity had assembled around my box; and even in the streets of the metropolis, I scarcely ventured to enter a shop without experiencing the greatest inconvenience."

An attractive vignette of the happy mistress was drawn by John T. Smith, then an apprentice in the studio of Sherwin, the engraver. "I saw all the beautiful women of the day; and being considered a lively lad, I was noticed by several of them," he wrote. "Here I received a kiss from the beautiful Mrs. Robinson."

One morning, as young Smith waited upon the visitors, Mary came into the studio singing. Mrs. Darby accompanied her daughter and for safety carried the miniature of the Prince. Mary asked to see a sketch of her that Sherwin had made, and when Smith answered that it was in an upper room, she replied: "Do try to find the drawing for me, and I will reward you, my little fellow."

Little or not, Smith, who had seen Rosetta in *Love in a Village* on the preceding evening, went upstairs humming suggestively: "With a kiss, a kiss, and I'll reward you with a kiss!" Finding the sketch, the youth trotted down the stairs. "I had no sooner entered the room with the drawing in my hand, than she imprinted a kiss on my cheek, and said, 'There, you little rogue.'"

Sherwin perfected the design for Mary's carriage: a basket of five buds, surmounting a rose wreath around the initials M.R., the whole seeming to form a ducal coronet. Although of humble origin, the son of a woodcutter, he was a votary of fashion and the most popular artist in London. He fitted in the Bohemian camaraderie around Mary and was a frequent guest at the Great Piazza. One evening they sat discussing his plans for an engraving that would present Mary as Abra kneeling at the feet of Solomon. Who should stand for the young Prince of Israel? A hint that a certain high personage would be perfect for Prince Solomon fell on astonished ears—even though the Princess Royal had posed as Pharaoh's daughter in Sherwin's *The Finding of Moses*. The artist hesitated and then suggested another. Mary's eyes flashed: "Kneel to him? I'll die first!"

Another glimpse is even more intriguing. In her *Memoirs*, dour old Miss Laetitia Hawkins wrote a chapter entitled "Ladies of Various Descriptions." After paying her respects to Kitty Fredericks, Mrs. Dorothy Jordan, and Lady Emma Hamilton, she wrote: "If I paid, indeed, due respect to rank, there is one lady of very superior claims, who ought to have had precedence of all my fair acquaintance of the tribe of iniquity."

That Mary was unquestionably very beautiful, Miss Hawkins admitted, "but more so in the face than in the figure; and as she proceeded in her course she acquired a remarkable facility in adapting her deportment to her dress. When she was to be seen daily in St. James's Street or Pall Mall, even in her chariot, the variation was striking. Today she was a *paysanne*, with her straw hat tied at the back of her head, looking as if too new to what she passed to know what she looked at. Yesterday, perhaps, she had been the dressed belle of Hyde Park, trimmed, powdered, patched, painted to the utmost power of rouge and white lead; tomorrow she would be the cravated Amazon of the riding-house; but be she what she might, the hats of the fashionable promenaders swept the ground as she passed."

But let no daughter of Eve count herself happy until time has closed her account with fortune. "The period now approached that was to destroy all the fairy visions which had filled my mind with dreams of happiness." Mary found that *Je ne change qu'en mourant* spelled only *Inconstant Florizel*.

As plans for the establishment of the Prince in a wing of Buckingham House went forward, Mary expected a home fit for a duchess. The Prince had promised her such an establishment as soon as he should have his. Instead she had been settled in a small house in Cork Street, Burlington Gardens. She remonstrated, but the Prince could do no better: King George controlled the royal purse. Misunderstanding followed disappointment. As autumn faded into winter, the idyl of the summer faded forever.

"We must meet no more," wrote Florizel. Mary replied. He failed to answer; she wrote again. Wretched and emboldened by fear, she drove her pony phaeton to Windsor Castle. "On my arrival the Prince would not see me. My agonies were now undescribable."

On Hounslow Heath a footpad had frightened Mary by snatching at the reins of her ponies and then running after the phaeton. But her terror was slight in comparison to that she felt upon returning to Old Windsor. There she beheld Mrs. Elizabeth Armstead.

Elizabeth Bridget Cane had once been personal maid to the famous Mary Robinson of Drury Lane. But wit and beauty removed her from the servant class. Like many fashionable ladies of the eighteenth century, as soon as she had lost her virtue, she assumed her widowhood and posed as the beautiful Mrs. Armstead.

"My foreboding soul instantly beheld a rival," cried the deserted Perdita, "and with jealous eagerness, interpreted the, hitherto, inexplicable conduct of the Prince, from his having frequently expressed his wish to know that lady."

Rumor and gossip that Florizel had been estranged from Perdita sped through London. Borrowing lines from the *Philaster* of Beaumont and Fletcher, on November 11, 1780, the *Morning Post* inquired of Mary:

> Now, Lady—where's your honour now?
> Can no man fit your palate but a Prince?

"Mrs. R——n is affirmed to have publicly professed an intention to visit Germany within a few weeks after Christmas," said the *Morning*

Post on November 20. "A riddle is therefore got into circulation at the west end of the town respecting the truth of her ardour."

The *Morning Herald*, a new daily which the Reverend Henry Bate had established on November 1, 1780, now turned scandal reporter. The reverend editor, whose friendship with Mary provided a reliable source of gossip, reported that Mrs. Robinson, dressed in a brown Capuchin cloak and hood, and accompanied by Lord Malden, had spent the evening of November 21 at a masquerade in the Pantheon.

Lord Malden was acting as mediator, and he brought the lovers together at his house in Clarges Street. The Prince was exceedingly happy. He slipped his arm around Mary and declared that never for a moment had he ceased to love her. "I began to flatter myself that all our differences were adjusted. But what word can express my surprise and chagrin, when on meeting his Royal Highness *the very next day* in Hyde Park, he turned his head to avoid seeing me, and even affected *not to know me.*" The amour had ended.

The Reverend Mr. Bate received clandestine information about the separation. On January 8, 1781, the *Morning Herald* announced the cause: "A certain young personage and Lord M—— are not now on those terms of intimacy which made them more like brothers than Prince and subject."

14

Prelude to Battle

"*H*IS MAJESTY was pleased to express his sense of Major Tarleton's services in very flattering Terms, but did not think proper to give him any additional rank, he having very lately only been appointed to the Rank of Major," said Lord Amherst, Secretary for War, on November 6, 1780, in a letter to Lord Cornwallis.

The Green Dragoon, keeping vigil beside Broad River, was extremely disappointed. He felt that he had earned promotion. He had sweltered under Carolina sun. He had ridden through thunderstorms and forded icy streams. He had suffered from malaria. He had nearly died of yellow fever. And he *had* chased the King's enemies from South Carolina. To Lieutenant Henry Haldane, who had become aide to Lord Cornwallis after the death of Money, Banastre wrote manfully: "The more difficulty, the more glory."

The rains had turned the roads to Woodward's lowland plantation into a quagmire. Wagons bogged down and horses floundered. So Tarleton moved several miles upland on December 18 and pitched camp at Daniel's plantation. But even though he hastened to inform Lord Cornwallis that his new camp lay the same distance from Brierly's, in his removal he missed Captain Kinlock bearing a letter from his Lordship with information about the appearance of Brigadier General Daniel Morgan among the militia of South Carolina.

From Brierly's, Captain Kinlock forwarded the letter:

Wynnesborough, Dec. 18th, 1780

Dear Tarleton

Lord Rawdon has received intelligence, which, however, he does not credit, that Morgan's Corps and the Cavalry had passed the Catawba. I have sent out everybody that I could engage to go, but the friends here are so timid & so stupid that I can get no intel-

ligence. I have heard nothing from 96, but a man who came here
from Broad River says that Gen'l Cunningham has beat Clarke
and wounded him mortally. I shall be glad to hear a confirmation
of this. I apprehend we must first dislodge Lacey etc. from Turkey
Creek & then march up the West Side of Catawba to some of the
fords above Tuckaseege. I wish you would take pains to inform
yourself as thoroughly as possible of the state of the roads, Provisions, forage, Mills, etc. I hear a good account of the Recruits in
general. I hope to march from here 3500 fighting men barring
those I mentioned to you upon the frontier.

Lord Rawdon very readily agreed to undertake Watson so we
shall be relieved of that plague.

I trust you will make every possible shift rather than go much
further back, as I should in that case be uneasy about McArthur,
and as soon as you have been able to get information about the
Country, I should be glad to see you to talk over our march.

I am Dear Tarleton
Very Sincerely Yours
Cornwallis

There was disturbing intelligence about the American army Gates
had assembled at Charlotte after the British withdrawal. On December 2 Major General Nathanael Greene had reached Charlotte and
relieved Gates. Among the most active Partisans he had found Daniel
Morgan. Having arrived from Virginia in September, on October 1
Morgan had assumed command of a legion formed from the surviving
Continentals of Delaware and Maryland under Lieutenant Colonel John
Eager Howard and seventy Continental dragoons under Colonel Washington.

Lord Rawdon's intelligence report had basis in fact. On December 16
Greene had written Morgan: "With these troops you will proceed to
the west side of the Catawba river, where you will be joined by a body
of volunteer militia, under the command of Brig. Gen. Davidson, of
this state, and by the militia lately under the command of General
Sumpter."

From Charlotte on December 20 Greene marched his army in two
divisions. The main body moved to Haley's Ferry on the Pedee, crossed,
and on December 26 encamped on Hicks Creek, nearly opposite
Cheraw. The detachment under Morgan moved into the country between the Broad and Pacolet rivers. By means of these pincers Greene
hoped to pin Cornwallis in Winnsboro by threatening both Camden
and Ninety-Six.

Morgan's appearance among the militia was immediately reported to
the British. From Williams' on December 24 Brigadier General Cunningham wrote Tarleton: "From the best authority am convinced the

Rebels are embodying at Ramsours Mill, in all probability intend moving their operations towards this Quarter."

As Ramsour's was high up the Catawba, the British rested and enjoyed Christmas day. But on December 26 intelligence was so disturbing that Lord Cornwallis twice wrote Tarleton. In the forenoon he wrote: "A man came this morning from Charlotte town; his fidelity, however, very doubtful; he says, that Greene marched on Wednesday last towards the Cheraws, to join General Caswall, and that Morgan, with his infantry and one hundred and twenty-four of Washington's light horse, crossed Biggar's ferry, on Thursday and Friday last, to join Lacey. I expect more certain intelligence before night, when you shall hear again from me."

That evening, after he had received all the reports from his spies, scouts, and expresses, Lord Cornwallis again let Lieutenant Colonel Tarleton hear from him:

> I send you the reports of the day. First, Morgan and Washington have passed Broad river; secondly, a brig from Cork says, that a packet had arrived there from England, and that accounts were brought, that six regiments were under orders for embarkation, supposed to be destined for Carolina; thirdly, and worst report of all, if true, that one thousand French are got into Cape Fear, who will probably fortify themselves at Wilmington, and stop our water communication with Charles town with provisions; fourthly, that an embarkation was taking place, under General Phillips, from New York, said to be destined for the Chesapeak.
>
> Lord Rawdon mentions, that by a letter from M'Kinnon to England, he is afraid that the accoutrements for the 17th Dragoons are coming up by the slow process of General Leslie's corps. Try to get all possible intelligence of Morgan.

On December 27 Lieutenant Haldane wrote Tarleton: "If it would not be inconvenient, His Lordship would wish to see you tomorrow." Next day Colonel Tarleton rode twenty miles across the rolling hills of Fairfield to visit the commander in chief at Winnsboro.

Lord Cornwallis confided to him the plans of the winter campaign into North Carolina. After the destruction of the corps under Ferguson his Lordship had ordered Major General Alexander Leslie and his troops from the Chesapeake. They had arrived in Charleston on December 13 and were collecting wagons in preparation for the march to Winnsboro. His Lordship anticipated great success after the arrival of these reinforcements, especially the Guards under Brigadier General Charles O'Hara. But he had one problem. Even though the fortifications around Ninety-Six were in condition to withstand direct assaults, he was afraid of the punishment that Morgan and the militia might inflict upon the Loyalists.

§

The most trusted British spy beyond Broad River was David George. Known for Loyalist sympathies, George had once been hauled off to a rebel camp, only to be freed for lack of evidence of spying. But the Whigs were watching him, and he ended one of his letters: "Brandon's Men is always scouting about the Bearer is Very uneasy awaiting for me I hope your Excellency will Excuse Hast I am your Earlships Most obedient Humble Servant."

Despite surveillance by Brandon's militia, on December 30 David George wrote a long letter to Earl Cornwallis:

> My Wifes sister Last Night came to my house out of strong Rebel Settlement up at Princes fort; by her I have heard the Design & Intention of the Rebels; as far as their Captains have any Knowledge; as she came she Informs me that she got into some of their Camps on the south side of the Pacolate River at one Grimses Mill about Ten or Twelve Miles below the Iron Works on Lasons Fork—she understood from Captain Francis Princes and Henry Princes Wives; That they were waiting for Colonel Morgan & Colonel Washington who was on their March; in order to Join Them Morgan with five or six Hundred Light horse had Crossed broad River at Smiths ford a few Dayes agoe; and Washington with their artilliry and foot men was to Cross broad River at the same ford yesterday; That they intend to march against Ninety Six and agusta; they say they will have Three Thousand men; to go against Them places: but I have always observed that they always make the Most of There men.

George concluded his report with advice about rivers, fords, and strategic points. But before his bearer appeared, the spy wrote a second letter with even more alarming news for the noble Earl:

> I have sot down to acquaint you with what I have Heard a few Moments agoe Morgan & Washington Had Joind the party that Lay at Grimes Mill yesterday & they all moved to Colonel Henderson Plantation about a mile this side of the mill and I am well Informed that they Intend to March as fast as they can to Ninty Six I don't believe they have as many men at it is Reported to my Wifes Sister.

That night the bearer set out on the eighty-mile ride to Winnsboro. He arrived late in the afternoon of January 1, 1781, almost simultaneously with a courier from Major McArthur. From Brierly's the Major had written: "General Cunningham & his people quitted the fort on Saturday night & mounted for 96 & the Rebels took possession of it ye Sunday morning at eight o'clock."

There was consternation at British headquarters in the mansion of Colonel Richard Winn. McArthur's report crushed all hope for an effective Loyalist militia. Colonel Washington, operating in the van of Morgan's Corps, had decided to strike at Williams', and for that purpose he had sent forward a troop of forty dragoons under Colonel Joseph Hayes. Upon hearing rumors of their approach, Cunningham's militia had fled.

In the center of a rich farming section filled with food and provender, Ninety-Six was of great strategic value. Its bastion protected some of his Majesty's most loyal subjects. Alert and ready under the command of Lieutenant Colonel J. Harris Cruger, it lay astride the high road to Augusta.

Lord Cornwallis called his aide, Lieutenant Haldane, and told him to ride for Tarleton's camp and order the Green Dragoon to move at once for Ninety-Six. Haldane and his guide rode all through the cold night, over wet and slippery roads. At five o'clock in the morning he reached Daniel's plantation and found Tarleton's marquee.

Banastre was already astir, and his bugler began sounding the call to boots and saddle. "Lt. Col. Tarleton proposes moving immediately," Haldane scribbled in a note to McArthur, "and will join your battalion at the ferry. Lord Cornwallis desired you would leave your heavy baggage at the encampment of the Legion."

At seven o'clock that morning Lord Cornwallis sent an express galloping westward to Brierly's with orders for Tarleton to push Morgan to the utmost. And the General offered to bring the whole army if it were needed to protect Ninety-Six:

Dear Tarleton,

   I sent Haldane to you last night, to desire you would pass Broad river, with the legion and the first battalion of the 71st, as soon as possible. If Morgan is still at Williams', or anywhere within your reach, I should wish you to push him to the utmost: I have not heard, except from M'Arthur, of his having cannon; nor would I believe it, unless he has it from good authority: It is, however, possible, and Ninety Six is of so much consequence, that no time is to be lost.

                                                         Yours sincerely,
                                                               Cornwallis

Let me know if you think that the moving the whole, or any part of my corps, can be of use.

Taking the British Legion, whose cavalry and infantry now numbered only 550, and 200 men of the 71st Regiment, with two threepounders, Tarleton moved to Brierly's Ferry. He sent his infantry over the Broad River in flatboats and his cavalry across the ford. Westward into the Dutch Fork he marched, his dragoons riding patrol and his scouts seeking intelligence. But the reports from David George and Major McArthur were faulty. Morgan was nowhere near Ninety-Six.

At Somer's plantation, six miles beyond Brierly's, Tarleton's troops went into bivouac. Long before daylight next morning they were ready to march again. By candlelight the Green Dragoon wrote his commander:

> Somers Plantation
> Jan'y 3 ½ past 6 a.m.
>
> My Lord
> I am well here—I move *directly toward Monses Mill* a proper course *as I have no Intelligence*
> I have the Honor
> to be
> Your Lordships
> Most Devoted Serv't
> Ban. Tarleton
>
> If the 7th or 71st
> Battalion was at Byerly's
> it would be well

Immediately Cornwallis replied: "I received yours of this morning. I suspect that the enemy are retired. If so, I would lose no time. Which side of Broad River do you think it best for you to march? The 7th regt are ordered to Byerley's." And in a postscript he said: "Be quite sure that 96 is safe. 7th reg't will take your old gun to Ninety Six."

Realizing that Cornwallis dared not advance, leaving a powerful enemy in his rear, Tarleton decided to march far to the west, head off Morgan, and drive him back over Broad River. Such a campaign, far from the main army, needed the sanction of the commanding general. In the early afternoon Banastre outlined his proposed strategy in a letter to Lord Cornwallis:

> Monse's Mill
> Jan'y 4 2 p.m.
>
> My Lord
> Morgan, with upwards of one thousand two hundred men, being on this side Broad river, to threaten Ninety Six, and evade your lordships army whenever you may move, I beg leave to offer my opinion how his design may be prevented.
> I must draw my baggage, the 71st and legion's are deposited at my old camp, to me. I wish to be escorted by the 17th light dragoons, for whom horses are ready; by the Yagers, if to be spared; and by the 7th regiment. The 7th I will send, as soon as I reach Ennoree, with the field piece, to Ninety Six. My encampment is now twenty miles from Brierly's, in a plentiful forage country, and I can lay in four days flour for a move.

When I advance, I must either destroy Morgan's corps, or push it before me over Broad river, towards King's Mountain. The advance of the army should commence (when your lordship orders this corps to move) onward for King's mountain. Frequent communication by letter can pass the Broad river. I feel myself bold in offering my opinion, as it flows from zeal for the public service, and well grounded enquiry concerning the enemy's designs and operations.

I have directed Captain M'Pherson, the bearer of this letter, who is going on the recruiting service, to deliver a letter to Lieutenant Munroe, whom I left at my camp, to bring up my baggage, but no women.

If your lordship approves of this plan, Captain M'Pherson may give my order to Lieutenant Munroe to escort to me three puncheons of rum, and some salt; and, upon their arrival, I will move.

> I have the Honor
> to be
> Your Lordships
> Most Devoted Serv't
> Ban. Tarleton

Tarleton's letter emphasized four points in the plan. Later he made these clearer in the *Campaigns*: "He mentioned the mode of proceedings to be employed against General Morgan: He proposed the same time, for the army and the light troops to advance: He explained the point to be attained by the main body: And he declared, that it should be his endeavor to push the enemy into that quarter."

Winter rains had begun falling again, and the soldiers needed their heavy clothes. So Tarleton decided to remain at Monse's Mill, twenty miles from Brierly's, and request Lord Cornwallis to send forward his baggage. In reply his Lordship wrote:

> Jan 5, 1781
>
> Dear Tarleton,
>
> I received your letter sent yesterday 7 o'clock a.m. I have ordered the baggage of your Corps to Byerley's Ferry, under the care of the 7th Regt. I propose marching on Tuesday next. You will continue to correspond with me, keeping on my left Flank, either on the east or west of Broad River, as you will judge best according to the intelligence you may receive. McArthur will of course march with you.
>
> Yrs.
> Cornwallis

At two o'clock that afternoon Captain McPherson reached headquarters with the outline of Tarleton's proposed campaign.

Cornwallis approved the plan, for he felt that it would carry out his strategy perfectly. In his reply he promised to cooperate by moving on the following Sunday:

Wynnesborough, January 5, 1781
eight o'clock P.M.

Dear Tarleton,

Since I wrote you this morning, I received yours, dated yesterday, two P.M. You have exactly done what I wished you to do, and understood my intentions perfectly. Lest my letter of this morning miscarry, I repeat the most material paragraph.

Your baggage is ordered to Brierley's, under care of seventh regiment. I propose marching on Sunday.

Yours sincerely,
Cornwallis

"I heard from Tarleton last night," his Lordship then wrote Balfour. "Morgan has retired & has got too far to give any hope of overtaking him; so that I shall march as soon as possible, I believe on Sunday & Leslie will follow on Tuesday."

Next morning he added: "I shall not march till Monday, as I find that Tarleton will not be quite ready."

In Morgan's camp on Pacolet all was not well. To Greene, on January 4, 1781, Morgan wrote: "My situation is far from being agreeable to my wishes or expectations. Forage and provisions are not to be had. Here we cannot subsist, so that we have but one alternative, either to retreat or move into Georgia. A retreat will be attended with the most fatal consequences. The spirit which now begins to pervade the people, and call them into the field, will be destroyed. The militia who have already joined will desert us, and it is not improbable but that a regard for their own safety will induce them to join the enemy."

Greene was more cheerful. Conditions in his camp on Pedee were worse than those in Morgan's on Pacolet. But from his spies he knew the straits of the British. Balfour and his occupation troops had to remain in Charleston. With his own corps Greene had Rawdon and the Volunteers of Ireland pinned down in Camden. Cruger and his regiment dared not leave Ninety-Six. The force under Cornwallis had been so depleted that Sumter, rapidly recovering from his wound, had been imploring Greene to strike directly at Winnsboro. Leslie had begun floundering in the swamps of Santee.

"It is my wish also that you should hold your ground if possible," Greene replied on January 13; "for I foresee the disagreeable consequences that will result from a retreat. If moving as far as Ninety-Six, or anywhere in the neighborhood of it, will contribute to the obtaining more ample supplies, you have my consent. Col. Tarleton is said to be on his way to pay you a visit. I doubt not but he will have a decent reception and a proper dismission."

Escorted by fifty troopers of the 17th Light Dragoons and by the 200 recruits of the 7th Regiment commanded by Major Timothy Newmarsh, the wagoners hauled Tarleton's baggage to Monse's. They were burdened with equipment, for at last the British had begun their campaign to subdue North Carolina.

As Tarleton moved westward, he learned that the American militia were swelling the ranks of Morgan's corps. Somewhat alarmed, on January 5 he asked permission to retain the recruits of the 7th Regiment originally scheduled for garrison duty at Ninety-Six. Then on Saturday, January 6, his corps began a slow advance. They crossed King Creek and Indian Creek, both flooded by the continual rains. They came to rest at Duggin's plantation on Indian Creek.

Like a proud and indulgent father, Lord Cornwallis sent his favorite officer everything he asked for, even when he had scarcely enough for himself. In the evening of January 6 his Lordship wrote: "I received yours of yesterday. You will see that some part of your wishes are already anticipated. I am told that you have already received three of the Q'r, Master Gen'ls waggons at Byerleys. I sent another two loaded with rum and salt; you will easily conceive that we have not many to spare. I shall march on Monday & direct my course for Bullock Creek. Leslie will march on Tuesday by the river road for the same place. I approve of your proposal relative to the 7th reg't. I shall send orders to the comm'g officer accordingly."

Perhaps Lord Cornwallis was too indulgent and his commander of horse out of hand. On January 7 his Lordship wrote an angry letter: "Your Q'r M'r. Newland has outraged me exceedingly. He went to the Congarees, where he pressed all the Q'r Master Gen'l's waggons to which I trusted for getting off this ground. In vain the Commissaries represented that they were the hussars of the Army employed by my order in the Public Service. He swore he did not care; that he had Col. Tarleton's orders to press waggons & he would have them & appealed to the *ratio ultimo* of the Broad Sword. You must be sensible that unless he is severely dealt with the conducting of this Army through the Country will be impracticable. What he has done with the waggons, or where they are, God knows!"

In spite of his anger at Quartermaster Newland, Lord Cornwallis somehow assembled wagons at Winnsboro and got his army off the ground on Monday morning. By night he had reached McAlister's plantation and from there he answered the report from Tarleton:

McAlister's Plantation,
January 8, 1781 7 P.M.

Dear Tarleton,

I have just received yours, 7th January, three o'clock P.M. I shall remain here tomorrow, march to cross roads on Wednesday, halt Thursday, and reach Bullock's creek meeting house Saturday. I have no news.

Yours very sincerely,
Cornwallis

Next day Cornwallis received his report from Tarleton and filed a routine reply:

M'Alister's, January 9, 1781
three P.M.

Dear Tarleton,

Nothing new since yesterday; some of Washington's cavalry, who had been escorting prisoners to Charlotte town, returned over Broad river. I have taken every means in my power to find out Morgan's movements, and whether he repasses Broad river.

I received yours January 8th.

Yours very sincerely,
Cornwallis

On January 9 the Green Dragoon remained at Duggin's, waiting for the rains to stop and the Enoree to fall. He sent his daily report to Cornwallis, but conditions were so bad that his courier failed to get through until late the following afternoon. As he waited, Cornwallis wrote Lord Rawdon: "I think it prudent to remain here a day or two longer, otherwise by the corps on my flanks being so far behind, I should be in danger of losing my communication. I have not heard from Tarleton this day, nor am I sure whether he has passed the Enoree."

The flooded rivers now completely disrupted communications. On January 12 Cornwallis wrote Leslie: "I have not heard from Tarleton since Tuesday, I believe he is as much embarrassed with the waters as you are."

With liaison gone, his Lordship deviated from the plans for the campaign and slowed his march toward King's Mountain. To Balfour on January 12 he wrote: "The Rains have put a total stop to Tarleton and Leslie, & I do not think it right to advance too far with a large train of provision waggons and so small a corps."

From these considerations, Lord Cornwallis completely changed his strategy. Instead of rushing forward to trap Morgan, he decided to await the arrival of Leslie and then to march northward with a powerful army. But he did not know the location of his left wing and he failed to inform Tarleton of the change in the plans for the campaign.

To Lord Rawdon on January 12 Cornwallis wrote: "The Rains have impeded all operations on both sides. Morgan is at Scull's Shoals on Pacolet, & Tarleton I believe still on the south of Ennoree unable to pass either that River or the Tyger. The Broad River is so high that it is with difficulty a canoe can pass. If Leslie had not been likewise detained, I might have tried to stop Morgan's retreat, but the Corps I have with me altho' very good, will not afford a strong detachment to take care of Baggage & Provisions."

As Tarleton lay at Duggin's, his scouts brought intelligence that Morgan was encamped at Grindal Shoals. By five o'clock on the morning of January 12 the Green Dragoon had roused his troops. As usual he had lost track of time, and he misdated his report January 11, 5 a.m. Unaware of his Lordship's change of strategy, he was soon marching rapidly forward, looking for practicable fords over the Enoree and Tyger rivers.

Still intent upon turning Morgan and driving him directly into the path of the British army, Tarleton wheeled his corps northward on January 14. He crossed the Enoree at Musgrove's Mill. By cutting footlogs for his infantry and swimming his horses he crossed the Tyger above the Cherokee Road. By evening he had learned that, after posting militia detachments to guard the fords over Pacolet River, Morgan was retreating from Grindal Shoals toward Burr's Mill on Thicketty Creek.

Cornwallis, with all communications broken down, was unaware that his dragoon had advanced miles beyond Duggin's or that he had located his quarry. In midmorning his Lordship wrote him a sleepy letter:

Bull Run, Jan'y 14, 1780, 10 p.m.

Dear Tarleton

I received yesterday morning your letter dated Duggins, Indian Creek, Jan'y 11, 5 a.m. By report however of the man who brought it I conceive it ought to have been dated Jan'y 12 as he assures me that he left you on Friday morning.

I shall march tomorrow to the head of Tardy River & the next day to Hillhouse near Bullock Creek Meeting House. Leslie is at last got out of the swamps & reached this day the neighborhood of Rocky Mount. I have not heard of Morgan's moving, but conclude he will now cross Broad River, as I hear it has fallen very much.

Yrs. sincerely
Cornwallis

Tardy River undoubtedly furnished an excellent camp site, for the British had covered only thirty miles in the six days since leaving Winnsboro. In his own difficulties Lord Cornwallis had dismissed all fears about Tarleton and turned to coaxing Leslie from the swamps. He felt exactly as he had in writing Balfour just before receiving Tarleton's first report from Blackstock's. "I have as yet heard no news from Broad River, but I always trust that where Tarleton is things will go on well."

The army dragged slowly along, as Cornwallis waited for Leslie. Finally it encamped at Hillhouse plantation on Turkey Creek, some forty miles above Winnsboro. From Hillhouse's, on January 16, Cornwallis wrote Tarleton his last letter of the campaign: "I have not heard from you since the 11. I fear Morgan has too much the start of you. I have ordered meal to be ground & propose marching in three or four days to Beatty's Ford. Leslie will join me tomorrow or Thursday."

Then, on the eve of the battle of Cowpens, at Hillhouse plantation on Turkey Creek some aide wrote a memorandum, made many duplicate copies, and broadcast them wholesale above the signature of Lord Cornwallis. Among other gems was this brilliant nonsense: "The banditte under the chiefs, who style themselves Colonels, such as Bratan, Brannon, Wynn, Clarke, Few, etc., etc., have betaken themselves to their hiding places & the power is now totally in our hands."

While the aide of Cornwallis was dreaming up fiction, Morgan wrote Greene from Burr's Mill on Thicketty Creek, on January 15, disavowing any intention of fighting Tarleton. "The enemy's great superiority in numbers, and our distance from the main army, will enable Lord Cornwallis to detach so superior a force against me, as to render it essential to our safety to avoid coming to action."

Greene had wanted Morgan to stand and fight. Morgan answered: "My force is inadequate to the attempts you have hinted at. I have now with me only two hundred South Carolina and Georgia, and one hundred and forty North Carolina, volunteers. Nor do I expect to have more than two-thirds of these to assist me, should I be attacked, for it is impossible to keep them collected."

Morgan was discouraged: "It is beyond the art of man to keep the militia from straggling. These reasons induce me to request that I may be recalled with my detachment, and that Gen. Davidson and Col. Pickens may be left with the militia. . . . They will not be so much the object of the enemy's attention, and will be capable of being a check on the disaffected, which is all I can effect."

Morgan concluded: "Col. Tarleton has crossed the Tyger at Musgrove's Mill; his force we cannot learn. It is more than probable we are his object. Cornwallis, by last accounts, was at the cross-roads near Lee's old place."

At that moment intelligence arrived that Tarleton's troops were British regulars and Morgan added a chilling sentence: "We have just learned that Tarleton's force is from eleven to twelve hundred British!"

Tarleton had already begun probing for a passage over the Pacolet. At every ford he discovered Morgan's troops. So, in the evening of January 15, he used a stratagem. Setting off rapidly as if to go to Wofford's Iron Works high up the river he marched for three hours. Then silently he went into bivouac. Morgan's troops collected and marched up the east side of the Pacolet, but they ran past the silent camp. Next morning before daylight, Tarleton wheeled his troops back and crossed the river at unguarded Easterwood Shoals, six miles below Morgan's troops.

Immediately he sent patrols to reconnoiter and to seize several log buildings constructed by the troops of the late Major Ferguson. As he later wrote: "Tarleton intended to take post, with his whole corps, behind the log houses, and wait the motions of the enemy; but a patrole discovering that the Americans were decamped, the British light troops were directed to occupy their positions, because it yielded a good post, and afforded plenty of provisions, which they had left behind them half-cooked in every part of the encampment."

After his troops had finished the breakfast left by the frightened Americans, Tarleton wrote Cornwallis for the first time since marching from Duggin's. His letter expressed the two convictions that had animated his campaign: that Cornwallis was in a position to cut the Cherokee Road; and that Morgan would not stand and fight. On both counts he was wrong.

Pacolet Jan'y 16th
8 a.m.

My Lord
   I have been most cruelly retarded by the waters.
   Morgan is in force and gone for Cherokee Ford.
   I am now on my march. I wish he could be stopped.

I have the Honor
to be Your most Devoted Serv't
Ban. Tarleton

15

Cowpens

$\mathcal{D}$ANIEL MORGAN hated the British. As an eighteen-year-old lad, freshly run away from his home in New Jersey and settled in the Shenandoah Valley, he had joined as a wagoner in the disastrous march of General Edward Braddock. In 1756 he thrashed a British lieutenant for cursing him and striking him with the flat of his sword. For this offense he received 500 lashes, applied so vigorously to his bare back that blood trickled down into his shoes and chunks of flesh the size of his thumb hung down on ribbons of skin.

After the close of the French and Indian War, Morgan again settled in the Valley of Virginia. He married and prospered. He became a leader in the militia. When the Revolution started, Captain Morgan recruited a company of Virginia riflemen and in twenty-one days marched them from Winchester to Boston. He volunteered for the expedition to Canada and became the hero of Benedict Arnold's unsuccessful attack upon Quebec.

In 1776 Congress gave Colonel Morgan command of a regiment of Virginia Continentals. But his love was the rifle, and in 1777 he received command of a regiment of 500 sharpshooters just being organized. With Morgan's Rifles he wreaked a bloody vengeance for his scarred back. From Boston to Saratoga to Philadelphia he was in the hottest of the fighting.

But the political intrigues of Gates disgusted him. He refused to join in the cabals, and he was not promoted. Consequently, when he had a severe attack of sciatica in 1779, he retired from the army.

In 1780 Congress righted its injustice by making the retired colonel a brigadier general. Immediately Morgan rode from Virginia to join the Southern army under Gates. In North Carolina he contracted malaria and during the autumn was desperately ill of chills and fever.

When Greene sent him across the Catawba, Morgan was still so weak he could scarcely campaign. During the cold, rainy weather at Grindal's Shoals he got wet, and his sciatica became acute. On the ride from the Pacolet to Cowpens he was so wracked by pain that he could not bear to trot his horse.

As Morgan retreated from Pacolet on January 16, Tarleton doubled his efforts. "Patroles and spies were immediately despatched to observe the Americans," he said in the *Campaigns*. "The dragoons were directed to follow the enemy till dark, and the other emissaries to continue their enquiries till morning, if some material incident did not occur. Early in the night the patroles reported that General Morgan had struck into byways, tending towards Thickelle creek."

The Loyalist militia captured a colonel who had straggled from the American militia and brought him before Tarleton. "The examination of the militia colonel, and other accounts soon afterward received, evinced the propriety of hanging upon General Morgan's rear, to impede the junction of reinforcements, said to be approaching, and likewise to prevent his passing Broad River without the knowledge of the light troops, who could perplex his design, and call in the assistance of the main army if necessity required."

The British had little sleep that night. By two o'clock the buglers were sounding reveille. By three o'clock the troops were ready to march. Calling in his pickets and telling his wagoners to follow after daybreak, Tarleton set out on the road to Thicketty Creek. In his van marched the light infantry supported by the Legion infantry. In the center came the 7th Regiment, then the artillery, and then the 71st Regiment under McArthur. Tarleton brought up the rear with his Green Horse.

The march was slow and tedious, for the night was dark and the road rough. About an hour before dawn they reached Thicketty Creek, and from there Tarleton sent forward a cavalry patrol. Soon these horsemen clashed with an American patrol under Captain Inman. Learning that Morgan was encamped only five miles in front, Tarleton ordered Captain Ogilvie to reinforce the advance guard with two troops of dragoons, then to move up and begin harassing the Americans.

When Captain Inman, having escaped in a running fight with the green horsemen, dashed in with the alarm over Tarleton's night march, Daniel Morgan was surprised. He had not expected an attack at dawn. But it was too late to retreat. The British would cut his rear to pieces if he attempted to ford Broad River.

Morgan called in everyone who could give him personal observation of the tactics of the Green Dragoon. He asked Colonel Winn, who had commanded Sumter's reserve at Blackstock's: "Can you inform me of the manner Colonel Tarleton brings on his attacks?"

"I can. Tarleton never brings on the attack himself. His mode of fighting is surprise. By doing this he sends two or three troops of horse, and if he can throw the party in confusion, with his reserve he falls on and cuts them to pieces."

Turning from Winn, the veteran with the inflamed sciatic nerve pointed to the wooded eminence known as the Cowpens. "On this ground," he said, "I will defeat the British or lay my bones."

The country around Morgan was exceedingly rough and hilly. Before him ran a red clay byroad. Behind him for 350 yards the terrain rose toward a ridge, a slope of open wood of oak and chestnut where once a Loyalist named Saunders penned his cows from the range. For 80 yards behind this crest the ground dropped into a swale. Then from a smaller ridge the country leveled into a plain stretching toward Broad River. To the east stood Thicketty Mountain, and in the distant west loomed the Blue Ridge Mountains.

Across the crown of the ridge at Cowpens, among the oaks and chestnuts, in a line about a quarter of a mile long, Morgan deployed his seasoned troops. To his left he posted the light infantry commanded by Lieutenant Colonel John Eager Howard, a splendid contingent of some 290 Continentals. In line on his right Morgan posted Triplett's and Tate's Virginia militia and Beale's Georgians. These men were mostly veterans who had rejoined as volunteers after serving their enlistments in the Continentals. The command of this line, consisting altogether of about 450 troops, he also entrusted to Howard.

About 150 yards down the slope, in a thin line masking the main body, Morgan deployed 300 Carolina militia under Colonel Andrew Pickens who had marched in during the night. These Morgan ordered to deliver two deliberate fires at 50 yards and then to withdraw to a position on the left of Howard's Continentals. He also told them that in case of a charge by Tarleton's dragoons every third man should fire and the other two hold their fire lest the cavalry continue their advance. And he exhorted them: "Shoot for the epaulette boys!"

On the slope about 150 yards below Pickens, Morgan threw out an irregular line of 150 sharpshooters to act as skirmishers. The Georgians, commanded by Major John Cunningham, he sent to his left, and to his right he sent the North Carolinians, commanded by Major Charles McDowell. He told these riflemen to conceal themselves behind trees, to wait until the British had advanced to within 50 yards, and then to shoot from rest. After one fire, they should retire and take their places in the line commanded by Pickens.

"Let me see," said Morgan as he rode away, "which are most entitled to the credit of brave men, the boys of Carolina or those of Georgia."

In the swale behind the crown of Cowpens, Morgan posted Lieutenant Colonel Washington with 80 Continental dragoons and Lieutenant Colonel James McCall with 45 mounted infantry who had been armed with swords. These were his only reserve. He had already ordered the drivers of the baggage wagons to move on toward Broad River and the horses of the militia to be tied in the woods beyond the swale.

As his troops began forming, Morgan rode along their lines encouraging them. He saw that the men as well as the officers understood the battle plan. He cautioned each line against alarm: the men ahead were supposed to retreat—it was part of the plan. Then, like a country politician at a rally, he cracked jokes, inquired about wives and sweethearts, and promised that as sure as he lived the Old Wagoner would crack his whip over Ben Tarleton—as Morgan called Ban.

"I would not have had a swamp in the view of my militia on any consideration," Morgan said years later in justifying his choice of a battleground; "they would have made for it and nothing could have detained them from it. And as to covering my wings, I knew my adversary, and was perfectly sure I should have nothing but down-right fighting. As to retreat, it was the very thing I wished to cut off all hope of. I would have thanked Tarleton had he surrounded me with his cavalry. It would have been better than placing my own men in the rear to shoot down those who broke from the ranks. When men are forced to fight they will sell themselves dearly; and I knew that the dread of Tarleton's cavalry would give due weight to the protection of my bayonets, and keep my troops from breaking as Buford's Regiment did. Had I crossed the river, one-half of the militia would immediately have abandoned me."

∽

When Captain Ogilvie reached the foot of Cowpens, he sent a messenger galloping back through the half-light of dawn with an exciting report. Morgan was forming his lines for battle.

Immediately Tarleton called in his guides and consulted them "relative to the ground General Morgan then occupied, and the country in his rear. These people described both with great perspicuity: They said that the woods were open and free from swamps; that the part of Broad river, just above the place where King's Creek joined the stream, was about six miles distant from the enemy's left flank, and that the river, by making a curve to the westward, ran parallel to their rear."

With an immediate grasp of the enemy's position and a supreme confidence that his British regiments could drive these militia against Broad River, Tarleton hurried his troops forward. He halted them some 400 yards from the American front line. Then, that he might inspect the enemy's posture more closely, he ordered Ogilvie and his dragoons to drive in the skirmishers.

With a shout the Green Horse charged, their sabers flashing, the hoofs of their horses pounding up the gentle rise. Suddenly the rifles of the sharpshooters blazed. Dragoons screamed, cursed, fell from their horses. Shocked and demoralized, they recoiled. When the horses came back, fifteen saddles were empty.

Tarleton decided to make a frontal assault. Ordering the infantry to throw down everything save arms and ammunition, he began arranging his line. "The light infantry were then ordered to file to the right until they became equal to the flank of the American front line: The legion infantry were added to their left; and, under the fire of a three-pounder, this part of the British troops was instructed to advance within three hundred yards of the enemy," he wrote in the *Campaigns*.

When the Grasshopper, as the Royal artillerists called the little cannon sitting upon legs, started belching grapeshot into the woods, the American skirmishers fled. Some 300 yards below the line of Pickens' militia the center and the right wing of the British force paused. Here Tarleton completed his formation. To the left of the Legion infantry he emplaced another Grasshopper. Beyond that he deployed the 7th Regiment, commanded by Major Newmarsh.

"A captain, with fifty dragoons, was placed on each flank of the Corps, who formed the British front line, to protect their own, and threaten the flanks of the enemy," said Tarleton. "The 1st battalion of the 71st was desired to extend a little to the left of the 7th regiment, and to remain one hundred and fifty yards in the rear. This body of infantry, and near two hundred cavalry, composed the reserve. During the execution of these arrangements, the animation of the officers and the alacrity of the soldiers afforded the most promising assurances of success."

They formed a colorful line. Green-coated dragoons sat their horses, sabers in hand. Red-coated light infantry, muskets at rest, bayonets fixed, formed the right. The red-coated artillerymen stood to their cannon. The green-coated infantry of the British Legion formed the center. On the left stood Newmarsh's Royal Welsh Fusiliers.

Tarleton led the attack in person. At about seven o'clock he shouted a command, and the majors dressed their lines. At his command the drums rolled, the fifes shrilled, the artillery roared. The red and green line caught step and paraded. The Green Horse cantered. Several nervous recruits in the 7th started firing, but Newmarsh suppressed them. And, as their commander said in the *Campaigns*: "The troops moved on in as good a line as troops could move at open files."

But Pickens' riflemen were marking the epaulette boys. Coolly those sharpshooters tumbled officers and noncommissioned officers down the slope. The blended line of red and green began to sag. They quickly re-formed. Then with huzzas they charged, their officers shouting, "Give them the bayonet!"

Pickens' militia retreated without squandering. Those nearest bolted for the assigned position on the left of the Continentals. Those on the right, in perfect order for militiamen, began making a traverse of the quarter-mile front. Instinctively, Tarleton seized the opportunity. "The cavalry on the right were directed to charge the enemy's left," he later said. "They executed the order with great gallantry, but were drove back by the fire of the reserve, and by a charge of Colonel Washington's cavalry."

The collapse of Pickens' line seemed the beginning of the expected debacle. At about seven-fifteen Tarleton re-formed his line and threw it against the Continentals. American muskets boomed in volley after volley, but the red and green line never faltered. Rifles crackled. Epaulette men tumbled in the scrub. Said Tarleton: "The fire on both sides was well supported and produced much slaughter."

At about seven-thirty Tarleton trotted back to his reserve and ordered McArthur to move the 71st to the left and begin flanking the Americans. McArthur dressed his line. At his command the pipers stepped forward and the bagpipes began to skirl. The Highlanders pivoted and started on the left oblique for the American right flank.

Observing the movement of the Highlanders, Howard ordered the company on his extreme right to wheel to their left, come about, and face the flankers. Misunderstanding, they turned and marched in good order toward the the rear. The rest of the Virginia and Georgia militia quickly followed. Seeing their right wing crumble, the Continentals turned and began retreating also.

"What is this retreat?" Morgan thundered at Howard.

"A change of position to save my right flank," answered Howard.

"Are you beaten?"

"Do men who march like that look as though they were beaten?"

"Right!" snapped Morgan. "I'll choose you a second position. When you reach it, face about and fire!"

Sensing victory, Tarleton tried to throw everything into the action. In the wake of the Continentals his infantry surged, their line straggling and their ranks thronging in tumultuous disorder. They had become hopelessly entangled in their charge.

"They're coming on like a mob!" Washington sent word to Morgan. "Give them one fire and I'll charge them."

Morgan received Washington's message just as he reached his new position. To Howard he shouted: "Face about! Give them one fire, and the day is ours!"

At about seven-forty-five the Continentals came about and loosed a withering gunfire straight from the hip. The red and green staggered. The dead and wounded cumbered the ground. At that moment Howard yelled: "Give them the bayonet!"

Into the disorganized British troops charged the steady ranks in buckskin. "In all battles, a moment occurs, when the bravest troops, after having made the greatest efforts, feel inclined to run," once observed Napoleon. To this truth the Green Dragoon bore vivid testimony: "An unaccountable panic extended itself along the whole line."

The recruits prostrated themselves on the ground and bellowed for quarter. "Tarleton's quarter!" rang the reply. But Daniel Morgan was not a butcher. Howard checked his men and shouted: "Throw down your arms and we'll give you good quarter!"

Instead of surrendering, the light infantry and the Legion infantry ran toward the road leading back to the Pacolet. Seeing his center give way, Tarleton strove valiantly to rally his infantry. At the same time he sent an order for his reserve dragoons to go to the support of McArthur. "The cavalry did not comply with the order, and the effort to collect the infantry was ineffectual; neither promises nor threats could gain their attention," he said.

At about seven-fifty Washington's dragoons charged among the British foot soldiers. Some 200 yards from the battle front they corralled the leaders and rounded them up like stampeding cattle.

During the milling the Green Horse had not budged. Tarleton now galloped to bring them to the charge. Pickens' sharpshooters guessed his identity and opened with their rifles. He rode on, his life still charmed. But not that of his charger. Suddenly the beast collapsed. Banastre sprang up, sword in hand. He had heard the shouts of "Tarleton's quarter!"

At that moment Dr. Robert Jackson, assistant surgeon of the 71st Regiment, rode up and offered his horse to Tarleton. The Colonel refused to take another's means of safety. But Jackson insisted, exclaiming: "Your safety is of the highest importance to the army!"

Dr. Jackson whipped out his handkerchief, fastened it to the end of his cane, and with the jauntiness of an interne strolling along Rotten Row, headed for the Americans. To their challenge he answered: "I am assistant surgeon to the Seventy-first Regiment. Many of the men are wounded and in your hands. I therefore come to offer my services to attend them."

On the left McArthur and his Highlanders still fought valiantly. Against them Pickens now threw his re-formed militia, and the gallant battalion slowly began retreating. Howard wheeled his disciplined Continentals on their flank. Into the Scottish center charged Colonel James Jackson at the head of his Georgians. He snatched at their regimental flag but missed. Howard promised quarter; and locked in hand-to-hand fighting, but hopelessly surrounded, the Highlanders grounded their arms. Major McArthur stepped forward and presented his sword to Colonel Pickens.

The Highlanders had paid the toll of gallantry in blood and death. Of their 16 officers, 9 lay dead or wounded. And among the wounded, swearing vengeance upon the Green Dragoon, lay Lieutenant Roderick Mackenzie. He would never let Tarleton forget this day.

In the meantime Tarleton, riding Jackson's horse, was trying to bring into action the reserve of the British Legion. "The weight of such an attack might yet retrieve the day, the enemy being much broken by their late rapid advance," he said in the *Campaigns*; "but all attempts to restore order, recollection, or courage proved fruitless. Above two hundred dragoons forsook their leader, and left the field of battle."

But proudly he added: "Fourteen officers and forty horsemen were, however, not unmindful of their own reputation, or the situation of their commanding officer."

The Royal artillerists still fought their guns. Round after round they hurled at the victors. Captain Anderson and Captain Kirkwood selected a gun each, and with their Continentals rushed it with the bayonet. Seeing their assault, Tarleton charged with his fifty-four loyal dragoons. But the Americans seized the cannon, and he signaled a retreat.

The American dragoons now charged the retreating Green Horse. Some 30 yards ahead of his troops rode Washington. Tarleton and his horsemen turned back in defiance.

Washington slashed at the officer on Tarleton's right, but his sword broke near the hilt. The Britisher rose in his stirrups for the *coup de grâce*, but a lad named Collins rode past and dropped his sword-arm with a pistol ball through the shoulder. At that moment the officer on Tarleton's left cut at Washington, but the blow was deflected by Sergeant Major Perry.

The Green Dragoon charged, his enormous saber raised. Washington parried the slash with his broken sword. Reining his charger in a circle, Tarleton snatched his pistol and fired. The ball missed Washington but wounded his horse. Having fired the last shot at Cowpens, Banastre Tarleton galloped after his fleeing Green Horse.

∽

After an hour of fighting, Colonel Tarleton left approximately 100 dead, some 39 of them officers. In Morgan's hands he left 229 wounded and 600 prisoners, some 27 of them officers. He had also lost 2 cannon, 800 muskets, 100 dragoon horses, 35 wagons, the colors of the 7th Regiment, and all his music.

The Americans had only 12 killed and 60 wounded.

The British dragoons raced to their baggage. They found that the guards, learning of the defeat, had mounted the draft horses and fled, and the Tory guides were now pillaging the wagons. The green horsemen charged the Tories, killing and dispersing them for enemy spoilers. Quickly they burned the baggage. Then, unmolested, they continued their flight toward Broad River, while Colonel Washington and his horsemen followed a cold back trail toward the Pacolet.

After crossing Broad River at Hamilton's Ford, the defeated dragoons went into bivouac. They were exhausted and hungry. In his anguish over the loss of his troops Banastre Tarleton cast himself upon the cold, wet ground and lay open-eyed through the wintry night.

All through the night stragglers and fugitives poured into the rendezvous at Hamilton's Ford. Next morning, having collected about 200 of his dragoons, Tarleton rode into the camp of Lord Cornwallis on Turkey Creek, twenty-five miles from Cowpens, almost at the same time the reinforcements under General Leslie were arriving. In humiliation the Green Dragoon reported to his Lordship the loss of the effectives and the equipment of the light infantry, the Legion infantry, McArthur's battalion of the 71st, and the entire 7th Regiment—the worst British defeat since the surrender of Burgoyne at Saratoga.

All day there were reports, explanations, exculpations. Why, after a twelve-mile night march, had Tarleton gone into battle without resting his troops? Why had Cornwallis spent January 17 on Turkey Creek peacefully grinding corn? Why had Tarleton failed to report to his Lordship between January 12 and 16? Did his Lordship receive the Dragoon's letter saying "I am now on my march"? Why had Colonel Tarleton not backed Morgan against Broad River and waited for the army, with its infantry and artillery? Why was General Cornwallis not at King's Mountain, where he should have been according to the written plan of campaign?

In the evening, when Lord Cornwallis sat down to write his report to Sir Henry Clinton, he was sober and factual. He recounted his orders to Tarleton, the chase after Morgan, the battle of Cowpens, and the defeat of his Majesty's arms. He detailed the loss in men and equipment. He also wrote of the fifty-four dragoons "who, having had time to recollect themselves, and being animated with the bravery of the officer who had so often led them to victory," had rallied around Tarleton.

"It is impossible to foresee all the consequences that this unexpected and extraordinary event may produce," Cornwallis advised Clinton. But in forwarding a copy of his report to Lord Germain, Cornwallis wrote: "I shall only say, in addition to what I have said to Sir Henry Clinton, that this event was extremely unexpected; for the greatest part of the troops that were engaged, had, upon all former occasions, behaved with the most distinguished gallantry."

To Lord Rawdon, Cornwallis plaintively confessed: "The late affair almost broke my heart." Nevertheless, every career was at stake, and there was a note of formality in Lord Cornwallis' references to Lieutenant Colonel Tarleton. There was never again between them that free, spontaneous, almost father-son relationship.

Older officers, passed over in the rapid promotion of Tarleton, now enjoyed their revenge. Lieutenant Roderick Mackenzie, paroled after having been left among the wounded, charged the Green Dragoon with arrogance and complained that before the battle he did not consult Majors Newmarsh and McArthur, infantry officers who had been in the army before the birth of Banastre Tarleton.

As the wounded passed through Camden, Major George Hanger, slowly recovering from yellow fever, heard their bitter criticism and hotly defended his friend. In Charleston, Colonel William Moultrie, a prisoner since the fall of Charleston, noted that the British officers were saying angrily that their defeat "was the consequence of trusting such a command to a boy like Tarleton."

Others sneered at Tarleton and swore that his talents never exceeded those of a Partisan captain of light dragoons. "That he possesses personal bravery inferior to no man is beyond doubt," admitted Charles Stedman, civilian commissary to the army under Lord Cornwallis. But he accused: "During the whole period of the war no other action reflected so much dishonour upon the British arms. . . . Colonel Tarleton acquired power without any extraordinary degree of merit, and upon most occasions exercised it without discretion."

After ten days of humiliation and hounding and listening to the other officers grieve for their sixty-six messmates, Banastre Tarleton broke. To Lord Cornwallis he sent a written request that he be allowed to retire and that, after the pattern of the naval courts of inquiry, he be given a court-martial to determine the responsibility for the loss at Cowpens.

On January 30 Lord Cornwallis replied in a comforting letter: "You have forfeited no part of my esteem as an officer by the unfortunate event of the action of the 17th: The means you used to bring the enemy to action were able and masterly, and must ever do you honour. Your disposition was unexceptionable; the total misbehaviour of the troops could alone have deprived you of the Glory which was so justly your due."

Tarleton never understood what deprived him of his glory. After the bitterness had passed, he wrote dispassionately in the *Campaigns*: "The defeat of the British must be ascribed either to the bravery or good conduct of the Americans; to the loose manner of forming, which had always been practiced by the King's troops in America; or to some unforeseen event, which may throw terror into the most disciplined soldiers, or counteract the best-concerted designs."

General Morgan was restrained in his report to Greene. "The troops I have the honor to command have gained a complete victory over a detachment from the British army commanded by Lieut. Col. Tarleton," he wrote on January 19. "The action happened on the 17th inst., about sunrise, at the Cowpens." But after a detailed account of the battle, he remarked that Tarleton's retreat before Washington was not an act "which one would have expected from an officer of his splendid character."

Among the Americans all was huzza. "After this nothing will appear difficult," Greene exulted to Marion, and his troops at Hicks Creek celebrated with a *feu de joie*. Poignantly remembering Gates's flight from the Green Horse at Camden, Colonel Otho Williams congratulated Morgan: "I am much better pleased that you have plucked the laurels from the brow of the hitherto fortunate Tarleton, than if he had fallen by the hands of Lucifer."

So great was the rejoicing that on March 9 the United States through Congress thanked Brigadier General Morgan and the officers and men under his command for their fortitude and good conduct in gaining "a complete and important victory over a select and well appointed detachment of more than eleven hundred British troops, commanded by Lieut. Col. Tarleton."

Congress presented Morgan a gold medal. To Howard and to Washington it awarded a silver medal and a sword. To Pickens it gave a sword. Virginia honored Morgan with a horse and a sword, and Governor Rutledge immediately sent Pickens a commission as brigadier general in the South Carolina militia.

In London there was shocked silence. Finally, on March 29, after a full report of the affair at Cowpens, the *London Chronicle* said: "By all accounts Col. Tarleton was never more distinguished for spirit and gallantry than on this occasion."

16

The Mangled Hand

Near Turkey Creek, Jan. 19th, 1781

Sir

The action of the 17th instant having thrown into your hands a number of British Officers and Soldiers, I primarily request of you that Attention and Humanity may be exhibited towards the Wounded Officers and Men, for whose assistance I now send a Flag, Doctor Stewart and the Surgeon's Mate of the Seventh Reg't.

I secondly desire you to inform me the number and Inability of the Prisoners, which the Fortune of War has placed in your possession.

I have the Honour, etc.
B. Tarleton
Lt. Col. Comm'd'g. B. L.

Brig. Gen. Morgan

P.S. I have sent some money for the use of the prisoners.

But Dan Morgan was far from Cowpens. Within two hours of the end of the fighting he left Colonel Pickens and his militia under a flag to care for the wounded, and with the rest of his infantry and their able-bodied prisoners headed for Cherokee Ford. The night of January 17 he camped on the north side of Broad River.

Knowing that escape from Cornwallis would depend upon rapid movements, he resumed his march long before daylight. When the cavalry caught up, he placed the prisoners in Washington's charge and sent them across the upper fords of Catawba. With his main body he advanced rapidly toward Ramsour's Mill on Little Catawba. On the morning of January 23 he crossed the Catawba and took post at Sherrald's Ford.

On the day of the battle, when Dr. Jackson, waving his white hand-kerchief, had walked up to the Americans, they were suspicious and hauled him off to the compound. Colonel Washington sent for him and took him to Morgan. The General treated the doctor with great respect and set him tending the wounded.

Next morning Jackson wrote a letter to Morgan and sent it via the American surgeon, Dr. R. Pindell.

Jan. 18, 1781

Sir

As the wounded must suffer much for the want of necessaries, and even medical assistance, with your permission, I should wish to inform Lord Cornwallis of their situation; that if he thinks proper, he may order something for their relief; some surgeons of the general hospital, and some hospital appointments. From your very great politeness to me, I am confident you will grant every-thing that is reasonable and proper.

I have the honor, etc.
Robert Jackson, Surgeon's Mate,
1st Bat. 71st Reg't.

Dr. Pindell sent the letters from Jackson and Tarleton to Morgan at Ramsour's Mill. In his covering letter Pindell said: "I send a flag which arrived yesterday from Col. Tarleton. You will see his own requisitions, in addition to which, Dr. Jackson, in conjunction with the gentleman who came with the flag (finding it impossible to have their wounded properly provided for in this country) are desirous of having the men paroled, and to have permission to take them within the British lines." He added: "I am of the opinion, also, that they cannot be provided for here, and think their proposals of equal advantage to us."

Morgan accepted the proposal. The Americans took the paroles of the wounded, and the British loaded them on wagons and removed them to the base hospital at Camden. But so great was American admiration of the jaunty doctor that Morgan released Robert Jackson without his parole!

Whether from miscalculation or bad intelligence Lord Cornwallis marched northwest in pursuit of Morgan. Said Tarleton: "The 19th, the army, with the cavalry on their flank, moved toward King's Creek: The 20th, Lieutenant-Colonel Tarleton was directed to pass Broad river with the dragoons and the yagers, to obtain intelligence of Gen-eral Morgan, and to give protection to the fugitives who might yet have escaped the power of the victorious Americans. He recrossed the river in the evening, having received information that Morgan, soon after the action, had quitted the field of battle, to pass his corps and the prisoners at the high fords on Broad river, leaving the wounded under the protection of a flag of truce."

Acting upon Tarleton's information, on January 21 Cornwallis veered his march to the northeast and crossed Buffalo Creek and Little Broad River. On January 25, two days after Morgan had passed, he reached Ramsour's Mill. Because his wagon train was impeding his advance, his Lordship paused for two days at Ramsour's, burning his baggage and converting his army into a corps of light troops. Then with high hopes he set out again in pursuit of the Americans.

At sunrise on January 25, from his camp at Sherrald's Ford, Morgan sent a note to General Greene: "I am this minute informed by express, that Lord Cornwallis is at Ramsay's Mill, on their march this way, destroying all before them."

At twelve o'clock Morgan sent a second express to Greene. "The enemy encamped last night at Ramsour's Mills, in force; they marched near thirty miles yesterday," he wrote. "I am convinced Cornwallis will push on till he is stopped by a force able to check him. I will do everything in my power; but you may not put much dependence in me, for I can neither ride nor walk; a pain in the hip prevents me."

At two o'clock Morgan sent still a third express riding to Greene: "I receive intelligence every hour of the enemy's rapid approach, in consequence of which I am sending off my wagons. My numbers at this time are too weak to fight them." The Old Wagoner concluded his letter: "I have sent for Gen. Davidson to join me, which I expect he will do tomorrow."

When Brigadier General William Davidson had collected 500 North Carolina militiamen, Morgan posted him at Beatty's Ford on the Catawba. As more men drifted in, he set them felling trees into the public fords. But the action of the British at Ramsour's puzzled Morgan. "Am a little apprehensive that Lord Cornwallis intends to surprise me, lying so still this day or two," he wrote Greene. "If I were able to ride and see to everything myself, I should think myself perfectly safe; but I am obliged to lie in a house out of camp, not being able to encounter the badness of the weather."

In spite of his rheumatism, next day, January 29, Morgan visited Davidson at Beatty's Ford. "The enemy is within ten miles, of this place, in force; their advance is in sight," he wrote Greene after seeing Tarleton's advance guard. "I expect they will attempt to cross in the morning."

But the rains which had kept Morgan indoors nursing his sciatica had also flooded the Catawba. For two days, while the waters receded, the British camped in sight of Beatty's Ford. At one o'clock in the morning of February 1 Lord Cornwallis broke camp. As a feint he sent Webster with the 33rd Regiment toward Beatty's, with orders to begin a cannonade as if he meant to force a passage.

With the main body Cornwallis marched to a private ford at Cowan's, six miles below Beatty's. The campfires on the opposite bank showed the crossing to be heavily guarded. His Lordship called for O'Hara and the Guards. Into the icy, swirling Catawba plunged the light infantry of the Guards under Lieutenant Colonel Hall. They waded in platoons to brace each other against the swift water which reached nearly to their armpits. As they reached the middle of the river, an American sentinel shouted a challenge through the murky half-light. Receiving no answer he fired his musket.

The Tory guide fled. Colonel Hall waded straight across the river, but as he climbed up the bank a sniper killed him. O'Hara then plunged into the Catawba, but his horse rolled over in the rapid current. Leslie followed. His horse was swept downstream. As the grooms struggled to save the drowning horses, Lord Cornwallis plunged in to lead his troops. Davidson's sharpshooters opened on the red-coated commander in chief. They wounded his horse, which stumbled on and crumpled on the shore.

By then the Guards had formed and begun firing. The militia fled. As General Davidson swung into his saddle a Guardsman toppled him. Calling Tarleton and his dragoons, Cornwallis ordered a pursuit of the fugitives. Finding the Americans gone and Webster crossing unmolested at Beatty's, Tarleton sent patrols sweeping the country. They returned with intelligence that the fugitives and the militia from Rowan and Mecklenburg counties were to assemble at two o'clock at Tarrant's Tavern.

"Although the report of the distance and the numbers was contrary to his wishes," Tarleton felt "that the time was advantageous to make an impression upon the militia."

Riding through a chilling downpour, over ten miles of muddy roads, the Green Dragoon reached Tarrant's. "The militia were vigilant, and were prepared for an attack," said he. "In this critical situation Tarleton resolved to hazard one charge, and, if unsuccessful, to order a retreat. When at a proper distance, he desired his soldiers to advance, and remember the Cowpens."

Stung by the taunt the dragoons charged. The militia broke. As they ran, Tarleton sent small detachments to chase them. Said he: "This exertion of the cavalry succeeding the gallant action of the guards in the morning, diffused such a terror among the inhabitants that the King's troops passed through the most hostile part of North Carolina without a shot from the militia."

Marching on through rain and mud, late in the afternoon of February 4 the British reached Salisbury. Learning that Morgan was at Trading Ford on the Yadkin River, only seven miles in front, Lord Cornwallis sent forward O'Hara and the Guards, Bose's regiment of Hessians, and Tarleton's dragoons. Wrote Tarleton: "Owing to rain, darkness, and bad roads, the troops did not arrive at the Yadkin till near midnight."

Morgan's rear guard had crossed in the evening, drawn the boats to them, and camped defiantly beside the flooded river. Impatient to get at the Americans, on February 6 Cornwallis sent Tarleton and his dragoons, supported by the 23rd Regiment, on a scouting sweep up the west bank of the Yadkin. Finding no opposition, Tarleton crossed at the high fords. Next day Cornwallis followed, and on February 9 the British marched into the Moravian settlement around Salem.

In the meantime, on receiving Morgan's letter announcing the victory at Cowpens, General Greene decamped from Hicks Creek. After sending his army northward under Brigadier General Isaac Huger, with orders to join Morgan's corps high up in North Carolina, Greene rode toward Morgan's camp. Escorted by only a squadron of dragoons, on January 31 he reached Beatty's Ford and was not far distant when Tarleton scattered the militia at Tarrant's. Then he rode ahead of Morgan's retreat, ready to assume command if the Old Wagoner's health should completely fail.

On February 5 Morgan reached Guilford Courthouse. On February 6 he wrote Greene: "I am much indisposed with pains, and to add to my misfortunes, I am violently attacked with the piles, so that I scarcely can sit upon my horse."

At Guilford Courthouse on February 9 Huger's troops overtook Morgan's. Greene assumed command. Next day he wrote a simple end to Daniel Morgan's campaign:

> Camp at Guilford C.H. Feb. 10th, 1781.
> Gen. Morgan, of the Virginia line, has leave of absence until he recovers his health, so as to be able to take the field again.
> Nathanael Greene

Greene then headed for Boyd's Ferry on the river Dan, with Cornwallis in pursuit. Along the way Tarleton's advance troops skirmished with the rear guard under Light-Horse Harry Lee.

On the evening of February 12 the Green Dragoon camped ten miles beyond Guilford. From there he wrote Cornwallis:

> Iron Works Feb'y 13, 5 a.m.
> My Lord
> I sent out spies to find the Enemy position—They only retired five miles. My Patrols took a militia man who says Green passed High Rock yesterday—The two corps will meet at the Fork of the Roads twenty miles from here & ten from Duke's Ferry—Every exertion shall be made to obtain Intelligence today.
> I have the Honor
> To be Your Lordship's
> Most devoted Serv't
> Ban. Tarleton

In a desperate effort Cornwallis lashed his troops forward, and they marched forty miles in the next twenty-four hours. But when Tarleton's patrols reached Boyd's Ferry on February 14, they found only "some works evacuated, which had been constructed to cover the retreat of the enemy, who six hours before had finished their passage, and were then encamped on the opposite bank."

After Greene's escape across flooded Dan River, Lord Cornwallis marched slowly back to Hillsboro. Here he issued a proclamation inviting all loyal subjects to repair to the King's standard. The militia between the Haw and Deep rivers began assembling under Colonel John Pile. On February 23 Cornwallis sent Tarleton with 450 troops to protect these Loyalists. That night the Dragoon reported:

Feb'y 23 1781

My Lord
    Hint of your Lordship's billets stops me. George Johnson & John Justin bear this—They wish to come out of Town tonight— Their property is near me—They may be trusted—
    I hear nothing of the Enemy.
I have the Honour
To be your most devoted Serv't
Ban. Tarleton

Although Tarleton had heard nothing of him, on February 21 Colonel Lee and his Legion had recrossed the Dan and were riding to crush the insurrection along the Haw. At O'Neil's plantation, about a mile from Tarleton's camp, Colonel Pile and about 600 militiamen met a squadron of green-clad dragoons whom they saluted with "God save the King."

The Loyalists were marching along a road between two rail fences. Before they realized their mistake, the green dragoons of Light-Horse Harry Lee were among them, their sabers flashing. In cold blood the dragoons killed 90 Tories. They left 150 more slashed and bleeding. The quality of Lee's mercy here was far worse than Tarleton's at the Waxhaws.

As Tarleton roused his troops to punish Lee, a courier dashed in with a letter which sent him hurrying back to Hillsboro:

Hillsborough, Feb. 24th, 1781
three p.m.

Dear Tarleton,
    I have received intelligence from two persons, that Greene passed the Dan on the 22nd and was advancing to Dobbyn's. They mentioned so many particulars, that I cannot help giving some credit: I therefore wish you to join me as soon as possible.
Yours sincerely,
Cornwallis

After the massacre of Pile's militia neither the Tories nor the Whigs would rise to support their friends. Both Cornwallis and Greene rested the outcome of the campaign upon the operations of their respective armies.

Lord Cornwallis withdrew from Hillsboro and on February 27 encamped near Allemance. General Greene immediately encamped between Troublesome Creek and Reedy Fork. On March 2 Tarleton sent Captain Hovenden and his Philadelphia Light Dragoons to forage about three miles from camp. Near one of the plantations Hovenden saw American dragoons, supported by infantry, and galloped to report the presence of the enemy.

Advising Lord Cornwallis of the approach of Greene's troops, Tarleton led out the whole advance guard. As the British neared the plantation, the Americans began firing from thickets on both sides of the road. But an advance by Captain Francis Dundas and the Guards, supported by Webster's infantry, routed them out; and a charge by the Legion cavalry then put them to flight.

After a week of marching and countermarching in an effort to break away to Wilmington, Lord Cornwallis decided to fight. At daybreak on the morning of March 14 he started his advance toward Greene's army at Guilford Courthouse. As usual he sent forward Tarleton and his dragoons. After proceeding seven miles along the highway from Salisbury, they struck the pickets of Colonel Lee. There was sharp conflict between the advanced parties of the two armies.

Tarleton's forces drove back the Americans, but every sign, including acknowledgment by the prisoners, indicated the immediate approach of Greene's army. Said Tarleton: "The King's troops moved on till they arrived in sight of the American army. An engagement was now become inevitable, and both sides prepared for it with tranquility and order."

In the skirmish Banastre was wounded in the right hand by a rifle ball, but he continued to ride and lead his troops. That afternoon Colonel Lee sent a flag, requesting information on the condition of certain prisoners from Lee's Legion. 'Tarleton very politely answered by an amanuensis, that he would, with pleasure, execute the request; and apologized for not writing himself; saying that he had received a ball in his right hand in our morning rencounter," Lee wrote in his *Memoirs*.

As the armies prepared for battle, Lord Cornwallis formed his right wing of the corps under General Leslie; his center from the brigade commanded by Colonel Webster; his small left wing from the light infantry of the Guards and the Hessian yagers. The reserve consisted of the grenadier company of Guards under Brigadier General O'Hara.

"Lieutenant-colonel Tarleton was ordered to keep his regiment in reserve till the infantry could penetrate through the woods to the open ground, near the court house," said Tarleton in the *Campaigns*.

The British opened the battle by cannonading the center of the American line. Cornwallis then ordered the entire British line to advance. "The order and coolness of that part of Webster's brigade which advanced across the open ground, exposed to the enemy's fire, cannot be sufficiently extolled," said Tarleton. The American militia could not stand the shock of the British bayonet. But the Continentals held, and the battle raged for two hours. The outcome remained in doubt until Webster maneuvered around and drove back the right wing of the Americans.

Along the road Tarleton's cavalry kept pace. Said Tarleton: "Earl Cornwallis did not think it advisable for the British cavalry to charge the enemy, who were retreating in good order, but directed Lieutenant colonel Tarleton to proceed with a squadron of dragoons to the assistance of Major-general Leslie."

As they moved to the right, the dragoons saw some prisoners being led off. "The prisoners were quickly rescued from the hands of their captors, and the dragoons reached General Leslie without delay," said Tarleton. "As soon as the cavalry arrived, the Guards and the Hessians were directed to fire a volley upon the largest party of the militia, and, under the cover of the smoke, Lieutenant-colonel Tarleton doubled round the right flank of the guards, and charged the Americans with considerable effect."

In this action the Green Dragoon received another wound.

When Banastre Tarleton led his dragoons into battle, his right hand in a sling and his bridle reins held in his left, a boy could have knocked him from his charger with a quarter staff. Without protection of any kind he faced death at the head of his Legion. He was magnificent. His action was sheer courage. In his Order of the Day, Lord Cornwallis gave his warmest praise "to Lieutenant Colonel Tarleton for the spirit and ability shown by him in the conduct of the Cavalry, which so greatly contributed to the final success of the glorious day."

In his report to Lord Germain, Earl Cornwallis wrote of the dragoon: "Lieutenant-colonel Tarleton's good conduct and spirit in the management of his cavalry was unexceptionable."

After the battle Dr. Stewart amputated a part of Banastre's right hand, including the fore and middle fingers.

The British remained encamped around Guilford for four days. Then on March 18 Lord Cornwallis started on the long march to Wilmington. In his Lordship's retreat from his Pyrrhic victory, Tarleton commanded the rear guard. As the British army was crossing Deep River, Tarleton rode up with information that Greene and the American army were in hot pursuit. Then he destroyed the bridge. Greene halted, and Cornwallis continued undisturbed to Cross Creek.

As he rode through the swamp and sandy pine barren of eastern Carolina, the Green Dragoon was despondent. His swollen hand lay useless in a sling. He had shown his courage. He had vindicated his honor. Now was the time to retire.

Ban went to Cornwallis and declared his intentions. But his Lordship was firm. Ban Tarleton with one hand was better than most of his other officers with two.

So the Green Dragoon set about reordering his life. He practiced writing with his left hand. He exercised with his saber in his left hand. By the time he reached Wilmington he had become cheerful again.

Knowing that the London newspapers would announce his wound and frighten his family, on the day that his advance guard rode into Wilmington, Banastre wrote a note to his brother John:

> North Carolina Apr ye 6 1781
>
> My Dear Brother
> You will excuse my writing long Letters—The public print will tell you how I was wounded—This I think will declare that I was shot in ye right hand; half of which has been amputated—the wound will soon heal.
> I thought of coming home; upon reflection I find it impracticable at present, as there will be nobody to command the light Troops, of Lord Cornwallis' army—Lord Cornwallis interests himself warmly about my promotion. He insists upon it. I shall write to Collyer. I wish the Legion may be established & he agent. Adieu.
>
> Ban. Tarleton

As soon as John received Ban's letter, he appointed Nathaniel Collyer, Esquire, his brother's agent, to confer with Lord Germain about placing the British Legion on the American Establishment. Lord Rawdon's Volunteers of Ireland and Simcoe's Queen's American Rangers had been placed upon an American Establishment with the same privileges as the regular regiments on the British Establishment. Both Cornwallis and Clinton had urged that the same reward be given the men and officers of the British Legion.

To Collyer, John wrote: "I shall be glad if you will immediately inquire from Gov. Martin or Capt. Broderick which part of the hand has been amputated, whether the two first fingers, or the two last, be particular and inform me as soon as possible—Also give me your opinion and Sentiments with respect to its effects—will it prevent him from being active in his Profession? Considered as a Commander of Cavalry."

John's solicitude was unnecessary. Collyer found that on March 7 after reviewing the record of the British Legion, without knowledge of their flight at Cowpens, Lord Germain had concluded a letter to Sir Henry Clinton: "Upon these considerations, and as a mark of His

Majesty's Royal Approbation of the Gallant Behavior of this Corps, and of the Services of that very deserving Officer, Lieutenant Colonel Tarleton, who commands it, the King has been graciously pleased to approve of Your Recommendation of the British Legion for permanent Rank in America, and the officers will be recommended to Parliament for Half Pay whenever the Corps shall be reduced."

Lord Cornwallis was doing all in his power to reward the wounded dragoon. On April 18 his Lordship wrote Lord Amherst a letter such as a Secretary for War seldom receives from a field commander. He said: "Lieut. Colonel Tarleton's Services have been throughout eminent and distinguished: It is true, he was once unfortunate, but by no fault of his. He never showed more ability than in the maneuvers which compelled Morgan to fight him, and his disposition was unexceptionable. The fate of that unfortunate day was one of the events to which War has been ever liable. It will give me the most sensible mortification if his Majesty should still think him unworthy of the Rank of Lieutenant Colonel."

What did King George think? The *Morning Herald* of May 15 said:

We have it from the first authority that a *certain great person-age* did particularly require of Lord Cornwallis, that he would send him the military character of Colonel Tarleton, as it might appear to his Lordship in the course of service; and that in consequence, his Lordship has transmitted an *eulogium* to his M——y, which contains the following words:

"He is indefatigably laborious and active, cool and intrepid in action, discerns as by intuition, seizes with rapidity, and improves with skill the short, but favorable and decisive moments of victory."

On June 15, 1781, his Majesty promoted Banastre Tarleton to be the lieutenant colonel of the 79th Regiment of the British Army.

As he rested at Wilmington in the warm spring weather, and his right hand slowly healed, Banastre wrote a teasing letter to his sister Bridget, recently betrothed to Edward Falkner.

N'Carolina Apr Ye 15 '81

My Dear Sister

I long to see you—but I am afraid I shall be kept here till I am reduced to the situation of Col. Tamper—I write now so ill that I shan't be able to write a legible love letter, I must court personally (for I am a handsome fellow yet) or be obliged to my friends for a Wife—Pray Madam write me long Letters—young Misses have nothing else to do—Liverpool must be so changed that I should lose my way between Hanover Street and the Play House— Pray have you any handsome Faces of great Fortunes now in Town let me know express; I may come Home & marry such a one—

None but the brave deserve the Fair—I shall try when I have lost an Arm, an Eye, & a Leg—But my dear Bridget (a horrid name) my Lady must have a swinging Fortune for I have still a taste for every pleasure—& my imagination is a good deal heightened by all my fighting and Quixotism—Still gay as usual—you read, smile and tell Mama—I never mean to be grave till I can't help myself which I do now to everything most plentifully—Tell me honestly Sister are you going to be Marryd, a Soldier you know is a man of Honour therefore I may be confided in—Pray how is Parson Clayton, how is our good Mother; How is the large family of our Bro. Tarleton; Tho last, not least, how is John—Is he to be a Bachelor or a Benedict—The paper is at an End, so I must end with what I shall be to the End of my life.

Your Affect. Bro.

Ban. Tarleton.

17

The Long Retreat

As HIS ARMY rested at Wilmington, Lord Cornwallis began debating whether to advance into Virginia or retreat into South Carolina. In December Sir Henry Clinton, to cooperate with his Lordship's northward march, had sent Brigadier General Benedict Arnold and a large detachment of both regular and Provincial troops to Virginia. Among them were Lieutenant Colonel Thomas Dundas and Lieutenant Colonel Simcoe and his Queen's Rangers. Hoping to capture Benedict Arnold—and have a quick hanging—Washington had dispatched the Marquis de Lafayette and 1200 Continentals into Virginia. As a check to Lafayette, Clinton sent 2600 additional troops under Major General William Phillips. On March 26 Phillips arrived at Portsmouth.

Lord Cornwallis could obtain no reliable information about Phillips. Nor could he hear from Lord Rawdon. After halting briefly at Deep River, Greene had turned and begun a rapid march southward. Since then the Americans had captured every dispatch sent northward from Camden.

As he hesitated, Cornwallis called a conference of his principal officers. To his Lordship's question Tarleton replied that either march was feasible. He volunteered, if his Lordship embarked the infantry, to cut his way down the Waccamaw with his dragoons, cross Winyah Bay at Georgetown, and meet him in Charleston.

Suddenly Cornwallis decided. Ordering his officers to prepare the army for a long march, he sent Tarleton and the Legion to collect boats on the northeast bank of Cape Fear River. On April 25 the Royal Navy ferried the army across Cape Fear, and with Tarleton leading the van, Lord Cornwallis began his long retreat to Yorktown.

For ten days the British marched through barren country without incident or hindrance. But the strain began showing in the actions and

174

letters of the commander. He ordered that there be no looting, pillaging, or disturbing of the inhabitants, with the penalty of death for violation.

With his dragoons a day's march ahead of the main army, Tarleton was again swift, vigilant, and bold. He confided to Lieutenant Colonel Hamilton that the march to Virginia was his idea. As usual he began misdating his letters.

Lord Cornwallis became angry and wrote him a sharp letter:

> Nahunta Creek, May 5, 1781
>
> Dear Tarleton,
>
> You must be sensible that, in the present instance, I put the greatest confidence in you. I trust to your discretion my honour and future happiness. I am convinced you will be on your guard against the sanguine opinions of friends and your own prejudices. Above all things, attend to dates, and distinguish between is and has been. You will read my letter. Send as many messages or notes as you can; but all conveyed in the same *cautious language. I confide in the correctness of your report as to the practicability of passing, and the certainty of a speedy communication with Phillips: If it won't do, take care not to stay too long.*
>
> Yours sincerely,
> Cornwallis
>
> *My letters to Phillips are in the new cypher; he has not the old one.*

Tarleton took the reproof without sulking. By now he had crossed the Tar River into a fruitful region. He ordered the inhabitants to provide great stores of food for his troops and for the approaching army. He then asked permission to ride thirty miles farther ahead and seize Halifax, thus opening a passage across Roanoke River into Virginia.

From his camp at Nahunta Creek, Lord Cornwallis replied: "*If it appears from your information that General Phillips is certainly within reach of joining, you may go on to Halifax to secure a passage, reporting to me the state of things, to direct the movements of the infantry; forward the enclosed by different hands.*"

As Tarleton and his 300 troops pushed forward, the American militia began assembling. At Swift Creek and later at Fishing Creek they attempted to stop his advance. With a whoop his dragoons charged them, killing without mercy. After the defenders had fled, the Green Horse trotted into Halifax.

In his report Tarleton requested that Cornwallis send him the light company of the Guards "on horseback to assist him in the defense of his present post, till he could procure authentic information from James River, as it was rather hazardous for a corps of light dragoons, without carbines, and sixty infantry, to remain on the same ground many days and nights, nearly fifty miles from the army, in a populous and hostile country."

The British army lumbered on and finally came to rest at the Tar. Still without word from Phillips, Cornwallis wrote him another letter and sent it to Tarleton to forward by one of his spies.

> Camp at Crowell's plantation, near
> Tarr river, 8th May, 1781
>
> Dear Tarleton,
>
> *I cannot venture to pass the Roanoke without some certain information of Phillips, or of the state of things in Virginia. You will read and forward the enclosed letter: Not having been able to mount the light company of guards, I think they would only embarrass you. You may stay two or three days at Halifax, if you think it safe: If in that time you hear any certain or favorable news of Phillips, let me know it, and I will move forward immediately: if not, return by whatever route you please, and join me near Cobb's or Vivaret's Mill, fixing every possible channel of intelligence at any price.*
>
> I understand that General Butler is at Wake Courthouse with a few militia. Our accounts of Lord Rawdon's success continue to be confirmed.
>
> Faithfully yours,
> Cornwallis
>
> *I look forward, if possible.*

That morning emissaries from Phillips finally reached Tarleton. From his advanced position he sent an express galloping toward the Tar. After learning that Phillips and Arnold were still south of the James River, his Lordship relaxed. In the evening he wrote a polite note:

> Crowell's plantation, May 8, 1781
> eight P.M.
>
> Dear Tarleton,
>
> I have just received yours of this date with more satisfaction than that of yesterday. The light company of the Guards *shall proceed immediately; I will follow as fast as possible: you will of course secure the opposite bank when Sutherland arrives.*
>
> I am, very sincerely, yours
> Cornwallis

As soon as Lord Cornwallis reached Halifax, he ordered Tarleton and his dragoons, with two companies of mounted infantry, to cross the Roanoke, ride northward, and inspect the fords and bridges over the next two rivers. At Armstead's Bridge on May 14 the cavalry crossed the Meherrin. Next day, as they approached the Nottoway, Tarleton learned that Simcoe and the hussars of the Queen's Rangers had passed that river and were riding southward to meet Cornwallis.

Turning back over another route, Tarleton overtook Simcoe at Hicks Ford over the Meherrin. As he came galloping up, with his troops dressed in white, the Queen's Rangers were surprised and prepared for a fight. But Simcoe recognized the Green Dragoon, and there was a joyful reunion. That night the horsemen bivouacked on the Hicks plantation.

Tarleton reported his position. Before day he received a note from Lord Cornwallis: "I am making all possible expedition, and hope to be at Nottoway on Friday evening. I would have you proceed tomorrow to Nottoway, and remain near Simcoe's infantry."

Tarleton and Simcoe had removed all impediments between the two armies. On May 20, 1781, after a hazardous march of 225 miles in twenty-five days, Lord Cornwallis rode into Petersburg and took command of all the King's troops in Virginia.

ↄ⅁

Before entering upon a campaign, Lord Cornwallis sent out spies and patrols to learn the strength and the situation of the American troops. Hearing of a concentration of about 400 militiamen at Warwick Courthouse, he sent Tarleton and his dragoons to investigate. They galloped through a heavy rain, surprised, and dispersed the Virginians.

Cornwallis had determined to cross the James River and move against Richmond. He marched the army to Mead's across the James from Westover and began swimming his horses. That evening he sent a note to Tarleton:

Bird's plantation, May 25, 1781

Dear Tarleton,

The swimming has succeeded very well, not withstanding the high winds; the waggons are the most tedious part of the business. I trust, however, that everything will be ready for your passing early tomorrow morning; in the meantime, you will patrol towards the Appomattox, and do everything you can to procure intelligence. You may venture to swim all your horses, except the very best. I have ordered the 43rd regiment to land at Brandon's tomorrow morning, and march to Mead's to join the army: Should you hear anything material, you will communicate it to Major Ferguson.

Yours, very sincerely
Cornwallis

As soon as the British crossed the James, Lafayette abandoned Richmond. On May 24 he wrote to Washington: "Were I to fight a battle,

I should be cut to pieces, the militia dispersed and the arms lost. Were I to decline fighting, the country would think itself given up. I am therefore determined to skirmish."

Cornwallis followed Lafayette to Hanover and on June 1 sent Tarleton to scout the Americans. But Lafayette had retreated to Dandridge's on the South Anna River to await the arrival of Continentals under Baron von Steuben and Mad Anthony Wayne. The Legion found his camp, drove in his pickets, and caused a general call to arms.

During the excitement a patrol of dragoons struck the rear of the American camp, captured an express and his dispatches, and brought him to Tarleton. Among his papers was a letter from Lafayette to Thomas Jefferson, governor of Virginia. Learning from this that Jefferson and the General Assembly of Virginia were meeting at Charlottesville, Cornwallis suggested that Tarleton and his dragoons attempt to capture the author of the Declaration of Independence.

With his hand decently healed and his spirits buoyed by the friendship of Simcoe, the Green Dragoon was eager to go governor-hunting. But suddenly there was an echo from Cowpens: Cornwallis had ordered Captain Hutchinson to mount the 2nd battalion of the 71st Regiment and ride with Tarleton; but Hutchinson and his officers signed a *remonstrance* against joining the Dragoon who had left McArthur and the 1st battalion on that bloody slope. Instead, they asked to join Simcoe who had orders to harass Von Steuben.

Mounting 70 infantrymen of the 23rd Regiment under Captain Champaigne and choosing 180 dragoons from the Legion and the 17th Light Dragoons, before daybreak on June 3 Tarleton galloped away on the high road between the North Anna and the South Anna rivers. The weather was hot, and he paused to rest his men and horses in the middle of the day. In the afternoon they pressed forward. At eleven o'clock they went into bivouac near Louisa Courthouse.

On that hot Sunday afternoon Captain John Jouett, of the Virginia militia, sat in the Cuckoo Tavern in eastern Louisa County. As the horsemen galloped past the Cuckoo, Captain Jouett recognized the uniforms of the British dragoons. He guessed Tarleton's destination and prepared to thwart his mission. After nightfall he set out on the fleetest nag in seven counties, and while the British slept he passed them on a back road and raced toward Charlottesville.

At two o'clock Tarleton was in the saddle. Before dawn he overtook and burned twelve wagons loaded with arms and clothing for the troops under General Greene. A half-dozen miles from Charlottesville the raiders divided. Tarleton rode to Castle Hill, the home of Dr. Thomas Walker, and demanded breakfast. The others rode on to Belvoir, the home of Mr. John Walker. Both parties routed from their beds some of the leading patriots of Virginia.

At Belvoir, Francis Kinlock, son-in-law of Mr. Walker and member of Congress from South Carolina, sprang out of bed and fled in his nightshirt. As he was streaking through the orchard, he heard a shout, "Wait, cousin Francis, I could always beat you in a race!"

The Congressman recognized his kinsman, Captain David Kinlock. He surrendered. Francis had been educated in England, and before David left for America the women of his family begged him not to kill Francis. "No," he said, "but I will be sure to take him prisoner!"

After stopping half an hour to refresh his horses Tarleton approached the Rivanna River, at the foot of the hill on which Charlottesville was built. "The advanced dragoons reported that the ford was guarded; an attack was nevertheless ordered; the cavalry charged through the water with very little loss, and routed the detachment posted at that place," said Tarleton in the *Campaigns*. "As soon as one hundred cavalry had passed the water, Lieutenant Colonel Tarleton directed them to charge into the town, to continue the confusion of the Americans, and to apprehend, if possible, the governor and the Assembly."

Tarleton hurried Captain McLeod and his dragoons off to apprehend Thomas Jefferson. But while Tarleton had breakfasted at Castle Hill, Captain Jouett had reached Monticello. Jefferson escaped less than ten minutes before the arrival of Tarleton's Green Horse.

In spite of Jouett's warning, the British captured seven members of the Assembly. Brigadier-General Scott and several officers and men were killed, wounded, or taken. After destroying large quantities of military stores, Tarleton headed back to the main army.

ο‍ω

After the dragoons had rested from their dash to Charlottesville, Cornwallis decided to return to Richmond. As the army marched, Tarleton commanded the rear guard. Marquis de Lafayette followed with the American army, powerfully reinforced by General Wayne's troops of the Pennsylvania line, Von Steuben's Corps, and some detachments of Virginia militia.

How closely he crowded Tarleton was reflected in the Dragoon's report to Cornwallis:

> Colonel Adam's plantation
> June 13, 1781, half past four P.M.

My Lord,

I believe that La Fayette passed the South Anna, or Pamunkey, this morning, for the mountain road, at Bird's ordinary. He lay at Bird's Mill yesterday evening. I have been on the three notched road all day; I have left it for this place for the benefit of forage and communication with your lordship; I shall strike it again tomorrow morning, and go by Napier's to Pier's Mill. I cannot yet learn what water it stands on. La Fayette's design is to follow. I will immediately inform your lordship if he does not keep a proper distance; any detachment I shall strike at.

I have the honour to be, etc.

Ban. Tarleton

When the Royal army reached Richmond, they encamped, with Simcoe posted at Westham and Tarleton at Meadow Bridge. During this pause Lafayette's light troops skirmished with Tarleton's patrols.

On June 20 Lord Cornwallis evacuated Richmond. As he moved toward Williamsburg, both Simcoe and Tarleton guarded the rear of the army, but Lafayette continued to hang upon their trail. When the British marched from New Kent Courthouse, the main army of the Americans was within twelve miles. Unruffled, Cornwallis retreated and on June 25 reached Williamsburg.

As the Royal army lay around the capital of Virginia, constantly harassed by the light troops under Lafayette, Lord Cornwallis received a curious letter from Sir Henry Clinton. After a recapitulation of the number of troops he had sent south, Sir Henry ordered Cornwallis to return certain regiments to New York. He concluded: "I beg leave to recommend to you, as soon as you have finished the active operations you may now be engaged in, to take a defensive station, in any healthy situation you chuse, (be it at Williamsburg or Yorktown)."

Judging Sir Henry's call for troops to be positive, Lord Cornwallis marched toward Portsmouth for their embarkation. On July 4 the Royal army reached James Island. Simcoe crossed the James River with the Queen's Rangers and possessed Cobham. Tarleton swung back eighteen miles from Williamsburg and dislodged some American riflemen from a church. Then with bravado, under a screen of heavy rain, he rode on to the camp of Lafayette at Tyre's plantation, insulted his pickets, and spread a general alarm.

Returning to his station near James Island, Banastre waited all next day. On the morning of July 6 his foragers returned with the news that Lafayette was charging down the road, spoiling for a fight. Giving money to a British dragoon and a Negro to pretend that they were deserters, Tarleton sent them back with the false information that the British army had crossed and that only the British Legion and mounted infantry of the rear guard remained on the north bank of the James.

Late that afternoon Lafayette approached the ferry, and the American riflemen began driving in the British outposts. Lord Cornwallis ordered Tarleton's cavalry to support the pickets. Just before sunset Lafayette passed the swamp, over which were several narrow causeways, and advanced with 1500 soldiers.

Upon the first cannon shot from the enemy the concealed British army formed and charged. The clash was bitter. After dark the Ameri-

cans abandoned their cannon and retreated across the swamp. Then
Lafayette rallied his troops and marched away to Green Springs. Next
morning Tarleton scouted his position. In spite of Ban's pleas for his
Lordship to turn back and finish the Marquis, Cornwallis left Lafayette
licking his wounds and moved his army across the James.

Then, to keep his dragoons employed, Cornwallis tossed the rein to
Tarleton and sent him raiding. In his orders his Lordship told him to
ride to Prince Edward Courthouse and from thence to New London in
Bedford County, "making the strictest inquiry in every part of the
country through which you pass, for ammunition, clothing, or stores of
any kind." He also wrote: "All public stores of corn and provisions are
to be burnt."

Loading their equipment and a puncheon of rum on three light
wagons, the Green Horse left Cobham on July 9. The July sun was
scorching, and they moved in early morning and late afternoon. Soon
they reached Petersburg, then Prince Edward, and swept on to Bedford. As they marched, Tarleton Shermanized south-central Virginia.

The dragoons encamped for two days in Bedford County. For cavalrymen the grassy region at the foot of the Blue Ridge Mountains was a
bonanza. They made off with some of the best-blooded horses in
America.

In the meantime, hearing the cries of the pillaged and seeing the
impotence of the militia, Lafayette sent Wayne and his Pennsylvanians
into Amelia County. And to cut off Tarleton's return, he posted a
strong detachment under Dan Morgan, healed and returned to duty, at
Goode's Bridge, near Petersburg.

Acting on information from Cornwallis, Tarleton burned his wagons
and wheeled into southern Virginia. As he rode, his Green Horse
ravaged. In Lunenburg County he burned the Reverend James Craig's
mill at Flat Rock Creek and then compelled the good old parson to take
off his black coat and assist in slaughtering his pigs for roasting.

"Let me inform you," David Garland wrote Governor Thomas Nelson on July 23, "Col. Tarleton and his legion came through this county
last week, and considering his rapid march (thirty or forty miles a day)
has done considerable damage in destroying the public grain etc., as
also wounding three persons & carrying off some others as prisoners. He
threatened to return immediately after the 16th of next month, when
he assures us that he will carry the sword & fire through the land, not
sparing any persons but such as hath or may take parole before that
time."

Even General Washington heard of the raid. He wrote in his *Diary*:
"A letter from Marqs. de la Fayette (commanding in Virginia) informs
me that after Lord Cornwallis had crossed James River he detached
Tarleton with a body of horse into Amelia County with a view, as was

supposed, to destroy some stores which had been deposited there, but which had been previously removed."

Moving at thirty or forty miles a day and outrunning any news of their approach, the Green Horse passed unmolested near the American army. After crossing the rivers Nottoway and Blackwater on July 24, they rejoined Cornwallis at Suffolk. But an expedition of 400 miles in fifteen days, during a sweltering July, left the Dragoon from the cool Mersey exhausted. In the *Campaigns* he wrote bitterly: "The stores destroyed, either of a public or private nature, were not in quantity or value equivalent to the damage sustained in the skirmishes on the route, and the loss of men and horses by the excessive heat of the climate."

As soon as Tarleton had returned to camp, Lord Cornwallis ordered the Royal army to march to Portsmouth. He had already dispatched the troops destined for Sir Henry Clinton. They had gone aboard ship, but before they could sail an express arrived from Sir Henry, countermanding the embarkation. His letter ordered Cornwallis not to cross the James River, or if he had crossed, to return to Williamsburg Neck, in order to secure Old Point Comfort and Hampton Roads.

But General Leslie, chief engineer Lieutenant Sutherland, and the captains of the Royal navy examined Old Point Comfort and disapproved it as a station for the navy. Therefore, Lord Cornwallis embarked several regiments and sailed up York River to secure Gloucester and Yorktown.

During this confusion Tarleton passed the British Legion over the ferry to Norfolk and marched into Princess Anne County. On August 14 Lord Cornwallis ordered the dragoons to follow him to Yorktown. He wrote: "We had a passage of four days, but made good our landing without opposition on either side. I have no positive accounts of the enemy. Fayette is said to be marching toward the Pamunkey, and I am not quite easy about our post at Gloucester. Wayne had certainly advanced to Goode's bridge; but I suppose he will be recalled."

While Lord Cornwallis superintended the building of fortifications around Yorktown and Lieutenant Colonel Tarleton frightened the militia, Sir Henry Clinton began assembling reinforcements in New York. He anticipated no danger, for the Royal Navy controlled the coastal waters between the commands.

Suddenly on August 30 Count de Grasse, with a French fleet of twenty-eight ships of the line, sailed into the Chesapeake. He anchored the principal part of his flotilla in Lynnhaven Bay, from which he had decoyed the British fleet under Admiral Graves. He then dispatched three ships of the line and several frigates to seal off the mouth of the York River. He disembarked some French troops under Count de St. Simon, and they marched to join the Americans under Lafayette.

Lord Cornwallis decided to give battle. "Lieutenant-colonel Tarleton was desired to reconnoitre the position of Lafayette and St. Simon, and to use every expedient to obtain exact intelligence of their numbers," wrote Tarleton. "After spies were sent out, the British dragoons and two companies of mounted infantry advanced toward the enemy. A picket of Militia, at the mill dam on the Hampton road, was dislodged, and the cavalry were led on to the left of the main route, in order to force another detachment, who commanded the shore of the James river, by being posted on the cliffs which overlooked it. This being accomplished, and a disposition being made to secure a retreat, Lieutenant-colonel Tarleton selected three officers and six men, well mounted, to proceed with him, at half speed, to the right of the encampment at Williamsburgh, whence, after discovering the situation of the enemy, who had taken ground near the college, he returned unmolested to Yorktown."

Lord Cornwallis decided to march his army by night and strike at daybreak. To his misfortune, an express arrived from Sir Henry Clinton bringing a letter, dated at New York on September 2, which said: "By intelligence which I have this day received, it would seem that Mr. Washington is moving an army to the southward, with an appearance of haste, and gives out that he expects the cooperation of a considerable French armament: Your lordship, however, may be assured, that if this should be the case, I shall either endeavor to reinforce the army under your command by all means within the compass of my power, or make every possible diversion in your favor."

While Lord Cornwallis waited for reinforcement or diversion under Sir Henry, Tarleton and the British Legion gathered discouraging information. "The pickets of the militia at the mill dam, on the Hampton road to Williamsburgh, were often insulted and drove in by the British dragoons, that Lieutenant-colonel Tarleton might confer with a spy, who resided beyond them," said Tarleton. "By this means, and by sending boats in the night up York river, constant intelligence was obtained. On the 26th Earl Cornwallis was informed that a large body of troops had arrived in James river from the head of Elk and Baltimore, and that the forces of France and America were assembling at Williamsburgh."

As the Americans assembled, the British lay snug in their fortifications at Yorktown. Tarleton and the British Legion lay in front of the left wing. On September 28 a picket in front of the right wing gave notice that the enemy were approaching. By noon the French chasseurs and grenadiers appeared and formed across the main Williamsburg road. By four o'clock they were extending toward the left flank of the Legion. Sounding the call to mount, Tarleton formed the Green Horse. All afternoon he sat and watched, but the Americans and French contented themselves with cannonading the fortifications.

Next morning the combined French and American forces pushed nearer. Both armies continued their cautious sparring. In the evening an express boat arrived with a letter from Sir Henry Clinton, advising Lord Cornwallis that he would sail with large reinforcements on October 5. Said Tarleton: "To this letter is attributed the order for the British troops to quit the outward, and to retire to the inner position, which was accomplished before daybreak."

On October 1 advanced detachments of the Allies reconnoitered the British lines. As these moved into position, Lord Cornwallis decided to transfer his cavalry from the besieged town. During the evening of October 2 Tarleton and his Green Horse passed over the York River.

At daybreak on October 3, 1781, Lieutenant Colonel Dundas, who commanded at Gloucester, led out detachments from all the regiments in the garrison to forage the country in his front. About three miles from town the wagons and bat-horses were loaded with Indian corn, and at ten o'clock the troops covering the foragers began to return. As they moved through the woods, with a rail fence on either side of the road, Lieutenant Cameron dashed up with information that the enemy was advancing in force. Out of a column of dust rode the hussars of the Duke of Lauzun.

Tarleton turned back in defiance. His black stallion screamed and reared. Tarleton fired his pistol at the charging Duke. At that moment a French uhlan drove his lance through the horse of a British dragoon. The stricken beast careened against the stallion, overthrowing both him and his rider. The fighting days of Banastre Tarleton were over.

18

A Prince's Ransom

$\mathcal{T}$HE SCANDALOUS ROMANCE of Florizel and Perdita lasted exactly a year. The Prince first saw Mary on December 3, 1779, and their final break occurred about December 15, 1780. Mary's heart was not broken, but she was desperate. In the eyes of the law she had deserted Thomas Robinson. She had ruined a brilliant stage career. She was £7000 in debt and facing captivity for the rest of her life. But she returned his jewels to the Prince. She kept only the bond for £20,000 signed by the heir to the English throne and stamped with the royal arms, and scores of the most passionate letters an unwitting man ever left with a scorned, humiliated, and vengeful woman.

"A certain illustrious young personage is said to have promised that Mrs. R——'s establishment should immediately succeed his own; which, however, remaining still unsettled, though the former arrangement is made, has occasioned some severe reproaches on the part of the now suspicious Perdita," reported the Morning Herald on January 4, 1781.

Editor Bate loved scandal. A preacher's son, he had been reared in a pious family and educated at Queen's College, Cambridge. As a young curate to the Reverend James Townley, author of the titillating farce entitled High Life below Stairs, he had become interested in writing. After accepting a living at North Fambridge he became one of the first editors of the Morning Post. The sharpness of his pen and the excitability of his temperament so frequently embroiled him in fisticuffs and duels that he became notorious as the "Fighting Parson."

After the reverend scandalmonger had been sentenced to a year in jail for libeling the Duke of Richmond, he was dismissed from the Morning Post. He retaliated by founding the Morning Herald. From the King's Bench Prison he made his newspaper a paragon of yellow journalism.

Bate had an affinity for the theater. In 1775 he published *The Rival Candidates*. In the following February Sheridan produced Bate's *Blackamoor Washed White*, a comic opera which was withdrawn when disapproving patrons of Drury Lane broke into riot. In 1779 his *The Flitch of Bacon*, set to music by William Shield, was staged with considerable success in the Opera House at the Haymarket.

In 1780 Henry Bate married Mary White, sister of Mrs. Elizabeth Hartley, the celebrated Shakespearean actress of Covent Garden. Mary assisted her husband in his writing. In the early days of his newspaper, she was the one who knew the actresses, the reigning sultanas, and the Fair Cyprians of the West End, and who filed the gossip for Henry's column in the *Morning Herald*. And perhaps it was she who wrote the announcement of the end of *L'affaire Perdita* in the *Morning Herald* of January 5, 1781: "A certain *amour royal* is now totally at an end; a separation has taken place a *thora* for more than three weeks, and a settlement worthy of such a *sultana* is the only thing now wanting to break off all intercourse whatever. Mrs. R——n, thinking the adjustment of this part of the *divorce* too essential to be trifled with, has roundly written to her once *ardent lover* 'that if her settlement is not duly arranged within the space of fourteen days from the commencement of the new year, his —— must not be surprised, if he sees a full publication of all those *seductory epistles* which estranged her from *virtue* and the *marriage vow*.' "

As Mary Robinson surmised at Windsor, the inconstant Florizel had transferred his affections to Mrs. Armstead. For the next six months this amour furnished the newspapers with piquant gossip. On January 18 the *Morning Herald* reported: "Mrs. Arms——d has taken care to have it pretty repeatedly intimated to the celebrated Perdita, that 'a certain young personage's absence from her is owing to the *superior influence of certain charms* in another quarter, at the altar of which he still continues to sacrifice.' "

In its "Masquerade Intelligence" for February 3 the *Morning Herald* informed its readers of the latest skirmish: "The fair *Perdita* seemed to be upon a reconnoitering party royal; but the cruel Damon did not so much as cast one longing look behind."

On February 8 the *Morning Herald* reported: "Mrs. Arm——d has certainly been gratified at last in an amour with a certain young personage; and now flatters herself that her charms will not be so soon unrivetted, as were those of the once exalted, and enviable Perdita."

On Saturday evening, February 17, the Prince went to the Opera to hear *Mitridate*. According to the *Morning Herald* of February 19 all of the devotees of the Cyprian Goddess were present. "Mrs. R——n sat in a box almost over the P——'s; Emily took her station almost opposite—from which side Mrs. A——d also directed her *artillery*. His Highness, in surveying them round, met in an upward glance the eyes of Mrs. R.

They scarce exchanged a look, when his attention was rivetted by Mrs. A——d, who during the momentary victory over her competitor, drew a glove from a beautiful hand, and seemed to hold it as a gauntlet to her R—l admirer." And then: "The pensive Perdita every now and then sent down an unavailing sigh, which unfortunately for her, was dispelled by the Goddess of Inconstancy before it reached the ear of the royal enamorata."

A month later the *Morning Herald*'s reverend editor felt the issue was decided: "Notwithstanding all the interested assertions to the contràry, Mrs. Armst—d is inidisputably the reigning *Sultana* of a certain royal paramour."

But on April 10 the cud of scandal was worth further chewing: "The Armstead and the Perdita are grown such implacable rivals, that the most serious consequences are to be apprehended from a personal meeting, which the partisans of either are anxious to avoid."

Other scandalmongers entered the new fracas. Hidden in the *Morning Post* of April 11, was a fetching advertisement:

> *The Budget of Love*
> or
> *Letters Between Florizel and Perdita*
> To which are prefixed some anecdotes of the Fair Heroine
> Should I now see my father
> He would not call me son.
> *Winter's Tale*, Act 4, Sc. 2, Flor.
> Printed for J. Bew, No. 28, Paternoster Row.

"The Budget of Love" was an innocuous poem, but it spawned a malicious volume entitled:

> LETTERS FROM PERDITA TO A CERTAIN ISRAELITE
> AND
> HIS ANSWERS TO THEM

In heavy-handed humor the author published a serious of fictitious letters between Mary and a moneylender. The Shylock offered to cancel her debts for a certain *quid pro quo*.

To the Reverend Henry Bate immediately came a letter:

Mr. Editor:
The determined and premeditated attacks daily made on the reputation of a certain lady lately retired from the stage, call forth the serious interposition of every man of honour or feeling. It is hoped, for the credit of human nature, those *infamous* and *disgraceful* publications are the production of a female pen. I am no flatterer, neither do I pretend to justify Mrs. R——'s conduct, any further than common candour and decency suggest. The sub-

ject is become a matter of universal conversation. The treatment that lady daily receives, is base and disgraceful to the liberty of the press.

Had the authors dealt out their envenomed slander with a less severe hand, the obscure part of the world might have in some measure credited their groundless assertions; but the disguise is too thin to cover the design, to escape the least observation. Even had Mrs. R—— been the character they describe, the illiberal and scurrilous treatment she has received, would entitle her to the pity and protection of every enemy of *wanton persecution*.

I am, Mr. Editor
Your humble servant
Y. Z.

"The Perdita, finding all arts and devices fail in attempting the recovery of the inconstant Florizel, has at length abandoned the pursuit, and is now certainly preparing for her re-entry on the stage," reported the *Morning Herald* of April 3. Next morning it announced that Mary would open the season at Covent Garden in the character of Jane Shore.

On June 2 the *Morning Herald* was aghast: "The Perdita is said to have declared herself *pregnant* and desired the great event to be announced to R—l ears in form." Then it added: "The declared pregnancy of the Perdita has alarmed the Armstead beyond expression!"

In late spring Mary took a spacious house in Old Windsor, "where she proposes enjoying the rural sweets of retirement the ensuing summer, unallayed by domestic jars, or jealous inquietude."

On June 8 she returned to London and attended a masquerade at the Haymarket Theatre. Her friends were all there: the Prince of Wales, the Duchess of Devonshire, Earl Cholmondeley, Lord Malden. "The Perdita in a most becoming military attire (scarlet faced with apple green), with her usual supporters, C——y and M——n, for a short time illumed the gloomy scene," reported the *Morning Herald* of June 11, "but early sought domestic quiet from the *solitary throng*."

The gay companion of Cholmondeley and Malden was flying high. On June 12 Henry Bate pointed out to his readers that "Fortune has again smiled on Perdita; on Sunday she sported an entire new phaeton, drawn by four chestnut-coloured ponies, with a postillion and servant in blue and silver liveries. The lady dashed into town through Hyde Park turnpike at four o'clock, dressed in a blue great coat prettily trimmed in silver; a plume of feathers graced her hat, which even Alexander the Great might have prided himself in."

Next morning the reverend editor reported sarcastically that Thomas Robinson had returned to Mary. "In all this dissipation she is not unmindful of her marriage vow. Her accommodating spouse participates in all, and yields implicitly the connubial bed, or drives her *petit* ponies black or grey, just as the moment suits without a murmur or regret."

The Robinsons were living on creditors. The security for the extravagant sums Mary was borrowing consisted in negotiations for the return of the letters of the Prince of Wales. Mary's asking price was £25,000. The Prince could not raise £25,000. The negotiators then turned to his father!

In the meantime, according to the *Morning Herald* of June 21, "The creditors of a once admired Sultana of R—l fame, are become of late more *restive* and *impatient* than heretofore, from a discovery that certain arrangements which have been sedulously reported to be in agitation, are proved to be no more than the fairy fancies of the deluded fair one!"

A whole train of danglers and dependents then deserted. Nor were Mary's possessions safe. On July 18 the *Morning Post* reported: "Perdita's carriage was stopped in the streets last Wednesday and the pretty bauble *touched* on an execution; but we are happy to hear that it was soon restored, through the *pecuniary* interest of a noble friend."

The litigation over the letters of Florizel dragged through the summer. On August 14 in scintillating double-talk the *Morning Herald* announced its end. The Reverend Henry Bate's informant was undoubtedly Mary herself, for his story carried her exaggerations and her plans. Having collected the ransom, she intended to visit France until the end of the furor:

> It is beyond dispute that Perdita has succeeded in her *amourous litigation* with her hitherto tardy Banker in Wales. Not less than twenty thousand pounds were the stipulated *doceur*, which sum she is to be put in immediate possession of, on condition of certain mansucripts being surrendered to the *Custos Rotulorum* of the Principality, and to which having acceded, there remains only to name the *plenipos*, who are interchangeably to confirm the indissoluable bond, and to return with full credentials to the original *consideration* to their respective principals.
>
> The Perdita, having completed the sum of her *worldly* wishes with the *Treasury Bench*, and *apparently* attained to the summit of all future expectations in this, or indeed the succeeding reign (should she live so long), has resolved to bid adieu to this hapless land, and to transplant the British Rose into the more genial soil where grow the Lilies of France.

There was secret confirmation of the scoop in the *Morning Herald*. Like any other worried father, King George, on August 28, 1781, wrote his Prime Minister:

> My eldest son got last year into a very improper connection with an actress and woman of indifferent character through the

friendly assistance of Lord Malden; a multitude of letters passed, which she has threatened to publish unless he, in short, bought them of her. He had made her very foolish promises, which, undoubtedly, by her conduct to him she entirely cancelled. I have thought it right to authorize the getting of them from her, and have employed Lieut. Col. Hotham, on whose discretion I could depend, to manage this business. He has now brought it to a conclusion, and has her consent to get these letters on her receiving £5,000, undoubtedly an enormous sum, but I wish to get my son out of this shameful scrape.

ᐒ

In the week that Colonel Hotham paid over the £5000, Mary Robinson ordered a portrait and a carriage. On August 25 the *Morning Herald* noted that she was sitting for Gainsborough, little dreaming that her portrait would one day be numbered among the masterpieces of the artist.

"The Perdita's new *Bove de Paris* coach bids fair to kick the poor brimstone-coloured equipages quite out of doors," said the *Morning Herald* of September 11. Two days later Mr. Bate editorialized: "It has been universally remarked, that the Perdita, since her fracas with her *illustrious amorata*, has preserved a line of conduct so irreproachable and prudent, that even her most rancorous enemies cannot stigmatize her with the smallest reflection."

As tongues wagged, Mary whispered a secret to her reverend friend. On October 19 the *Morning Herald* reported: "This morning the Perdita sets off for Margate, in order to embark for Ostend, in her route to Paris, where she means to spend the months of November and December. She is to be accompanied only by her little daughter and a necessary suit of domestics."

In the French capital Mary was welcomed as a heroine. Sir John Lambert, resident English banker, realized the value of a client just come into £5000. He secured her a commodious apartment and a box at the Opera. The venerable chevalier then introduced *la belle Angloise* to Philippe, Duke of Chartres.

Duke Philippe, possessor of the largest private fortune in Europe and a harem of concubines, immediately laid siege to Mary's affections. He had always taken what he wanted, and the Parisians eagerly watched the sparring between the actress and the rake whose profligate Orleans ancestors inspired the word *roué*. The *Morning Post* kept Mary's supporters alerted: "She was much admired at the French Opera, and never appeared there without drawing his Royal Highness, the Duke de Chartres, and several other leading men of fashion into her box."

Philippe was swarthy and pimpled. His nose was flat, and he wore rings in his ears. He was haughty and his person contrasted garishly with that of the Prince of Wales. Mary disdained his advances.

On October 22 Marie Antoinette bore the Dauphin. As soon afterward as possible, she and King Louis dined in public at Versailles. Having heard of the English siren, Marie asked Duke Philippe to bring her to this *grand couvert*. Excited by a royal hint, Mary dressed in the height of splendor: a gorgeous dress with pale green lustring train and body, festooned with delicate lilacs, and a tiffany petticoat. For the occasion she bought a chapeau of white feathers from Mademoiselle Bertin, hatmaker to her Majesty.

The royal diners were protected from the public by a crimson cord drawn across an alcove in the palace. When Mary appeared in the crowd, the Duke left the side of King Louis and placed the lovely foreigner under the gaze of Queen Marie. After dinner, as Marie Antoinette drew on her gloves, she noticed Mary admiring her queenly arms. She uncovered them again and leaned for a few moments on her hands. Queen and adventuress understood each other.

Mary wore upon her bosom the diamond-circled miniature of the Prince. To this the Queen paid particular attention. Next day she sent Philippe to borrow it, and when he returned he brought a purse, netted by the hands of Marie Antoinette, a gift to *la belle Angloise*.

After the queenly head had rolled from the guillotine, Mary wrote in her "Monody on the Death of the Queen of France":

> Oh! I have seen her, like a Sun, sublime!
> Diffusing glory on the wings of Time!
> And, as revolving seasons own his flight,
> Marking each brilliant minute with Delight!

On her birthday, November 27, Philippe made a final effort to seduce the inexorable *Angloise*. "A rural *fete* was appointed in the gardens of Mousseau, when this beautiful pandamonium of splendid profligacy, was, at an unusual expense, decorated with boundless luxury," wrote Mary in her *Memoirs*.

Every tree bore M.R., the initials of *la belle Angloise*, woven in wreathes of artificial flowers and illuminated by colored lamps. But to no avail. As precaution Mary clung to the arm of the venerable chevalier Lambert.

Rumors of Mary's conquests drifted back across the Channel. On December 7 Bate's *Morning Herald* fluttered pulses with its prediction: "The Perdita is expected to arrive from France in the course of the next week, with such a train of first rate fashions that cannot fail to set the whole female world 'a madding.' "

In the month's of Mary's absence from England the affections of
the Prince had drifted from the lovely Mrs. Armstead to Mrs. Grace
Dalrymple Elliott, known as "Dally the Tall." As early as July 27 Mr.
Bate had predicted the departure for Paris of this sometime mistress
of Philippe, since Dally "finds the Princely object which occasioned her
return not likely to bow before her beauteous altar."

By October 19 the *Morning Herald* could report Dally's boasting
about a visit and a kiss from the Prince. In announcing Mary's plans to
return to London, the *Morning Herald* concluded: "The expected
arrival of Perdita from Paris planted an agonizing thorn in the pillow
of Dally the Tall, who has declared to her unsuccessful *Puff in Ordinary*,
that she is determined upon quitting the Kingdom the moment she is
assured of her rival's return." Sneered Henry Bate: Mrs. Elliott has
"always discovered a penchant for the Princely leavings of the more
enchanting Perdita."

On December 24 he reported: "The Dalrymple has declared herself
pregnant, and taken care to have it well understood that Lord C——y
cannot possibly lay claim to a single feature of the amourous produce,
be it what it may; solemnly averring on her *honour*, that his Lordship
was totally effaced from her memory before she had the faintest conception of the bliss that now awaits her! However difficult it may be to
ascertain its *real sire*, one is already named for it, who is said to be
extremely flattered by the *novelty of the title*, and has already given
orders that the *ceremonies of the straw* be supported with the utmost
magnificence and eclat."

Dally was pregnant. In spite of denials by George, Prince of Wales,
she had the baby christened Georgiana. Perhaps the ceremonies of the
straw were not supported with princely magnificence. Dally returned to
the protection of Duke Philippe and settled in a rose-covered cottage
beside his castle.

Georgiana fell to the care of Earl Cholmondeley. When he married
Charlotte Bertie, sister of the late Robert of Ancaster, Georgiana was
in the litter of surprises his Lordship brought home to his bride.
Around their home in Piccadilly and in their palace at Houghton
Georgiana played, becoming in time like a sister to little Susan Priscilla
Bertie.

On the day that Mary left London for Paris, at faraway Yorktown
Lord Cornwallis surrendered his army. Next morning Count Rocham-
beau selected the Duke of Lauzun to bear the tidings to the King of
France. Brave Lauzun or mad Lauzun the men of France called him.
Handsome Lauzun or divine Lauzun their women called him. Duke
Philippe introduced handsome Lauzun to beautiful Mrs. Robinson.

"She was gay, lively, frank, and goodnatured," wrote Lauzun in his
Memoirs. "She did not speak French. I was an object of attraction for
her, a man who had brought great news, who had returned from war,

who was about to go back to it: he had suffered a great deal, he still suffered much—she thought she could not do enough for him. I therefore had Perdita."

Having succeeded where Philippe had failed, Armand Louis de Gontaut, Duc de Lauzun, spent a delighted fortnight with Mary. "Perdita left for England and was so desirous that I accompany her to Calais, that I could not refuse," wrote the Duke. In exquisite oblivion they dallied from Paris to the Channel.

Years later, in the beginning of the Reign of Terror, "Mad Lauzun" was enmeshed in the struggle in La Vendee. He was sentenced to death. On the bleak morning of December 31, 1793, when his jailers came to lead him to the guillotine, they found him breakfasting on raw oysters and white wine. Armand Louis greeted them with a smile. And as he went to his final assignation, perhaps the man who had slept with the Queen as well as the Perdita remembered them both, and wondered still which was the lovelier, Marie or Mary.

"Last night the divine *Perdita* visited the opera for the first time since her return from Paris," reported the *Morning Herald* of January 9, 1782, "and sat in one of the third tier of boxes on the King's side. She was dressed in white satin, with purple breast bows, and looked supremely beautiful! Her head dress was in a style that may be called the *standard of taste:* the cap, composed of white and purple feathers entwined with flowers, was fastened on with diamond pins. Upon her breast she wore no cross, but the image of a *Royal Martyr,* over which waved a brilliant plume: and still above, far more refulgent, two lovely eyes shot forth a lustre that seemed to give animation to the picture."

19

Ban and Mary

*T*HE RETURN OF Banastre to his home in Liverpool was a triumph, but he did not tarry long. Off to London he hastened. On February 28, 1782, there was a brilliant midwinter Assembly at the Pantheon. Among the 800 masqueraders were the fashionables of England. They danced and they watched floor shows: Signor Delphini treading Italian measures and Mr. Bannister reciting his favorite roles. At one o'clock the company supped on roast fowl, cold roast beef, and jellied tongue, washed down with sherry, port, madeira, and Rhenish wines. Then in pre-Lenten joy they danced until six in the morning.

Among the revelers were the Prince of Wales and Viscount Malden; Colonels Lake and St. Leger; and gallant Colonel Tarleton. Next day the *Morning Herald* observed: "The chief constellation of the pleasurable sphere was the lovely Perdita, in a domino and mask that did not quite conceal her dimples!"

But the hero and the dimpled Cyprian did not rush into each other's arms. There was none of the poetry of love, no spontaneous overflow of powerful emotions. Like stately galleons they passed, but they dipped their colors in salutation.

Mary already had enough trouble for one evening. The *Morning Herald* reported that while she and Lord Malden were chatting a Frenchman sat beside her. When Mary said a few words to the Frenchman, her lord became piqued and unmasked, inviting the foreigner to unmask also. Upon his refusal, there was a heated exchange. The reporter expected a duel. The young bloods guarded their mates like beasts in season: Lord Malden would kill or be killed by anyone stealing the affections of beautiful Mrs. Robinson!

The shock unnerved Mary and sent her to bed with high fever. But on March 1 the *Morning Herald* reported: "Perdita is again in the *beau monde* perfectly recovered from her late alarming indisposition."

A week later the Reverend Mr. Bate told her admirers: "The lovely Perdita's dress last night at the Opera was a beautiful rainbow green of the slightest shade, with carmelite bows and trimmings. Her hair was ornamented with braided wheat ears fastened with diamond pins."

With the dress of beautiful rainbow green Mary wore the jaunty creation of Mademoiselle Bertin. On April 13 the *Morning Post* described it in detail: "The cap in which the beautiful Perdita has lately appeared is a *chef d'oeuvre* of elegance; it is ornamented with plumes of feathers and a wave of artificial roses, interspersed with various flowers, on a ground of sea green, and is fastened on with brilliant pins."

On April 19 London's fashionables went to the masquerade at the Pantheon. "Mrs. Robinson was present but did not unmask," reported the *Morning Herald* on April 22: "She wore a dress of white crepe, decorated with festoons of white flowers, and a cap trimmed in a similar manner. She was much admired for the elegant simplicity of her dress. The Colonels North, Tarleton, Mr. Windham, and Mr. Pitt wore the uniforms of Light Hussars."

That morning Mary had launched what the *Morning Herald* called "another new elegant coach, that far eclipses all the various equipages of the *bon ton*." It was lined with white satin and trimmed with broad silver fringe!

Upon his return from Liverpool, Banastre had rented a house in St. James's Place, almost in the shadow of Brooks's Club and only a couple of blocks from St. James's Palace. He hired John Shaw as his valet. He bought two saddle horses and soon was cantering about the West End. Then he picked up two old race horses which in high humor he renamed Adrastus and Antiquity. Riding or strutting around in his green jacket, tan trousers, boots, and helmet of nodding black swan's feathers, with his mangled hand carefully tucked in his pocket, he became one of the best-known figures in London.

He went back to the Cocoa Tree, to the boisterous life he had led as a student in the Middle Temple. He went the rounds of the clubs: to Weltjie's, to Daubigney's, and to Brooks's when he could wangle an invitation from Charles Fox. Soon he was gambling more recklessly than before the losses he had paid with the legacy from Aunt Parker.

As he rushed from the Pantheon to private receptions and round about town, Banastre found welcome in the home of John Murray, Earl of Dunmore. The Scottish lord had served as the last royal governor of Virginia. He was eager to talk of the campaign along the James and the York.

Lord and Lady Dunmore had resided in the Governor's Mansion in Williamsburg. Lady Augusta, their oldest daughter, had loved the colonial capital. She had been courted by the local gentry. She had attended balls in Norfolk. She had danced with the Tidewater gallants. So she had much to talk over with the hero fresh from Yorktown.

Soon Ban was Augusta's constant escort. From party to theater to opera they went, while the grande dames whispered and Bate watched. On April 26 the reverend gentleman's *Morning Herald* printed an exclusive story: "Among the couples paired off for matrimony are Lady Augusta Murray and Colonel Banastre Tarleton!"

But something chilled the romance between the dragoon and the freckled daughter of Lord Dunmore. Although she flirted with Tarleton in '82 and danced away the Queen's Birthday Ball with Hanger in '84, Lady Augusta tarried. Then to her heartbreak, in 1793 she married Augustus Frederick, Duke of Sussex, the sixth son of King George and Queen Charlotte.

The courting was done and the marriage solemnized in Rome. Then the ceremony was repeated by the Reverend Mr. Gunn of the Anglican Church at St. George's, Hanover Square, London. Doubly in vain! In August 1794 the King, with Farmer George's discrimination in selecting heifers and bulls for breeding, under the infamous Marriage Act of 1772, voided the marriage of Augustus and Augusta. They clung together for a while in the wreckage, but the tide was too strong. From a noble Italian ancestor their children, Augustus Frederick and Ellen Augusta, took the surname of d'Este.

 oↄ

During these hectic weeks Banastre found time to sit for Sir Joshua to finish his portrait. He also sat for Gainsborough, who painted him on his black charger. "The picture of my Brother at Gainsborough's will not measure with the frame less than 12 feet 6 inches," John wrote their mother.

When the Royal Academy opened its annual exhibition on April 29, each artist exhibited his portrait. In the evening Sir Joshua, as president, conducted King George through the gallery. Perhaps his Majesty winced. On the walls were portraits of the Prince of Wales and of Mrs. Robinson.

The critic for the *Morning Herald* adjudged the portraits of the Prince of Wales and of Colonel St. Leger the best of Gainsborough's work. Then he asserted: "Colonel Tarleton is likewise a spirited, very masterly performance, but the painter has evidently sacrificed too much for the full speed idea of a spirited martinet."

The portrait of Tarleton by Reynolds outshone Gainsborough's. "The portrait of Colonel Tarleton is a highly finished painting," commented the *Morning Herald* on the former. "The principal figure is finely disposed, and the ground and sky described in a glow of colouring admirably suited to a martial subject."

Immediately Peter Pindar, laureate of mirth and scandal, had a verse for the artistry of Sir Joshua:

Lo! Tarleton dragging on his boot so tight!
   His horses feel a godlike rage,
   And long with Yankees to engage—
I think I hear them snorting for the fight.

Behold with fire each eyeball glowing!
I wish, indeed, their manes so flowing

Were more like hair—the brutes had been as good
   If, flaming with such classic force,
   They had resembled less that horse
Call'd Trojan—and by Greeks compos'd of wood.

∽

At the King's Theatre on May 2 society held the most fashionable masquerade of the season. The supper was lavish and the music royal. Sheridan introduced Monsieur Lepique, who danced *Apollo and the Muses*. Reported the *Morning Herald* of May 4: "The Prince of Wales, during the performance of Lepique, sat between the Duchess of Devonshire and Lady Jersey, in her Grace's box, and continued the remainder of the night in company with Major St. Leger and Colonel Tarleton."

On May 10 the Prince of Wales, with 1600 of the social ragtag, danced through another masquerade at the Pantheon. "Not a woman of rank was to be seen," commented the *Morning Herald*. Lady Worsley and Mrs. Elliott marched around arm in arm the whole evening: "The Perdita was likewise in a domino, attended by her noble gallant."

How Lord Malden enjoyed parading his beautiful Cyprian. He loved her. He trusted her. In fact he was so certain of Mary's faithfulness that one evening in early spring, as he sat with Tarleton and several other rakes in St. Alban's Tavern, he began boasting. With libertine cynicism Ban demurred. Suddenly the Lord offered to bet one thousand guineas that the Colonel could not win the affections of Mrs. Robinson.

"Win her and jilt her," cried Tarleton as they shook hands.

While Viscount Malden and Colonel Tarleton strove for Mrs. Robinson's affections, a dashing London rake named Pugh, who wholly misunderstood the character of the beautiful actress, entered the contest. But he used a different approach. He wrote a note offering her twenty guineas for a ten-minute conversation.

Mary accepted the proposal. She appointed an hour for young Pugh to visit her at her home in Berkeley Square. Upon his arrival he was ushered into the sitting room where he found her chatting with Lord Malden and Colonel Tarleton.

At his entrance Mary detached her watch from her side and laid it on the table. Leaving her companions she devoted her conversation entirely to Pugh. From the chuckles of her friends he realized that they were privy to the joke. When the ten minutes had passed she took up her watch, rose from her chair, rang for her maid, and requested her to escort Mr. Pugh to the door. She divided the twenty guineas among four of her favorite charities.

With Pugh annihilated, the Colonel and the Lord settled down to sedulous courting. Heroism strove with titled nobility. Banastre's handsome features, elegant manners, and dashing conversation outrivaled those of the bumbling, roly-poly future Earl of Essex. Mary fell passionately in love with the rakish colonel. In late May they slipped away from London for an assignation at Barrow Hedges, near Epsom.

Two weeks later the Colonel sneaked back to London to collect his wager. Lord Malden's frustration was complete and ludicrous. Mary's fury scarcely knew bounds. She refused to speak to her betrayers. Three squibs from the pen of the Reverend Henry Bate told a startling sequel.

"Monday afternoon a very serious accident befell Mrs. Robinson, while taking an airing in Hyde Park. A phaeton being driven with violence against her chariot overturned it. In the fall she was so dangerously wounded, that she was conveyed in a state of insensibility to her house in Berkeley Square," said the *Morning Herald* on June 5.

"The Perdita, by one of those fatalities which the wanton God of Love can only account for, was carried to the house of Lord M——, in Berkeley Square, immediately after the late alarming accident, where she was received with all becoming humanity." But the *Morning Herald* of June 7 concluded: ". . . his Lordship left home and now resides in St. James Street!"

Ban rushed to the side of Mary. As he comforted her, she cried. But she forgave him. Said the *Morning Herald* of June 8: "The Perdita so far from having returned to her former Lord, as stated in some of the prints, is certainly divorced from him a *mensa et thoro*, and now cohabits with her military seducer Col. T—— at his house in Hill Street, Berkeley Square."

Scarcely a day passed without the *Morning Herald's* homage to the Fair Cyprians: Mrs. Armstead, the Farrenelli, Dally the Tall, the Bird of Paradise, the Blue-eyed Nun, and the Perdita. Its gossip column usually began with a review of the opera at Covent Garden or the play at Drury Lane, descended to chit-chat about actors and actresses, sank to the demireps, and, as on July 23, hit bottom with a juicy tidbit: "The Perdita and her noble lover are now separated forever—it occasioned some convulsive pangs on either side, but at last *les noeuds d'amour* were torn asunder."

Perhaps *les noeuds d'amour* was the subject of the "Poetical Address" Mary published in the *Heliconian*. Her confession of love proved such a popular poem that a jest started the rounds that the fair author would do up her hair in no paper except the *Heliconian*. "When this was told Mrs. Robinson, the other day, she burst into a loud laugh, and said she consoled herself with this reflection, that Perdita would not long have an opportunity of continuing this practice, as her Poetical Address sold so fast, that a copy, in a few days, would scarcely remain to be purchased."

In the *Morning Herald* of July 6 the Reverend Henry Bate moralized: "To the disgrace of this Kingdom, and the subversion of all virtuous principles, her speech is but too true."

"Lover of Virtue" wrote an indignant letter to the *Morning Herald* of July 31, castigating it for filling its columns with the doings of these "fashionable prostitutes." He exclaimed, "In what degree of low scandal is a certain morning paper now held! Whole columns of it filled with Mrs. Robinson's green carriage."

∽

"Colonel Tarleton is of late become the constant companion of the Duke of Bedford, a circumstance which augurs well for a young grandee," commented the *Morning Chronicle*. Bedford's companion next turned his genius upon the Prince of Wales.

He discovered that the Prince was an enthusiastic turfman and he soon won entree into the group of gentlemen riders around his Royal Highness. Among these Sir Harry Featherstone bore the oriflamme. Sir Harry had the qualifications: an income of £10,000; a private race course on the Harting Downs behind his home at Up Park in Sussex; and old Rockingham, the greatest horse ever foaled in England. By the middle of summer the Prince, the Duke of Dorset, Sir John Lade, Colonel Lake, and Colonel Tarleton were eager for the silken fray.

Before riding from London with the Prince, Banastre wrote his plans to Thomas. There was lighthearted news of Mrs. Robinson. The Perdita was being courted by handsome, rakish Charles James Fox. A former junior lord of the Treasury in Lord North's cabinet, Charles was famous for his oratory and for his love of cards, race horses, and beautiful women. Ban showed no jealousy:

St. James's Place July 29, 1782

My dear Brother,

If you will let me know when you will be at home you will oblige me for by that information I shall plan my journey.

This place is very stupid and empty. I remain in it at present to get an answer to a memorial I have presented relative to the estab-lishment of my regiment.

Brighthelmstone I returned from yesterday, I went there from Lewes.

Write to me as soon as you receive this, as I have promised to go for a few days to Sir Harry Featherstone's previous to my departure for Lancashire and Cheshire. Politicians say that this country is in a bad condition—Divisions at home, weakness abroad etc. etc.

Have you room for four horses and can I give them some grass in the house? Or must I send them to Liverpool?

Pleasant John is very angry with me but I suppose he is always keenest in his anger with his best friends. The Secretary is now my rival with the Lady in whose cause and in defense of whose disinterested conduct John first took umbrage against me. The Fox will not be so fortunate in his association as I am fortunate in separation. I shall ever applaud the Perdita as the most generous woman on earth.

Please present my best love and compliments. If Mrs. Tarleton can employ me in any way before I leave this place, assure her of my intention and wish to serve her.

God bless you says
Your affectionate Brother
Ban. Tarleton

On the Up Park race course on Monday, August 5, Colonel Tarleton's Adrastus beat Sir Harry Featherstone's Dasher for 1000 guineas, post and pay, each horse carrying 11 stones, 10 pounds, over the course. By afternoon Adrastus had rested enough to carry the same weight over the course and beat Colonel Monson's Conundrum for 1000 guineas, post and pay.

But Banastre did not have Charles Fox's skill at handicapping and on Tuesday raced tired Adrastus, carrying 11 stones, 10 pounds, against Dasher, carrying only 11 stones, 2 pounds, over the course, for 1000 guineas, post and pay. Sir Harry won.

Sir Harry then organized a sweepstakes race over the last quarter mile of the course. Each entrant posted 25 guineas for prize money. Sir Harry swept the field on Rockingham, closely followed by Tarleton on Antiquity. Sir Harry on his Don Joseph then beat Banastre on Adrastus, for 50 guineas, post and pay, to close the season at Up Park.

The *Morning Post* of August 16 laughed: "*Tam morte quam mercurio* is not quite applicable to Colonel Tarleton; his success at the Up Park Races was by no means a counterpart to his military career."

Upon his return to London Banastre again wrote Thomas:

St. James's Place
Aug 13th

My dear Brother

I am just returned from Sir Harry Featherstone's—

I wrote to you a fortnight since, desiring you would let me know whether you was at home; and requesting of you to inform me, if I should send my horses to your house or to Liverpool—

If I can do it with propriety, I shall certainly go with Stewart to the relief of Gibraltar. It is the imagined destination of the grand fleet.

In consequence of my intention I have wrote to my Lord Cornwallis to decide upon the propriety or impropriety of the step in my present situation—

If I don't go I will write to you immediately, but you must write first—

My best respects attend Mrs. Tarleton and all your family—

As ever dear Brother
Ban. Tarleton

Said the *Morning Herald* three days later: "A correspondent of the *Ton* says Mr. Fox has entirely chased the Provincial Lieutenant Colonel from the suite of the amorous Perdita."

Mary screamed. Next morning Henry Bate recanted: "The present intimacy subsisting between the ex-minister and the Perdita is said to be perfectly political on the part of the Lady, who probably foresees *in imagination* her oratorical associate once more seated on the *Treasury Bench* in the hallowed chapel of St. Stephens."

As the gossip-mongers wrangled over Charles and Mary and the Provincial Lieutenant Colonel, the cartoonist Gillray entered the lists. On August 20 he published "The Thunderer."

The Thunderer, as Gillray christened Banastre, stands in his resplendent uniform before the Whirligig chophouse. He has drawn his sword and is boasting his exploits. Beside him stands a headless figure wearing the Prince's plume of three feathers, and above the door a happy but diminutive Perdita in the form of a Whirligig is receiving the Army's treatment for prostitutes.

The sign of the Whirligig aroused sympathy for Mary. Even the *Morning Post* found its conscience and on August 29 accorded her a titillating profile:

Hasty Sketch of Perdita
By a Gentleman over Head and Ears in Love

Formed by the hand of nature for almost every opposite pursuit to that in which the whirl of life has engaged her, Perdita but half enjoys her present situation; yet she gives to it every grace and embellishment of which it is susceptible. She has frequent recourse to splendour, more than a necessity to forget what is most dear, than to remember the brilliance by which she is surrounded. The meteor which dazzles for a moment, and affords the bright illusion she seeks, too often evaporates, even while she hails it as a friend, and the gloom of profound despondence succeeds. 'Tis in this disposition that the generous sigh heaves from her bosom, the gentle tear starts to her eye, and she regrets the absence of those trifling joys which the cross rubs of life, in gay disguise of some

imagin'd elegance, have rob'd her of. Then it is that her soul
turns unsatisfied away from whatever princes can bestow! Were
her talents mean, her fancy less elevated, her heart less animated,
her passions less vivid, she would derive a more constant pleasure
from the gaieties which are now her occasional consolation. Her
temper is by nature quick, impatient, excursive, and romantic;
and makes her equal to every thing which is uncommon, adventurous, and unpremeditated. There is nothing enthusiastically
great of which she is not capable, when she obeys the unresisted
impulse of the moment; and love or generosity would carry her
from pole to pole. There is a *pride* in her spirit which bids it revolt from its obligations, and the idea of an *unequal* connection
extirpates tenderness in proportion as it excites gratitude. Her
love is the child of nature, nurs'd by the heart; and the genius or
grandeur which enforces her wonder and admiration, have often
failed to create her fondness, or kindle her affections. Deprived of
many comforts in society of which she is worthy, she becomes
less reconciled to herself, and less comfortable to others, than, in
a state less subject to the caprices of fashion, she would be. She
has taste & feeling which fit her for the retreats of life. Simplicity
has charms for her. Attached to her, by nature, are the soft dejec-
tions of a pathetic spirit, a tender friendship with the Muse, and
a soul that aches for the softness of unstraying love. In her earliest
day, budded these flowers. Though they have been stopped from
blowing; though the deflated blossoms were beaten off by the
weather of the world, though the vegetation has been checked,
yet the tender plants have forced their way, and borne the fruits of
generosity, liberality and charity. There are times when Perdita
had rather warm the chilled bosom of poverty, imprint a kiss on
the lip of untitled merit, and drop a tear on the wounds of misfortune, than hold converse with the most distinguished of her
train. It is to be deplored that she is not the happiest, because she
has a heart to be the best; yet to her should be adjudged the highest praise, who in a difficult situation shews, by her sensibility, that
she deserves a better.

Charles Fox, gambling and penniless, sympathized with Mary. He
asserted that the Prince should provide security for the ruined actress.
Upon Fox's advice she surrendered the bond for £20,000. After this gesture of good will he secured the settlement of an annuity of £500 upon
her with an annuity of £200 to continue during the life of Maria Elizabeth.

"I hear Charles saunters about the streets and brags that he has not
taken a pen in hand since he was out of place," wrote Fox's aunt, Lady
Sarah Napier, to Lady Susan O'Brian on September 11. Lady Napier
did not believe the intimacy perfectly political. "*Pour se desennuyer,*
he lives with Mrs. Robinson, goes to Sadler's Wells with her, & is all
day figuring away with her. I long to tell him he does it to show that

he is superior to Alcibiades, for *his* courtezan forsook him when he was unfortunate and Mrs. Robinson takes *him* up."

While Lady Napier chortled, on September 21 the *Morning Post* announced the triumph of the Provincial Lieutenant Colonel in one of the most magnificent paragraphs of scandal ever penned:

SHIP NEWS

Yesterday, a messenger arrived in town, with the very interesting and pleasing intelligence of the Tarleton, armed ship, having, after a chace of some months, captured the Perdita frigate, and brought her safe into Egham port. The Perdita is a prodigious fine clean bottomed vessel, and had taken many prizes during her cruize, particularly the Florizel, a most valuable ship belonging to the Crown, but which was immediately released, after taking out the cargo. The Perdita was captured some time ago by the Fox, but was, afterwards, retaken by the Malden, and had a sumptuous suit of new rigging, when she fell in with the Tarleton. Her manoeuvering to escape was admirable; but the Tarleton, fully determined to take her, or perish, would not give up the chace; and at length, coming alongside the Perdita, fully determined to board her, sword in hand, she instantly surrendered at discretion.

The hero had lost interest in Gibraltar. He was constantly with beautiful Mrs. Robinson. To escape the eyes of the prying, they tripped off to Old Windsor.

"Colonel Tarleton has lost the hard idea of *defending* Gibraltar, in the soft and delightful hope of attacking *Fort Perdita* and carrying it by a *coup* before the class of the present season," said the *Morning Post* on September 26. "For this purpose he has pitched his tent in the environs of Windsor, where the object of his wishes now parades in the pride of charms and universal conquest."

Next day the *Morning Herald* published the latest dispatch from the campaign: "The Bush at Staines, a few days ago, was converted into a temple of the Cyprian Goddess; the fair Perdita took up her residence there for a few days, attended by a worshipper of military appearance, who was observed to be uncommonly devout in all his addresses to her *divinity*."

The *Morning Herald* squeezed this scandal dry: "The Perdita and her once enamoured Colonel have at length ceased to lay rural snares for the wanton heart of each other," it mocked on October 19. "Both, sufficiently gratified, have returned to town and its more delightful mazes of fashionable inconstancy."

Mary loved elegance. On the walls of her home were portraits of her by Cosway, Romney, Gainsborough, and Reynolds. She had a retinue of liveried servants. Her ponies and phaeton were the envy of even Sir

John Lade. Her ambition was to seize the crown of fashion worn by the Duchess of Devonshire, and in her aid she enlisted the couturiers and milliners of France.

"The Perdita has received a dress from Paris, which was introduced this autumn by the Queen of France, and has caused no small anxiety in the fashionable circles," said the Morning Herald of October 30. "It is totally calculated for the Opera, where it is expected to make its first appearance."

The dress was a sensation. "Ladies of the first style adopt it, and gentlemen patronize it," smirked the Morning Herald of November 20. "The chemise de la Reine, in which Mrs. Robinson appeared at the Opera, is expected to become the favorite undress among the fashionable women."

Every paper was filled with comment on this latest of fashions. At last the Morning Chronicle of November 28 said flatly: "The Queen's Chemise is the most unbecoming dress that was ever projected among the vagaries of fashion, except for those whom nature has distinguished with a slim and elegant form." And it warned that unless the wearer was endowed with a bosomy figure like Mary's she would "look better in a linsey-woolsey nightgown."

The gold-clocked stockings introduced by the "lark-heeled Perdita" caused disputes in fashionable circles and the fair inventor was reviled for extravagance. Her clothes were imitated by the virtuous who scorned her. But the Morning Herald noted: "There is a neatness and decency in the dress of Perdita that challenges universal admiration."

While Mary kept the fashionable circles in an uproar with her imported clothes, Ban ducked the reporters. But their estimate of the romance was tucked away in a corner of the Morning Post of November 21, disguised in the words of Othello:

> Perdition catch my soul, but I do love thee,
> And when I love thee not, chaos is come again.

Mary gloried in a succession of phaetons: "Mrs. Robinson now sports a carriage which is the admiration of all the charioteering circles in the vicinity of St. James," said the Morning Post on December 4. The new carriage by Benwell of Long Acre was gorgeous: "the body carmelite and silver, ornamented with a French mantle, and the cypher in a wreath of flowers: the carriage scarlet and silver, the seat-cloth richly ornamented with silver fringe. Mrs. Robinson's livery is green, faced with yellow, and richly trimmed with broad silver lace; the harness ornamented with stars of silver, richly chased and elegantly finished. The inside of the carriage is lined with white silk, embellished with scarlet trimmings."

The *Morning Herald* of December 3 reflected: "The Perdita has set a very splendid example to her impure sisters in the charioteering style which few of them will be able to follow." On December 5 it said: "Yesterday the Perdita sported her new carriage in various parts of town, accompanied by the gallant Tarleton."

As the gallant Colonel and his beautiful lady paraded unabashed in the vicinity of St. James's Palace or rushed hand-in-hand to the opera, Preacher Bate was watching. Before Christmas he had his reward. On December 21 he told the readers of the *Morning Herald*: "The Perdita appeared on Saturday night at the Opera with her own *caro sposo*."

Thomas Robinson had turned up to plague Mary. On December 23 Bate enlarged the scandal: "The Colonel, it seems, is dismissed, not that he is declared unfit for service, but he is only rich in laurels and martial trophies."

Laurels and martial trophies won. Mary drove her phaeton to Old Windsor for the Christmas holidays, and Ban followed with his saddle horses. The royal family spent Christmas at Windsor Castle. Thus it was ordained, said the *Morning Herald*, starting another year of gossip on January 2, 1783, that Mrs. Robinson should be reconciled with the Prince:

"Perdita and her Colonel have taken up their residence at Old Windsor, and are perpetually on horseback. The beautiful fair one was coming from her morning exercise of riding, at the time his R. H. came through this town from the chase; they met near the market place on horseback. His Royal Highness stopt when he came near her, and pulling off his glove, shook her by the hand; the blushing *Perdita* holding one of her hands at the same time across her face,—Oh, modesty in the extreme!"

Quipped the *Morning Herald*: "The beautiful Perdita's momentary interview with a certain heir, was said by the astronomers in the neighborhood of Windsor, to be a transit of Venus over the *Georgium sidus*."

Mary had been foolish. After her unhappy marriage with Thomas Robinson, she had grasped at the affection of the Prince. Then she had followed her fancy from Malden to Lauzun to Malden to Tarleton, and perhaps to Sheridan and Fox. And she had paid for her frailty in tears.

Nor had Banastre been wiser or more virtuous. At first Mary had been just another conquest. But as the months passed he found in her the fulfillment of his needs and fell passionately in love with her. He had the figure, the gallantry, and the elegant manners of the perfect soldier. She had the beauty, the wit, and the charm of the perfect actress. They were the handsomest couple in London.

On January 16 the *Morning Chronicle* broke its reserve and gave the Colonel a dignified profile by quoting Shakespeare's *Henry IV*:

Colonel T——n

I do not think a braver gentleman,
More active valiant, or more valiant young,
More daring, or more bold, is now alive,
To grace this latter age with noble deed.

∾

During the summer and fall Tarleton had been busy with the affairs of the British Legion. He and the other officers and men captured at Gloucester were on parole. They still received the pay of their ranks. But the British Legion was a Provincial corps, and since his return to England, Tarleton had sought to have it recognized and placed on the regular British Establishment.

"The King having been pleased to direct that the cavalry of the British Legion lately serving in North America, should be placed on the British establishment," on December 25, 1782, the War Office ordered this done. "I am to signify to you His Majesty's pleasure that you do take the necessary steps for placing the said Regiment upon the British Establishment," Lord Townshend wrote Tarleton. He also requested him to send "names of such officers at present serving in the British Legion as you may think proper to recommend for commissions on the British Establishment."

The Green Dragoon submitted the names of the officers who had commanded the cavalry of the Legion during the march from Tybee to Yorktown: Lieutenant Colonel Banastre Tarleton, commandant; Major George Hanger; Captains Richard Hovenden, David Ogilvie, Thomas Gildart, and Thomas Miller; Lieutenants Moore Hovenden, Duncan Munro, Michael Largen, and Acttan Cameron; and Cornets Davis, Miller, Chapman, Stapleton, and Hovenden. The Reverend John Lott Phillips was named chaplain and Dr. John Smith surgeon for the Legion.

With his regiment on the British Establishment and his rank and half-pay assured, Banastre began looking forward to the conclusion of the treaty of peace and the end of his parole. Then another exciting assignment was offered him. In May 1782 Lord Shelburne, Secretary for Colonial Affairs in the Rockingham cabinet, asked Lord Cornwallis to go out to India as governor general and commander in chief. In January 1783 Shelburne renewed the offer. The appointment needed only confirmation by Parliament.

Lord Cornwallis offered the command of his cavalry to the Green Dragoon. Immediately Banastre wrote Thomas:

St. James Place,
Jan. 21, 1783

My dear Brother

I received your letter last night, and by this day's coach send you the books you desire—Thank you for the Pheasants which I have accepted—

Your letter dated Coventry, arrived a few days ago, I deferred answering it, as its principal contents were relative to my going to the Indies, I postponed my reply till I could give you more satisfactory accounts in that head, but I am sorry to say that I am ignorant, till this business is undertaken by Parliament, & my Lord Cornwallis is invested with his powers—I apprehend the voyage to that quarter of the world is near; for whether the negotiations turn to peace or war, it is to take place. The season for the Voyage is very near; and I know it will be the immediate attention of the House of Commons, as soon as they meet after the recess, to consult and finally determine on the business.

I saw my Lord Cornwallis yesterday, he is of the same opinion—

The Regiment that I had in America is placed on the British Establishment as Dragoons, the Officers take rank 25 Dec. 82.

Hard to say! I have not yet effected any exchange—If peace ensues from the Treaty on foot, I am free; if War is the result I must obtain leave to act in the East Indies—But I shall know more in a few days—

Make my affectionate respects to Mrs. Tarleton, and my kindest compliments to Mr. and Mrs. Stanley.

Believe me to be
Yours most affectionately
Ban. Tarleton

20

All for Love

As BANASTRE began preparing for the voyage to India, Mary clung
tighter than ever before. The handsome couple were seen together
everywhere. Sighed the Morning Post of January 24: "All for Love is
Colonel Tarleton's motto." The paragrapher concluded: "Mrs. Robinson's popularity renders her apparently the properest woman in the
world for the situation in which she is placed, and to which every part
of her conduct does the highest credit."

At the masquerade that evening they were oblivious of others. Henry
Bate spied them and in the Morning Herald reported: "The Perdita
marching all night with her gallant colonel."

As he waited for Parliament to confirm the appointment of Lord Corn-
wallis, Banastre tried to put his affairs in order. During the year in
London he had exhausted all his resources. He had run up extravagant
bills. From Drummond the banker he had borrowed a sum equal to a
year's pay. He had won and lost large sums in gambling, and he owed
Louis Weltjie a large sum advanced for play. So he wrote his brother
Thomas, seeking means of pacifying his creditors before sailing for the
East:

St. James's Place—January 28th 1783

My dear Brother,

I received your letter last night informing me that on this day
you proposed to return to Gayton. I thought I should have seen
you in London. I yesterday wrote acquainting you of my long
wished exchange having arrived.

I wish you good diversion in the country, and believe me to be
with every tender wish for the happiness of your family.

Your most affectionate Brother

Ban. Tarleton

The Tarleton family was proud of Banastre and was willing to pay his debts and help him get ready for the voyage to India. Promptly Ban started closing down his establishment. He put his horses in Richard Tattersall's sales stables, but he offered his brothers first option on them.

There was now only one possibility of failure—the real possibility behind the talk of dropping Lord Shelburne from the Cabinet. Ban wrote Thomas:

St. James's Place, Febr 11. 83

My dear Brother

I have received your letter from Gayton enclosing information of the manner of supplying me with the money, I stand in need of—I am much indebted to you and my mother for your readiness and goodness on this occasion—Your enquiry about the time allowed to raise the 1200£ is answered by requesting you to do it as soon as you can with convenience—The form proposed in your letter, is very proper and acceptable & I readily subscribe to it—

I have this day spoken to Tattersall about the Hounds—He says there have been none yet proper for you exposed to sale since he received the order—The first good ones he will send to you. I have ordered all my horses to be put up Monday week at his repository —there are two very good hunters able to carry 14 stone and well bred—I ask 150£ for one and £100 for the other. They are to be bought in for 20£ under that price—If you have any wish about them let me know & your desires shall be complied with.

The India Business I am assured comes on next week—but departure must soon follow it.

Some people talk of a change in Administration. The preliminaries of peace are displeasing to most people & will be most severely combated on Monday in the House of Commons—

I send by this days Coach Lord Cornwallis's Answer to Sir Henry Clintons narration—

Take my assurance of my duty & sense of obligation to my Mother & give my sincerest respect & love to the rest of the Family—

Yours most affectionately
Ban. Tarleton

The change in administration came quickly. On February 14 Lord Shelburne resigned from the Cabinet. With the fall of Shelburne, Lord Cornwallis lost his sponsor for the post in India. In a coalition government the Duke of Portland nominated Lord North for Home secretary and Charles Fox for Foreign secretary. Both the Whigs and the Tories now had to wait for the action of the King.

As he waited, Banastre was constantly with Mary. "The Perdita's box at the Opera house is fitting up in the most elegant style; the chairs, etc., etc., are pink satin, and it is ornamented with glasses in the Parisian taste," said the Morning Herald of February 20. Soon the newspapers were in an uproar over the train of beaux, ex-treasury secretaries, and martial heroes in Mary's splendid box.

Extravagance was second nature to Mary, but she also had an innate kindness, a delicacy of sentiment, a sympathy for the less fortunate. On February 22 the *Morning Herald* published a story that helped balance the popular impression. A carpenter, while repairing her house in Berkeley Square, fell to his death. He left his family destitute. Out of her dwindling funds Mrs. Robinson set aside a small annuity for his widow and children—an example, the reverend editor exhorted, that the prudish of London might well emulate!

That evening Ban and Mary went to the masquerade at the Pantheon. Next day the *Morning Post* observed: "The Perdita and the Tarleton paired off very early."

They went happily to the next masquerade at the Pantheon. On March 5 the fashion reporter for the *Morning Post* observed: "Various elegant and fancy dresses were sported on this occasion, at the head of which must be ranked that of the Perdita, composed of brown and pink, which was relieved and decorated with the greatest taste: Col. T——, on whose arm she reclined the greatest part of the evening, appeared as an Huzzar."

Mrs. Bate in the *Morning Herald* set a new standard for fashion reporters. After noting Mary's brown and pink costume, she devoted her column to Ban's uniform. "Col. Tarleton and the Perdita were arm in arm the whole night; the Colonel was dressed in a similar uniform to that which he wore at the head of his legion in America, only more superb; a blue jacket and waistcoat embroidered with silver, and small sugar-loaf silver buttons, not unlike a hussar; a pair of buckskin breeches likewise embroidered, and a pair of neat boots of uncoloured leather, which joined close to the breeches knee, and fitted as tight as a silk stocking; he wore a buff belt over his jacket, from which was suspended a very large scymetar, and a helmet on his head. The uniform was very striking, and the colonel being a handsome figure, it had a very pleasing effect."

The expensive finery did not escape the scrutiny of Tarleton's creditors. They began presenting their bills. On March 8 he wrote Thomas: "My departure has been so publicly announced in the Newspapers—that all my bills have been presented—some rather rudely. I wish you would let me draw upon you for three or four hundred pounds at a month or two months date till the loan business is adjusted."

Ban was now constantly with the noble and titled gamblers around the Prince of Wales. Play was high in that golden circle. In two years his Royal Highness had squandered £800,000. The Duke of Bedford, with £70,000 a year, could afford to lose. The Duke of Chartres, with and annual income of £600,000, set a staggering pace on his visits to London. Charles Fox, whose father, Lord Holland, had already paid

£140,000 in gambling debts for his sons, was insatiable: he roomed in St. James's Street in order to be near Brooks's Club.

The *Morning Herald* reported that the Prince was said to have lost £30,000 "to a certain popular character." Then Ban's luck changed. On March 19 he again asked permission to draw upon his older brother for £400. Next day the *Morning Herald* exclaimed: "A certain Colonel is said to have lost lately at Brooks's upwards of £30,000 and a great part of it to a would be Minister."

On April 2 the would-be Minister entered the Cabinet. King George accepted Charles Fox as Foreign secretary in the Portland administration. But even in a coalition government there was wrangling enough to postpone the confirmation of Lord Cornwallis. As Tarleton waited orders from his Lordship, he sank deeper into debt.

Finally he could go no further and retain honorable place among the friends of the Prince. His only recourse was another appeal to his family. So he wrote Thomas:

> St. James's Place
> May 5th 1783
>
> My dear Brother Tarleton
> To you, as the Head of the family I address this letter; to which, I desire you will after consulting my Relations give a serious, quick, and definitive answer—
> Before I plunge deeper into play which may be my destruction, I make this earnest proposal: If my friends will lend me money to pay my debts, which amount to near three thousand pounds: I most solemnly pledge myself to them to quit London and my present connexion instantly, to come into the country till I imbark for the E. Indies and never to play again for more than five pounds during my life—
> The money I hope I shall be able to pay again if I go to India; that I trust will produce it: If I stay in England Marriage or some other event may—
> If my friends do not assent to my request: I must endeavor to sell my Commission and play on. This road is dark and I wish not to be a traveller but in case of refusal to my proposition, I must—
> I shall not write more to varnish or mislead, weigh this last thought well—
> If I quit my present plan of life now by my high rank in the Army and my reputation as a military man, I may be saved; If I persevere and am unfortunate I am destroyed—
> God bless you,
> I wish an answer by express
> I am your affectionate & obliged Brother
> Ban. Tarleton

Ban's plans to quit London and his "connexion" prostrated Mary. On May 6 the *Morning Post* reported: "Mrs. Robinson has been for some days past extremely indisposed at her home in Berkeley Square, but is now in a fair way of recovery."

The newspapers reported that Secretary Fox called at Mary's home daily. They also reported that the Prince was disturbed and made constant inquiry about her.

Into this chaos Mr. Benwell of Long Acre delivered Mary's new carriage. "Great praise is due Mr. Benwell for the neat and elegant style in which he has executed the design of this matchless and superb equipage," exclaimed the Morning Post of May 29.

The superior and wonderful taste Mrs. Robinson has displayed in her new vis-a-vis exceeds the utmost limits of fanciful elegance, at the same time that it is perfectly neat even in the minutest article. The body is brown richly ornamented with a border of mosaic painting of straw and silver. In the middle of the door panel is a mantle of pink and silver, lined with ermine, which encloses an oval, in which the cypher half appears amidst the rays of the rising sun. Beneath rests a lion couchant. The side panels are similar to the doors, leaving out the mantle. The lining is straw coloured silk, ornamented, and superbly decorated with pink & silver lace, embroidered with singular magnificence. The hammer-cloth is entirely composed of the embroidered lace, and pink & silver fringe alternately so as to cover the whole of the festoon. The carriage is straw and silver, sumptuously ornamented with large silver buckles, joints, springs, &c. &c. &c. Mrs. Robinson may now, with infinite propriety, lay claim to a title she justly deserves, and without flattery, be proclaimed the Priestess of Taste.

The newspapers noted that Ban had gone into hiding. On May 29 the Morning Post snickered: "An irresistible Colonel, it is said, is at present non est inventus, at least in public." Next day it added: "On Thursday last Colonel Tarleton arrived at Liverpool from London."

∽

Banastre had gone to plead with his family. The widow and sons of John Tarleton were wealthy and highly respected. Thomas and John were provincial businessmen who had never lost a fortune across a faro table. Mrs. Jane Tarleton hated gambling and she loathed Mary Robinson. The family was adamant.

So Ban galloped back to London. He was in serious trouble. His note for £320 with Drummond was coming due on June 9. The India business had collapsed, and Lord Cornwallis had gone to his home at Culford.

In a desperate mood Banastre wrote his mother:

St. James Place, Saturday, May 31st, 1783

My dear Madam,

I travelled without stop till I arrived here—I have been very busy since my arrival, and after revolving each circumstance & trying every possible means in my power I find my Situation almost desperate—My Lord Cornwallis is out of town for a few days—His assistance & advice I cannot have in time to proceed against a *disagreeable event* which must happen: a note of mine for £320 to Messrs Drummond the Bankers becomes due the 9th of next month—the money was lent me, upon my promissory note —If you can assist me with the above sum, you will much oblige me—I will endeavor to do all in my power, not to trouble my friends in regard to my *other* affairs, and acquaint them how they are likely to turn out—

I'm really sorry to make this application being fully sensible of all past favors—

Believe me your much obliged & affectionate Son

Ban. Tarleton

Colonel Tarleton's chaotic affairs were now a general topic of conversation. Someone started a rumor that he had committed suicide. This came to the attention of the Prince and he told Banastre.

A doleful letter went off to Thomas:

St. James's Place. June 3, 1783

My dear Brother

I am at a loss what to do & what to say—Weltje is very importunate for his money and I can at present devise no way to satisfy him—It is lucky I returned when I did to this place for a report was prevalent (the Prince of Wales told it me) that I had shot myself—God forbid!

If I had 1000£ I could do something, propose something—at present I can do nothing—I'm going to try the Secretary of War —I am afraid at last all my commissions must go—I can say no more.

Adieu Dear Brother

Ban. Tarleton

I wrote to my Mother soon after I arrived—Drummond & Weltje must be paid.

After a week Banastre again appealed to his mother:

St. James's Place, June 7th

My dear Madam

I wrote to you this day week immediately after my arrival in town—

My affairs wear a very gloomy aspect—I have asked leave to sell my commission & retain my rank; have yet received no answer—

I mentioned in my letter to you that 320£ would be very serviceable—I hope to God you have complied with my request. Mr.
Drummond's note is now due. I wrote likewise to my Brother—
if he could assist me to pay Weltje; something might be done, or
else destruction is inevitable—

I can say no more because I cannot give you comfort by anything I have to say at present—Adieu—

Your most
affectionate & obliged Son
Ban. Tarleton

When Lieutenant Colonel Tarleton attempted to sell his commissions in the Army and in the British Legion, he received an unexpected
setback. On June 9 General Fitzpatrick sent him an order "for disband-
ing the Regiment of Light Dragoons under your command." He was
reduced to half-pay of £173 a year. But the maneuver by the War
Office, in creating a British regiment of Americans, most of whom
Major Hanger had already settled in Nova Scotia, allowed the Green
Dragoon to be gazetted in the Army List as lieutenant colonel of the
American Dragoons.

Old Mrs. Jane Tarleton had great moral courage. She loved Banastre
as a mother often loves a wayward son. She was proud of his friendship
with the Prince of Wales, but she knew that the Prince was profligate.
She also thought that the heart of Ban's trouble was Mary Robinson.

She would pay Banastre's debts only if he would settle on the Continent:

1783

My dear Son

I have already answered your Letter you wrote in the Morning
of the 7th instant. Your last unwelcome favor of the same date I
only received Yesterday & am truly distressed & alarmed at the
representation you have given me of the state of Your affairs
which I find still wear the same gloomy aspect, without the least
appearance of an alteration for the better were the measures pursued, which I have been under the disagreeable necessity so earnestly & repeatedly to recommend to Your serious consideration—
I am still inclined to think They would extricate you from Your
present difficulties but nothing (in case you entertain no expectation of going in a Military Capacity to the Indies) but a determined resolution on Your part to abandon Your present scene of
folly & dissipation & retire to France or Germany & there to live
in the Most economical & frugal plan will ever keep you independent where you will one day find the greatest blessing in life—
being perfectly acquainted from *Experience* with Your unfortunate turn for *expense & the inclination You have for play*—After
Your retreat to the Continent which *I hope will not be deferr'd,*
if your Attorney will prepare a Schedule of Your affairs & when

the nature & extent of the demands against you are properly explained & in what manner they can be compromised the most to Your advantage: Your friends here will exert themselves in Your favor as far as prudence & their own situation will permit, but I must once more beg leave to assure You of the moral impossibility to pay near the amount of Your debts, as I fear they are much more considerable then you have at present any conception of. When your affairs are liquidated & You can return with safety to England, I must insist on Your residence in the country with your Friends, who will be always happy to see You & endeavour to render Your stay amongst them as agreeable as possible, as they are convinced, if after Your return You was to be permitted to live in town, that no fortune could support Your boundless extravagance—I shall be glad to hear that You have laid down Your carriage & dismissed that useless train of Men Servants & also that you have given up your House in St. James's Place & have taken less expensive Lodgings—in one word I wish to see a thorough reform in Your conduct before You go abroad that I may place some confidence in Your promises—You may easily imagine what heart felt sorrow & the pain & distress of mind it gives to be reduced to the dreadfull necessity of expressing myself in this manner to one who I once flattered myself would have proved so great an ornament to himself & comfort to me & all his *Friends.*

God bless You & believe me

Your truly affectionate Mother

The gentleman you intrust Your affairs with I hope will be one of those that was mentioned to You here—

Banastre had borrowed money from Weltjie to pay his debts of honor. If he should flee to the Continent without repaying him, Weltjie would tell the Prince and Ban would be disgraced in the eyes of his future king. He refused to leave and wrote another appeal to Thomas, begging the family to save him from debtor's prison: "If you & my Mother acquiesce I bind myself to my first letter on the subject if desired—Any bills at distant date might be discounted—Weltjie or Drummond—Write definitively I beseech you for my being in the King's Bench I imagine would not be a pleasant circumstance I presume to you or my Mother—"

Banastre's attempt to frighten his family aroused his mother. After deliberation she answered:

June 16, 1783

My dear Son

I was much surprised at the receipt of Your Letter of the 13th instant, which was wrote in a stile I by no means approve of—everything in my power has been attempted to save you from the situation to which unfortunately for your connections Your im-

prudence has reduced You to, & to which it is unnecessary to inform You they have not by any means been instrumental in—You
must also in justice to Your friends confess what they have done
on different occasions: they have endeavored to save You from
that fate which has been the certain consequence of Your many
indiscretions, not to call them by a harder name.

Mr. Drummonds Note I should have little objection to pay if
You would quit & retire out of the Kingdom till some steps could
be taken to compromise Your other affairs which I still think cannot with propriety be done whilst You are on the spot. I shall not
bind myself to a specific sum with a view to a composition as that
measure must & will depend on the real state of Your Circumstances when they are thoroughly investigated, nor shall I entrust
You with any Authority for that purpose—Your brother has absolutely refused to pay Weltjie's debts or to hear his name mentioned except on the footing of Your other Creditors—You cannot surely plead ignorance of the situation in which You know
the best of Fathers & Husbands left me, when he bequeath'd me
£5000 to dispose of by will amongst my children—You have
already had from me near £2000—the remaining £3000 I wish
to divide amongst the other four who have all ways behaved with
the greatest affection—& you cannot wish to deprive me of the
little comfort which I enjoy in Life or reduce me to poverty.

Your truly affectionate
Mother

As Banastre waited to hear the decision of his family, he turned to
Lord Cornwallis. He wrote a proposal for settling his debts and showed
it to his Lordship. Then he posted it to his family:

New Bond Street—June 16, 1783
My dear Friends

After very serious deliberation and anxious reflexion on the state
of my affairs, I shall state the result of such thoughts as my ulti-
mate proposition—My friends are able, and inclined to assist me;
they know my embarrassments; the amount of my debts has been
made known to them; and the sums I have borrowed without
interest, I have most repeatedly mentioned—

They have likewise had communicated to them my design
of travelling, in case of their acquiescence to my request; which
journey I promise to undertake, not like a young man of pleasure
but as Lieut. Col. Tarleton whose Regiment is now ordered to be
disbanded in America: But before, I can possibly with honor to
myself, put *this* scheme into execution, every just effort should be
made to arrange my affairs, which are distracted by dissipation
and play; lest loss of reputation attend me wherever I go—

In order that the pecuniary part may be as easy as possible to
my friends and that they may have a hold upon my future con-

duct, I make the following proposal—As no composition can be offer'd for money borrowed, suppose, past payment now, or bills at 3 months were given for half the amount of the 1000 gs. and a promise for a total liquidation within the year if my conduct is such as to merit the approbation of my friends during that period —perhaps this mode might accommodate all parties—a total and immediate payment would please me most—because my gratitude is concerned—

As to my other affairs, play debts &c I will give any attorney you are pleased to name the list and amount; that they may be settled in the most convenient way and agreeable to your directions—

The impatience of my creditors cannot be temporized with any longer than in receiving an answer to this letter—from that instant I shall take steps for an honorable & proper journey—or give my preference to a prison or a flight.

This letter must be shewn to Lord Cornwallis, and as he does me the honor to interest himself in my welfare, I shall ask his mediation in this business.

I take my leave, beseeching you to consider my dear friends, that tho' my reputation by my late actions, may be slightly sullied, it is not so tarnished but you have power yet to restore it—

Believe me with the greatest
Affection and regard,
Ban. Tarleton

Lord Cornwallis sympathized with the man he had raised from an obscure cornet to a national hero. His Lordship knew that an officer must settle his debts, even those of honor, and he had seen other soldiers entangled with women. He knew the great temptations in the society around the Prince. So he wrote Thomas, begging the Tarleton family to rescue Banastre and give him one more chance:

Mansfield Street, June 16th 1783

Sir

The very sincere regard which I have for your Brother, and my earnest desire of rescuing him, if Possible, from ruin, has induced me to take a liberty which I fear you will think unjustifiable, but as his friends have given so many proofs of their affection for him, I hope they will in this instance pardon my interference.

The plea for the payment of the borrowed money was suggested by me, and I cannot suppose my friend so divested of all sense of honour and gratitude as not to perform his part of the agreement, after a years probation he will not surely again plunge into those follies which have so nearly destroyed him.

I am sensible that his past conduct has not merited your confidence, yet when I consider that his reputation, and all the future prospect of character in the world is at stake, I cannot help flatter-

ing myself that you will give him one more trial. I must again beg
that you will excuse the part which I have taken in this business,
and am, Sir,

> With great esteem
> Your most obedient
> & Most Humble Servant
>   Cornwallis

Immediately Thomas replied to Lord Cornwallis:

                                                    June 22
My Lord

I was honored on Friday last by the receipt of your Lordship's
most obliging letter in behalf of my Brother. I have this day layed
the state of his affairs as far as I have the least knowledge of them
before all his Friends. We are all willing that upon his immediate
quitting the Kingdom to pay his Note to Messrs. Drummond &
afterwards to call a meeting of his Creditors & to offer them the
best composition that it is in our power to make—The Col. must
be sensible that his friends have already paid very considerable
sums for him, more than prudence can justify in their situation.

Permit me my Lord to ask you if there is the least probability
of the Col. going out in any military capacity to India—that being
the scheme that for some time past has been held out to his
Friends by him.

> I am your Lordship's
> Most ob't and most humble servant
>   Thomas Tarleton

By the same post Mrs. Jane Tarleton wrote her beleaguered son:

                                                    June 22
My dear Son

We have now to acknowledge the receipt of Your Letters of the
16th instant, also one from Lord Cornwallis the contents of which
have been seriously & minutely considered—Your Friends have
neither ability nor can you suppose they have ever intertained the
most distant idea of pursuing the line of conduct which has been
pointed out by you respecting the final settlement of Your Affairs,
the impossibility of which is to obvious to every person the least
conversant in business nor can we think of advancing so large a
sum as £1000 without obtaining some security that You shall not
be molested by Your other Creditors till some method can be
adopted to extricate You from every difficulty that at present attends You. As we are fully persuaded partial & unjust payments
never remove the difficulties which you suffer but only prolong
them, We must again advise Your immediate retreat from this
Kingdom tho we are entire Strangers to the plan You may have on

the Continent or what you mean by travelling as Col. Tarleton. All that we insist on is that You live on Your pay as it is impossible after this effort ever to attempt to relieve You more. When we are acquainted with Your arrival abroad You may depend that not a moment shall be lost'd in procuring a real state of Your affairs with a view to compromise them in the best manner we can. Drummond's Note we exclude from this General observation as that shall be paid directly. We could have wished that You would have been more explicit in Your Letter as to Your future prospects You have in Life for if You have no other dependance than Your half pay, Your conduct must be the reverse of what it has been or You will be plunged into the same distress again.

Your Brother T has wrote by this post to Ld. Cornwallis to which I refer You. God bless You & send You peace of Mind—

Your truly affectionate
Mother

On June 29 Mrs. Jane Tarleton confirmed the family's offer. With breaking heart but with great integrity she laid down the conditions to Banastre. "London cannot, nor must not, be your place of residence."

Hereafter she could give him only "a hearty welcome to my house, there to live on the most frugal scheme, for you have reduced me to this alternative."

Then Jane Tarleton disposed of the woman she hated: "I must also add before I conclude this letter that it will give me real pleasure & satisfaction to hear that Your connection with Mrs. Robinson is at an end; without that necessary step all my endeavors to save You from impending destruction will be ineffectual."

∽

As his family concerted plans to drive Banastre from England, he was in the excitement around the Prince of Wales. On August 12, 1783, his Royal Highness would come of age. Secretary Fox proposed that the Prince be granted £100,000 a year. In June the Duke of Portland submitted this proposal to the King. After acrimonious negotiation, King George granted his son £62,000 a year, £50,000 from the Civil List and £12,000 in revenue from the Duchy of Cornwall. Then Parliament voted £60,000 to establish his residence at Carlton House.

As plans for Carlton House went forward, the Reverend Henry Bate said in an editorial in the *Morning Herald* of June 30: "The Prince of Wales will never have a better opportunity of evincing his attention to valour and military worth than by providing in his new establishment for Colonel Tarleton. That officer's merit will, when the history of America is read by posterity, throw a reproach on those who neglect him during the present hour."

Lord Cornwallis did not wish to see Banastre provided for at Carlton House. He knew that hope of reformation lay only in getting him away from the Prince and out of the kingdom. Again he wrote Thomas.

Mansfield Street. July 1st, 1783

Sir,

I received the favor of your obliging letter of the 22nd, & am much pleased to find that you did not take in ill part my officious concern on behalf of your Brother.

It was intended by the late administration that I should go with the supreme command both civil & military to India, if that event had taken place I intended that your Brother should accompany me; so that he had grounds for his assertion that there was a probability of his going to India.

It is a painful task for me again to enter upon the state of his affairs, when I must begin by acknowledging that his friends have already done more than he had a right to expect; But I am very anxious for a last trial to save him, which can only be done by getting him out of this Country. When I wrote last I thought that his debt to Mr. Drummond for money lent to him without interest or security had amounted to about a thousand pounds. I now find that I had misunderstood your Brother, & that he owed to Mr. Drummond about three hundred & near seven hundred of the same species of debt to Mr. Weltjie, the man who keeps one of the principal Clubs in St. James' Street. His quitting England without either paying or giving some security to Mr. Weltjie, would undoubtedly do the Col. infinite discredit, effectually blast his reputation to the whole world: If part of these two debts could be paid & the remainder secured he may be saved from a disgrace from which he can never recover, and, I flatter myself, from a conviction that there is much goodness of heart at bottom that he could not be so lost to all sense of honor & gratitude as to involve himself in past difficulties from which he could never hope honestly to extricate himself.

I must again ask pardon for the liberty which I have taken at the same time that I indulge a hope that his friends may be able for this once to settle the business so as to preserve him from irrecoverable disgrace.

I am Sir, with great esteem
Your Most Obed. &
Most Humble Servant
Cornwallis

Banastre again visited Lord Cornwallis. Then he wrote his mother:

London, July 3, 1783

My dear Madam

I have seen my Lord Cornwallis since I last wrote to you—His Lordship had mistaken the description I had given him of my debt of £1000: He understood it to be all due to Drummond, whereas the greatest part of it was due to Weltjie.

The impossibility of my quitting the Kingdom, with the calumny that would fall upon me by such a borrow'd debt, struck Lord Cornwallis as forcibly as myself, and I promised to write to my friends on the subject—I hope to God his & my application may meet with success—

My Friends are anxious to know what I mean by travelling as Lieut. Col. Tarleton? A plain answer solves the question. My object is economy, to perfect my knowledge of the languages and obtain science as a military man—

My plan of destination and my views I will hereafter communicate—I shall always attend to your wishes

With the utmost gratitude
I remain
Your affectionate Son
Ban. Tarleton

After a week Mrs. Jane Tarleton answered. There had been a family consultation. As a businessman who believed that debts for food and clothes and lodging came ahead of gaming debts, Thomas had refused to join in any measures which would pay Weltjie before the other creditors. So she would pay both Drummond and Weltjie:

July 11

My dear Son

I have now to acknowledge the receipt of Your Letter of ye 3d instant, also one from Ld. Cornwallis, to your Brother which his absence from home has prevented him from answering, but I don't doubt he will reply to it by tomorrows post at which time I expect his return to this place.

I have repeatedly addressed You respecting the situation of Your affairs & pointed out in the strongest manners the only line of conduct that ought to be pursued to extricate You from the difficulties to which Your follies & independence have reduced You to. That is to make a fair & impartial distribution amongst all Your creditors without exception of the money which I am obliged to advance, Your Brother I must again inform you having absolutely refused to concur in any mode of payment by which Weltjie will have a preference to the rest of Your creditors, as that Debt must have originated from play or from money borrowed with that view to which You cannot be ignorant of my great aversion to & also my final resolve not to pay any engagements of that nature for the future. Ld. Cornwallis & Yourself having laid so great stress upon the discharge of Drummond & Weltjie's demand, I am induced to consent to it on the Express condition that I am not again troubled or called on for the payment of the rest of Your debts now or at any other period & if

You are determined to put this plan into execution, I shall be deprived of giving You any farther assistance as my Circumstances will be greatly reduced by this measure—

I must also beg leave to observe that in acquiescing to this scheme I am still of opinion that this partial and unjust payment will reflect disgrace & tend to blast Your reputation infinitely more than calling Your Creditors together & distributing £1000 equally amongst them. As I shall be obliged to give six months notice to call in money from Interest to the amount above alluded to I shall not be able to pay Weltjie & Drummond before that time—they may then depend on having their demand against You punctually discharged with which proposal I make no doubt they will be glad to comply.

I am much surprised You have not yet made me acquainted with your view or intended destination on the Continent or taken the least notice of the paragraph in my last Letter in regard to Mrs. Robinson—I must desire in Your next You will be more explicit on both these subjects.

Your truly affectionate
Mother

After his mother had written Banastre, Thomas drafted his reply to Lord Cornwallis:

July 13

My Lord

I had the honor of finding Your Lordship's obliging Letter on my return here—after a few days' absence—I have laid your Lordship's kind favor before the Col.'s Friends, who are willing to engage themselves to pay the amount of his debts to Messrs. Drummond & Weltjie in Six Months provided that he will instantly quit the Kingdom—for I am very sorry to add that little reliance can be placed upon him during his stay in this Country— His Friends, my Lord, are extremely anxious to hear of his departure but he has never informed them of the place of his destination or the style he means to travel in—

I am my Lordship's
Most obt. & most hum. Svt.
Thomas Tarleton

Thomas sent his letter to John for approval. John was more direct. He wanted Lord Cornwallis to know that his plea had moved the family to rescue Banastre: "I think the above very proper but it would not be amiss if you was to inform Lord C. that his Friends are resolved not to advance more than £1000 to pay the debt above ment., & that even this measure was adopted owing to his Lordships intercession on behalf of Ban.".

The promise of Mrs. Tarleton to pay Ban's promissory note for £320 satisfied Drummond. But knowing that the Tarletons were wealthy,

Weltjie threatened legal action unless he received security for his £700. Ban knew that his mother would never give written security for money lost in gambling.

He called upon Lord Cornwallis for advice. His Lordship understood the nature of debts of honor. He knew that Weltjie was a confidential servant of the Prince and that unless he were satisfied he would ruin Tarleton's reputation with the heir to the throne. So he signed Tarleton's bond for £700.

Two weeks later his Lordship wrote Thomas:

Mansfield Street, August 5, 1783

Sir

If I had not been obliged to quit London suddenly on account of my Son's illness, I should have informed you sooner that in consequence of your letter of the 13th ult. the Col. has agreed to quit England immediately & has most solemnly promised me to live in a retired manner in some country town in France, and apply himself to learning the French language, and the study of his profession. I cannot believe that it will be possible for him to depart so far from all sense of honor as to break his word with me.

Mr. Drummond was perfectly satisfied with your assurance but Mr. Weltjie threatened to proceed to the utmost extremities unless he had some written security—I have, therefore, to prevent anything injurious to his reputation joined in a Bond with the Col. for the payment of Mr. Weltjie's debt in six months.

I am, Sir,
Your most obdt. & most Humble Servant
Cornwallis

∽

While Ban had been struggling with his debts or badgering his family, Mary had almost dropped from sight. Many wondered how the Cyprian priestess could have afforded such a luxurious cabriole. To its readers the *Morning Post* confided: "The Perdita's new *vis-a-vis* is said to be the aggregate of a few stakes laid at Brooks's which the competitors were not able to decide. Mr. Fox, therefore, proposed that as it could not be better applied than to the above purpose, that the *Perdita* should be presented with an elegant carriage. The illnatured call it *Love's Last Stake* or *The Fools of Fashion*."

Her admirers expected to see Mary parading *Love's Last Stake* in the charioteering circles of Hyde Park. She failed to do so, and her absence soon evoked comment. The *Morning Herald* of July 8 said: "The Perdita so seldom appears in public that her presence excites universal admiration."

Mrs. Bate was watching. Soon she had the secret that kept Mary from charioteering. She learned why Ban had failed to answer his mother's

questions about Mrs. Robinson. Said the *Morning Herald* on July 12:
"The Perdita is pregnant!"

The *Public Advertiser* was less than chivalrous. On July 24 it railed:
"The Perdita very properly has determined for the present not to figure
away in her conspicuous carriage made by Benwell: she, not without
reason, bears the Scorn and Indignation of the insulted Public. For
surely that such Infamy may be at all tolerated, it should be latent
altogether. The moment it becomes obvious and obtrusive, it becomes
intolerable. To Virtue and good Order the Provocation is great: and
the resentment, to be at all appropriate, should be great also."

As soon as his principal creditors had been satisfied, Banastre started
packing for his trip to the Continent. He told Mary of the action of his
family. She was nervous and irritable, and there was an agonizing scene.
He begged her to go with him, but she proudly refused. She was in no
condition to travel.

Left alone, Mary became desperate and decided to borrow the money
and pay Weltjie. She sent her footman to Brooks's Club with a note
asking Charles Fox to lend her £800. He sent her £300 and promised
to send £500 next morning.

In the meantime, after the Treaty of Paris the Duke of Lauzun had
turned the French army in America over to subordinates and on
March 11 had sailed for France. After reporting to the King and his
ministers, Lauzun rushed over to London. That evening he was with Mary.

When Banastre failed to appear, they became alarmed. They hastened to Mary's box in the Opera and waited there. Finally she sent her
footman to Ban's favorite haunts. He returned with the news that Colonel Tarleton had started to Dover.

Torn by fear and love, Mary determined to follow him. She wanted
only to keep him with her, for with the £300 he could safely return
to London. At two o'clock she hired a post chaise and set off for Dover.

The horses seemed to creep along the Dover Road and even though
the coach lurched and rumbled she fell asleep. Suddenly she awoke
with a scream. She realized she was in labor and immediately turned
back to London. Somehow the midwifery was bungled, and in the
ordeal she was paralyzed. Mary had paid her forfeit to love.

Banastre had gone to Southampton rather than Dover for his passage
to France. Without knowledge of the tragedy in his wake, on July 25
he wrote his mother from Hampshire: "You desire me to write more
fully about Mrs. Robinson—the connection is closed. She is too proud
to follow me and she has long been too generous, always I should have
said to encrease the poverty of any man—I most solemnly assure you
she has not been the occasion of my bankruptcy—Play alone which I
abjure, has—I won't now complain of my bad fortune, it is too late—"

The news of Mary's miscarriage spread. On July 31 the *Morning
Herald* reported: "Mrs. Robinson lies dangerously ill at her house in

Berkeley Square; the envious part of her own sex attribute her indisposition to chagrin at the declining influence of her charms; if that is really the case, the name of Perdita will soon be too truly applied to this once all-conquering impure."

The *haut ton* as well as the *demimonde* were interested in the recovery of the invalid. On August 13 in a letter from Brighton, Lord Pembroke wrote Lord Herbert in Calais: "About Mrs. Robinson—her face is still pretty, but illness has brought on a disadvantageous additional scowl to it; & as to her body, she is quite defaite, *se trainant a piene*, a perfect Sciondolana. She may possibly come about again, but she must not go any more to an opera on the day of miscarriage."

21

Ode to Valour

THE PRINCE OF WALES drove down for the summer to Brighthelm-stone, a sleepy little town on the coast of Sussex. Crowds followed: lords and ladies, heroes and Cyprians, panders, quacks, and money-lenders. On August 22 the *Morning Herald* advised its readers: "Some days since the Perdita flew off like a comet from her house in Berkely Square and headed for the coast of Sussex!"

At Brighton, as Brighthelmstone was soon renamed, there was an Indian, a former surgeon of the East India Company, who had opened a hospital in which he treated rheumatics with scented steam baths and massage. Mary wanted an excuse to follow the gay throng, and her physician recommended that she try these vapor baths. Where was her gallant Colonel? "Tarleton is at this instant with Mrs. Robinson," Lord Pembroke wrote Lord Herbert in Calais on August 25. "Why do you suppose him on the Continent?"

Unknown to Lord Pembroke, and in accordance with his promise to his family and to Lord Cornwallis, Ban had wandered into exile. On September 8 the *Morning Herald* published an account of one of his parting escapades:

> About ten days ago Col. T—l—n, when at one of our watering places (Margate) famous for its *Faro Bank*, received a letter from a person who signed himself D——. The letter desired a private meeting about three quarters of a mile from the Town on par-ticular business.
>
> The Colonel neither knew the writer, nor could he conceive any idea of what nature this particular business was. He showed it to two other officers who happened to be present, General —— and Major ——, and they agreeing that it was a challenge ad-vised the Colonel to take his pistols, go to the place, and said they

would attend him. He accordingly went and met the person un-
attended, whom he accosted with the very natural question of
"Pray what do you want with me?" The person replied "We are
not alone, Sir," "Nor shall we be" said the Colonel. "for I know you
not; and you can have nothing to say to me which can be improper for these gentlemen to hear—" The stranger then took the
Colonel aside, and told him that all concerned with the Faro
Banks were sharpers; and that if the Colonel would follow his,
the stranger's directions, he would teach him how to rob them all.
The indignation of the Colonel rose, as may be imagined, and he
would have put the fellow to death, had not the General and
Major interposed, and mitigated the rascal's punishment to a
severe kicking.

On enquiry he proved to be D——, the noted foreign sharper &
blackleg. The story circulated immediately and our Germanic
Chevalier was obliged to decamp the next day.

After Banastre crossed the Channel, he tried to follow the advice of
Lord Cornwallis to settle in a village in southern France and devote
himself to professional studies. As he moved inland, he received news
of Mary's illness. Conscience stricken, he tortured himself for the tragedy
he had brought upon her. From Douai on September 23 he confided to
his brother Thomas:

. . . I have been miserable & now not happy—Wisdom & fortitude ought to teach Philosophy—I trust I shall attain it soon, for
I have had adversity enough to chase away all passions.

I reveal to You I have not forgot Mrs. R—— Oh God such a
conflict I hope never again to encounter—I hear she is dangerously
ill—But no more—I shall grow distracted.

Hoping to learn more about Mary, Ban turned back to Calais. Here
he joined the colony of English exiles who had escaped debtor's prison
by flight. Then he wrote his mother:

Epains Calais Oct 6th, 1783

My dear Madam

I am return'd to this place to await supplies & letters from England. I shall, I hope soon receive letters from the Commander-in-
Chief & Lord Cornwallis.

I shall inform you of my plan as soon as it is arranged—At
present I give all my time to attain a perfect knowledge of the
language & to professional studies—

I must lament for ever that my country has done nothing for
me since my return from America—The fatigues I have undergone,
the perils I have encountered, and the military honor I have won
certainly deserve compensations from England—Other people's

services of much inferior nature have met with reward—Mine are cruelly, tho of very brilliant nature, at present, neglected.

I return You Madam many many thanks for your proof of kindness, affection & generosity. They are dear to me as the inattention of my native country is disgustful—

> I am dear Madam
> Your most dutiful & obliged Son
> Ban. Tarleton

Thomas refused to answer Ban's letter. Again the remorseful hero reminded his brother of his sacrifice:

Calais, Oct. 25, 1783

My dear Brother

I have wrote twice to You since I left London in the summer, once from Sir. H. Featherstone, & my last from Douay—I am sorry I have no answer—I shall not enlarge upon the anxiety I feel on this occasion, or mention the conflicts of mind I have undergone, to please my friends—The sacrifice I have made & the services I have rendered my country certainly merit other treatment—But no more—Adversity or Philosophy may teach content & resignation—I wrote to my dear Mother some time since from this place: I told her that I waited here for letters—I still am in the same situation & except that my servt. Shaw, feeling my situation altered and his place & profit diminished, joined the rest of the world & abandoned my service—His accompt was a long one: He brought me in debtor as you may imagine; I had no other mode of settling it but giving almost all the money I had: A draught upon my agent for the arrears of pay of 79 Regt. for £35, & two draughts upon my mother for 50 & 40 each—

I gave him a letter to Brotherton who owes me money to take up the two draughts upon my Mother which I sincerely wish he may do—If he does not, I shall be chagrined—for my Mother has certainly conducted herself very affectionately towards me notwithstanding her present silence: I do not now wish her to trouble herself with the above mentioned bills—I had no other resource to get quit of ingratitude—I live cheap—I devote my time to study which cannot soothe a mind agitated as mine is & has been— Whatever is my fate I sincerely wish yours a happy one.

> Adieu
> I'm yours affectionately
> Ban. Tarleton

Still angry over Ban's behavior, Thomas did not answer. But with a mother's love, Jane Tarleton wrote her unhappy son a letter filled with kindness. He answered:

Calais Nov. 21, 1783

My dear Madam

I had the pleasure of a letter from you ten days ago. I was sorry to be obliged to give John Shaw the draughts I did upon you. I had no other resource—they must meet their fate—If I had had money I would have paid them & left this place a long time ago. Which now I hope to be able to quit in a few days & direct my route towards Tours—No amusement, no exercise have I had here, save what I found in my study—I have received a letter lately from Lord Cornwallis—He presses me much to leave Calais—

One thought strongly implanted in my breast no retirement or length of time will get the better of & that is that *I have been infamously used by my country*—

Believe me, dear Madam
Your most affectionate
Ban. Tarleton

In the meanwhile, after the fashionable world had returned to London, Mary lingered at Brighton. The steam baths limbered her stiff joints, and slowly she came about again. She regained some use of her limbs, but she was never again able to stand alone nor to completely flex her fingers.

Without Banastre, Mary was lonely. The crying gulls over the deserted summer resort and the whistling gales of autumn filled her with depression. She longed for the gay sounds of the city; she wanted to go home.

On November 28 the *Morning Herald* announced her return to London: "The *Lybian Lions* that lie couchant under the burning sun of the *vis-a-vis* of the *all subduing* Perdita, after having been concealed from the public for some time, range abroad with a fierceness equal to that of the tyger which drew, of old, the chariot of Cupid."

Mary went back to their old haunts. But London seemed empty to her, and she was pathetic. Miss Laetitia Hawkins preserved a doleful vignette of one of her visits to the opera: "On a table in one of the waiting-rooms of the Opera House was seated a woman of fashionable appearance, still beautiful, but not in the bloom of beauty's pride; she was not noticed except by the eye of pity. In a few minutes two liveried servants came to her, and they took from their pockets long white sleeves, which they drew on their arms; they then lifted her up and conveyed her to her carriage; it was the then helpless paralytic *Perdita!*"

Yet Mary never complained, never spoke of her tragic ride. Wrote Maria Elizabeth: "Mrs. Robinson consoled herself with having affected the service she proposed by this unfortunate journey and never once was known peevishly to lament the irreparable consequences."

She now remembered only Ban's laughter and kindness. In her imagination he became the most dauntless of Britons, his attributes godlike. And so during her long wait for his return from France, Mary sang her love and admiration:

ODE TO VALOUR

Inscribed to Colonel Banastre Tarleton

Transcendent Valour!—godlike Pow'r!
Lord of the dauntless breast, and steadfast mien!
    Who, rob'd in majesty sublime,
    Sat in thy eagle-wafted car,
    And led the hardy sons of war,
    With head erect, and eye serene,
    Amidst the arrowy show'r;
        When unsubdued, from clime to clime,
    Young Ammon taught exulting Fame
O'er earth's vast space to sound the glories of thy name.

In long strophes Mary sang of "Valour." In Miltonic phrases she
hymned "chaos," "creation," and his "Word Supreme" which awoke
the "Human Form" sublime. She praised man for taming the steed and
subduing the lion by *Valour* alone.

From age to age on Fame's bright roll,
        Thy glorious attributes have shone!
        Thy influence soothes the soldier's pain,
    Whether beneath the freezing pole,
        Or basking in the torrid zone;
            Upon the barren thirsty plain,
    Led by thy firm and daring hand,
    O'er wastes of snow, o'er burning sand,
    Intrepid Tarleton chas'd the foe,
    And smiled in *Death's* grim face, and brav'd his
                                        with'ring blow!

Mary closed her hymn with an apostrophe to the man who had now
become the soul of all her thought and being.

Tarleton, thy mind, above the Poet's praise
Asks not the labour'd task of flatt'ring lays!
As the *Rare Gem* with innate lustre glows,
As round *the Oak* the gadding Ivy grows,
So shall *Thy Worth,* in native radiance live!
So shall the *Muse* spontaneous incense give!
Th' *Historic* page shall prove a lasting shrine,
Where Truth and Valour shall *Thy* laurels twine;
Where, with thy name, recording *Fame* shall blend
The *Zealous Patriot,* and the *Faithful Friend!*

∽

In late fall Ban left Calais. In his idleness he had thought of a way to pass the time and increase his reputation. He would write a history of the campaigns of 1780 and 1781. He wrote his plans to his mother:

St. Omer Dec. 15, 1783

My dear Madam

I have rec'd your kind letter & heartily congratulate you & rejoice at the additional laurel branches about your table.

I'm sorry to inform you that all prospect of war is over on the continent which is a great mortification to my ambition & a total defeat to my plans.

I should have retired to some village in France away from the sea coast but still in a daily expectation of a Box of maps & papers which are necessary for the sketch of the Campaigns of 80 & 81 which I have in hand—The package has pass'd several times between Dover & Bologne but never yet has arrived at Calais.

Another reason likewise will keep me some time near the sea coast of France which is, a rumour I have got that all the accompts in America will be again overlooked which will perhaps call me for a day or two in England—I hope my presence will be dispens'd with; let them call upon the rich & not upon the poor—I wish every Englishman will put his hand upon his heart & exclaim with as much truth as I can, that *he had served his country well & honestly—*

I shall endeavour to evade all calls to London upon this business, if I can do so & preserve my reputation—I think it very hard that I receive no promotion or no offer of service either civil or military—Patience begins to fail me—I hope Lord Cornwallis is my friend—I hate idleness, & should like employment any where.

Believe me with the greatest affection

Your obliged Son

Ban. Tarleton

Best love to Mrs. Falkner—continue my address as before

Banastre did not wish to offend Lord Cornwallis, especially in the matter of the bond to Weltjie. In early December he wrote Nathaniel Collyer, asking him to write Mrs. Jane Tarleton about meeting the payments to Drummond and Weltjie. Collyer did not know how to approach Mrs. Tarleton.

Tarleton wrote him:

France—Dec. 29th, 1783

My dear Sir

You say you are at a loss how to open a correspondence with my Mother relative to the payment of the 320£ to Drummonds, & the bond to Weltjie—You know the circumstances & can communicate them by letter at the same time declaring that I author-

ized you in such an undertaking—The time for the settling of
these affairs was appointed in Jan. By calling if you do not recollect
you can inform yourself of the date—It would be better to antici-
pate the payment than be behind hand with it, as my Lord Cornwallis may be called upon else, about the Bond—
    If you please you may inclose this letter.

Believe me
Yours
Ban. Tarleton

In London Mary spent a weary December and Yuletide. The new
year brought no respite. On January 22, 1784, Henry Bate said: "Envy
is generally foiled by its own weapons. The idea that Mrs. Robinson
can suffer an inconvenience for the want of a few thousand is the
greatest compliment that can be paid her—she could command the
purses of half our nobility—but she will not sacrifice her delicacy at the
shrine of avarice."

The reverend editor believed in justice. He dared champion those
overwhelmed by tragic circumstance. "The gallant Tarleton may with
an eye of sympathy and pity look upon his brave and wounded soldiers
just returned from America and exclaim 'We have served those who
neglect us. We have gained laurels, though we have not earned the
gratitude of those we fought for.' "

༄

In early January Banastre was joined by Major George Hanger. Much
had happened since these Legionnaires had parted in New York. After
the articles of peace had been signed, Hanger had obtained permission
to visit the Duke of Lauzun. Yet he feared to cross the ferry into Philadelphia wearing the uniform of the British Legion, "a corps not much
esteemed by the Americans," as he admitted. To his surprise, however,
he had been treated with the utmost courtesy, not only by the Duke of
Lauzun, but also by the leading families of Philadelphia. He had even
been invited to dine by the president of the Congress.

Sir Guy Carleton sent Hanger to Nova Scotia to supervise the settling
of the soldiers of the British Legion. When Sir Guy evacuated New York
on November 25, 1783, the Major sailed for home. Apprehensive about
his finances, he assigned the power of attorney jointly to Colonels
McMahon and Tarleton. Upon their advice he skirted debtor's prison
by landing in France rather than in England.

Many Englishmen besides Henry Bate were dismayed by the government's indifference to the veterans returning from defeat in America.
Richard Tattersall, of the famed waistcoat and horse fancy, whose auction mart had become the rendezvous for London's sporting bloods,
became interested in Hanger. "You have been robbed and plundered,"

he wrote the Major, advising him to come home. "I will bail you from everybody who may arrest you; and, if you cannot pay, I will."

Hanger immediately returned to London, and Tattersall invited him into his home at Hyde Park Corner. There the Major lived for nearly a year. He was arrested for debt, but Tattersall put up bail. When the case was heard, the jury, without leaving the jury box, returned a verdict for him. Free at last, he joined the gay set around the Prince of Wales.

Lord Cornwallis was pleased and on April 9 wrote Colonel Ross: "I saw George Hanger today; he has settled his affairs and tells me that he has between £400 and £500 to live on."

As soon as his mother had paid Drummond and Weltjie, Banastre began planning to return to England. Rumors had spread that Parliament was to be dissolved and a call issued for a general election. He wished to return to Liverpool and stand for Parliament.

John called upon Lord Cornwallis for advice and on March 3 wrote his mother:

> . . . I have this instant left Lord Cornwallis who assured me that he has given up all ideas of taking any command whatever in India, & that the Colonel on that account has not the most distant chance of being sent there & that he most strenuously advises you on no pretense to advance Banastre any money, or to pay any debts that in future he may contract, he condemns his conduct for still residing in Calais & Boulogne which places are cluttered with English Refugees, & are the most expensive on the Continent—
>
> Lord Cornwallis reprobates all thoughts of the Colonel's coming into Parliament, which he is of opinion would only compleat his ruin, without a glimpse of hope, of that measure being attended with any advantage to him, either in a military or political career, besides the utter impossibility of being able to support his extravagance in Town during the Session of Parliament, Lord C. has promised to write to him on these subjects, & to beg of him to leave his present situation, & to determine finally to settle at Tours, where he may have an opportunity of making himself master of the French & German Languages & where he may also improve himself in the knowledge of his profession.

In spite of his Lordship's advice, Banastre returned to London. Quietly he moved into Mary's home in Berkeley Square. "As he had just returned from Calais from spending his holidays whither the late change in administration forced him; having destroyed his military hopes, and even rendered his return to England in some degree problematical; though the present much indulged idea of a new parliament has brought him over, he now figures in the polite circles," said the anonymous *Memoirs of Perdita*.

"The Colonel's finances are insufficient for both, as his late trip to France serves to prove," continued the *Memoirs*. "During his absence Perdita has been confined by an illness, for which a severe rheumatism was the assigned cause. . . . Since the return of her admirer her appearance in public has been announced by some friendly hand 'that it was a pleasure to see this truly elegant creature once more abroad, after so many months absence.' It is also insinuated that her house in Berkeley Square is new painting, with elegant meritricious embellishments, and that she intends to write over the door *Qui Cunque Vult*."

Ban's family was dismayed. On March 25 John wrote his mother: "I have not seen Lord Cornwallis since Banastre's arrival in Town. I cannot, nor can you be ignorant of his Sentiments, respecting him, therefore it is unnecessary to wait upon his Lordship for further explanation. Parliament is dissolved, the proclamation being published for that purpose this morning."

The *London Chronicle* on March 30 informed its readers: "There are, it seems, no less than seven candidates started for Liverpool, at the head of which is Col. Tarleton."

Tarleton's return was the result of the defeat of Charles Fox's India Bill. As Foreign secretary Fox had tried to counteract the high-handed actions of Warren Hastings in governing India. He proposed that the administration of the East India Company be subordinated to a supreme body of seven commissioners appointed by Parliament.

The House of Commons passed the India Bill. But the King wrote a note with his own hand and sent it to the House of Lords: anyone voting for the Bill is "not only not his friend but would be considered by him his enemy." The bill failed. Fox wrote: "We are beat in the House of Lords by such treachery on the part of the King."

Parliament was dissolved on March 25. The Tories, led by William Pitt, and the great Whig aristocrats, led by Charles Fox, now joined in a struggle for power. Both parties appealed to the electorate.

Charles Fox stood for election in the borough of Westminster. Admiral Lord Hood and Sir Cecil Wray opposed him. The contest was rough, but the Prince of Wales canvassed the borough with "dear Charles." The great Whigs followed his example. Among the most effective canvassers was the Duchess of Devonshire, who purchased a vote from a plumper with a kiss!

With Tarleton campaigning in Liverpool, Mary threw her talents into the struggle for the election of Fox. Squibs, paragraphs, and songs flowed from her pen. But Lord Cornwallis wrote Colonel Ross: "Fox is, however, 288 behind Sir Cecil Wray, notwithstanding the assistance of the Duchess, Mrs. Bouverie, and Mrs. Robinson."

In Liverpool the real contest for the two seats in Parliament was between Bamber Gascoyne, Jr., Lord Penrhyn, and Lieutenant Colonel Tarleton. Bamber Gascoyne, grandson of Sir Crisp Gascoyne, Lord Mayor of London, had been elected in 1780. Very wealthy, very genteel, and very popular, he stood at the head of the poll. Lord Penrhyn, christened Richard Pennant, son of a Liverpool merchant, and now an industrialist recently created a baron in the Irish peerage by Secretary Fox, stood second. A Whig, Lord Penrhyn had first been elected for Liverpool in 1767, but in 1780 he had lost his seat to Henry Rawlinson.

His family forgave Ban. Their greatest ambition was to seat a Tarleton in Parliament. They poured out their money, and the struggle between him and Lord Penrhyn became very bitter. Heeding the tutelage of Fox and using his great popularity, the Colonel appealed to the common people: the carpenters, the shipwrights, the sailors, the market women. He rode his horse into the market place and kissed every market girl. On the Hustings he used for the first time what was to become a famous gesture. When words seemingly failed him, he held aloft his right hand mangled at the battle of Guilford Courthouse and cried, "For King and Country!"

But military service and popular manners were no match for the fascinations of Lady Penrhyn. She had extensive hereditary Liverpool connections and made the utmost possible use of them. Influence prevailed over popularity.

After a poll of six days, in which 1950 freemen voted, the tally stood: Gascoyne, 960; Penrhyn, 869; Tarleton, 856; and Meredith, 36. As soon as the election committee declared the results, Tarleton demanded a recount. In a short speech he said that out of justice to the friends who had supported him during the election, he thought himself honor-bound to demand a scrutiny.

The request was granted, but after three weeks of checking, the ballot stood: Gascoyne, 960; Penrhyn, 853; and Tarleton, 844. "The scrutiny at Liverpool is over," the London Chronicle announced on May 8, 1784, "and Lord Penrhyn, to the general satisfaction of the electors, is returned. Colonel Tarleton gained only four votes by the scrutiny."

Thanking his friends and bidding his co-workers farewell, the defeated Colonel hurried off to London to join in the rejoicing over the election of Fox. The Prince celebrated the triumph of "dear Charles" on a scale of extravagance unusual even for Carlton House.

About 600 of the most distinguished persons in the kingdom assembled in the beautiful gardens at two o'clock. "Preparations for the occasion were full of taste and magnificence," wrote the reporter for the London Chronicle of May 20, 1784. "Covers were laid under nine extensive marquees for 250, and the entertainment consisted of the finest fruits of the season, confectionaries, ices, creams, emblematical designs, ornamented with mottoes and other devices, in honor of the triumph which they were to celebrate. Four bands of instruments were placed at different parts of the garden, and the company were entertained with various novelties of a comic kind."

Then came dancing on the lawn. The Prince of Wales, with the Duchess of Devonshire, led the country dances, with the dancers frequently changing partners and at times grouping into cotillions. The gentlemen wore the buff and blue of the Whig Party, and the ladies were in morning dresses, "fancied in all the varieties of cultivated taste." Said the reporter: "We do not believe that a more superb exhibition of beauty was ever seen."

At six o'clock the ladies retired to dress for the ball given by Mrs. Crewe. About thirty gentlemen remained to dine with the Prince: Mr. Fox, Admiral Pigot, General Fitzpatrick, Colonel North, Colonel Onslow, Colonel Tarleton, and others. "The Prince was in uncommon spirits at dinner, and besides singing several songs in very pleasing stile, also joined in some catches and glees."

The Portland ministry had fallen because of Fox's India Bill, and in the election some 180 Whigs, known as "Fox's Martyrs," lost their seats in Parliament. William Pitt and the Tories began negotiations to send Lord Cornwallis to India.

On May 15 the *London Chronicle* reported: "Earl Cornwallis is now in treaty with Ministers to go out to India, to succeed Mr. Hastings as Governor-General of Bengal." Rumor spread that Colonel Tarleton would accompany Lord Cornwallis.

As he waited, Banastre joined the Prince and his friends in outdoor sports. With his tennis racket in his left hand he was more than a match for his Royal Highness, and in true sporting fashion he pocketed handsome sums with each win.

But cricket was Tarleton's enthusiasm. He helped organize a club with playing fields near the White Conduit House in Islington. Said a news reporter on May 29: "Thursday a grand cricket match was played in the White Conduit Fields. Among the players were the Duke of Dorset, Lord Winchelsea, Lord Talbot, Col. Tarleton, Mr. Howe, Mr. Damer, Hon. Mr. Lennox, and the Rev. Mr. Williams. A pavillion was erected for refreshments, and a number of ladies attended."

Even while the Colonel enlivened the royal tennis courts and capered with the gentlemen cricketers his prospects declined. In his late political campaign he had become one of the most violent of Whigs. No disciple of Charles Fox would ever find haven in the territory of the East India Company! On July 10 the *London Chronicle* announced the company's decision: "Colonel Tarleton does not accompany Lord Cornwallis to India, nor is he to have any military appointment in the service of the Company."

∾

By late spring the Tarleton-Robinson partnership was in financial chaos. Creditors began threatening foreclosure and replevin. On May 10,

1784, the *Morning Herald* said: "Mrs. Robinson's vis-a-vis, of which such various reports have prevailed, still appears to be in the service of its fair mistress in spite of rumour."

Mary began retrenching, economizing, dismissing servants. The *Morning Herald* advised: "Perdita has left off her carriage one of her flaunting footmen." Sneered the *Morning Post* of July 13: "The cyprian divinity of Berkeley Square is said to be on her last legs."

During all this misfortune Ban held his place in the gaming circle around the Prince. In early summer the Duke of Chartres had come over from Paris, bringing Dally the Tall, and he was now staggering the English nobility with his card playing. Finding the Prince of Wales up to his ears in debt, his Serene Highness offered to lend several hundred thousand pounds to the heir to the English throne.

With Chartres came the Duke of Lauzun. Handsome Lauzun visited Mary. Brave Lauzun followed gallant Tarleton about London. On July 19 the *Morning Herald* reported that the Prince of Wales, the Duke of Chartres, and the Duke of Lauzun had gone down to Brighton for the season. With them went Colonel Tarleton. On July 23 the *Morning Post* featured an item saying that a noted courtesan of Berkeley Square, who had intended to recuperate during the summer at Bristol Hot Springs, "from causes that we cannot exactly ascertain, has begun to take her course toward the coast of Sussex." Mary had gone to Brighton, too.

From the Ship Inn, Perdita made her last appeal to Florizel. In spite of his faults—and they were great—Prince George was warmhearted. Immediately he replied:

Dear Mrs. Robinson:

I have received your letter, and it really quite overcomes me, the scene of distress you so pathetically paint. I will certainly wait upon you, but I am afraid it will be late before I can come to the Ship, as I have company with me. Should it be within the compass of my means to rescue you from the abyss that is before you, and for which you mention Mr. Brent, I need not say that the temptation of gratifying others, and at the same time and by the same means making one's self happy, is too alluring to be neglected a single moment; however, you must allow me to be that explicit and candid, that it must in great measure depend upon the extent of what will be necessary to be done for your service, and how far my funds may be adequate, as well as my power equal to attain that object. In the meantime only rest assured of my good wishes and good intentions.

I am, dear Mrs. Robinson, very sincerely yours,

George

To Mrs. Robinson, Ship Inn, Brighton

The Prince came to the Ship Inn. Despite his gallant offer, Mary's affairs were hopeless. The sheriff of Middlesex had placed an execution upon her possessions. Her clothes, jewelry, furniture, and other effects, including the beautiful portrait by Gainsborough, were carted off for auction to the rooms of Messrs. Hutchins, Boulton, & Philips, King Street, Covent Garden. Before starting the sale, the auctioneer stated that if anyone would pay or give security for £250 the goods would be returned to the owner. There was no response.

The painting by Gainsborough sold for 32 guineas. Mary's famed cabriole also sold for 32 guineas. Of all her amorous treasures Mary saved only the diamond-studded miniature of the Prince of Wales. Said the Morning Post righteously: "Sic transit gloria mundi!"

Laetitia Hawkins was pleased: "As for Perdita, I saw her on one day handed to her outrageously extravagant vis-a-vis, by a man whom she pursued with a doting passion; all was still externally brilliant; she was fine and fashionable, and the men of the day in Bond Street still pirouetted as her carriage passed them: the next day, the vehicle was reclaimed by the maker; the Adonis whom she courted, fled her; she followed—all to no purpose."

As criticism of Mary grew louder, on August 5 the Reverend Henry Bate in his Morning Herald gave his rivals a lecture on editorial charity: "It has lately been the fashion to slander and abuse Mrs. Robinson in a certain Morning Paper; the motive for so doing is now become evident to the meanest capacity. It ought to be remembered that though private pique may be gratified by public and unmerited slander, injustice will ever meet contempt in the minds of those who are able to judge from conviction. To defend Mrs. Robinson is almost unnecessary; her propriety of conduct, both in public and private places, is far, very far, above the necessity of fulsome panegyrics."

In early August, while Mrs. Robinson lingered at the Ship Inn, Colonel Tarleton, Major Hanger, and the Prince rode to the silken fray at Up Park. Sir Harry Featherstone opened the season by losing a quarter-mile race for 100 guineas to the Prince. Then Sir Harry beat Sir John Lade, each riding his own horse. The third race was between Colonel Tarleton and Major Hanger, each riding his own horse. Tarleton won. Not satisfied, the old cavalrymen raced again: Tarleton on Sir Harry Featherstone's Speranza beat Hanger on Colonel Sheldon's Bustard, over the course, for 50 guineas.

The climax for the day was the grand match for 500 guineas between the Prince and Sir John Lade, the Prince's horse ridden by Peter Delme and Sir John's by Colonel St. Leger. The Prince won.

Next day seven horses were entered in the two-mile race for the sweepstakes. Sir Harry Featherstone as usual swept the field on old Rockingham. Colonel Tarleton followed closely behind on Colonel

Batten's Balloon. Trailing in sixth place came Major Hanger on Colonel Sheldon's Longitude.

Then the turfmen began planning for the races at Up Park in 1785, drawing up the regulations for the sweepstakes: 10 guineas each, with 100 guineas on the cup, for the best of three two-mile heats, the horses to have been the bona fide property of the subscribers six months before starting, and "to be rode by gentlemen." To these regulations were affixed the signatures of the Prince of Wales, Sir Harry Featherstone, Lord Grosvenor, Sir John Lade, Mr. Delme, Mr. Onslow, Colonel Tarleton, and Major Hanger.

From Up Park, Tarleton returned to Brighton. Mrs. Robinson's despair had lessened. Handsome Lauzun had never forgotten their ride to Calais, and he had offered her a haven in southern France. Quietly Ban and Mary packed. Tenderly he lifted her into a rented carriage, and they set out on their long wanderings.

"Mrs. Robinson has been obliged within these few days to leave England for the Continent for the recovery of her health," reported the *Morning Herald* on August 14. "She has lost almost the use of her limbs, and upon her journey was lifted in and out of her carriage. Her disorder is a rheumatic gout of so obstinate a nature that her recovery is doubtful."

The *Morning Post* also thought the end was near: "Of the Perdita's recovery there is little hope, though her physician is Sir John Elliott: which, with the cooperation of a warmer climate, is not a little in her favor. There is further hope from the youth of her constitution: for, after all, she is yet a few months under thirty."

News of the invalid and her protector dribbled back to London. "Mrs. Robinson has gone to the Continent, from whence her present fortune does not promise a speedy return," said the *Morning Herald* of September 22.

As soon as Ban and Mary had crossed the Channel, John Tarleton went off to rescue his famous brother from ruin and Mrs. Robinson. On October 8 he caught up with them at L'Hotel de Russie in Paris. Ten days later he wrote his mother: "The Colonel & myself have met several times, & we seem to be on friendly terms—I have dined with him & he has returned the compliment.

"Mrs. Robinson is in a bad state of health & cannot in my opinion survive the Winter, as she is most dreadfully afflicted with the Rheumatism. I had the satisfaction of dining with him on Friday last, & was informed that she intended to reside here the whole season if her health would permit her."

Ban and Mary left Paris on November 3. Soon afterward John returned to London. On November 10 the *Morning Post* informed its readers: "The gallant Colonel, whose chief boast is that he has killed more men, and ruined more women, than any other man in Europe, can never be in want of honours, whilst he has the honour to accompany the lovely Perdita, on the Continent, by way of Ciscisbeo."

On December 1 the *Morning Post* reported: "The Perdita fails in finding the spring of rejuvenescence in any foreign fountain. Her led Captain, as may be expected, improves in the principles and practices of a *bravo*."

Henry Bate was far kinder. On December 15 the *Morning Herald* said: "The lovely, though ill-fated Mrs. Robinson, the now too verified *Perdita*, winters in the south of France, upon the scanty *pittance* gleaned from the Remnant of her amourous treasures."

The new year brought little news from the wanderers. On February 1, 1785, the *Public Advertiser* sermonized: "The poor Perdita yet continues without hope of recovery, both as to constitution and fortune, a salutary beacon against the gaiety that ends in heaviness of heart."

But the Reverend Henry Bate knew Mary's friends. On February 11 the *Morning Herald* had definite news: "Mrs. Robinson is with the Duc de Lauzun, much invalided, at his chateau in the country."

22
Old Wounds

$\mathcal{F}$ROM THE CHÂTEAU OF LAUZUN Ban and Mary wandered on to Villefranche. The *Morning Post* got wind of their move and said on February 15, 1785: "Among the new plays to be brought forward this season will be *The Wandering Lovers, Col. T. and Mrs. R.*"

Mary recovered amazingly in the sunshine of the Côte d'Azur. Her spirit soared, and she began planning to visit her brothers in Leghorn. But Sir John Elliott, her physician, recommended that instead she try the warm springs of Aix-la-Chapelle.

Off to Aix went Ban and Mary, making a leisurely journey across France. They stopped in Paris and he visited his friends. He tried cards, but his three fingers turned up the deuce. He wrote John, confessing another state of "play and gambling." Then he crossed over to Brighton for a meeting with the moneylenders.

As Banastre started back to Paris he wrote John a sharp letter:

Brighthelmstone. May 29, 1785
My dear Brother—

I am setting off for France—I need not explain to you or my Friends my Situation—I was obliged to sell part of my half pay to go. I have presented a Memorial to the King—I mean to stay abroad till something is done for me—I hope my friends will make me some allowance or I must starve. I will write to you once more to tell you where I am to be found.

Yours affectionately,
Ban. Tarleton

John wrote his bitter thoughts to Clayton, now a rising young businessman who had to be consulted about family affairs: "Annexed I send you a Letter which I rec'd. last night from Col. T. the Contents

of which I had every Reason to expect from his late bad luck at play &
his extravagant & absurd Turn of Mind. I sho'd make no Objection if
the rest of the family concurs with me in opinion to allow him at the
rate of £200 to 250 pr An. encluding in that amt. his half pay, I mean
that part of it which remains unencumbered & taking the entire Management of it into our own Hands—What that may produce, I am
ignorant of, but I shall wait on his late Agent tomorrow to render myself perfectly Master of the Subject & write you again, being at present
confin'd to my Chamber by a relapse of my former Complaint the
Gout which preys upon my Constitution & seems determined not to
leave a reduced invalid. The above plan I mean to adopt if the rest of
the family are willing to subscribe their Quota, which cannot I imagine
amt. to any large Sum—I am not for encouraging or supporting Extravagance which I shall write in plain terms to the Col: I am only
inclined to save consequence if we refuse to make a provision for him
on the present urgent Occasion."

Clayton forwarded the unwelcome letters to his older brother,
Thomas, saying: "I shall make no Comments on the above Letters,
but whatever is done for him I beg may be after his leaving Brighthelmstone as the papers say the Prince is going down there, & I fear any
money advanced for his Expence to France, wou'd certainly be dissipated in that place & the plea of starving would again find its way into
Lancashire. I shall not acquaint my Mother today—I think you had
best come over: I shall drop John a line that whatever is thought reasonable for me to do must absolutely be withheld till He is on the
Continent."

But Clayton confessed, "I am at a loss how to communicate it to my
mother as she is unprepared by her not having seen John's last letter.
At all events I shall not acquaint her today as she is engaged in Company."

∽

While the Tarleton brothers conferred by letter, the *Morning Herald*
of July 15 reported: "Mrs. Robinson is at Spa— by the late advices her
health is said to be so much recovered that her return to England next
spring is spoken of as a certainty."

The news from Spa was stale to the brothers. They knew Ban and
Mary were in Aix. That was the problem. How could they disentangle
their scapegrace brother from that Robinson woman? How could they
shake that three-fingered hand loose from a deck of cards? In a letter
to John, Banastre had given them some hope. He had indicated that
he planned to settle down and finish the story of his campaigns in
America. He wished to clear himself of the responsibility of "the unfortunate day at Cowpens."

Lieutenant Colonel Tarleton had already suffered much in the bitter Clinton-Cornwallis controversy. This war of pamphlets had been both personal and political, and it had been rancorous. The surrender at Yorktown had caused the downfall of Lord North's ministry. The disastrous campaign of 1781 had apparently ruined the prospects of the two generals who conducted it, and Lieutenant General Sir Henry Clinton, whom public opinion censured, had made every effort to throw the blame on Lieutenant General Cornwallis.

When Lord Cornwallis had arrived in New York from Yorktown, his meeting with Sir Henry had been acrimonious. Their arguments had centered around three points: (1) the authority for the march into Virginia; (2) the responsibility for selecting and fortifying Yorktown and Gloucester; and (3) Clinton's delay in trying to relieve Yorktown.

But the enthusiastic reception Lord Cornwallis received upon his arrival in England and the kind attitude of King George had softened his rancour. He began to take a philosophical view of his defeat—it was the fortune of war. But not so Sir Henry Clinton. In New York late in the year 1781 he published *Correspondence between His Excellency General Sir Henry Clinton, K.B. and Lieutenant General Earl Cornwallis.*

Sir Henry mailed copies of this pamphlet to friends and officials in England early enough to arrive ahead of Lord Cornwallis. To clear himself Cornwallis urged a general investigation. On February 7, 1782, the House of Lords resolved "to enquire into the causes of the great loss." Among the many papers ordered laid on its table were "Copies or Extracts of all Instructions or Orders from any of His Majesty's Ministers to Lieutenant General Sir Henry Clinton and Lieutenant General Earl Cornwallis in the years 1780 and 1781." The debate in Parliament lasted until March 6, but the fall of the ministry prevented resolution or action.

During the summer of 1782, as Tarleton had paraded around London with the Duke of Bedford, he had come under attack. With patent hostility the *Morning Chronicle* had opened its columns to his enemies and on August 6 printed a letter assailing his military and personal integrity:

For the *Morning Chronicle*

To Lieutenant Colonel Tarleton
of the
Provincial Legion

Sir,
    This letter is addressed to you by a military man, who has had the honour to serve his country fourteen years, in rank not inferior to yourself; has served in America since the commencement of the

unhappy disturbance, and has with pleasure been a witness on several occasions where you have distinguished yourself by the lucky opportunities which fortune throwed in your way.

It was highly becoming the character of a truly spirited young man, when a cornet in Meyston's Horse, to get leave to go out a volunteer in the 16th regiment of light dragoons in the year 1776, then under orders for America. It was lucky at this period that cash run low, and the tables proved unfortunate, which, in the event, has been attended with good consequences to yourself, which the country may thank for your voluntary service.

The late Mr. Tarleton, your father, who as a very respectable character, and Master of a *Guinea trader*, had acquired a pretty fortune by disposing of his houses in the West Indies, and afterwards, settled in Liverpool, from whence he originally traded to the Coast of Africa; were he now alive, it must give him infinite pleasure to have a son who has gained so much eclat in the military world.

It is much to be lamented that you are deprived of the fore and middle finger of the right hand, by an unlucky rifleman, the loss of which I am afraid disenables you from using the broad sword, with which you were wont to make so formidable an appearance.

Elevated with two several successes, the first *Ninshan*, or Indian Chiefs party of the Stockbridge tribe of Indians, at Kings bridge, where the brave veteran Colonel Simcoe, with the Queen's Rangers, broke the corps who then dispersed, two troops of the legion, with you at their head, finished the business.

Unluckily for you, in the conflict your broad sword was *top heavy*, and having over lunged, you were dislodged out of the styrrup, and falling to the ground in an Indian corn-field, one of the Ninshan's party was just going to put a period to your life, when a lucky dragoon came up at that instant, and cut him down.

This, Sir, was a lucky escape, and I wish you may always meet with such in time of danger; but at the same time I am sorry with many more gentlemen who know this matter, *that this brave soldier was poorly rewarded for this generous action.*

Preserving life or common safety being a first principle of nature, if such a thing could be bought in time of danger, what would not be given to purchase it? This I believe every one will allow.

That he got no reward at all I will aver; what I call no reward, is that he was not provided for in the service as it lays in your power to do, and no provision made for him in any other department. The paltry sum of a guinea, and appointing him your orderly man, was a poor reward indeed.

As an old soldier, I beg leave to tell you that you ought not to overlook merit in a private soldier; for you will find that Xenophon, the greatest General and Statesman of antiquity has condescended to rank gratitude to deserving private men among the many merits he has ascribed to his General Cyrus, when he says immediately after the action, in which it was observed any common soldier, distinguished himself, was promoted, and properly rewarded, according to his merit; but when it happened that a private soldier by an uncommon exertion saved the life of his officer, he was loaded with rewards. Your second success in America will be the subject of another letter, no ways derogatory to your character as a military man.

I am, Sir,

Your most obedient and very humble servant
An Officer of the Army

Portland Place, Cavendish Square
August 1, 1782

"An Officer of the Army" was perhaps Lieutenant Roderick Mackenzie of the gallant 71st Regiment of Highlanders. He had never forgiven the Green Dragoon for the debacle at Cowpens. On August 9 the Morning Chronicle published a second letter from "An Officer." In this he assailed Tarleton's handling of his troops on "the unfortunate day":

To Lieutenant Colonel TARLETON, of the Provincial Legion.

SIR,

The second, and the last success you had in America, was in the surprise of Colonel Beaufort, on the borders of South Carolina, whom you luckily attacked when cooking their dinner, by the side of a wood, many hundred yards from their arms, or ammunition. Their numbers were inferior to your party, and it would have been as easy for you, and much more honour, which has ever distinguished the brave commander of his country, to have made that small party prisoners, without making so much use of your broad sword, which providence now has rendered you incapable ever of useing.

In every sphere of life, as well as in that of war, destructive weapons are seldom used to naked men begging mercy, the few officers of this small force, with the Colonel, made their retreat good on horseback, though you were so well mounted, not having time to form their men. This was not the victory in which you gained all your eclat, and which was certainly conducted with address, by the cavalry and infantry of the legion, which in your account of the affair to the Commander in Chief, you term blended, and I wish sincerely for the honour of this country, as well as for your own, they had not continued afterwards to be blended, and not mixed with other corps; as it must be obvious to the world, evil consequences must ensue, without the oldest officer, as is justly allowed in war, has the command of the detachment.

This unfortunately was the case with the detachment, consisting of the 7th and 71st regiments, joined with your provincials, when improperly ordered under your command by Lord Cornwallis, to attack General Morgan.

The party of the 7th was commanded by an old Captain, who had been a Lieutenant in the service when you were at school, who also commanded the party of the 71st, was ordered to put himself, in conjunction with the legion, for this intended enterprise. This veteran was much surprised on receiving orders from a Provincial Lieutenant Colonel, whose highest rank then in the army, was a Captain *newly made*, but however, like a good soldier, he punctually obeyed your orders, preferring his country's good to the indignity he then laboured under, and I wish for your sake, as well as our country, that he had not been so very implicitly good natured, or that he had not obeyed your orders at all.

You got yourself and the party completely ambuscaded, completely surrounded, upon all sides, by Mr. Morgan's rifle men. What was the consequence? The two detachments of British were made prisoners after a great slaughter was made among them, your legion dragoons were so broke by galling fire of *rifle shot*, that your charging was in vain, till prudence, on your side, with about twenty more, who were well mounted, made your retreat good, by leaving the remains of the poor blended legion in the hands of Mr. Morgan, who I must say, though an enemy, shewed great masterly abilities in this manoever.

Thus fell, at one blow, all the Provincial Legion, with about *three hundred veterans!*

> I am, Sir,
> Your very humble servant,
> *An Officer of the Army*

So abusive did "An Officer" become that the editor of the *Morning Chronicle* took "the liberty of omitting the reflection which concluded the manuscript:—He does not think himself warranted to publish any reflection that tends, in any degree, to depreciate the character of an officer specifically addressed by name."

While Tarleton was smarting from these diatribes, Sir Henry Clinton, who had arrived in London on June 14, was busily preparing a lengthy defense of his actions as commander in chief in America. In early January 1783 he published *Narrative of Lieutenant General Sir Henry Clinton, K.B. relative to his Conduct during part of his command of the King's Troops in North America: Particularly to that which respects the unfortunate Issue of the Campaign of 1781.*

In his *Narrative* Sir Henry Clinton asserted "that none of the misfortunes of the very unfortunate campaign of 1781 can, with the smallest degree of justice, be imputed to me." But perhaps the *Gentleman's Magazine* of February 1783 spoke for the nation when it said: "An impartial reader, on perusing this Narrative, will hardly think that Sir Henry Clinton has exculpated himself from directing the Earl to take post at York and Gloucester."

Lord Cornwallis received his copy of the Narrative on January 15, 1783. He soon issued a rebuttal: An Answer to that part of the Narrative of Lieutenant General Sir Henry Clinton, K.B. Which relates to the Conduct of Lieutenant General Earl Cornwallis, during the Campaigns in North America, in the Year 1781. His Lordship asserted that "I acted under positive orders, pressing contingences, or discretionary power." He admitted that Tarleton's defeat at Cowpens was the turning point of the campaign, but he denied responsibility for it. "The disaster of the 17th of January cannot be imputed to any defect in my conduct, as the detachment was certainly superior to the force against which it was sent, and put under the command of an officer of experience and tried abilities."

An Answer by Lord Cornwallis so completely refuted the arguments in Clinton's Narrative that Sir Henry published a rebuttal: Observations on some parts of the Answer of Earl Cornwallis to Sir Henry Clinton's Narrative. In his Observations he contended: "I left his Lordship in the Carolinas, with every power, civil or military, which I could give him, to carry on such operations as he should judge most likely to complete their reductions."

Then Sir Henry reopened the old wound: "But after the unfortunate day of Cowpens, which diminished his Lordship's acting army nearly one fourth . . ."

An unknown commentator now entered the controversy with a pamphlet entitled A Parting Word: or, a Summary Review of the Controversy between Sir Henry Clinton and Earl Cornwallis. The author redefined the question: Did or did not the conduct and opinions of Lord Cornwallis result in Yorktown? He summarized the entire campaign from King's Mountain to Yorktown. He concluded by saying that Sir Henry wanted all the credit for success, but wanted Lord Cornwallis to take all the blame for failure.

Among his proofs he asserted: "Now, it is evident from this passage, that until the unfortunate day of Cowpens, which was it seems the 17th of January, 1781, Sir Henry certainly approved of Lord Cornwallis's design to march into North Carolina."

As the controversialists continued to roll off the phrase "the unfortunate day of Cowpens," the impression grew stronger and stronger that on the 17th day of January, 1781, Lieutenant Colonel Banastre Tarleton lost the battle that lost the campaign that lost the war that lost the American Colonies!

In February 1785 while Prime Minister Pitt was urging Lord Cornwallis to go out to India, Sir Henry fired his final salvo. He published the seventh edition of his *Narrative*. The Clinton-Cornwallis controversy flared up again.

Banastre Tarleton now determined to exculpate himself of "the unfortunate day of Cowpens." He still possessed his order books, his memoranda, and the original copies of at least thirty letters from Lord Cornwallis. He had the pamphlets of the controversy. He had Dr. David Ramsay's *History of the Revolution of South-Carolina* to serve as a model. And he had a gifted pen: Mary had so far recovered that she could help in writing *A History of the Campaigns of 1780 and 1781 in the Southern Provinces of North America*.

But Tarleton did not wish to offend Lord Cornwallis. The Dragoon, though he had become Radical Whig, a follower of Charles Fox and an associate of Fox's Martyrs, still hoped to go to India with his high-Tory Lordship. When Ban finally wrote from Aix-la-Chapelle, he asked John to inquire if Lord Cornwallis objected to his using their official correspondence in the *Campaigns*.

John immediately posted off to London to consult Major Hanger. But that enthusiastic horseman was riding in the silken fray at Up Park. The *London Chronicle* of July 26 reported that Sir Harry Featherstone's private race course "has been the rendezvous of all that is gay and fashionable in the country. Duc de Chartres, Duke of Queensbury, Lord Grosvenor, and a number of other distinguished persons accompanied the Prince."

Hanger was riding the horses of Lord Grosvenor, but Sir Harry was unbeatable. In the final race he whipped Epaminondos over the West Harting Downs to win the gold cup for the sweepstakes.

Then came a thrilling innovation for these salacious young coxcombs. Girl runners were brought in. The Prince bet 100 guineas "on a well-shaped, buxom girl against the field; but, unfortunately, the favorite fell down, and though his Royal Highness instantly flew to her assistance, yet she was distanced." Ah, sighed the *Morning Herald* of August 3, these were truly "Sporting Girls."

When John finally reached Hanger, the Major observed that Tarleton's request required delicate handling. "Lieutenant-Colonel Tarleton was in Germany when he wrote his history," Hanger said later in his *Address to the Army*. "Mr. John Tarleton, brother to the Colonel, called on me some time previous to Earl Cornwallis's departure for India, and showed me a letter which he had received from Lieutenant-Colonel Tarleton, dated Aix-la-Chapelle, in which he desired particularly that Earl Cornwallis might be informed that he had then begun, and intended to publish, a history of the campaigns of 1780 and 1781, in the Carolinas and Virginia."

The Major called upon Lord Lothian, a close friend of Cornwallis, and Lothian agreed to broach the subject. Cornwallis was sympathetic.

ᐁ

During the fall of 1785 and winter of 1786 Ban and Mary remained at Aix-la-Chapelle, weaving together the threads of the complicated march from Tybee to Yorktown. He relied upon memories of the campaigns, but she corroborated these from letters and dispatches in newspapers and magazines, especially the *London Gazette*, the *Remembrancer*, the *Annual Register*, and the *South Carolina Gazette*.

The writing was slow, but the authors were happy. Through the long afternoons and evenings they sat together composing and revising. In the year and a half spent on the *Campaigns*, Mary experienced the most peaceful moments of her troubled life. As Maria Elizabeth, at this time an eleven-year-old girl, wrote long afterward in completing her mother's *Memoirs*: "During her sojourn at Aix-la-Chapelle, a dawn of comparative tranquility soothed her spirits. Secure from the machinations of her enemies, she determined, though happiness seemed no more within her reach, to endeavor to be content. The assiduities and attentions shown her by all ranks of people presented a striking medium between the volatility and libertine homage offered her at Paris, and the persevering malignity which had followed her in her native land . . ."

The family and friends of the Duke and Duchess of Châtelet, attracted by Mary and affected by her illness, showed every kindness to the fair invalid.

> Balls, concerts, rural breakfasts, succeeded each other in gay and attractive variety. . . . When compelled by severer paroxysms of her malady to seclude herself from their society, a thousand kind stratagems were planned and executed to relieve her sufferings, or soften the dejection to which they unavoidably gave rise.
>
> Sometimes, on entering her dark and melancholy bath, the gloom of which was increased by high grated windows, she beheld the surface of the water covered with rose-leaves, while the vapour baths were impregnated with aromatic odors. The younger part of the family, when pain deprived Mrs. Robinson of rest, frequently passed the night beneath her windows, charming her suffering and beguiling her of her sorrows, by singing her favorite airs to the accompaniment of the mandolin.

Mary devoted her spare time to poetry. Proud of her Welsh ancestry, she read John Williams' prose translation of a poem written by Taliesin, in the vale of Ben Batridd. She transformed the tale into a stirring ballad with an eerie final stanza:

> Thrice did he ope the lattice grate
> And thrice he bade adieu,
> When, lo! to join the parting shade
> The Maiden's spirit flew!

She sent the poem to the *London Chronicle*, which published it on November 22 as "Llwhen and Gwyneth." The following day the *Morning Herald* announced: "Mrs. Robinson has lately written a comic opera: the scene lies at Villa Franca, and the principal character is a pretended experimental philosopher, who is visited by Ladies of all nations to learn the effect of animal magnetism."

Mary had begun to draw upon her experiences and her travels for literary material. In this she was in the advance guard of the romantics. But her opera was not promising, and on December 10 the *Morning Herald* announced Sheridan's decision: "Mrs. Robinson's opera will not be brought out this season."

Mary's father, who had become a captain in the Russian Navy, died on December 5, 1785, and was buried with full military honors. To her John Darby had been a shadowy but revered figure. His death stirred her deeply and she cried in a long elegy:

> He lives no more!
> Far on a foreign shore,
> His honour'd dust a laurel'd grace receives
> While his immortal soul in realms celestial lives!

ono

On February 23, 1786, Lord Cornwallis accepted Pitt's offer of the post of governor-general and commander in chief in India. The news reached Tarleton in Aix. The time had come for action.

Leaving Mary in their cottage near the Baths of the Rose, Banastre hastened to London. On March 16 the *Morning Herald* reported: "Colonel Tarleton is arrived from France. Lord Cornwallis, who has been the generous patron of this enterprising young officer, will no doubt extend a wing of protection over him in his Oriental department."

For a month Banastre remained in London. He applied to Lord Cornwallis for the promised command. But Tarleton's behavior since their return from Yorktown had alienated his Lordship. There was also a political impediment. Prime Minister Pitt would allow no follower of Charles Fox any command in India.

On April 17 John wrote his mother an eloquent report on the failure of Ban's mission:

> Col. Tarleton left London for Dover late last night, after the fruitless exertions we had made to endeavor to prevail on Lord Cornwallis to permit him to accompany his Lordship to India— no interest was neglected for that purpose, but it proved on the present of little moment & efficacy, he has been extremely ill used by Lord Cornwallis, who has abused the confidence placed in

him by Colonel Tarleton, who had he not relied on that noble Lord's promises, & professions, might have been in a different & even in an enviable situation of life.

I was obliged to advance £100 the amount of the annuity you & I agreed to allow Col. Tarleton till he has some preferment from his Majesty, the hopes of which I think are not far distant notwithstanding the late check we have received, to Enable him to that amount I was also reduced to the necessity of farther being bound with him to the amount of £100 more for debts he had contracted which I shall pay myself—I wish Tarleton would agree to allow Ban the same annuity we do, it would then take away the pretence of his being obliged to exceed his income, & would be quite sufficient till he gets some employment—

So back to Aix went the Colonel, his disappointment turned to bitterness. Friends tried to dissuade him from publishing the *Campaigns*. His book would be regarded merely as a part of the Clinton-Cornwallis row.

Banastre wrote Sir Henry Clinton for advice, and the old General replied:

Dear Tarleton,

That I was averse to any Publication of yours making its appearance at this Time you know full well. My Motives were liberal to the Earl and friendly to you. But I am free to own that after the Steps you took to make known your Intentions (which may be thought rather precipitate) I now think it absolutely incumbent upon you to proceed. And so far from impeding your Wishes, I would be happy in forwarding them by furnishing you with every Thing I can with Propriety. But not having had any Conversation with you on the Subject since your Resolution was taken, I am at a loss to know wherein I can best assist you. For as to the Plan of the Siege of Charles Town which you asked me for, it does not immediately strike me what use you can make of it, as your Operations were higher up the Country—and the only one in my Possession (having sent those of Moncrief to the King by Lord Lincoln or Brace) takes in only the approaches to the Town & the works around it. The Importance of your success against Washington's Cavalry at Biggin's Bridge will best appear by my Instructions to Coll. Webster which was so completely executed by that splendid stroke. And the many other Services derived from the active and spirited Excursions of your Cavalry are noticed with every Attention to your Merits in My Letters to the Ministry detailing that Siege. I submit to you to make Use of these two papers. The Plan however is very much at your Service and will be delivered to you by Capt. Gaylor. But as it is the only one I have I request you will take care to return it to me as soon as you have done with it.

I understand Faden has or is about publishing a Plan of the Siege of York Town by Major Girlack Dep. Q. M. Gl. to the Brunswick Troops. I subscribed 5 Guineas to it. I suppose it will come out with your Book as it relates to the Siege on which you can speak more fully & properly than that of Charles Town. Your Conversations with me on that Subject have convinced me that had your Advice been taken when La Fayette attacked Lord C——— Rear Guard early in July, or when you recommended to him the move against St. Simon or La Fayette or both on the 12 Sept. 81, and after beating in detail the Army which was coming to besiege him, to retire to the station he left in Carolina contrary to my Orders, we should not have suffered the Mortification which followed, nor would America have been to this Hour independent. What then, my dear Tarleton, would have been the Situation of this Country? Instead of trembling whenever France pleases to frown on us, lest her Junction with America should one day rob us of our Islands, a Reunion with our Colonies, become by the War soldiers & sailors ripe for anything, would have not only removed all apprehension for our West Indian Possessions, but might have enabled us in a single Campaign to have taken those of our Enemies!!

> I have the honor to be, etc.,
>   H. Clinton

While Ban collected maps and other materials, Mary wrote steadily. They were quiet and their critics had apparently forgotten them. On June 29 the *Morning Post* observed: "Of Mrs. Robinson, once so famed, the world hears nothing."

Then the *Morning Post* of July 14 shocked London with a full-column story:

DEATH OF MRS. ROBINSON

Mrs. Robinson, the once famous *Perdita*, died a few days ago at Paris. This woman, who was possessed of most of the amiable qualities, that make time glide easily on was ushered early into life. She was the natural daughter of a gentleman, who held a commission in the army, and was married, when at a boarding school, to a Mr. Robinson, clerk to an attorney, before she attained her seventeenth year. Their finances for some time were low, and she being possessed of stage abilities, was recommended to the late Mr. Garrick. Her first appearance, on the boards of Drury Lane Theatre, was in the character of Juliet; but that which brought her into notice, and gave her the name of *Perdita*, was Shakespeare's *Winter's Tale*. In this dramatic romance, she attracted the notice of a Royal Personage, who soon became enamoured of her, and took her from a public station. The various situations she has since been in, her amours with Lord M——, Col. T———, etc. are all well known. Her admirers of the *Ton* having worn her out

of fashion, she retired to France, where her fame had gone before
her, and having lived for some years there, and finding several of
the engagements of *honour* that had been entered into by her
admirers, broken, her circumstances straitened, and her reputation, as a *Cyprian devotee* gone, she is said to have sunk into a
state of despondency for several months ere she died.

This Lady, had she walked in the paths of virtue and peace
would have been an ornament to her sex, and a peculiar happiness to him of whom she was the *better half*. But a spirit of levity,
and strong propensity to dissipation, and the *haut ton*, overcame
her virtue and her sense, and not guarded by the *sturdy oak*, but
leaning on the *feeble bending twig* as a protector, she easily gave
way to the flatteries, the follies, and the vices of those who paid
their court to her.

She was possessed of literary abilities. A farce of her own writing was brought out for her benefit at Drury Lane Theatre; and
several other practical productions have at different times appeared
in public prints, of which she was the author. Her abilities, as an
actress, were above mediocrity, but did not place her as the first of
her profession. She was genteel in her manners, delicate in her
person, and beautiful in her features. Her heart was open to the
feelings of humanity, of which the late Mrs. Baddeley was a striking example; Mrs. Robinson relieved her when in Chelsea, in the
most deplorable and wretched situation that the helpless woman
could be in—having the cravings of nature without the means of
supplying them, added to the pangs of labour, and all the horrors
of an outcast and forlorn wretch to combat.

Mrs. Robinson was born in Illminster, in Somersetshire; her
mother's name was Derby, and formerly kept the George Inn in
that town.

The public accepted the report. Perhaps a few readers smiled wanly
over the *Morning Post's* spiteful little obituary:

"As a good natured hint to the Cyprian multitude, we insert the
following lines on the death of Mrs. Robinson, the once famed Perdita:

> Let coxcombs flatter, and let fools adore,
> Here learn the lesson to be vain no more!"

Three weeks later the *Morning Post*, without a word of explanation
or retraction, printed a letter from an angry reader:

Aux Bains de la Rose
Aix la Chapelle, Germany, July 20, 1786
Sir,

With astonishment I read in a *Morning Post*, of the 14th instant, a long account of my *death*, and a variety of circumstances
respecting *my life*, equally void of the smallest foundation.

I have the satisfaction of informing you, that so far from being dead, I am in the most perfect state of health; except for a trifling lameness, of which, by the use of the baths at this place, I have every reason to hope, I shall recover in a month or six weeks. I propose passing my winter in London, having been near two years upon the continent, though not at Paris half the time.

Lest it should be received and understood in the world that the account of my life is genuine, I beg leave to contradict two very material circumstances, respecting my family connections. In the first place, my father, Captain Darby, whose legitimate daughter I had the happiness of being, died six months since, on board his own ship, of 74 guns, in the Russian service—beloved and regretted by all his connections and acquaintance. My mother is of Welsh extraction, and descended from the Seys's of Boverton Castle in Glamorganshire, a family truly respected and well known in that part of the world. I was born at Bristol, and received my education under the care of Miss Hanna More: Illminster is a place to which I am a total stranger.

As a man of feeling, I request you to contradict the report, with candour, and all possible expedition. I have brothers in Italy, who will experience the greatest anxiety, should such a detail reach their ears; and I am fully convinced, that your knowledge of the world, and liberal sentiments, will induce you to render justice to a person, whose absence requires an advocate, and who has the honour to subscribe herself,

Sir, with esteem,
Your obliged and
obedient servant,
Mary Robinson

23

The Campaigns

"C OL. T. IS WELL. I have received a Letter from him this morning—
he returns to England on the 7th December—with me," John wrote
his mother from Paris on November 20, 1786.

Banastre was now too busy to write his mother, but John, knowing
that she would see the Colonel's name in the newspapers, on December 26 wrote to assure her that the moneylenders had agreed not to throw
Ban into the King's Bench Prison: "The Colonel is very well and I have
the pleasure to acquaint you that he will not be molested by his Creditors; he intends publishing the history of the two campaigns in North
America this Winter; it will be one volume in Quarto; and it is with
that view that he is now in Town."

Colonel Tarleton showed his manuscript to friends. They were impressed. On January 8, 1787, the *Morning Herald* informed his admirers:
"Lieutenant Colonel Tarleton's *History of the Campaigns in Virginia,
and the Neighboring Provinces,* is well spoken of by those who have
seen the manuscript. And on this occasion we may say with Shakespeare
'What, the sword and the pen,—do you study both, Mr. Colonel?' "

The *London Chronicle* observed on January 11: "Yesterday Colonel
Tarleton was present at the Levee at St. James for the first time since
his return from France."

But there were those who were not impressed. On the day of the levee,
Lieutenant General James Grant wrote Lord Cornwallis: "Tarleton has
advertised a History of the two last campaigns to the southward, to be
immediately published; as far as I can learn he does not mean—or rather
the author to whom he lends his name does not mean—to compliment;
nothing is to be imputed to you directly, but reflections by implication;
whatever they may be, I am sure they cannot affect you, but they must
fall heavy upon himself, and I shall have a very bad opinion of our pro-

fession, if any man of character and rank ever takes notice of him afterwards: but I only mention the tale of the day, and do not give it to you,
from any authority, but your friends wait for the publication with impatience. Sir William Howe is astonished at the intention, and thinks
just as I do about it."

Ban spent the winter reading proof, supervising the preparation of
maps, and getting ready for the publication of the *Campaigns*. On
March 17 the *London Chronicle* carried an advertisement:

> This Day was published
> Elegantly printed in One Volume Quarto
> And illustrated with a Map of the Country, and
> Plans of the Sieges and Battles, price £, 6s in Boards
> A History of the Campaigns of 1780 and
> 1781, in the Southern Provinces of North America
> By Lieutenant Colonel Tarleton
> Commandant of the late British Legion
> Printed for T. Cadell, in the Strand

Thomas Cadell had produced a handsome volume, neat, well printed,
and attractively bound in leather. The title page read:

> A
> HISTORY
> of the
> CAMPAIGNS
> of
> 1780 and 1781
> in the
> SOUTHERN PROVINCES
> of
> NORTH AMERICA
> By
> Lieutenant-Colonel Tarleton
> Commandant of the Late British Legion
> London
> Printed for T. Cadell, in the Strand
> M. DCC. LXXXVII

"Colonel Tarleton's *History of the Campaigns in America*, like Caesar's *Commentaries*, has not a single line, more than the title page, to
precede it," exclaimed the *Morning Herald*. "Not a word of preface,
advertisement, or introduction is given to prepare the reader for the
subject: in fact the battle begins without a drum being beat or a word
of command given."

As soon as possible after Cadell's publication, Mr. Colles and others
in Dublin brought out an octavo edition. It was hastily thrown together,

abounded in misprints, and lacked maps. But it was cheap and sold in quantity. In time it became the better known of the editions.

Critics were divided over the merits of the *Campaigns*. The review in the *Monthly Review* of July 1787 was favorable. "In most of the transactions here recorded, Colonel Tarleton was personally concerned; so that their authenticity, the most material circumstance in all historical narratives, cannot (we suppose) be called into question; and, in order to confirm what he has advanced, he has regularly inserted, at the end of each chapter, and in connexion with the preceding details, many original letters from the commanders in chief, and other officers. Of these, the dispatches to government, which have been published in the Gazettes, with proclamations, general orders, etc. make the most considerable part, though there is likewise a great number of private letters, especially from Lord Cornwallis to Colonel Tarleton, which have not before been published; most of them contain temporary directions and private intelligence, relative to the marches, disposition, detachments, etc. of the two armies, and other communications, which tend to explain the several plans of operation. . . . The volume is handsomely printed, and, on the whole notwithstanding some imperfections, which good judges have hinted to us, does credit to the Author as an Officer."

The reviewer in the *Critical Review* of May 1787 had been less favorable. "The author, lieutenant colonel Tarleton, enters into a very minute detail of his own services, and makes a very free comment on those of others, and in particular of Lord Cornwallis. His conclusions are not, however, always logically deduced, nor, as we conceive, warranted by military science."

After quoting and analyzing several passages from the *Campaigns* the reviewer continued: "It will be obvious, that colonel Tarleton is unfortunate in the period of his publication. The observations, whether just or unjust, are such as must have occurred to him on the spot, and previous to the conclusion of the war. If they were ever to have been made public, they should have been so while Earl Cornwallis was in England."

To many readers the *Campaigns* seemed a continuation of Mary's "Ode to Valour." In Tarleton's defense of himself and in Mary's adulation of him, the commandant of the British Legion became too heroic. Concluded the *Critical Review*: "On the whole, we cannot praise this History: it is diffuse, laboured, and tedious. The author appears everywhere, forward, on the canvas; and, when his importance is estimated by the weight of his own remarks, we are tempted frequently to remove him to the background."

The critic for the *Monthly Review* noted this overestimation of the importance of the author. In a second notice he tartly observed: "As we did not rank Col. T. with a Caesar or a Frederick, we confined our notice of his *Commentaries*, if we may so style his publication, within the compass of a page."

The politicians scoffed. Mr. Storer wrote William Eden: "Mr. Tarleton, the Colonel that writes commentaries, is to walk today for a wager; he is to walk five miles in an hour. Which way will you bet?"

The friends and relatives of Lord Cornwallis were furious. They asserted that Tarleton had attacked an absent benefactor. To Lord Cornwallis in India they sent a copy of the *Campaigns*.

From Calcutta on December 12, 1787, his Lordship wrote his brother, the Reverend Dr. James Cornwallis, Bishop of Lichfield and Coventry: "Tarleton's is a most malicious and false attack; he knew and approved the reasons for the measures which he now blames. My not sending relief to Colonel Ferguson, although he was positively ordered to retire, was entirely owing to Tarleton himself; he pleaded weakness from the remains of a fever, and refused to make the attempt, although I used the most earnest entreaties. I mention this as a proof, amongst many others, of his candour. I know it is very foolish to be vexed about these things, but yet it touches me in a tender point."

The *Morning Post* was waiting for the appearance of the *Campaigns*. Soon afterward it printed a series of twelve letters of stricture. They were immediately amplified and published by Lieutenant Roderick Mackenzie as *Strictures on Lt. Col. Tarleton's History of the Campaigns of 1780 and 1781 in the Southern Provinces of North America*.

Mackenzie dedicated the *Strictures* to the Right Honorable Francis, Lord Rawdon, aide de camp to the King, for "the attention shown by your Lordship to the officers wounded at the disastrous affair at Cowpens." His *Strictures* were intensely personal and charged with hatred: "Whether in actions of importance, or slight skirmishes, I everywhere can trace the exaggereated accounts of this author's prowess." Said he sarcastically: "Lieutenant Colonel Tarleton landed in America in the year 1777, with the rank of Cornet of Dragoons, and in the beginning of January, 1781, we find him the *primum mobile*, the master spring which puts the whole machinery of the army in motion!"

He condemned from his own knowledge and opinion: "His mode of reasoning, in the present instance, is invidious in the extreme, with respect to the General, and equally contemptuous of every officer in his army."

The stricturist ripped and destroyed wherever possible: "In our author's description of the action at Hanging Rock, the partiality which he entertains for his own corps, is evident: the gallantry of officers, and of a detachment with which he was not immediately connected, is consigned to oblivion."

Perhaps Mackenzie was ignorant of the fact that among the papers in the War Office was an eloquent testimonial to Tarleton's reason for partiality: "That the Right Honourable Lord Rawdon, for one instance of the good behaviour of the Infantry of the British Legion, at Hanging Rock in South Carolina in August 1780, offered them colours, and the officers upon the spot medals, which were declined by the direction of Lt. Colonel Tarleton."

Mackenzie quoted the account of the engagement at Blackstock's from Ramsay's *History of the Revolution of South-Carolina.* After accepting the American report, he said: "The dispatches of Earl Cornwallis, with respect to the action at Blackstocks, has bestowed a laurel on Lieutenant Colonel Tarleton, which should have adorned the brows of General Sumpter, but then, as now, his Lordship drew his information from a corrupted fountain."

Of the 137 pages of *Strictures* devoted to the *Campaigns,* Mackenzie devoted 40 pages to the battle of Cowpens. He began with the appearance of Morgan west of the Catawba River, gave a running account of Tarleton's chase of the Americans, analyzed the disposition of the British troops, and then related what he saw of the battle.

In the eyes of Lord Cornwallis the *strategy* used to bring Morgan to battle had been unexceptionable. In those of Roderick Mackenzie the commandant of the British Legion made four errors in his *tactics.* Although the British troops had been marching since two o'clock that morning and needed food and rest, Tarleton did not halt them when he saw Morgan's troops drawn up in line of battle. Tarleton directed his line to advance before it had been properly formed, with resultant confusion and dismay. Tarleton failed to give discretionary powers to Major McArthur, an experienced infantry officer. And Tarleton ordered Lieutenant Ogilvie and forty dragoons to charge Colonel Washington's cavalry.

The Green Dragoon had defended himself by quoting Cornwallis' "total misbehaviour" of the troops. Said Mackenzie: "I was upon the detachment in question, and the narrative which I now offer has been submitted to the judgment of several respectable officers, and it has met with their entire approbation." He then pointed out that of the 16 officers in the 71st Regiment 9 were killed or wounded: "Few corps, in any age or country, will be found to have bled more freely."

The Lieutenant cried: "I leave Lieutenant Colonel Tarleton all the satisfaction which he can enjoy, from reflecting that he led a number of brave men to destruction, and then used every effort in his power to damn their fame with posterity."

The *Monthly Review* of February 1788 said of the *Strictures:* "A more severe piece of criticism we have seldom seen. Your periodical Reviewers are nothing to this military critic, who seems inclined to give no quarter; at least it does not appear that he has afforded any to Col. Tarleton."

Tarleton's friends were furious. Major George Hanger began drafting *An Address to the Army in Reply to Strictures by Roderick Mackenzie.*

Exclaimed the Major: "Any author who can daringly assert so base a falsehood, as that only twelve Americans fell in the action of the Cow Pens, has totally forfeited all claim to belief in his report of *that*, or any action."

After the lie direct, the former vice commandant of the British Legion began tearing the *Strictures* apart. "Though I may be obliged to assert and to prove that his whole production is unfair, uncandid, and unsupported by military knowledge; and though I may shew, that while he assumes to declare, 'that Tarleton's assertions are absurdities hitherto unparalleled,' he opposes nothing to these *absurdities* but vain attempts at ridicule, vainer *assertions* of his own, and an endless string of vague *ipse dixits*."

Continued Hanger: "Whenever an opening is found for detraction, or reflection on Lieut. Col. Tarleton as an officer, Roderick Mackenzie is sure to come forward; but as cautiously does he avoid touching on particular events to which the most envenomed pen must render a tribute of praise: as for instance, the action at *Monk's Corner; Lenou's Ferry; Colonel Beauford's defeat* in the upper part of Carolina; and *Sumpter's defeat near Camden*. Not one single comment has this *candid* Stricturist made on either of these actions."

Major Hanger, recuperating from yellow fever, had been with Lord Rawdon at Camden on January 17, 1781. He had talked with the wounded brought to the hospital. "I had an opportunity of obtaining every information relative to that unfortunate action, by daily, nay hourly, conversing with various officers who had been present at that action, and many of whom were uninfluenced by prejudice of *Party*."

In *An Address to the Army*, Major Hanger again did his best. He defended Colonel Tarleton's *Campaigns* point by point, stricture by stricture. Why? "My trifling observations result from a real affection for a man with whom I am most intimately connected, and who, by the author of the *Strictures*, has been most grossly represented and aspersed. I am acquainted with his abilities, his honor, his courage, and his real zeal for the cause in which his country was engaged."

An Address to the Army relieved the tension. Hanger's wit set the friends of the disputants chuckling. "Major Hanger's Work is exactly what was to be expected," observed the *World*. "It is frank and spirited —very zealous for his friend—often whimsical, but always sincere."

Then the *World* ended its notice of the controversy:

> Hanger's new *Book* is worth your reading—
> In authorship a new proceeding!
>   First, he reprints what has been seen:—
>   Then of his own you take a sup,
> *Strictures*,—he proves, should not have been,
>   And then he—stops the Strictures up!
> Concluding, in the way of Hanger—
> "My dear Mackenzie—that's a Banger!"

24

Sons of King George

$\mathcal{T}$HE PUBLICATION OF the *Campaigns* regained for Lieutenant Colonel Tarleton some of the prestige he had dissipated in the five years since his return from America. But even at twenty-six shillings a copy the book would make no money, and the author could not live as befitted his taste on his annual half-pay of £173. So he turned to the only thing in which he had any skill. He became a professional gambler.

With Captain Hardy of the Guards as partner he set up a faro bank at Daubigney's Tavern. "Faro is become a matter of business, as well as a game of chance in the polite world, and almost all the houses of fashion are now dealers and chapmen in this lucrative concern," said the *Morning Herald* of March 19, 1787. "In a more professed way of this infatuating amusement is just opened a new house under the dashing firm of Tarleton and Co!"

Tarleton had precedents in opening a faro hell. In the closing decades of the eighteenth century, London society went mad over this game. Men and women of the highest rank prostituted themselves to it. Charles Fox, when out of office and destitute, joined General Fitzpatrick in setting up a faro bank at Brooks's Club. When the Whigs again came into power, Fox assigned the bank to Lord Cholmondeley, Thomas Stepney, and Mr. Thompson. Under their management it ruined half the members of Brooks's.

The members did not trust the waiters to be croupiers, but dealt the cards themselves. The dealers received three guineas an hour, and at this rate Lord Cholmondeley and other noblemen of highest rank slaved away like menials. The gains were fabulous. As banker, Lord Cholmondeley realized £300,000 to £400,000.

Lord Robert Spencer, so nearly bankrupt that he sold his collection of paintings, turned banker and in one year won £100,000. With this he purchased Woolbedding, near Midhurst, Sussex, and never again did he touch a card.

Tarleton chose Daubigney's Tavern because it was patronized by military men, especially by officers of the Guards. He was a member of Daubigney's Club and a close friend of Colonel St. Leger who presided over it. In order to be near Banastre, George Hanger, the reigning bully of the Scavoire-Vivre Club, moved his headquarters over to Daubigney's. Here he lounged around the entrance, nursing a huge rattan, which in grim playfulness he had christened "the Infant."

Customers feared the Infant. Hanger was noted for duelling, and so they tried not to offend him. But soon there came to issue an antagonism that had carried over for two years. While the Major was at Brighton in the summer of 1785, there had been a disagreeable incident at the Prince's table. Captain Lloyd was made the butt. He began to feel that the royal favor toward him had abated and he frequently complained that his conduct had been misrepresented to the Prince.

At the Cocoa Tree on Sunday evening, June 17, 1787, Lloyd met Hanger and William Beckford. He addressed Beckford with cordiality, but did not speak to Hanger. He told Beckford: "I suspect that some scoundrel or another has prevailed on the Prince to withdraw his Highness's countenance from me."

Although Captain Lloyd had not mentioned Major Hanger, everyone present knew he was referring to Hanger. Immediately the Major asked him: "Am I alluded to by this insinuation? If so, I must insist on a meeting."

The Captain accepted the challenge, and the duellists chose their seconds. Lloyd asked Captain Morrice to stand with him, and Hanger chose Colonel Tarleton. The seconds began preparing for the meeting. They inspected and tested the hair-triggered pistols. They agreed on a distance of twelve paces. They rehearsed the intricate formulae of the code duello.

But Tarleton hated affairs of honor. Since no one could question his courage, no one imputed his hatred to cowardice. Said he later: "It was my good fortune at that period of my life, as is universally known by my friends, to have often engaged as a pacificator; as a duellist—never."

So the seconds arbitrated. They persuaded Lloyd to write a declaration of intent. The document in no way satisfied Hanger. On June 19 the seconds sat until the early hours of morning trying to "devise some honourable mode of accommodation."

Colonel St. Leger also held various interviews with the offended officers. "The point of honour seemed to outweigh every consideration or reason that the mediators could propose." But on June 21 the *London Chronicle* was happy to inform its readers: "The serious misunderstanding between the Hon. Major Hanger and Captain Lloyd is at length, by the unremitting toil of the arbitrators, brought to a satisfactory and honourable conclusion."

Next day Tarleton and Hanger joined the other members of the White Conduit Cricket Club to witness a test match between White Conduit and All England. Each team had posted 1000 guineas—winner take all. Such enthusiasts as the Duke of Bedford, the Earl of Derby, Lord Galloway, and the Duchess of Ancaster, Lady Aylesford, and Lady Willoughby de Eresby saw All England win.

While Ban led a restless life around London, Mary remained quietly at Aix-la-Chapelle. Then she decided to try the hot mud baths at St. Amand. "At length, solicitude for the restoration of her health, added to the earnest remonstrances of her friends, determined her on making the effort," said Maria Elizabeth. "For the purpose of being near the baths, which must be entered an hour before the rising of the sun, she hired a small but beautiful cottage near the spring, where she passed the summer of 1787."

During the summer Mary found a decaying tree in the woods of St. Amand. To her it became a poignant symbol, and she poured out her grief in a poem:

> Often do I seek thy shade dear withering tree,
>   Sad emblem of my own disast'rous state;
> Doom'd in the spring of life, alas! like *Thee*
>   To fade, and droop beneath the frowns of Fate;
> Like *Thee*, May Heaven to me the need bestow,
> To shelter Sorrow's tear, and sooth the Child of Woe.

The mud baths were soothing. The little foreign colony at Spa was optimistic, and in England friends were delighted. On October 30 the *World* said: "Last letters from Aix-la-Chapelle mention that Mrs. Robinson's health is entirely recovered."

Mary's health improved so much that she felt strong enough to return to England. Ban went for her. They lingered through the mellowing autumn days at St. Amand and then started for London.

The *World* of December 10 reported: "Colonel Tarleton, on his return home, traveled through France with Lord Winchelsea. Mrs. Robinson did not accompany Colonel Tarleton any part of the way. She stays at Paris a little longer, in the Hotel d'Angleterre."

The *Morning Post* of January 14, 1788, began another year's chronicle: "Mrs. Robinson, the celebrated Perdita, has published in France, several pieces of poetry which have been well received."

Ban's star had also begun to rise again. On January 15 the Duke of York mustered and paraded the Coldstream Guards. The *Morning Post* noted that Lieutenant Colonel Tarleton was among the military men approving the address of the royal colonel.

From friendly sources Henry Bate learned the truth about Mary's health and plans. The *Morning Herald* reported on January 24: "The return of Mrs. Robinson to England is an event that may be expected in a week or little better. She has appealed without success to every remedy on the continent for the restoration of her limbs, and now has the contemplation to try the Bath waters."

About the middle of January, Mary and Maria Elizabeth left Paris. During the last week of the month they arrived in London. On January 31 the *Morning Post* satisfied the curiosity of its readers: "Mrs. Robinson, though better than when she left England, has returned in a very weakly situation, and appears deeply affected and oppressed in spirits."

Mary's friends were happy over her return and tried to cheer her. "On her arrival in London she was affectionately received by the few friends whose attachment neither detraction nor adverse fortunes could weaken or estrange," said Maria Elizabeth. With her family and a suite of domestics, Mary settled at 42 Clarges Street. Ban settled near her at 30 Clarges Street.

Their conduct made people recognize their love and accept their illicit relationship. Even the Tarleton family stopped bullying them. Mary's friends began to call, and Ban's frequented her home. Among these were the sons of King George: the Prince of Wales, the Duke of York, and the Duke of Clarence.

Banastre was now one of the closest favorites of the royal brothers. They were attracted by his elegant manners, lively conversation, and high spirits.

The Clarges Street fellowship enjoyed their cakes and ale. In a letter to Lady Eliott, Sir Gilbert Eliott wrote: "Fox drinks what I should call a great deal, though he is not reckoned to do so by his companions, Sheridan excessively, and Grey more than any of them; but it is a much more gentlemanly way than our Scotch drunkards, and it is always accompanied with lively clever conversation on subjects of importance."

At one of their parties the Duke of York, rising abruptly from the table, fell prostrate upon the floor. The Prince, getting unsteadily to his feet, surveyed his fallen brother and solemnly declared: "There lie, as our Royal father says, the hopes of the family!"

The royal drunkards would wager on anything, and some of their gaming losses were carefully engineered. As early as 1756 Horace Walpole had recorded the story of a race between a flock of geese and a flock of turkeys. Major Hanger had heard of the race and one night introduced the subject into the gay talk at Carlton House. Hanger asserted that the turkey would outstrip the goose, and the Prince backed his judgment. It was decided to race twenty turkeys against twenty geese for ten miles on a wager of £500.

The Prince sent Hanger to select twenty of England's finest turkeys. At the appointed time and place the Prince with the turkeys met Mr. Berkeley with the geese. The race began at four o'clock in the afternoon. By seven o'clock the turkeys were two miles ahead of the geese. As the shadows lengthened the turkeys began flying up to the lower limbs of the trees along the road. Vainly the Prince urged them onward. Hanger dislodged one from its roosting place, only to find three or four others comfortably perched among the branches. Berkeley drove his waddling geese past the roosting turkeys, and the turkey party conceded the race.

About this time the roisterers were joined by Richard, the seventh Earl of Barrymore. At the age of five this descendant of the "Great Barries"—Burrach Mohr—inherited an earldom covering thirty parishes in Ireland. At the proper age he matriculated at Eton and promptly proved remiss in his studies. During the Easter vacation in 1785 he visited Newmarket for the Second Spring Meeting. The main event was a match between Rockingham and Sergeant over the Beacon Course. At odds of seven to four, the sixteen-year-old Etonian bet enough on Rockingham to win 1000 guineas. When the bookmaker handed him a thousand pounds, he coolly demanded another fifty, knowing that racing bets are paid in guineas. So great was the young Earl's admiration for Rockingham that he paid 2500 guineas for the aging champion.

Barrymore lived at Wargrave, a manor house named for a burial mound of Anglo-Saxon warriors, near Twyford-on-Thames. Here he surrounded himself with friends and retainers. He installed Henry Angelo as swords-master. From London he brought Signor Delphini and John Edwin to direct the dancing and acting at his private Wargrave Theatre. He appointed Anthony Pasquin his poet laureate.

At Wargrave he maintained a group of the best prize fighters in England. At one time in the cottage near his manor house he supported Johnson, Big Ben, Hooper the Tinsman, William and Joseph Ward, and Jackson. He ate at the table with them, led them in pranks, promoted their fights, and backed them with extravagant wagers. Bully Hooper, who came to the ring from the trade of tinsmith on Tottenham Court Road, was his favorite. Under Hooper's training the Earl became as skilled as a professional boxer.

His Lordship's character was perverse and not a little violent. His favorite diversion was to drive a closed carriage along Oxford Street, mimicking the screams and sobs of a woman in distress. When a gallant rescuer rushed to the carriage Barrymore would alight and thrash him for his impertinence. The Prince nicknamed the noble scamp "Hellgate."

The Prince of Wales had been invited to become a member of Brooks's Club without the formality of a ballot. Upon the return of the Duke of York from his military education in Germany, in August of 1787, the Prince introduced him into Brooks's. "The Duke of York never misses a night at Brooks's, where the hawks pluck his feathers unmercifully, and have reduced him to the vowels I.O.U.," wrote a contemporary. "The Prince attends very often and takes very kindly to play."

But when the Prince proposed Tarleton and Captain John Willet Payne of the Royal Navy for membership, not everyone in Brooks's was overjoyed. General Grant wrote a summary to Lord Cornwallis: "At the Irish Club we have been honoured with the presence of the Prince of Wales and the Duke of York, who are reciprocally obliged to one another: the Prince has taught the Duke to drink in the most liberal and copious way, and the Duke in return has been equally successful in teaching his brother to lose his money at all sorts of play,—Quinze, Hazard, etc.,—to the amount as we are told, of very large sums in favour of India General Smith and Admiral Pigot, who both wanted it very much. These play parties have chiefly taken place at a new Club, formed this winter by the Prince of Wales in opposition to Brooks's, because Tarleton and Jack Payne, proposed by His Royal Highness, were blackballed."

In a huff the Prince set up a rival club under Louis Weltjie, now chief steward at Carlton House. On February 27 the *Morning Post* observed: "A club at Weltjie's under the Prince and the three Royal Dukes is establishing on the most familiar and accommodating footing with respect to conversation and play."

Dover House never became a serious rival of White's or Brooks's, but Weltjie did his best. When Hellgate Barrymore was proposed for membership, there were two more black balls in the box than members in the room. Weltjie was called in. He admitted, "I did put in two black balls myself, lest he should come in, and ruin my club."

The newspapers began reporting wild gambling at Dover House. One said the Duke of Bedford had lost £70,000 to the Prince. Several days later another announced: "Colonel Tarleton has plucked a fat pigeon."

The *Morning Herald* of March 28 reported that "Colonel Tarleton's new vis-a-vis made its appearance last Monday:—it is a very beautiful and striking vehicle." For readers who wondered about the Colonel's finances, on April 5 the *Morning Herald* reported: "A certain *Colonel* of *dashing* memory in America, has made a few successful skirmishes against the YOUNG DUKE:—And to compensate for the rugged toils of war, it is thought he will hereafter be enabled to repose on a *pillow* of *pigeon's feathers.*"

On April 9 the *Morning Post* announced cryptically: "Perdita is said to be about town. Colonel Tarleton, after his late success, may be a good pigeon. Lord Malden is wiser."

The *Morning Herald* concluded its financial report on April 19: "The Perdita, notwithstanding her long indisposition still keeps her good looks: she sports an elegant vis-a-vis, and her dress and liveries are in corresponding style."

Truly the recent fugitives had struck it rich!

Mary now devoted all of her talent to poetry and published a series of sonnets in the *World*. Ban was still banker for his faro game at Daubigney's. In his gayer moods he attended the parties at Weltjie's or lounged with the Prince of Wales at Carlton House. For relaxation he took to the tennis court or cricket field. He still loved to follow the races and in April went with the Prince to Newmarket.

On April 23 Mr. Braddye, riding the Prince's colt Pegasus, defeated Lord Barrymore, riding Sweet William, for the Macaroni Stakes. But on April 26 Hellgate's horses won every race.

By now a handicapper second in skill only to Charles Fox, Barrymore raced Rockingham, with an eight-pound handicap, against Sir George Armitage's Stargazer, Jockey Jewison up. Three mounted jockeys had been stationed along the four-mile course to point the way to the Earl. At the starting gun, Rockingham bolted, and by the time he had crossed the flat, he was leading Stargazer by a quarter of a mile. Fearing injury to the noble scion of the Great Barries, attendants closed the doors of the stables. But old Rockingham pulled up and stopped at the winning post.

On May 2 the *Morning Post* exclaimed: "Even the enemies of Rockingham now allow him to be the best horse that ever came to Newmarket—four miles over the Beacon Course in seven minutes and a few seconds!"

Hellgate continued to match his horses and skill against those of the noted veterans of the turf: the Duke of Queensbury, the Duke of Bedford, Sir Harry Featherstone, Sir John Lade, Charles Fox, and the Prince of Wales. With Rockingham he won the King's Plate and the Jockey Club Plate, and then he purchased Highflyer, Rockingham's sire, and sent father and son to his breeding paddock.

After the Spring Meeting the betting fraternity at Carlton House turned to prize fighting. The Prince, the royal Dukes of York and of Clarence, the Duke of Hamilton, Earl Barrymore, General Fitzpatrick, Colonel Tarleton, Major Hanger, and Alderman Coombe began patronizing Hellgate's stable of pugs. Soon bloody, bare-knuckle fighting became the most popular sport around London. On June 9 the *Morning Post* noted that his Royal Highness, the Prince of Wales, had been in the numerous company witnessing the bout between Jackson and Fawtrell.

Cricket, however, remained Tarleton's choice. On July 7 the *Morning Post* noted: "Colonel Tarleton has received a hurt in his groins in playing at cricket which the medical faculty pronounce to be extremely dangerous." Ban set off for Brighton to recuperate, and Mary went with him.

The seaside resort had become an international favorite. To it came the royal and the noble, the statesman and the beau, the scholar and the idler, the rich and the beggar. The heir apparent to the throne and the royal dukes walked freely along the Steine among their father's subjects. In the gay, courtly throng with Ban and Mary at Brighton were the Duke and Duchess of Cumberland, the Duke and Duchess of Marlborough, the Dukes of Norfolk and of Bedford, and the Dukes of Chartres and of Lauzun. And they were joined by Pitt and Burke, Fox and Sheridan, the Barrymores, Sir John and Lady Lade, Major Hanger, Lady Jersey, and Mrs. Maria Fitzherbert, the secret wife of the Prince.

ๆๅๅ

About the end of July politics sent Tarleton and Hanger rushing back to London. Lord Townshend and Lord Hood were standing for Parliament in a by-election in Westminster, and the Whigs needed some hatchetmen. The Duke of Bedford put up the money for Lord Townshend, and Tarleton enlisted Hellgate's pugilists. The canvassing was rough. "The bludgeon men in the suite of the new candidate received a week's pay yesterday," observed the *Morning Post* of August 1. "Hanger and Tarleton are Quarter Masters to this honourable legion."

The *Morning Post* of August 2 continued: "On Monday next, at three o'clock, the three regiments of banditti, with Colonels Stanhope, Tarleton, and Hanger at their head, will march from the parade at Froome's round Covent Garden, with all the honors of blood and courage, from their electioneering campaign."

Men of both parties were beaten up. By August 11 the *Morning Post* could name dozens of Lord Hood's followers who had been wounded. Soon the Tories began singing a caustic song:

> There's a gallant Tarleton, he that once
>   A Legion did command—
> Legions of Devils now he leads,
>   With bludgeons in their hand.
> And a Knocking Down we'll go, etc.
>
> And there's blaspheming Hanger, too, who
>   Knows the art of War,
> He'll beat a Blackguard at a Blast,
>   Mendoza at a Spar.
> And a Sparring we will go, etc.

Upon Lord Townshend's election, the Whigs met at the Crown and Anchor Tavern to celebrate. On August 13 in post-election spleen the *Morning Post* reported that for the purpose of encouraging the useful arts the Buff and Blue Society had distributed election medals. For ghost-writing Townshend's speeches Sheridan received a gilt medal. For the man who had split the greatest number of skulls there was a gold medal, or two guineas. "This was warmly contested by Ward, Colonel T——, Johnson, M— H-g-r, and Ting. T-l-t-n was convinced he merited it, but wishing to encourage the useful arts, ceded in favor of Ward."

In discussing contributions to the campaign the *Morning Post* of August 21 credited:

Major Hanger: 10,000 oaths and 15,000 curses.
Colonel Tarleton: four paving stones for the demolition of Martin the publican's windows.
Mrs. Robinson: the use of her vis-a-vis.

The poetaster for the *Morning Post* then hymned a Victory Ode:

Burke, Tarleton, Hanger, Ward, and Ting,
All boxers tried, the next I sing,
Who Martin's windows bravely shattered,
Knocked down the doors, and shutters battered!

During the shouting and the fighting, some wag thought of a series of inscriptions for fictitious tombs in Kilkhampton Abbey. On September 6 his epitaph for Colonel Tarleton's monument appeared in the *World*:

Colonel T*******

Coach-builders, Curricle-builders,
Harness-devisers, and Wheel Patentees
Deplore your loss. Your Colonel is no more!
Here beneath this rough-hewn Stone,
Called from Life without a groan,
In piteous case he lies at length!
Sunk in all his manly Beauty,
Perish'd all his Martial Duty,
Wither'd all his prosperous Strength.

Colonel T*******

Was one of those unhappy few, in whom the
General, the Sergeant, the Drummer, and
The suttling Wench had set their Seal,
To certify to the World that he
Was a Soldier!

Campaigns had he seen many, Dangers had he
  Fought with there, Troubles had he made easy,
  Achievements had he crowned with Conquest,
      And the Enemy's Musquets had he
          Brought into Contempt!
Yet why? He was sentenced to die, like Sisera,
      By the hand of a Woman, and, in
              Consequence of that Destiny
Expired at Midnight of the 1st of Jan. 1796
  In the Arms of Mrs.———, with his
  Head where his Heels should be.

On September 19 Henry Bate announced in the *Morning Herald*:
"Lieutenant Colonel Tarleton is at this time employed in an active
campaign at Liverpool, for which borough he proposes himself again
at the next general election."

During the heat of the canvassing in Westminster, Ban and Mary
quarreled. She was jealous of his passions, his wandering fancy, and
she threatened to go to her brothers in Italy. While he was in Liverpool, she turned her threat into a confession of love and published
it in the *World* of October 31 as "Lines to Him Who will Understand Them." Mr. Bell, editor of the *World*, did not understand the
poem. He wrote: "More fanciful and pathetic lines are scarcely to be
found in the whole body of English Literature."

LINES
To
HIM WHO WILL UNDERSTAND THEM

Thou art no more my bosom's FRIEND;
Here must the sweet delusion end,
That charm'd my senses many a year,
Thro' smiling summers, winters drear.—
O, Friendship! am I doom'd to find
Thou art a phantom of the mind?
A glitt'ring shade, an empty name,
An air-borne vision's vap'rish flame?
And yet, the dear deceit so long
Has wak'd to joy my matin song,
Has bid my tears forget to flow,
Chas'd every pain, sooth'd ev'ry woe;
That Truth, unwelcome to my ear,
Swells the deep sigh, recalls the tear,
Gives to the sense the keenest smart,
Checks the warm pulses of the Heart,
Darkens my Fate and steals away
Each gleam of joy thro' life's sad day.

BRITAIN, Farewell! I quit thy shore,
My native Country charms no more;
No guide to mark the toilsome road;
No destin'd clime; no fix'd abode;
Alone and sad, ordain'd to trace
The vast expanse of endless space;
To view, upon the mountain's height,
Thro' varied shades of glimm'ring light
The distant landscape fade away
In the last gleam of parting day:
Or, on the quivering lucid stream,
To watch the pale moon's silv'ry beam;
Or when, in sad and plaintive strains,
The mournful PHILOMEL complains,
In dulcet notes bewails her fate,
And murmurs for her absent mate;
Inspir'd by Sympathy divine,
I'll weep her woes—for they are mine.
Driven by my Fate, where'er I go
O'er burning plains, o'er hills of snow,
Or on the bosom of the wave,
The howling tempest doom'd to brave,
Where'er my lonely course I bend
Thy image shall my steps attend;
Each object I am doom'd to see
Shall bid remembrance turn to Thee.

Yes; I shall view thee in each Flow'r,
That changes with the transient hour:
Thy wand'ring Fancy I shall find
Borne on the wings of every wind:
Thy wild impetuous passions trace
O'er the white wave's tempestuous space:
In every changing season prove
An emblem of thy wav'ring Love.

Torn from my country, friends, and you,
The World lies open to my view;
New objects shall my mind engage;
I will explore th' historic page;
Sweet Poetry shall soothe my soul;
Philosophy each pang controul:
The muse I'll seek, her lambent fire
My soul's quick senses shall inspire;
With finer nerves my heart shall beat,
Touch'd by Heaven's own Promethean heat;
ITALIA's gales shall bear my song
In soft-link'd notes her woods among;
Upon the blue hill's misty side,

Thro' trackless deserts waste and wide,
O'er craggy rocks, whose torrents flow
Upon the silver sands below.

Sweet Land of Melody! 'tis thine
The softest passions to refine;
Thy myrtle groves, thy melting strains,
Shall harmonize and soothe my pains.
Nor will I cast one thought behind
On Foes relentless, Friends unkind;
I feel, I feel their poison'd dart
Pierce the life-nerve within my heart;
'Tis mingled with the vital heat,
That bids my throbbing pulses beat;
Soon shall that vital heat be o'er,
Those throbbing pulses beat no more!
No—I will breathe the spicy gale;
Plunge the clear stream, new health exhale;
O'er my pale cheek diffuse the rose,
And drink OBLIVION to my woes.

25

Fighting Blood

$\mathcal{I}$N LATE OCTOBER 1788 there was an announcement that King George was slightly indisposed. Sir George Baker, the King's physician, diagnosed the malady. The Prince rushed up from Brighton. During the evening of November 4 the King became violent. He flew at his son, seized him by the collar, and threw him against the wall. The Queen went into hysterics. The Princesses began an agony of weeping. The Prince fled, and the insane King sat and babbled all night.

An account of the scene was relayed to the Prime Minister on November 6. Pitt waited all evening for a messenger from Windsor Castle with news of the King's death. The Whigs among the Prince's friends waited, too, but they were leaderless: Charles Fox had chosen this autumn to tour Italy with Mrs. Armstead. Meanwhile they sent the Duke of York to Lord Loughborough, the chief justice, to say that his Royal Highness looked to him alone for guidance. During the evening of November 6 Captain Payne, secretary to the Prince, posted a letter to Lord Loughborough from Windsor Castle: the King's "state is so bad, that I fear dissolution is almost the best that can be hoped. The *last* stroke, as I hear from the *best* authority, cannot be far off. It is what everybody, in a situation to see, is obliged to wish, as the *happiest possible termination to the melancholy scene*. The event we looked for last night is *postponed*, perhaps for a short time."

But King George, who seemed so near death at midnight, dropped into a profound sleep and awoke out of immediate danger. Those with a kingdom almost in their grasp were now forced to settle for a regency, and for even that they had to negotiate with Pitt and the Tories. Captain Payne wrote Sheridan: "I have had correspondence enough myself on this subject to convince me of the impossibility of the Ministry managing the present Parliament by any contrivance hostile to the Prince. Dinner is on the table."

The Prince's party intended to sweep every Tory from office. Sir William Fawcett, adjutant general, wrote Lord Cornwallis that the Whigs planned to appoint 4 field marshals, including the Prince, the Duke of York, and the Duke of Gloucester. There would be 31 generals, 12 lieutenant generals, and 12 major generals. All colonels down to and including Lord Rawdon were to be promoted to major generals. Captain Payne was to be Lord of the Admiralty, and Sheridan, Secretary of the Navy. Fox was to be Secretary for Foreign Affairs, and General Fitzpatrick, Secretary for War. The Duke of York was to be commander in chief. On February 6, 1789, the *World* announced that in the reorganization being planned the aide to the Duke would be Lieutenant Colonel Banastre Tarleton.

Parliament met on November 20, but action was polite and formal, for neither Whigs nor Tories were ready for battle. The Whigs were without word from Fox until he stumbled into Thomas Hotel, Berkeley Square, on November 24. He had reached London from Bologna by post chaise in nine days. When he walked into Parliament his appearance shocked everyone. His body was emaciated, his face sallow and sickly, his eyes swollen. His stockings hung upon his legs, and he rather dragged himself along than walked up the floor to take his seat.

The conflict now became desperate. Meetings were secret and mysterious. Letters were written in cipher. Accusations of unscrupulousness, disloyalty, and treason were bandied to and fro. The showdown came on December 10, when Prime Minister Pitt moved "that a committee be appointed to examine and report precedents."

Fox dragged himself to his feet. For what useful purpose does the Minister propose to search for precedents? "There exists no precedent whatever that will bear upon this case."

Warming to his subject the great Whig orator thundered: "In my firm opinion, his Royal Highness the Prince of Wales has as clear, as express a *right* to assume the reins of government, and exercise the power of sovereignty during the continuance of the illness and incapacity with which it has pleased God to afflict his Majesty, as in the case of his Majesty's having undergone a natural demise. And as to this right, which I conceive the Prince of Wales has, he is not himself to judge when he is entitled to exercise it, but the two Houses of Parliament, as the organs of the nation, are alone qualified to pronounce when the Prince ought to take possession of, and exercise this right."

Pitt saw the blunder, slapped his thigh, and whispered to a friend: "I'll *unwhig* the gentleman for the rest of his life!"

In his reply Prime Minister Pitt rejected the doctrine of the right of the Prince. The doctrine is little less than treason to the Constitution. The heir apparent has no more *right* to the executive power than any other person in the realm. In the case of the incapacity of the sovereign it falls upon the two remaining branches of the Legislature to make provision for the interregnum. Said he: "Let not the House, therefore, rashly annihilate and annul the authority of Parliament, in which the existence of the Constitution is so intimately involved."

The leading Whigs seemed set on self-destruction. "The day was closed by such a blunder of Sheridan's as I never knew any man of the meanest talents guilty of before," wrote Grenville. "During the whole time that I have sat in Parliament, in pretty warm times, I never remember such an uproar as was raised by his threatening us with the danger of provoking the Prince to assert his right, which were the exact words he used."

Pitt calmly rejected "so indecent a menace," and warned that "the House will do its duty, in spite of any threat, however high the quarter from which it may come."

Fox's blunder had ruined any chance for the immediate creation of a regency. "At White's, all was hurrah and triumph; at Brooks's all was despondency," William Grenville wrote to the Marquis of Buckingham. "Fox's declaration has done no small service to us. Is it not wonderful that such great talents should be conducted with so little judgment?"

On December 16 Pitt introduced into Parliament resolutions setting up a restricted regency. Fox and the Whigs fought stubbornly, but Pitt, with addresses of support pouring in from the towns and cities, remained steadfast, winning vote after vote.

The Regency Bill became the law of the land. "Mr. Pitt," wrote Mr. Storer, "is so powerful that he can do as he pleases. Had he known his own power at the beginning of this business, perhaps he would never have thought of the Prince of Wales as Regent."

A limited regency had almost incited the Prince's party to assert his right. "Meantime, nothing was equal to the violence of the party, de part et d'autre, but most the Prince's side, because disappointed," wrote a contemporary. "The Duke of Portland has declared to the Prince his determination not to act with Mr. Sheridan in council, who is just now Prime Minister at Carlton House. He and his wife live with Mrs. Fitzherbert, having no other habitation. Charles Fox, besides ill-health, is plagued to death all day long, dissatisfied with Mr. Sheridan's supremacy."

While England teetered on the edge of anarchy the indefatigable sportsmen pursued their games. On January 1, 1789, the *World* reported that on the day before, on Knavestock Common in Essex, Ward had defeated Wood in a spectacular prize fight. Among the spectators were Sir Peter Burrell, Mr. Damer, Mr. Aston, and Colonel Tarleton.

Ban was deeply involved in the scheming at Carlton House. Like most of the friends of the Prince, he waited while Fox, Sheridan, and Lord Rawdon guided the party. From his friendship with the sons of King George he expected promotion and active duty when the Prince's party should come into power.

That party had an unexpected opportunity of measuring its popularity. On February 7 died Sir Thomas Halifax, member of Parliament for Aylesbury. Smarting from their defeat in 1784 and hopeful of imminent rise to power, the Whigs sent Colonel Gerard Lake, now first equerry to the Prince, to stand for the vacant seat.

A couple of days later the Carlton House set was startled by the appearance of a letter purportedly signed by stammering German-born Louis Weltjie:

> To de Gendelmen, de Abbes, and de Freholders of de Comte of Ailsbri.
>
> My frind Gerri Lake havin offurd his sarvis's, to repreprepresent you in parlialialiament, I presum to tak de friddom to recummind um to you, bein my frind, and grate frind of my master de Prince. He is ver clever gendelmen, and kno de horse ver vell, how to bi for de Prince, and how to sel for himselv. But if you tink him two poor, and send him to de divl, I beg to offer miselv to his intrist, havin got plenti of munny in de honrable stasion I holds undur de Prince. I am naturalise Inglisman and Wig, and was introduce to de Wig Club by Lord Stormant and Jak Payne. My public sentiments are dat I vil give you ver good dinnurs and plenti of munni, if you wil lect me your representatatavive. My frinds and connuxions are de Duk of Quinsbri, Lord Lodian, Lord Lubbro, Lord Malmsbri, Lord Clurmunt, Lord Cartrit, Sheridan, Gerri Lake, Jak Payne, Geo. Hangre, Burke, Singel Spict Hambledon, Eglintown, Master Lee, Trevis de Jew, yong Gray, all de Convays, Harri Standup, Tarletun, and Tom Stepni. My principles are God dam de King and de Quin, de Pitt, and de Rustricsuns; and God bles de Prince and all his broders, and de Duk de Cumberland. I say agen and agen dat de Prince be our lawful suvring, and not his fader.
>
> I am, gendelmen,
Your frind and sarvant,
W. Velshie

While the Weltjie letter, a hoax supposedly written by Thomas Onslow, was ruining the Whigs at Aylesbury, the Prime Minister and the Tories marked time. Pitt was gambling on the advice of Dr. Francis Willis, a physician skilled in the treatment of insanity. He maintained that the King would recover.

Signs of returning reason became numerous. King George began recognizing and talking with members of his family. On February 20 Princess Augusta Sophia wrote Miss Goldsworthy: "I have the pleasure, my dearest Gooly, of telling you we had the happiness of a Visit from my dear Papa. Last night he came up stairs at 7 and staid till ½ past 9. Thank God, my dearest Goully, for this Comfort. Thank God for his great mercy to us. I am so very happy that I really could hardly believe my eyes when I saw him, he was so composed, so kind, so exactly what you and all our real friends could wish."

The Prince of Wales and the Duke of York were not happy. "I have not heard yet," wrote Lord Bulkeley to William Eden on February 24, "but conclude they were both rioting and drunk at the masquerade, as they were at one a week ago. The truth is that they are quite desperate, and endeavor to drown their cares, disappointments, and eternal chagrin, in wine and dissipation."

This was the melancholy state of affairs General Richard Grenville, governor of the household of the Duke of York, described to Lord Cornwallis. Said he of the Duke: "I am sorry to say that he still continues in the same style of life which has lasted the whole winter, and which if he does not soon change, neither his constitution or pocket can hold out, and we shall be obliged, as the sailors call it, to cut and run for the Continent; in short, my dear Lord, we take a long time to sow our wild oats, and I am sadly afraid we shall never have a good crop, unless something turns up in our favour, to remove us from this scene of riot and eternal dissipation."

Other correspondents kept Lord Cornwallis informed of the moves in this scramble for power. Lord Rawdon, who had been promised the post of Home secretary in the prospective Cabinet, on February 28 wrote a confession to his old commander: "I, as you probably would suspect, have taken part decidedly with the Prince on this question, thinking the combination attempted to be marshalled against him the most mischievous in its necessary effect upon the constitution, that could possibly be conceived. By this means I have slidden into a kind of alliance with the D. of Portland. Had a new administration been formed, I should have had a seat in it! This ground having, however, been stipulated by me, and admitted by them, that I should never be considered as absorbed into the Duke's party, but should remain with my particular friends a distinct body. This the Prince guaranteed; and that condition would have lodged in my hands a check upon the intemperance of some of that set that would have been very useful."

Rawdon's letter reached India in August. Lord Cornwallis, said by his enemies to stutter merely because the King stuttered, was mortified. He replied in a bitter letter:

In regard to the political part which you thought it right to take in the late melancholy situation of affairs, I cannot avoid acknowledging that few things could have given me greater concern.

I know you to have the nicest sentiments of honour and integrity, and I greatly respect your judgment, yet I am not entirely without apprehension that on that occasion it was somewhat warped by pique and ill-humour on one side, and persuasion, open arms, and a laudable desire to provide for some friends on the other. Had I been upon the spot I should have thought it the duty of a friend to have stated my sentiments to you, and to have represented what the impartial world would probably say upon your relative situation to the poor sick King, whose crown would undoubtedly have been torn virtually from his head, or at least must have sat very uneasy upon it, after his recovery, if a Regent had been appointed without restrictions.

The die is now cast; and although I thought our old friendship and your letter called upon me to say so much, I shall be very delicate in troubling you in future with my sentiments on political subjects; for I know from experience, that when people arrive at so great a degree of difference of opinion, both in regard to men and measures, as I am much afraid is the case at present between you and myself, frequent discussions of that nature seldom fail to irritate, and hardly ever succeed to convince.

This can however make no kind of alteration in our private friendship, as I am persuaded that we mutually possess each other's esteem. On my part I shall always have a pleasure in giving the warmest proofs of it on every occasion that may offer through life.

Finally the Prince wrote Lord Cornwallis, seeking approval of the conduct of the Duke of York during the King's illness. The Earl refused his approbation and said that had he been in his seat in the House of Lords he would have voted against the Regency.

Undeterred, the Prince and the Duke continued roaring around London. One evening on the way to the opera they rode in the Prince's coach. In one of the narrow streets their carriage was stopped by traffic. A mob began shouting: "God save the King!"

The Prince lowered his window and shouted back: "Long live the King!"

One ruffian shouted: "Pitt forever! God bless Pitt!"

The Prince answered: "Damn Pitt. Fox forever!"

The ruffian jerked open the coach door. The Prince attempted to spring upon the man, but the Duke held him back with one hand and struck their attacker with his fist. At that moment the coachman lashed his horses, and off they went, the crowd booing and the coach door flapping wildly.

ᝳ

Because the Duke of Richmond supported Pitt on the Regency Bill, the animosity of the royal brothers fell upon all members of his family. It was especially heavy upon Richmond's nephew, Lieutenant Colonel Charles Lennox of the Coldstream Guards. At Daubigney's Club the Duke of York said that he had heard Colonel Lennox stand for language "which no officer or gentleman ought to have tolerated." Then he sneered: "The Lennoxes don't fight."

During inspection on May 15 Colonel Lennox left his station, approached the Duke, and demanded to know whether his Royal Highness had said "that he had put up with language unfit for a gentleman to hear." The Duke ordered the Colonel back into the ranks.

At a conference in the orderly room of the Horse Guards, in the presence of all the officers of the regiment, the Duke answered Lennox: Yes, he had heard the improper language, and had said he heard it; but he declined to name the speaker. As the exchange became heated, he told Lennox: "I desire to derive no protection from my rank as a Prince, or my station as commanding officer. When not on duty, I wear a brown coat, and shall be ready, as a private gentleman, to give you satisfaction."

Colonel Lennox wrote each member of Daubigney's, asking if he remembered hearing him take abusive language. Their letters were unsatisfactory, so Lennox sent a letter to the Duke by the Earl of Winchelsea demanding a public retraction. The Duke's answer was both unsatisfactory and verbal, and the Colonel sent the Duke a written challenge.

For his second the Duke chose Lord Rawdon. The Colonel chose Lord Winchelsea. The seconds set the duel for sunrise next morning. The Duke was living at Carlton House, and to prevent the Prince from discovering his absence, he left his hat and wore one belonging to a servant. With Lord Rawdon he drove to Wimbledon Common in a hired post chaise.

The seconds measured twelve paces and instructed the principals to fire at the signal. Lennox aimed at the Duke's forehead. He fired, and the ball cut a side curl from the royal head. But the Duke did not fire. Winchelsea requested the Duke to fire. Lord Rawdon replied that the Duke had no intention of firing. The Duke had come out to give the Colonel satisfaction—he had no animosity against him. Would the Duke, then, retract his statement? The Duke would not: if Colonel Lennox was not satisfied, he might fire again. Now Lennox refused, whereupon both parties left the ground.

Lords Rawdon and Winchelsea wrote a long account for the newspapers. They concluded: "The seconds think it proper to add, that both parties behaved with the most perfect coolness and intrepidity."

As a member of Daubigney's Club, Colonel Lennox heard much of the talk about the duel. He did not like Tarleton's spirited support of the Duke. So he wrote him an upbraiding letter.

Ban thought that Lennox had sent him a challenge. Immediately he replied:

No. 30, Clarges Street, May 18

Sir,

In answer to the very extraordinary letter I have this moment received, I must as a member of *Daubigney's* observe, that if any part of my private or political conduct has given you offense, I am ready to maintain it.

> I have the honor to be, Sir,
> Your most obd't humble Serv't
> Ban. Tarleton

Lt. Col. Lenox

Both cooled off and nothing came of the exchange. A few days later a convention of the officers of the Coldstream Guards found that "subsequent to the fifteenth of May, Lieutenant-Colonel Lennox had behaved with courage, but, from the peculiarity of the circumstances, not with judgement." He exchanged places with Lord Strathhaven of the 35th Regiment.

It would have been happier for Charles Lennox had he dropped lifeless on the field of honor. Though he lived to become Duke of Richmond and to usher in Waterloo with the most famous ball in the annals of British society—

> There was a sound of revelry by night,
> And Belgium's capital had gather'd then
> Her Beauty and her Chivalry—

—under the ramparts of Quebec he died, like a mad dog, writhing with hydrophobia.

When he learned of the duel, King George became dangerously agitated. He closed the door, threw his arms around the Duke, and cried: "My dear Frederick, Heaven has miraculously saved your life and mine!"

Even so, King George suffered no relapse. By June 4 he was normal, and his birthday was celebrated with unusual splendor. Crowds thronged St. James's. They were ushered in one door and out through the opposite. Everyone was happy.

During the evening there was dancing in the palace. In high spirits the Prince called the figures to a lively tune, "Tarleton's Delight." But as he was dancing a country dance with the Princess Royal, and turning each couple, the Prince came to Colonel Lennox and Lady Catherine Barnard. As the Princess reached her hands toward Lennox, the Prince grasped them and led her out of the dance.

The Duke of York did not hesitate to turn the Colonel and Lady Catherine. But the Duke of Clarence followed the example of the Prince.

"Are you tired?" the Queen asked the Prince when she saw him leave the dance.

"Not at all," he answered.

"Do you find it too hot?"

"In such company it is impossible not to find it too hot."

"Then," said the Queen, "I suppose you mean that I should break up the ball?"

"It's the very best thing you can do," replied the Prince.

Queen Charlotte gave the signal for retiring.

෴

As the hopes of the Prince and the schemes of the Whigs oozed away, Colonel Tarleton continued his gaming. On April 9 a reporter for the *World* saw him in company with Sir Peter Burrell and other boxing enthusiasts on Blackheath, where George the Brewer and Miles the Drover fought for the prize.

Banastre was living by his wits. But he was living well, and in a style befitting a companion of the Prince. He had a full retinue of servants, horses, and carriages. The *World* of July 7 said: "Colonel Tarleton, by his green livery, still keeps up the remembrance of his famed Legion."

During the summer Ban followed the Prince to Brighton. "The Duke of Bedford, Sir H. Featherstone, Major Churchill, Lord Egremont, Lord Barrymore, C. Wyndham, Colonel Tarleton, and George Hanger have already arrived," reported the *World* of July 17. "The Dukes of York and Clarence are expected next week."

Mary was with Ban. Secretly writing under the name of "Laura," she was winning popularity with her melancholy verse. She was also living in high style, with a suite of liveried attendants and all the accouterments of wealth. "Mrs. Robinson on Friday launched an elegant Phaeton, and four beautiful grey ponies," said the *Oracle* of August 24. "She was attended by Colonel Tarleton, her constant and *cher ami*. Mrs. Robinson is daily recovering."

Tarleton was constantly with the royal brothers. Cricket, horse racing, musicals, and card playing consumed their time and energy. "Last Friday a match at Cricket was played, on the Flat near Brighton: the Duke of York on one side, and Colonel Tarleton on the other; who chose eleven each," said the *Oracle* of August 20. "The Duke's side fetched in their innings 292; Colonel Tarleton's 7, having five wickets to go down." The game was not played out for lack of time, but "The same gentlemen will play again on Wednesday for 100 guineas; Colonel Tarleton is to have Street the Miller."

As the season drew to a close, the Prince of Wales gave a sumptuous dinner for his friends. Places were laid for fifty-four—among them the Duke of York, the Duke of Clarence, the Duke of Cumberland, Lord Clermont, Lord Robert Spencer, Mr. Fox, Mr. Sheridan, Colonel St. Leger, and Colonel Tarleton. Then the *Oracle* of August 24 reported: "Saturday Colonel Tarleton set off for the York Races with the Prince of Wales and the Duke of York."

After the York meeting, Ban returned to London and waited for the next prize fight. Lord Barrymore had promoted a match between Johnson and Perrins, the Birmingham giant. They were scheduled to meet on Thursday, October 29, near the town of Banbury. Opposition to these bloody spectacles, especially to the class of patrons who flocked around the prize ring, was developing throughout England, and on Wednesday the county magistrates met in Oxford determined to prevent the match. But as Banbury lay outside their jurisdiction, they could do nothing.

Colonel Tarleton and Mr. Meadows, innkeeper of Birmingham, served as umpires. Perrins had his brother for bottle holder and another boxer named Pickard for his second. Johnson had the brothers William and Joseph Ward for second and bottle holder. Major Hanger represented the interests of Lord Barrymore, who lay ill at Wargrave.

The promoters had secured an enclosed space large enough to hold several thousand spectators. In the center they had erected a platform four feet high and twenty feet square. Over the floor they had laid a covering of turf and over that a layer of sawdust. They sold tickets at one-half guinea each, but long before the fight local sportsmen shoved over a wall and crowded out the gentlemen from London.

The fight was desultory and lasted an hour and twelve minutes. There was much dodging and slipping. Johnson proved to be the cleverer boxer and superior ring man. He danced around Perrins, keeping the sun at his back, and flicked away at the squinting eyes of the Birmingham giant. When Perrins became too exhausted to raise his guard, Johnson knocked him out.

Johnson received £800 prize money, and one half of the gate receipts. A Mr. Bullock won £20,000 and gave Johnson £1000. He left Banbury in a post-chaise and four, with gay ribbons fluttering from the postillions. The men from Birmingham made up a purse of 300 guineas for Perrins.

Hanger sent a messenger galloping toward Wargrave. As he rode he shouted at every open tavern: "Johnson beat Perrins! Johnson beat Perrins! Johnson is champion of the world!"

With his enormous winnings, Hellgate went on a splurge. One afternoon he met Charles Fox outside White's. Fox suggested they kill time by playing for small stakes. They chose quinze, for a guinea a game. Barrymore won every farthing in Fox's wallet. Then he arose, saying, "I can't waste my time like this."

Nettled by the run of bad luck, with his sporting blood rising, Fox exclaimed: "Name it!"

"One thousand guineas a game," replied the Earl.

Barrymore won the first game. Again he won. And again and again. After winning 7000 guineas, Barrymore stood up and said that he had to go home. Fox protested that he should be given a chance to win back some of his money. Hellgate would have none of it. "I won't win any more from a dead flat," he said.

Fox handed his Lordship a draft for the 7000 guineas and followed him to the door, still arguing strenuously.

"No, I won't win any more from a dead flat," repeated the Earl.

Infuriated by the phrase, "dead flat," Fox demanded to know what it meant.

"A dead flat," shouted Hellgate, swinging into his carriage and heading toward Wargrave, "is a person who wears silver buttons so highly polished that they reflect the faces of his cards."

Having bet heavily on Johnson, Colonel Tarleton was also flush, and he began throwing his guineas around. On January 9, 1790, *The Norfolk Chronicle and the Norwich Gazette* reported a bet—but no winner: "Colonel Tarleton is to run fifty yards with Lord Mountford on his back, in less time than the Duke of Queensbury trots a hundred and ten with any horse, mare, or gelding he chooses to ride. Both are to start at the same moment: Beacon Course, on the second day of the next Newmarket Meeting, play or pay, for 500 guineas. The odds are laid as five to four that the Colonel wins, and considerable sums have been betted on this curious race."

A week later the Colonel was at Seaford, in Sussex, one of the Cinque Ports, canvassing the voters. "Colonel Tarleton is not canvassing Seaford on his account; but as the representative of his brother, Mr. John Tarleton," the *London Chronicle* announced on January 14. "The Colonel means to offer *himself* for Liverpool."

26

To the Hustings

*A*NTICIPATING A dissolution of Parliament, in the spring of 1790 Lieutenant Colonel Tarleton prepared *An Address to the Freemen of Liverpool*. This pamphlet of 58 pages, printed in London and distributed through the booksellers in Liverpool, set forth the political issues involved in the coming election, judged the character and work of Lord Penrhyn and Bamber Gascoyne, and pleaded for the election of Colonel Tarleton—all this in a style that savored more of Richard Sheridan's oratory than of Mary Robinson's prose.

Upon Prime Minister Pitt, who had prevented Tarleton from going out to India with Lord Cornwallis, the pamphleteer poured his wrath. He impugned the Minister's conduct on the India Bill and on the Westminster election. He stated that Pitt, "during the discussion of the African Trade, exhibited a species of duplicity unsuspected and unprecedented."

He attacked Pitt's handling of the Regency Bill. He pointed out that "Mr. Fox, at whose name corruption startles, and at whose wisdom the subordinates and hireling agents of administration tremble, defended the rights of the constitution and his Prince."

He said that under Prime Minister Pitt "the bravest and most deserving characters have been doomed to obscurity, inaction, and neglect." He went on to ask why, when all nations have honored their heroes, has not our worthy, intrepid, and patriotic townsman, Colonel Tarleton, "reaped the well earned fruits of military fame? Have intrepid courage, active vigilance, and distinguished qualities, been rewarded with patronage, preferment, or even attention?"

He asked his townsmen: "To whom shall we impute this scandalous omission, this disgraceful inattention?"

He answered himself: "An illiberal Minister who holds the reins of authority with the absolute austerity of a Roman Dictator."

The cause of this neglect? "Defamation may assert, that the Colonel, by an attachment to the Whig interest, has forfeited his just and merited claim to preferment." But "As a soldier, a Briton, and a good subject, he reverences the Crown, yet will not yield to the stern commands of any Minister."

The writer made a direct appeal. He pointed to the extensive commercial concerns of the firm of Tarleton and Backhouse. He eulogized the manner in which their business was conducted. "There exists not a tradesman in this large and populous town, who is not anxious to enter into their service. The private virtues and excelling qualities of the family are too deeply implanted on your memories to require any observation."

Then he turned from the family to himself. "The Colonel has the air, manners, and address, of a man of rank; dignity without affectation, and politeness without pride: His breast is the seat of those passions, that warm our nature and exalt human reason: his disinterested integrity, incorruptible heart, and his invariable attachment to the interest of his country, justly entitle him to your patronage and support."

He detailed his own military record—forgetting to mention Cowpens: a grateful public has acknowledged these services, but his Gracious Sovereign has not rewarded them. And he ended *An Address* with a summons: "It remains, therefore, for you, my fellow townsmen, to perform this enviable duty, by electing him one of your Representatives."

Tarleton had thoroughly canvassed the borough. Failing of election by only a dozen votes in 1784, he had brought the knowledge and techniques learned in the Westminster elections in 1784 and 1788. He had kissed the girls in the fish market. He had dazzled honest carpenters and whalers along the Mersey with his courtly manners. He had brought a sheaf of campaign songs fresh from the pen of Mary Robinson.

From the home of his mother he formally announced his candidacy:

Bold-street, June 14th, 1790

To the Worthy and Independent FREEMEN of Liverpool.

Gentlemen,

The Dissolution of Parliament affords me a second Opportunity of tending you my Services: My ill success on a former Occasion I cannot ascribe to any want of spirit or affection on your part, but to the too great security exhibited in the early part of the Poll: Confiding in your good opinion, which I am not conscious of having done any thing to forfeit, I again solicit your Votes; and should I be so happy as to obtain a seat in Parliament for Liverpool, which I shall ever consider as the greatest honor that can be conferred on me dur-

ing my existence, be assured I shall continue unremittingly attentive to the interest and prosperity of my Brother Townsmen.

I have the honor to remain,

With the greatest Regard and Respect,

GENTLEMEN,

Your most obedient,

And most humble servant,

Ban. Tarleton

Mayor Thomas Smyth and bailiffs Henry Blundell and John Shaw
issued a call to the merchants and tradesmen of Liverpool. They met
at the Exchange at noon on June 16 to consider the proper persons to
represent the borough in Parliament and to concert such measures as
might appear best calculated to meet the wishes of the Freemen. At the
meeting Penrhyn and Gascoyne jointly announced that a decided majority of gentlemen and tradesmen were desirous that "We should
again have the Honor of representing this truly respectable Borough
in Parliament. Permit us thus jointly to take the Liberty of requesting
the Favor of your votes and interests at the ensuing election."

When John Bolton placed Colonel Tarleton's name in nomination,
and Mayor Smyth called for a show of approving hands, the Corporation and the coalition were surprised at the Colonel's strength. Mayor
Smyth and his bailiffs, aside from wishing the election of the old members, were honest in trying to avert strife and rioting. They knew about
the Whig Legion, the split skulls, and the shattered windows of Martin the Publican. But in forming a coalition of Whigs and Tories and
trying to freeze out the popular Colonel, they had made a political
blunder of great consequence.

Signs of indignation flared up. Handbills began to appear. "Little Q
in the Corner" wrote: "Our worthy Corporation, seized with the most
violent compunctions of distress, for their own security" in retaining
the coveted privilege of sending two representatives to Parliament, have
convened a meeting today to avert the evil by joining in the support of
the two Old Members. This was an accumulation of arrogated power,
he asserted; and then he declared his love and respect for "brave Tarleton who comes from the bloody Field to wear out that Body in your
Service, a part of which he has already buried to attest his zeal."

Another wrote, signing his letter "Andrew Marvel": "At a time when
three Candidates are upon the spot, and have publickly addressed you,
is it not the highest degree of arrogance and presumption for the Mayor
and Bailiffs to call a meeting of the Freemen? What right have they
to judge for you?"

"Amor Patriae" wrote that the meeting was for the purpose of adver-
tising that a decided majority of the Freemen wished to unite the interests of the other candidates to the injury of the brave Colonel. Wit-

nesses were convinced that the assertion was false, for at the meeting the show of hands was two to one in the Colonel's favor, which completely threw the coalition into confusion. He continued:

"In this instance, it is particularly to your interest to oppose this Coalition, as by encouraging it, you make yourselves ridiculous, joining Men of Opposite political Principles, Hand in Hand, to vote against each other in Parliament, and thereby take away in the Senate the consequences of this great and commercial Town, render your Representation a Nullity, and make you Englishmen of no Consideration by selling your Birthrights.

"But you may rest assured, that your gallant Townsman, the Liverpool Hero, with the firmest reliance on your disinterested support, will boldly stand forth unconnected with any other Candidate," *Amor Patriae* continued, stating that Colonel Tarleton wished only the "Honour of representing his Native Town in Parliament, as the summit of his ambition, and the first Honour you can distinguish him by for services rendered his country."

That evening Colonel Tarleton addressed a letter to the Electors:

Bold-street, Wednesday Evening,
June 16, 1790

To the Free and Independent ELECTORS of the Borough of Liverpool.

Gentlemen,

Accept my warmest Gratitude for your kind Attendance and generous Support, at the Meeting of this Morning—The avowed purpose for which it was called is extremely laudable.

The Peace, Harmony, and Welfare of the Town I shall ever behold with the most heart-felt Satisfaction.—When I had last the honor of offering you my Services to represent you in Parliament, your great Exertions in my Favor made an Impression on my Mind, which Time can never efface.

The Experience of this Morning has plainly shewn you that the Interest of my two Opponents is one.—I shall stand alone and unconnected with any Party.—No one will more cheerfully pay the due Tribute of Applause to your late Representatives, than myself. They have done their Duty. I need not assure you, how sincerely I lament that I was unfortunately excluded from the possibility of exerting an equal degree of Zeal in your Service.

Agreeable to my promise at the last Election, I have once more made you a humble offer of my Services; and from the general favourable reception with which I have been honored, I cannot doubt my Success.—I have too great a confidence in the Freedom and Independence of your Principles, to think I have any thing to apprehend from any attempts to circumscribe that Constitutional Liberty, which is your Birth-right, the noblest Inheritance of Mankind.

As to my pretensions, I shall observe a total Silence.—Of those you, Gentlemen, are the judges.—Were they multiplied an hundred fold, I should hold it presumptuous, in the highest degree, to demand that as a Right, which is the greatest Favor you can bestow, and an Honor equal to the proudest ambition.—It remains, Gentlemen, for me to solicit your firm Support to the end of the Contest, and to assure you how truly I am, in all Events, and in every Situation of Life,

GENTLEMEN,
Your affectionate Fellow-Citizen,
And most faithful and devoted Servant,
Ban. Tarleton.

Next morning the prospects of their affectionate fellow citizen were far from bright. The incumbents had begun an attack upon Tarleton's connection with the Prince and the recent unpleasant contest over the Regency.

Andrew Marvel rallied to the defense of his hero: "See your gallant Townsman solicits your Support. The Brave Son of a worthy Father: He has fought your Battles—But some youthful levities are alleged against him—Pitiful attack!—Who is perfect? Are there not spots on the Sun? Depend upon it, after what Malice can invent, he will be found as a Soldier, a Senator, and a Man—no way inferior to either of his Antagonists."

But their gallant townsman knew when to sound retreat. He wrote a letter to the Freemen withdrawing his candidacy:

June 17th, 1790

To the Worthy FREEMEN of Liverpool

Gentlemen,

With deep and unfeigned Regret I am obliged to inform you, that I cannot rescue you from the tyrannical Effects of a late Coalition. A Junction between Interests, which were thought uniformly discordant as Lord Penrhyn's and Mr. Gascoyne's, must, for the present, overweigh the Liberty of the People, or produce a Contest that would be attended with Consequences highly ruinous to a commercial Town like Liverpool.

Actuated, therefore, by Sentiments of the purest Regard for the Happiness of my native Town, although at the same Time conscious that I have the Hearts of the Majority of my Brother Freemen, I beg Leave to sacrifice my feelings and Pretensions, for the Quiet of the Public.

To the Independent Freemen who have joined me on this Occasion, I offer up my warmest Thanks that a Heart filled with the liveliest Sensations can inspire; and most solemnly assure them, that my Gratitude will never cease but with my Existence.

> I have the Honour to be,
> With the greatest Regard,
> GENTLEMEN,
> Your most obedient humble Servant,
> Ban. Tarleton.

He then mounted his horse and reined his head toward London. The coalition could now rejoice. Gascoyne and Penrhyn prepared a long letter to their constituents: "Colonel Tarleton having (by public Advertisement) declined to offer himself at the approaching Election, we take the Liberty not only to congratulate you on so desirable an Event, and one so likely to maintain the Peace of the Town, but also to return our warmest Thanks for that firm and powerful Support we have received during our joint Canvass."

"Countryside" wrote: "I wish our brave Townsman, the Colonel, may meet with every promotion he can deserve in the line of his profession." And "Common Sense" added: "I acknowledge our brave Townsman, the noble colonel, is a Valuable Man in the Military Line; and there he shines as much as Penrhyn and Gascoyne in the Parliament-House."

Rumors began to circulate. The hero of the British Legion had been bought off. Denial, recrimination, and more rumors followed. Then a clarion sounded.

"To Arms!" cried an "Independent Freeman." " 'Tis now the cause of Freedom calls upon you to assert your rights, and independently vote in the Noble Colonel, who is driven by the Mayor and certain great Men, with a heavy heart, from his native Town."

"Little Q" trumpeted from his corner: "Is not your Townsman, your own elect BANISHED? Is not HE, Whom Your Town, as well as Your Whole Country, glories to boast of, DEGRADED and FORCED FROM YOU, like a wretched EXILE and an OUTCAST? Your noble Brother, who came with hard-earned Laurels blooming on his Brow, that you might add to it the Civic Crown, and who had achieved such Feats, as the Romans of old would have been proud to honour him with a triumph for, SPURNED and marked with INFAMY and NEGLECT!"

Cried he: "Is there ONE who will yet represent the COLONEL, and demand a POLL in his Name:—if any such can still be found, the Freemen may still return him, in *Defiance of every Coalition!*"

And to the tune of "I've Kissed and I've Prattled" the Tarleton supporters sang:

> Come all ye brave fellows, in Liverpool born,
> Come hither and listen to me;
> Come all ye brave fellows, in Liverpool born,
> Come hither and listen to me;

I'll tell you the way to be wealthy and gay,
　　Content, independent, and free;
I'll tell you the way to be wealthy and gay,
　　Content, independent, and free.

Here's TARLETON your townsman, a friend at command,
　　Who fought for his country and you;
Here's TARLETON your townsman, a friend at command,
　　Who fought for his country and you;
Who bled in the cause of your freedom and laws,
　　Oh TARLETON's the gallant true blue.
Who bled in the cause of your freedom and laws,
　　Oh TARLETON's the gallant true blue.

A branch of your rearing, a Lancashire tree,
　　Should flourish in Lancashire soil;
A branch of your rearing, a Lancashire tree,
　　Should flourish in Lancashire soil;
Let your laurels divine, his temples entwine,
　　The rewards of his perils and toil.
Let your laurels divine, his temples entwine,
　　The rewards of his perils and toil.

During a political campaign, it was the custom for certain pubs like the Black Horse, the Angel, the Talbot, and the Rainbow to remain open so that the candidates could supply drink. In the Black Horse and the Rainbow, near the Exchange, were large rooms in which men—and women—were kept drunk until they were needed at the Hustings. Thinking that Tarleton's departure had meant the end of the campaign, the Corporation now made a second blunder. They restricted these pubs to normal hours and shut off the free liquor.

George Crump, a solicitor of eminence, saw their error; and "availing himself of the excitement occasioned by it, called together a number of electors at the upper end of Water Street, and caused a cask of ale or porter to be rolled into the street, the head to be knocked out, and the contents to be distributed; and harangued the electors upon the injustice of the coalition and the expediency of supporting Colonel Tarleton."

They drank and sang their "Lancashire Laurels" to the tune of the·"Little Plough Boy."

Come all ye noble Freeman,
　　Who love an honest soul,
Brave citizens and seamen,
　　Come fill the flowing bowl;
Let's drink our British Hero
　　Of courage fam'd afar,

> Who fought for honor bravely,
>> Amidst the smoke of war,
>>> You'll ne'er forget your townsman
>>> Who oft with sword in hand,
>> Conveyed the name of Liverpool,
>>> Thro' many a foreign land.

By Saturday, June 19, a groundswell had set in for the Lancashire hero. Heelers were canvassing and orators were talking. "To preserve the Harmony of your Town, that Hero who fought your battles midst Clouds of Smoke and Streams of Blood, has with regret bid you farewell."

They urged, "If now you dare act for Yourselves, elect, without Solicitation or Hesitation, that Hero, and thereby Show to a Junta formed to oppress you, that you are not to be led like Oxen to the Slaughter, or fools to the Correction of the Stocks. Dare to be Men! Dare to be Englishmen!"

There issued a call from Tarleton's committee headquarters on Brunswick Street: "You are desired forthwith to call at the Committee Room, and give your names as supporters of the oppressed (though Gallant) Colonel Tarleton."

By noon on Saturday wrangling and rumor had swept Liverpool. "An insidious and false Report having been industriously circulated, that a Poll will not, or cannot be demanded in Favor of Colonel Tarleton, on Monday next," wrote the Committee for Tarleton, "This is to inform the Noble and Independent Freemen that a Poll will be demanded, and the Colonel will stand the contest 'till the last."

The journeymen had been aroused. One of their number admonished them that "altho' your Gallant Hero, the Colonel, be not among you, March boldly to the Exchange early on Monday morning, demand a poll in his behalf, and see who dare be hardy enough to refuse it."

> All ye who love a gallant blade,
>> Come here and learn my song, Sirs!
> My voice I'll raise, in Tarleton's praise,
>> And sure I can't be wrong, Sirs!
>> Then come and poll, each honest soul,
>> For *Tarleton*, Britain's glory,
> His name shall rise above the skies,
>> So fam'd in warlike story.

"The future ages will say 'That the Freemen of Liverpool have set a glorious example to the whole Kingdom: that they have not sold their birthright for guzzle, nor been lured from their purpose by Beef and Pudding.'"

The Tarletonites set new words to "A Hunting We Will Go!"

> See Tarleton comes, your truth to prove,
>   His native town to cheer,
> He loves the Cause, of Freedom's Laws,
> He loves the Cause, of Freedom's Laws,
> You'll find his heart sincere,
> You'll find his heart sincere.
>   A voting let us go,
>   A voting let us go,
>   A voting let us go,
>   A voting let us go.

"Sully not the Brave Colonel's Cause, by Riot or Disturbance; but join Firmness to Decorum, and the Cause is your own."

All day Sunday, June 20, the canvassers worked. A backfire of rumor was spreading: "Lord Penrhyn's friends have made overtures to Colonel Tarleton, for the Free and Independent Partisans to form a Union." From Lord Penrhyn's committee room: "No such overtures have been made by Lord Penrhyn, or by any Person or Persons on his Behalf."

The Independents and Whigs were deserting Lord Penrhyn, for many felt that "Lord Penrhyn has sullied his honor by joining a Man of diametrically opposite Principles."

On Sunday night "Independent Burgess" issued a handbill: "Colonel Tarleton, in order to shew his disposition for peace, made a sacrifice of what has long been his greatest ambition, and quitted the town." Therefore, said he, "I shall this evening give my name (as 780 have already done) to vote a plumper for him." "Independent Burgess" had promised to vote for Lord Penrhyn, but felt absolved from his promise because of the coalition—as had 167 others.

"Colonel Tarleton is sent for Express, and will undoubtedly present himself to his liberal and generous Supporters the moment of his Arrival," said the Tarleton committee in a card on Sunday night. "The Friends of Colonel Tarleton are requested to meet in Bold-Street, at 8 o'clock in the morning and proceed from thence to the Hustings."

At about eight o'clock on Monday morning a large body of people paraded the streets, headed by William Riggs of the counting house of Tarleton and Backhouse. They then joined the crowd in front of the home of Mrs. Tarleton. There the Tarletonites formed and with colors flying paraded down Church Street, up Lord Street, across Castle Ditch, and through Castle Street, and on to the Hustings. Their leader was Ellis Leckonby Hodgson, Esquire, late of Lisbon, sitting a gallant dun gelding. Unfortunately, Mr. Hodgson appeared very fatigued and was supported by a freeman who occasionally ministered water and smelling bottle, thus preventing him from alarming the party with a swoon.

Lord Penrhyn and Bamber Gascoyne, Jr., met at the Golden Lion and, preceded by a band, marched up Lord Street and through Castle Street to the Hustings. In their parade were Mayor Smyth and the officers of the Corporation and nearly all of the merchants and principal tradesmen of the town. With them went several clergymen, for five Liverpool preachers, the Reverends Thomas Dannett, John Davies, George Hodson, Thomas Maddocks, and Robert Roughsedge, voted in unison against Tarleton, Sin, and Mrs. Robinson.

The action of the clergymen stirred more wrath among Tarleton's followers than any other event during the election. "When I see Clergymen at the Head of a Mob, with their Hats waving in the Air, vociferating Huzza!" wrote "Anti-Corporate," "I own I poignantly feel the Self-violation of Respect due to the Cloth. An Active Part in an Election ill suits the Reverential Dignity—not even the mild placidity of a H—n; though in him it seems less monstrous, as it strikes in Unison with the general tenor of his Conduct; and, as he was never known to blush but with the radiance of the Vine, it would be a Pity to deprive him of the only Opportunity he has in showing his Gratitude for the many good Things of this Life he has enjoyed at the Gascoynian Table."

The coalition was not idle. Rumors about Tarleton's mode of living were flying. Finally, the select committee from Tarleton's headquarters issued a card cautioning the independent electors "to shut their EARS against the Poison of any Man, or Set of Men, who may dare to report any Thing to the Prejudice of his truly brave and distinguished conduct."

As Monday drew to a close the Colonel was weakest in the balloting: Penrhyn, 76; Gascoyne, 72; and Tarleton, 71. Hoping to stem the tide until the return of their candidate, his managers threw in their staunch votes, commonly called *yards of broad cloth*: John Sparling, former high sheriff of the County; John Brown; Thomas and Edward Parr; and Clayton Tarleton. This maneuver gave 76 votes each to Penrhyn and Tarleton.

That evening Banastre rode into Liverpool, too tired to speak or canvass, and issued a bulletin:

Bold-street, Monday Evening,
June 21, 1790.

"Colonel Tarleton presents his respectful Compliments to his Brother Townsmen, and begs they will not impute any Neglect or Want of Affection to him, if he does not pay each Individual a personal Visit:—The Business of the Hustings, and the Committee-Room must necessarily occupy all his Time:—And Colonel Tarleton, therefore, feels persuaded that his Friends, in the great Cause of Liberty, will act immediately with Vigour, and dispense with the common Forms of Ceremony."

The return of their candidate revived the zeal of Tarleton's followers. Crump, Corie, and the Tarleton brothers fanned the excitement among the laboring class, and a small riot was mounted on Monday night. Next morning there circulated a handbill: "The Committee formed for the Conducting of Colonel Tarleton's Election most heartily request the Freemen not to carry sticks, or offensive weapons of any kind."

Colonel Tarleton, dressed in the uniform of the British Legion, first appeared at the Hustings near the Exchange on Tuesday morning. The crowd was eager to hear him speak. They "listened with delight to the manly, soldier-like and popular speeches" of their townsman "whose elegant manners and fascinating conversation caused his society to be courted by princes of the royal blood, and by the great and noble of the land."

The candidate addressed himself to the free and independent voters. He thanked them for their support in the general election of 1784. He repeated his opinion that his loss was due to lack of effort in the earlier days of that contest. He scored the forming of a coalition and he charged it with tyranny in trying to prevent a free election. Again and again he cried: "The point we struggle for is freedom of election."

He asserted that the coalition had invaded the dearest rights of Freemen. He incited his followers to act with vigor. And drawing to a climax, the disciple of Burke, Sheridan, and Fox held aloft the hand shorn of two fingers at Guilford Courthouse and cried: "These gave I for King and country!"

Throwing back his sleeve to show the scars where the sword had ripped his arm, he ended with the flaming lines from Shakespeare's *Henry V*:

> He that shall live on this day, and see old age,
> Will yearly on the vigil feast his neighbors,
> And say, Tomorrow is Saint Crispian:
> Then will he strip his sleeve and show his scars,
> And say, These Wounds had I on Crispians's day.

By Tuesday morning Gascoyne had enough of coalition. He took to his bed and sent his friends a card to "most respectfully inform them that his indisposition prevents him the honour of attending upon the Hustings."

But not Lord Penrhyn: he had one day of fight left. On the Hustings he declared that the friends of Tarleton had violated the Rights of the Election: they had taken one of his voters by force from young Lord Murray.

"Not true," cried Tarleton's friends. They had seen Lord Murray forcing a man along Castle Street who, without intermission, was shouting "Tarleton Forever! Tarleton Forever! Tarleton Forever!" All the while the man's wife kept pulling him by the coat, begging him to be true to his promise to give his vote to the Colonel.

At that moment a party of Freemen, seeing their comrade, endeavored to rescue him, accusing Lord Murray of having stolen their property. "In the scuffle, Lord Murray struck one of the party, when a small species of bruising ensued, in which, it must be confessed, Lord Murray displayed the character of a common Porter, *much to his credit.*" "Anti-corporate" ended: "What a wonderful thing it is to be a *Man of Quality:* even theft passes with impunity under the all-fascinating Letters LORD."

With Gascoyne ill, the coalition disrupted, and riot and disorder everywhere, Lord Penrhyn hauled down his colors. Tarleton had won!

The contest at Liverpool excited interest everywhere. The London newspapers reported the daily tally of votes and the provincial newspapers repeated them. On Saturday, June 26, the *World* reported: "The accounts last night in London were, that in consequence of the very alarming riots which threatened even the burning down of Liverpool," Lord Penrhyn had retired from the race.

Upon Lord Penrhyn's withdrawal Tarleton issued a letter:

Liverpool, June 23, 1790

To the Worthy and Independent FREEMEN OF LIVERPOOL

Gentlemen,

Professions are ill calculated to express the fullness of my heart; your glorious exertions, however, must not relax; vigilance and vigour are requisite to finish your glorious and patriotic undertaking.—But, GENTLEMEN, suffer me to solicit one, in addition to the multitude of favours you have already conferred on me.—Let not any spark of resentment, blown up from the defeated hopes of the expiring Coalition, lead us to commit any action contrary to the peace and harmony of the Town, and the prompt and quick continuation of the Election.

I have the Honor to Remain,
GENTLEMEN,
With the greatest affection and gratitude,
Your most obedient servant,
Ban. Tarleton

The mobs that Banastre's presence and oratory had inflamed now grew quiet. The Hustings were silent. In came the common folk, from Edward Abbott, saddler, to William Youd, mariner, to plump their single votes for the colonel in the uniform of the Green Horse Troop. Richard Roe came with John Smith. Large clans, like those of Bankes, Duttons, Lyons, Parr, and Wilson voted solidly for him. So did the Tarletons: Clayton, John, John, Jr., and Thomas. Daily his lead increased. On Monday evening, June 28, the poll ended. The final vote stood: Tarleton, 1269; Gascoyne, 888; and Penrhyn, 716.

Immediately the Colonel wrote his followers:

Bold-street, June 28, 1790

To the Worthy and Independent FREEMEN of Liverpool.

Gentlemen,

You have compleated your Victory, and I take the earliest opportunity of congratulating you on your Success—The important Cause in which you engaged with such patriotism and perseverance, required conduct and Courage, like yours, to rescue you from Oppression. The invasion made upon your dearest Rights, which is sending your own Representatives to Parliament, alarmed your Feelings, and aroused your independent Minds to resistance. You have boldly asserted, and nobly maintained your FREEDOM. Amidst the numerous Elections throughout this extensive Empire, none will be more distinguished for Harmony, Independence, and Patriotism, from the Commencement to the Conclusion. The respectable Majority you have acquired on the Poll, emblazons the Cause, and will evince your Sentiments and Exertions to the latest Posterity. The Situation you have raised me to, GENTLEMEN, will always be remembered with Gratitude, and I trust you will believe me, when I assure you, that my future Life shall be uniformly devoted to the Service of my Brother Townsmen.

I have the Honor to remain,

GENTLEMEN,

With the greatest Regard,

And Affection,

Your most obedient Servant,

Ban. Tarleton

"Colonel Tarleton's Committee request, that all demands against them may be delivered into the Committee-Room on Thursday between the Hours of Ten and Two," said a notice. His friends met and paid the claims. The Colonel stood at the head of the poll free of cost.

On Thursday evening his friends gave him a dinner at the King's Arms Hotel, formerly the Tarleton house in Water Street. In accordance with an ancient custom, they chaired their new representative and bore him in triumph through the principal streets in Liverpool. In their celebration there were healths, and draughts, merriment, wit, and rejoicing.

From a long triumphal ode "Cantabrigiensis" read:

Yield ye triumphal chariots—yield the Prize—
Our Hero comes, whose warlike deeds shall rise,
And stand recorded in the Historian's page,

Firm and unshaken thro' each varying age,
And lo! our Con'or comes, whose noble soul,
No factious ties, or ranc'rous bonds controul;
Spite of Oppression's frown, now FREEDOM reigns;
Superior still her sacred pow'r maintains;
'Twas his to vindicate his Townsmen's cause,
Assert their Rights, and guard their injur'd laws;
Now Freedom triumphs, now she shines confest,
In her own noble sphere, a Soldier's breast.
But see, he comes! with what majestic gait,
The Hero onward bears his manly state,
Commanding firmness, smoothed with cheerful grace,
Sit on the open features of his face,
Whilst Courage, Goodness, Honor, are his claim,
And every Virtue speak a right to fame,
Whilst Patriot zeal and Loyalty combin'd,
Mark the brave subject and the honest mind.

Then the Chairman read the eulogy:

The Unanimity of a Multitude, in the electing a Person to a Place of Public Trust, is undoubtedly (if not a Criterion) a Proof of the Ability of such Person to act with Propriety in such Office. Such, in my Opinion, is the general Choice of a grateful and unbiased Public in the late Election of Colonel Tarleton. A patriotic Member should always represent a great commercial and populous Town; but, when the Hero and Honest Man are evidently united in the same Person, the Right of Election indubitably belongs to such an eminent Character. The Colonel has acquired Laurels in the Field; and, as a Senator, will transmit those Laurels to Posterity, emblazoned in Glory! He has acted the Hero, and will act the Man of Honor, and patriotic Senator. Born and bred amongst you, he fully confided in his Townsmen's Attachment to his Interest; and now, with Gratitude, acknowledges the very great Honor you have conferred upon him.

To you young Freemen, he is more immediately attached, for your Candour, Unanimity and spirited Zeal in his Behalf, lately so eminently displayed. Enlisted under your Colonel's Banner— under the Banner of Freedom and Loyalty—your most sanguine Hopes will be fully gratified, in your valiant Representative's faithful Discharge of his Duty, both as a Soldier and as a Senator. His Laurels, which cast a verdant Bloom on your elective Regimentals, shall never fade; but with Time shall assume a more vivid Green, and flourish through the countless Gradations of Time!—ever blooming!—and ever victorious!"

Next morning, when Lieutenant Colonel Banastre Tarleton, newly elected Member of Parliament, swung into his saddle and rode off on the road toward London, he was proud and happy. Several Tarletons had served as mayor of Liverpool. He would be the first Tarleton to sit in the sacred hall of St. Stephen.

He went home to Mary, to the Prince and his friends at Carlton House, to days of roistering and nights of gambling. And he was in a fracas almost before he alighted in Clarges Street.

On Saturday evening, July 10, the Prince and his friends attended the play at Haymarket Theatre. After the play, at about ten-thirty, when the carriage of the Duke of York was driven toward the portico of the theater, it collided with the carriage of Mrs. Benfield. The drivers quarreled and began a war of whips. The Prince and the Duke rushed forward to quell the disturbance.

Colonel Tarleton, Colonel St. Leger, and Colonel Monson ran forward to protect the Princes. They attempted to stop Mrs. Benfield's coachman, J. Hetherstone, from driving his carriage so violently against the Duke's carriage; and moreover to show him that he should have paid proper respect for precedence in the first place. But, tipsy and angry, Hetherstone lashed his own horses, the Duke's horses, and even the persons of the colonels, the Duke, and the Prince. The colonels finally shoved him off the box, and Hellgate Barrymore backed the carriage out of the line.

"The Prince of Wales lost his watch, and was heard to say that he was never before involved in so disagreeable a dilemma," said the *London Chronicle* of July 10–13. "The Duke of York also had his watch snatched at, but the fellow who made the attempt had the honor of receiving a severe drubbing from his Royal Highness."

The following day a constable brought Hetherstone before Justice Hyde where he was indicted by Colonels Tarleton, St. Leger, and Monson for "an insult committed against his Royal Highness, the Prince of Wales, by forcing a precedent for his mistress's carriage." The colonels "each severally indicted him for assaulting them."

Soon after this affair the Prince and his friends set off for Brighton for racing, cricket, and card parties. Play was not as steep as in former years, and dress occupied more time. Lady Elizabeth Lambert and Lady Maria Carr set a new style by wearing their sashes hung loosely across the shoulder like the ribbons of the Knights of the Garter. During August the Prince adopted the French fashion of wearing trousers instead of knee breeches in the morning.

All of the friends of the Prince were at Brighton except George Hanger. The quondam major of the British Legion had reached the end of his finances and joined the recruiting service of the East India Company.

Hellgate Barrymore was with the Prince, cavorting around and bragging about his private theater at Wargrave. His Lordship frequently acted in the productions. When someone wrote a letter to the newspaper criticizing his acting, the Earl suspected Mr. Fox, manager of the Royal Theatre of Brighton.

Strolling with his comrades along the Steine on July 27, Barrymore caught sight of the son of the manager. Bolstered by the presence of friends, he decided to pick a fight. He jostled young Fox. He snatched off his hat. He kicked his shins. Overawed by the presence of noblemen, Fox tried to escape. Finally he put up his fists in self-defense.

Spectators quickly gathered. Colonel Tarleton was strolling along the Steine with the Duke of York and the Prince of Wales, and they ran forward to join the throng. Some boxing enthusiasts formed a ring and persuaded the Prince to act as referee. Thus protected from the vengeance of Barrymore's thugs, young Fox beat the tar out of Hellgate. Forgetting the impartiality of his office, the Prince shouted: "Damn me, Barrymore, behave like a man!"

27

Song of the Nightingale

SOON AFTER HER RETURN to London, Mary met Robert Merry, just back from Florence where he had been a member of the ancient Scuola della Crusca. Soon they joined in a poetical correspondence through the pages of the *World*. One Saturday she received Merry's "Laurel of Liberty." Twelve hours later she finished her reply, a 350-line poem entitled "Ainsi va le Monde." On the following Tuesday the *World* published it under the pen name of Laura Maria.

"Ainsi va le Monde" received favorable criticism, and Mary was soon making regular contributions to the *World*. Often her work filled the poetry column. But who was she—this Laura or Laura Maria who was fast becoming the ornament of the Della Cruscans? Robert Merry, Bertie Greatheed, Mrs. Hester Piozzi, and Mrs. Hannah Cowley were well-known. "Of the Della Crusca school, of the *World*, the public is acquainted with all the writers except the plaintive Laura, who doubtless will be tempted by the example of her successful associates to discover her real name," said the *Morning Post*. "Mr. Merry and Mrs. Cowley exult in their poetic fame, while the elegant Laura continues to charm the town under a fictitious signature."

Provincial newspapers reprinted the poems by Laura and Laura Maria. As they continued to excite interest, with people in the highest society memorizing and reciting them, Mary decided to test public reaction to one under her proper signature. She sent her next poem, signed Mary Robinson, to the *World*. She also claimed authorship of all lines signed Laura and Laura Maria.

Mr. Bell replied that the poem with which Mrs. Robinson had honored him was vastly pretty; but that he was well acquainted with the author of the productions alluded to. Thoroughly angered by editor Bell's mendacity, the invalid sent for him and cured him of his skepticism.

Mr. Bell published "Ainsi va le Monde" as a 16-page booklet. It ran through several editions and was translated into French. Said the *Monthly Review* of February 1791: "This poetic address to Mr. Merry gives us a favourable opinion, in a general view, of the literary abilities of the fair writer, Mrs. Robinson."

As the popularity of the Della Cruscans mounted, William Gifford, afterward the merciless editor of the *Quarterly Review*, attacked the movement in a satirical poem called *The Baviad*. Said he: "It is scarcely necessary to observe that Yendas, and Laura Marias, and Tony Pasquins, have long claimed a prescriptive right to infest most periodical publications."

His "Introduction" concluded: "The fever turned into a frenzy: Laura Marias, Carlos, Orlando, Adelaide, and a thousand other nameless names caught the infection; and from one end of the Kingdom to the other, all was nonsense and Della Crusca." And in a footnote he added: "Kingdom. This is a trifle. Heaven itself, if we may believe Mrs. Robinson, took part in the general infatuation."

> See Cowley frisk to the ding-dong chime,
> And weekly cuckold her poor spouse, in rhyme;
> See Thrale's grey widow with a satchel roam;
> And bring in pomp laborious nothings home;
> See Robinson forget her state, and move
> On crutches tow'rds the grave, to "Light o'Love"—

ぐ

Impatiently Banastre had waited for the convening of Parliament. On Thursday, November 25, 1790, with the other newly elected representatives, he followed the old members through the traditional ceremonies. He followed the Black Rod to the Bar of the House of Lords and heard the Lord Chancellor call for the election of a speaker in the House of Commons. The House elected Henry Addington.

Election to Parliament quickly enhanced Lieutenant Tarleton's military career. On November 18 he was promoted to the rank of colonel in the army. His half-pay was raised to £320.

On Friday he followed Speaker Addington again to the House of Lords, where he heard the Speaker lay claim to the ancient rights and privileges of the Commons. After receiving royal approbation, the Speaker returned to the House and reminded the representatives that they must take the oath. After having been sworn in, Tarleton took his place beside Mr. Clement Taylor on the benches of the Opposition.

Ban was among friends. From his days at University College were William Plumer and James Bland Burgess. There was John Scott, who had also been a young don when his brother William was Ban's tutor at Oxford. From their years of soldiering in America were Colonel Nisbet Balfour, Colonel Gerard Lake, Colonel John Graves Simcoe, and old General Sir Henry Clinton. There was Sir Harry Featherstone from Up Park. Members from among his London friends were Charles Fox, Richard Sheridan, and Lord Robert Spencer. And from Yorkshire was William Wilberforce, the Tory member who would be his most consistent opponent.

Since 1787 Wilberforce had been the spokesman for a militant group of Abolitionists headed by Thomas Clarkson. On Friday, December 10, he introduced one of his many bills against the slave trade.

For the first time in his career Banastre Tarleton rose from his seat and called, "Mr. Speaker!" He was handsome, proudly dressed in the uniform of his American Dragoons, and he surveyed the House with calm. In a clear voice which betrayed his Lancashire origin he stated the opposition of the slave traders in Liverpool. His maiden speech concluded: "I venture to predict, that the common sense of the Empire will strangle this modern attempt at mistaken philanthropy."

While Banastre was launching his career in Parliament, Mary was busy writing. After reading her poems in the *World*, Sir Joshua Reynolds urged her to publish them in a book. So did Edmund Burke, editor of the *New Annual Register*.

Selecting John Bell of the *World* to publish her *Poems*, Mary opened a subscription list. She asked Sir Joshua to paint her portrait for a frontispiece; and as he painted she composed a tributary lyric to him. Always her warm friend and counselor, the old artist wrote:

Leicester Square,
Dec. 18, 1790

Dear Madam:

I am quite ashamed of not having returned my thanks before this time for the obliging notice which you have taken of me in your truly excellent poems: it was my intention to have done it in person, though I am not much in the habit of going out. I confess I am surprised at the wonderful facility (or *handling*, as we painters call it) which you have acquired in writing verse, which is generally the result of great practice. Were I to say all I think, even to yourself, it would, I fear, look like flattering; and perhaps to others, as proceeding from the high style in which I have been bribed. I shall comfort myself therefore with saying, that I hope what you intend to publish will not be inferior to this specimen; if so, you will long remain without an antagonist in the field of poesy.

I am, with great respect,
Dear Madam,
Your most humble and obedient servant
J. REYNOLDS

P. S. The Picture is ready, whenever Mr. Burke calls for it.

∾

On January 19, 1791, Ban deserted the hall of St. Stephen to attend the long-anticipated fight between Johnson and Big Ben. For this occasion, to Wrotham, in Kent, boxing enthusiasts streamed from London in carriages, on horseback, and afoot, in crowds "never before seen on such an occasion, if such an occasion ever before occurred."

The meeting took place on a piece of ground enclosed within walls which appeared to be those of an old abbey. This arena could hold some 5000 men. But about eleven o'clock the crowd shoved one of the walls down, injuring nearly 100 spectators, and then surged through the opening, jamming the enclosure beyond safety.

In the center of the old abbey grounds, the promoters had erected a platform 21 by 20 feet. This they had covered with turf and sawdust. "About 10 minutes after 12 o'clock Colonel Tarleton, as promoter, appeared on the stage." Johnson's second, Joe Ward, and his bottleholder, Mendoza, followed the Colonel. Five minutes later Harry Aston, Esquire, as arbitrator, entered the ring, followed by Big Ben's second, Bill Ward, and his bottleholder, Humphreys. They were followed by Mr. Wharton, the referee.

Johnson appeared first and received an ovation befitting the five-to-two favorite. Big Ben then came on the stage. Johnson walked around and around his opponent, viewing him contemptuously from head to foot.

At twelve-thirty sharp the fight started. Each round went to a knockdown. In the eighteenth round the contest reached its climax. "Both parties were so desperate and striking so furiously as to threaten each other with instantaneous death. Many of the spectators were compelled by their feelings to turn away from the horror of the scene . . . both of them were bleeding so much that it was difficult to distinguish the face from the hind part of the head. Johnson fell. The spectators appeared almost petrified."

In the twentieth round Johnson seized Big Ben's hair and at the same moment struck him in the face. Between rounds Ben's second cropped off his hair. Johnson won the next three rounds. In the twenty-fourth round Big Ben recovered and carried the fight to Johnson. "Receiving a dreadful blow under the ear, he fell like a sparrow." Wharton raised Big Ben's hand in victory.

"We are clearly of the opinion that Ben was not victorious by accident," said the Cambridge Chronicle and Journal of January 22, "but by real superiority, as a boxer. He strikes equally well with both hands, strikes with greater quickness than Johnson, and with greater force, his blow being always straight forward. Johnson, in rallying, is best but a round fighter. We will hazard a conjecture, that if they fight again upon the same terms, Ben will win again."

But Banastre had lost his love for boxing: never again would he promote a match. On January 29, the Cambridge Chronicle helped to explain his sudden aversion: "Colonel Tarleton and Mr. Ogden are the greatest losers by the defeat of Johnson on Monday."

The member for Liverpool was again broke. At Wrotham had vanished the remnant of the feathers plucked from the fat pigeon.

∾

In Parliament the new year opened with more wrangling over the abolition of the slave trade. On February 4 William Wilberforce moved that the House of Commons form a Committee to sit Upstairs on the question. Mr. Cawthorne complained of the long drawn-out inquiry.

Colonel Tarleton rose from his seat, not to object to the Wilberforce motion, but to give notice of a motion he intended to make in six weeks. He complained of the injury already done to the merchants, manufacturers, and planters by the antislavery agitation. "By now every man must surely have made up his mind on the subject. If the Gentlemen want to show philanthropy, why not investigate the Poor Laws, which would afford them scope for their Humanity, or the state of our infant settlement in New South Wales."

On April 18 the House formed a Committee of the Whole to consider a bill to prevent the further importation of slaves into the British Colonies in the West Indies. Wilberforce led the fight against a system of labor "contrary to every principle of religion, morality, and sound policy." He cited the cruelty of the slave hunters, the miserable conditions aboard the slave transports, the inhuman lot of the slaves on the large plantations. "Never, never," he cried, "will we desist until we have wiped away this scandal from the Christian name, released ourselves from the load of guilt under which we labor, and extinguished every trace of this bloody traffic."

Banastre began his reply with a tribute of "gratitude toward those constituents who have sent me so honourably to this House." Then turning to Wilberforce, he said: "The ingenuity, the amplification, and the pathetic eloquence, of the honourable gentleman, having worked no conviction on my mind, I shall proceed to arrange the arguments I have against the Abolition of the Slave Trade."

He then delivered the longest, best-prepared, and most eloquent speech of his early parliamentary career. Like a schoolboy debater he began by listing the main heads for his speech:

The beginning of the slave trade.

The sanction given to it by government.

The manner of conducting the trade on the coast of Africa.

The transit to the West Indies.

The employment and treatment of Negroes in the West Indies.

The amount of property engaged in the trade.

The value of the West Indian islands to England.

The eagerness which other nations have discovered to enlarge their slave trade.

And the importance of the trade as a nursery for seamen.

"The Africans themselves have no objection to the trade," he said. "Many people who are prejudiced against it have been carried away by mistaken humanity and often by misrepresentation."

As the representative of Liverpool, and of a family with large shipping interests and valuable property in the West Indies, Tarleton answered Wilberforce from experience: "The number of deaths in passage in the Liverpool ships has never exceeded five out of a hundred, whereas, in regiments sent to the West Indies or America, the average is about ten and a half in the hundred."

Appealing to members with mercantile interests, he pointed out the government's interference in their commerce. Then he turned sarcasm upon Wilberforce and the Clapham sect of Evangelicals.

"Gentlemen, your success in trade has of late years been so prodigious, that it seems necessary to suspend your activity, by cutting off one of the principal branches of your commerce, for the sake of humanity and the honour of the nation. You are to have no further respect for, nor future confidence in Acts of Parliament. The sanction of the Legislature is nothing. A few of the Ministerial side of this House have been gifted with religious inspiration, and the revelation has been extended to certain eminent personages on this side of the House; and these enlightened philanthropists have discovered, that it seems necessary, for the sake of humanity, and the honour of the nation, that all British merchants concerned in the African trade, should have their designs harassed, their property injured, and their reputations traduced; notwithstanding such persecution must undoubtedly foster, encourage, and aggrandize the surrounding nations of Europe, who rival Great Britain in her commerce and in her navigation."

And, as a member of the Opposition, he put the onus on Prime Minister Pitt. "I cannot bring myself to think this a convenient Time, the country in an eligible situation, or the Minister serious in his inclination to make an experiment which presents a certain prospect of loss, and no probability of advantage. An abolition would instantly annihilate a trade, which annually employs upwards of 5,500 sailors, upwards of 160 ships, and whose exports amount to £800,000 sterling."

Then, shaking his three-fingered right fist at the Prime Minister, he cried: "And the same experiment would undoubtedly bring the West India trade to decay, whose exports and imports amount to £6,000,000 sterling, and which gives employment of 160,000 tons of additional shipping, and sailors in proportion; all objects of too great magnitude to be hazarded on an unnecessary speculation, which, in all probability, would prove ruinous to the commercial consequence, the national honour, and the political glory of Great Britain."

Whether the three-fingered fist alarmed or amused William Pitt and his Tories, the eloquence displayed by the Colonel cheered the Whigs. Charles Fox rushed over to Brooks's Club and nominated the orator. On the evening of April 18 Banastre Tarleton was elected to membership.

During these months Banastre's life with Mary had been orderly and tranquil. They lived in elegant style, with their carriages, their coachmen, and their servants. Her home was the meeting place for many of the scribbling fraternity: John Taylor, James Broaden, Peter Pindar, General Burgoyne, Robert Merry, S. J. Pratt. Many of his friends called, among them the sons of King George. Fox's jest about Lord Robert Spencer and Mrs. Bouverie applied equally well to the Colonel and his lady: "They make adultery respectable."

By spring Mary had succeeded in financing the publication of her poems. In sixteen weeks she secured some 600 subscribers. At a guinea a copy, her book was a best seller even before publication.

Poems, by Mrs. Mary Robinson, was published on May 12, 1791. It was a beautiful book: bound in mahogany-brown leather tooled in gold, set in exquisite typography, and illustrated with Burke's engraving of Reynolds' painting. The dedication was elaborate: "The illustrious, and distinguished names that appear in the list of subscribers will Prove lasting testimonies of the liberal sentiments of a Polished nation—*To Whom They are Dedicated with the most Profound Respect.*"

The names of the most illustrious subscribers were printed on a separate page:

Subscribers

His Royal Highness
George, Prince of Wales

His Royal Highness
Frederick, Duke of York

His Royal Highness
William Henry, Duke of Clarence

His Royal Highness
William, Duke of Gloucester

His Serene Highness
The Duke of Orleans

His Serene Highness
Prince Ferdinand, Duke of Wurtemberg

The rest of the 600 distinguished names were arranged in alphabetical order, from the Duchess of Ancaster to Mrs. Uniacke. Among them were the Duke and Duchess of Bedford, the Duke and Duchess of Devonshire, the Earl and Countess of Cholmondeley, Sir Peter Burrell and his wife Lady Willoughby, Charles Fox, and Mr. and Mrs. Richard Sheridan.

Among her military friends subscribing were General John Burgoyne and Major General Gerard Lake. There were many personal friends, too: Sir Joshua Reynolds, the Reverend and Mrs. Henry Bate, Mrs. Dorothy Jordan, S. J. Pratt, Robert Merry, John Taylor, and Dr. John Wolcot (Peter Pindar). The list included 4 preachers, 36 students and professors at the University of Cambridge, and 21 of Tarleton's friends and relatives in Liverpool.

Poems was a moral triumph for Mary, for Banastre's family no longer were ashamed to have his name linked with hers. His mother subscribed for a copy. Clayton subscribed for a copy, and John took two. Both Mr. and Mrs. Thomas Tarleton took a copy, and even in Eton College, Thomas Tarleton, Junior, subscribed for a copy, to set the young Etonians goggle-eyed over the "Ode to Valour" that Mrs. Robinson had inscribed to his Uncle Ban.

Advertisements in the newspapers requested the subscribers to pick up their copies from Mrs. Robinson's home at 42 Clarges Street, Piccadilly. Undoubtedly some sent servants for their copies, but many of the fashionables of London society received *Poems* from the hand of the crippled author.

The reviewers were kind. The *Monthly Review* for December 1791 was personal and flattering. "This ingenious and celebrated lady has attracted the attention of the public, both by her personal and her mental accomplishments; and who can withstand the united powers of beauty and wit?"

The *Critical Review* of July 1791, in a review which treated poetry generally and Mrs. Robinson's *Poems* specifically, summarized the beginnings of the literary mood known as Romanticism. "Within a very few years, a race of versifiers has sprung up, determined to claim at least the merit of novelty in expression, in unusual figure and striking metaphor. Rejecting the accustomed modes of description and phraseology, these fastidious writers seem fond of introducing uncommon terms and ideas, to provoke attention and to excite admiration."

The poems of Mrs. Robinson, the reviewer continued, belonged to this school. There were odes, elegies, sonnets, and stanzas, and "these compositions abound with vivid exertions of genius, pathos, and sentiment." And: "It is certainly an elegant and original work, which coming from the pen of one person, and that person a woman, is entitled to singular approbation."

To the general praise for the fair author, editor Boaden modestly added the voice of the *Oracle*: "We, as it may be supposed, participate in the praise of those elegant productions, for it is in the *Oracle* that they have appeared for the most part: and effusions of similar excellence are frequently continued to us by the friendly zeal of the same lovely Muse."

 oⱥᴑ

In recording the whisperings of Romanticism, Mary developed a specialized vocabulary. Her choice of words set a pattern later followed by Keats. She seemed to exult in words like *forlorn, foamy, fancy, starry, orb, vision, casement, viewless,* and *ecstasy.*

Both she and Keats used the same kind of subject matter. She wrote "The Adieu to Fancy," and he wrote "Fancy." Both wrote an "Ode to Melancholy" and an "Ode to the Nightingale."

Poems included Mary's "Ode to the Nightingale" and "Second Ode to the Nightingale." Both were autobiographical and intensely emotional. In "Ode to the Nightingale" the poetess dimly outlined her life: her sorrow, her trip to France, her travel through foreign realms, her vain attempts to break the bonds of affliction, her search for happiness in Paris, her return to England, and her discovery that friendship and love are delusive.

ODE TO THE NIGHTINGALE

Sweet BIRD OF SORROW!—why complain
    In such soft melody of Song,
That ECHO, am'rous of thy Strain,
    The ling'ring cadence doth prolong?
Oh! tell me, tell me, why
Thy dulcet Notes ascend the sky,
Or on the filmy vapours glide
Along the misty mountain's side?
And wherefore dost Thou love to dwell
In the dark wood and moss-grown cell?
Beside the willow-margin'd stream—
Why dost Thou court wan Cynthia's beam?
Sweet Songstress—if thy wayward fate
Hath robb'd Thee of thy bosom's mate,

Oh, think not thy heart-piercing moan
 Evap'rates on the breezy air,
 Or that the plaintive Song of Care
Steals from THY Widow'd Breast alone.
Oft have I heard thy mournful Tale,
On the high Cliff, that o'er the Vale
Hangs its dark brow, whose awful shade
Spreads a deep gloom along the glade;
Led by its sound, I've wander'd far,
Till crimson evening's flaming Star
On Heav'n's vast dome refulgent hung,
And round ethereal vapours flung;
And oft I've sought th' HYGEIAN MAID,
In rosy dimpling smiles array'd,
Till forc'd with every HOPE to part,
Resistless Pain subdued my Heart.

Oh then, far o'er the restless deep
 Forlorn my poignant pangs I bore,
Alone in foreign realms to weep,
 Where ENVY's voice could taunt no more.
I hop'd, by mingling with the gay,
To snatch the veil of Grief away;
I hop'd, amid the joyous train,
To break Affliction's pond'rous chain;
VAIN was the Hope—in vain I sought
The placid hour of careless thought,
Where Fashion wing'd her light career,
 And sportive Pleasure danc'd along,
 Oft have I shunn'd the blithesome throng,
To hide th' involuntary tear,
 For e'en where rapt'rous transports glow,
From the full Heart the conscious tear will flow.
 When to my downy couch remov'd,
 FANCY recall'd my wearied mind
 To scenes of FRIENDSHIP left behind,
Scenes still regretted, still belov'd!
Ah, then I felt the pangs of Grief,
Grasp my warm Heart, and mock relief;
My burning lids Sleep's balm defied,
And on my fev'rish lips imperfect murmurs died.

 Restless and sad—I sought once more
 A calm retreat on BRITAIN's shore;
 Deceitful HOPE! e'en there I found
 That soothing FRIENDSHIP's specious name
Was but a short-liv'd empty sound,
 And LOVE a false delusive flame.

Then come, SWEET BIRD, and with thy strain
Steal from my breast the thorn of pain;
Blest solace of my lonely hours,
In craggy caves and silent bow'rs,
When HAPPY mortals seek repose,
By Night's pale lamp we'll chant our woes,
And, as her chilling tears diffuse
O'er the white thorn their silv'ry dews,
I'll with the lucid boughs entwine
        A weeping Wreath, which round my Head
Shall by the waving Crescent shine,
        And light us to our leafy bed.—
Yet, ah! nor leafy beds nor bow'rs
Fring'd with soft MAY's enamell'd flow'rs,
Nor pearly leaves, nor Cynthia's beams,
Nor smiling Pleasure's shadowy dreams,
Sweet BIRD, not e'en THY melting Strains—
Can calm the Heart where TYRANT SORROW REIGNS.

28

Bounding Billow

*A*FTER THE WORK of editing *Poems*, Mary was exhausted. Her friends persuaded her to spend the summer at Bath, and she and Maria Elizabeth left London in early June. Ban skipped the gaiety at Brighton, and after a short visit to Liverpool, where on June 21 he and his friends dined together on the anniversary of his election to Parliament, he joined Mary.

"Colonel Tarleton is returned from Bath, where he has been for some days past, and is now enroute to Paris," reported the *Oracle* of July 12. "Mrs. Robinson is expected at her house in Clarges Street in the course of the month, greatly benefited by the Bath waters."

As a member of the Whig Party, its Buff and Blue friendly to the Revolutionists, Tarleton was welcomed in Paris. He watched the militant French people: heard them sing "Ca Ira" and the "Carmagnole." He listened to their orators in the National Assembly. He visited the Marquis de Lafayette and developed a greater admiration for the Frenchman with whom he had skirmished along the James River. Then he went to the palace of Philippe of Chartres, now the Duke of Orleans, and tried his luck in a friendly game of faro. In September he returned to London.

Something had turned up to remove the Duke of York from "the scene of riot and eternal dissipation." On November 23 his Royal Highness married Princess Frederica, daughter of King Frederick William of Prussia. It was a long and elaborate affair. At one o'clock the King came from Buckingham House to St. James's Palace and commenced the levee about two o'clock.

The *Oracle* of November 24 noted that the levee "was more numerously attended than had been remembered for some time." Beginning with the Prince of Wales, the Duke of York, the Duke of Clarence, Prime Minister William Pitt, and the Archbishop of Canterbury, it listed hundreds of guests. Then it observed: "Among the Duke of York's friends who attended the Levee yesterday, the following were observed who are not constant in their visits at the Court—the compliment may therefore be attributed to the Duke's nuptials." In the list of leading Whigs were Lord Rawdon, Lord Melbourne, Lord Robert Spencer, the Right Honorable Charles Fox, and Colonel Tarleton.

Next day at Buckingham House the Queen received in the Drawing Room for the young Duchess of York. All of the Duke's friends were invited. The *Oracle* was amused that the first guest to arrive at the Palace was Colonel Tarleton, but it wasted no tolerance on another courtly visitor: "George Hanger, on his passage to and from the Levee at St. James's, paid not the least attention to the surrounding pickpockets—'Who steals my purse steals trash.' "

Although there was revelry in the palace, in Clarges Street something was amiss. Ban's fancy had begun to wander. After his return from Paris, some "Low Caprice" had lured him into a gaudier bower than Mary's.

In the *Oracle* of December 12 Mary recorded their separation:

> To ——————
> "I will instruct my Sorrows to be Proud."—
> —Shakespeare—

> 'Tis past! and now, remorseless Fate,
> Thy Victim braves thy direct hate,
> My mind resists thy poison'd dart,
> And conscious pride sustains my heart;
> Behold my placid smiles disclose,
> The pang is past that seal'd my woes!

> Since now, no more to grief a prey,
> My tranquil hours shall glide away;
> Since Reason from my sated brain
> Shall tear the records of past pain;
> Since warring passions sink to rest,
> And fierce resentment leaves my breast;
> Since from the wreath fond Fancy made
> Hope's transient flow'rs for ever fade;
> One proud indignant tear shall prove
> The signal of expiring love.
> Sweet offspring of long cherish'd woe,
> No more thy glittering fount shall flow;
> But trembling in its azure cell,
> Conceal'd in haughty silence dwell;
> Or if, perchance, one drop should steal,
> The pangs of memory to reveal,
> On my cold bosom shalt thou shine,
> A peerless gem—on Feeling's shrine!

Ban paid little heed to Mary's sorrow. He idled away his time at Brooks's. He ran to any excitement in the West End and on December 19 was among the first on the scene when fire broke out in Richmond House, Privy Gardens. The Duke of York ordered out the Coldstream Guards, and about 300 of them kept order and assisted the fire fighters. The Duke of Clarence arrived early with the floating fire engines and spent much of the day up to his knees in water. Among other noblemen and gentlemen who lent a hand were Colonels Lennox, St. Leger, Stanhope, and Tarleton.

ભ્

During the fall Mary wrote her first novel. Having experienced literary fame and financial success from her *Poems*, she undertook one of those extravagant Gothic romances so popular in the closing decade of the eighteenth century.

On February 2, 1792, she published *Vancenza or The Dangers of Credulity*. "The whole edition of *Vancenza* was sold in one day!" exclaimed Maria Elizabeth. "The work has since gone through five editions."

The Analytical Review of March 1792 complained: "We expected to have met with more passion and character in the production of a female who has not been an idle spectator of life." Yet there was in *Vancenza* something of that confession which became a stock characteristic of Mary's novels. She could write from personal experience: "There remained not a shadow of hope in her breast that the Prince was unacquainted with the imprudent interview at the cottage . . . she knew that from the moment a woman places her reputation in the power of an undeserving object, she is no longer mistress of her own happiness; as perpetual dread of disgrace is worse than even the full conviction of the most atrocious crimes, she becomes the wretched and fearful dependent upon the mercy of her enemy, at all times liable to the contempt and shame he may draw upon her."

In *Vancenza*, too, Mary began her long exposition of the philosophy of the royal mistress. "Small is the triumph of chastity that has never been assailed by the cunning of the seducer. The snows of Lapland preserve their whiteness and solidity, as long as they escape the dissolving glances of the burning orb. The female heart has little right to exult in its resolution, 'till it has resisted the fascinations of pleasure, the voice of insidious flattery, and the fatal allurements of pernicious examples. No woman can say, I will venture so far and then recede; for Chastity, exposed to the breath of Slander, is like the waxen model placed in the rays of the meridian sun: by degrees, it loses its finest traits, till at length it becomes an insipid mass of useless deformity."

The plot of *Vancenza* involved love, seduction, assassination, and lingering death, all within the grisly old Castle of Vancenza in Spain.

Of "the solemn glooms of Gothic piles" James Boaden wrote in his
"Sonnet to Mrs. Robinson, upon reading her *Vancenza*":

> VANCENZA rises—o'er time-touch'd spires
> > GUILT unreveal'd hovers with killing dew,
> Frustrates the fondness of the VIRGIN's fires,
> > And bares the murd'rous CASKET to her view.
>
> The thrilling pulse creeps back upon each Heart,
> And HORROR lords it by thy fascinating Art.

"Vancenza, it is true, is not written in the simple style," said the
Monthly Review of March 1792, "but it is written, and in our opinion
well-written, in the style of elegance peculiar to Mrs. R. The richness
of fancy and of language, which the fair author had so successfully displayed in her poetical productions, she has transferred to prose narration, and has produced a tale, which, we venture to predict, will be
much read and admired."

The popularity of *Vancenza* was but a withered laurel: Ban still con-
sorted with his "Low Caprice." There had come no hint of reconciliation. Into a poem for Saint Valentine's Day 1792 went all the grief of
the forsaken mistress.

Stanzas
Written on the 14th of February

To My Dear Valentine

> Come, Hope, and sweep the trembling string;
> > Drop from thy pinions balm divine;
> While, drooping o'er my lyre, I sing
> > The graces of my VALENTINE.
> Ah! Graces, fatal to my peace,
> > Why round my heart your mischiefs twine?
> Say, barb'rous Love, can aught increase
> > The triumphs of my VALENTINE?
>
> No more about my auburn hair
> > The sparkling gems shall proudly vie;
> The cypress, emblem of Despair,
> > Shall there a faded chaplet die.
> Young dimpled Pleasure quits my breast
> > To seek some gaudier bow'r than mine,
> Where low Caprice, by Fancy drest,
> > Enthrals my truant VALENTINE.
>
> The frozen brook, the mountain snow,
> > The pearls that on the thistle shine,
> The northern winds, that chilly blow,
> > Are emblems of my VALENTINE.

Pale Sorrow sheds the quiv'ring flame
    That gleams on Truth's neglected shrine,
Fann'd by those sighs which still proclaim
    How much I love thee, VALENTINE!

Whene'er the icy hand of Death
    Shall grasp this sensate frame of mine,
On my cold lip the fleeting breath
    Shall murmur still—"DEAR VALENTINE!"
Then o'er my grave, ah! drop one tear,
    And sighing write this pensive line—
"A FAITHFUL HEART lies mould'ring here,
    That well deserv'd its VALENTINE!"

The vision of the icy hand of death was real. Tortured by the truancy of Banastre, Mary had become desperately ill. The *Oracle* of February 15 reported: "Mrs. Robinson has been confined to her bed these three weeks, under the care of Dr. Moseley."

On the same day the *Oracle* observed: "The rapid sale of Mrs. Robinson's novel of Vancenza has taken all of the second edition already. This distinguished encouragement cannot but prove highly flattering to the Authoress, and will doubtless tempt her to pursue with increasing and ardent zeal the paths of Literature."

On February 27 Mary published the third edition. In a long dedication she said to her readers: "The sale of two Editions of *Vancenza*, within one month after its publication, is too unequivocal a proof of protection, to allow me a silent gratification, where my heart prompts me to acknowledge the gratitude of its feelings."

But she declared: "I disclaim the title of a Writer of Novels; the species of composition generally known under that denomination, too often conveys a lesson I do not wish to inculcate." Then she concluded: "To that Public, by which my literary productions have been so warmly received, I embrace this occasion of expressing my sense of obligations, and of respectfully dedicating the volumes of *Vancenza*."

∾

While Mary lay ill and despondent, Ban spent much of his time in Parliament. On March 9 William Wilberforce gave notice that on Thursday, March 29, he would present his motion "respecting the abolition of the slave trade." Tarleton replied: "I hope that the majority of this House on that day will teach Mr. Wilberforce to abandon a project so injurious to our important commerce, and to employ his talents in future in some pursuit less destructive to the interest of their country."

On March 29 the House became a Committee of the Whole to consider the motion made by Wilberforce. After listening to several speeches,

Banastre rose and began: "Though other Gentlemen have dealt largely in violent invective, and consumed much of the time of the House in attempting to affix an indelible stigma on the African trade, and almost a general crimination on all persons who have ever been concerned in it: as I do not envy them their feelings, I shall not adopt their example by entering minutely into every branch of the question of abolition."

Then the Colonel summarized the investment in Liverpool: "With regard to the capital engaged in the African trade at Liverpool, my own local knowledge will, I trust, give me the attention of the House, and carry with them some weight and consideration. One hundred and ten to one hundred and twenty ships sail annually from the port of Liverpool alone, from 120 to 500 tons burden, constructed peculiarly for the African trade, and unfit for any purpose of carrying."

After emphasizing that these vessels carried cargoes manufactured in the Midlands, he concluded: "In Liverpool, besides the merchants, many masters of vessels and inferior officers would lose their lucrative stations, and many industrious mechanics, who have served regular apprenticeships to, and have, for many years, continued in, a particular line of business, for the fabrication of articles exclusively required in this trade, would lose both the capital they have acquired in their present stores, and their future employment."

In an editorial on the debate, the *Oracle* of April 4 remarked: "Colonel Tarleton also displayed very laudable talents; and was uncommonly animated in the defense of his constituents. We think his reproof of the Minister rather harsh and indiscreet."

After pointing out that "Colonel Tarleton made a strong impression on the House and aroused the attention of the West India planters," the *Oracle* concluded: "The Colonel's efforts deserved and received the highest plaudits. The pleasure we derived from his oratorical powers, induces us to wish that he would oftener appear prominently in the senatorial scene of action."

Mary saw Ban's fame growing and her heart swelled with pride. Ill as she was, she brought her supreme talent to bear on him. She wooed him through poetry:

> *The Adieu to Fancy*
> Inscribed to the Same
>
> When first I knew thee, Fancy's aid
> A mine of peerless worth display'd,
> A thousand graces hourly stole
> In melting visions o'er my soul.
>
> For Fancy guides the shaft of Love,
> And bids fantastic visions move

In mystic mazes round the breast,
In Hope's delusive colours dress'd.

'Tis Fancy wings the Poet's thought,
With classic Taste sublimely fraught;
And bids the fount of Reason flow,
With smooth delight, or ruffled woe.

Full oft the gentle Sylph I've seen,
With soothing smile and sportive mien,
When, wand'ring to her fairy bow'rs,
She bound my grateful breast with flow'rs.

And oft with flatt'ring Hope she came
To twine a wreath of promis'd Fame;
Yet 'midst the laurel'd gift I found
Full many a thorn my breast to wound.

Oh! then she brought, my mind to calm,
Persuasive Friendship's soothing balm;
And Sympathy, with throbbing breast,
In Pity's specious semblance drest.

Yet Friendship's beauteous form I found
Would start aghast at Sorrow's wound;
And Sympathy's slow trickling tear
Would cease to flow when Grief was near.

Then let me own the tranquil scene,
The constant thought, the smile serene,
And know myself supremely blest!
DECEITFUL FANCY—TAKE THE REST!

Ban was now spending much of his time at Brooks's, chatting and gaming. Politics, abolition of the slave trade, and the progress of the French armies were subjects for friendly controversy, and he backed his opinions with guineas. Soon the name of Ban Tarleton led all the rest in the plump leather-bound *Betting Book.*

"Colonel Fitzpatrick bets Col. Tarleton 10 gns. that the slave trade is abolished before Episcopacy."

"Col. Tarleton bets General Smith five guineas that the news of Mons being taken by the French arrives in London before Intelligence is received of the taking of Syringapatam by the British Army."

Mary wrote other verses to her estranged lover:

When Fortune, smiling on my lot,
Illumined with joy my favour'd cot;

When sportive Love a wreath entwin'd,
The Graces of my breast to bind;
When Youth rush'd forward to bestow
On my ripe lip, the Ruby's glow;
When health spread Rapture o'er my cheek,
That bade the Blushing Roses speak,
And gave my eyes the spark divine—
Say, were not all these treasures thine?

There was no reply. *The Betting Book* carried another wager: "Mr. Sheridan bets Col. Tarleton one hundred guineas to fifty that Mr. Pitt is first Lord of the Treasury on the 28th of May, 1792."

Mary now leased the house at 13 St. James's Place, only a couple of blocks from Brooks's Club. But proximity brought no reconciliation. On July 23 Mary wrote a pitiful letter to Richard Sheridan:

"You will perhaps be surprised to hear that, after an irreproachable connection of more than *ten years*, I am suffered to depart in *Exile* from my Country, and all my hopes, for a few paltry debts. I sail this evening for *Calais*, *alone*, broken-hearted.

"My state of health is too deplorable to bear description, and I am depressed in spirits beyond what my strength can support. I conjure you not to mention this letter to anyone. I am sufficiently humbled by the base ingratitude of the world, without the additional mortification of public exposure. Since Colonel Tarleton has suffered me to be thus driven a wanderer upon the mercy of an unfeeling world, after having endured every insult from his present low associate, I am resolutely determined never to accept any favor from him. Will you, my dear Sheridan, do me the kindness to lend me one hundred pounds? I will pay you, upon my honour."

And in a postscript she added, "Pray, don't tell Tarleton—he will triumph in my sorrows."

Richard Sheridan, never more than a few jumps ahead of the sheriff himself, probably did not have £100. But somehow he raised the money.

On the next evening Mary, Maria Elizabeth, and Mrs. Darby crossed on the packet from Dover to Calais. Mary had the steward place her on deck, where she watched the receding coastline of England. With spirits depressed almost beyond bearing, she gave voice to a grief-stricken "Farewell to Tarleton."

STANZAS

WRITTEN BETWEEN DOVER AND CALAIS, JULY 24, 1792

Bounding billow, cease thy motion.
    Bear me not so swiftly o'er;
Cease thy roaring, foamy ocean,
    I will tempt thy rage no more.

Ah! within my bosom beating,
    Varying passions wildly reign;
Love, with proud Resentment meeting,
    Throbs by turns, of joy and pain.

Joy, that far from foes I wander,
    Where their taunts can reach no more;
Pain, that woman's heart grows fonder
    When her dream of bliss is o'er!

Love, by fickle fancy banish'd,
    Spurn'd by hope, indignant flies;
Yet when love and hope are vanish'd,
    Restless mem'ry never dies.

Far I go, where fate shall lead me,
    Far across the troubled deep;
Where no stranger's ear shall heed me,
    Where no eye for me shall weep.

Proud has been my fatal passion!
    Proud my injured heart shall be!
While each thought, each inclination,
    Still shall prove me worthy *thee!*

Not one sigh shall tell my story;
    Not one tear my cheek shall stain;
Silent grief shall be my glory—
    Grief, that stoops not to complain!

Let the bosom prone to ranging,
    Still by ranging seek a cure;
Mine disdains the thought of changing
    Proudly destin'd to endure.

Yet, ere far from all I treasur'd,
    T . . . . , ere I bid adieu;
Ere my days of pain are measur'd,
    Take the song that's still thy due!

Yet, I believe, no servile passions
    Seek to charm thy vagrant mind;
Well I know thy inclinations,
    Wav'ring as the passing wind.

I have lov'd thee,—dearly lov'd thee,
    Through an age of worldly woe;
How ungrateful I have prov'd thee
    Let my mournful exile show!

Ten long years of anxious sorrow,
    Hour by hour, I counted o'er;
Looking forward, till to-morrow,
    Every day I lov'd thee more!

Pow'r and splendour could not charm me;
    I no joy in wealth could see!
Nor could threats or fears alarm me,
    Save the fear of losing thee!

When the storms of fortune press'd thee,
    I have wept to see thee weep!
When relentless cares distress'd thee,
    I have lull'd those cares to sleep!

When with *thee*, what ills could harm me?
    Thou couldst every pang assuage;
But when absent, nought could charm me;
    Every moment seem'd an age.

Fare thee well, ungrateful rover!
    Welcome Gallia's hostile shore:
Now the breezes waft me over;
    Now we part—To Meet No More.

Mary Robinson hated Calais, with its little colony of English expatriates, mostly fugitives from debtor's prison, living just beyond the fingertips of English law. But there she had to remain while planning ways of reaching her brother in Leghorn. The wrath of the French Revolution blocked the road through France, and before she could cross to Germany fighting broke out in Flanders.

"We are allowed to say that the town through our means will still be gratified with the elegant Communications of our Laura Maria," said the *Oracle* of July 25. On July 30 it reported Mary's supposed destination and hinted that she would return in about two months to bring out her newly composed opera at Drury Lane.

The curious gossiped about Mary's flight, and the vindictive turned on Maria Elizabeth, now a lovely girl of seventeen. In *The Female Jockey Club*, the author repeated a lie: "We have lately heard, with unfeigned sorrow, (so fugitive are lover's joys) that there at present exists a serious difference between them, the *Liverpool hero* having betrayed certain symptoms of amorous fondness for Perdita's fair daughter."

While Mary languished in Calais, there came from Dover the man she wanted least to see—Thomas Robinson. For years Mary had wanted a divorce, but she was a valuable property to the sordid little gambler— too valuable to relinquish merely on her own request. Now he brought with him his brother, Commodore Robinson, recently returned from the East Indies. The Commodore wished to meet Maria Elizabeth and to save her from her scandalous situation. He offered her a wealthy and comfortable home, but on one condition: she must forever renounce Thomas and Mary Robinson. The daughter who had nursed Mary through nine years of agony scorned the offer.

The *Oracle* of August 3, 1792, published "Bounding Billow." There Banastre Tarleton read Mary Robinson's public confession:

> Ten long years of anxious sorrow,
>   Hour by hour I counted o'er;
> Looking forward, till to-morrow
>   Every day I lov'd thee more!

Finally he could bear no more. He spurned his "Low Associate"—oblivion spread a veil over her name—and crossed over to Calais. There were tears and weeping and renewed promises. Back to London he sent Mary, Maria Elizabeth, and Mrs. Darby. Then with a show of bravado he rode on into seething, revolutionary Paris.

"Mrs. Robinson is detained on her route to England by extreme and dangerous illness, and is at Calais, where her physician bade her remain," said the *Oracle* of August 28. Three days later it added: "Mrs. Robinson's Opera goes into Mr. Sheridan's hands the moment that the malady so far yields to physic as to permit her crossing the Straits of Dover. Her spirits seem excessively depressed by the natural influences of her complaint."

Mary and her family left Calais on September 2. She knew what lay ahead in London—gaiety beyond her finances, a few friends of the highest rank, gossip, and condemnation. But she would be with Banastre.

In *The False Friend* Mary repeated the question that now confronted her: "I think it is Rousseau who says, that the bravery of battle is mechanical: If then, the mind can be brought to bear up against the dangers of annihilation, why can it not be self-steeled against the perils of existence?"

As she lay in the cross-channel boat, she answered her own challenge in a sonnet which ended:

> Yet, why should Fancy other's woes reveal?
>   Have I not felt the rudest storms of Fate,
> And prov'd each pang the helpless breast can feel?
>   Then, Fortune, I defy thy fiercest hate!
> Henceforth each sensate nerve be hard as steel;
>   For where Despair resides, Reflection comes too late!

On September 2, the day the party escaped from Calais, the French Revolution reached the peak of its fury. Mobs tore open the prisons and slew 1200 Royalist prisoners. The Robinsons sailed only a few hours before the arrival of a decree for the arrest of every English subject in France.

In Paris, Banastre now heard the "Ca Ira" sung with fury. On September 2 as he walked along the Rue de la Paix he met the mob—still in a frenzy from slaughtering the Royalist prisoners. They began shouting "A la lanterne!" Seizing his only chance to escape swinging from a lantern post, he ran to join them, shouting as loudly as any: "A la lanterne!"

Next day Ban dined with the Duke of Orleans. "During the meal there was a great hubbub in the street and the guests got up from the table to look out at its cause. They beheld a head carried aloft on a pike. Philippe said coolly: 'Ah! C'est la Lamballe; je la connais à ses cheveux.'" For refusing to sign the oath against monarchy, red-headed Princess Lamballe had been torn to pieces by the mob. In her fate the noble dinner guests read their own. A year later Banastre Tarleton was the only one of the twelve who had not been guillotined.

"Colonel Tarleton is at Paris," the Oracle reported on September 7. On September 10 it added: "Mrs. Robinson is returned to her house in St. James Place from France, with her elegant and accomplished daughter."

"Colonel Tarleton is expected in England every day. He has left Paris," said the Oracle. He arrived in London on September 29 and rushed to Mary's home at 13 St. James's Place. Then, in defiance of the gossips and the gaping newshawks, he lifted Mary in his arms, placed her in her carriage, and drove with her to the Haymarket Theatre.

The Oracle of October 1 reported: "Colonel Tarleton, who by repeated report was Lamballed in Paris, has returned to London, and when needful, for the honour of his native country, to fight another day. He arrived in town on Saturday, and in the evening accompanied Mrs. Robinson and her party to the Hay Market Theater." It concluded: "Mrs. Robinson never looked better."

Mary was radiantly happy and she was flaunting her triumph, each sensate nerve as hard as steel. She was again by the side of the only man she ever truly loved, and he had publicly shown that he considered her his wife.

Why had Tarleton not been Lamballed? With war clouds gathering, the government had sent Colonel St. Leger to Vienna to report on the condition of the Austrian Army. Perhaps Tarleton was also on a secret mission, for after his visit with Mary he rushed down to Brighton. "Yesterday morning Colonel Tarleton had an audience of the Prince," said the General Evening Post of October 2, "after which he left Brighton for London."

As they settled into a semblance of love, Mary placed a symbolic golden ring upon the finger of her handsome graying colonel. For the joyful occasion she wrote her own epithalamium:

Stanzas

Presented With a Gold Chain Ring to a Dear Friend

Oh! take these little easy chains,
    And may they hold you while you live;
For know, each magic link contains
    The richest treasure I can give!

An *Emblem*, earnest, of my Love!
    Pure as the gold that forms the toy;
The more 'tis try'd, the more 'twill prove
    Beyond the touch of base alloy.

As *Even* as these *Links* shall be
    The giver's *Mind*, that scorns to range;
And, like the *Heart* ordain'd for thee,
    They may be *Broke!* but cannot change!

Then, take the little shining toy,
    And may it never quit thy sight;
And let it be my proudest joy,
    To know *My Chains*, tho' *lasting, Light!*

∽

Tarleton's visit to Paris having aroused the general curiosity, on October 6 the *World* ran a profile of the Liverpool hero:

Col. Banastre Tarleton

Intrepid TARLETON chas'd the foe,
    And smil'd in Death's grim face,
And brav'd his withering blow!
    —Mrs. Robinson's *Ode to Valour*

The glorious exploits performed by military heroism, are worthy of being transmitted to later posterity. To record the actions of the *military Hero*, when fighting in defence of his country, when endeavoring to crush unprovoked rebellion, or seditious legions, raised to oppose just laws, and good government, is just and proper. The faithful page of history has recorded the brilliant actions of HANNIBAL, SCIPIO, CAESAR, and POMPEY, in ancient times; and those of MARLBOROUGH, TURENNE, and SAXE among the moderns.

Few persons have exhibited greater valour and intrepidity in the field of battle than Colonel TARLETON. To enter into a detail of his military actions, is not the design of this Sketch; they are well known, and justly applauded.

Mr. TARLETON is a native of *Liverpool*. His family have resided there for some years, and are highly respected. Young TARLETON evinced in his earliest years an heroic disposition, and gave pleasing evidences of that courage and prowess which have rendered him so justly celebrated.

The American war excited Mr. TARLETON's attention, and having learnt the principles of *Military Tactics*, he resolved to embark for *America, having* already received a commission as an officer.

The brilliant and splendid successes which he gained over the American forces, raised him high in the estimation of the Commanding Officers of the British army. He was advanced as his valour and courage were exhibited, to that degree of military honour which he now enjoys.

When the operations of the British arms in America were closed, Col. TARLETON came over to England, and soon after paid a visit to his native place. He was received at *Liverpool* with the most unequivocal marks of esteem and gratitude; the inhabitants were eager to view the gallant hero, and he was carried in triumph amidst the acclamations of numerous spectators. The inhabitants of Liverpool have since expressed their grateful sense of his military services, by electing him a Representative in Parliament for that town. Mr. TARLETON has shewn himself not unworthy of the confidence reposed in him.

During the debates on the *Abolition of the Slave Trade*, Colonel TARLETON took a decided part against the Abolition. In his speeches, he selected those arguments which appeared the most calculated to support what in reality was indefensible: but the Colonel spoke the language, and adopted the arguments of his constituents. For taking so active a part in opposing the Abolition of the *Slave Trade*, he has become the object of partial censure.

When the *Revolution in France* took place, Colonel TARLETON went over to *Paris*, and was present at the *Grand Federation* in the year 1790. He with some other English gentlemen attended the Marquis DE LA FAYETTE in the *Champs de Mars*. Since that time, Colonel TARLETON has paid several visits to that Metropolis, and was present during the horrid *massacres* which, to the disgrace of human nature, have lately taken place in that capital. He was preserved amidst the general carnage. But found extreme difficulty in procuring a passport to return to his native country.

Colonel TARLETON has favoured the public with an interesting "*Journal of the Millitary Operations of the British in America.*" This work (published in quarto) was very favourably received, and does credit to the Author.

In private life, Mr. TARLETON is open, generous, and humane.

> With TARLETON's name, recording FAME, shall blend
> The warlike *Hero*, and the faithful *Friend*.

The *Oracle* now outsmarted the *World*. On October 10 it railed at the French princes for continuing to live in luxury, with numerous attendants and mistresses. "These unhappy men are in the most lamentable state of infatuation." Obviously the Revolution had taught them nothing. "These deplorable facts may be corroborated by Sir James Murray, Colonel St. Leger, and Colonel Tarleton."

The editors of the *Oracle* thought they knew the secret of Tarleton's trip to Paris, and Daniel Stuart threw his harpoon: "These Gentlemen now mentioned, with a spirit of emulation highly honorable to soldiers, repaired to the Continent to offer their services to the Duke of Brunswick."

The reaction of the half-pay Colonel was furious. He stormed into the office of the *Oracle*. When Stuart glanced up from his desk a three-fingered fist was shaken in his face and a thick Lancashire voice shouted: "I did not go to the Continent to offer my services to the Duke of Brunswick!" The Colonel did not wish to be called a mercenary.

That afternoon Banastre set out for Liverpool to visit his mother. He wished to tell his family of the Reign of Terror and to talk politics with his brothers, especially Clayton, now mayor of Liverpool. He hoped to still the rising clamor for war against France.

In the *Oracle* next day Stuart printed a retraction:

COLONEL TARLETON

We have authority to contradict the article in our paper of yesterday, which says that Col. Tarleton's late visit to the Continent, was to offer his Services to the Duke of Brunswick. Colonel Tarleton's motives in visiting Paris, were merely those of curiosity, without any political views whatever, and without the smallest ideas of offering his services to either party; neither did the colonel pass the Frontiers during his short residence on the Continent.

Somewhere in this shifting chaos the Prince befriended Mary, perhaps with the £100 she had borrowed from Sheridan. That fond muse repaid him with a poem. On October 20, under her pen name of Julia, she published her tribute in the *Oracle*.

SONNET

TO THE PRINCE OF WALES

From Courtly Crowds and empty joys retir'd
Adorn'd with Heaven's best gift, a Lib'ral Mind!
Still shall thy grac'd perfections be admir'd,
Thy *polished Manners*, and thy sense refin'd.

Oh! form'd to decorate each varying Scene,
To smile, the darling of the *mirthful train!*
Or, with Sage Precepts, of the mind serene,
To *prove* all trivial, empty Pleasures, Vain!

From the fond Muse, accept a Wreath Sublime!
A Wreath, not deck'd with Fancy's transient fires;
Truth shall record the Virtue she admires,
And mock the withering hand of ruthless Time!

So through the chilling veil of horrid Night,
The Burning Orb darts forth, A World Of Living Light!

After a stay with family, friends, and constituents, Ban returned
leisurely to London. On October 23 the *Oracle* said: "Colonel Tarleton
has left Liverpool and is now at Lord Melbourne's, from whence he is
expected in town tomorrow."

On October 23 the *Sun* entered the controversy. It had never been
friendly to Tarleton and was predisposed to believe he had gone to
Paris to seek a commission in the French Army. "Colonel Tarleton is
enjoying his well deserved reputation for having relinquished pursuits,
upon conviction of their danger, that threatened ruin to his Country."

To which the *Oracle* rejoined: "Colonel Tarleton has never been violent in his Political Sentiments; and from the general tenor of his conduct, we have every assurance that his principles are such as will induce
him to act, upon all National questions, with honour to himself, and for
the Glory and Prosperity of his Country."

Four days later the *Sun* returned to its irony. "Some of Colonel
Tarleton's *pretended* Friends are endeavoring to deprive him of a degree of credit with his Fellow-citizens to which we know him to be well
entitled. To use his own words 'He went to France a violent Democrat,
but in consequence of what he saw there, he has returned a confirmed
Aristocrat!' The inference to be drawn from this declaration we leave
with the Public."

The *Sun's* attitude was part of the spirit of intolerance sweeping England. Feeling against revolutionary France was running high. Pitt and
the Tories were preparing for war. On December 1 the War Office
ordered the militia embodied. Throughout the kingdom mayors were
arousing their townsmen. In Liverpool, Mayor Clayton Tarleton, a
Whig, was trying to still the clamor.

Realizing the ruin that war could bring to a commercial people,
Banastre wrote to Clayton:

Dec'r 6th, 1792

My dear Brother,
    I wish I had been at your elbow when you put the invitation you
enclosed to me to the press—Pray look at the reports of the city

meeting yesterday. Their resolutions breathe the true spirit of Moderation—you may rest assured that the flame of loyalty (which I trust in God will never die in this country) is now artfully kindled to precipitate these Kingdoms into War—A good citizen, a good Whig, and a *good* subject ought to look at measures with calmness and moderation and strive to balance the political machine which will soon after the commencement of hostilities, be kickt up by despotism or democracy—I do not now speak as a soldier. I should have every dazzling expectation in my professional character, but I speak from observation and the sincerity of my Soul, as representing a prosperous commercial people; therefore as a friend, a brother and a chief magistrate I conjure you to weigh these things unadorned.

From
B.T.

Be moderate in your address and I will explicitly the moment I have time give you my reasons.

Parliament convened on December 13. To forestall the Tory plans for war the Whigs pressed for the recognition of the government of France. During the debate on Fox's motion, on December 15 Tarleton defended himself against the recent attacks in the press. He professed a strong attachment to the Crown and the Constitution. Said he: "If this counry should unfortunately be plunged into war, I am ready to use my utmost exertions in defense of my King and country."

He lamented the scenes which had taken place in France: some that he had witnessed would have brought tears to the eyes of the hardest-hearted man. "I am convinced, however, that this country ought to negotiate rather than go to war, for there is no saying how or when a war with France may end. I do not think Great Britain is so deeply concerned in continental transactions as to be obliged to go to war, secured as she herself is in her insular situation." Then with a flourish he cried: "*Penitus toto divisos orbe Britannos?*"

29

The Betting Book

ARLETON UNDERSTOOD the nature of the French Revolution. He had enjoyed the hospitality and seen the excesses of the nobility; he had inspected the revolutionary army and witnessed the frenzy of the Paris mob. He also understood the aims of Pitt and the Tories: he had watched them readying the Navy and embodying the Militia, and had seen them beat down the conciliatory proposals of Charles Fox.

Into *The Betting Book* at Brooks's Club on January 6, 1793, went his opinion at odds of twenty-one to one: "Col. Tarleton bets Mr. Clopton one hundred and five guineas to five gns. that Great Britain is at war with France within Six Months from the above date."

While peace and Banastre's 105 guineas hung in the balance, on January 26 the *Oracle* reported: "Colonel Tarleton has been confined for some days past with a rheumatic fever, of which he still continues much indisposed."

Six days later the Colonel's prophecy came true. On February 1 France declared war against England.

Great was the excitement as the nation began mustering her fighting men. King George appointed the Duke of York his field commander, and on February 25 Frederick sailed for Holland, taking with him General Lake and Colonel St. Leger and three battalions of the Foot Guards.

Enviously yet helplessly, Banastre watched his friends depart. Reported the *Oracle* on March 22: "Colonel Tarleton, with that zealous ardour which has ever distinguished his Military Character, has offered to raise a Regiment of Light Cavalry."

Mary took Banastre to Old Windsor. With understanding born of her own affliction, she nursed him, consoled him in his disappointment, and tried to cheer him with a garland of verses:

328

STANZAS

Inscribed to a Dear Friend, when confined by
Severe Indisposition, in March, 1793.

Ye glades that just open to greet the blue sky,
　　All encircled with woodlands bespangled with dew,
From your borders, once cherish'd, disgusted I fly;
　　For your beauties are faded, and sadden'd your hue.

O! soft gliding river, whose banks I behold
　　Undelighted and mournful, no longer you please;
Nor the deep azure bells, nor the cowslips of gold
　　Nor your smooth glassy bosom o'ershadow'd with trees.

Yon mountain, whose breezes enliven the soul,
　　Never more will I climb at the dawning of day;
Never more to the turf-cover'd meadows I'll stroll,
　　Or on beds of young primroses carol my lay.

For, glades, to your sod with my love I've retir'd
　　When the red beams were rushing the foliage among,
When the last glowing shadow of Evening expir'd,
　　And the rocks rung responsive to PHILOMEL's song.

And thou, lucid river, I've sat by thy side,
　　To behold his dear form in thy clear glassy breast,
When the Moon spread her light o'er thy soft rolling tide,
　　And the wise were content with the dulness of rest.

And thou, craggy mountain, where oft I have stray'd,
　　To behold from your summit the thatch of his cot;
Like the slow-winding river, the dew-spangled glade,
　　And the thick-woven woodlands—be ever forgot.

See! Nature is sadden'd by Sympathy's tears,
　　Since my Lover no longer enlivens the day;
And forlorn shall she be till her darling appears,
　　As the ROSE droops its head when the SUN FADES AWAY.

During Ban's illness Mary published a thin book of verse entitled
Sight, The Cavern of Woe, and Solitude. She dedicated it to John
Taylor of Hatton Garden. Said the *Monthly Review* of August 1793:
"*Sight* manifests great pathos, feeling, and tenderness in the fair writer."

Both the poetry and the poetess were in high popularity. A few volumes of *Poems* were taken out to India and sold at three and four guineas each. "Lines to him Who Will Understand Them" had been set to music and become a popular drawing-room number. On March 21 the *Oracle* reported that Westall had painted Venus from Mary's "Cupid Sleeping," written in honor of the Duchess of Devonshire, and that the poetess, *with permission* had dedicated an engraving of it to the Prince of Wales.

During the fall Mary had written an opera which she called *Kate of Aberdeen*. After reading the manuscript, Sheridan returned it with his regrets. She then tried the Haymarket Theatre. On March 30 the *Oracle* noted that she had completely withdrawn the work.

So passed the winter—Mary writing and nursing, Ban fretful and impatient. On April 23 the *Oracle* announced: "Colonel Tarleton continues extremely indisposed."

But Mary and the April sunshine were winning. On May 27 the *Star* observed: "Mrs. Robinson's health is hourly mending; she looks as lovely as ever." She turned her happiness into verse:

TO THE SAME

On his recovering from a long indisposition, in May, 1793.

Go, balmy gales, and tell LISARDO's ear,
 That Health comes smiling on the wings of Morn;
Tell him, that sweet Repose approaches near,
 To banish fev'rish Days, and Nights forlorn.

Brightly the sun-beams on the mountains break,
 And whisp'ring Zephyrs shake their wings around;
The Day-star steals away in lustre meek,
 And spreading glories gild the dewy ground.

Exulting FLORA opes her varying hues;
 The Valley smiles, the verdant Hills look gay;
From her abundant store Profusion strews
 The buds and tints of rosy-bosom'd May.

The lofty woodlands wave their leafy heads,
 To wake the plumy trav'llers of the air;
The low-born lilies, on their humid beds,
 Expand their spotless bosoms, fresh and fair.

Slow winds the brawling river through the vales;
 Down the rough rock the roaring torrents flee;
The high-pois'd lark on floods of ether sails,
 To greet the Lord of Light with songs of glee.

Soft is the perfume of Morn's beauteous breast,
 And soft the murmurs of the insect train;
While Nature's hand, with pearly lustre drest,
 Leads tip-toe Pleasure o'er the glitt'ring plain.

> For thee, LISARDO, she unfolds her store,
>> For thee she weaves a garland, proudly gay;
> Come then, my Friend, the lib'ral Nymph adore,
>> And own that Rapture is the child of May.

> And while returning Health pervades each nerve,
>> As April suns disperse the wintry gloom,
> The sad rememb'rance of past "woe shall serve
>> FOR SWEET DISCOURSES in our TIME TO COME."

On June 4 the Guards paraded in honor of King George's birthday, and next morning the *Star* rejoiced that Colonel Tarleton had so far recovered as to be among those viewing the parade.

The Duke of York had begun the siege of Valenciennes. There was talk that the French would soon surrender. The veteran who had watched Washington strangle the British army at Yorktown knew how long a siege could last. *The Betting Book* recorded his opinion: "Mr. Stepney bets Col. Tarleton 20 guineas that Valenciennes & the citadel is taken in twenty one days from the date of this bet. June 10, 1793."

But the Colonel was still weak, and his physician ordered more rest. He and Mary quietly slipped into the country. On July 23 the *Oracle* reported: "Mrs. Robinson has been some days in the neighborhood of Windsor."

Soon rumors spread that Colonel Tarleton had joined the Duke of York in Flanders. "Colonel Tarleton is not at the Camp before Valenciennes, as stated in a morning paper; but by order of Dr. Warren, traveling in the neighborhood of London, for change of air, being still in a very precarious state of health," said the *Oracle* of July 27. "Mrs. Robinson has been for some days at Cobham, in Surrey, in the delightful and muse inspiring vicinity of Painshill, employed in the gentle offices of consoling her sick friend."

As the golden days of summer passed and the excitement of war and mobilization continued unabated, other rumors began flying. On September 12 the *Star* announced that Colonel Tarleton would decline to stand for re-election at Liverpool. His brother John, "whose commercial interests render him popular, will probably succeed him."

James Boaden knew the lovers were at Old Windsor. The editor sent Ban a query and on September 14 the *Oracle* relayed his answer to his constituents: "We have authority to say that their gallant Representative will never relinquish what on both parts is attended with so distinguished an honor."

There was other news from Old Windsor. Shuffling awkwardly around on her crutches, Mary had fallen and injured herself. But the editor informed the readers of the *Oracle:* "Mrs. Robinson is perfectly recovered from her late accident and is expected in town in a few days, having a second volume of poems ready for publication."

In Flanders on August 18 General Gerard Lake and the Guards defeated the French at Linselles. The action was the most brilliant of the campaign, and the Duke of York wrote to the Prince: "You will have been pleased with the bravery and spirit of our friend Lake and the Brigade of Guards."

But the Duke retreated to Dunkirk where he was hard-pressed. The War Office began readying reinforcements. The public had begun wondering if it would send out the distinguished Dragoon. On September 17 the *Oracle* said: "The Colonel is we hear daily recovering from his long indisposition, under the care of Dr. Warren."

Then, to clear up his military status, the *Oracle* said: "Colonel Tarleton was expressly requested by Sir William Erskine to accompany him on his present expedition. His well known services and rank in the army will prevent his accepting any inferior situation whatever."

An accident delayed his return to London. On September 20 the *Star* reported: "Colonel Tarleton, so recently recovered from his long indisposition, had the misfortune to sprain his knee so violently that he is still confined in the country, from whence he is at present incapable of removing."

On October 5 the *Oracle* said: "Mrs. Robinson returns to town as soon as her house in St. James Place is ready to receive her." Soon afterward she returned from Old Windsor.

Under the pseudonym of Horace Juvenal, Mary published a satire called *Modern Manners.* In it she lampooned such fashionable vices as dandyism, faro, and prize fighting:

> O ye *box-lobby heroes!*—men of shops!
> Bravoes in *buckskin*—Hannibals at hops!
> Did ye but know what wretched things ye are,
> Despis'd by men—and laughed at by the fair,
> You'd shrink to grubs, and from grubs you'd fade away,
> The short liv'd insects of a short-liv'd day!
> With men of might, when Truth no more prevails,
> A *knock-down* argument—but seldom fails.
> Humphries and Johnson, fill'd with British *Spirit,*
> Whose strong pretensions knock down timid merit;
> (More pow'rful than the magic force that lies
> In Hanger's bludgeon, or Fl—z—l's eyes)
> Attend each sporting club throughout the Town,
> Not to make speeches—but to knock ye down;
> E'en Dukes will sometimes condescend to box;
> And many an orator's *knocked down* by Fox.
> Fair Ladies, too, o'er whelmed by Faro's frown
> *Knock up* their Lords, till Christie knocks them **down!**

"Could Horace and Juvenal have descanted thus eloquently, on Heroes and Bravoes and Buckskin, on box-lobbies, hops and shops?" laughed the *Monthly Review* of October 1793. But *Modern Manners* had "roused a nest of hornets," said the *Oracle* of November 9. "A Reviewer never suffers one author to chastise the malice of another."

In early fall Banastre returned to London. Everyone congratulated him on his recovery. The *Oracle* said in an editorial on October 31: "Every lover of his Country must rejoice in the recovery of Colonel Tarleton from his long and dangerous illness. The services of this Gallant Officer during six years in America gained him the love of a nation, that can never forget them. Though the Colonel often bled in the field and lost two fingers in the service of Great Britain, he is too good a soldier, not to wish for the opportunity which may place him, with the rank he deserves, in a situation, he can fill, but with *honour to himself* and to *his Country*."

Two weeks later the *Oracle* publicly asked a question that many of its readers had asked in private. "Is it not singular that Colonel Tarleton, who has given so many memorable proofs of his loyalty and gallantry, has not yet been called upon to fight the battles of his King and Country?"

Could King George have forgotten him? The Colonel went to the levee in St. James's Palace to find out. "He was at court on Wednesday last," said the *Oracle* of November 23, "and was even honored with Royal congratulations on having at length triumphed over so threatening an indisposition."

It would have been a just reward if Mary had been at Banastre's side during King George's congratulations. Despite the pains of her own rheumatic body, often dulled with laudanum, she had nursed him, cheered him, supported him, and paid his bills. But her only reward was to see him head for Brooks's Club, to argue and bet and drink with Charles Fox and Richard Sheridan. Said the *Oracle* on November 29: "Colonel Tarleton, with perfect health and spirits, is *longo post tempore* returned to the fashionable circles. We believe his late indisposition was the most obstinate foe the Colonel ever encountered."

Yet Mary was happy. She had Ban's love, and the public was applauding her poetry. At Sheridan's Drury Lane Theatre the distinguished Stephen Kemble was reciting her somber *Cavern of Woe* "with the happiest effect and distinguished applause."

In the *Oracle* of November 28 editor Boaden praised and warned: "Mrs. Robinson ought to be highly flattered, when her poetry is become the subject for painters—musical composers—translators—public recitation—and theatrical remark. She must expect all the shafts of ENVY to assail her, and arm herself against them accordingly."

After Kemble's recitation, John Taylor carried his copy of *Sight, The Cavern of Woe, and Solitude* when he called on painter Joseph

Farington. On December 1 Farington recorded in his *Diary*: "Taylor of Hatton Garden called on me this morning and sat for a considerable time. He brought with him some poems by Mrs. Robinson, one of them on sight dedicated to him. He says Mrs. Robinson is about 38 years of age. Colonel Tarleton does not now live with her, but is very often at her house in St. James Place."

Mary hailed the new year with more poetry. On January 4, 1794, she published the second volume of her *Poems*. "We rarely, indeed, meet with elegance equal to the language of this work," observed the *Oracle* on January 8. But the *Critical Review* was hostile to Mary's *Poems*: "We find in them more words than ideas, and a splendour of diction with little discrimination or choice of figures. Many relate to incidents in her own connections, and are *proudly plaintive*."

Mary had violated the *Critical Review*'s eighteenth-century canons of poetry. "We could wish that a fancy naturally brilliant, and numbers so flowing might, by careful cultivation, be improved into poetry, able to stand the test of criticism." And the reviewer sneered because she had written for money—"calls more pressing than the impulse of genius or the desire of fame."

Mary sent *Poems* to John Taylor. Back came a tributary "Impromptu," which opened graciously:

> Ah! fair, dearest Laura, my thanks would I pay
> For the treasure of *Genius* thy friendship bestows.

And after several stanzas it closed more graciously:

> Then take, dearest Laura, the tribute sincere,
> From a friend who admir'd thee in life's early hour;
> Who beheld in thy *bloom*, the sweet promise appear,
> That time has matur'd to so lovely a flow'r.

Mary's old friend from Hatton Garden then turned to prose:

Dear Madam,

It is not because you have paid so very flattering a tribute to my professional character, as to dedicate to me one of your most beautiful Poems, that I am induced to lay the following trifles at your feet. I am too sensible of the merit of that Poem, to make so inadequate a return. My object on this occasion, is at least to tender my thanks, and to indulge myself in the pleasure of boasting that I have for many years enjoyed the friendship of one of the most accomplished women of the present age.

I am,

Dear Madam,
Your Sincere Friend,
JOHN TAYLOR

In December Ban was able to return to Parliament. When not in the House, he was usually at Mary's or around the corner at Brooks's. He was now forty years old, in poor health, and graying rapidly. He had given up riding and cricket and tennis and boxing. He delighted to sit in the spacious rooms of Brooks's and talk.

Chatter about the war frequently led to argument, which in turn usually led to *The Betting Book*. On January 17 was recorded: "Mr. Stepney bets Colonel Tarleton 10 gns. that the French republicans do not attack any post maintained by the allies between the Duchy of Luxemburg & the port of Ostend with a corps consisting of 2,000 men before the 15th of Feby next."

On January 20 another opinion: "I bet Mr. Grey 1 guinea that Cyprus is in the possession of the French on or before this day three Weeks. Ban Tarleton."

Occasionally these bets were wild whims: "Col. Tarleton bets Mr. T. Thompson 100 gns. to 10 that Mr. Horne Tooke is not first or second on the Poll for Members for Westminster at the next General Election. P.P. Feby. 4, 1794."

In Parliament, Wilberforce began his attack on slavery by moving that the trade carried on in English ships in supplying foreign territories with slaves be abolished. Tarleton was immediately on his feet to voice the sentiment of the Liverpool slavers.

"I consider the change specified as a dangerous interference with trade, which I must oppose, because I think it an unequivocal attack upon private property," he cried on February 7. "As to the trade in question, if it had to commence *de novo*, I should have no difficulty in declaring decided opposition to it. But as circumstances stand at present, I must consider the measure proposed as a violent aggression upon property, which will produce the most serious consequences."

Meanwhile Mary was working on another novel. Rumors spread that she had drawn her characters from life and would reflect the fashionable vices of society. On February 13 the *Morning Post* reported: "All the fashionable Widows are up in arms against Mrs. Robinson and wonder how a woman without rank dares take such liberties with great people."

Next day Mary published *The Widow, or A Picture of Modern Times*. Using an old and acceptable novel form which Fanny Burney had revived in *Evelina*, she developed her plot through a series of letters. Exclaimed the *Oracle*: "As the characters are drawn from life, there are some striking resemblances!"

Although noting that Mary had had difficulty in passing from verse to prose, the *Monthly Review* of May 1794 found merit in *The Widow*. "In the present novel, however, she has succeeded better than in her former prose productions, in attempting to throw off the pomp of poetical diction and to reduce her style to the tone of polite epistolary correspondence. But the principal merit of these volumes is their exhibiting a picture of *Modern Times*, in which the features of fashionable folly and depravity are drawn with skilful hand, and with such strokes of deformity as are well adapted to excite contempt and indignation."

As in *Vancenza* Mary's passions and attitudes were strikingly confessed by the title character in *The Widow*:

> We are all subject to error, and the feeling, considerate mind readily embraces every occasion to commend, rather than depreciate. Let those who censure, examine their own heart; let them, before they condemn, prove themselves immaculate. The fraility of our sex depends on a thousand circumstances, and ought to claim the tenderest indulgence. A woman may be weak without being vicious; a variety of events may conspire to undermine the most powerful rectitude; and the severity frequently exercised by relations in the education of youth, gives an habitual discontent, which renders every scene of life dull and insipid. The mind, so tinged with peevish indifference, shrinks from the energies of virtue, and easily becomes a prey to the designing. There are women who have no opportunities to wander from the paths of propriety; peculiar deficiency in personal attractions will often shield the weakest heart from the attacks of the seducer; others are placed on such an eminence of delight, so surrounded by all the comforts, the luxuries of life, blessed with the attentions of amiable kindred, (while every wish is anticipated by the affections of a worthy husband) that to deviate from virtue would be unpardonable. But let the unprejudiced observer turn to that woman, who, perhaps, tenderly educated in the bosom of afluence, with a mind exquisitely sensible, driven upon the mercy of an unfeeling world; young, beautiful, stricken with poverty, shrinking under oppression, assailed by flattery, and allured by splendor; surely the most obdurate heart must sigh for such a wanderer, and confess that, if anything can palliate indiscretion, it is the combination of such circumstances. But, alas! how few will examine with candour, or judge with lenity! How few will look back upon past provocation, in order to extenuate present culpability! For my own part, I confess I never behold the blush of contrition, without feeling an involuntary impulse to bathe it with a tear of pity! The *happy* do not want the aids of compassion, and I trust I shall cease to exist when I withhold a sigh from the unfortunate.

The first edition of 3000 copies of *The Widow* was quickly sold. Mary began preparing a second edition. But the labor was too great. Reported the *Oracle* of March 8: "Mrs. Robinson has been several weeks indisposed with a nervous fever."

As Mary lay on her sickbed, she found hope and comfort in Maria Elizabeth. Her heart swelled with pride when she read an account of the masquerade at Brandenbourg House. Society's great and fashionable were there: The Prince of Wales, Lord and Lady Melbourne, Richard Sheridan, and a host of others. On February 26 the *Oracle* said that the prettiest women present were "Miss Jerningham, Lady Asgill, and Miss Robinson."

∽

In Parliament, Ban fought the Tories. Prime Minister Pitt had expressly declared that the English were engaged in a war with France only in so far as it related to the defense of England. Yet the Whigs assumed a more limited ground of complaint. On March 17 General Fitzpatrick moved an address to the throne on the detention of General Lafayette and two other members of the French Constituent Assembly who had been captured at Liége and turned over to the Prussians.

Colonel Tarleton seconded the motion for the address. He told how General Lafayette, accused of disloyalty, had left his army and appeared before the French Assembly. Although he was acquitted, his troops had embraced Jacobin principles and refused to obey him when he returned. "He therefore departed from France with a few followers, intending to go to Holland, and from thence to America, that asylum of liberty and peace."

Banastre told of Lafayette's capture in neutral territory and imprisonment in the Castle of Olmütz. "I would desire the House to consider the impolicy of such conduct; and I hope, that at a time when we are treating with Prussia, possibly for the purpose of parting with our treasure, we will interfere, and endeavor to rescue Lafayette from those hardships to which he has been unmeritedly doomed to suffer; and that his Majesty's Minister will lose no time to wipe away the foul stain that has blurred the ermine of Majesty."

He concluded: "I could, from my personal knowledge of the unfortunate general during my residence at Paris, say much of his virtues, his integrity, his attachment to the cause of true and temperate liberty, his tenderness to his wife and children, his universal benevolence, and his admiration for this country."

The move was popular. The *Oracle* of March 22 expressed the general attitude: "Colonel Tarleton's having been the antagonist of LaFayette in America gives him the more credit for his manly and eloquent defense of the unfortunate General in the House of Commons."

The Robinson household was that day in happy excitement. On March 22 Maria Elizabeth's *The Shrine of Bertha* was published. Mary's hand was evident in the structure of her daughter's first novel, and the author credited her mother with the songs in it.

The *Critical Review* dismissed *The Shrine of Bertha* with a two-sentence sneer: "Novels, as their sole purpose is entertainment, must either be the most amusing or the most insipid of publications. We cannot say that the two volumes before us belong to the former class." But readers liked *The Shrine of Bertha* and it ran through several editions.

∿

By now it had become apparent to even his best friends in the Horse Guards that the Duke of York was less than brilliant as a field commander. So Pitt turned for guidance to Lord Cornwallis who had returned to England, his military ability vindicated by the successful war against Sultan Tippoo Sahib of Mysore. Soon afterward the War Office announced that the Earl of Moira (the former Lord Rawdon), who had been promoted to major general, would lead an army to the Continent.

Would Lord Cornwallis use his influence to advance the famed Green Dragoon? In its editorial on April 4 the *Morning Post* said: "The independent spirit of our gallant Tarleton has perhaps deprived him of the gew gaw of a court, but while he can press his mutilated hand upon a heart devoted to the services of mankind, he need not envy those who bear 'their blushing honours thick upon them'."

Banastre was not noticeably sanguine about his chances for active duty. In *The Betting Book* he wrote: "I have given Mr. Sheridan one guinea to receive one thousand in case I command the advanced party at any of the suburbs of Paris on or before the 25th of Decbr. next. Ban Tarleton. R. Sheridan."

The odds were sound. Pitt disliked the radical disciple of Charles Fox. Undoubtedly Charles Pigott voiced the sentiment of a large segment of the Tories in a satirical sketch called "Colonel Tarleton," published in *The Whig Club* in 1794. The sketch put the blackest construction on every event and motive in Tarleton's career. With great cruelty but equal truth the satirist wrote of the precarious finances of the Colonel: "To this he could lately call Perdita to Witness; but that elegant frail one remains now only a melancholy ruin of her former beauty; and is reduced to beguile her hours, and prop the Colonel's tottering finances, by weaving novels and fineering sonnets."

Then Pigott damned the Dragoon:

. . . But with the war his glories ended: the brave soldier degenerated into a vain boaster: in every company his own exploits were his constant theme; and those who were inclined voluntarily to have paid him the tribute of applause he merited, were fatigued into silent disgust by his endless repetition. The esteem of the more rigid were alienated by the dissipation into which he plunged; race horses and mistresses, his gaming and high feasting, soon exhausted the spoil of six successive campaigns; and on the appointment of his former patron to the most important command this country can bestow, he cast a look of impatience toward the east, in the hope of restoring his shattered fortunes by the plunder of the rich banks of the Ganges.

But that noble Lord, pure in his own conduct, was determined that those who accompanied him should be pure also; nor would he suffer the rapacity of a needy dependent to strain his reputation for integrity. The Colonel was mortified by an absolute refusal; in the refusal was buried all remembrance of former obligations; and that he might record his ingratitude to futurity, the Colonel published his history of the American campaigns, which was an open and malignant attack on the military conduct and skill of his benefactor.

The *Campaigns* had ruined any hope for active duty Tarleton may have had. As long as Lord Cornwallis remained a military power, Ban would remain on half-pay. On April 7 the *Morning Post* noted the animosity: "Our brave Countryman Tarleton was in one of the streets at the West End of the Town when Lord Cornwallis proceeded in the City Cavalcade on Saturday. The *People* did say that a blush suffused the cheeks of the noble Marquis."

30

The Devil's Walk

*P*RIME MINISTER PITT now relied on the advice of Lord Cornwallis. As the coalition with Austria, Prussia, and Holland began showing signs of collapse, Pitt and Dundas sent Lord Cornwallis to visit the Prussian army. On his way out, Cornwallis reached British headquarters in Holland on June 6. Here he found many friends from his campaigns in America.

Earl Harcourt, with whom Cornet Tarleton had ridden to capture General Lee, was second in command. Sir William Erskine, who had made Captain Tarleton his brigade major, was next in seniority. Earl Moira, who as Lord Rawdon fought beside Lieutenant Colonel Tarleton at Camden, commanded a wing of the army. Lord Cathcart, once colonel of the British Legion, was with Moira. Major General Nisbet Balfour commanded a division. General Lake had already won eternal glory at Linselles. Dundas was with the Duke, and Ross was with Cornwallis. Only Major General Simcoe, now lieutenant governor of Upper Canada, and Colonel Tarleton were absent from the struggle.

After negotiations with the Prussians, whom he found more interested in the dismemberment of Poland than in the defeat of France, Cornwallis started for London. On the way home he again visited the army in Holland. He was dispirited. Lieutenant Colonel Henry Calvert wrote: "Cornwallis goes to England without a plan, and declares he knows not what can be done."

But the Austrians had a plan: recall the Duke of York and make Cornwallis commander in chief. Count Mercy, Austrian minister to the Hague, conveyed this suggestion to Pitt. After reviewing the Count's proposal, the Prime Minister wrote Cornwallis: "He is persuaded that if you had the command of our army with the local rank of field marshal there would be no difficulty in so arranging it that you might have the virtual command of the whole army, Austrian as well as British."

But even as he dangled the rank of field marshal in front of Corn-wallis, Pitt knew the real problem. Ministers could not sack the favorite son of the King. Pitt admitted as much to his Lordship: "I am fully aware of the apparent difficulty in superseding the Duke of York's command."

Cornwallis was reluctant, but replied that he was prepared to assume the post. Pitt then wrote the King. His Majesty agreed, and in a long letter wrote manfully: "But I own, in My Son's place, I should beg my being allowed to return home if the command is given to Lord Cornwallis."

Meanwhile Colonel Tarleton was devoting himself to his duties in Parliament. Even though he had shrugged off Pigott's attack in *The Whig Club*, he was bitterly disappointed. As he saw his old comrades in command in Holland, he suffered; and as he suffered he grew more radical in his politics.

He was still warmly attached to the Prince and the dukes. But now, plunging on after Fox, he was seldom with his royal friends. He no longer followed the Prince down to the royal pavilion at Brighton.

The Prince himself was in a bad way. His debts amounted to some £630,000. The only possible relief seemed to be a marriage settlement. So, one afternoon in August, as the King was returning from the chase, the Prince approached him and said abruptly: "I wish to marry."

The King was delighted. According to the Marriage Act of 1772 the union between the Prince and Mrs. Fitzherbert was void. Now he could end his son's unlawful connection. Immediately he thought of a buxom princess beyond the Rhine. From Weymouth he wrote on August 24: "Agreeable to what I mentioned to Mr. Pitt before I came here, I have this morning seen the Prince of Wales, who has acquainted me with his having broken off all connections with Mrs. Fitzherbert, and his desire of entering into a more creditable line of life by marrying; expressing at the same time that his wish is that my niece, the Princess of Bruns-wick, may be the person."

Lord Malmesbury headed a matrimonial mission to Brunswick. The appearance of this plenipotentiary threw the little German court into a dither. The Duchess was overcome and the Princess greatly affected. After some haggling the plenipotentiary matched the Prince and Princess. On December 4 he signed the contract.

While these negotiations were in progress, affairs in London were far from encouraging. Mary Robinson was bitter over Banastre's re-verses—not only for his own sake, but because he was her remaining link with the world of power and of fashion. She did her utmost to cheer him, lacking cheer herself. *The Widow* was selling well. But the sales did not bring in enough to support Mary's fashionable home; and Banastre's half-pay of £320 per annum was not even one night's stake to a gamester who would hazard £100 on the turn of a card. Mary gave him her literary earnings, provided for him out of her £500 annuity, but she could not earn enough to feed his rapacity. How she hated gambling! Her novels became such polemics against the vice that on May 2 the *Oracle* observed: "The Daughters of Pharaoh are highly offended by the liberties taken with their honorable employment by Mrs. Robinson in her new novel."

Then, in the summer of 1794, cash ran low. Ban and Mary quarreled, and she packed up and moved out to Old Windsor.

At once she missed him, and as summer drifted by she yearned for him more and more. To soothe her loneliness she began fineering a sequence of sonnets. Under the guise of recounting the unhappy love of Sappho for Phaon, she poured out a torrent of love and despair.

"Why do I shrink from that crisis which will decide my fate?—Why? Because the deceiver Hope still bids one linger on the wreck, though the yawning gulf around me menaces destruction. Because the feeling heart must *love*, or it must *perish*," she wrote in *The False Friend*.

In Sonnet XXV Mary pleaded:

> Canst thou forget, O! idol of my soul!
> > Thy Sappho's voice, her form, her dulcet lyre!
> > That melting ev'ry thought to fond desire,
> Bade sweet delirium o'er thy senses roll?
> Can'st thou, so soon, renounce the blest control
> > That calm'd with pity's tears love's raging fire,
> > While hope, slow breathing on the trembling wire,
> In ev'ry note with soft persuasion stole?
> > Oh! sov'reign of my heart! return! return!
> For me no spring appears, no summers bloom,
> > No sunbeams glitter, and no altars burn!
> The mind's dark winter of eternal gloom
> > Shews 'midst the waste a solitary urn,
> A blighted laurel, and a mould'ring tomb!

Once again a lover heeded the magic of poetry. On September 10 the *Oracle* reported: "A certain *Literary Female* has good humoredly received a gallant Colonel into those habits of friendly attendance, so reciprocally gratifying, and which misconception alone could have broken off."

In Sonnet XX Mary sighed:

> Away, false fear! nor think capricious fate
> Would lodge a demon in a form divine!
> > Sooner the dove shall seek a tyger mate,
> Or the soft snow-drop round the thistle twine;
> > Yet, yet, I dread to hope, nor dare to hate,
> Too proud to sue! to tender to resign!

But the quiet of Old Windsor oppressed the Colonel. The Berkshire hills did not seem as pleasant now as when he was recuperating during the previous summer. Soon he and Mary quarreled and again separated. A political forecast in *The Betting Book* marked his return to London: "I bet Mr. Sheridan 5 gns. to 10 that Lord Spencer does not go Lord Lieutenant to Ireland on or before the 12 July '95."

To Old Windsor in late September came George Darby, Mary's younger brother. He had made the trip to England on business for his firm in Leghorn. Finding Mary in tears, he made her promise to go with him to Italy—perhaps in the sunshine of the Riviera her rheumatism would abate. On September 27 the *Oracle* announced her plans for leaving England.

Mary steeled herself to give up Banastre forever. But at that moment he reached the pinnacle of all his present hopes. On October 3, 1794, the War Office announced the long-delayed promotion of the senior colonels. In the *London Gazette* Mary read that Banastre was now Major General Tarleton.

Yet Ban's promotion brought little consolation to her. In Sonnet **XVIII** Mary cried:

> Why art thou chang'd? O Phaon! tell me why?
> > Love flies reproach, when passion feels decay;
> > Or, I would paint the raptures of that day,
> When, in sweet converse, mingling sigh with sigh,
> I mark'd the graceful languor of thine eye
> > As on a shady bank entranc'd we lay:
> > O! eyes! whose beamy radiance stole away,
> As stars fade trembling from the burning sky!
> > Why art thou chang'd, dear source of all my woes?
> Though dark my bosom's tint, through ev'ry vein
> > A ruby tide of purest lustre flows,
> Warm'd by thy love, or chill'd by thy disdain;
> > And yet no bliss this sensate being knows;
> Ah! why is rapture so allied to pain?

In *The False Friend* she answered herself: "The delirium of love is scarcely curable. We cherish it in silence; and we nurse it with false hopes, till it masters our resolution, and sets philosophy at defiance."

The day after Ban's promotion, Mary wrote a long letter to John Taylor of Hatton Garden:

I was really happy to receive your letter. Your silence gave me no small degree of uneasiness, and I began to think some demon had broken the links of that chain which I trust has united us in friendship for ever. Life is such a scene of trouble and disappointment that the sensible mind can ill endure the loss of any consola-

tion that renders it supportable. How, then, can it be possible
that we should resign, without a severe pang, the first of all human
blessings, the friend we love? Never give me reason again, I conjure you, to suppose you have wholly forgot me.

Now I will impart to you a secret, which must not be revealed.
I think that before the 10th of December next I shall quit England forever. My dear and valuable brother, who is now in Lancashire, wishes to persuade me, and the unkindness of the *world*
tends not a little to forward his hopes. I have no relations in England except my darling girl, and, I fear, few friends. Yet, my dear
Juan, I shall feel a very severe struggle in quitting those paths of
fancy I have been childish enough to admire—false prospects.
They have led me into the vain expectation that fame would attend my labours, and my country be my pride. How have I been
treated? I need only refer you to the critiques of last month, and
you will aquit me of unreasonable instability. When I leave England—*adieu* to the *muse for ever*—I will never publish another line
while I exist, and even those manuscripts not finished I WILL
DESTROY.

Perhaps this will be no loss to the world, yet I may regret the
many fruitless hours I have employed to furnish occasions for
malevolence and persecution.

In every walk of life I have been equally unfortunate, but here
end my complaints.

I shall return to St. James's Place for a few days this month to
meet my brother, who then goes to York for a very short time,
and after his return (the end of November) I DEPART. This must
be secret, for to my other misfortunes pecuniary derangement is
not the least. Let common sense judge how I can subsist upon
£500 a year, when my carriage (a necessary expense) alone costs
me £200. My mental labours have failed through the dishonest
conduct of my publishers. My works have sold handsomely but
the profits have been theirs.

Have I not reason to be disgusted when I see him to whom I
ought to look for better fortune lavishing favours on unworthy objects, gratifying the *avarice of ignorance and dulness*, while I, who
sacrificed reputation, and advantageous profession, friends, patronage, the brilliant hours of youth, and the conscious delight of correct conduct, am condemned to the scanty pittance bestowed on
every indifferent page who holds up his ermined train of ceremony?

You will say, "Why trouble me with all this?" I answer, "Because when I am at peace you may be in possession of my real
sentiments and defend my cause when I shall not have the power
of doing it."

My comedy has been long in the hands of a manager, but
whether it will ever be brought forward time must decide. You
know, my dear friend, what sort of authors have lately been patronized by managers; their pieces ushered to public view, with all the

advantages of splendour; yet I am obliged to wait two long years without a single hope that trial would be granted. Oh, I am TIRED OF THE WORLD and all its mortifications. I promise this shall close my chapters of complaints. Keep them, and remember how ill I have been treated.

Mary wrote to Taylor again on October 13: "In wretched spirits I wrote you last week a most melancholy letter. Your kind answer consoled me. The balsam of pure and disinterested friendship never fails to cure the mind's sickness, particularly when it proceeds from disgust at the ingratitude of the world."

Later she repeated her sentiments in a poem entitled "To John Taylor, Esquire":

> Then think not the praises your kindness bestows,
>   Like the zephyrs, pass over my bosom, and die;
> For, I know, 'tis from friendship the bright current flows,
>   That reflects the small flow'ret with tints of the sky!

Banastre's friends crowed: his promotion was only a prelude to active duty. Now Major General Tarleton would get his command of dragoons. Observed the *Morning Post* of October 13: "Our gallant Countryman, Tarleton, is promoted to the rank of major general. This looks as though his military services are not quite forgotten."

On October 22 the General attended the first levee of the season. The assemblage was brilliant. The ambassadors from England's allies and from most of the other nations of Europe were present. There were the Archbishop of Canterbury and his nephew, Lord Cornwallis. Prime Minister Pitt headed the members of Parliament. There was the nobility of England: dukes, marquises, earls, viscounts, barons, baronets, knights, bishops, admirals, and generals. Among the recently promoted generals presented to King George none stood more proudly than Banastre Tarleton.

The King's son, a duke who would one day rule Britain and all her possessions overseas as William IV, was the first to record a bet with the new general:

> H.R.H. the Duke of Clarence bets Major Gen'l Tarleton 5 gns. that peace will be concluded with France under an administration in which Mr. Pitt bears a share. Oct. 30, 94.
> > William
> > Ban. Tarleton

∽

As the tempo of the war with France increased, so did the passion for gambling. White's, Brooks's, and Almack's clubs were a continuous round of play: faro, macao, hazard, or roulette. Excluded from these precincts, the women organized gambling parties in their homes. The mansions of Lady Buckinghamshire and Lady Archer became notorious. Watching from her window in St. James's Place, Mary had seen the flow of high life to these fashionable routs. Her hatred of play had driven her to write a stinging satire on the gambling of her neighbors. Innocently she named it *Nobody*.

She sent the comedy to Sheridan, who kept it for two years. Finally he put it in rehearsal in the fall of 1794. For the production he chose an all-star cast, headed by Barrymore, Bannister, and Elizabeth Farren. After rehearsals began, rumor ran that there would be trouble if the play appeared at Drury Lane. Alleging that the play ridiculed a friend, Miss Farren dropped the lead.

Sheridan next secured Mrs. Dorothy Jordan, favorite of the London stage, for the lead in *Nobody*. Dorothy Jordan was afraid of nothing. Unmarried mistress of the Duke of Clarence, she was mother of fourteen children, most of them little Fitzclarence grandchildren of King George. She lived in splendor with her lord at Bushy Park, delighting in the close friendship of the Prince and all the royal dukes. Wrote James Boaden: "I remember the warmth with which Mrs. Robinson chanted the kindness of Mrs. Jordan in accepting the principal character."

The prospect of having *Nobody* produced at Drury Lane aroused Mary's hopes. And the sonnets of the English Sappho brought back her Phaon. Ban returned and asked forgiveness. She cancelled her plans for going to Italy.

Sheridan was now Tarleton's closest friend, and during the weeks in which Mary's play was in rehearsal the cronies sat around Brooks's talking, drinking, and making opinionated entries in *The Betting Book*. "Mr. Sheridan bets General Tarleton five guineas that the Opposition on the first Day of the ensuing Meeting of Parliament divide as many in proportion to the number on the Ministerial Side as They did on the first Day of the last Session of Parliament, Nov. 13, 1794."

Two days later: "General Tarleton bets Mr. Sheridan two guineas that the shortest way from Debrets Shop in Piccadilly to No. 4 in Old Burlington St. is through Bond St. & not thro. Sackville St."

The General and the playwright were on a spree; it was not their first nor their last, but it was memorable. Indeed Tarleton's drinking, like Tarleton's charging his dragoons, was unforgettable. Samuel Taylor Coleridge and Robert Southey, two young poets wandering about London in search of material, saw the General aflame. They cherished the memory of his wine-reddened face and after a season published their tribute in the *Morning Post* as "The Devil's Thoughts."

Southey whipped up a second version which he named "The Devil's Walk." He pictured Old Nick sauntering around London, well pleased with human behavior. Just before returning to Hell he stepped into a fashionable gambling house, chuckled, and turned to go:

> But just before he could get to the door
> A wonderful chance befell.
> For all on a sudden, in a dark place,
> He came upon General ——'s burning face;
>
> And it struck him with such consternation,
> That home in a hurry his way did he take,
> Because he thought by a slight mistake
> 'Twas the general conflagration.

Soon after the fashionable houses had opened the faro season the *Morning Post* of November 26 editorialized: "The Lady Gamblers have commenced their Winter Routs, but this Monstrous Violation of Propriety and Decency has not yet come under the cognizance of the Magistrates, who seem asleep to their Duty."

Unfortunately, Sheridan had scheduled the presentation of *Nobody* to coincide with the commencement of the ladies' routs. On November 26 he advertised in the *Morning Post*: "The Theater Royal, Drury Lane, presents the *Mourning Bride*, to which is added for the First Time, a New Comedy, in Two Acts, called *Nobody*."

Just before the opening, Mrs. Jordan received a letter saying: "*Nobody* shall be damned." Maria Elizabeth said that "The author received likewise, on the same day, a scurrilous, indecent, and ill-disguised scrawl, signifying to her that the farce was already condemned. On the drawing of the curtain, several persons in the galleries, whose liveries betrayed their employers, were heard to declare that they were sent to do up *Nobody*. Even women of distinguished rank hissed through their fans."

The first act passed off well, but as a song in the second act was being encored, the clapping got out of hand and a modest riot followed. The gallant Mrs. Jordan quailed. She forgot her lines and stumbled through the "Epilogue" in incoherent fashion.

Mary was humiliated. From exaggerated hopes she fell into despair. But not before she had vented her indignation on manager, actress, and public alike.

Nobody "was really a pleasant portrait of the manners of the higher ranks," said the critic for the *London Chronicle*. "The first act was favourably received, but an air by Mrs. Jordan, somewhat too long, being encored, the audience were thrown into ill humor, and the performers disconcerted. The piece then met with some opposition, but, however, was heard with applause and murmurs to the end."

Sheridan sent Mrs. Jordan back on the boards the next evening. The play had lost its novelty so quickly there was no disturbance. Said the *London Chronicle* of December 1: "Last night *Nobody* was brought forward a second time, and Somebody was found to applaud it, although Nobody appeared to be entertained."

Mary revised her comedy, making several alterations and additions. On December 6 Sheridan tried it a third time. The play failed and he withdrew it. Scoffed the Morning Post: "Instead of Nobody we advise her to call it St. James Square in an Uproar!"

∽

Meanwhile Pitt and Dundas were scheming. After the recent military reverses, they realized that they had to get rid of the Duke of York. But Lord Cornwallis had changed his mind. He came up to town and told the Prime Minister that he would never consent to being placed over the Duke.

Pitt again wrote the King on this painful subject: "Your Majesty's servants flatter themselves that His Royal Highness's zeal for Service will lead him to consent to act under the command of Lord Cornwallis."

But the Duke dissented. The proposal touched his honor. To Pitt he wrote: "Should His Majesty be pleased to appoint Lord Cornwallis to the command, as it is now proposed, I trust that His Majesty will graciously consent to my request for permission to return to England."

On November 27 the King gave his consent. Dundas wrote his letter of recall. The Duke turned the command of the army over to Earl Harcourt. On December 2 he left for home and on his arrival in England joined the Duchess at Oatlands.

Many of the Whigs were jubilant. They swore that the recall of the Duke proved the bankruptcy of Tory policies. But not Tarleton: he was angry at Pitt's removal of his royal friend. However, there was nothing he could do about it.

He went home to Mary for the Christmas season. After the uproar over Nobody, she had moved from St. James's Place to a less fashionable house in Burlington Street. In spite of her disappointment over her comedy and her resolution to stop writing, she began a long novel centered around a heroine named Angelina.

Banastre was now high in the counsels of the Whigs in their opposition to the war. In early January some 50 merchants in Liverpool drew up a petition asking the mayor to call a meeting to address the King in favor of peace. The honorable mayor refused. He replied that he knew 200 merchants who believed it would be mischievous to petition the King. Yet General Tarleton voted in favor of negotiation with France.

"In the House of Commons we are weak in numbers, but not in argument," wrote Fox; "nor, I think, in credit, for notwithstanding Pitt's great majorities, it is evident that the House is very far from sanguine about the war, if not altogether disgusted with it."

In their rebellious mood some of the Whigs began leaving powder off their hair. The more radical had their hair cropped in the French fashion. Fox and the Duke of Bedford were among the first crops, but Tarleton did not immediately follow their example. Perhaps former Mayor Clayton Tarleton was a restraining influence upon the representative from Liverpool.

The Opposition thought the situation deplorable. They felt that the people would soon rise, and that only a change in the ministry could avert disaster. When would the change come? Into *The Betting Book* went a prophecy: "I bet Mr. E. Fawkener 10 gns. to 30 that the navies of France, Holland, and Spain act in union & that Mr. Pitt ceases to be Minister on or before the 1st of Jany. 96. Jan. 18th 95   Ban. Tarleton."

With glee the leader of the Whigs wrote: "Mr. Fox bets the same with General Tarleton."

Mr. Fox correctly estimated the Whig chances of unseating Pitt. He smiled when the General wrote: "I bet Mr. Fox 50 gns. that Mr. Pitt ceases to be Minister on or before April 96. B. Tarleton."

Even then Pitt was sealing the immediate fate of B. Tarleton. He had proposed that Lord Cornwallis be promoted to master general of Ordnance with a seat in the Cabinet. The King consented. The power over the Army passed completely into the hands of Cornwallis.

At the same time King George promoted his son. On February 10, 1795, he made the Duke a field marshal. In his letter to William Windham, Secretary for War, his Majesty wrote: "At the same time he is to have a letter of Service placing him on the Home Staff, which will give him the command." As senior officer, Field Marshal the Duke of York was still nominally commander in chief.

⁓

Scarcely had King George rescued the Duke from his hassle, before his Majesty was engulfed in the wedding of the Prince of Wales. After the negotiations had been concluded by Lord Malmesbury, on December 29 Princess Caroline left Brunswick. But the rapid advance of the French armies through the Low Countries imperiled her journey, and nearly three months passed before she sailed for England.

Commodore Jack Payne, with Mrs. Harcourt in attendance, brought the Princess to Gravesend aboard the 50-gun warship *Jupiter*. Here she transferred to a royal yacht and sailed happily up to Greenwich. Cornet Beau Brummell, with a detachment of the Prince of Wales Regiment, escorted her from Greenwich to St. James's Palace.

When Princess Caroline was for the first time ushered into the presence of Prince George, she kneeled. The Prince gracefully raised her and then embraced her.

"Harris," he cried to Lord Malmesbury, "I am not well. Pray get me a glass of brandy."

"Sir, had you not better have a glass of water?" asked Malmesbury, noting his flushed countenance.

"By God, no! I will go directly to the Queen." He staggered off.

"Mon Dieux!" gasped the bewildered Princess. "Is he always like that?" A moment later she added: "I find him very fat, and not at all like the picture sent me."

King George asked Lord Malmesbury, "Is she good-humored?"

"I have never seen her otherwise, Your Majesty," replied Malmesbury.

"I am very glad of it," nodded the King.

Arrangements were completed, and the royal wedding was celebrated on April 8, 1795. "I could not help remarking how little conversation passed between the Prince and Princess during the procession," said the Duke of Leeds.

During the wedding ceremony the Prince was so drunk he seemed dazed. He kept his eyes on Lady Jersey with whom his name had been linked even before his marriage with Mrs. Fitzherbert. Before the ceremony was half over he rose impatiently from his knees. The Archbishop of Canterbury stopped. The King stepped forward, settled the Prince again, and then stood behind him whispering the responses.

As the newlyweds drove from the chapel, they broke into a sullen row. After a few days at Windsor, they drove to the Prince's country place at Kempshot. Only her lady in waiting accompanied the Princess, but many of his friends went with the Prince.

Years later Caroline complained that when she came downstairs in the mornings during her honeymoon, she found many of the "blackguard companions of the Prince, who were constantly drunk, and sleeping and snoring on the sofa."

Banastre was not in this snorting charivari. He was fighting the Tories in Parliament. On April 25 the Morning Post reported that Lord Lauderdale had given an elegant dinner party on Good Friday. Among the distinguished guests were Mr. Fox, Mr. Sheridan, and General Tarleton.

In the House of Commons Tarleton was firm in demanding the prerogatives of a member of Parliament. He was also quick to demand that members live up to their code of honor. Having learned that Sir Benjamin Hammet had delegated to his son the privilege of franking letters, he moved that Sir Benjamin be ordered to be in his seat in the House on April 10. On that day the offender was in his seat, bearing a letter from his doctors saying that he had been ill. He pleaded that he never franked a letter while his son used the privilege.

Tarleton replied: "It is palpable that there is a mistake or misuse in the exercise of the privilege of franking. The Act says that only bodily infirmity can justify deputation.

"It is certain that abuses have existed to an enormous extent. In times like the present it is peculiarly incumbent upon us to defend the dignity of this House."

The General then moved "that it appears to this House that Sir Benjamin Hammet has deputed a person to exercise the privilege of franking for him, not being in such state of bodily infirmity as to entitle him to take advantage of the clause in the said act for that purpose, and that he has delegated that trust for two years to his son."

The master of the rolls said that the "honourable mover deserves the thanks of the House for having brought this forward," but it appears that "the Honorable General has not brought evidence" before the House. So the House dropped the charge.

As one of the ranking army officers in Parliament, General Tarleton joined in most of the debates on matters relating to the military. His views became regarded as those of an expert. He said that the Army needed more subaltern officers. On May 29 the *Oracle* commented favorably: "Much attention is due the assertion of General Tarleton, that the service is now, and was during the American War, very insufficiently furnished with subaltern officers."

In late spring, when the question of a loan to the Emperor of Germany came before the House of Commons, the Whigs fought it on the principle of embarrassing Pitt and the Tories. Fox spoke against the bill, calling it a profligate expenditure of English treasure.

On June 10 Tarleton opposed the loan for the same reason and added his opinion that the stipulations by the Emperor were not likely to be fulfilled. "I think that it is vain to attempt the conquest of twenty-four millions of people, and that with a view to destroy their republic." He concluded: "It would be better to make peace."

ᕤᕦ

After the adjournment of Parliament, Banastre remained in London, spending his time at Brooks's or with Mary. She was writing another novel, but constant hard work had worn her thin. In late summer she left for Bath and took rooms at 10 North Parade.

Mary loved the warm springs at Bath. Perhaps the warm water had no effect on her withered legs, but residence in Bath, away from the strain of London, had a soothing effect upon her nerves.

"Mrs. Robinson has been at Bath, and thence round the Country. She goes back again in a few days and the latter end of October comes up to town. Her purpose is to publish another novel," observed the *Oracle* of September 4. "General Tarleton is at Hampton-Court invigorating for the ensuing Parliamentary Campaign."

In late September Mary returned to London. She spent a couple of weeks with Banastre at Weybridge, in Surrey. Then they went on to Bath.

Soon after their arrival, as Mary was hobbling along North Parade, a vicious mastiff attacked her. She was about to fall victim to him when her screams brought Banastre running. Said the *Oracle* of October 16: "General Tarleton was fortunately on the spot, and by the timely effect of great activity and strength, rescued her from a situation, which in the helpless state of the lady, was perilous indeed."

A week later the lovers returned to London. She placed her novel in the hands of Hookham and Carpenter and for the next few weeks read proof and prepared for its publication. He returned to Brooks's and waited for the opening of Parliament.

King George opened Parliament on October 29. On his way to the House of Lords he was hissed and hooted. In St. James's Park an unknown assailant fired a bullet through a window of the carriage, but he arrived unhurt. "My Lord," he said to the Lord Chancellor, "I have been fired at."

That evening there was debate on "An Address of Thanks to the Throne"; and notwithstanding the attempt on the King's life, Tarleton led a bitter attack on the King's ministers. "The prospect of affairs is, indeed, most gloomy," he said. "The numerous army which the French have lately obliged the King of Spain to bring into the war on their own terms, will now be employed in the invasion of Italy, while our efforts against the French possessions in the West Indies will probably be frustrated, as they have been on the coast of France, through misconduct on our side, and the difficulty of the very attempt itself. It is vain to repeat exertions that have been so successfully foiled. Ministers are no longer deserving in confidence. Their evident incapacity requires their immediate dismissal, and the trial of new men, as well as new measures."

Tarleton's call for the dismissal of the King's ministers lessened his small chances for an active command. Now he must content himself with fighting Pitt and the Tories. And he fought for the sheer love of battle.

The attempted assassination of the King prompted Pitt to introduce bills against treason and sedition. The first extended the ancient Treason Laws of Edward III and the second placed strict regulations upon all public meetings. These proposals to curb freedom of discussion aroused all of the energies of the Opposition.

The Whig Club called a meeting of the voters of Westminster for November 16 to hear an address by Charles Fox. Early in the morning the crowd began filling Westminster Hall and overflowing into New Palace Yard. They were good-natured and boisterous, but the authorities, fearful of the effect of Fox's oratory, deputized scores of special constables to prevent riot and violence.

"On one side of the Hall a Hustings was erected for the speakers. A little after Eleven General Tarleton came on the Hustings and having requested the attention of the people, stated that the Lord Chancellor had informed His, the General's friends, as the courts of Law were then sitting, no meeting could be held in Westminster Hall without great interruption of public business. That on that account the Hustings would be removed to New Palace Yard, and the opinion of the people taken in that place. He concluded by exhorting them to observe a peaceable conduct, and retired with much applause," wrote Farington in his *Diary*.

As workmen shifted the speaker's platform from the hall to the palace yard, the crowd watched the great Whigs through a window of the King's Arms Tavern: the Duke of Bedford, Charles James Fox, Lord Lauderdale, Lord Derby, Grey, Whitbread, Tierney, Sheridan, Tarleton, and others. Continued Farington: "A little after 12 the Hustings being prepared, the duke of Bedford, etc., came upon it. Much hallooing and clapping on their appearance. The Duke was dressed in a Blue coat & Buff waistcoat with a round hat. His hair cropped and without powder. —Fox also cropped, & without powder, His Hair grisly grey.—Fox first came forward to speak, Sheridan on his right hand and Tierny on his left. The Duke of Bedford immediately behind him.—The Hustings was much crowded. Hood was there, as was Lord Belgrave and many friends of government. After much acclamation Fox addressed the multitude stating the loss of the liberties of the people, if the Bill passed, and calling upon them to come forward and support a petition to the House of Commons against it."

As reaction against Pitt's bills spread, there seemed an upsurge among the Whigs. So on December 7 General Tarleton announced his candidacy for re-election as a member for Liverpool. He had the support of the Whigs in London. He expected the backing of his brother Clayton. And he also expected financial aid from his brother Thomas.

Three days after his announcement, Tarleton attacked Pitt's bills on treasonable practices. The General did not fear treason. He knew about the Corresponding Societies that aped the French. He had listened to their tawdry orations mimicking the harangues in the French Convention. But he had also seen the government fail to convict those charged with treason. On November 21, 1794, the *Star* had reported seeing him with Fox and Sheridan at the trial of John Horne Tooke in Old Bailey.

"The reasons, in my mind, which induced Ministers to bring in the bill, were the acquittals in Old Bailey and the present ruinous war," Tarleton cried. "The bill will prevent the people from canvassing the conduct of the ministers with respect to the war, and other domestic circumstances of a distressing nature. The security of the Monarch lies in the hearts of his subjects, and no monarch was ever deeper rooted in the affections of his people than the Prince who fills the throne at present. A sufficient evidence of this appeared when his Majesty went to St. Paul's shortly after his recovery."

He concluded by iterating a favorite theme: "We have attacked France wantonly and unprovokedly because we did not choose that twenty-five millions of people should settle their internal government without our interference."

During the Christmas recess the member for Liverpool devoted himself to play. On the last Sunday evening in December he visited Mrs. Concannon's fashionable faro hell on Grafton Street. "General Tarleton lost £800 at Mrs. Concannon's; Mr. Hankey, £300," said a reporter. "The Prince was to have been there, but sent a late excuse."

On Monday, despite Banastre's heavy loss, all was serene and gay. That evening, according to the *Oracle*, the Sheridans, the Bouveries, Lord Robert Spencer, General Tarleton, Mrs. Robinson, and a long list of patrons of the drama were at Drury Lane to see *Alexander the Great*.

Banastre closed the old year with politics. Said the *Oracle* on December 31: "General Tarleton has everything to expect from his Liverpool interest, having been brought into Parliament by his fellow townsmen. He is as independent a member as any in the House of Commons. We are surprised at his attaching himself to Party. The services he has rendered his country would have insured him everything honorable and lucrative, had his politics been of different description."

Mary opened the new year with literature. On January 4, 1796, Hookham and Carpenter published *Angelina*. The length, three volumes containing 1030 closely printed pages, surprised her readers. Many said that the story would have filled four handsome volumes. Nevertheless, they snapped up the first edition, and on February 1 the *Oracle* reported: "Mrs. Robinson is preparing a second edition of *Angelina*."

But Mary had attempted to paint too large a canvas. "The story is altogether destitute of unity," observed the *Monthly Review* for March 1796. "The suffering Angelina, who gives name to the novel, the persecuted Sophia, the impetuous Belmont, the romantic Fairford, and Lord Acreland, together with a multitude of interesting under characters, cause such a confusion that, as soon as attention is excited for one, it is immediately called to another—such appear to us to be the defects of a work, which with all its faults we are little inclined to condemn; for we are persuaded that it cannot but excite a lively interest in those who read it."

The *Critical Review* of April 1796 was unsympathetic. "Were we permitted to consider this novel as a burlesque upon the extremes of romantic absurdity, we should certainly pronounce it a work of considerable merit. We have seldom seen the nonsensical jargon of mock sentiment, and overstrained hyperbole, more happily exposed to ridicule."

As soon as Mary's best sellers began bringing in money, Ban headed for the faro tables. On Sunday evening, January 17, he again visited Mrs. Concannon's. The music was excellent and the faro bank was surrounded by the most dashing adventurers. Reported the *Oracle* on

January 26: "General Tarleton at one time was out £ 800, but afterwards recovered £ 312 on one card."

During the previous winter Mary had written a blank-verse tragedy called *The Sicilian Lover*. A producer let the manuscript lie on his desk for months before returning it with a promise of production during the next season. Learning that "one of the most striking situations had been pilfered for another tragedy," Mary rushed *The Sicilian Lover* to Hookham and Carpenter. The play was published immediately in order to promote its sale through the popularity of *Angelina*.

The *Oracle* of January 26 observed that Mary's move to forestall piracy followed the example Horace Walpole set in publishing his *Mysterious Mother*. And remembering *St. James Square in an Uproar*, it concluded: "Thus her friends will have the benefit of her pen, while it will evade the malice of her enemies."

The criticism of *The Sicilian Lover* in the *Monthly Review* of March 1796 was encouraging. The critic noted that the story "is fraught with horror, and abounds too much with slaughter and death. On the whole, however, he who can read its incidents without sympathy, and its imagery without delight, must have an unfeeling heart and a depraved taste. We congratulate Mrs. Robinson that she has discovered the true bent of her talents; and we advise her to apply herself in the future to the improvement of them in the same walk. With powers as hers, cultivation will soon produce excellence."

Mary sent a complimentary copy of *The Sicilian Lover* to the Duke of Leeds. He was delighted:

Madam,

Permit me to thank you for the favour you conferred on me, by sending me your Tragedy: I trust you will not deem me guilty of flattery when I assure you that few productions of the present poetical age have afforded me more pleasure, than the perusal of the *Second Act*: the scene between Honoria and her father is very well managed, and capable of much affect; as is the scene with the Banditti in the third.

I imagine many will unite with me in observing how much your continuing to persevere in this species of composition would increase your profit, and enhance your poetical reputation; which has already much signalized itself in the rich field of English literature!

I have the honor to remain,
Madam, etc., etc.,
Leeds

St. James Square
Friday morning

The old Duke, whose first wife had eloped with Mad Jack Byron, father of the poet, was still gallant. He composed a little *jeu d'esprit* and enclosed it in his letter to Mary:

Impromptu

When sensibility and truth unite
    To give thy thought with sweet poetic art,
'Tis genuine nature dictates what you write,
    And ev'ry line's a transcript of your heart!

'Tis grace and feeling, polish'd by the Muse
    To claim applause and charm the wond'ring throng!
Then who the sacred laurel shall refuse
    To her whom *Nature* hails the *Queen of Song?*

31

Brother Against Brother

*A*s THE DATE for the general election approached, General Tarleton devoted all of his energy to the affairs of his Liverpool constituents. In Parliament he tried almost single-handedly to block Wilberforce's movement to abolish the slave trade.

"The Liverpool traders have suffered more than any others by the war, as the African coast has been swept by the enemy's forces," he said on February 18, 1796, in reply to Wilberforce's motion to change the order of the day and take up the question of the slave trade.

> There are two propositions in my mind that are insurmountable: the inexpediency of the measure, and the time for carrying it into execution. In 1793 the House was decidedly in favour of gradual abolition; and while this country was in peace, they all along entertained this idea. But if we compare the present with the past, it must be confessed, that no time could be more unfit for coming to a resolution of abolition than the present. The honorable gentleman has looked at the West Indian islands and has concluded that the circumstances existing there justify such a measure. I am of a very different opinion. The progress of the French manners there will show that it is necessary to oppose them—to save our possessions in that quarter. We ought rather to endeavour to increase the population, since it adds to our defense, than depress it by stopping the importation of Negroes.
>
> The discussion of the question may have such effect on the slaves as to turn them against their masters and to induce them to pursue the practices inculcated by Jacobin principles and the doc-

trine of the rights of man. With regard to the commerce itself, there is less cruelty in it than gentlemen imagine. It engages the attention of the petty princes and prevents mutual wars and massacres.

I am convinced of the impropriety of the measure and therefore move "That the order of the day be now read."

Even Tarleton's friends on the *Oracle* on March 1 lamented his opposition to abolition: "Though General Tarleton cannot be excused for voting against abolishing the Slave Trade, yet he has a most philanthropic heart, as those who served with him in America will attest."

On March 7 Wilberforce again brought up the question of abolition. Tarleton was ready. From his seat on the back bench of the Opposition, he rose and delivered a sharp reply:

Many classes of the community are deeply affected by the war and the adoption of this measure will aggravate their distress. A variety of articles of manufacture are made merely for carrying on this commerce, which supports numerous bodies of mechanics. If it is abolished, their means of living will go along with it.

The merchants of Liverpool, have at great expense, built ships of a peculiar construction for the convenience of trade, and if the bill is passed, these ships will lie idle on their hands. Hence it will be incumbent upon Government, should the bill pass, to indemnify them for their losses. The encouragement given the seamen by the Liverpool merchants is a great source of naval strength to this country.

Ministers have given commissions to many gentlemen for raising black regiments. By the bill these regiments will be emancipated. The disturbances in the West Indies renders the present period very unfit for abolition. The war has greatly reduced West Indian property, and the bill, if passed, will inevitably bring it to utter ruin.

Wilberforce was determined to push through his bill; Tarleton was just as determined to prevent a vote. Amid repeated cries for the question, he again called the attention of the House to the great injustice that would be done to the commerce of Liverpool if the trade were abolished.

"The dry docks there," he said, "have been built principally on account of the African trade. From authorities which I can depend on, the Americans, the Spaniards, and the Swedes are offering the greatest encouragement for the prosecution of this trade. I am sure both Spain and America will encourage the traffic of slaves. So will Ireland, which will rise on the ruin of Liverpool."

Tarleton's success in postponing the triumph of Wilberforce's principles was well received in Liverpool. Plans for the coming election were completed. Mayor Thomas Naylor swung the Corporation to the General. The support that had seemed so monstrous when given Gascoyne and Penrhyn in 1790 was welcomed by the General and his independent political friends. On May 13 the *Oracle* said: "Liverpool will doubtless keep the zealous and indefatigable townsman who has so labored for his constituents."

Banastre opened his campaign with a letter:

Gentlemen:

As it is generally believed a dissolution of Parliament is approaching, I deem it respectful to inform you, that I intend to offer you my services, when that period shall arrive. The cause of my absence from Liverpool, I hope, is sufficiently known and understood.

My parliamentary duties have not ceased, nor will my desire to protect and defend the interests and rights of my brother townsmen, terminate or diminish but with my existence.

I have the honor to be,
Gentlemen,
With the Greatest regard and affection,
Your obliged and obedient servant
Ban. Tarleton

London, May 13, 1796

Bamber Gascoyne, mindful of the mud flung upon his proxy in the chairing in 1790, pleaded ill health and retired. The Tory Party, under the powerful interest of Thomas Clarke, Esquire, selected his younger brother, Colonel Isaac Gascoyne, as their candidate. The election now seemed only a matter of form.

On May 21 the *Oracle* said: "Among the most active and attentive members of the House of Commons, may be named Messrs. Pitt, Fox, Sheridan, General Tarleton, Mr. Grey, Mr. Dundas, and Mr. Francis—all of whom stand a fair chance of being returned in the ensuing contest."

But this easy estimate of the General's chances was shortly to be upset by a maneuver involving—of all people—John Tarleton. Although Banastre had campaigned vigorously for John at Seaford, his brother was not elected in 1790. In a by-election in that borough John won in 1795 and entered Parliament.

John was a Tory, a staunch friend of Pitt. He abhorred the radical politics of Banastre. He sat on the opposite side in the House of Commons, but he lived with the General at 30 Clarges Street. In spite of their politics, Ban was fond of John and introduced him to his friends at Brooks's.

The senior representative for Seaford was Sir Godfrey Webster. He and John were not congenial, and the £3000 cost of John's seat had started a dispute between them. Sir Godfrey became acrimonious and even threatened a challenge. Not a duelist, John had the Baronet placed under a bond to keep the peace. The row disgusted voters of Seaford.

The Prime Minister then made a stunning move. He decided to split Banastre's following by throwing John Tarleton into the contest in Liverpool. Immediately after John's announcement, the *Oracle* sent a reporter to Banastre. On May 26 it informed its readers: "The General declared his brother's politics to be *ministerial* and his opposition not *personal*. It is difficult at present to form any conjecture as to the issue. The General advertises that this new candidate was totally unexpected. They both declare themselves unconnected with any other candidate. *Tant mieux* for Mr. Gascoyne, who is expected to cut in between the two."

Angered because Pitt had set John against him, Banastre hastened to Liverpool the moment Parliament adjourned. With him he carried the blessing of Fox and the Whigs and, perhaps, the financial backing of the Duke of Bedford. Upon arrival at his mother's home in Bold Street on May 25, he found his friends waiting.

"Britannic" had composed an ode:

Lines

Written on the arrival of our Patriotic Representative
General Tarleton

See, from his Native Town the Hero claim,
The proud distinction of his well earn'd fame!
He whose undaunted breast so bravely stood,
Like a strong bulwark 'midst a sea of blood:
Still to his country dear, defends her cause,
And vows to live the Champion of her Laws!
Where Senates thunder, he with honest grace,
Courts not a bribe, nor flatters for a Place;
No sycophantic guile, nor sordid praise,
He to the abject, or the venal, pays.—
Loyal and free, he props the Public Weal,
With Reason's Eloquence, and Patriot Zeal!
With Nature's Language mocks the pow'r of Art;
Truth on his Tongue, and Freedom in his Heart!
And though this busy scene of life shall face,
And Power and Splendour prove an empty shade,
Still shall his Name adorn our grateful shore,
And *Tarleton* live till Time shall be no more!

If General Tarleton had "truth on his tongue and freedom in his heart," he also had bad news in his ear. John was showing surprising strength, and Thomas and Clayton had decided not to aid either candidate. After issuing a card thanking his "Brother townsmen for their kind attention since his arrival in his native town," he drafted a letter:

To the Worthy and Independent Freemen of Liverpool

Gentlemen,

Allow me to congratulate you on the arrival of that period, when the inestimable right reverts into your possession of sending your representatives to parliament. If my attention to your interests during the course of nearly six years, entitles me in any degree to your approbation, I may safely affirm, that an increased knowledge of parliamentary proceedings joined to unabated zeal and undiminished health, will render me a more useful delegate in future for this truly respectable commercial place; in case I should enjoy the honor of reaching that desirable point of distinction.

I think it my duty explicitly to declare, that I stand alone, and most distinctly apart from any other Candidate whatever: From the first of the gentlemen, who have already solicited your favour, the Opposition is natural.—From the other it is unexpected.

Of my political principles I shall briefly say, that I view all the component parts of the English constitution, as settled by our ancestors at the Revolution, with veneration and affection, and I consider loyalty as well as liberty essentially necessary, for the preservation of public order and individual happiness.

I have the honor to be,
Gentlemen,
With gratitude and respect,
Your obedient townsman
Ban. Tarleton

May 25, 1796

With the Gascoyne and Tory interests behind him, Colonel Gascoyne was assured of election. So the struggle lay between the Tarletons, Whig Banastre and Tory John. They maintained that their opposition was not personal. "Junius" scotched that idea. "You cannot doubt it, when you consider how absurd the idea must be, that this great, opulent and commercial place, would submit to have its two representatives, however unexceptional in character, out of one family."

From the Gascoyne headquarters at Childwall came songs and handbills for the Tories. Equally active were the General's headquarters at his mother's in Bold Street and at the mustering place in the yard of the Angel Inn in Dale Street. But the most active were John Tarleton's Tories in Brunswick Street. They issued blast after blast against the incumbents.

"Frater" raged most unfraternally against the General's military record: "Let us not disgrace ourselves by again returning a man to represent us in Parliament, who has ingloriously remained inactive, at a time when his military talents, if he has any (but which any man, who will take the trouble to read Lieut. McKinsey's 'Strictures on General Tarleton's History of the American War,' will at least doubt, if not disbelieve) might have been usefully employed in the field!"

To John's followers there could be no doubt that the General was a Jacobin. He had traveled unimpeded in revolutionary France. He had reviewed troops in the Field of Mars with Lafayette and then had defended him before the English Parliament. And in imitation of those vile regicides he wore his hair in the French crop!

From their camp "Humanus" warned that all the dire calamities and distresses which had so long lacerated and harrowed the bosom of distracted France would be the fate of England. The good and virtuous part of the community would be sacrificed: "Your wives, mothers, daughters would fall victims to the brutality of lawless ruffians; your property would be seized upon by triumphant robbers, and your habitations stormed—open Massacre would be the order of the day, and Assassinations the order of the night."

"Philotas" attacked the General for "His uniform opposition to every measure of administration, good or bad—his attachment to the French politics—his excursion to Paris to see the beauties of the Revolution and particularly that patriotic scene, where the amiable Comtesse de Lamballe was dragged naked through the streets and torn to pieces by the independent, public spirited Patriots of France—his various senatorial attempts to justify the conduct of the regicides respecting the war with England, and to make England appear the aggressor."

Even his loyalty was impugned by "Frater": ". . . if administration could have confided in his loyalty or principles, he would not have been passed over" for military command.

> 'Tis Bedford's weak party, with Tarleton and Fox
> Who to imitate Frenchmen have cut off their locks;
> A democrat practice which nothing avails:
> Old England stands firm spite of dogs without tails!

John's followers dragged Mary's name into their propaganda. They prepared a handbill purporting to be from General Tarleton:

"Lost: A large packet of papers containing D - - e of B - - - - - d's draft upon him in favor of Mrs. R - - - - - - n, for sundries, for five hundred and eleven pounds, four shilling. N.B. this draft is due 1st June, 1796."

Also from John's headquarters came a vicious personal attack:

"Not stolen, but strayed from his Kennel in the Jacobin Society of London, a remarkably Fierce looking Animal of the Cur kind, with his Tail cut off, answers to the name of Crop, wears a black collar around his neck, and has two Claws missing from his right fore Paw. Whosoever

Jane Tarleton, by Wright of Darby   John Tarleton, by Wright of Darby

(Photos courtesy of Mrs. H. M. Fagan)

Cornet Tarleton, by Allan Ramsay

(Photo courtesy of Mrs. H. M. Fagan)

Lieutenant-Colonel Tarleton, by I. R. Smith after a
painting by Sir Joshua Reynolds

Mrs. Robinson—"Perdita" by Thomas Gainsborough

Georgiana, Duchess of Devonshire, by J. Cook after a painting by Sir Joshua Reynolds

Richard Brinsley Sheridan, by John Russell

J. Roberts del.   Publish'd for Bells British Theatre Dec.r 1777.   Thornthwaite Sc.

M.rs ROBINSON in the Character of AMANDA.

I'll not trouble you Sir, yonder's my Cousin
Wellbred I'll beg his Protection.

Mrs. Robinson in Quaker dress, by George Romney

Charles, Lord Cornwallis, by Thomas Gainsborough

Francis Rawdon Hastings, Earl of Moira, artist unknown

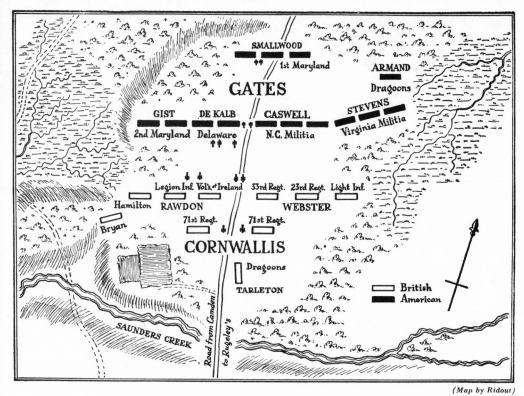

(Map by Ridout)

The Battle of Camden, August 16, 1780

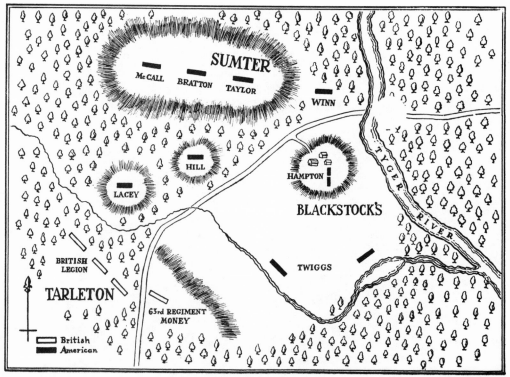

(Map by Ridout)

The Battle of Blackstock's, November 21, 1780

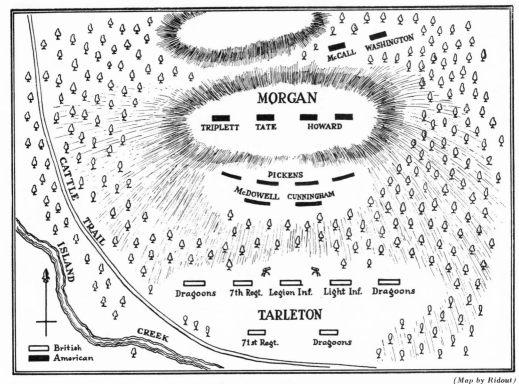

MORGAN

TRIPLETT TATE HOWARD

PICKENS

McDOWELL CUNNINGHAM

McCALL WASHINGTON

CATTLE TRAIL

ISLAND

CREEK

Dragoons 7th Regt. Legion Inf. Light Inf. Dragoons

TARLETON

71st Regt. Dragoons

British
American

(Map by Ridout)

The Battle of Cowpens, January 17, 1781

Guilford Courthouse
GREENE

HUGER
Virginia

WILLIAMS
Maryland

STEVENS
Virginia

LAWSON
Militia

LEE
Cavalry

WASHINGTON
Cavalry

KIRKWOOD LYNCH

BUTLER
N.C. Militia

Singleton's guns

EATON

CAMPBELL
Rifles

Legion Inf.

33rd Regt. 23rd Regt.
WEBSTER

Yagers
Light Inf.

Gren. Co. 2nd Bat. Guards

O'HARA

CORNWALLIS

71st Regt. Bose
LESLIE

1st Bat. Guards

Dragoons
TARLETON

British
American

(Map by Ridout)

The Battle of Guilford Courthouse, March 15, 1781

The new Vis-a-vis, or Florizel driving Perdita.

Lord Malden, Earl of Essex

George IV, by the studio of Sir Thomas Lawrence

William IV, by Sir Martin Archer Shee

(British Museum photo)

Major George Hanger—"Georgey a' Cock-horse"

(British Museum photo)

The Great Subscription Room at Brooks's Club

Charles James Fox, by Karl Anton Hickel

Duke of York, by Sir David Wilkie

BOUNDING BILLOW

Words by
Mary Robinson

Music by
Thomas Welsh

BOUND--ING BIL----LOW CEASE THY MO--TION. BEAR ME

NOT SO SWIFT----LY O'ER.____ CEASE THY____ ROAR----ING

FORM-----Y O-CEAN. I WILL TEMPT____THY RAGE NO

MORE.____ I WILL TEMPT____THY RAGE __ NO MORE.

Sir Banastre Tarleton, by Lady Susan Priscilla Tarleton

will return him to his Keeper, Mrs. R - - - - - - n, in C - - - - - - - Street; to any of the Gaming Houses in Covent Garden, or to any of his Grace of B - - - - - -'s Grooms, shall be rewarded with a Fraternal Embrace for his Trouble."

From Banastre's headquarters his friends replied: "General Tarleton is known to you! He never run from an enemy's sword, nor run after a ministerial purse. In the field, and in the Senate, he performed his duty as a true Briton."

> Sure ingratitude ne'er can your bosoms defile,
> To your Hero then ever be true,
> Nor e'er let a brother's malevolence vile
> Be approved of and sanctioned by you.

Seeing the idle sailors, the blackened hulks, and the rotting quays of Merseyside, many applauded the General for uniform opposition to the war. Cried one: "Uncontrouled, without fear, he has braved the storm in opposition to a war, he foresaw at the commencement, would be detrimental to your interest, and the happiness of thousands of families."

Many admired the General for checking abolition. In the streets they were singing:

> A few months ago, oh! did you not hear,
> The slave trade would fail, which made us to fear;
> That now it's all over, you need not repine,
> For the General has baffled Wilberforce's design!
>
> O rare Tarleton, well done, General,
> We'll vote for you again and again.

The vote was very light. On May 31 "Aristides," noting that John was 179 votes behind, wondered "whether by a continuation it may not be candidly inferred, that he does mean a personal opposition to his brother." As expected, with Colonel Gascoyne well ahead, the brothers were contesting the last seat; and John did indeed seem out of it.

The sons of Great T were confounded. Thomas and Clayton refused to vote. Banastre also refused to vote. John voted. He cast his ballot for Banastre. Then came the small T's: for Colonel Gascoyne; Robert, ropemaker, and Gilbert, tanner; for General Tarleton; Robert, shipwright, and John, cooper.

At the close of the poll on June 1 the vote stood: Colonel Gascoyne, 672; General Tarleton, 516; and John Tarleton, 317. During the day John Tarleton had not secured a single vote. His friends agreed that there was no chance of success. He withdrew.

The moment John struck his colors, Ban issued a letter that sounded more like a lament than a song of triumph:

Gentlemen,

I seize the earliest opportunity of returning you my most cordial thanks for the honor you have conferred upon me, by sending me a second time to parliament. With respect to the contest which has invaded the peace and interrupted the labour of this important place, I briefly say, that I most heartily wish every circumstance appertaining to it consigned to oblivion. And now, Gentlemen, give me leave honestly to declare, that I will to the utmost of my power, protect your Commerce and defend your Rights.

With greatest respect and attachment,
I remain,
Your affectionate Brother Townsman
Ban. Tarleton

June 1, 1796

Banastre had ended the political career of his favorite brother. Never again was there cordiality between them. He had also alienated Thomas and Clayton and brought sorrow to Bridget and his mother. So he closed his headquarters and left Liverpool as soon as possible. In farewell he published a letter refuting the charges that had been brought against him and pledging allegiance to his King and country.

To the Worthy and Independent Freemen of Liverpool

Gentlemen:

In taking my leave of you to attend my duty in that honourable station to which you have again elected me, I cannot refuse myself the pleasure of expressing once more my grateful thanks for the confidence which you have placed in me, and that too at a period the most serious and alarming which this country has ever known.

Conscious that my parliamentary conduct, however opposite to the favorite opinion of the day, and frequently sanctioned only by the concurrence of a small minority in the House of Commons, raised me at least beyond the imputation of being actuated by any interested motives; I did not stoop to justify that which my adversaries could not impeach. Trusting that my Constituents were too well informed to be misled either by ostentatious professions, or groundless accusations, I reposed my cause fearlessly on your judgment; Your approbation has justified my confidence, and has returned me free and unshackled to adopt the line of parliamentary conduct which, to the best of my apprehension, the welfare of the community, and the welfare of this important town may require.

Those sentiments of loyalty for which my Constituents so generally gave me credit, it now becomes my duty to avow; nor could I have, even upon the minds of those who have unsuccessfully opposed my return to Parliament, an idea, that my attachment to the King and Constitution of these realms, is surpassed by any of those who have offered themselves to their notice. That artifice of almost every administration of representing the opposers of their measures as enemies of their country, has never been carried to so dangerous an extreme. But the cloud of prejudice is dissolving, and a short time will perhaps demonstrate who are the true friends of their country: those who have taken advantage of the alarms of the timid, and the prejudices of the weak, to increase the public burthens, to abridge the constitutional rights of the subject, to extend the system of corruption and undue influence, and to involve these Kingdoms in a most ruinous and destructive war; or those whose endeavors have been faithfully exerted to secure the rights and privileges which have been for ages the boasts of Britons, and to terminate a contest whose object yet remains undefined, but which has been attended with an unexampled profusion of British treasure and of British blood, and which if farther persevered in, seems the most likely of all other measures to occasion those very calamities which the promoters of it appear so desirous to avert.

I have the honor to be,
Gentlemen,
Your affectionate Townsman
Ban. Tarleton

"Farewell, General Tarleton! You are a brave, but not a wise man," answered a "Fellow Burgess." "Your personal popularity has for once befriended you; but you will find that even amongst the men who have reelected you, the majority detest your political conduct, and lament your being at the fag end of a contemptible party."

32

Heartbreak

*W*HEN BANASTRE TARLETON left Liverpool he was deeply disturbed. On April 25 Jane Tarleton, fearful that she might not live through the political strife between her sons, had made her will. To her other children she had allotted various properties and then she had listed the sums of money advanced to pay Ban's gambling debts. These she had forgiven and had then bequeathed him £1500.

The pleading and generosity of his mother, together with the refusal of Clayton to throw his powerful Whig following against John and the violence of John and his Tories, had shaken the devil-may-care General. He reached his home in St. James's Place a thoughtful man, a man of unexpected determination. Never again did he sign his name in *The Betting Book*.

Banastre began rehabilitating himself. Well aware of the power of literary fame, through which Mary had risen above the charges of moral turpitude, he began thinking of the *Campaigns*. Its publication had been a turning point, from which followed social recognition, election to Parliament, and promotion in the army. He now decided to publish a second edition. After making arrangements with his publishers, he began writing a "Preface."

This Preface would not have been written, if the American War had been considered by those who were principally instrumental to its origin, as a failure in politics, as well as in arms. But, since the arts of commerce and of peace have again been fatally interrupted, it seems the natural, as well as the moral obligation of any man, who has the good fortune to be born in a land of liberty, to lose no opportunity of pointing out the causes and effects of those events, which touch the interest and happiness of the governors and the governed.

That the times in which we exist, are seriously alarming, and pregnant with important events, no impartial person will deny, and every informed one can explain. We are engaged in a war whose consequences threaten equally the power and constitution of England: Nor is the present, or future prospects, confined to ourselves; in its career it desolates the fairest portion of the earth, and may ultimately reach and affect the principles, property, and condition of every inhabitant of the globe.

In exploring and balancing the causes of this convulsion and devastation, the mind irresistibly and invariably points to the American revolution: from that centre all the political phenomena appear to diverge: and their influence might have been diverted from this country, if example could have informed, or adversity corrected, that busy, meddling, domineering spirit, which may indeed arm despotism with terror, but which robs monarchy of half its beauty and respect.

As the knowledge I have of the American war, which I obtained in America, and the course of reading and observation I have practised since that period, enable me to cast some light upon the revolution and its consequences, I shall endeavor to arrange all the links of the connection, which may be disjointed and scattered, before time or rust consign them to darkness and decay: And my next attention shall be employed in portraying the characters of those men, who filled the principal situations in the Western hemisphere.

Then Banastre summarized the campaigns from 1776 to 1781, but he did not mention Cowpens. He was psychologically unable to admit that he had lost the largest body of troops that he ever commanded in battle. Yet like one constantly struggling to forget a bad dream, he found that the struggle itself reminded him of the unfortunate 17th of January.

He did mention Yorktown, and then wrote of "the magnanimity and patriotism of Washington—the virtues and unmerited sufferings of Lafayette, and the perseverance and ability of Rochambeau, and other French and American generals, whose courage, energy, and talents, contributed materially to the independence of the United States."

In criticizing the British generals, Tarleton was generous to Sir William Howe and praised Burgoyne. He defended Clinton, and after pointing out the difficulties of his command, wrote: "Sir Henry Clinton became the victim of his own feelings."

But Lord Cornwallis, his former friend and partisan, Tarleton mentioned without praise: "Of the noble Marquis, other historians or eulogists may give a more ample biography." After noting his Lordship's assignment in India, he grudgingly added: "He has been as successful in that climate as any of his predecessors."

After reviewing the American War and its consequences, Tarleton turned to the war with France. He praised "the eloquence, wisdom, and patriotism of Mr. Fox." He condemned the Tories: "That the present administration should urge on their bloody career, amidst blunders, misfortunes, and disgraces, unparalleled in the history of man, yet still have the smiles of the court—the majority in parliament—and the lives and fortunes of millions of people at their disposal: And that no circumstance, however adverse or ignominious, seems likely to rouse this besotted nation, till it is about to experience the same accursed calamities of war, which it has occasioned and provoked in other countries."

On August 27 Tarleton finished and signed his *Preface*. He was enjoying his competition with Mary. That morning the *Oracle* had said: "Mrs. Robinson's works are so highly esteemed on the Continent, that of the selection of novels now printing at Leipzig (chosen as specimens of English literature), hers is the first to be printed."

On September 8, Cassell and Davies advertised in the *Times*:

This Day is published, in Quarto, price £1.15. in boards
the 2d Edition of The SOUTHERN CAMPAIGNS IN AMERICA
With a Preface, containing Thoughts on Military
and Political Subjects
By Major General TARLETON
Printed for T. Cassell, jun. and W. Davies (Successors
to Mr. Cadell) in the Strand.

The second edition of the *Campaigns* was well received. Said the *Oracle* on October 1: "General Tarleton must expect abuse, in proportion as he becomes popular in the political world. His *Preface* is well written and, what is almost as good, well received in literary circles."

When Parliament convened on September 27 Tarleton showed a new independence. "I do not think a more eligible person to fill the high office of Speaker can be found within the walls of the House of Commons," he declared in supporting the Tory nomination of Henry Addington. "The right honorable gentleman is liberally endowed by nature and adorned with valuable and classical attainments. The House has had ample experience of the urbanity of his manners, his attention to the business of the House, and his adherence to the principles of the Constitution. These are powerful recommendations. For in the forms of the House and in the dignity of the Chair those who sit on my side of the House will find the best protection against insolent majorities and the attachments of power."

Upon his election, Speaker Addington thanked Lord Campbell, who had nominated him, and Mr. Powys, who had seconded the nomination. And then, turning to the Opposition, he concluded: "Neither can I be insensible to the liberal manner in which the motion has been supported by the honorable General."

When on October 2 William Windham, Secretary for War, set forth the Army estimates, Tarleton was even more vehement than Charles Fox among the Opposition spokesmen who condemned Tory confusion and inefficiency in the conduct of the war. Moreover he saw the situation with the eye of the military man: "I do not think there is much subject for boasting. Whether we look at the general state in the West Indies or at particular islands, there is not much room for satisfaction or exultation. The caribs in St. Vincents are still in a state of insurrection. The troubles in Guadaloupe, and various other islands, still interrupt the industry of the inhabitants. Victor Hughes has not been dislodged, nor his operations disconcerted. In Santo Domingo the melancholy ravage which has been made by disease affords no satisfaction."

On October 22, as the great debate raged, Hookham published Mary's *Sappho and Phaon, in a Series of Legitimate Sonnets.* After long neglect, the sonnet had regained popularity among the Romantic poets, and Mary defined as *legitimate* those with Petrarchan form.

"Sappho's passions are expressed with tenderness and harmony," observed the *Analytical Review.* The *Critical Review* spoke with understanding "of the heart which is under the influence of the tender passion."

∾

Having rejected indirect overtures, the French Directory intimated that it would give passports to any envoy for direct negotiation. In October Pitt sent Lord Malmesbury to Paris. Someone suggested that because of bad weather and broken roads his Lordship's journey would be slow. Roared Burke: "It must indeed be slow. He must go the whole way upon his hands and knees."

Then Pitt called upon Parliament for authority and money to recruit an additional 100,000 soldiers. In urging the passage of this Cavalry Bill the Tories hinted at grave danger of invasion. Now Tarleton saw a chance to use his knowledge of military history to enhance his reputation. For days he and Mary worked together, and on November 2 he rose from his seat in the Opposition and began:

"As I conceive the country to be arrived at the most critical and awful period of its history, and perhaps of its existence, as a free country, as there does not appear to be more than one step to intervene, before we descend from liberty to slavery, I shall now claim the indulgence of the House, while I enter my conscientious and solemn protest against the system of measures now under consideration.

"When a menaced invasion is loosely intimated to the House—when large quotas of money or personal services are called for—when a considerable addition is to be made to the army—I think it both the business and the duty of its members to resort to the practice of their ancestors in similar situations, if similar situations can be found."

After disclaiming any ability as an historian, the General searched Britain's history for similar threats of invasion. He dwelt especially on the actions of the King and Parliament. When he came to the house of Hanover, he cited the rebellion in 1715 and showed how Parliament acted against the Old Pretender. He detailed the preparations made in 1743 to repel the Young Pretender. Then, returning to the present threat, he said: "What is the situation of Great Britain in the year 1796? There does not exist, the House is convinced, a Pretender to the Throne. We have upwards of 100,000 men at this moment embodied within the island, and the army, we all know, is well affected to the Government of the country. We have besides this regular force, some thousands of volunteer infantry and yeomanry cavalry—a description of persons very unlike those mentioned in last night's debate. We have a fleet unequalled in numbers, and with pride and pleasure I boast, unequalled in gallantry and skill, if we ever resort to the glorious pages of our national naval history. And instead of being menaced at a time of peace and in an unprepared state, activity and preparation pervade every part of this island."

The General then gave a detailed account of the situation of the French armies, their reverses since July, the state of their morale, and the seeming impossibility of preparing them for invasion. Finally he attacked Pitt.

"Whilst the operations in Germany were favourable to the French, when they threatened the destruction of our bravest ally, when his fate seemed almost inevitable, when the season of the year was particularly favourable to the French for extending their victorious career, and pointing their full force against the shores of this country: What line of conduct did His Majesty's Ministers then adopt or pursue? Did they then take any decisive or effectual measure? Did they issue out any proclamation? Did they call Parliament together?

"No! But now when the danger is past, when the designs of the French are frustrated, when their armies have suffered considerable losses, when the season of operation is almost over, and what remains of it will be employed in securing their communications upon the Upper and Lower Rhine, in reinforcing their armies, in re-establishing discipline, this country is called upon for an additional force of 103,000 men to ward off invasion. In this dilemma I shall leave them: either that the danger was greater in October, or that they were guilty of supineness in July!"

It was the most powerful speech of Tarleton's career, and it left the Tories on the horns of dilemma. But now Banastre had a dilemma of his own. The Prince's desertion of the Princess had become the universal theme of gossip. His Royal Highness was condemned by duchesses and fishwives alike. Snapped the *Oracle*: "Lady Jersey has not reached the age of discretion."

Mary had once wept for an inconstant Florizel, and in this *esclandre* her sharp tongue was seldom still. She reviled the Prince for his treatment of Caroline.

To the friends of the Prince, Mary's censure was treason. Anthony Pasquin exclaimed in *The New Brighton Guide*: "It cannot be supposed that Mrs. Robinson, or the Perdita, or the *Lame Sappho*, or what you will, would in the moment that she is receiving an annuity of £500 from the bounty of the Prince, unite in the interested cabal who labor to tarnish his good name—she should have remained, at least, inactive during the crooked course of the floating falsehood. How lamentable it would be to admit that the force of *any species of jealousy* can awaken impertinences, and convert *ideal events*, for the unwarrantable purpose of suppressing an unoffending individual whom we envy, but whom it was intended by Truth and Nature we should respect! But it is not possible—Mrs. Robinson's morality cannot be so far unhinged."

Mary's attitude aroused Ban's resentment, and he began asking himself whether she was a liability. But there was no break between them. As he attended Parliament, she continued her writing. During the spring and summer she had written a sweeping tale of Gothic horrors. On November 26 Hookham published her romance under the title of *Hubert de Sevrac*.

"Mrs. Robinson's *Hubert de Sevrac* is a romance upon the plan of Mrs. Radcliffe," said the *Oracle* on December 12. "The grateful terrors of the first volume are displayed with infinite address and the greatest force of language."

The *Monthly Review* of January 1797 equivocated over *Hubert de Sevrac*: "This work possesses many of the beauties & some of the faults, which characterize that species of modern novels called *Romances*. The mysterious, the horrible, the pathetic, and the melancholy, are the leading features of this kind of writing. We could point out many parts of these volumes that are delineated with strength and spirit: but, as a whole, the composition rather fails in effect, owing to the multiplicity of characters & incidents and to the frequent change of scene."

The critic for the *Critical Review*, having already reviewed Mrs. Radcliffe's *The Mysteries of Udolpho* and *The Italian* and Matthew G. Lewis' *The Monk*, was discouraging. "The character of Mrs. Robinson's novels being generally known, it is perhaps sufficient to say that *Hubert de Sevrac* is inferior to her former productions," he wrote. "There are detached parts, however, of which we may speak with approbation; and, during the prevalence of the present taste for romances, the whole may afford amusement to the supporters of circulating libraries."

In spite of this critical faultfinding, Mary's Gothic romance was popular, and with the new year came continental recognition. On January 27, 1797, the *Oracle* reported: "Mrs. Robinson's *Hubert de Sevrac* is already in the Press in Paris, translated by an able and popular pen."

M. André Cantwell, translator of Mrs. Radcliffe's *Le Voyage en Hollande*, had turned Mary's romance into *Hubert de Sévrac, ou Histoire d'un émigré*. But in *La Décade philosophique, littéraire et politique*, a critic who signed himself "A. F. C." wrote: "*L'ouvrage nous a semblé très faiblement écrit.*"

On the Continent, Mary's fame spread. From the press in Halle in 1797 came the German version of *Hubert von Sevrac*. Later in the year, as the German readers developed a taste for Gothicism, the press in Leipzig, accepting a manuscript for which Mary could find no English publisher, brought out *Julie St. Laurence*.

ᚱ

Clayton died on December 4, 1796. Popular, distinguished, and a political disciple of Ban's, he had been the flower of the Tarleton family. As the stagecoach rumbled toward Liverpool, Banastre rode in manly sorrow and severe self-appraisal.

After his return to Parliament for the winter session, the news from Liverpool became distressing. Old Mrs. Jane Tarleton would scarce survive the winter. Ban knew that his mother's greatest wish was to see him separated from Mary. All winter he wrestled with his conscience. Loyalty struggled against loyalty.

Long ago Mary had warned him:

> Ah! tell me not that jealous fear
> > Betrays a weak, suspicious mind;
> Were I less true, and thou less dear,
> > I should be blest, and thou be kind!

> But while, by giddy Fancy led,
> > In search of Joy you wildly rove,—
> Say, can my *Mind* be free from dread,
> > When ev'ry sense is chain'd by love?

> Yet, soon my anxious fears shall cease,
> > Since I am doom'd from Thee to part;
> That day will give me lasting peace;
> > For oh! that day will Break My Heart!

For fifteen years Mary had cherished their attachment. In spite of her paralysis, she had nursed him in sickness and supported him in health. And yet from their union had come only sorrow. She had lost her beauty. She was haggard and shrewish and almost helpless, a tragic wisp who kept herself alive through will power and laudanum. Perhaps her love for Ban had become merely platonic.

"Man is only constant, while he feels the flame of affection burn vividly within his bosom: he is not the creature of our dominion, but of his own passions," she wrote in *The False Friend*. "He will love as long as he is pleased, and he will please as long as he can love. Sentiment forms no part of his attachment; all the claims of esteem, generosity, and friendship, sink subdued before the ruling power of self-gratification."

Mary was £1200 in debt. Much of it came from supporting Banastre. She felt that he should pay some of her debts when he came into his inheritance. He scorned the idea, and she accused him of ingratitude. They quarreled violently. So just before leaving for the bedside of his mother, he went to her and told her that their connection was at an end.

Too proud to plead with him or to let friends see her weep, Mary fled London. On April 26 the *Oracle* reported: "Mrs. and Miss Robinson set out from their house in Burlington Street on Sunday morning for Bath, for the spring season."

But Mary did not reach Bath. Her agony was too great.

> Say not, that minutes *swiftly* move,
> When blest with those we fondly love;
> Also! each moment seems to me
> An *age of Bliss*—when blest with Thee!
>
> But torn away from Thee, my friend,
> The weary scene would *quickly* end;
> For like the lightnings, fraught with ill,
> The pang, though Short, Would Surely Kill!

On May 8 James Boaden announced in the *Oracle*: "Mrs. Robinson is confined on the Bath Road by a violent fever."

Hubert de Sevrac was the rage in Paris, and a German translation was rushing through the press in Halle. Yet in her fever and delirium, in a rented bed on the road to Bath, Mary Robinson cared nought for *Hubert*. Her tortured fancy cried only for Banastre.

But Ban did not come. On May 23 Jane Tarleton died. As Ban grieved for his mother in the surroundings of his youth, Mary wept. "The chamber of sickness is the school of meditation. There the mind, abstracted from trivial occupations, weighs in the even scale of justice all the pains and pleasures of existence. Reason there predominates over Prejudice, and we shake off her deceptive visions, as the light of truth expands by rumination," Mary afterward wrote in *The False Friend*.

Finally she dried her tears. "The moment that the spell which chains the senses is broken, the phantom of love takes flight, leaving no substitute but regret and indignation."

Into "Lines Written on a Sick Bed, 1797," went her indignation and despair:

> I see Deceit in sainted guise
>   Of holy Friendship, smile;
> I mark Oppression's eager eyes,
>   And tremble as the breath of Guile
> Assumes Affection's sighs.
>
> Then, bed of sickness! thou to me
>   No keener pangs canst bring;
> I have familiar grown with thee;
>   And while the scorpion sorrows sting
> My soul no joy can see.
>
> Yet, bed of sickness! while my breast
>   In fev'rish throbs shall rise
> My cheek shall smile—and endless rest
>   Anticipating Hope supplies
> Hereafter—with the blest!

In London, Mary's friends learned of her heartbreak. In the *Oracle* of May 30 James Boaden confirmed the parting: "General Tarleton has lost his mother; if we mistake not, this is not the only loss he has recently sustained, in that which comes nearest the heart, cherished by many years of social intercourse."

Finally Mary grew calm. After fifteen tumultuous years with Banastre she had been cast aside. "What a curse is memory to those who have outlived the sustaining power of hope!" she cried in *The False Friend*. "Why are we destined to retrace the paths of pleasure, in imagination, while our weary footsteps tread on the thorns of disappointment?"

Nothing now survived but her sorrows and her memory, and these flowed together into her valediction:

The Sorrows of Memory

> In vain to me the howling deep
>   Stern Winter's awful reign discloses;
> In vain shall Summer's zephyrs sleep
>   On fragrant beds of budding roses;
> To me, alike each scene appears,
>   Since thou hast broke my heart, or nearly;
> While Mem'ry writes in frequent tears
>   That I have lov'd thee very dearly!
>
> How many summers pass'd away,
>   How many winters sad and dreary,
> And still I taught thee to be gay
>   Whene'er of life thy soul was weary;

When ling'ring sickness wrung thy breast,
    And bow'd thee to the earth, or nearly,
I strove to lull thy mind to rest—
    For then I lov'd thee, Oh! how dearly!

And tho' the flush of joy no more
    Shall, o'er my cheek its lustre throwing,
Bid giddy fools that cheek adore,
    And talk of passion—ever glowing;
Still to my mind should time impart
    A charm to bid it feel sincerely,
Nor idly wound a breaking heart,
    That lov'd thee long and lov'd thee dearly.

Could gold thy truant nature bind,
    A faithful heart would still content me,
For oh! to keep that heart unkind,
    I gave thee all that Fortune lent me!
In youth, when suitors round me press'd,
    Who vow'd to love, and love sincerely;
When wealth could never charm my breast,
    Tho' thou wert poor I lov'd thee dearly.

Seek not the fragile dreams of love,
    Such fleeting phantoms will deceive thee;
They will but transient idols prove—
    In wealth beguile, in sorrow leave thee.
Ah! dost thou hope the sordid mind
    When thou art poor will feel sincerely?
Wilt thou in such that friendship find
    Which warm'd the heart that lov'd thee dearly?

Tho' fickle passions cease to burn
    For her so long thy bosom's treasure,
Ah! think that reason may return
    When far from thee my steps I measure;
Say who will then thy conscience heal,
    Or who shall bid thy heart beat cheerly?
Or from that heart the mem'ry steal
    Of her who lov'd thee long and dearly?

When war shall rouze the brooding storm,
    And horrors haunt thy thorny pillow;
When fancy shall present my form
    Borne on the wild and restless billow;
Or where wilt thou an helpmate find
    Whose pulse, like mine, shall throb sincerely?
Or who thy heart in spells shall bind
    When hers is broke that lov'd thee dearly?

I will not court thy fickle love
    Soon shall our fates and fortunes sever;
Far from thy scorn will I remove,
    And smiling, sigh adieu for ever!
Give to the sordid fiend thy days,
    Still trust that they will act sincerely,
And when the specious mask decays,
    Lament the heart that lov'd thee dearly!

For time will swiftly journey on,
    And Age and Sickness haste to meet thee;
Friends prov'd deceitful—will be gone
    When they no more with smiles can cheat thee.
Then wilt thou seek in vain to find
    A faithful heart that beats sincerely;
A passion cent'ring in a mind
    Which, scorning int'rest, lov'd thee dearly.

When in the grave this heart shall sleep,
    No soothing dream will bless thy slumber,
For thou perchance may'st wake to weep,
    And with remorse my sorrows number!
My shade will haunt thy aching eyes,
    My voice in whispers tell thee clearly
How cold at last that bosom lies
    WHICH LOV'D thee LONG, and LOV'D thee DEARLY!

33

Youth and £20,000

MARY NOW PLUNGED AHEAD on her novel, trying to forget her suffering and her sorrows. Too feeble to go out, she sold her carriage. Painfully she shuffled between bed and couch. Through the bright summer days of 1797 she lay prone and drove her stiff fingers across page after page of paper.

She grew weary, but she scarcely paused. To ease her trembling nerves she dabbled away at poetry. Occasionally Peter Pindar or William Godwin came to tea, and their radical society was congenial. Godwin was writing a tragedy; his bride, Mary Wollstonecraft, had nearly finished *The Wrongs of Women*.

"This is the age of novel writing," exclaimed Boaden in the *Oracle*. "This and the last years have produced several of superior excellence: Dr. Moore's *Edward*—Mrs. Robinson's *Hubert*—Madame D'Arblay's *Camilla* —Mrs. Radcliffe's *Italian*—and Mr. Pratt's *Family Secrets*."

By the middle of October, Mary had finished writing *Walsingham*. Longman's, alive to the popularity of the author, outbid Hookham and purchased the mansucript at what the *Oracle* called "a price almost unequalled for a work of the same species."

The sale of Mary's *chef-d'ouevre* relieved her of immediate financial worries. But she paid the price of her security in pain and tears. "The work which Mrs. Robinson is now finishing will probably be her last," said the *Oracle* of October 17. "Her health declines rapidly. The sting of ingratitude wounds deeply in a sensitive heart."

The *Morning Post* expressed the same opinion: "Mrs. Robinson's ill state of health measures a period to the effusions of a muse, which has acquired the proudest celebrity, and which will build a monument to her memory, in spite of envy, persecution, and ingratitude."

On December 7 Longman published *Walsingham*. Mary's readers were waiting eagerly for her exposition of high life. Nor were they disappointed. Reported the *Oracle* next morning: "Mrs. Robinson's *Wal-singham* has literally set the fashionable world in an uproar. Lord Kenyon should thank her for the scenes she has developed respecting the female faro banks. She must expect that every critic pen will be dipped in gall, in return for the keen sarcasm with which she has exposed the general criticism."

On December 8 the editor of the *Morning Post* took the view that "Her reputation as a poet and novelist is now too high for the thunders of retaliating criticism to reach it." Ten days later he quoted "One of our most able critics," saying that *Walsingham* had "a striking moral tendency, and is written in a forcible and elegant style, with copious imagery, and an incessant display of a fine and teeming fancy."

Mary's portrayal of society was "ill calculated to abide the ordeal of criticism," said the *Analytical Review* of January 1798. "We must suppose Mrs. R. to be acquainted with the manners of fashionable life. Yet if her portraits be not *caricatures*, the extremes of society appear to meet: her noblemen use the slang of the stable, and the language of her fine ladies somewhat resembles the dialect of certain females who deal in acquatic productions at the east end of town."

Walsingham was Mary's confessional. There was no mistaking it, even though her lines were spoken by the young hero:

"I was born to sorrow; I was nursed with tears: Solitude was the silent cherisher of affliction; and I rushed into the busy world trembling, fearful, suspicious, and disgusted: prejudice my companion and wounded pride the inmate of my bosom. From such a being what could be expected? The elastic nerve which conveys energy to the human heart, was strained by persecution till its powers of action were nearly annihilated. I shrunk, I yielded, before I had learnt to exercise the virtue of resistance."

The details as well as the attitudes came from the author's own experience: "Since my residence on the continent, I have endeavoured to mingle with society: I am forlorn but not misanthropic: dejected but not splenetic: there is an infinite difference between the uncomplaining sadness of despondency and the peevish inquietude of a capricious imagination. What are the sensations I excite: curiosity and pity."

Noting that "no publication of this kind has made so much noise in the literary and fashionable world for many years past," the editor of the *Morning Post* began filling its columns with poems and striking passages from *Walsingham*. On December 19 he announced: "We purpose continuing the extracts from *Walsingham*. The interest which this work continues to excite will render our intention pleasing to the classical and philosophical reader."

Editor Boaden of the *Oracle* had missed the opportunity to serialize extracts from *Walsingham*, but he continued to report the furor it created. On December 23 he said: "*The Faro Furies* have burnt Mrs.

Robinson's *Walsingham* by the hands of the common *Dealer*. Their midnight incantations breathe nothing but revenge." On December 30 the *Oracle* closed the old year with prophecy: "Mrs. Robinson's *Walsingham's* animadversions on Box-Lobbies, Bull-dogs, Polygraphs, and Old Women will probably cause a revolution in the taste for those eccentric sources of amusement."

Noting the upswing in Mary's popularity during this excitement, Hookham thought it proper to launch a second edition of *Angelina*. In Halle the publishers issued a second edition of *Hubert von Sevrac*. At the head of popular reading in Ireland stood *Hubert de Sevrac* and *Walsingham*.

In Paris, from the *Imprimerie de Rabaut le jeune, Place de Carrousel No. 527, traduit de l'Anglois* and *orné de gravures*, came *Walsingham ou l'Enfant des montagnes, par Marie Robinson, auteur D'Angelina, D'Hubert de Sévrac, De La Veuve*, etc., etc., etc. And in Berlin a translator was working on *Walsingham oder das Naturkind. Mit Musik*.

By New Year's Day the second edition of *Walsingham* was sold out. Mary was working feverishly on the third edition. Said the *Morning Post* on January 11, 1798: "Mrs. Robinson and Mr. Lewis share the literary fame of the day. The run of the *Castle Spectre* and the rapid sale of *Walsingham* have established their reputations in the front ranks of Literature."

But Mary was giving way under the strain. On January 15 both the *Morning Post* and the *Oracle* reported that she was ill. On January 18 the *Morning Post* enlarged its comment: "Mrs. Robinson's disorder is a nervous fever, attended by a depression of spirits, which all the attention of her friends cannot alleviate."

In her sorrow Mary seemed almost to have relinquished the desire to recover. Said the friendly *Oracle* on January 25: "Mrs. Robinson has been confined to her bed these last ten days with a nervous fever—the vein of melancholy which pervades *Walsingham* bespeaks an inquietude of mind, which in some measure proclaims the cause of her present indisposition."

While Mary lay ill, Banastre did not visit her once. And on February 5 the *Morning Post* avowed: "A CERTAIN NOBLEMAN is very much offended at Mrs. Robinson for having ridiculed fashionable pursuits of the day in her last novel!"

Florizel, too, had turned his back on Perdita.

ᖇᖇ

Although Banastre had followed Charles Fox in boycotting Parliament, he now abandoned secession and returned to his seat in Opposition. One by one the Whigs were coming back. Only Fox remained aloof, frittering away his talents at St. Anne's Hill, cultivating roses and Mrs. Armstead.

But around Tarleton a storm was now raging. In his enthusiasm for the Whig Club he had roused his political enemies. "General Tarleton's association with the gang of Thelwell, Jones & Co. at the Crown and Anchor has been the means of procuring him at least one promotion— that of Steward of the Whig Club," said the *True Briton*. "What circumstance could afford a plainer proof of the principles and views of this wretched relic of a once respectable Society?"

Banastre was sincere in his Whig principles. He had not forgotten his experiences in America, and more than any other of the British officers defeated by the American he had embraced the ideas of liberty against which he had fought. His friendship for Lafayette was notorious, and during the summer he had formed another with a volunteer who had fought beside Washington. General Thaddeus Kosciusko, badly carved up in fighting against the forces dismembering Poland, had stopped in London to recuperate before completing his voyage to America.

Kosciusko had been with Greene's army on Hicks Creek on that unforgettable 17th of January. He had fought at Guilford Courthouse. And so when this former enemy arrived in London, Tarleton sought him out. He was fascinated by the old patriot. Said the *Oracle*: "General Tarleton is a constant visitor to Kosciusko, who is confined to his sofa, with wounds not yet healed."

Tarleton introduced Kosciusko into the Whig Club, and members decided to present the distinguished warrior with a sword. At their monthly dinner at the Crown and Anchor, as presiding officer, Banastre presented the sword to Kosciusko. In the presentation he said "that in the hand of this brave and gallant man, it will always be wielded for freedom."

The Tory newspapers became sarcastic, and on December 7 the usually friendly *Oracle* struck with venom: "A certain renowned Hero and Patriot, well known for his manly exploits in America, has written an admonitory letter to Kosciusko, in which he implores him never to draw the Whig Club Sword against the Liberties of men struggling for their Freedom—never, in the plenitude of his heroism, to mow down helpless Women and Children—never to cut up defenseless men when they are running away—and never to render himself famous for his flight from Cowpens!"

During the debate on the Defense Bill, on March 27, 1798, General Tarleton gave ministers some military advice: "Formerly the enemy sent an army to Ireland. But now that Ireland has been put in a proper state of defense, and measures taken for preventing a repetition of attacks in that quarter, where is this country most open to danger? On the eastern coast, which is not far distant from the capital.

"If the French should march thither, their march will be as rapid as possible. They know that there are no fortified towns to be left behind them. They will not encumber themselves with heavy baggage and provisions, which, by retarding their movements, would afford time to render their efforts ineffectual. Did Buonaparte do so when he marched to Vienna? No, no. I would therefore advise that so many troops should not be left in the southern, the western, and the northern extremities of the Kingdom, but that the best of our troops, both infantry and cavalry, should be drawn to the neighborhood of London, where our force should be concentrated, detachments being left to protect the principal towns, such as Newcastle, Hull, Liverpool, and Bristol."

But in the heat of his oratory the Whig general made a slip. Said the *Oracle*: "Of Buonaparte, with whom he hoped to have the pleasure one day of talking over battles, he spoke much as a great and distinguished general."

The idea of the loser at Cowpens talking over battles with Napoleon was funny. It set both friends and enemies laughing. It brought the ridicule of the newspapers down upon the head of the luckless orator:

"Should the *conversatione* which General Tarleton promises himself with General Buonaparte really take place, it will not be like that between Scipio and Hannibal," observed the *Oracle* of April 7. "Buonaparte, we know, is a General, and all the World knows Tarleton to be, at least so he is set down in the *List of the Army*. But Buonaparte, however he might hail Tarleton as a brother General, would perhaps question his Civism, after the support which he has given to the Slave Trade."

The *Oracle* then became personal: "It is not wondered that General Tarleton should wish to talk with Buonaparte. Talking has ever been known to be his strongest propensity."

Knowing that Mary had helped write Ban's speeches, editor Boaden chided him for remaining silent during the recent debate on abolition. "General Tarleton, 'abandoned by the Muse,' was not prepared with any touches of the beautiful to whitewash the Negroes in the late Debate."

Again the *Oracle* twitted the General: "Mrs. Robinson has written a spirited Ode to Gratitude, which she dedicates to a disbanded officer." And then James Boaden, with his knowledge of the private lives of Ban and Mary, on April 21 said with candor: "Mrs. Robinson's *Walsingham* has done much to overturn Faro and his Host. If report may be credited, no one has more reason to execrate a gaming table than this lady."

During the heckling of Banastre, Mary was so nervous that she could not begin another novel. Instead she began editing her poems. Bitter, with love turned to scorn, she began erasing Ban's name from her poetry. All lines inscribed "To a dear friend" were changed to read "To a once dear friend." From the "Ode to Valour" she removed the inscription and the apostrophe to Tarleton.

As Mary revised and rearranged her poems, she realized that she had enough to fill three volumes. So on April 20 she announced the opening of a subscription list to finance the publication of her *Poetical Works*. Said the *Morning Post* grimly: "And a certain ungrateful character hears of her intention without a blush."

Subscriptions began flowing in. From friendship, pity, or charity, the wealthy gave their patronage. Within a week the list included the Duchesses of Devonshire, Northumberland, Gordon, and Hamilton; the Marchioness of Hertford; and the Countesses of Bessborough, Fitzwilliam, Guildford, Cholmondeley, and Oxford.

"Mrs. Robinson, this time, wisely receives her own subscription to the new edition of her *Works*," said the *Oracle* of April 27. "She thus arms herself against a General Envasion."

ᏇᎶ

In Parliament the General was cast in the role of peacemaker. During the debate on a Bill for Manning the Navy, on May 25, George Tierney spoke against hurrying the bill through the House. In his sarcastic rejoinder, Pitt suggested that Tierney was trying to obstruct the defense of the country.

Tierney appealed for protection to Speaker Addington. He then asked the Prime Minister to soften the tone of his remarks. But Pitt had taken enough from the Radical Whigs. He refused. Tierney immediately challenged him. They met at Putney Heath on the morning of May 27. Both fired twice, but neither was wounded.

"Tarleton has told me he tried to prevail on Tierney to forbear, but in vain," wrote Wilberforce to a friend; "and I have reason to believe that there was a good deal of talk about it amongst the party before the meeting took place."

In editorializing on the affair in the *Oracle*, Boaden observed: "The Duke of Norfolk, the Duke of Bedford, General Tarleton, Mr. Tierney, and all the others whom Government has dismissed or refused the command of a regiment happen to be crops."

The Whigs became violent. With Fox at St. Anne's Hill, Sheridan attempted to assume his mantle. Tarleton backed Sheridan. That their oratory at least rankled the Tories showed through the heavy-handed report in the June 21 *Oracle*:

"The mighty General Tarleton, swollen with vanity by the friendly panegyric of Mr. Sheridan on Tuesday, came forward yesterday with a prepared speech against the Ministry. In the frenzy of his skirmishing, he attacked them on the Expedition against Ostend, which he attempted to prove betrayed a total want of skill and capacity. This little David, who with his sling and his stone, put himself in the most formidable position, was completely silenced by the plain and manly statement of Mr. Dundas, that the whole expedition was undertaken by the expressed desire of Sir Charles Grey, whose military genius was at least equal to that of the honorable general."

As Tarleton's rebuff hung in the air, an old friend reached the end of his resources. George Hanger left off skulking around London and gave himself up to the Court of King's Bench. In reward for high living and general improvidence he was imprisoned within the rules for debtors. But his confinement was an accidental piece of good luck. George had ample time to write *The Life, Adventures, and Opinions of Colonel Hanger*. He was released a few months later, newly accomplished, totally unpenitent, and very well rested.

With his last £40 Hanger turned coal dealer. He worked hard, and although the newspapers taunted him for becoming a black diamond merchant, he prospered. One day the Prince rode past his coal yard and yelled, "Hey, George, how go coals today?"

"Black! Black, your Highness, black as ever!" retorted the irrepressible wag.

Mary, too, had resumed writing. Now only a frail wisp, who had to be helped from bed to couch, with her mind almost like an eager unembodied spirit, she lay and dreamed over her life with Banastre. Friends tried to effect a reconciliation. Finally Ban came to her home on Curzon Street. They talked and talked, but not even friendship could be rekindled from the ashes. However, he promised to return.

Into a poem went all the hopes and fears that now became Mary's alpha and omega.

LINES

Written on the 9th of September, 1798

Ah? Why should Grief bid Fancy's visions fly?
And dark'ning clouds obscure yon azure sky?
Last night, as blest with thee the moments flew,
And Hope's fair scenes seem'd opening to my view;
When Fate, relenting at my sorrows past,
Seem'd to my wishes to accede at last,
And grant at least *a portion of thy heart;—*
She strikes the blow—and says that *we must part!*
Part did I say? Rather may welcome Death
This form dissolve, and snatch this fleeting breath;
So I from future sorrows may be free,
Nor bear *ten thousand deaths* in losing THEE!

How can'st thou unconcern'dly give me pain?
Retract, retract, that cruel word again!

Nor suffer thus the dreadful thought to rend,
And wound the bosom of thy tend'rest Friend.—
Or if (avert it Heav'n) the die is cast,
And our approaching meeting be our last,
One parting sigh, one tender tear, bestow,
And seem at least unwillingly to go!
So shall that sigh repay me for my fate,
That tear for all my sorrows compensate.

Tarleton fled London. From Woolbedding, the beautiful estate bought with winnings at gambling, he wrote on September 15: "I have retired to Lord Robert Spencer's friendly mansion, to read and subsist free, being very, very poor."

At Woolbedding Major General Banastre Tarleton read and reflected. He was forty-four years old, gray, worn-out, and gouty. He was indigent. He was estranged from the woman who had loved and cherished him for fifteen years. And he was, as his enemies had said, "at the fag end of a contemptible party."

Sympathetic to Mary, the newspapers were still ridiculing him. "Colonel Hanger seems now fond of walking near the Obelisk in St. George's Fields," chivvied the *Oracle* on November 17. "To make a complete pair, he should have his friend Tarleton with him."

When Banastre returned to London, the news reporters gasped. He had let his gray hair grow long again! They wondered if he had renounced his Jacobin principles as well. Had another Radical Whig deserted Fox, or was the General contemplating active service?

There was now an opportunity. In June, Lord Cornwallis had gone to Ireland as Lord Lieutenant. Ban's friends had begun overtures to the Duke of York. In early November, from his headquarters in the Horse Guards, Frederick sent for Banastre:

> Horse Guards
> Friday 3 o'clock p.m.
>
> Dear Tarleton,
>
> I wish you should come to me here for a moment as I have something to mention to you.
>
> Ever yours most sincerely,
> Frederick

Bonaparte was mustering the French troops for an attack on Spain. A cry for help had come from Portugal. After a long conference, the cavalry general walked from the Horse Guards in triumph.

With light heart Ban returned to his friends at Brooks's. Lord Cholmondeley invited a group of them up for a week of shooting at Houghton in Norfolk. They went, for Houghton was considered the finest country seat in all England, and Tarleton wanted a go at the pheasants.

At Houghton lived Susan Priscilla Bertie. She was "the most spirit-
uelle and clever person I ever met with," wrote Lady Frances Shelley.
"She was very handsome and attractive. Lord Villiers had wished to
marry her, but poverty, and perhaps family pride, made this impossible."

At Houghton, too, lived Georgiana, the daughter of the Prince of
Wales and Mrs. Grace Dalrymple Elliott. "Georgiana Seymour and
Harriet Cholmondeley were the bright stars in that firmament. The
latter was the daughter of Lord Cholmondeley and afterwards married
the great parti of the day, Mr. Lambton. She and Priscilla," continued
Lady Frances, "were adopted daughters of the Cholmondeleys, and
were brought up with Lady Cholmondeley's own children. They certainly made Houghton the ple ʒantest house I ever stayed at. Its society
was like that of an old French chateau, where every lady laid out her
best accomplishments to please the assembled guests. It was there that
I first met Beau Brummell!"

Susan Priscilla made Houghton as pleasant a place as Ban Tarleton
had ever known. With Lord Villiers and handsome Buck Brummell
hovering dangerously near, the gray-haired dragoon, old enough to be
Susan's father, decided upon an all-out campaign. He talked, he courted,
he persuaded. He told her the secret from the Duke of York.

Susan was fascinated by the famous General with the elegant manners
and scandalous reputation. She believed that he had stopped gambling.
She was willing to believe that he had broken off with Mary Robinson.
She wanted to believe that he had been converted from his radical
politics. And so, when he rode off to London and Parliament, there was
a sparkle in her eyes. And in his stride there was a spring which had
been conspicuously absent for a long while.

The Duke of York again sent for Banastre:

Oatlands, December 2d, 1798

Dear Tarleton,

I have many thanks to return you for your letter.

The Subject upon which I wish to speak to you, will, I trust not
be disagreeable. At the same time it will very well keep till I return to Town on Tuesday when I shall be very much obliged to
you if you will call upon me at the Horse Guards at 12 o'clock.

Ever yours most sincerely,
Frederick

Major General Tarleton
Brooks's
St. James's Street

From Houghton the Cholmondeleys rushed down to their home in
Piccadilly. On December 9 Lady Willoughby de Eresby entertained the
Princess of Wales. Countess Cholmondeley started for her sister's home

in Whitehall, but enroute her carriage broke down. The Prince sent his carriage for her.

That night in the House of Commons, General Tarleton presented a petition from the Mayor and the Corporation for the improvement of Liverpool. During the debate he let slip a hint: "I believe I shall have an opportunity for making up in my professional line for lost time."

The *Oracle* seized upon the hint and on December 11 wrote an editorial of well-wishing. "General Tarleton appeared last night anxious in the House of Commons to inform the public, that he was about to be employed by the Government. The Honorable General pledged himself that his Country should derive great advantage, if not greater security from his efforts. Not withstanding that we have differed widely from his political line of conduct, we hope that he will soon justify his professions, solemnly made in the face of the nation."

Then the news broke. Major General Banastre Tarleton had been appointed to command his Majesty's forces in Portugal. King George held a levee on December 12, and General Tarleton was presented to his sovereign on the occasion of his appointment. After the levee he was granted a long interview by the King.

The next day the *Oracle* had a scoop: "Miss Bertie, a beautiful and accomplished young lady, will on Monday be led by General Tarleton to the altar of Hymen. Rumour states that they became acquainted at Lord Cholmondeley's. Forgetful of the General's peccadillos, we hope him all the happiness afforded by youth and twenty thousand pounds."

The newspapers were all rumor, gossip, and speculation. "General Tarleton became accidently acquainted with the lady when he lately went upon a shooting party into Norfolk," reported the *Sun*. "In three days the match was settled, and the lady was content to resign all the luxuries of the fashionable life to attend her military husband abroad on his professional duties. According to report, she is not critically handsome, but possesses a very animated countenance, and is highly accomplished, especially in music."

The *Morning Post* spoke on December 14. Its voice was that of publisher Daniel Stuart, but its words were those of the forsaken woman who edited the poetry page. Mary Robinson remembered handsome young Robert Bertie and Rebecca Krudener. Said the *Morning Post*: "The Lady to whom General Tarleton is to be married is named Krudener, and not Bertie, as has been stated by mistake."

Almost every newspaper reader in London knew the story of hell-raising Robert Bertie, Marquis of Lindsay and Duke of Ancaster. On the morning of the wedding day the Reverend Henry Bate's *Morning Herald* informed it readers: "The Miss Bertie, whom General Tarleton is to espouse, is a natural daughter of his late friend, the young Duke of Ancaster."

The *Morning Post* printed a short vignette: "The young lady to whom the General is to be united is Miss Bertie, daughter of the late Marquis of Lindsay. Her age is about two or three and twenty. She is rather below the middle stature, but very pretty; her looks, however, are not more engaging than the accomplishments of her mind. She has had a most finished education, speaks several languages with great grace and fluency, draws with much taste and fancy, is a skilful musician, and has studied with great attention and success the more useful sciences: she is mistress of Astronomy, Geography, etc., having had a perfect, polite education. Miss Bertie is much caressed by Lady Willoughby, Lady Cholmondeley, and their circle. Her father left her some property; but we believe her fortune will not amount to £20,000 though it is a handsome sum."

Estimates of the fortune Tarleton would win with his bride varied. Some said £12,000, some £20,000, and others as much as £30,000. The staid *Observer* printed the facts and left its readers to speculate over investments and compound interest: "The late Duke of Ancaster left to the charming bride of General Tarleton £3000 and £300 a year, which have been accumulating ever since."

Banastre Tarleton and Susan Priscilla Bertie were married at eight o'clock in the evening of December 17, 1798. The Reverend Mr. Western of Canterbury by special license performed the ceremony at Lord Gwydyr's home in Whitehall. His Lordship gave the bride in marriage, and she was attended by Miss Walls, Miss Lisle, Miss Clitheroe, and Miss Seymour as bridesmaids. After a large reception, the newlyweds left for Langley Broom, the Gwydyrs' country home, to spend their honeymoon.

After Ban and Susan had retreated to spacious Langley Park, the editors of the newspapers began speculating on how the Radical Whig general had won the command in Portugal. Twitted the *Morning Herald*: "The Minister now seems to be pursuing a new method of getting rid of the Opposition gentlemen, by sending them abroad."

After his joke the Reverend Mr. Bate said editorially on December 19: "Colonel Tarleton is allowed on all hands to be an officer of great vigor and courage, a consideration which has very commendably prevailed with his Majesty's Ministers over that of party prejudice in the appointment of that Gentleman to the command of the British troops in Portugal."

The *Morning Herald* then stated that General Tarleton owed his appointment "solely to the patronage of the Duke of York."

The *Morning Post* said that the appointment had been "at the particular request of Marquis Cornwallis," and immediately issued a denial of its story. But Daniel Stuart, astute publisher of the *Morning Post*, soon hit on the right answer: "It now proves that Lord Gwydyr is the artist of General Tarleton's fortune, his Lordship having obtained the Portuguese appointment."

General and Mrs. Tarleton returned to the West End for a gay Christmas season. Susan Priscilla began rushing from the Gwydyrs' home to the Cholmondeleys', to the shops and back again—planning, buying, preparing for the trip to Lisbon. Nor was she alone. Said the *Oracle*: "Miss Lisle, who is about to give her hand to Mr. Arbuthnot, the new Consul General of Portugal, is an *élevée* of Lady Cholmondeley and the bosom friend of Mrs. Tarleton."

Banastre was just as busy. He was frequently at the Horse Guards. So that he might receive the pay and allowances of a major general, the Duke of York appointed him colonel of the Durham Regiment of Fencible Cavalry. For his aide, Ban selected his nephew, Captain Thomas Tarleton, Jr. Tom had been educated at Eton and Oriel College, Oxford, and had already served several years in the army.

Captain Tarleton hastened to London. Lord Gwydyr took charge of uncle and nephew and on January 8, 1799, escorted them to St. James's Palace for the first levee of the new year. His Lordship presented General Tarleton to King George on the occasion of his recent marriage and Captain Tarleton on his becoming aide-de-camp to his uncle.

"General Tarleton has been hunting with the Duke of York this week at Langley Park," observed the *Morning Post* of January 12. "The zeal of Lord Gwydyr for the welfare of Mrs. Tarleton is certainly an amiable feature of his character."

Ban and Susan spent seven exciting weeks in London. Marriage had restored him to the close company of the royal brothers, and he hunted with the Duke of York and visited him at Oatlands. He visited the Prince at Carlton House. Susan flitted about the West End, visiting among her titled and powerful relatives, concluding her shopping, and packing for the voyage to Lisbon.

The sons of the King gave Ban a royal send-off. The Prince presented him with a beautiful dress sword to wear on state occasions during his foreign service. Ban christened it "Sweet Lips."

After the farewells, on February 5 General and Mrs. Tarleton and Captain Tarleton left London for Portsmouth. By then the full story of the expedition to Portugal had been revealed. A rumor that the French planned an attack upon this tiny ally of Britain had brought an appeal from the Portuguese Court for a suitable British officer to train the Portuguese army. For this the Duke of York had ordered General Tarleton to active duty.

After ministers had duly reflected, they added to the mission to Portugal the name of General Cornelius Cuyler. Said the *Star*: "In addition to the force which this country may spare for the assistance of the Portuguese, it will be of great importance that time should be given to organize and animate the troops of our ally, a task for which the talents of the Commanders are peculiarly adapted."

Next day the *Star* woke up to the trick of the Tories. Cuyler was senior to Tarleton. "General Cuyler is going out to Portugal as Commander-in-Chief of the British Forces in that Kingdom. General Tarleton, who is destined for the same place, is to command the cavalry."

In Portsmouth the Tarletons waited and waited, while the warships of the convoy gathered off Spithead and the troops of the expedition embarked in the transports at Southampton. Finally the General's bride went aboard the frigate *Hyena*. But contrary winds and wintry gales prevented the fleet from sailing.

◌◌

After her dreams of reconciliation had faded, Mary began a novel about Banastre. During the fall she wrote steadily, and her publisher rushed the book through the press in time to catch the excitement over the marriage of her former *Cher Ami*. "Mrs. Robinson makes the hero of her new novel perish on his voyage to Lisbon," said the *Morning Post* of February 18. "Poets are generally thought prophets, and Mrs. Robinson has in more than one instance been correct in her predictions."

Mary's friends were not distressed by this prediction, for they now execrated Banastre. In retaliation, his friends condemned her. But everyone sympathized with Susan Priscilla. She was an innocent bride caught in the backwash of her husband's scandalous life.

On February 19 Longman and Rees published Mary's *The False Friend*. Her revenge was terrible. Readers of *The False Friend* recognized Banastre at once. Said the *Oracle*: "The character of Treville in Mrs. Robinson's new novel is said to be drawn from an original. For the honour of human nature, we hope the anecdotes are not authentic."

The *Morning Post* observed: "The sable habits in which Mrs. Robinson has disguised her *False Friend* does not conceal the glaring traits of the character she means to delineate."

The gales still blew, and in the harbor at Portsmouth the *Hyena* rocked and swayed. Finally Susan Priscilla had enough of the storm-tossed frigate and on February 24 Ban took her ashore. In their hotel the newlyweds ran into the literary storm. The newspapers were almost turning T-r-e-v-i-l-l-e into T-a-r-l-e-t-o-n.

"Mrs. Robinson's charming new book has a very ancient title, and is on a very old subject," said the *Oracle* of February 28. "Even King David complained of a False Friend, with touching eloquence; and as the days of chivalry are no more, *Bravery in the Field* is not always accompanied by *Fidelity in the Closet*."

The False Friend was written in a series of letters, "a form the most favourable for the ardency of expression which is to be found in the compositions of this lady," said the Monthly Magazine of September 1799.

The plot was rambling. Sir William St. Leger returned from India and learned that Lord Densmore had seduced his wife. He challenged and killed Densmore. In the meantime there were five elopements, several rencounters, duels, and suicides. Seven persons were killed or drowned. Treville, the clergyman, having caused the death of an unmarried as well as of a married woman, eloped with another man's wife, and with his companion was drowned while sailing from Yarmouth to Lisbon. After noting that the story was of a melancholy cast, the reviewer observed: "The conversations, of which there are many, and most of them among people in high life, abound in coarse and ill mannered repartees."

In the character of Treville, Mary sketched vignette after vignette of Banastre: "Too polite to be religious; too witty to be learned; too youthful to be serious: and too handsome to be discreet."

Susan had known Ban intimately for only about four months. As she read The False Friend in a warm hotel room in rain-swept Portsmouth, she might well have believed some of the things written by her husband's cast-off mistress. But in her bride's optimism Susan Priscilla could hardly accept Banastre as "a libertine of the most dangerous species; a dissembling sycophant; a being who hovered round the wealthy and the high born, to poison domestic happiness, and to tarnish reputation under the sacred habit of virtue and religion: a coxcomb by education; a deceiver by practice; a flatterer by profession; and a profligate by nature."

As Mary had written, creating Treville out of the detritus of Tarleton, her wrath had risen. Susan could only have shuddered at the bitter invective in which Mary had embalmed the man whom they both loved:

> I look back upon my short intercourse with the busy world, and I shudder; for the folly and duplicity of mankind disgust the heart, and I begin to consider society as the bane of sentiment, the poison of felicity. Even the acrimony of a misanthropic spirit is less pernicious than the honeyed mischief of deceit extracted from the selfish mind, and dressed in the fair semblance of friendship and affection. I have seen villains sanctioned by high patronage, even in the avowal of crimes, for which the lower orders of society would be eternally dishonoured. I have beheld men, without sentiment, feeling, rectitude, or character, upheld in infamy; countenanced by the exalted, and even by the virtuous; their enormities concealed beneath the brazen mark of arrogance, and their violations of honour excused as the ebullitions of a glowing fancy; while their unblushing licentiousness is considered as the warmth of passion, and their ingratitude placed to the account of fortune's unkindness.

Yet such men will watch, like ravenous wolves, for prey; they will cajole the simple, deceive the innocent, defraud the credulous, and insult the unprotected; they will borrow from the wealthy, cheat the believing, ruin a friend, or calumniate a patron; associate with those they despise and ridicule; court, and even flatter, the exalted fool who admits him to his confidence; and at the same moment, debauch his wife, or intrigue with his mistress. In his political character he is equally insincere, and no less successful. He will be, for a time, the most servile adulator, the most sycophantic courtier; till his hopes are disappointed, and his merit justly appreciated. He *then* becomes a zealous partisan; the fawning, servile lacquey of his patron; he will say and unsay with the most convenient facility; profess an independent mind, and at the same moment avow himself the tool of party. Thus viewing both sides of the road to preferment, and by weighing popular clamour in the scale against private worth, he assumes a consequence which he is not entitled to, either by birth or abilities; and, with the aid of unabashed effrontery, takes precedence of truth, talents, and integrity! Such a man is the profligate, unprincipled, mean, insidious, self-interested, ungrateful Treville!

Finally the winds changed and the skies cleared. On March 5 the transports dropped down the Solent and picked up their convoy at Spithead. The Tarletons sailed off in the *Hyena*. After them the paralyzed, dying novelist sent another malediction:

> In vain you fly me! on the madd'ning main
> SAPPHO shall haunt thee 'mid the whirlwind's roar;
> SAPPHO shall o'er the mountains chaunt her strain,
> And Echo bear it to thy distant shore!
> No scene upon the world's wide space shall be
> A scene of rest, ungrateful man, to thee!

34

Old Windsor

HE FIRST EDITION OF *The False Friend* was quickly sold. By May 24 the second edition was on sale. Rumors of Mary's revenge had reached the Continent, and her readers were eager. In Paris, "*traduit de l'anglais sur la 2eme edition*," the firm of Migneret was rushing publication of *Le Faux Ami*. And in Rudolstadt, Herr von Schenk was translating *Der falsche Freund*.

But again Mary found little satisfaction in literary success. Her anguished mind was still under the afflatus of vengeance. She felt she had a score to settle with Susan Priscilla. And realizing that the character of the vivacious young wife was above reproach, she decided to broadcast to the world that Mrs. Tarleton was a natural daughter.

Mary's pen flew until she sank into lethargy. On June 20 she sent her manuscript to Longman and Rees, and on August 29 they published *The Natural Daughter*. "Those who have read Mrs. Robinson's *False Friend* will probably be gratified also in knowing the *Natural Daughter*," said the *Oracle*. Next day it summarized the book: "Mrs. Robinson's *Natural Daughter* visits all the Watering Places, and notwithstanding her birth, is reckoned one of the most agreeable companions to be met with for a sentimental *tete-a-tete*."

Susan Priscilla's piety had shielded her. Not one whisper of past misconduct could Mary hear. And so, after a false beginning in which she turned a real person like Peregrine Bertie into an imaginary Peregrine Bradford, Mary had abandoned her plans and written a thin, novelized autobiography.

Martha Morley, the heroine, had suffered wrongs. "She had been deeply wounded, but the blow was given by a vulgar hand; she had been treated with scorn, but it was the low scorn of recreant ignorance; she had been neglected, and there was distinction in the neglect of unenlightened beings. She had been hurled from affluence to indigence, from the sunny smiles of flattering folly, to the stern and darkening frown of unequivocal adversity."

Mrs. Morley's experience on the stage was an idealization of Mary's career at Drury Lane. Her fame as a poetess was Mary's as Laura Maria. "Are you Ann Matilda, or Della Crusca, or Laura Maria? Comical creatures! They have made me shed many a tear, though I never more than half understood them."

And Mrs. Morley cried with a voice that was Mary's: "Of all the occupations which industry can pursue, those of literary toil are most fatiguing. That which seems to the vacant eye a mere playful amusement, is in reality an Herculean labour; and to compose a tolerable work is so difficult a task that the fastidiously severe should make the trial before they presume to condemn the humblest effort of imagination."

After publishing *The Natural Daughter*, Mary felt called upon to defend publicly her own conduct in deserting Thomas Robinson. In November 1798, under the pseudonym of Anne Frances Randall, she had published *Thoughts on the Condition of Women, and on the Injustice of Mental Subordination*.

"Supposing that destiny, or interest, or chance, or what you will, has united a man, confessedly of a weak understanding, and corporal debility, to a woman strong in all the powers of intellect, and capable of bearing the fatigues of busy life: is it not degrading to humanity that such a woman should be the passive, the obedient slave of such a husband?" Mary asked her readers. "Is it not repugnant to all the laws of nature, that the feelings, actions, and opinions should be controlled, perverted, and debased by such a helpmate?"

Condition of Women was only a reflection of the arguments of her friends William Godwin and Mary Wollstonecraft, but it was animated by Mary's spirited defense of her own conduct.

"Supposing that a WOMAN has experienced every insult, every injury, that her vain boasting, high-bearing associate, man can inflict: imagine her, driven from society; deserted by her kindred; scoffed at by the world; exposed to poverty; assailed by malice; and consigned to scorn; with no companion but sorrow, no prospect but disgrace; she has no remedy. She appeals to the feeling and reflecting part of mankind; they pity, but they do not seek to redress her: she flies to her own sex, they not only condemn, but they avoid her. She talks of punishing the villain who has destroyed her; he smiles at the menace, and tells her, *she* is a WOMAN."

During the summer of 1799 a French publisher brought out a translation of *Condition of Women*. Then Mary determined to avow the authorship. On September 11, 1799, under the signature of Mary Robinson, Longman and Rees republished *Thoughts on the Condition of Women, and on the Injustice of Mental Subordination*. The cost was almost death. Mary lay on her bed, exhausted and ill—her indisposition, the *Morning Post* said, "brought on by mental labors."

At Englefield Cottage, Old Windsor, she lingered through autumn. In her destitution she threw her remaining physical and mental energy into editing the poetry page of the *Morning Post*. But on December 13 her editorial chief reported: "Mrs. Robinson is very dangerously ill, and is attended twice a day by a physician."

ᔕᕬ

Major General and Mrs. Banastre Tarleton were returning to England. Assignment to Portugal had been dreary. Nothing had happened in that quarter. Instead of attacking Spain, Napoleon had sailed to Egypt. The British generals had been readying troops to ward off an invasion that no longer threatened, and they had found lethargy and lack of enthusiasm throughout the Portuguese army. Tarleton's task of disciplining the Portuguese cavalry had been impossible. A cavalryman whose conception of the training of dragoons had been derived from the practices of Baron Friederich von der Trenck, he had found that the Portuguese cavalry horses had been subleased to draw hacks about the streets of Lisbon. There was graft and corruption everywhere.

Besides, Banastre had been ill, and a dragoon wracked by gout was worse than useless. On July 31 the *Morning Post* noted: "General Tarleton's health is said to be much broken since he left England." Then it snickered: "He has probably discovered a *good constitution* more valuable than he thought it." It was laughable: a middle-aged man with a young bride and the gout!

The General's domestic life was not quiet. Susan Priscilla, the spoiled darling of her aunts Countess Cholmondeley and Lady Willoughby de Eresby, was imperious. She brooked no interference in her plans to ride her black stallion with spurs and blind bridle.

Nor did she convenience the London gossips who had lifted their eyebrows hopefully as the graying General, his pretty young wife, and dashing Captain Thomas Tarleton had left for foreign duty. Tom and Susan did not like each other. "Happily perhaps for all parties, the imperious little lady and the handsome A.D.C. were much more given to squabble than to flirt—and the General wisely left them to settle their own quarrels," Tom's daughter Mary naïvely wrote in her *Journal* years later.

To the relief of all, the War Office recalled the mission. General and Mrs. Tarleton and Captain Tarleton arrived at Falmouth on October 22 —ironically enough on a ship with the name of *Walsingham*. They hastened to Lord Gwydyr's home in Whitehall. When the King and Queen held a drawing room at St. James's on October 30 they attended, and General Tarleton was presented to their Majesties on the occasion of his return from Lisbon.

Busy with his reports and conferences, Banastre remained in London until about the middle of December. After celebrating their wedding anniversary at Lord Gwydyr's, Ban and Susan spent the Christmas season with her foster sisters and brothers. "Houghton, in Norfolk, is exhibiting its Christmas Festivities, and never with more grace and elegance," reported the Oracle of December 31; "to whose visitors are now added General Tarleton and his Lady."

Directly the Tarletons returned to London. The social season opened on January 18 with the Queen's Birthday Ball. Ban and Susan were there, in the very heart of England's society. In describing the costumes of the ladies of highest rank, the fashion reporter for the Oracle said: "Mrs. Tarleton wore a dress with a yellow striped satin body and train, with petticoat of white crepe, with stripes of applique in brown and yellow, with broad dark fur between."

Many were watching closely the activities, the conduct, the military career, and the politics of the Whig general. Would he turn renegade? Would the Tories foster his career in the Army? On January 11, 1800, the Oracle speculated: "It is imagined that General Tarleton will be employed in the meditated expedition. The general may as well forget Service if he is suffered to remain inactive."

The Oracle answered one question on February 5: "General Tarleton took his seat on the Opposition Bench, near Mr. M. A. Taylor." Soon afterward it said: "General Tarleton, since his return from Portugal, continues to take his seat on the Opposition side of the House of Commons, but beyond that 'Mum is the Word!'"

Lord Gwydyr and his wife, Lady Willoughby de Eresby, sympathized with the Princess in her estrangement from the Prince. They worked consistently for a reconciliation. The Tarletons also belonged to the Reconciliationists. "Her Royal Highness the Princess of Wales dined yesterday with Lord Gwydyr and Lady Willoughby, at their home in Whitehall," said the Morning Post of February 22. "General Tarleton and his Lady were of the party."

On March 31 the Oracle reported that "Lord Gwydyr, Lady Willoughby, General and Mrs. Tarleton, Mr. Cholmondeley and Mr. Crewe dined yesterday with the Earl and the Countess of Cholmondeley." Next day the Gwydyrs gave a dinner for General and Mrs. Tarleton, to which came the Prince of Wales.

Even as the General and the Prince chatted, forgetful of the actress who had once been so dear to them both, Mary Robinson was recovering. Her withered legs had grown thinner, her fingers stiffer. The last trace of bloom had faded from her cheeks, and her eyes were luminous with a hectic light. But somehow she had lived and was facing life with renewed courage.

Critics had ignored or condemned *The Natural Daughter*, and it sold poorly. Mary's finances were low and she worked almost endlessly on her poems for the *Morning Post*, whose editors considered them "one of the principal embellishments and supports of their journal." Conducting the poetry page of that newspaper threw Mary more than ever into the company of the scribbling crew. From this association blossomed a warm friendship with Samuel Taylor Coleridge, whom Daniel Stuart had employed to write editorials for the *Morning Post*.

To Robert Southey, compiling the second volume of his *Annual Anthology*, Coleridge wrote on January 25: "I have inclosed a poem which Mrs. Robinson gave me for your 'Anthology.' She is a woman of undoubted genius. There was a poem of hers in this morning's paper which both in metre and matter pleased me much. She overloads everything; but I never knew a human being with so *full* a mind—bad, good, and indifferent, I grant you, but full and overflowing. This poem I *asked* for you, because I thought the metre stimulating and some of the stanzas really good. The first line of the twelfth would of itself redeem a worse poem. I think you will agree with me, but should you not, yet still put it *in*, my dear fellow! for my sake, and out of respect to a woman-poet's feelings."

Mary realized that her conduct had been partly justified by *The False Friend, The Natural Daughter*, and *Condition of Women*. Could she fully justify having become the mistress of the Prince of Wales? Dare she tell the truth about the romance between Florizel and Perdita?

With the remorseless honesty of the condemned, who have nothing to lose or gain, she began her autobiography. "These pages are the pages of truth, unadorned by romance, and unembellished by the graces of phraseology," she wrote. Mary was too poor to buy writing paper, so she wrote her story on the covering sheets of old letters from great folk in the world of wit and fashion. Among the signatures were those of the Duchess of Ancaster, the Earl of Jersey, the Marquis of Lothian, the Duke of Grafton, and of his Royal Highness, the Duke of Clarence.

With a scrapbook of her triumphs open beside her, she worked steadily all winter. On April 5, 1800, the *Morning Post* noted that she was completing her *Memoirs*. But Mary had traced her life only to that point where she was being pursued by the relentless Florizel. Then, as she reached the struggle in her conscience over the husband and the Prince, she suddenly broke off. She had been arrested for debt.

"In vain she applied to those, on whom honour, humanity, and justice gave her undoubted claims," wrote Maria Elizabeth. Among those was the Prince of Wales, now some £250 in arrears with Mary's annuity.

April 23, 1800

My Lord,
    Pronounced by my physician to be in a rapid decline, I trust that your lordship will have the goodness to assist me with a part of the

sum for which you are indebted to me. Without your aid I cannot make trial of the Bristol waters, the only remedy that presents to me any hope of preserving my existence. I should be sorry to die at enmity with any person; and you may be assured, my dear Lord, that I have none towards you. It would be useless to ask you to call on me; but if you would do me the honour, I should be happy, very happy, to see you, being,

My dear lord,
Yours truly,
Mary Robinson

The Prince declined to aid or to visit. On May 30 she poured out her bitterness to William Godwin, who in his grief over the death of Mary Wollstonecraft had become Mary's tenderest friend:

The fact is simply this, were I to resist the action as a *married woman*, I might set it aside, and recover damages from my prosecutor, because the arrest is for necessaries, and my husband is therefore by law obliged to pay the debt, there being no kind of legal separation between us. But then, I should involve my husband, and act, as I should feel, dishonestly towards my creditors. I therefore submit patiently. I have had various proposals from many friends to settle the business, but I am too proud to borrow, while the arrears *now due* on my annuity from the Prince of Wales would doubly pay the sum for which I am arrested. I have written to the Prince, and his answer is that there is no money at Carlton House —that he is very sorry for my situation, but that his own is equally distressing!! You will smile at such paltry excuses, *as I do*. But I am determined to persist in my demand, half a year's annuity being really due, which is two hundred and fifty pounds, and I am in custody for sixty-three pounds *only!* So circumstanced I will neither beg, borrow, nor steal. I owe very little in the world, and still less to the world—and it is unimportant to me where I pass my days, if I possess the esteem and friendship of its best ornaments, among which I consider you.

Mary's detention caused a flurry among her friends. From Keswick, on May 21, Coleridge had written Godwin: "Have you seen Mrs. Robinson lately? How is she? Remember me in the kindest and most respectful phrases to her. I wish I knew the particulars of her complaint. For Davy has discovered a perfectly new acid, by which he has restored the use of limbs to persons who had lost them for years (one woman nine years) in cases of supposed rheumatism. At all events, Davy says it can do no harm in Mrs. Robinson's case, and if she will try it, he will make up a little parcel, and write her a letter of instructions, etc."

If Godwin did not persuade the crippled disciple of Mary Wollstonecraft to try Davy's miraculous salve, at least he remembered Coleridge to her in the kindest phrases. He himself always remembered Mary kindly. In *Fleetwood* he used her as the original for Mrs. Kendrick, of whom he wrote: "She was of exquisite beauty, tall, graceful, and captivating. Her tastes were expensive, and her manners gay. Her demeanor was spirited and impressive, her passions volatile, and her temper violent. With all this, she was by no means destitute of capacity. She was eloquent, witty, and sarcastic; exhibiting, when she pleased, the highest breeding, and delivering her remarks with inexpressible vivacity and grace. Thus endowed she was surrounded, wherever she appeared, with a little army of suitors. Every youth of fashion, who had the courage to look up to her, became her professed admirer; and, among these admirers, it was pretty universally believed that all had not offered up their incense in vain."

So that Mary should not spend the little remainder of her life in debtor's prison her friends paid the debt of £63. Ban Tarleton was not among the subscribers. With his rich young wife, he was enjoying the highest social life. They went to dinner after dinner and from ball to ball.

On June 12 the Duchess of Devonshire gave a grand ball at Devonshire House. The most brilliant part of London society attended. During the rout a hungry mob surged around the house. Tarleton stepped to a window and shouted: "My good fellows, if you grow riotous, I shall be really obliged to talk to you!"

To the astonishment of all, the crowd dispersed.

Richard Sheridan was amused at the reformation of his quondam crony. Like a character from *The School for Scandal*, he bantered:

"Well, Tarleton, are you on your high horse still?"

"Oh! higher than ever: if I was on a horse before, I am on an elephant now."

"No, no, my dear fellow, you were on an ass before, and you are on a mule now!"

That Tarleton should devote himself to social duties, hunting, and fishing was not treated so expansively by the hard-bitten newspapermen. On July 11 the *Morning Post* jibed: "In these war-like times it is recorded that General Tarleton in the space of one hour, killed and took—thirty-seven gudgeons!"

A week later the *Morning Post* touched another sensitive chord: "It is remarkable that General Tarleton has not made one speech of importance since his desertion of the Muses."

The Prince of Wales and his set spent the summer season at Brighton. There were the Duke of Bedford, Lord Egremont, Lord Clermont, Sir John and Lady Lade, Mr. Delme, and many of the old turfmen. But not the Tarletons. Lord Gwydyr, who had made his own fortune as Peter Burrell, did not propose to see the money of his niece disappear across a faro table, not even in the Brighton pavilion of the Prince of Wales.

On July 29 the Tarletons left London for a vacation. Said the *Morning Post* of September 5: "General Tarleton has retired from busy life to an old house of Lord Gwydyr's, near Llanwrest, in North Wales, upwards of 250 miles from the metropolis."

In the *Morning Post* Daniel Stuart embellished his earlier remark: "It is strange that, in these warlike times General Tarleton should be consigned to a *mountain obscurity*: popularity is a mere vapour, which dazzles, but evaporates."

ono

Still proud, still determined not to beg, borrow, or steal, yet too frail to write another novel, Ban's former Muse was trying to live by writing poetry. Mary published a stream of poems in the *Morning Post* above her pen names of Julia, Laura, Laura Maria, and Tabitha Bramble.

In the course of ten days during the month of July, she began and concluded a translation from the German of Dr. Hager's *Picture of Palermo*. But this proved "an exertion by which she was greatly debilitated," wrote Maria Elizabeth. And so with great reluctance she laid aside her blank-verse translation of Klopstock's *Messiah*.

Despite her almost helpless condition, Mary tried to move around in her Englefield cottage. According to the *Morning Post* of September 15, she fell and injured her head severely.

Her friends tried to cheer her. Coleridge wrote her a long letter telling of the birth of his son Derwent. Mary wrote an ode of nativity to the baby. In the apostrophe she prayed:

> Sweet Baby Boy! accept a Stranger's song;
>   An untaught Minstrel joys to sing of thee!
> And, all alone, her forest haunts among,
>   Courts the wild tone of mazy harmony!
> A Stranger's song! Babe of the mountain wild,
> Greets thee as Inspiration's darling child!
> O! may the fine-wrought spirit of thy sire
> Awake thy soul and breathe upon thy lyre!
> And blest, amid thy mountain haunts sublime,
>   Be all thy days, thy rosy infant days,
> And may the never-tiring steps of time
>   Press lightly on with thee o'er life's disastrous maze.

Coleridge sent Mary a manuscript of "Kubla Kahn" for her criticism. She was delighted with its wild romantic imagery and wrote a lengthy counter poem containing echoes:

Now by the source, which lab'ring heaves
  The mystic fountain, bubbling, panting,
While gossamer its net-work weaves,
  Adown the blue lawn, slanting!

I'll mark thy "sunny dome," and view
Thy "caves of ice," thy fields of dew!
Thy ever-blooming mead, whose flow'r
Waves to the cold breath of the moon-light hour!

Mary's covering letter to Coleridge spoke charmingly of Englefield: "My little Cottage is retired and Comfortable. There I mean to remain (if indeed I live so long) till Christmas. But it is not surrounded with the romantic Scenery of your chosen retreat: it is not, my dear Sir! the nursery of sublime thoughts—the abode of Peace—the solitude of Nature's Wonders. O! Skiddaw! I think if I could but once more contemplate thy Summit, I should never quit the prospect till my eyes were closed for ever."

"O Poole!" cried Coleridge in a letter to his dearest friend, "that the woman had but been married to a noble Being, what a noble Being she herself would have been."

Toward the end of November he sent Mary a glowing love poem entitled "Alcaeus to Sappho." She published the *jeu d'esprit* in the *Morning Post*, perhaps a little vain over the concluding stanza:

Then grant one smile, tho' it should mean
  A thing of doubtful birth;
That I may say these eyes have seen
  The fairest face on earth!

Ban and Susan had left Llanwrest and arrived in London on October 30. On November 17 the *Oracle* said: "General Tarleton and his amiable consort, since their return from Wales, have been on a visit to Lord Gwydyr and Lady Willoughby at Langley Park. The General and his Lady have left Whitehall for Houghton, on a visit to Lord and Lady Cholmondeley."

As the Tarletons waited for Christmas at Houghton, Mary was dying at Englefield in Old Windsor. She was now so weak that she could no longer bear the pain of being carried from bed to sofa, yet "she retained a perfect composure of spirits, and, in the intervals of extreme bodily suffering, would listen, while her daughter read to her, with apparent interest and collectedness of thought, frequently making observations on what would probably take place when she had passed that *bourn*, whence no traveler returns."

About December 1 she completed the arrangement of her *Poetical Works*. On December 18 Longman and Rees published her *Lyrical Tales*. Next day the *Morning Post* published "All Alone," which Daniel Stuart called "one of the most affecting productions that has lately issued from the English Press."

In it the poetess lamented:

> My father never will return,
>   He rests beneath the sea-green wave;
> I have no kindred left, to mourn
>   When I am hid in yonder grave;
> No one! To dress with flowers the stone:—
>   Then—surely I am left alone!

The news from Englefield was grim. Peter Pindar wrote the invalid a painfully cheerful letter, filled with chatter and whimsy. "I have just heard that you have been exceedingly unwell: for God's sake do not be foolish enough to die yet, as you possess stamina for an hundred years, and a poetical mind that cannot be soon replaced. Leave Englefield-green then for London, and let us enjoy our usual laugh and whim. I am much older than you, and yet, I think the Devil at a great distance."

The whimsy helped, but did not cure the dropsy. The accumulation of water on Mary's chest threatened to suffocate her. Maria Elizabeth and a young friend supported her in their arms or propped her up on pillows.

On Christmas Eve she asked "How near is Christmas Day?" They told her.

"Yet I shall never see it," she said.

Toward midnight Mary cried, "O God! just and merciful God, help me support this agony!"

Next evening she sank into a lethargic stupor, from which, when Maria Elizabeth approached, she roused herself to whisper, "My darling Mary." In a few minutes she fell into a coma.

She breathed her last at noon on December 26, 1800.

"Mrs. Robinson, the well known Perdita and long noticeable in this and other papers for her poetical effusions, report states as having died at Englefield Green on Friday last. For some years she is said to have been in indigent circumstances," was all James Boaden could say in the *Oracle*. But some friendly pen prepared a long obituary, containing the outward facts of Mary's life, and published it in both the *Courier* and the *Morning Post*.

The *Sun*, in its final tribute on December 31, 1800, said: "Mrs. Robinson certainly possessed great poetical powers. Her imagination was vivid, and fraught with a variety of imagery. Her language was rich and glowing. If she had obeyed the impulse of her own genius, her compositions would have displayed a beautiful simplicity, but she was unluckily ensnared by the DELLA CRUSCA School, and was often betrayed into a gaudy luxuriance of expression. Several of her Poems are, however, wholly undebased by this ornamental extravagance, and are indeed simple, interesting, and beautiful."

Mary Robinson's dearest memories centered around Old Windsor. Here she had laughed away time's viewless wings with the only man she ever loved. "Let me be buried in Old Windsor church-yard," she requested just before her death, adding that she wished to be buried with all possible simplicity. Her wishes were respected. Through the rows of majestic elms they bore her to a grave near a spreading larch. But of all the great world of art and fashion that she had known, only two came to walk behind her coffin: William Godwin and Peter Pindar.

A day later two persons received each a lock of auburn hair that once fell over a pair of laughing blue eyes. If there was poetry and justice these two were a General and a Prince.

Her friend and fellow poet, the Reverend Samuel Taylor Coleridge, pronounced a benediction upon her memory. In a letter to Maria Elizabeth he said: "In this Feeling I cultivated your Mother's acquaintance, thrice happy if I could have soothed her sorrows, or if the feeble Lamp of my friendship could have yielded her one ray of Hope or Guidance— your Mother had indeed a good, a very good, heart—and in my eyes, and in my belief, was in her latter life—a blameless Woman."

Friends erected a simple monument over Mary Robinson's grave. On one side of it they engraved these verses she had written for her tomb:

> O Thou! whose cold and senseless heart
> Ne'er knew affection's struggling sigh,
> Pass on, nor vaunt the Stoic's art,
> Nor mock this grave with tearless eye.
>
> Far oft when evening's purple glow
> Shall slowly fade from yonder steep
> Fast o'er this sod the tear shall flow
> From eyes that only wake to weep.
>
> No wealth had she, no power to sway;
> Yet rich in worth, and learning's store:
> She *wept her summer hours* away,
> She heard the wintry storm no more.

Yet o'er this low and silent spot,
Full many a bud of Spring shall wave,
While she, by all, save one, forgot.
SHALL SNATCH A WREATH BEYOND THE GRAVE!

On the other side they placed a simple legend:

Mrs.
Mary Robinson,
Author of Poems,
and other literary works,
died the 26th of December, 1800,
at Englefield Cottage,
in Surrey,
aged 43 years.

35

Recall to Siberia

*B*ANASTRE TARLETON was happy, well-to-do, and reformed. Recognition was his, both social and military. On January 1, 1801, the day after they had paid their last tribute to Mary Robinson, the newspapers announced his promotion to the rank of lieutenant general. A week later the War Office announced his appointment as the colonel of the 22nd Regiment of Light Dragoons. He would receive full pay and allowances as long as his regiment remained in active service. Newspapers hinted that Lord Gwydyr was still the artist of Tarleton's fortune.

On January 15 the *Oracle* noted: "Lord Gwydyr's park at Langley is supposed to contain more game than any other enclosure of the same size in the Kingdom." On January 28 it reported: "The Duke of York and friends went yesterday on a shooting party to Langley. His Royal Highness and Lord Gwydyr are first rate shots. Lord Villiers and General Tarleton were of the party."

All winter and spring Ban and Susan remained in London enjoying the hospitality of Lord Gwydyr and Earl Cholmondeley. On January 18 they went with Susan's great kinfolk to the Queen's Birthday Ball. And on February 4 the Duke of York was back with Tarleton for another go at the pheasants of Langley Park.

During the winter session Banastre was regular in his attendance in Parliament. As befitted a reformed Radical Whig in the service of the Tory government, he remained silent. He avoided his former cronies, visited Brooks's Club less frequently, and was careful to be seen at the King's levees. On June 4 he and Susan attended the King's Birthday Ball.

He was often at the headquarters of the Duke of York. Occasionally he visited Oatlands. So no one was surprised when the *Morning Post* announced on June 14: "General Tarleton, having been appointed to the staff in Ireland, has set off for that part of the United Kingdom."

On July 25 Ban and Susan reached Cork. Soon they were settled at an estate called Richmond, and he was afield with his troops. He took seriously his duties as commander of the Southern District of Ireland.

Perhaps, with discontent and disaffection rampant among the Irish, Napoleon might try invasion. The British staff remembered General Hoche's expedition to Bantry Bay in 1796. They remembered the French troops who landed with General Humbert and surrendered to Lord Cornwallis in 1798. Green was their memory of Wolfe Tone, and greener still that of the bloody uprising crushed at Vinegar Hill by General Lake.

So, after a tour of inspection, General Tarleton drew up plans to prevent rebellion and thwart invasion. A synopsis of these he sent to the Duke of York:

Richmond, Sept. 4, 1801

If an enemy should effect a landing from this time to the 25th of March between Younghall and Renmare river with 5-6-7 or 8000 men, I shall endeavour to beat him to the southward of Cork, using every precaution in the operation, risking nothing too far, but maintaining those advantages & that ascendency which we possess over an invading army. All possible information of the proceedings of both parties shall be regularly transmitted to Headquarters.

If the Enemy's forces should amount to a larger number, and extend to 15 or 16 thousand men, I shall throw every obstacle in his way, and endeavour to preserve Cork, not however hazarding to an extreme the general safety of the country, or the good of his Majesty's Service. In case it is not advisable under the existing circumstances to enter upon a general action for the protection of Cork, I shall measure back my way to the Black Water river (which within the months I have described will not have a great variety of practicable fording places) using upon my route all possible expedients to delay the enemy, whilst the King's forces and loyal inhabitants may concentrate their strength in that part of the District, and derive advantage & security from the talents and presence of the Commander of the Forces.

I trust this general outline is properly traced—and it would be adhered to by me, if nothing unforeseen occurred—at the same time I am sensible that the operations of the Enemy must in a great measure direct the proceedings of the General Officer in command.

With respect to Secret-intelligence which is generally obtained with great difficulty, and expense, but which, if properly conducted, affords the surest and cheapest road to success, I shall leave that subject to the different General Officers in command, throughout the Southern District, and trust to their information, until disaffection begins to Embody or the menaced invasion takes place. In either of these cases I shall take a leading and active part in that branch of the Service, which I consider as highly essential to the general Safety of the Army, and the advancement of military glory.

As soon as the weather settles, and I hope, before the arrival of the enemy, I shall esteem it my duty to make frequent promenades with the troops in marching order. I shall assemble the garrisons of Cork, Bandon, Kinsale, Mallow and Fermoy, between their respective quarters, in order to accustom them to the features of the Country, and the mode of taking post always remembering that sufficient time is allowed for their return to their own cantonments in the evening.

I have thus stated very briefly my general ideas upon the military points subject to my present inspection. If explanation or alteration, should either be wished or required, I shall most readily append to the demand or conform to the order.

Ban. Tarleton
Lt. Genl.

From the Horse Guards on September 20 the Duke replied that Tarleton's letter had given him some "ideas" and asked for amplifications of the plans for using light dragoons. In a friendly vein he concluded: "Pray give my compliments to Mrs. Tarleton. I hope the air of Ireland agrees with her."

Immediately Banastre replied:

Richmond, Sept. 28th, 1801.

Sir

Your Royal Highness wishes me to detail my reasons relative to the useful employment of Cavalry in Ireland. Without trespassing much upon your Royal Highness's time, I think I can advance and support propositions, which are so clear and conclusive that they appear to me to be irresistible. The face of the country, which I have seen, and as far as I can learn from others, throughout the Southern district, is bold and commanding—The hills and vallies are extensive—The roads in every direction are more numerous and harder, than any I have ever seen in any country—The enclosures are larger in general than those of the maritime counties of England, Norfolk excepted—And the sight of the Eye is not interrupted or restrained by woods or a barren expanse. In such a country as I have described, most military men will allow, that an army composed of infantry, artillery, and cavalry, if it is directed with skill and quickness, must have the advantage over one, which is deficient in the two latter arms. A superiority of *cavalry* (which word according to my idea of it I will hereafter explain) will enable the officer commanding such an army to advance his posts—cover the country—and consequently increase all the wants and difficulties of an invader. Whilst it must be obvious if his force consists almost entirely of infantry, that he meet the foe, as the foe would wish, namely, upon equal terms. In the meantime uncurbed disaffection may hover on his flanks, and in his rear, and in a country like this the communication with the Enemy would be unrestrained, except the King's infantry was quadruple to that of the enemy, and even then the division of such an army might expose the public cause to ruin because the invader would have the option to select his own operations, if he was unmolested and unrestrained by the maneuvre of the cavalry.

By the word Cavalry, I not only mean Light Dragoons, but I include mounted riflemen, & companies of infantry mounted on horseback, the latter never to act on their horses, but to accompany the two former in all their movements. The utility of such an institution (especially in Ireland) would equal the wishes of the warmest friend to his country—Lord Cornwallis cannot forget the Services he received from a Corps composed in this manner, but of bad materials, in America, and such a corps or corps, with the addition of the mounted artillery might be employed to more advantage in this country—because the extent of view is greater, the roads better—and the forage in Ireland abundant to excess.—

Why Light Dragoons have been unemployed in this country, or rather debased by being moved only as Marechausse—mail coach men, I cannot explain to myself? Even that disgraceful business has been ill done—the rebels having succeeded in every attempt made upon the coaches—whilst the expense to the public has been enormous, and the whole of the cavalry by such an application of it, has nearly lost its discipline—its vigour, and that self confidence which good cavalry always possesses. Why the cavalry has been posted in the interior of the island, I am equally at a loss to guess? But I beg your Royal Highness's pardon, I do not mean to criticise the conduct of others, but merely by explaining my own conceptions upon the advantageous employment of cavalry in Ireland.— The face of the country is the Enquiry which cavalry officers pay attention to, before they decide upon the question whether a country is good, bad, or indifferent for cavalry movements. I have exhibited above, what I think of the features of this country, I will now proceed to compare it with those in which I have either lived or served—or even visited—I cannot however, help observing here, that fox-hounds and hare-hounds are kept all over the country. Cannot light troops be employed where the young and old take their amusement? I follow this question then by saying, that this country, according to my judgment, is more fit for cavalry operations, than that part of Germany situated on the banks of the Rhine,—is better than any part of Holland, except just about Maestricht—better than America, better than Portugal—better than Wales—and equal to most parts of England, especially since the latter country has been so much intersected by canals.

If, therefore, it is only conceded to me, that this is an indifferent country for the operations of cavalry, I must request your Royal Highness to take a survey of the different objects, with which, in such a situation, the officer in command, may have to contend, and by which he may be assailed. In the first place it is his duty to prepare himself against an active and skilful invading enemy. If he has not a good cavalry—and the enemy comes with a larger force of infantry than his own—the affair is soon over—communication being immediately opened with the country—not so—if he can keep the country in ignorance by restraining him with his cavalry.

Secondly he must look to the numerous inhabitants of this country who unfortunately for us, are considered, and I am afraid with truth, as disaffected. By disaffected, I mean that they look upon themselves (with justice or otherwise I shall not pretend to say) as oppressed by the upper classes of Society, and are ready for any change. If he cannot contain the enemy's parties, how will he be able to keep them in order? In short if his cavalry, for with that aim it must principally be done, cannot serve the double purpose of restraining the enemy and intimidating the inhabitants, how desperate would the public cause become in four or five days, if the enemy effected a landing with a force exceeding 12,000 men, in any part of Ireland? I believe I need not press this argument any further having trespassed too long already on your Royal Highness's time, I shall conclude then by saying, that I think I have shewn that the face of the country in general in this island is favorable to cavalry, and that successful consequences must arise from a proper application and combination of artillery, infantry and cavalry.

Ban. Tarleton
Lt. Gen.

ↄ№

But Lieutenant General Tarleton never had an opportunity to use cavalry in Ireland. Prime Minister Pitt found terms offered by Napoleon acceptable, and England ended the first phase of her struggle with France. On March 25, 1802, Lord Cornwallis, as envoy plenipotentiary for Great Britain, signed the treaty of the Peace of Amiens. His task accomplished, Pitt resigned.

Great Britain immediately began demobilizing. There were too many troops in Ireland. After long deliberation, the Duke of York, Prime Minister Addington, and Speaker Hobart decided on "removing all the Lieutenant Generals from the Irish Staff, as a means not only of economy, but as tending to facilitate future arrangements."

In accordance with this decision, on June 10 the War Office notified Lieutenant General Tarleton of his recall from Ireland. In the meantime King George had acceded to the wishes of his weary people and dissolved Parliament. The Whigs and Tories began squaring off for a general election. Instead of returning to London, on June 25 Ban and Susan left Cork for Liverpool.

In the three and a half years since Tarleton's return to active duty, his politics had become confused. During his service in Portugal and Ireland he had been absent from Parliament, and during the brief periods of his attendance, he had not made a single speech of importance. He had deserted Fox, but he had disdained to join Pitt.

For a time he was a member without a party. He had long admired Henry Addington and, as the general election approached, he solved his dilemma. He pledged his support to the new Prime Minister.

Immediately upon his arrival in Liverpool Tarleton announced his candidacy. He appealed to the Independent voters, and few cared whether his change of political views was a matter of conscience or a return for military promotion. After nine years of war, the people were tired, and the Hustings was peaceful.

The election began on July 6, with Lieutenant General Tarleton, Major General Isaac Gascoyne, Joseph Birch, and Francis Chalmer standing the poll. At the close of the first day Gascoyne led the poll with 115 votes. Tarleton was second with 55 votes. Birch was third with 51 votes, and Chalmer trailed with only 16 votes. The light voting disappointed all the candidates.

Tarleton immediately issued a card:

Brother Townsmen:
    The figures of the poll express the present state of it; but the experience of your kindness, and a consciousness of the faithful discharge of my public duties, raise in my mind the hope of a speedy and flattering alteration.
                        I have the honor to be,
                        Brother Townsmen,
                            Your faithful and Affectionate Servant,
                                Ban. Tarleton
July 6, 1802

During the evening Ban canvassed the Whigs and Tories. Everywhere he found floating rumors. His enemies were predicting that soon after election, General Tarleton would return to his command in Ireland.

Next morning he addressed a letter to the Independent voters:

Brother Townsmen,
    In the course of my canvass yesterday evening (which was highly satisfactory) I met with several reports amongst the freemen, relative to my holding a high position in Ireland. I beg leave to lay before the public eye an official letter upon that subject.
                        Royal Hospital Dublin, June 10, 1802

Sir,

I am commanded by the commander of the forces to acquaint you, that your appointment as Lieut. Gen. upon the staff will cease on the 24th inst.

F. Beckwith, Military Secretary

I leave the fabricators and reporters of such tales to the contemplation of their own designs, and the benefit they will derive from them, when the truth is presented to my brother townsmen. With the highest respect and affection I remain your faithful servant,

Ban. Tarleton

Liverpool, July 7, 1802

That evening the figures of the poll showed Gascoyne still leading, with 381 votes. Tarleton had 228 and Birch 182, a gain of 42 votes for the General. Satisfied with this speedy alteration, he issued another card:

Brother Townsmen,

The advantage we have gained, and our present superiority at the poll, evinces our strength; but we must not relax our exertions in order to secure a respectable majority tomorrow.

I have the honor to be,
Brother Townsmen,
With the highest respect
and gratitude
Ban. Tarleton

July 7, 1802

In came all the Tarletons, great and small, Whig and Tory, and voted for Banastre. The wounds of the bitter campaign of 1796 had healed, and Thomas and John gave their brother their financial backing as well as their votes. On the third day he pulled farther ahead of Birch.

On July 9, the fourth day of balloting, Birch and Chalmer struck their colors. After a listless campaign an apathetic general election had ended. From the Tories, Gascoyne had received 884 votes. From his Independent friends among the Whigs and Tories, Tarleton had received 600 votes. The disorganized Whigs had given Birch 447 votes, and some 31 protest votes had gone to Chalmer.

For the third time Ban Tarleton's Independent friends had elected him to Parliament. On July 12 many of them paid 15 shillings each to dine with him at Bate's Hotel. Gaily they sang:

> In the midst of these dangers did Tarleton appear,
> A friend to his country, a stranger to fear;
> His monarch, approving the deeds he has done,
> Promoted his rank, for the laurels he's won!

But something was lacking. Gone was the enthusiasm of former years. Banastre was still popular. His manners were still elegant and his talk was still charming. But had the Whigs nominated a man like William Roscoe, Tarleton would have been defeated.

Ban and Susan returned to London and settled in Grosvenor Street. Under her tutelage he had become thoroughly respectable in both public and private life. He had even stopped badgering the King's ministers. Between December 2, 1802, and March 6, 1804, he kept profoundly silent in Parliament. Newspapers remarked on the elegance of their horses and carriages and everyone admired the emeralds surrounded by diamonds which Ban had given Susan in memory of his Green Horse. They attended the rout of the Duchess of Marlborough and were among the guests at the rout of the Countess of Derby. So was the Prince of Wales.

As he followed Susan into society, everyone began noticing that the graying General was jealous. No matter whom they visited, nor at whose table they dined, he insisted on sitting beside his wife. Amused, Lady Morpeth wrote her sister: "General and Mrs. Tarleton are thought too conjugal as they always sit on the same chair and eat out of the same plate."

But events were shaping that would remove the Tarletons from London social life. Napoleon had become so threatening that on May 18, 1803, Great Britain declared war. During the summer the British mobilized and deployed their forces. On September 25 the Duke of York ordered Lieutenant General Tarleton back to Ireland, as second in command to General Henry Edward Fox.

Knowing that the Duke planned to recall General Fox for duty on the Continent, Tarleton sailed over to Cork confidently expecting to succeed to the command. But on October 20, even before he and Susan could get settled, the War Office ordered him to relieve the Duke of Cumberland as commandant of the Severn Military District in western England. The Duke sent Lord Cathcart to command in Ireland.

"General Tarleton, agreeable to the etiquette of the Army, could not serve under Lord Cathcart, who is a junior officer," said the *Morning Post* of October 26 in speculating on the abrupt reassignment. The *Oracle* refuted this statement. It proved Cathcart the senior by citing the history of the British Legion.

On October 27, just one month after they had left for Cork, Ban and Susan trailed back into London. He was disappointed and angry. In Parliament he said bitterly: "I was second in command in Ireland and had expected to succeed to the chief command in that Country. When appointed to the command I at present hold, I considered myself as sent to Siberia."

But Tarleton's recall was not demotion. At Boulogne, Napoleon had begun massing men and material for an invasion of England. The British expected to fight the French on the beaches somewhere between Dover and Plymouth. To command the home defense the Duke of York chose Lieutenant Generals Moore, Simcoe, and Tarleton: he sent Moore to Dover; Simcoe to the Southern Military District, with headquarters at Plymouth; and Tarleton to defend western England and Wales, where the French had landed Colonel Tate's brigands in 1797.

In selecting his commanders perhaps the Duke followed the advice of Lord Cornwallis. As young officers the three had fought in the American War and had seen militia defeat veterans. They had learned guerrilla tactics and they could be trusted to work with the volunteers and to create fencible regiments. And their reputations as fighting men would inspire the militia.

Nor did these defenders lack advice. That old military analyst Colonel George Hanger, between naps in his easy chair in the Sol Arms in Tottenham Court Road, wrote *Reflections on the Menaced Invasion and the Means of protecting the Capital by preventing the Enemy from landing in any Part contiguous to it.*

The Severn Military District covered the counties of Gloucester, Monmouth, Brecknock, Radnor, Carmathen, Cardigan, and Pembroke. In his general orders the Duke instructed Tarleton to be sedulous in watching the anchorages in Bristol and St. George's channels and in guarding against surprise landings. He instructed him to establish all necessary fortifications along the coast and to train and maintain the volunteer and militia regiments.

Ban and Susan left immediately for Bath and settled in York House. As there were 16,000 volunteers in the Severn District, he began field inspections as soon as possible. On November 18 he rode over to Bristol and reviewed the Royal Bristol Volunteers. They were commanded by Major General Fisher, who was old, easygoing, and lax in discipline. Tarleton was critical in his report, and a feud sprang up between the two generals. Many letters passed between them. On January 8, 1804, Banastre wrote him:

Sir,
I am sorry you receive so many applications for leave of absence at this juncture. As I am, however, aware that Officers of the Militia have local concerns of great importance to themselves, I shall endeavour to indulge them as far as I can do with propriety —I am certain I need not remind the Officers of the Militia, that we have a public duty at this crisis, paramount to every private consideration whatever, and on the first signal of alarm how necessary it will be for each individual to repair to his regiment.

Ban. Tarleton
Lt. Gen.

"General Tarleton reviewed the Bath Volunteers," reported the *Morning Post* of January 9. By the end of February he had finished his inspection, and with Susan he returned to London for the remainder of the session of Parliament. On March 6 he spoke twice on Yorke's Bill for the Consolidation of the Volunteer Troops.

Immediately after the adjournment of Parliament, the Tarletons returned to Bath. Nothing of consequence happened in the Severn District, and Ban disappeared in the routine of a small command. He spent his time in writing letters, holding conferences, and reviewing troops. Small but vexing problems came to him:

Bath, July 24

My dear General,

As your letter of yesterday's post is not pleasant—let us both try at least to render it as palatable as possible—I have no objection to Major Mitchell, but on the contrary, I hear an excellent Report of him—but I confess that I part from Power with Regret—He has rendered himself highly useful to me—by the knowledge he has acquired of the District—& his mode of doing business has recommended him to everybody about me.

For these reasons & the very advanced state of Mrs. Power's pregnancy I beg the longest indulgence that can be granted with regard to his removal from the Staff of the Severn District.

Yours Dear General
Very truly
Ban. Tarleton

The situation at Bristol worsened, and during the summer and fall many letters of complaint passed between Tarleton and Fisher. Finally the old general allowed his troops to become mutinous. On December 13 Tarleton wrote a letter to General Calvert reporting the condition: "I feel it an imperious duty to state to you for the information of the Commander-in-Chief, that Maj. Genl. Fisher either on account of his age or the feebleness of his character as a military man, falls so much daily in the estimation of the Militia Officers, that serious apprehensions may reasonably be entertained in the Corps now at Bristol losing considerably in point of discipline—I was obliged to go over to Stapleton Prison yesterday to check a spirit of insubordination in the S. Devon Regiment."

Left to herself by her busy husband, Susan Priscilla passed the long days in reading and singing, playing the spinet and painting. She attended church and reflected at length on religious matters. She lavished affection upon her pets. Her greatest joy was the return to London for Parliament. She could again mingle in society with the Cholmondeleys and Gwydyrs.

In Parliament, General Tarleton was quiet until Wilberforce revived the issue of the slave trade. On February 15, 1805, he spoke vigorously in defense of the trade. His arguments were familiar: "There are in Liverpool alone above 10,000 persons completely engaged in this trade, besides countless numbers who are in some way or other affected by it. I have received instructions from my constituents to oppose the honorable gentleman's intentions with all my power."

As the members wrangled over questions far removed from the war effort, Napoleon was rushing his preparations for invasion. At Boulogne 130,000 troops waited only a favorable opportunity to cross the English Channel. Should the French Navy seize control of the sea for only a few days there would be fighting on the beaches of southern England.

But the defenses against invasion were in readiness. The General told the House: "The militiamen, as I have convinced myself by a very close inspection, are highly disciplined, and want to be accustomed a little to the regular service, to make them as good soldiers as any in it."

During the debate on the Irish Enlistment Bill, Tarleton criticized members for their lack of realism: "In the third year of a war, like the present, of the most formidable description ever known, it is rather extraordinary to hear gentlemen speak as if it were a mere *guerre de pots de chambre*, as an illustrious character denominated one of the petty civil wars of France!

"The effect of having a large disposable force would be to change the nature of the war from defensive to offensive, to free the country from the apprehension of becoming itself the scene of war, a calamity which every man who is acquainted with war and the scenes that accompany it, will wish to remove far from any place he has affection for."

Upon their return to Bath, Ban and Susan settled into their routine. In early September came a diversion. His sister Bridget came down from Fairfield to spend some time at the mineral springs at Clifton. On September 11 they drove over to visit her.

Apprehensive that this unannounced trip to Bristol might have been misunderstood by old General Fisher, Tarleton wrote him next day:

My Dear General,

It may appear strange to you to have heard that I was at Bristol yesterday, and to find that I did not pay my respects to you—

My visit was of a domestic kind—a dear sister of mine has been sent to Clifton to seek health by drinking the waters of that place— To her therefore, my attentions were solely confined and I returned immediately after I had seen her to Bath—

Your feelings, I am convinced will sympathize with mine on this occasion and render every apology unnecessary—

I purpose seeing the three regiments of Militia at 12 o'clock on Wednesday the 18th at Durdham Down.

Yours Dear General
Very truly
Ban. Tarleton

ᏬᎾ

Meanwhile in far-off India old Lord Cornwallis was on his last campaign. After signing the Treaty of Amiens, his Lordship had spent three happy years at Culford. William Pitt, who had resumed the office of Prime Minister, had then asked him to go out to India again, to relieve Marquis Wellesley and his brother, General Sir Arthur Wellesley, as governor-general and commander in chief.

Although sixty-six years old and in declining health, Cornwallis had obeyed the summons of his King. In March 1805 he sailed for Calcutta. The day after his arrival he wrote General Gerard Lake: "It is my earnest desire, if it should be possible, to put an end to this most unprofitable and ruinous warfare."

Soon he started inland to take command of the British troops. As his barge was being towed slowly up the Ganges, he became desperately ill. Carried ashore, he died on October 25 and was buried at Ghazipur.

Close friends succeeded to the commands he had held. Earl Moira was appointed master general of Ordnance and constable of the Tower of London. Lieutenant General Simcoe was appointed commander in chief in India, but he died at Exeter before sailing for the East. Sir Arthur Wellesley became colonel of the 33rd Regiment and with it there seemed to come the mantle of Cornwallis.

But nothing came to the dragoon who was once highest in his Lordship's estimation. In the Severn District he struggled to keep the Home Defenses alerted. But for a lieutenant general the scope of affairs continued to be discouragingly limited. His correspondence dealt with petty details or with individuals. Shall a deserter be flogged or sent overseas unwhipped? To Lieutenant Colonel Roy he wrote:

Bath, Octbr. 20th 1805

Sir,

I have received a report thro' the proper channel relative to the death of a deserter—As the Corporal only performed his duty I beg every protection may be afforded him—The Coroner's inquest, I make no doubt, will bring in a verdict of justifiable homicide.

Ban. Tarleton
Lt. Genl.

Next day, October 21, 1805, came one of the great climaxes of the war. Off Cape Trafalgar on the coast of Spain, Admiral Lord Nelson defeated the combined fleets of Spain and France. Tarleton realized the significance of the victory. In the House of Commons he later assured the nation: "The late memorable and glorious victory at Trafalgar has put an end to all apprehension of invasion."

The strain of the war, however, continued its toll. The health of William Pitt became so wretched that Sir Walter Farquhar, his doctor, advised him to try the waters of Bath. Leaving London on December 7 he reached Bath on December 11 and went to Lord Harrowby's residence in Laura Place.

As commanding general in the Severn District, Tarleton paid a courtesy visit to the Prime Minister. Pitt was affable and conciliatory. Soon these political enemies found that their views on the war coincided. Both realized that there could be no lasting peace with Napoleon. The war had to be fought until victory. For this the General pledged his support to the Minister. Banastre Tarleton joined the Tories.

Then came the news of Napoleon's victory at Austerlitz. Pitt sickened, and his doctors rushed him to London. For a few days he seemed to mend. On January 12, 1806, he wrote Marquis Wellesley: "I am recovering rather slowly from a series of stomach complaints, followed by severe attacks of gout, but I believe I am now in the way of real amendment."

But despite his optimism, Pitt had just a handful of days left him. Sir Arthur Wellesley came to see him, and during their talk Pitt fainted. Soon he began sinking. As he lost consciousness, he whispered to Stanhope: "My country! How I leave my country!"

William Pitt died on January 23, and his sorrowing country accorded him a grave in Westminster Abbey. Addressing the House on the occasion of Pitt's funeral, General Tarleton said in eulogy: "The last six months of his administration were the most brilliant in his life."

Charles Fox was now the most distinguished man in English public life. When King George asked Lord Grenville to form a ministry, his Majesty raised no objection to the selection of Fox as Secretary of State for Foreign Affairs. From the leading Whigs and Tories, Fox and Grenville chose a Cabinet which gained popular favor as All-the-Talents.

When news of Tarleton's defection reached Liverpool there was consternation among the Whigs. One of their leaders, signing himself "Ignotus," on February 8 published "A Letter Addressed to the Earl of Sefton." Of Tarleton he said: "Attached to Mr. Fox by a similarity of habits, he always blindly voted in opposition, except on the grand question of the Slave Trade, when he thought himself obliged to support the interests of his constituents, a mode of conduct which was persisted in till the Addington administration was formed and the Peace of Amiens affected."

After mentioning Tarleton's visit to Pitt, Ignotus continued: "General Tarleton, by having, in the first place, abandoned the cause of Mr. Fox, and his adherents, and ultimately attaching himself to Mr. Pitt, and supporting those measures which he had so long decried, has become completely a *Political Weathercock*."

During the ministry of All-the-Talents the Weathercock from Bath was without a leader. He followed neither Grenville nor Fox. In the debates he confined himself largely to military affairs.

"I disapprove highly of encroaching upon the Volunteer System," he said on April 14, in discussing the bill to reduce the volunteer force. "No less than 300,000 men have voluntarily come forward, and have already proved themselves extremely serviceable to the country, and are by this change totally unfixed and unhinged. Is this the proper time for such dangerous experiments, when the enemy may attempt invasion during the course of the summer?"

Secretary Fox was dying of dropsy. From his unfinished work he chose the project nearest his heart, and with a final display of influence he moved that Parliament abolish the slave trade.

General Tarleton had the greatest objections to this bill. He spoke of the rise of the commercial city of Liverpool. He told again of her ships in the African trade. Again he proclaimed Liverpool the nursery of England's seamen. And again—and for the last time—he lamented the value of her property about to be destroyed.

The final vote on the bill came on June 10. Just before Parliament abolished forever the slave trade, Tarleton turned upon Fox. With all the bitterness of a former friend he cried to the members of the House: "This resolution is wholly uncalled for in any part of the country, and was introduced seemingly for no other purpose than to show he has the power to carry his point."

The breach never healed. Soon Fox was too ill to attend Parliament and retired to the house of the Duke of Devonshire at Chiswick. There he died on September 13. The nation mourned his death and buried him beside Pitt in Westminster Abbey. But from Bath came no eulogy from the General who had once blindly followed Charles James Fox.

36
The Weathercock

$\mathcal{T}$HE DEATHS OF Pitt and Fox and the elevation of Addington to the peerage as Lord Sidmouth freed Tarleton of all political allegiance. He chose to remain Tory. As soon as the date for a general election had been set, he announcd his candidacy:

> Brother Townsmen,
>
> A report has just reached me, that *Parliament is immediately to be Dissolved*, and I seize the earliest opportunity of announcing to you, that as soon as I can be exonerated from the punctilios of my military situation, I will hasten toward my native town, in order to present myself to you, as a candidate for the high honor of again Representing You.
>
> After four contests, and three successive returns to Parliament, there is nothing unknown between us. I am thoroughly and gratefully impressed by your Kindness and confidence, and with all humility, I offer to your remembrance and consideration, my Parliamentary conduct, during the last four years.
>
> I have the honor to be,
Brother Townsmen
Your obliged and devoted Servant
Ban. Tarleton
>
> Bath, 17th October, 1806

Lord Charles Grey had succeeded Fox as the leader of the Whigs. He had long been a personal friend of Tarleton, both in the House and in Brooks's Club, but in partisan politics friendship remained an illusion. Grey encouraged the Whigs in Liverpool to support the candidacy of William Roscoe.

Roscoe was a wealthy banker of Liverpool, a man of pure principles and simple manners. As a scholar and author he had won an international reputation with his *Life of Lorenzo de Medici* and his *Life and Pontificate of Leo the Tenth*. In politics, however, Roscoe was an amateur.

The Whig Party had sent Lord Stanley, the Earl of Sefton, and Admiral Sir Isaac Coffin to canvass the voters in his behalf. "Little expecting an opposition in the outset," wrote a historian, "the friends of the old members had neglected to secure the out-voters who were very numerous, and indeed fully adequate to turn the scale in any arduous contest."

The Whigs quickly spotted the weakness in the strategy of the Tories. They provided funds and transportation for the out-voters supporting Roscoe. They then published a broadside which detailed Tarleton's desertion of their party.

The broadside reported Pitt's visit to Bath and said that the General had greatly desired to see the Minister, "but having uniformly opposed the measures of his administration, he was doubtful how he should be received. He determined, however, to wait upon the Minister, and bid him Welcome to Bath." It said that Pitt was polite, and Tarleton quickly came to the point. The gentleman holding the stamp office in Liverpool was ill and not expected to recover, and the General wished to name his successor. "To this proposition Mr. Pitt, without hesitation acceded; but on the express condition, that he should immediately renounce all connections with his old political adherents. Accordingly, the General addressed a letter to an *Illustrious Personage*, in which he expressed his sincere regrets that he should find it necessary to desert 'that illustrious band of Patriots.' "

Unfortunately, the stamp distributor recovered, and Pitt died. "And the General's letter has been handed about in the higher political circles —the avowal of his own perfidy—and the record of his own disgrace!"

Among the pasquinades issued by the Whigs was a handbill announcing a performance of the celebrated magician, Mr. Banastre, "who has had the honor of playing his tricks before the imperial Parliament of Great Britain."

1st. He will, to the astonishment of his audience, turn his coat 16 times in one minute.

2nd. He will, by his extraordinary powers, display the manner in which, in the summer of 1802, without any visible means, he led by the nose 600 persons in a populous town in the north.

3rd. He will produce his patent leaping Pole, with which he will take a surprising leap from the Exchange to the Stamp Office.

4th. He will likewise exhibit his wonderful tricks of Parliamentary Legerdemain which he had the honour of performing at Bath.

Currently William Roscoe was writing verse for children, to be collected in *The Buttefly's Ball and the Grasshopper's Feast*. With a fine disaffection for Tarleton to warm him, perhaps he also wrote:

> My three-fingered hand I keep constantly showing
> But the once blind electors are all grown too knowing,
> Of Roscoe and freedom they're constantly crowing;
> O! I fear I shall nevermore say Aye or No.
>
> O! My poor wounded hand, and all my fine clack, sirs,
> Will serve no more Obi or three-fingered Jack, sirs;
> For Roscoe and Freedom they shout, 'tis a fact, sirs;
> Alas! I shall never more say Aye or No.

The poll was serious, but there was an occasional chuckle. As a Freeman of Liverpool, Tarleton had the right to vote. During a slack period he stepped up to his bar and voted for himself. Immediately the Roscoeites hung out a placard:

> I have voted for myself. Tarleton for Ever. Huzza

Since Roscoe had no vote, the Tarletonites replied:

> I wish I could vote for myself. Roscoe

General Gascoyne took the lead on the first day. Their failure to distance Roscoe aroused Tarleton's followers, and on November 4 there was a riot.

> As the condidates were preparing to leave the hustings . . .
> . . . the tallies of General Tarleton which consisted in a considerable degree, of persons who follow the occupation of butchers, were led to the hustings by a man on horseback, brandishing a sham sword, and with a real sabre at his side, in defiance of decency, if not of law, and accompanied by one of their own craft carrying a butcher's axe.
> When the friends of Mr. Roscoe brought forward the chair in which it was intended to convey him to his own house, its admission was resisted by the party of General Tarleton, and an affray ensued, which for about half an hour threatened the most alarming consequences.

When the factions had cooled off, Roscoe told his followers: "What has just happened I shall regret to the last day of my life. But it gives me pleasure to say that it did not originate with us. It originated with those who cannot bear with patience the mortification of defeat.

"To expect that you would suffer yourselves to be attacked and murdered without resistance is more than the most peaceable candidate could expect of you. Be assured that a strict enquiry shall be made into this most disgraceful transaction, and that I shall not rest satisfied until the authors and actors shall be submitted to the animadversions of the insulted laws of our country."

Roscoe appealed to the magistrates, and Tarleton requested his followers to leave off swords and butcher knives. The popular cry now turned so completely in favor of Roscoe that one had to shout back his name to a passerby on the street at night as the countersign to prevent a ruckus.

About midday on Friday, November 7, Roscoe passed Tarleton in the poll. The Whigs broke into great bursts of applause. Their band paraded the streets playing "Oh, dear, what can the matter be?" At twelve o'clock on Saturday Roscoe passed Gascoyne and went to the head of the poll. Recognizing that he had been defeated, Tarleton withdrew from the Hustings.

At the close of the poll, after his friends had expended £12,000, Roscoe had 1151 votes—more than £10 a vote! Gascoyne's friends had spent only £3000 for his 1138 votes. And after his friends had expended £4000, Tarleton had 986 votes.

In a farewell letter to the Independent Freemen of Liverpool, the defeated candidate assigned two causes for his failure:

Gentlemen,
Before this address reaches your hands, you will have received the professions and acknowledgments of those who were my rivals, for the honor of representing you in Parliament.

They cannot, however, tell you of marked professional, or long public services. They cannot display a contempt for personal emolument, which, my almost general, yet constitutional opposition, to every minister, has evinced.

They cannot show, what my public conduct does, that your property, both as individuals and a body, was my unremitting aim and practice for upwards of sixteen years.

You, Gentlemen, are the best judges of why you elected me; you are the best judges why you have deprived me of that distinguished honor!

As my Parliamentary deeds have testified, and without contradiction, a regard for my constituents, I must look for the political sin, which has brought upon me this severe mortification. I am not conscious of any.—For it surely cannot be regarded as a crime, that I dared to think, about twelve months ago, and have continued constant in the thought, that peace could not be made with Bonaparte; as the assigned reason for the recent dissolution of Parliament, is a proof that the ministers have at last adopted that opinion.

In loose and general charges, which are always ascribed to the feeling of disappointment, I shall not meddle. I should have experienced (I confess the patriotic thought) the highest gratification, in rescuing my native town from the interference, in popular elections, of the nobility in its neighborhood, and of opulent strangers who inhabit it.

My intention has been frustrated, and may another freeman of the town prove more successful upon a future occasion. The wealth of my opponents has been the cause of my discomfiture, and corruption the means of their success.

To my friends who have nobly supported me, I offer thanks, the genuine dictates of my heart: their labours, their patriotism, their perseverance have carried us a long way upon the poll—and our defeat cannot be ascribed, to the badness of our cause, but to the unconstitutional proceedings of our enemies.

Under these circumstances, I bid Liverpool farewell, and although no longer a public servant of it, I shall never cease to be a well-wisher of my native town.

I have the honour to be,
Gentlemen
Your most respectful and Obedient servant
Ban. Tarleton

Fairfield, 8 Nov. 1806

ᔕᔑ

The grace with which Tarleton took his defeat won respect among all classes in Liverpool. The skill with which he had served his constituents during the past sixteen years would stand in sharp contrast to Roscoe's ineptitude in Parliament.

For better prosecution of the war the Whigs and the Tories, under Lord Grey and Lord Grenville, continued their coalition government. When King George demanded that the ministers not bring up the simmering question of Catholic emancipation, they refused. Their Cabinet resigned, and the King dissolved Parliament.

Confronted with another election, a group of 130 of the most influential citizens of Liverpool sent Tarleton an invitation to return and stand for Parliament. In their letter they said: "We are induced to express our hopes that you will again offer yourself to represent your native town, under the firm persuasion that your exertions in promoting the trade, and advancing the general interests of this borough, during a sixteen year service in Parliament, has secured to you a powerful interest, which if properly directed, cannot fail of being ultimately successful."

Ban and Susan were visiting friends near Oxford when he received the invitation. Immediately he accepted and announced his candidacy:

Gentlemen,

Your requisition was faithfully delivered to me at a great distance from my native town. The sentiments it contains, and the respectable signatures attached to it, must impress me with indelible gratitude. I accept your invitation, and will hasten to pay my personal respects to you with all possible diligence.

If it should be my lot, on this occasion, to be elected one of your representatives, I will enter upon the important and serious charge, with a full determination to attend to your interests collectively and individually; being thoroughly sensible, that few questions can occur in the Imperial Palace, in which the rights and prosperity of Liverpool are not intimately blended.

> I have the honour to be, Gentlemen,
> With the Greatest respect and attachment,
> Your most devoted Servant
> Ban. Tarleton

Coleshill, Wardwickshire,
April 29, 1807

Even before the arrival of Tarleton's letter, his friends had published the first squib of the campaign:

Liverpool, April 30. This day arrived here, H.M. ship of war Favorite, Capt. T——n, from Bristol Channel, where she has been a guard ship these six months past. On her last voyage to this port she received considerable damage in a violent squall of wind, being run on board of by the private ship *Pope-Leo*, Capt. R—e; she within these few days has been minutely inspected, and found perfectly sound in her timbers and upperworks; a great number of hands are employed in preparing her for another cruize.

Three days later Banastre and Susan were at the home of his sister Bridget. In his opening salvo he would have the electorate know that he was a Tory, standing in the Party of Church and King:

Gentlemen,

Six months have not elapsed since I quitted you, after receiving from your hands bitter mortification. The just exercise of the Royal Prerogatives have brought us together again. His Majesty's gracious Speech plainly unfolds to you the causes which have produced the present Dissolution of Parliament. The appeal of an old and virtuous Monarch to his People, will, I trust not be in vain, in a Country hitherto celebrated for its Loyalty.

It is almost unnecessary for me to express to the Inhabitants of Liverpool that I am Loyal to the King—am devoted to the Country, Aye in the strictest sense of the word, am ready to devote my Life in so holy a service. And that I am indissolubly attached to the interests and happiness of the Spot, where I first drew my breath.

On these terms, I offer you my services, and ask your votes at the ensuing Election. Giving you a Pledge, which I will preserve in-

violate—not to connect myself with any other candidate whatso-
ever.

I have the honor to be,

Gentlemen,

With unfeigned respect and attachment,

Your faithful Servant

Ban. Tarleton

Fairfield, 2nd May, 1807

Again the Liverpuddians were singing of the Liverpool hero. The
sentiment was animated, even if the rhythm of their songs was not so
smooth nor the rhyme so exact as in the days of Mary Robinson.

> Come, cheer up, my Lads, 'tis for victory we cheer,
> To gather fresh Laurels for Tarleton to wear,
> Our plumpers will gain them—then who can say NO?
> So brave Brother Freeman, a Plumping let's go!

> Chorus

> The Church and the King is the Doctrine we boast,
> Come, let us be ready, to plump up so steady
> And then, as our Member, Brave Tarleton, we'll toast.

> In spite of our Foes, who would wish us away,
> We'll stick by brave Tarleton, by Night and by Day;
> Yes, we'll stick to the man who to Georgey is true,
> Till the Foes of our Church shall all cry *Marbleu!*

> Chorus

> But though dear to our hearts is the Deed that we claim,
> We yet ne'er possessed an intolerant Flame;
> We wish well to all Sects, as the Law has decreed,
> But wish not our King from his Oath to secede.

> Chorus

One term in Parliament had been enough for William Roscoe. He
announced that he would not stand for re-election. But his supporters
ran him anyway. They set up a subscription list, and the poorer voters
contributed their shillings and half crowns. After about £100 had been
raised, several men of means took charge of the movement and on the
opening day of election nominated Roscoe.

The supporters of Roscoe did not sing. They attacked Tarleton. In a
handbill one cried: "What regard can a Man who has been guilty of
every vice, have either for his *King,* his *Country,* or his *God?*"

The issues were now joined: Church and King *versus* scandal, defamation, and character assassination. Poor Mary Robinson, deserted these

nine years and dead these seven, was dragged into the campaign in "A Hint to the Tarletonites."

"The following lines were addressed to General Turncoat by the late beautiful but unfortunate Mrs. R——n, on his cruelly forsaking her, when she found she was no longer able to maintain him, having been attacked with a violent fever, occasioned by traveling in a damp post-chaise, hastening to relieve this valiant General from *pecuniary distress*."

After several stanzas of "Bounding Billow" the stricturist exclaimed: "Where shall we find a heart so callous, as not to pity the sufferings of this ill-fated woman, and to execrate the unfeeling and ungrateful being, who could thus abandon so helpless and forlorn a female, who supported him for several years?"

William Roscoe was gentle and amiable in character, but the Roscoites were violent. For the only time in Banastre's political life his enemies dragged in the name of Susan Priscilla. In a handbill they inserted under "Lost and Found":

Found: Pocketbook with following memorandum: Mrs. T—le—n requests the *Professor of Mendacity* will do her the favor to accept her small Watch and Seal, as a proof of her sincere acknowledgement for the Professor's *important services* to her dear General.

In a squib called "The Liverpool Races," Susan's husband had become "The well built black stallion, Ban. This Horse has long kept the whip hand on the Liverpool course, and, on account of his spirit and propensity for Mares, has been highly esteemed by all the *blacklegs* in town. His disposition is vicious."

The customs officer in Liverpool had seized a large shipment of French lace, to the profit of himself and the General, said the Whigs. In their vilification they named him "Receiver General and General Receiver."

> The senior of these Generals
> Did always prove, *True Knight* in love:
> Was Perdita's *kind* General.
>
> Of this redoubted General,
> Ye Ladies fair! Ah! pray beware!
> He'll prove a *recreant* General.
>
> How comes it that this General's
> So well received? It is believ'd
> He is—Receiver General.
>
> Besides, you know this General
> Is Tender, kind, *possesses Mind*
> *And all that grace a General!*

> You must return this General:
> He's not afraid to praise your Trade,
> He's been himself—a General!

"An ass in a Lion's hide" the angry Tories dubbed poor Roscoe, turning disdain upon the gentle old man for his scholarly life of Leo X. The angrier Whigs replied in a scurrilous handbill attacking the leading Tory candidate:

Lieut. Gen. Banastre
Receiver General and General Receiver

Extremely concerned to hear that several men and women, of some character, in his interest are ashamed of his Ribbons and Cockades in consequence of their being worn by all the *Whores, Rogues, and Vagabonds* in the town, earnestly entreats, that no divisions may take place among his friends on account of any little difference of character of respectability amongst them; and he begs this the more anxiously, as he firmly believes, from his reception among the fair—*that every woman is at least a rake;* and from his own disposition, that *every man is at heart* a swindler.

In spite of the desperate electioneering of the Whigs, Tarleton the Tory stood at the head of the poll. General Gascoyne stood second. And Roscoe, running a poor third, decided to withdraw and stop the rioting.

Banastre Tarleton was proud and happy. His political conduct had been vindicated. He now stood at the pinnacle of his Parliamentary career. Never before had a Liverpool candidate been so popular with all classes; never before had any candidate received 1461 votes.

The victor started back to the Severn District. At the home of his sister Bridget he paused and wrote to his constituents:

Gentlemen,
The proud preeminence to which you have raised me on the poll demands my earliest and warmest acknowledgements, at the same time I am conscious, that the course, in which we so cordially concurred, was the grand momentum of my elevation: From the established and recorded Loyalty of Liverpool, I anticipated the effect, of the appeal of an old and virtuous Monarch of his People; and amidst the various elections of this extensive Empire, none can be more justly celebrated, if we consider the poll or the conclusion of it, than the one I have just witnessed in my native town.
To his Majesty's present Administration I am warmly attached, and one of the principal reasons for that attachment is, that it is not formed of discordant materials; I believe the present Government will improve our foreign relations:—will increase and usefully employ our disposable force—will attend to our navigation

laws—will enlarge and augment our commercial resources—will rigidly (in spite of the unfounded clamour recently raised) correct the abuses in the expenditure of public money:—will not enter into fruitless negociations, which only lead to degradation and dishonour—and will not tarnish the British Flag. As long as they continue in that career of public utility, the Ministers shall have my cordial support.

With respect to the local interests of Liverpool, which I am fully convinced are various and important, I will exercise the best talents I possess, and attend to the application of my constituents with scrupulous punctuality. And now my Townsmen and Friends, allow me to close this address, with the strongest assurance of my gratitude for your protection and favor, because no words can do justice to the many offices of kindness which I have received, since I have returned amongst you, from all classes of the respectable Inhabitants of Liverpool.

I have the honour to be, Gentlemen,
With the Greatest attachment and respect,
Your obliged and faithful Servant
Ban. Tarleton

Fairfield, 15 May, 1807

But the General made an error in strategy that would come back to haunt him. His friends circulated a handbill saying: "General Tarleton's Committee particularly requests all Persons who have any demands against them, will immediately bring their Accounts to the Committee Room, that they may be examined and paid before the General leaves Liverpool."

In the shouting and rejoicing few heeded the notice. Many who had signed the requisition failed to pay their pledges. Others forgot to submit their accounts. And Banastre left Liverpool before his committee had paid his election debts.

He spent a quiet term in Parliament. He and Susan enjoyed the social season, and on June 4 they attended the King's Birthday Ball. After the adjournment of the House, they returned to Bath.

During the fall of 1807 Ban and Susan visited the Cholmondeleys at Houghton in Norfolk. From there they drove to Lord Gwydyr's Grimsthorpe Castle in Lincolnshire. They were at Buxton, the home of the Duke of Devonshire, when they heard that the army under Lord Cathcart had captured Copenhagen. In their enthusiasm the Tarletons gave a ball which scandalized their friends: ". . . discretion was thrown to the winds and regardless of social status everyone was invited."

By December 1 the Tarletons had reached Edinburgh. Ban wished to consult Lord Moira now commanding in Edinburgh, for the Earl had great influence at the War Office. After his visit to Edinburgh Castle, he and Susan set off for London.

During the session of Parliament, Banastre was busier than usual. On February 23, 1808, the reason for his recent activity was revealed: he was appointed governor of Berwick and Holy Island. For routine inspection of the garrison at Berwick the governor received an annual stipend of £568, 15s, 10d. One of the sweetest sinecures in the gift of ministers, this seemed a fitting reward for a renegade Whig who could bring 1461 voters into the Tory Party!

Banastre now had the occasion to urge security for the family of one of his oldest friends. After a brilliant career in India, General Gerard Lake had returned home. A grateful nation had made him Viscount Lake, but he did not long enjoy the honor. He caught cold while attending the court-martial of Lieutenant General Bulstrode Whitelocke and died on February 20, 1808.

Unlike many of the conquerors of India, Viscount Lake died poor; and it was moved that Parliament settle a pension of £900 upon his family. "There can be nothing, in my opinion, more honorable to the noble Lord's character than that he returned from India a poor man," said Tarleton in supporting the motion. "There was not a greater idol throughout the whole army than the late Lord Lake."

Only occasionally did the Tarletons now appear in London society. On March 3 Banastre attended the King's levee and was presented to his Majesty on his appointment as governor of Berwick. On April 11, as an influential Tory, he went with a distinguished group to dine with the Chancellor of the Exchequer.

Banastre and Susan attended the King's Birthday Ball on June 4, but she was no longer among the best-dressed women in the kingdom. Deepening religious convictions now forbade lavish display. In ten years of married life she had matured beyond the vanity of fashion. Once she had been happy to go to London, but now she was happier to return to Bath and the Severn District.

After a quiet half year spent drilling volunteers whose enthusiasm waned as the probability of invasion receded, Banastre returned to London for the opening of Parliament. If he could have foreseen the painful nature of the session, he would have remained in Bath.

On January 9, 1809, G. L. Wardle, a retired militia colonel in extreme Opposition, moved an inquiry into the conduct of the Duke of York, commander in chief of the British Army. Colonel Wardle's charges were tantamount to indictment for graft, corruption, and the selling of promotions.

As a close friend of the Duke, Tarleton knew the background against which the charges were made. He had visited Oatlands. He knew of the estrangement of the Duke and the Duchess. He also knew that York had taken as his mistress a pert little strumpet named Mary Anne Clarke.

The Duke had settled Mary Anne in a house in Gloucester Place and lavished upon her his affections and £1000 a year. Like most fancy women she became extravagant. She needed money for clothes, carriages, and entertaining. So she began boasting of her control over the Duke and peddling her influence.

The Duke finally discarded Mary Anne, but he allowed her an annuity of £400, the going price for discarded mistresses. In 1808 he discontinued the annuity, and she threatened to publish his love letters.

Failing of blackmail, Mary Anne took all of her correspondence to Colonel Wardle. In her letters he found that there were seven military promotions for which she had been paid. He concluded: "The Duke was aware that she had been paid for her services and must have indirectly benefited thereby."

During the investigation, which dragged along for two months, Mrs. Mary Anne Clarke was brought before the bar of the House of Commons twelve times. She read forty-one of her letters, and they seemed to indict the Duke. But she overplayed her hand and, as the *Annual Register* commented, "carried her ease, gaiety, and pleasantness to a degree of pertness which was reprehensible."

During the parliamentary inquiry into the conduct of the Duke, Banastre faced one of the major crises of his life. For twenty years he had been a warm friend of Frederick. He owed his active military career largely to his influence. His attachment to the royal family was through the Duke rather than through the Prince.

After a week of debate, on March 17 the motion came to a vote. With anguish of soul, and yet with great courage, Banastre Tarleton voted against the Duke. But by a vote of 364 to 123 the House acquitted Frederick. Next day he resigned from the Army. In his place as commander in chief, Ministers appointed doddering General Sir David Dundas.

The animosities engendered by the affair of Mary Anne turned into a feud between Tarleton and General Sir Arthur Wellesley. Honest old Lord Cornwallis had complained of the extravagance of the Wellesleys in India. Tarleton was said to have given Sir Arthur the nickname of the "Sepoy General." By that name he was known in the Duke's headquarters in the Horse Guards.

After the death of Sir John Moore at Corunna, Ministers gave the command of the forces in Spain and Portugal to Sir Arthur. Tarleton's professional jealousy flared against the Sepoy General. When Wellesley's mistakes came under attack in Parliament, Tarleton sided with the Whigs. He voted for Lord Henry Petty's motion that the "Convention of Cintra" of August 30, 1808, and the "Maritime Convention" of September 3, 1808, "appear to this House to have disappointed the hopes and expectations of the Nation."

Said the *Oracle* for March 4: "General Tarleton rose, and, in a speech of great length and ability, took a review of the late campaigns in Portugal and Spain, pointing out in what particular cases, the Government and the commanding officers had been in error."

Wellesley was in his seat in the House, but Tarleton did not spare his feelings. He blamed Sir Arthur for not having opposed the armistice and the Convention of Cintra. He charged him with having involved the Army in operations of great danger.

Sir Arthur replied with considerable heat. He recapitulated his arguments used before the court of inquiry. He denied that the Army had been in such danger as Tarleton had represented. "Had the honorable General been in my place, he would not have hesitated to act as I did," he exclaimed. "I am sure his conduct would have been better in the field than his advice in the Senate!"

The Convention of Cintra now became a main topic of debate. On April 20 Tarleton again castigated Wellesley. On the motion to affirm the armistice in Portugal, he said: "Although I will not object to the motion, I cannot help thinking it will not have any beneficial effect in justifying this disgraceful Convention, nor any of those connected with it."

The quondam disciple of Charles Fox had had enough of Prime Minister Perceval and the Tories. He decided to return to the Whigs. Like the blackest radical he cried: "We have had nothing like the Convention of Cintra in the annals of British history. God forbid that we shall ever look upon it in any other view than most disgraceful!"

37

General of the Army

$\mathcal{D}$URING THE VIOLENT DEBATES over the Peninsular Campaign there was frequent mention of a Colonel de Charmilly. He was a Santo Domingo renegade who had surrendered to the English and been rewarded with a colonelcy. In the early stages of the campaign he had attempted to serve with the British, but finding him an unsavory character Sir John Moore had expelled him from Spain.

In Parliament on April 27, 1809, Banastre told of a chance experience with De Charmilly, "whom I do not recollect to have seen—of his private or public life I know nothing." Some time before Colonel de Charmilly was a guest at a dinner given at the Star and Garter by Mr. Devereux, representative from Ireland. After dinner the gentlemen engaged in a game of faro. De Charmilly won and took from the table several guineas. He then lost a considerable amount to his host. Several days later, when asked to pay, he pleaded drunkenness and ignorance of the transaction. He even threatened to challenge Devereux.

As a member of Brooks's Club, Devereux sought the advice of Tarleton. "My detestation of private play, and my slight acquaintance with Mr. Devereux, made me refuse in a decided manner to be the bearer of any message," declared Banastre, "but I undertook to officiate as an arbitrator."

To Tarleton's speech about Colonel de Charmilly came an unexpected reply:

Lisbon, May 20, 1809

General Tarleton,

I inform you that the newspaper, printed in French, called the *Courier de Londres*, impute to you a ridiculous and false story, as by you said publicly, entirely foreign to the matter in consideration; he says, it was then represented to you to be so; but that

431

your answer was, that you did it to prove that the person whom
you mentioned, did not deserve *to be believed*; this was giving to
an absent person a public lie; that is too much of an ungentleman
and of an unofficer-like conduct, to have been said, by such a *great
General* as you. As I am the person whom the paper says you was
speaking of, I denounce to you that paper, that you may have the
printer punished, the more, so, that you know better than anybody, that it was a swindling affair, in which I was tried to be
made a victim: the name of Count de Vandreuil mentioned by
you will prove to the world that certainly his friend who was one
against two, and offered to fight with both, was not the person to
whom blame could be attached; this business shall be made public at my arrival in England, and I hope to hear from the gallantry
of General Tarleton, that he has had the printer, imputing to him
an insulting conduct, punished; for my part, I beg to assure General Tarleton, that no swindler nor their friends, will ever intimi-
date me. I depend upon the generosity of the English nation, not
to be condemned unheard; as a man of honour and an Englishman, denised for his services, I engage to claim and solicit justice
against my calumniators till I have obtained it: for all the calumnies, cowardly invented against me; the rank, the fortune, and the
number of calumniators do not frighten me, as an honest man is
always morally stronger than several villains. When I shall be in
England, you'll hear of my arrival, that I may be informed in what
manner I may *help you to obtain justice* against the printer who
has used your name so ridiculously. In the meantime, I am,

General Tarleton,
Your most obedient humble servant
De Charmilly
Colonel of Cavalry

Did this mean a challenge? Afterward Banastre wrote De Charmilly:
"As the rank of Colonel entitled you to a meeting with the most exalted
of his Majesty's subjects, I considered myself the last person to refuse it
to you: and as the words referred to, were spoken in Parliament, I never
would retract them, out of respect for that Assembly, during my existence: Nor did I allow that any person or persons, except my constituents, had even a shadow of a right to call for an explanation of my
parliamentary conduct."

Rumor spread that De Charmilly had followed his letter to London.
So Banastre prepared for the meeting. For his second he chose an officer of the Guards, and together they concerted a double plan: "First
that I should remain out of the limits of my Military Command, as
long as I could find any pretext for so doing, in order to give Colonel
de Charmilly an opportunity of carrying his declared intention into
effect. Secondly, that I should consider any insult offered me, or challenge delivered, whilst in the exercise of my military command, as a

breach of discipline, which would necessarily compel me to place the person so offending in close arrest, until report had been made to the Commander in Chief."

For five weeks after the adjournment of Parliament, Tarleton waited for De Charmilly. Hearing nothing from the challenger, about August 1 he and Susan drove on to Bath. Neither the Colonel nor his second trespassed on the Severn Military District. Said the General: "Colonel de Charmilly never did with due anxiety, seek the means to discover the honour I designed him."

During the fall Ban devoted himself to his military duties. Then he returned to London for the opening of Parliament. He had almost forgotten De Charmilly when, on the evening of February 24, 1810, someone left a thirty-five-page pamphlet on his doorstep in Berkeley Square. It bore the title:

To the British Nation
Is Presented By
Colonel Venault de Charmilly
Knight of the Royal and Military Order of St. Louis
The Narrative of his transactions in Spain
with
The Rt. Hon. John Hookham Frere
and
Lt. Gen. Sir John Moore, K. B.
Being a Refutation of the Calumnies Invented against him

In *To the British Nation* Colonel de Charmilly told of his activities in Spain. He explained his misunderstanding with Sir John Moore and reproved Lieutenant General Tarleton for his attack upon him from the floor of the House of Commons.

Banastre immediately began a *Reply to Colonel de Charmilly*. He summarized his correspondence with Sir John Moore. He repeated his remarks in the House. He published De Charmilly's letter and told of his preparations for a duel. And then with a flourish he ended his reply: "I shall refer to legal opinions, the correctness of his last pamphlet, as well as of any future publications, which may appear in the world upon this subject."

Tarleton's *Reply to Colonel de Charmilly* ended the affair. It also revealed the character of the author. In it was the creed of the man whom Mary Robinson had once pilloried as "The Gamester":

It would be unbecoming in me to trespass upon the public, by endeavouring to attribute to myself, upon such an occasion as this, a better character than I deserve. In the world—in the British Army—in the circle of a large acquaintance—and to a few friends, in a closer or more remote degree, I am known. During a life like mine—I must have created some enemies, and committed many faults. With respect to play itself, from the practice of which, I have for some time withdrawn myself, I always thought that liberal allowances, to the various actors upon that scene, were to be made. I constantly discouraged private play, whenever an opportunity for so doing presented itself: and I never hesitated to declare, that the person who sheltered himself by the plea of intoxication from a play debt, and appealed to decision of the sword, was guilty of first-rate delinquency in civilized society. With this creed and by this practice, I have undoubtedly created enemies, but I have the pleasing reflection to console me, of having passed my fiftieth year without one private quarrel.

ᗡᖇᓇ

Nothing of importance ever happened in the Severn Military District. There were only a few companies of militia left in western England and these took care of themselves. Life in Bath was pleasant and York House was comfortable. But both Ban and Susan looked forward to the opening of Parliament as an escape from monotony.

Banastre was never more active in the House than in the closing years of his service. He hated the Peninsular Campaign. It was a source of constant argument between him and Sheridan. On January 23, 1810, he told the House that a diversion in Italy would have been better than fighting in Spain and Portugal. But he admitted that his idea of attacking the soft underbelly of Europe "might not have been agreeable to the Wellesleys."

Tarleton thoroughly disliked the Wellesleys. His scorn for the Sepoy General mounted when Sir Arthur was raised to the peerage as Lord Wellington. In reply to the report of the Lords Commissioners on January 25, he said: "The Merit of Lord Wellington is still unequivocal. Why, in cases of failure, should the merits of the officer not be enquired into as a matter of course, as is, in a great measure, the plan in the Navy?

"I blamed Lord Wellington, when he was in this House, for the Convention of Cintra. I now blame him for his rash advance into Spain."

On January 31 Banastre had his first collision with Prime Minister Perceval. "Perceval fought three pitched battles in naming the Finance Committee," said Thomas Creevy. "I saw the tellers count wrong by 3. I called to have the House told again, and again I saw them make the same mistake. I showed it to General Tarleton, who became furious; and the Speaker called him and me to order in the most boisterous manner."

Creevy and Tarleton were right, and on the third tally the mistake was corrected. But the Whigs could not prevent Perceval's vote of thanks to the commander in Spain. "All our indignation against Wellington ended in smoak," wrote Creevy. "Opposition to his thanks was so unpopular that some of the stoutest of our crew slunk away."

The House now began considering the Army estimates. Some members complained of the large number of generals on the staff. While debating staff expenditures on February 26 sarcastic Lord Leveson-Gower looked at Tarleton and said: "I cannot see the propriety of continuing the Honorable General, a member of this House, in command of the Southern District, where there are scarcely 2,500 troops, and these mostly militia."

The Chancellor of the Exchequer replied: "With respect to the staff expenditures, my noble friend has sufficiently explained himself." And glancing at the general of the Severn District again seated among the Whigs, the leader of the Tories observed: "Certainly the continuation of the Gallant General opposite, in the Southern District, cannot be considered as a return for any Parliamentary Services."

Stung by the remarks, Banastre rose to his feet. "The language of the Right Honorable Gentleman is as candid as that of the Noble Lord has been hostile," he asserted. And looking over the membership of the House, he asked: "Why should I be ashamed to hold a situation after having been 34 years in the Service?"

The Tories enjoyed needling the renegade. "I must believe that the command, which was so pertinaciously and painfully imposed on the Gallant General, was a kind of retributive vengeance for his uniform Opposition," said William Huskisson amid much laughter. "I presume that the Gallant Officer, much as he might be willing to suffer for his country, already finds the burden of his command so irksome, that he is longing to throw it off his feelings, in a sudden fit of impatience.

"Yet, I am credulous enough to think, that many officers might be found not unwilling to subject their feelings to insults quite as severe and of the same nature."

Undoubtedly Huskisson knew that the Gallant General's distinguished aide-de-camp, Lieutenant Colonel Henry E. Tarleton, was running the Severn District for his Uncle Ban.

Early in 1811 King George III relapsed into insanity, and on February 5, 1811, the Prince of Wales became Regent. There was little outward change: British diplomats worked on their alliances, the British fleets swept the seas, and the British army under Wellington plodded on after the French in Spain.

Then Wellington captured Badajoz, and on April 26 Parliament gave him a vote of thanks. "I concur most cordially in this vote of thanks," said Tarleton. "I opposed a vote of thanks for the battle of Talavera, but to this vote I will give my entire assent." He continued: "The affairs of the war are not yet finished. I trust that Lord Wellington will be successful in making the Peninsula rally around him and Europe make an effort for her own deliverance." And he ended: "No honors that the crown can bestow will then be too great for him."

As Wellington began driving the French out of Spain, he gave credit to the Duke of York for having built the magnificent British army. In the two years since his resignation, public attitude toward the Duke had changed, and now many wished to see him again commander in chief. Mrs. Mary Anne Clarke had written *The Rival Princes* in whch she tried to involve the Duke of Kent against the Duke of York. Then Francis Wright, the upholsterer whom Colonel Wardle had hired to furnish the home of Mary Anne and failed to pay, sued the Colonel.

In the trial Mary Anne was a witness. From her testimony it became evident that Wardle had engineered "one of the most foul, pitiful and unmanly plots *that was ever contrived.*" Public revulsion swept old General Dundas into retirement. The Prince Regent appointed his favorite brother commander in chief of the Army. General acclamation greeted the return of the Duke to his headquarters in the Horse Guards.

The vote to confirm the Duke as commander in chief came up in Parliament on June 6. Tarleton was anxious to state the reasons for his vote against the Duke two years before. "Standing as I do in a particular situation, and having partaken of the general feeling of the time of the enquiry," he said, "I then laboured under an impression, since removed, that some degree of blame attached to his Royal Highness.

"I then thought I had discovered a blot in the character of his Royal Highness, and notwithstanding the friendship with which I have been honored, I could not abstain from doing my duty in voting against him. That impression is now completely removed, and I can assure the House, that there is nothing more pleasant to the feeling of the Army, than the restoration of his Royal Highness.

"The situation of the country is such that it is fit that a Prince of the Blood should, if competent, have command of the army. The recognized merits of the illustrious Duke in a military point of view, entitle him to the thanks of the country."

Happy to serve again under the Duke, Ban spent the next months in the Severn District. Then he returned to Parliament. During the fall there were rumors of coming military promotions. Finally, on December 31, 1811, the *London Gazette* carried the announcement: "His Royal Highness the Prince Regent has been pleased, in the name and on behalf of his Majesty, to appoint the following officers to take rank by Brevet." Twenty-three lieutenant generals were promoted to the rank of general. Fifth in seniority among them was General Banastre Tarleton.

Among those promoted were four of Ban's old friends from the War of the American Revolution. There was William, Viscount Cathcart, once colonel of the British Legion. There was Oliver de Lancey, with whom young Captain Tarleton had ridden in the long-forgotten Mischianza, and Alexander Ross, who had carried the Cornwallis dispatches home from the battle of Camden. And there was Francis Dundas, beside whom Lieutenant Colonel Tarleton had fought at the battle of Guilford Courthouse.

But, while it brought promotions for her generals, England's struggle with Napoleon brought poverty, hunger, and misery. On February 6, 1812, General Tarleton gave Parliament a melancholy picture of Liverpool. "For now, whoever goes along the quays, not long since crowded with every species of Merchandise, will behold the melancholy and mortifying signal of a broom at the masthead of almost every other ship, to notify, alas! that it is to be sold."

In their distress the merchants of Liverpool had made an ominous decision: they had begun addressing their petitions to Parliament through Thomas Creevy. On March 23, in refutation of a report by Creevy, General Tarleton read a report from the mayor, bailiffs, and burgesses of Liverpool, saying that last year in constructing new docks on the Mersey, the contractors had imported Irish and Welsh labor and in slack times had established a soup committee for their relief. The report then went on to state that there was scarcely a British ship out of employment in the port of Liverpool, nor a ship carpenter out of employment who was worth it.

General Gascoyne realized the error in the report read by General Tarleton. "Most certainly there had been a dimunition in trade," he said. "When it was recollected that three-fourths of the trade in Liverpool was to America, could it be thought extraordinary that there was stagnation?"

Friction with the United States, arising from England's Orders in Council and desperate measures for manning her fleets by impressing seamen on American vessels, had ruined the trade of Liverpool. General Tarleton was caught in a dilemma: his military superiors had ordered these measures, and his Parliamentary constituents were in rebellion against them. On April 17 he attributed the distress in Liverpool to the Orders in Council. He declared "the highest and the lowest, the richest and the poorest, are equally aggrieved by them."

Ten days later General Gascoyne presented a petition to Parliament signed by 6560 of the most respected individuals in Liverpool pleading for a repeal of Orders in Council. Thomas Creevy spoke of the miseries of the people of Liverpool. General Tarleton observed that the accounts he had obtained and which he had communicated to Parliament on a former occasion, in opposition to the honorable gentleman, were derived from the most respectable authority. When the House ordered the petition to lie on the table, Henry Brougham rose and said that he had still another petition from Liverpool.

Was Banastre out of touch with his people? Why had Whig members begun showing solicitude for the miseries of Liverpool? Had Creevy and Brougham decided to try to wrest from Tarleton his seat in the sacred hall of St. Stephen?

In early May, Brougham and Creevy began consulting about standing for election in Liverpool. Creevy held a seat for Thetford, a pocket borough of the Duke of Norfolk. Brougham had received notice to seek another seat from the new proprietor of Camelford. William Roscoe invited both of them to come to Liverpool, assuring them that they could unseat Gascoyne and Tarleton. Brougham was inclined to stand without Creevy, lest he should "turn out poor Tarleton, who is as good opponent of the Tory Government as if he had been an out-and-out Radical."

Both candidates decided to await developments. They did not have long to wait. With distress and misery becoming visible everywhere, riots began sweeping the counties. As a measure of relief, on June 21, Parliament repealed the Orders in Council. But this was too late—the Orders had done their mischief. On June 18, driven by the American War Hawks, the United States had declared war against Great Britain.

In July Parliament rose; before it lay dissolution and a general election. Tired out, with rheumatism worrying him, Banastre sought rest at Lambton Hall. From there in early fall he wrote the Worthy and Independent Freemen of Liverpool:

"After a session, seldom equalled in the annals of Parliament, for the pressure both of public and private business, I had retired at the conclusion of it, to that situation, where I could best obtain retirement and repose. From this retreat I am suddenly called, by the reiterated, and I believe well-founded report, of the Dissolution of the Parliament. I shall not therefore, fail, Gentlemen, to present myself to you, with the confident expectation of again being elected one of your representatives."

Their representative at Lambton Hall did not realize the distress in the commercial circles of Liverpool. Nor was he aware of changing public sentiment. He was shocked when he learned that the manufacturers of Birmingham and Manchester were giving a public dinner in Liverpool to thank Brougham for his efforts in repealing the Orders in Council.

So disturbed was Banastre that on September 22 he rode over to Howick to consult Lord Grey. But the leader of the Whigs was secretly backing Henry Brougham, to whom his Lordship immediately wrote:

Tarleton came here yesterday, and left us again this morning. He is going first to Lowther, and then to Liverpool, on account of the dissolution.

I had a good deal of conversation with him, but when all is summed up it does not come to much. He is naturally, after his contests, annoyed at the idea of another. He seems to think the alarm taken by the Church-and-King people, and by the Corporation, at the attempt of Roscoe and his friends, as manifested at the dinner, to bring in two members, will produce a great deal of trouble, expense, and difficulty; that they certainly will start a candidate whose opinions are more congenial to their own; and that with this view an application had been made to Canning, who had answered that he was ready to stand if he could be insured against expense. I suggested the expediency of some communication between your friends and his. He professed himself personally well disposed towards it, but seemed to feel the same apprehension that you do of the consequence of taking any direct or public step for that purpose. He said naturally enough that he must look in the first place to his own interest; but that he would be glad to do anything he could consistently with that object, and without prejudice to it, to assist you. Roscoe he seems to think very hostile personally to him. All this, as you will see, comes to very little, and I did not think there was any use pushing the matter further, ignorant as I am of the local interests, and fearful as I must be, in a case of this nature, of doing more harm than good.

Lord Grey then ended his letter about Tarleton's visit by observing "He has not behaved well in politics."

∽

The Whigs now revealed their strategy. At a public meeting they decided to nominate both Creevy and Brougham and try to defeat both Gascoyne and Tarleton. On September 28 Brougham wrote Lord Grey a summary of their plans. "Respecting Tarleton, I feel exactly as you do, liking the man, and heartily grieved should he be turned out," he admitted. "Let but Creevey's case become desperate, as I have written to him, and if I can by any possibility show my predilection for Tarleton, both you and he himself may rely on my doing so. Could you contrive to let him know these my sentiments."

Lord Grey replied: "Tarleton has given me an opportunity of writing to him, and I said what you wished."

In the meantime the leaders of the Tory Party met at the Golden Lion on September 25 and decided to back General Gascoyne and George Canning. Already safe from defeat at Petersfield and at Sligo, Canning accepted on condition that his campaign be free of expense. On October 3 the Tories wrote him that they had already raised £6000.

"Gascoigne and Tarleton came here today, both indifferently supported, particularly the latter, who came on horseback with only two friends. They are neither of them popular," wrote William Roscoe to Creevy on October 4. "Canning, it is said, will make his appearance on Monday."

Then the candidates went to the Hustings. There were speeches and shouting and cries against war. There were songs and squibs and handbills. Some decried the press for the Navy. Others decried the poor rates. The Whigs advertised

Peace, Plenty, and Commerce
Vote for
Brougham and Creevy

In the voting Canning early took the lead, trailed closely by Gascoyne. Brougham and Creevy were third and fourth. At his bar, without the endorsement of either party, Tarleton stood almost alone.

"Why is Tarleton deserted?" cried a handbill. "The reason is plain: the Bills for the last Election are unpaid, and therefore those who shamefully refuse to pay their subscriptions, are fearful they would be called upon to pay their old scores. It is not the fault of the General— he handsomely came forward with a large sum!"

Because of the war and the stagnation of trade, all of the Tarletons faced bankruptcy, and the General had come to the end of his political finances. He could not match the £6000 of Canning.

At the close of the poll, Canning led with 1631 votes. Gascoyne had 1532. The Whigs were "beat to a mummy," as Creevy wrote his wife. "We had to do with artists who did not know their trade. Poor Roscoe made much too sanguine an estimate of our strength."

Tarleton received only five votes! He learned that Whig turned Tory cannot turn Whig again. Infuriated by the Whigs' bringing Brougham and Creevy to Liverpool, the quondam disciple of Charles James Fox asked his followers to vote for George Canning. In his political death, Banastre Tarleton was the staunchest Tory of them all!

After three days Banastre lowered his colors, closed his bar, and retired from the Hustings. With heavy heart he wrote a farewell to his political career:

To the Independent Electors of Liverpool

Gentlemen,
  In conformity to the declaration made to you, and dated from Lambton Hall on the 24 ultimo, I hastened to your town. I have now presented myself at your bar, the tribunal of Election: I have exhibited a true picture of my private and public parliamentary conduct: I have courted investigation on the important features of my votes and speeches during the last Parliament; and to the statement and reasoning offered to your attention in public Court, I have met with nothing but silent acquiescence. But I am penetrated with no common degree of grief and indignation, when I announce to you, that misrepresentation and slander, conveyed in whispers, have undermined my just claim to your confidence and protection. It is now easy to discover, as no public imputation has been thrown upon me, although called for and openly challenged,

that my political opinions are not the cause of the cold neglect, and unjust hostility, which I have experienced. The nucleus of the transfer of votes and interests, to another respectable individual, is derived from the profusion of some rich men, in carrying into effect a requisition, sent to me more than five years ago. I have in my possession that document, as well as clear evidence of the dissention arising amongst them, from that expenditure. An extract coupled with some names, the whole being too voluminous to publish in an address, lays the transaction open to the dullest eye, and the most besotted understanding. The dissension alluded to, commenced almost immediately upon the close of the Election (long, long, before I differed from the existing Minister) which involves in its consequences, a momentary destruction of my popularity, and an existing detriment to many suffering and ill used individuals.

By such arts and practices, the present triumph of those, who did style themselves my Political supporters, and now by an inversion of common sense, denominate themselves my personal friends, has been acquired. These delusions will pass away, and the light of truth will show their tendency and malignity. In the meantime, a separation, unexpected by the honest heart, is likely to take place between me and the inhabitants of Liverpool. It is grievous after so long a connexion to reveal to my Brother Townsmen, and to the World, an old and tried Representative, has been made the sacrifice of duplicity and ingratitude. These expressions may be attributed to mortification and vindictiveness. I boldly disclaim the charge: I give a narrative of these transactions with sorrow: as I am actuated only by a sense of justice, and the preservation of my own character.

To my sincere and upright friends, I offer the genuine thanks of a grateful heart, and as the prospect of a return for a seat, does not for the present appear brilliant, I am about to quit Liverpool, earnestly praying that her prosperity may be perpetual. I deem it right, however, to keep my bar open, as long as the law will allow, in order to show in the records of this great and opulent Town, that I have polled in two Elections within the space of six years, 1500 and 5 votes—without having my integrity impeached, or my diligence questioned.

> I have the honour to remain,
> Gentlemen,
> Your faithful Servant
> Ban. Tarleton

October 10, 1812

38

Sir Banastre

*L*ORD WELLINGTON finally drove the French from Spain and, marching the British army into southern France, began the campaign that ended in the abdication of Napoleon. As Tarleton had prophesied, no honors were too great for the General. He was created Duke of Wellington. On July 21, 1814, the Prince Regent honored the Duke with a grand fete at Carlton House. He invited 2500 guests, of whom 1800 came. Among these were General and Mrs. Tarleton, and Banastre became reconciled with the Duke.

Among the guests was Colonel George Hanger. Like almost everyone else, George had served in the war against Napoleon. In 1806 he had been appointed captain-commissary to the Royal Artillery Drivers, but in 1808 he had been allowed to retire on full pay, a scandal which brought severe remarks from the Commissioners of Military inquiry. In December 1814 his brother, the famed Blue Hanger, died, and George inherited the family estates, with an income of £3000 and the title of Lord Coleraine. But George always remembered his lean years. To anyone who called him "My Lord," he would say, "Plain George Hanger, if you please."

In late summer the Tarletons moved to Leintwardine House in the picturesque village of Leintwardine in Shropshire. Susan loved the quiet of the country, and Banastre enjoyed being a country squire. Together they fished in the Teme, and in the fall he hunted in the meadows. They were happy, and Ban forgot the ache of his rheumatism.

In honor of the uncle and aunt with whom he had served in Portugal, Captain Thomas Tarleton, Jr., named a son Banastre Henry and a daughter Susan. Ban and Susan Priscilla drove over to Cloverley for Susan's christening. Here Tom's daughter Mary first saw her Aunt Susan Priscilla.

Later she wrote in her *Journal*: "She was a talented, graceful, and accomplished and fascinating person—but also an eccentric one, setting conventionalities at defiance, alternating between the magnificence of the state of the Palaces she inhabited with her father's family, by whom she was acknowledged and brought up, and the absence of common comfort in her own home. On that visit to Cloverley, I well remember, she brought 4 lap dogs with her—and great was the surprise of us children on going down to dessert, to find our grand new Aunt sitting on the floor instead of at the table, with her dogs on her knee—I noted, moreover, a general impression of sweet music and most choice perfumes enticing me—and elegant work and beautiful albums which altogether drew a halo around Aunt Susan and gave her a place in our imagination apart from that of our other Aunts."

All went happily until the government began rewarding those who had overthrown Napoleon. On January 3, 1815, the *London Gazette* published a long list of generals and admirals who had been created Knights of the Bath. But the honor had been limited to those who had distinguished themselves since the beginning of the second war with Napoleon.

This excluded Banastre, and he was deeply wounded. Could anyone have distinguished himself training home guards in the Severn Military District? After three weeks of pondering he wrote a letter laying his grievance before Earl Bathurst, Secretary for War:

Leintwardine, Ludlow
27 January 1815

My Lord,

If something stronger than common report had not pointed out the Principal Secretary of State in the War Department as the chief engine in the new formation of the Military Order, I should not have made this address to your Lordship. And, although my feelings were severely smitten by that circumstance, I forebore to trespass upon your Lordship, until I had collected the best intelligence upon the subject.

I beg leave, my Lord, to premise, that I entertain no sentiments of hostility to your Lordship, and that I am solely actuated by a sense of injury; conceiving (I think with justice) that a great stigma has been fixed upon my professional life, by the Supplement to the London Gazette, dated 3rd of January, 1815. I could have been contented to have descended into my grave with the honourable rank of General in the British Army, earned by activity and courage, unassisted by money, noble birth, or powerful interest, if an instrument, to which I have alluded, had not given additional dignity to several of my contemporaries, and lifted into precedency many officers who had served under me.

Your Lordship's feelings will, if I am not mistaken, in this instance accord with mine, that this letter cannot be deemed an
intrusion or aggression upon you, or upon any other person whatso-
ever, but a fair vindication of my own conduct and character, to
which I am impelled by a laudable sense of honest ambition. What
is so dear to a soldier as his military reputation? Is not that reputation founded upon gallant exploits, honorable wounds, and military
records? If such foundation is valid, I appeal to the Government
Gazettes of my country, during the years 1780 and 1781. Sir H.
Clinton (the commander-in-chief) and Earl Cornwallis (the second in command) have mentioned my name with singular distinction, in every public despatch during that period; and I hope it
may, in this case, be esteemed venial, if I refer your Lordship to a
conversation held in the House of Lords, in which it was proposed
to thank me, as Lieutenant-Colonel-Commandant, such rank (according to usage) not allowing that honour.

If I had not nearly outlived the recollection of the American
war, it would be unnecessary to point out the different military
enterprises in which I have been personally concerned; but the object I have in view obliges me to go into a detail, irksome, perhaps,
to us both.

To the siege of Charleston I attended Sir H. Clinton; having
received the command of the cavalry upon that expedition, with
the rank of Lieutenant-Colonel-Commandant of the Legion. I pur-
posely pass over all my previous services—such as the direction of
the advanced guard of the party which captured General Lee in
1776—and intend to state my conduct after I had attained the
command of the cavalry.

During the siege of Charleston, three regiments of the enemy's
horse (Washington's horse, Pulaske's legion, Bland's or White's
dragoons) were surprised and destroyed at Monk's Corner and
Lenew's Ferry; and all communication with the country was cut
off by the light troops, although the place was not completely
invested by the army.

At the Wacsaws, on the frontier of North Carolina, the cavalry,
with part of the legion infantry on horseback, at the distance of a
hundred and thirty-six miles from Lord Cornwallis's army, defeated
a superior body of continental infantry, with great slaughter, and
took four pieces of artillery, five colors, and all the baggage of the
Americans, which contained valuable stores and clothing for the
garrison of Charleston.

At Camden, a charge of cavalry was made against infantry and
cannon, and a pursuit continued for upwards of twenty miles from
the field of battle, in which several prisoners, all the baggage, and
the last piece of cannon, were taken from the enemy.

At the Catawba River, General Sumpter was brought to action
two days after the battle of Camden: his force, of upwards of 1000
men, continentals and backwoodsmen, was surprised at mid-day;
two cannon, and many prisoners, and all baggage, fell into the pos-

session of a very inferior party. A considerable number of British soldiers were retaken, and loyal Americans redeemed from captivity.

At Blackstocks, on the Tyger River, General Sumpter, with superior numbers, was dislodged from blockhouses, in which position he threatened Ninety-Six, a British post; some prisoners taken, his corps dispersed, and the general placed *hors de combat* by a wound.

At the Cowpens, the British were defeated with loss, by superior numbers, consisting of continentals and backwoodsmen, under General Morgan. The reverse of fortune is principally attributable to the want of co-operative movements of Lord Cornwallis. (Vide *Tarleton's Campaigns,* c.iv.) In a letter which I have in my possession, Lord Cornwallis says, "Your movements in bringing the enemy to action were masterly—your disposition unexceptionable; nothing but the total misbehaviour of the troops under your command could have robbed you of the glory which was so justly your due."

At Guildford Court-House, the two armies were long and closely engaged, when the cavalry towards the end of the action, extricated the right wing from the enemy, which had surrounded it. In that charge I lost a considerable part of my right hand.

In short, all the movements of the British army were covered, through a woody and difficult country, by my legion from the fall of Charleston to the melancholy catastrophe at Yorktown, in Virginia. In that circuitous march of more that 1200 miles, many prisoners, cannon, and colours, fell into my hands, whilst detached from the main body of the army: a great proportion of the forage and provisions were provided for the British, and all risings and assemblies of the American militia were suppressed by the sword. The rank of Major and of Lieutenant-Colonel in the English army came to me for services in the field, by brevet, in 1780 and early in 1781.

That my deployment since the conclusion of the American war has not been upon the same active scale of operation, (having been only sent as a Major-General to Portugal, in 1798, a time of inaction; and as Lieutenant-General to Ireland, in 1803), is not imputable to me, as during my life, my professional talents have been cultivated by study, and my military zeal to distinguish myself in the cause of my king and country has not abated.

And now, my Lord, I will not detain you much longer; but a word or two upon the limitation to 1803, in the instrument I have already mentioned, I cannot omit. No rule or regulation of that kind can be supported by argument, as military services and military records must, at the tribunal of reason, be equally valid in the last or present century,—under the reign of his majesty George III or the government of the Prince Regent. The rule even hitherto has not obtained observance, as in various instances I can point out; those facts, however, I will not dwell upon, or discuss upon the present occasion. If the rule were literally observed, the article of exclusion is of so rigorous a nature, that it is morally impossible to carry it into effect. Look, my Lord, at the consequences it must eventually produce. If you exclude me as a veteran, you must come to the decisive avowal, that age incapacitates me from the enjoyment of any military distinction.

But, my Lord, I never can believe that a gracious and high minded Prince, after hearing a full exposition of the services of his military servants, can adopt or even countenance the decree of exclusion which tells me in plain language, that my toils and dangers are not regarded, and that the honours I have achieved, and the wounds I have endured, are neither remembered nor regretted.

I have, &c.,
Ban. Tarleton, General

After considering General Tarleton's letter for twelve days, Lord Bathurst replied:

Downing Street, February 8, 1815

Sir,

I have many apologies to make for not having acknowledged sooner the letter which you did me the honour to write to me.

No person can be more sensible that I am of your distinguished military services, and of the glory which attached to his Majesty's arms, in the American war, in consequence of the great zeal and activity which you uniformly displayed in that contest.

I am, therefore, much concerned that the regulation which it has been thought expedient to make on the present occasion has not enabled the government to mark their sense of your services, at the time when those of the officers who have served in the last war have been rewarded.

I have the honour, etc.
Bathurst

General Tarleton

Lord Bathurst's answer was no palliation, and General Tarleton's threat to appeal to a "gracious and high minded Prince" was not bluff. He went to London and laid his humiliation before the Duke of York. The commander in chief read the letter. The General's claims were just, but the government had already selected the Knights of the Bath.

Perhaps there were other ways in which the Prince Regent might remove the grievance. After two weeks of hesitation, Banastre wrote the Duke:

Berkeley Square
February 28, 1815

Sir,

As your Royal Highness has done me the honor of reading my letter to Lord Bathurst, it would be the height of presumption and folly to intrude for more than a moment upon your Royal Highness's valuable time. The circumstances of the year, impelled me to that address, and I now with great submission, solicit Your Royal Highness's gracious attention and interference with respect to the removal of the grievance of which I have complained.

If, therefore, I proceed to mention a Baronetcy as the panacea for my wounded feelings, I hope my abruptness will stand excused upon this occasion by Your Royal Highness; as I am certain, my selection of Your Royal Highness, as the person to remove pain and mortification from a Veteran, will receive the approbation of the army.

I have the honor to be
Sir
With sentiments of the highest respect
and attachment
Your Royal Highness's
Most obedient, and devoted servant,
Ban. Tarleton
General

To
His Royal Highness, Field Marshal
The Duke of York, Commander in Chief
Etc., etc., etc., etc., etc.

The Duke spoke to the Prince. The Prince spoke to Colonel MacMahon, his secretary, and there followed a considerable correspondence between MacMahon and Tarleton. Apparently to die without an heir, Banastre proposed collateral descent for the baronetcy: "General Banastre Tarleton, of the Parish of St. George's, London, to be created a Baronet, and in default of male issue, to descend to Thomas Tarleton, Esquire, of Bolesworth Castle, in the county of Cheshire, and heirs male of his body lawfully begotten."

As the descent of the baronetcy to the General's favorite nephew was being considered in the Herald's College, the Tarletons became excited. Would they at last become a titled family? Thomas urged pushing the matter vigorously, and Banastre replied with some irritation:

29 April

My dear Brother

From Drake I have learned with extreme concern that Tom has met with a serious accident. Pray let us know the result and give his address, as Drake could only mention Penley and not the Post town.

As the Prince has not held a levee I have not yet seen him—I did not want an interview until the whole business is concluded. My last letters (of which you have a copy) places the two points which have been obstructed, in a clear light, which a Royal conversation might obscure.

The indisposition and retreat of Ld. L. from business, prevents the interview with the P. and his Lordship. We must remain then, for a little while longer upon "our oars." At present, I am placed between the Devil and the Red Sea, and if my abstinence from the Royal Presence continues much longer, I should not be surprised if the Regent turned his back upon me, when I did approach his person.

As for what you say about the Patent do you take me for Goosey Gander? I mentioned having seen Bigland to you, and can you think I omitted any enquiries which would bring about an active completion of our joint wishes? The patent confirms, and does not dictate to the Gazette. Not one word, therefore can be entered into it, without Ministerial leave.

Drake dines with us today. He complains of the Archbishop's lengthening his stay in London.

We are sorry to hear Mary Anne has been ill and we hope the coming Spring (which is yet to come) will dissipate her aches & pains.

M. joins in best love

Affectionately Your Brother
Banastre Tarleton

The proposal of collateral descent was not accepted but with great pride Ban forwarded Colonel MacMahon's letter to Thomas:

Leintwardine Ludlow
Jan. 10, 1816

My dear Brother

I was truly sorry to hear of your indisposition, which I hope this open weather will remove. Eliza was lucky in having a short journey and finding a comfortable house. Our best love attends her. I annex a copy of a letter received from Colonel McMahon, the private Secretary to the Regent. Susan is only tolerably well. I have had a pain in my ear, and swelled face. But I now face the weather, and I receive plenty of fish and game.

Yours very affectionately
Ban. Tarleton

The letter from Colonel MacMahon announced the award of the baronetcy. Banastre hastened to London and on January 23 was created Sir Banastre Tarleton, Baronet.

Lady Tarleton often invited Tom Tarleton's daughters to London. She was very fond of Eliza. In her *Journal* Mary wrote: "My father went up to Town to meet Eliza on her return from Orleans. They stayed with Sir B. and Lady Tarleton in Grosvenor Place. My dear sister was pronounced by one of the fashionables who had the entree of my Uncle's house to be the most beautiful woman in London. Lady T. offered to keep her with her for the Season, but her extreme youth and delicacy toward Lady B— from whose care she had just been withdrawn prevented this offer from being accepted."

The rheumatism of which Sir Banastre had again begun to complain got worse: the exposure and dissipation in his youth claimed their reward. He and Susan avoided London society, but when Princess Charlotte, only child of the Prince Regent, married Prince Leopold of Saxe-Coburg on May 2, 1816, they attended the levee at Carlton House. Lady Charlotte Cholmondeley was one of the bridesmaids.

"Sir Banastre and Lady Tarleton left town yesterday for Grimsthorpe Castle, on a visit to Lord Gwydyr and Lady Willoughby," observed the *Star* on August 16, 1817. On August 26 Marquis Cholmondeley and his family left for Grimsthorpe Castle, and on September 8 the Gwydyrs, Cholmondeleys, and Tarletons moved to the Cholmondeley seat at Houghton.

From Houghton Sir Banastre and Lady Tarleton drove on into Scotland for a season of hunting and fishing. There they remained during the fall and winter, even though both suffered from the northern weather. From London on January 11, 1818, Charles Greenwood wrote to Ban: "I wish with all my heart that you were once more established in Lady Tarleton's old favorite place, Leintwardine. I had rather receive the poorest grayling from you there than the finest salmon from Scotland, which I cannot think is a country well suited to her Ladyship or to you, and I will flatter myself that you are now become of the same opinion, and that you will never again bend your steps that way."

Greenwood paused and then resumed his letter three days later: "I had wrote thus far on Saturday (the date of this) when I was informed of the death of Sir John Floyd, and as I knew the Duke of York's wishes to avail himself of every opportunity to serve you & thought it possible that he might think of you in succession to the 8th Dragoons I have therefore delay'd my letter; till I could be upon some certainty respecting the appointment, which however is still unsettled, but I am unwilling to delay writing any longer, or informing you that there never can be a better instance of the interest which the Duke of York takes in your welfare than upon the present occasion. In all probability you may hear again from me tomorrow. Ever, with my best Compliments to Lady Tarleton, and with great truth & regard, my dear Tarleton."

The 21st Regiment of Dragoons, of which Sir Banastre had been colonel since 1802, had been ordered home from the Cape of Good

Hope to be disbanded. Tarleton faced half-pay, but as Greenwood had intimated, on January 15 the Duke of York saved him by appointing him colonel of the 8th or Royal Irish Hussars. With the appointment the Duke sent a note of well-wishing. The regiment was in India under the command of Lieutenant Colonel Russell.

The emoluments from the colonelcy of the 8th Hussars were reckoned as £1443 a year. With this added to his annual pay of £583 as governor of Berwick, Sir Banastre now had a handsome income. He and Susan kept their house in Grosvenor Street, but spent most of their time at Leintwardine. His health had become wretched. Gout wracked him and arthritis began twisting his fingers. He suffered, too, from the troubles in his family. The war had ruined his brothers.

In 1815 John had filed a petition of bankruptcy. He died soon afterward, embittered and hostile. His widow was violent against Banastre. In 1818 Ban's beloved sister Bridget died, and on January 2, 1820, his brother Thomas died. None of the family had known that Thomas was also bankrupt. "They were unprepared for the complete wreck of fortune which his death disclosed," wrote Mary Tarleton in her *Journal*. Among the causes she listed "the cost of his brother Banastre's elections, and I rather think of some of his gaming debts."

Sir Banastre had tried to undo the damage to his family and "had come to our aid in pecuniary straits," continued Mary:

> Lady Tarleton never referred very much to her husband's early life. His active career in the American War was closed before she knew him, and the very enthusiastic religious views which she took up and with which she earnestly sought to imbue him prevented her dwelling with pleasure upon the "pomps and vanities" which surrounded him in middle life—the hollow unsatisfactoriness of which might well have struck a more sober-minded Christian than herself, for he owed much of his fame to the dashing and fascinating manner which won him the favor and intimacy of the Prince Regent. She was an excellent person, generous and self-denying to the last degree, bestowing (probably much more than) half her goods to feed the poor—doing all in her power for all those who would claim kindred with him—but withal evincing the peculiarities and small inconsistencies of one who has been in youth the spoilt darling of the world and of society, and in more mature age has earnestly turned to better things. The habits and influences still remained ranged on one side, long after the connections and aspirations had gone over to the other. She had been brought up in a hot-bed of exaggerated expressions of affection which however unsubstantial had been to her the daily bread, I should rather say, the salt and spice of her existence. She had been used to take people by storm with her grace and fascinations, and no respect and affection that she could secure to herself in grateful recognition of benefits conferred had any value for her compared with the unrea-

soning tribute of high flown words which had been the current coin of her little world.

As Sir Banastre aged, the royal brothers became more and more solicitous for him. In 1820 the Prince Regent succeeded his father as King George IV. In his coronation honors King George forever removed Sir Banastre's grievance by making him a Knight Grand Cross of the Order of the Bath. "In consequence of his infirmities" he was invested at his own house in Grosvenor Street by the Duke of York, acting as Great Master of the Order.

On June 7 the Duke of Gloucester, the King's younger brother, wrote Countess Derby: "I hasten to return my best thanks to your Ladyship for the very kind letter I had last night the pleasure of receiving from you, by which I truly lament to hear such a very bad account of my friend Sir Banastre Tarleton and to learn of the very alarming state of poor Lady Tarleton's health. May I request of you, at a proper moment, to have the goodness to express to her how sensibly I feel her attention and to assure her of the anxious solicitude I feel respecting herself and Sir Banastre."

Yet Sir Banastre and Lady Tarleton attended the Coronation of George IV. In spite of his rheumatism he proudly marched with the Knights Grand Cross in the Coronation procession of the King who had been his friend since January 18, 1782, when as Prince of Wales he came to meet the three colonels just arrived from America.

Sir Banastre never again appeared on a public occasion. He spent most of his time at Leintwardine. When the weather permitted he fished in the Teme and sent his catches to friends in London. From the Duke of York came a note thanking him for a "very fine salmon"; another thanking him for the grayling; and another saying that Princess Sophia had found the fish most excellent.

Through his secretary King George also sent his thanks for a mess of grayling:

Royal Lodge
Tuesday Sept. 19th

My dear Tarleton
Your six Grayling were not equally well hooked, one of them having by some means, broken away. Five, however arrived in very good condition, and were dressed on Sunday. The King eat his share, and thought them excellent; You must not however, imagine that we gave you all the praise of having caught them, knowing Lady Tarleton to be an Excellent Angler—I claimed, and obtained for Her, half the credit—the King has been for some time smarting under what is called the Shingles, which is both painful, and tedious. His Majesty is otherwise very well, I am sorry that I cannot say the same of the Duke of York, or had you to place any faith in the Paper Reports about him. Lord Cholmondeley has given up his Intention

of going to Houghton, he is however much better than he was some days ago—you may have heard that Lady Charlotte broke a Blood vessel, while, I believe, at dinner, about a week or ten days since. She is doing well, but it is yet too early, to pronounce her safe; Pray remember me most kindly to Lady Tarleton and I remain, my dear Friend

Most faithfully Yours
W. Ruppel

On Enquiry I find the number of your Grayling to be correct—
The King desires his Best Regards to You.

When King George IV died in 1830 and the Duke of Clarence succeeded him as King William IV, Sir Banastre was too feeble to attend the coronation ceremonies.

"My last personal recollection of the General," wrote Mary in her *Journal*, "is of a day when two of my sisters and I drove over from Broughton or Charlton (I think the latter) to see him and my Aunt whilst they were on a visit to Cholmondeley Castle—he was a fine, but rather stern and rugged looking old man, unshorn to a degree, which in those days was peculiar, confined by gout to his chair and his crippled hands further deformed by the loss of a thumb and forefinger of one of them in the American War."

Sir Banastre lingered on, suffering greatly, but in early January 1833 he began sinking. As soon as the news reached London, King William asked his secretary to send a letter to his old friend.

In great agitation Lady Tarleton replied:

Sir,
    When His Majesty's gracious message was delivered this evening, my poor husband was almost too ill to feel the full value of such a mark of this great goodness. He is seldom free from the effects of stupor, which greatly increases towards night; but in the morning however he is more himself, as I trust he will be, I shall revive him greatly with the delightful assurance that his sufferings are not disregarded by that gracious Sovereign in whose Service I feel certain that he would willingly sacrifice his life.
    I hope, Sir, His Majesty will graciously excuse any informality I may have been guilty of, and any mistakes that may have crept into these few lines—this house is at present the house of sorrow, this room very dark and 7 nights of watching and anxiety do not serve to clear the intellect—my heart however feels most sensibly and will treasure in its remembrance this proof of Royal favour bestowed on one so dear to me.

Believe me Sir
With great consideration
Your obedient and humble Servant
Susan Tarleton

Sir Banastre died on January 16, 1833. On January 25 Lady Tarleton, Thomas Tarleton, Jr., Dr. J. E. Tarleton, and other friends buried him in the churchyard at Leintwardine. Thomas hastened to London and delivered his uncle's insignia of knighthood to King William.

In London the newspapers paid little attention to his passing. But a reporter on the *Morning Chronicle*, remembering handsome Colonel Tarleton and beautiful Mrs. Robinson, wrote in the "Mirror of Fashion":

"General Banastre Tarleton, who died the other day at a very great age, was many years Representative in Parliament for Liverpool—in early life the boon companion and associate of George the Fourth, when Prince of Wales, and a staunch Whig. Previous to his marriage, which took place at an advanced period, he was the protector, friend, and intimate of "Perdita," the beautiful Mrs. Robinson, after the Prince of Wales had withdrawn from her. To the honour of General Tarleton, he remained faithful to that highly-accomplished female when she had lost the use of her limbs, and the General himself frequently sustained her from her carriage into the boxes of Covent Garden Theater, the house to which Mrs. Robinson was most attached, on account of its having been the scene of her early and successful personation of the character of 'Perdita' in Shakespeare's 'Winter's Tale.' The sweet simplicity she displayed in that personation first attracted the notice and won the affections of the Prince of Wales. General Tarleton was an active officer in the American War, relating to which he subsequently published, in a quarto volume, "A History of the Campaigns of 1780 and 1781." This work excited much controversy at the time. He was also a frequent debater in the House of Commons until he retired from Parliament. By the death of the General, another Regiment, falls into the gift of Ministers."

Sir Banastre left his sword, his trophies, and his papers to Thomas Tarleton, Jr. His earthly goods, including £7000 in bonds, he had willed to Susan Priscilla. She lived until 1864, an eccentric but gracious old aunt, always welcomed in the homes of the Tarletons and Gwydyrs and Cholmondeleys.

Sir Banastre's grave was soon neglected and forgotten, but Susan Priscilla had had a monument erected in Leintwardine Church and on it inscribed:

Near this place are deposited the mortal remains of Sir Banastre Tarleton—Baronet—General in the Army—Knight Grand Cross of the Order of the Bath, Governor of Berwick-on-Tweed, Colonel of the Gallant 8th Hussars—He represented his native town of Liverpool for seven Sessions and closed his distinguished career in this place Jan. 15, 1833.

He was a tender-hearted husband, an indulgent master and liberal benefactor to the poor. This monument is raised by his bereaved widow as a testimony of her affection. But he has a more imperishable memory for himself in the annals of his country, and in the hearts of many friends.

> He was a hero, his youth's idol, glory,
> He courted on the battlefield of war.
> England exulted in her valiant son
> And stamped his name for ever on her story.
>
> Time's trophy gained and sheathed the warrior's sword,
> He turned him sated from the world's renown
> To die the humble soldier of his Lord,
> And change earth's laurel for a heavenly crown.

Sources and References

CHAPTER 1

Return of the Hero

For the fighting around Yorktown see Tarleton, *Campaigns;* John Bell Tilden Phelps, "Extracts from the Journal of Lieutenant John Bell Tilden," *The Pennsylvania Magazine of History and Biography* (1895); *Journals of Captain John Montresor* (1882); *Memoirs of the Duc de Lauzun* (1912); James Brown Scott, *De Grasse at Yorktown* (1931); Cornelius Stevenson, "A Biographical Notice of the Duc de Lauzun," *The Pennsylvania Magazine of History and Biography* (1923); and "The Yorktown Campaign: The Journal of Captain John Davis of the Pennsylvania Line," *The Pennsylvania Magazine of History and Biography* (1881).

For Tarleton and the black stallion see James Parton, *The Life of General Andrew Jackson* (1861).

For the American treatment of Tarleton see George Washington Parke Custis, *Recollections and Private Memories of Washington* (1861); and Sallie DuPuy Harper, "Colonial Men and Times, Containing the Journals of Colonel Daniel Trabue," *William and Mary College Quarterly* (1948).

For Tarleton and the Duke of Clarence see James Grant Wilson, *The Life and Letters of Fitz-Greene Halleck* (1869); see also G. N. Wright, *The Life and Reign of William IV* (1837).

Tarleton's return to England was best covered by *Ruddiman's Weekly Mercury* and by *The Morning Herald and Daily Advertiser.* See also Isaac Schomberg, *Naval Chronology* (1802).

For Tarleton's reception in London see Lewis Bettany, *Edward Jerningham and his Friends* (1929); Peter Cunningham, *The Letters of Horace Walpole* (1857-59); Charles Robert Leslie, *Life and Times of Sir Joshua Reynolds* (1865); Mary Robinson, *The False Friend;* Winthrop Sargent, *The Life and Career of Major John André* (1861); Marguerite Steen, *The Lost One, A Biography of Mary (Perdita) Robinson* (1931); John Wolcot, *The Works of Peter Pindar* (1830); and Gore's *General Advertiser* (Liverpool).

CHAPTER 2

Banastre

For the Tarleton family see John Burke, *The Extinct and Dormant Baronetcies of England, Scotland and Ireland* (1841); and F. A. Crisp, "Pedigree of Tarleton," *Visitation of England and Wales* (Notes, Vol. 14) (1921). See also Thomas Baines, *History of the Commerce and Town of Liverpool* (1852); Richard Brooke, *Liverpool as it was during the last Quarter of the Eighteenth Century* (1853); and J. A. Picton, *Memorials of Liverpool* (1875).

For Banastre's education see *The Bursar's Book,* University College, Oxford, 1771; William Carr, *University College* (1902); William Edward Surtees, *A Sketch of the Lives of Lords Stowell and Eldon* (1846). H. A. C.

Sturgess, *Register of Admissions to the Honorable Society of the Middle Temple* (1949); and "Account of Lieutenant Colonel Tarleton," *The Political Magazine* (1781).

For Cornet Tarleton's career see *Muster Rolls, 1st Dragoon Guards*, Public Record Office, London; War Office papers, Public Record Office; and *The Norwich Mercury*. See also John Richard Alden, *General Charles Lee, Traitor or Patriot?* (1951); Erastus C. Benedict, *The Battle of Harlem Heights* (1880); Thomas W. Field, *The Battle of Long Island* (1869); Douglas Southall Freeman, *George Washington* (1946-1954) George Washington Greene, *The Life of Nathanael Greene* (1867-1871); Edward McCrady, *The History of South Carolina in the Revolution, 1775-1780* (1901); William Moultrie, *Memoirs of the American Revolution* (1802); David Ramsay, *History of the Revolution of South-Carolina* (1785); and *Journal and Orderly Book of Ensign Thomas Glyn*, manuscript, Princeton University Library.

Banastre's letter telling of the capture of General Lee is from the Tarleton family papers. An almost identical letter is in the Hardwicke papers in the British Museum.

The will of John Tarleton is in the Lancashire Record Office, County Hall, Preston. Thomas inherited the estate, but Banastre, John, William, Clayton, Bridget, and Mrs. Jane Tarleton each received £5,000.

CHAPTER 3

Mary

For Mary Robinson's early years see *Memoirs of the Late Mrs. Robinson, Written by Herself* (1801). See also "Account of the Late Mrs. Robinson," *The Monthly Magazine* (1801); "Mrs. Mary Robinson," *Literary Memoirs of Living Authors* (1798); and "Mrs. Mary Robinson," *Public Characters* (1801).

For fictional treatment see E. Barrington, *The Exquisite Perdita* (1926); Stanley J. Makower, *Perdita, A Romance in Biography* (1908); and Steen, *The Lost One.*

CHAPTER 4

The Mischianza

For movements of the British Army see Henry Clinton (William B. Wilcox, editor), *The American Rebellion: Sir Henry Clinton's Narrative of his Campaigns, 1775-1782* (1954); Bellamy Partridge, *Sir Billy Howe* (1932); and William S. Stryker, *The Battles of Trenton and Princeton* (1898).

For Captain Tarleton in Philadelphia see "Account of Lieutenant Colonel Tarleton," *The Political Magazine*; George Hanger, *An Address to the Army in Reply to Strictures by Roderick M'Kenzie (late Lieutenant in the 71st Regiment) on Tarleton's History of the Campaigns of 1780 and 1781* (1789); Henry Lee, *Memoirs of the War in the Southern Department of the United States* (1812); Sargent, *John André*; John F. Watson, *Annals of Philadelphia, and Pennsylvania* (1844); *The London Gazette*; and War Office papers in the Public Record Office.

For the Mischianza see "Letters of Major Baurmeister," *The Pennsylvania Magazine of History and Biography* (1936); *Journals of Captain John Montresor*; and Thomas Westcott, *Historic Mansions in Philadelphia* (1877). See also Oscar Sherwin, *Benedict Arnold, Patriot and Traitor* (1931); and Lewis B. Walker, "The Life of Margaret Shippen Arnold," *The Pennsylvania Magazine of History and Biography* (1900-1902); and *The Gentleman's Magazine* (1778).

John André's account of the Mischianza was published in *The Century Magazine* (1894).

CHAPTER 5

Susan Priscilla

For the Ancaster family see Burke's *Genealogical and Heraldic History of the Peerage, Baronetage, and Knightage* (1956).

There are a few references to Robert Bertie, Fourth Duke of Ancaster, in Cunningham, *Letters of Horace Walpole*; Sargent, *John André*; *The London Gazette*; and *The Morning Post*.

The will of Robert Bertie, fourth Duke of Ancaster, is in Somerset House, London. Banastre's letter is from the Tarleton family papers.

CHAPTER 6

The Green Horse

For the British withdrawal from Philadelphia see Isaac N. Arnold, *The Life of Benedict Arnold* (1880); H. B. Carrington, *Battles of the American Revolution* (1888); H. B. Carrington, *Washington the Soldier* (1899); Charles Lee, *Life and Memoirs of the Late Major General Lee* (1813); Sargent, *John André*; and William S. Stryker, *The Battle of Monmouth* (1927).

For the records of the British Legion see *A List of the General and Staff Officers under his Excellency, General Sir Henry Clinton, K. B.* (1779); Carlos E. Godfrey, "Muster Rolls of Three Troops of Loyalist Light Dragoons," *The Pennsylvania Magazine of History and Biography* (1910); and Lorenzo Sabine, *The American Loyalists* (1847). Manuscript sources include *Muster Rolls of the British Legion*, facsimiles from the Canadian Archives, Manuscript Room, Library of Congress; *Muster Rolls and Pay Lists of Tarleton's British Legion*, and *British-American Half-pay Lists*, Public Record Office; *Orderly Book of Captain Scott's Company of the British Legion*, de Coppet Collection, Princeton University Library; and miscellaneous letters and orders in the papers of the Colonial Office, the Home Office, and the War Office in the Public Record Office. See also *The Cambridge Chronicle and Journal*, *The London Chronicle*, *The London Gazette*, *The New York Gazette*, *The Pennsylvania Evening Post*, and *The Royal Gazette* (New York).

For early operations of the British Legion see *Simcoe's Military Journal, a History of the Operations of a Partisan Corps Called the Queen's Rangers Commanded by Lieut. Col. J. G. Simcoe, during the War of the American Revolution* (1844).

Banastre's letters to his mother are from the Tarleton family papers.

CHAPTER 7

Star of Drury Lane

For Mary Robinson's early writing see her Memoirs. See also Poems (1775); Captivity; The Natural Daughter; Songs, Choruses, etc., from the Lucky Escape; and The Monthly Review. A manuscript of the songs from The Lucky Escape in Mary's handwriting is in the British Museum.

For Mary's early stage career see The Gazeteer and New Daily Advertiser, The Morning Chronicle and London Advertiser, The Morning Post, and The New Morning Post or General Advertiser. See also J. Fyvie, Comedy Queens of the Georgian Era (1906); John Genest, Some Account of the English Stage from the Restoration in 1660 to 1830 (1832); and Edward Robins, Twelve Great Actresses (1900). For fictional treatment see Barrington, The Exquisite Perdita; Makower, Perdita; and Steen, The Lost One.

CHAPTER 8

Bloody Tarleton

For the invasion of South Carolina see Tarleton, Campaigns; Clinton, The American Rebellion; Alexander Garden, Anecdotes of the American Revolution (1865); William Dobein James, A Sketch of the Life of Brig. Gen. Francis Marion (1821); George W. Kyte, "British Invasion of South Carolina in 1780," The Historian (1952); Edward McCrady, The History of South Carolina in the Revolution, 1780-1783 (1902); Ramsay, Revolution of South-Carolina; Charles Ross, Correspondence of Charles, First Marquis Cornwallis (1859); The London Chronicle; and The London Gazette.

Banastre's letter to his mother is from the Tarleton family papers. The letters to André are from the Clinton papers in the Clements Library. Tarleton's letter of May 29 is from the unpublished Cornwallis correspondence.

All letters or portions of letters originally in cipher are printed in italic type.

The flag of Colonel Buford's regiment is in Sir Banastre's effects in the possession of Mrs. Helen M. Fagan. Buford was court-martialed, exonerated, and restored to command. James says that Captain Stokes, Lieutenant Pearson, and Ensign Cruitt recovered from their wounds.

"Tarleton's quarter", which meant no quarter, and "Bloody Tarleton" were American propaganda slogans.

CHAPTER 9

Along Black River

For the summer of 1780 see Tarleton's Campaigns; Anne King Gregorie, Thomas Sumter (1931); George Hanger, The Life, Adventures and Opinions of Colonel George Hanger (1801); James, Francis Marion; McCrady, South Carolina in the Revolution, 1780-1783; Lewis Melville, The Beaux of the Regency (1908); Harriott Horry (Mrs. St. Julien) Ravenel, Charleston, the Place and the People (1912); Ross, Cornwallis Correspondence; Schomberg, Naval Chronology; Benjamin Franklin Stevens, An Exact Reprint of Six Rare Pamphlets on the Clinton-Cornwallis Controversy (1888).

Banastre's letter to André is from the Clinton papers.

CHAPTER 10

Camden and Fishing Creek

See Tarleton, Campaigns; James H. Fitzgerald Brewer, History of the 175th Infantry, MNG, 1774-1955 (1955); Carrington, Battles of the American Revolution; Gregorie, Thomas Sumter; McCrady, South Carolina in the Revolution, 1780-1783; Samuel White Patterson, Horatio Gates (1941); Ramsay, Revolution of South-Carolina; Ross, Cornwallis Correspondence; David Stewart, Sketches of the Character, Manners, and Present State of the Highlands of Scotland (1827); Christopher Ward, The War of the Revolution (1952); and The London Gazette Extraordinary.

Banastre's letter to John is in the Picton Reference Library, Liverpool.

CHAPTER 11

The Swamp Fox

For Tarleton and Marion see Tarleton, Campaigns; Lyman C. Draper, King's Mountain and Its Heroes (1881); Gregorie, Thomas Sumter; Hanger, Life; James, Francis Marion; McCrady, South Carolina in the Revolution, 1780-1783; Ramsay, Revolution of South-Carolina; Ross, Cornwallis Correspondence; Sargent, John André; and unpublished Cornwallis correspondence.

CHAPTER 12

The Gamecock

For Tarleton and Sumter see Tarleton, Campaigns; Gregorie, Thomas Sumter; McCrady, South Carolina in the Revolution, 1780-1783; Ross, Cornwallis Correspondence; and especially the unpublished Cornwallis correspondence. Banastre's letter to his mother is from the Tarleton family papers. His letter to John is in the Picton Reference Library.

CHAPTER 13

Perdita

For the story of Florizel and Perdita see Mary Robinson, Memoirs; John Banvard, The Private Life of a King (1875); The Earl of Bessborough, Lady Bessborough and her Family Circle (1940); George Croly, The Personal History of George the Fourth (1841); Cunningham, Letters of Horace Walpole; Percy Fitzgerald, The Life of George the Fourth (1881); Laetitia Matilda Hawkins, Memoirs, Anecdotes, Facts, and Opinions (1824); Robert Huish, Memoirs of George the Fourth (1830); and Philip Lindsay, The Loves of Florizel (1951). See also Barrington, The Exquisite Perdita; Makower, Perdita; and Steen, The Lost One. Most of the scandal was carried in The Morning Herald and The Morning Post.

CHAPTER 14

Prelude to Battle

For the events preceding the battle of Cowpens see Tarleton, *Campaigns*; James Graham, *The Life of General Daniel Morgan* (1856); Greene, *Nathanael Greene*; Mackenzie, *Strictures*; and Ross, *Cornwallis Correspondence*. Of especial value is the unpublished Cornwallis correspondence.

Tarleton's letter of January 4 is printed in the *Campaigns* without salutation or close. The author has provided these in order that it may be printed in letter form.

CHAPTER 15

Cowpens

For the battle of Cowpens see Tarleton, *Campaigns*; and Graham, *Daniel Morgan*. Supporting accounts are from "A Journal of the Southern Expedition, 1780-1783. By William Seymour, Sergeant Major of the Delaware Regiment," *The Pennsylvania Magazine of History and Biography* (1883); "General Richard Winn's Notes," *The South Carolina Historical and Genealogical Magazine* (1942); Greene, *Nathanael Greene*; William Johnson, *Sketches of the Life and Correspondence of Nathanael Greene* (1822); Benson J. Lossing, *The Pictorial Field Book of the American Revolution* (1850-1852); McCrady, *South Carolina in the Revolution, 1780-1783*; Lynn Montross, *Rag, Tag, and Bobtail* (1952); and Ward, *The Revolution*.

For Tarleton's horse see Robert Jackson, *A View of the Formation, Discipline, and Economy of Armies* (1845).

For the fight between Tarleton and Colonel Washington see John Marshall, *The Life of George Washington* (1804).

For British reaction see Hanger, *Address to the Army*; Mackenzie, *Strictures*; Moultrie, *Memoirs*; Ross, *Cornwallis Correspondence*; Charles Stedman, *History of the Origin, Progress, and Termination of the American War* (1794); and the unpublished Cornwallis correspondence.

Stewart, *Sketches*, said that Fraser's Highlanders (the 71st Regiment) wore kilts in America.

Henry Mouzon's "An Accurate Map of North and South Carolina" (1775) shows Thicketty as Thickelle Creek. Kenneth Roberts, "900 Men Who Shook an Empire," *Collier's* (1956), Emphasizes that Morgan sent his wagons five miles to the rear toward Broad River.

CHAPTER 16

The Mangled Hand

For the campaign in North Carolina and the battle of Guilford Courthouse see Tarleton, *Campaigns*; Carrington, *Battles of the American Revolution*; Graham, *Daniel Morgan*; Greene, *Nathanael Greene*; Henry Lee, *Memoirs*; Ross, *Cornwallis Correspondence*; Ward, *The Revolution*; *The Morning Herald*; and unpublished Cornwallis correspondence.

Banastre's letters to John and Bridget are in the archives of the Virginia Historical Society. Some letters which he wrote with his left hand are in his unpublished correspondence.

CHAPTER 17

The Long Retreat

For the last phase of the British operations see Tarleton, *Campaigns*; L. C. Bell, *Old Free State* (1927); Graham, *Daniel Morgan*; "Kinlock of South Carolina," *The South Carolina Historical and Genealogical Magazine* (1926); Ross, *Cornwallis Correspondence*; Sherwin, *Benedict Arnold*; Simcoe's *Military Journal*; and W. E. Woodward, *Lafayette* (1938).

CHAPTER 18

A Prince's Ransom

See Mary Robinson, *Memoirs*. Also see *A Poetic Epistle from Florizel to Perdita* (1781); Grace Dalrymple Elliott, *Journal of My Life during the French Revolution* (1859); Fitzgerald, *George the Fourth*; Ronald Sutherland Gower, *Thomas Gainsborough* (1903); J. Heneage Jesse, *Memoirs of the Life and Reign of King George the Third* (1867); *Letters from Perdita to a Certain Israelite and His Answers to Them* (1781); *The Budget of Love, or Letters between Florizel and Perdita* (1781); *The Morning Herald*; and *The Morning Post*.

CHAPTER 19

Ban and Mary

The story of the early friendship between Banastre and Mary is derived from *The Morning Chronicle*, *The Morning Herald*, and *The Morning Post*.

For additional material see *Burke's Peerage*; Henry Hall Dixon, *The Post and the Paddock* (1856); The Countess of Ilchester and Lord Stavordale, *The Life and Letters of Lady Sarah Lennox* (1801); *Memoirs of the Duc de Lauzun*; *Memoirs of Perdita* (1784); Wolcot, *Peter Pindar*; and *The Racing Calendar*.

The letters of Banastre and John are from the Tarleton family papers.

Louis Weltjie was a German pastry maker who settled in London. He opened a pastry shop, then a restaurant, and finally "Weltjie's Club." He became a confidential servant of the Prince of Wales.

Banastre never paid Sir Joshua Reynolds for his painting. According to Sir Joshua's account books in Fitzwilliam Museum, Cambridge, the Tarleton family paid the executors of the Reynolds' estate. Gainsborough's Tarleton has never been seen since the exhibition of 1782. The author believes that Gainsborough refused to part with his painting until paid, and never being paid, eventually destroyed it.

The *Memoirs of Perdita* is most scurrilous. But its author knew Mary and Banastre, and much of what he wrote is substantiated by other evidence.

CHAPTER 20

All for Love

See Mary Robinson, Memoirs and Poetical Works. See also "Account of the Late Mrs. Robinson," The Monthly Magazine; Fitzgerald, George the Fourth; Lord Herbert (editor), Letters and Diaries of Henry, Tenth Earl of Pembroke (1939); The Morning Herald; The Morning Post; and War Office papers in the Public Record Office.

The letters of Banastre, Thomas, and Mrs. Jane Tarleton, and of Lord Cornwallis, are from the Tarleton family papers. Several of Mrs. Tarleton's letters are draft letters, and in order to print them in letter form, the author has appended her usual signature.

CHAPTER 21

Ode to Valour

See Mary Robinson, Memoirs; Poems (1791); and Poetical Works. See also An Alphabetical List of the Freemen who voted at the Contested Election for Members of Parliament to Represent the Borough of Liverpool (1784); Fitzgerald, George the Fourth; Hanger, Life; Hawkins, Memoirs; Memoirs of Perdita; Ross, Cornwallis Correspondence; The History of the Westminster Election (1784); The London Chronicle; The Morning Herald; The Morning Post; and The Racing Calendar.

CHAPTER 22

Old Wounds

Sources used are Mary Robinson, Memoirs; Poems (1791); Poetical Works; Stevens, Clinton-Cornwallis Controversy; The London Chronicle; The Morning Post; and The Morning Herald.

The letters of Banastre, Thomas, John, and Clayton are from the Tarleton family papers. The letter from Sir Henry Clinton is from the Clinton papers in the Clements Library. It is a draft letter, and the author has appended Sir Henry's usual signature.

CHAPTER 23

The Campaigns

Sources are Tarleton, A History of the Campaigns of 1780 and 1781 in the Southern Provinces of North America; Hanger, An Address to the Army in Reply to Strictures by Roderick M'Kenzie (late Lieutenant in the 71st Regiment) on Tarleton's History of the Campaigns of 1780 and 1781; Mackenzie, Strictures on Lt. Col. Tarleton's History of the Campaigns of 1780 and 1781 in the Southern Provinces of North America; Ross, Cornwallis Correspondence; The Critical Review; The Monthly Review; The Morning Herald; The Morning Post; and The World.

John's letters are from the Tarleton family papers.

CHAPTER 24

Sons of King George

See Tarleton, *Reply to Colonel de Charmilly;* and Mary Robinson, *Memoirs* and *Poetical Works.* See also John George Bishop, *The Brighton Pavillion* (1903); Fitzgerald, *George the Fourth;* Hanger, *Life;* Robert Robinson, *The Last Earls of Barrymore* (1894); Osbert Sitwell and Margaret Barton, *Brighton* (1948); *The Morning Herald; The Morning Post;* and *The World.*

CHAPTER 25

Fighting Blood

See Madame Frances (Burney) D'Arblay, *Diary and Letters* (1854); Fitzgerald, *George the Fourth;* Percy Fitzgerald, *The Lives of the Sheridans* (1886); Jesse, *Life and Reign of George the Third;* Robinson, *Last Earls of Barrymore;* Ross, *Cornwallis Correspondence;* John Russell, *The Life and Times of Charles James Fox* (1859); and Earl Stanhope, *Life of the Right Honorable William Pitt* (1867).

See also *The Cambridge Chronicle and Journal; The London Chronicle; The Norfolk Chronicle and Norwich Gazette; The Oracle;* and *The World.*

CHAPTER 26

To the Hustings

See Tarleton, *An Address to the Freemen of Liverpool;* and *The Poll for the Election of the Members of Parliament for the Borough of Liverpool Taken Between Colonel Tarleton; Bamber Gascoyne, Jr., Esq.; The Rt. Hon. Richard Lord Penrhyn; And Thomas Townley Parker, Esq.* (1790). See also Sitwell and Barton, *Brighton;* and *The London Chronicle.*

CHAPTER 27

Song of the Nightingale

See Mary Robinson, *Memoirs; Ainsi Va Le Monde; Poems* (1791); and *Poetical Works.* See also Willard Connaly, *The Reign of Beau Brummel* (1940); William Gifford, *The Baviad* (1794); Luke Hansard, *Parliamentary History;* Robert Isaac Wilberforce and Samuel Wilberforce, *The Life of Wilberforce* (1839); *The Cambridge Chronicle and Journal; The Critical Review; The Monthly Review; The New Annual Register;* and *The Parliamentary Register.*

CHAPTER 28

Bounding Billow

See Mary Robinson, *Memoirs; Poems* (1794); *The False Friend;* and *Vancenza.* See also Fitzgerald, *The Sheridans;* Hansard, *Parliamentary His-*

tory; *The Female Jockey Club; The General Evening Post; The London Chronicle; The Monthly Review; The Oracle;* and *The Sun.*

Mary Tarleton's journal and Banastre's letter to Clayton are from the Tarleton family papers.

The reasons for Banastre's trips to Paris during the French Revolution have never been revealed.

CHAPTER 29

The Betting Book

See Mary Robinson, *Memoirs; Modern Manners; Poems* (1794); *Sight, The Cavern of Woe,* and *Solitude; Poetical Works;* and *The Widow.* See also Alfred H. Burne, *The Noble Duke of York* (1949); James Greig, *The Farington Diary* (1923); Hansard, *Parliamentary History;* Charles Pigott, *The Whig Club* (1794); Maria Elizabeth Robinson, *The Shrine of Bertha* (1794); Russell, *Charles James Fox;* Stanhope, *William Pitt;* Wilberforce, *Wilberforce; The Critical Review; The Monthly Review; The Morning Herald; The Oracle;* and *The Star.*

CHAPTER 30

The Devil's Walk

See Mary Robinson, *Angelina; Sappho and Phaon; The False Friend; Poetical Works;* and *The Sicilian Lover.*

See also James Boaden, *Memoirs of the Life of John Philip Kemble, Esq.* (1825); Burne, *Duke of York;* Samuel Taylor Coleridge, *Selected Poetry and Prose* (edited by Elizabeth Schneider); Fitzgerald, *George the Fourth;* Greig, *Farington Diary;* Hansard, *Parliamentary History;* Seymour Harcourt, *The Gaming Calendar* (1820); Russell, *Charles James Fox;* Stanhope, *William Pitt;* John Taylor, *Records of My Life* (1832); *The Cambridge Chronicle and Journal; The London Chronicle; The Monthly Review; The Morning Post;* and *The Star.*

CHAPTER 31

Brother Against Brother

See Brooke, *Liverpool;* Hansard, *Parliamentary History;* Picton, *Memorials of Liverpool;* Wilberforce, *Wilberforce;* and *The Oracle.* For the election see *The Poll for the Election of Members of Parliament, for the Borough of Liverpool; taken between General Tarleton, General Gascoyne, and John Tarleton, Esq.* (1796).

CHAPTER 32

Heartbreak

See Tarleton, *Campaigns,* 2nd edition; and Mary Robinson, *Hubert de Sevrac; Sappho and Phaon; The False Friend;* and *Poetical Works.* See also

Hansard, *Parliamentary History;* Anthony Pasquin, *The New Brighton Guide* (1796); George Pellew, *The Life and Correspondence of the Right Honorable Henry Addington, First Viscount Sidmouth* (1847); Russell, *Charles James Fox;* Stanhope, *William Pitt: The Analytical Review; The Critical Review; The Monthly Review; The Oracle;* and *The Parliamentary Register.*

CHAPTER 33

Youth and £20,000

See Mary Robinson, *The False Friend; Poetical Works;* and *Walsingham.* See also Burne, *Duke of York;* Hansard, *Parliamentary History;* Richard Edgecumbe, *The Diary of Frances, Lady Shelley* (1912); Russell, *Charles James Fox;* Sargent, *John André;* Wilberforce, *Wilberforce: The Analytical Review; The Morning Herald; The Morning Post; The Observer; The Oracle;* and *The Star.*

CHAPTER 34

Old Windsor

See Mary Robinson, *Memoirs; A Picture of Palermo; Lyrical Tales; The Natural Daughter; Poetical Works;* and *Thoughts on the Condition of Women, and on the Injustice of Mental Subordination.* See also Ford K. Brown, *William Godwin* (1926); William Godwin, *Fleetwood* (1805); Earl L. Griggs, "Coleridge and Mrs. Robinson," *Modern Language Notes* (1930); Charles Kegan Paul, *William Godwin; His Friends and Contemporaries* (1876); John Russell, *Memoirs, Journal, and Correspondence of Thomas Moore* (1853); *The Courier; The Oracle;* and *The Sun.*

A microfilm copy of the journal and correspondence of William Godwin is in the Western Manuscripts, The Bodleian Library, Oxford.

CHAPTER 35

Recall to Siberia

See Cobbett, *Parliamentary Debates;* George Hanger, *Reflections on the Menaced Invasion and the Means of Protecting the Capital by preventing the Enemy from landing in any Part Contiguous to it* (1804); R. Grundy Heape, *Buxton under the Dukes of Devonshire* (1948); William Wilson Hunter (editor), *Lord Cornwallis* (1890); Pellew, *Viscount Sidmouth;* J. Holland Rose, *William Pitt and the Great War* (1914); and Russell, *Charles James Fox.*

For the election of 1802 see *A Complete List of the 1425 Burgesses who Polled at the Late Liverpool Election, with Songs, Squibs, Attacks, Etc.* (1802).

CHAPTER 36

The Weathercock

See Brooke, *Liverpool;* Cobbett, *Parliamentary Debates;* Henry Roscoe, *The Life of William Roscoe* (1833); Charles Duke Yonge, *The Life of*

Field Marshal Arthur, Duke of Wellington (1860); The Annual Register; and The Oracle.

See also A Compendious and Impartial Account of the Election at Liverpool, 1806; and A Collection of Addresses, Songs, Squibs, etc., Published at Liverpool, during the Election for the Members of Parliament in May, 1807.

CHAPTER 37

General Tarleton

See Tarleton, Reply to Colonel de Charmilly; and To the British Nation is Presented by Colonel Venault de Charmilly, Knight of the Royal and Military Order of St. Louis, the Narrative of his Transactions in Spain with the Rt. Hon. John Hookham Frere and Lt. Gen. Sir John Moore, K. B. Being a Refutation of the Calumnies Invented against him (1810). See also Mary Anne Clarke, The Rival Princes (1810); Cobbett, Parliamentary Debates; Thomas Creevy, The Creevy Papers (1904); John McGilchrist, The Life and Career of Henry, Lord Broughham (1868); George M. Trevelyan, Lord Grey of the Reform Bill (1920); Yonge, Wellington; The Annual Register; and The London Gazette.

CHAPTER 38

Sir Banastre

See Raymond Burt, The XXII Dragoons, 1760-1945 (1950); Melville, Beaux of the Regency; Robert H. Murray, The History of the VIII King's Royal Irish Hussars (1928); The London Gazette; and The Morning Chronicle.

See also J. B. Atlay, "Tarleton of the Legion," Cornhill Magazine (1905); A. G. Bradley, "Tarleton's Tomb," The Nation (1916); H. W. Pearse, "General Sir Banastre Tarleton," The Cavalry Journal (1910); "Sir Banastre Tarleton," The Gentleman's Magazine (1843); and "Tarleton's Portrait," The National Republic (1929).

The following obituary and biographical notices appeared: "Sir Banastre Tarleton," The Annual Register (1833); "Sir Banastre Tarleton," Blackwood's Magazine (1833); "General Sir Banastre Tarleton, Bart.", The Gentleman's Magazine (1833); and "Sir Banastre Tarleton," United Services Magazine (1833).

The letters used and Mary Tarleton's journal are from the Tarleton family papers. Information about Sir Banastre's induction into the Order of the Bath is from documents in the Central Chancery of the Orders of Knighthood, St. James's Palace.

The Works of Banastre Tarleton

A History of the Campaigns of 1780 and 1781 in the Southern Provinces of North America, by Lieutenant Colonel Tarleton. T. Cadell, London, 1787.

A History of the Campaigns of 1780 and 1781 in the Southern Provinces of North America, by Lieutenant Colonel Tarleton. Printed for Colles, Exshaw, White, H. Whitestone, Burton, Byrne, Moore, Jones, and Dornin, Dublin, 1787.

An Address to the Freemen of Liverpool. Privately printed, London, 1790.

A History of the Campaigns of 1780 and 1781 in the Southern Provinces of North America, by Major General Tarleton. T. Cassels, Jr., and W. Davies, London, 1796.

Reply to Colonel de Charmilly. Privately printed, London, 1810.

Substance of a Speech intended to have been delivered on the Vote of Credit Bill. Privately printed, London, 1810.

Substance of a Speech in a Committe of the House of Commons, on the Army Estimates. Privately printed, 1811.

The Works of Mary Robinson

A Letter to the Women of England, on the Cruelties of Mental Subordination, by Anne Frances Randall. Longman and Rees, London, 1799.

A Monody to the Memory of the Late Queen of France. Evans, London, 1793.

A Monody to the Memory of Sir Joshua Reynolds. Bell, London, 1792.

A Picture of Palermo, by Dr. Hager: translated from the German by Mrs. Mary Robinson, Phillips, London, 1800.

An Ode to the Harp of the Late Accomplished and Amiable Louise Hanway. Bell, London, 1792.

Ainsi Va Le Monde. Bell, London, 1790.

Alwine oder die Wiedergefundene Tochter. Basse, Quedlinburg, 1813.

Angelina. Hookham and Carpenter, London, 1796.

Angelina, Mit dem Bildniss der Verfasserin. Heyder, Erlangen, 1799.

Audley Fortescue. William Lane, London, 1795.

Captivity, a Poem, and Celadon, a Tale. London, 1777.

Der falsche Freund. Fleischer, Rudolstadt, 1800.

D'Harcourt ou L'héritier Supposé. Lepetit, Paris, 1798.

Die Witwe. Nauck, Leipzig, 1795.

Elegaic Verses to a Young Lady on the Death of her Brother. London, 1775.

Ellinda, or the Abbey of St. Ambert. Newark, 1800.

Hubert de Sevrac. Hookham and Carpenter, London, 1797.

Hubert de Sévrac, ou Histoire d'un émigré. Gide, Paris, 1797.

Hubert von Sevrac. Ruff, Halle, 1797.

Impartial Reflections on the Present Situation of the Queen of France. Bell, London, 1791.

Julie St. Laurence. Nauck, Leipzig, 1797.

Julia St. Laurence, A Novel. Nauck, Leipzig, 1812.

Le Faux Ami. Migneret, Paris, 1799.

Le Faux Ami. Renard, Paris, 1803.

Lyrical Tales. Longman and Company, London, 1800.

Martha, ou les Dangers du mariage précipité. Lenormand, Paris, 1801.

Mary Robinson: Memoiren von ihr selbst geschrieben. Brockhaus, Altenburg, 1802.

Memoires de Mistris Robinson, Célebrè actrice de Londres. Egron, Paris, 1802.

Memoires de Mistress Robinson. Ouvrier, Paris, 1802.

Memoirs of Mary Robinson, edited by J. Fitzgerald Molloy. Lippincott, Philadelphia, 1895.

Memoirs of Mary Robinson. Several printings of the edition by Molloy for the Grolier Society.

Memoirs of the Late Mrs. Robinson: A new edition with an Introduction. Cobden-Sanderson, London, 1930.

Memoirs of the Late Mrs. Robinson, Written by Herself, edited by Maria Elizabeth Robinson, Phillips, London, 1801; Bradford, Philadelphia, 1802; Phillips, London, 1803; and Phillips, London, 1805.

Memoirs of the Late Mrs. Robinson, Written by Herself. Hunt and Clarke, London, 1826; and 1827.

Memoirs of the Late Mrs. Robinson, Written by Herself, in Vol. VII of *A Collection of the Most Instructive and Amusing Lives Ever Published.* Whittaker, Treacher, and Arnod, London, 1829; and 1830.

Modern Manners. Evans, London, 1793.

Poems, by Mrs. Robinson. Parker, London, 1775.

Poems. Bell, London, 1791.

Poems. Vol. II. Evans and Becket, London, 1794.

Sappho and Phaon. Printed for the author, London, 1796.

Sight, The Cavern of Woe, and Solitude. Evans and Becket, London, 1793.

The False Friend. Longman and Rees, London, 1799.

The Natural Daughter. Longman and Rees, London, 1799.

The Poetical Works of the Late Mrs. Mary Robinson. Phillips, London, 1806; also Jones and Company, London, 1824.

The Sicilian Lover. Hookham and Carpenter, London, 1796.

The Songs in the Lucky Escape. London, 1778.

The Widow, or a Picture of Modern Times. Hookham, London, 1794.

The Widow or a picture of modern times. Nauck, Leipzig, 1795.

Thoughts on the Condition of Women and the Injustice of Mental Subordination. Longman and Rees, London, 1799.

Vancenza, or the Dangers of Credulity. London, 1792.

Vancenza oder die Gefahren der Leicht-Glaubigkeit. Sander, Berlin, 1793.

Walsingham, or The Pupil of Nature. Longman, London, 1797.

Walsingham oder das Naturkind, Mit Musik. Nicolai, Berlin, 1799.

Walsingham ou l'Enfant des Montagnes. Imprimerie de Rabaut le jeune, Paris, 1799.

Acknowledgments

The research for and the writing of *The Green Dragoon* has taken fifteen years, sixteen months of which were spent in Europe. During this time scores of people have given me information and encouragement. Especially am I grateful to Professors Henry H. Adams, John P. Boatman, Louis H. Bolander, J. H. F. Brewer, Paul E. Coletta, Allen B. Cook, James R. Cutting, Robert W. Daly, William A. Darden, Wilson Heflin, Neville T. Kirk, Richard E. Heise, William E. Jeffries, Douglas R. Lacey, Robert M. Langdon, Royal S. Pease, Don D. Thornbury, Herman O. Werner, Richard S. West, and Gerald E. Wheeler of the U. S. Naval Academy.

I am also grateful to Professors Francis W. Bradley and Robert L. Meriwether of the University of South Carolina; Mr. Colin Campbell; Dr. Henry H. Lumpkin, Command Historian, U. S. EUCOM, Paris; Colonel George R. Stephens of the U. S. Military Academy; Mr. Roger Thomas of the Maryland Hall of Records; and to Dr. Robert Wauchope of Tulane University.

Likewise am I grateful for the aid of Professors H. F. Brooks and Norman Callan and Director A. M. Parker of the Summer School of the University of London; of Professors W. S. Thatcher and W. W. Williams of Fitzwilliam House, Cambridge; and of Professors David S. Daiches and Basil Willey of Cambridge University.

To the Earl of Ancaster; the Marquis of Cholmondeley; Lord Adam Gordon, Secretary of Brooks's Club; Major Reginald Hargreaves; Mr. R. Harvey; Professor N. S. Marsh of University College, Oxford; Mr. G. G. Shiel; Mrs. Daphne N. Spiller, great-great-granddaughter of Thomas Tarleton; and to the late General G. W. Tarleton I am indebted for material and for permission to search and use documents.

To Lord Braybrooke I am most indebted for permission to search and print letters from the unpublished correspondence of Lord Cornwallis.

And to Mrs. Helen M. Fagan, daughter of Captain Alfred N. Tarleton, R. N., of Breakspears and great-great-granddaughter of Thomas Tarleton, I am extremely grateful for permission to use the relics of Sir Banastre Tarleton, to search the family papers and publish letters and other documents, and to reproduce pictures of members of the Tarleton family.

I wish to express my appreciation to the librarians in the following institutions: Bibliothèque Nationale; Bodleian Library; British Museum; Clements Library; Deutsche Staatsbibliothek; Duke University; Enoch Pratt Library; Huntington Library; Johns Hopkins University; Karl Marx Universitätbibliothek (Leipzig); Library of Congress; National Central Library (London); National Library of Ireland; New York Public Library;

Niedersächsische Staats und Universitätbibliothek (Göttingen); Picton Reference Library (Liverpool); Princeton University; University of Pennsylvania; University of Virginia; U. S. Naval Academy; and War Office (London).

For information and permission to use documents I am indebted to the director of the Central Chancery of the Orders of Knighthood, St. James's Palace; Clements Library; Fitzwilliam Museum; National Association of Archives (London); Public Record Office (Dublin); Public Record Office (London); and the Virginia Historical Society.

For permission to reproduce pictures I am indebted to the Directors and Trustees of the British Museum, the National Gallery, the National Portrait Gallery, and the Wallace Collection.

I wish to thank Mrs. Frances Barnes, my typist, and Miss Margaret Franklin, my research assistant in London, for their excellent work. I also wish to thank Mrs. Betty Ridout for drawing my maps and R. B. Fleming and Company for their photographic work.

My deepest gratitude, however, I owe to my family, Virginia, Robert, George, and Christine, and Mrs. Elizabeth Wauchope, for helping collect material and prepare the manuscript; and to Mr. Gerald M. Simons, editor for Henry Holt and Company, whose counsel and guidance have been invaluable.

Robert D. Bass

U. S. Naval Academy
Annapolis, Maryland
November 1, 1956

INDEX

Praise for Bass's brilliant biography

"It is exciting, colorful, fluent, highly entertaining. . . . Banastre Tarleton as a subject . . . has everything, including that most glamorous mistress in London, that a biographical (or movie?) hero ought to have. Here in his first full biography, decidedly, triumphantly, the swashbuckling Green Dragoon rides again."

—Ellen Hart Smith, New York Herald Tribune Book Review

". . . an extraordinary chronicle of high and low life, both equally tawdry, in the reigns of George III and George IV."

—Louis B. Wright, *New York Times Book Review*

". . . a book of surpassing interest and literary merit which can be recommended without reservations."

—Lynn Montross, *Washington Post*

"Mr. Bass's picture of British upper crust life is strikingly good and both Tarleton and Perdita emerge full-blown. Henceforth, no library of books on either the American Revolution or Georgean England will be complete without this chronicle."

—V. P. H., *Omaha World-Herald Magazine*

"This tempestuous biography—really two biographies in one—colorful, informative and brilliant, reads like a first-class historical novel."

—Scott O'Dell, Los Angeles *Mirror-News*